Effect Sizes for Research
Univariate and Multivariate Applications
Second Edition

Effect Sizes for Research

Univariate and Multivariate Applications

Second Edition

Robert J. Grissom

and

John J. Kim

San Francisco State University

Routledge
Taylor & Francis Group
New York   London

Routledge
Taylor & Francis Group
711 Third Avenue
New York, NY 10017

Routledge
Taylor & Francis Group
27 Church Road
Hove, East Sussex BN3 2FA

Printed in the United States of America on acid-free paper
Version Date: 20111017

International Standard Book Number: 978-0-415-87768-8 (Hardback) 978-0-415-87769-5 (Paperback)

Library of Congress Cataloging-in-Publication Data

Grissom, Robert J.
    Effect sizes for research : univariate and multivariate applications / by Robert
J. Grissom, John J. Kim. -- 2nd ed.
        p. cm.
    Includes bibliographical references and index.
    ISBN 978-0-415-87768-8 (hardback) -- ISBN 978-0-415-87769-5 (softcover)
    1. Analysis of variance. 2. Effect sizes (Statistics) 3. Experimental design. I.
Kim, John J. II. Title.

QA279.G75 2012
519.5'38--dc23   2011023926

Visit the Taylor & Francis Web site at
http://www.taylorandfrancis.com

and the Psychology Press Web site at
http://www.psypress.com

This book is dedicated to those scholars, who are amply cited herein, who during the past four decades have worked diligently to develop and promote the use of effect sizes, confidence intervals, and robust statistical methods, and to those who have constructively critiqued such procedures.

In memory of a beloved son, Philip R. Grissom.

Contents

Preface..xiii
Acknowledgments...xvii

Chapter 1   Introduction 1

Introduction 1
Null-Hypothesis Significance Testing..................................... 1
Statistically Signifying and Practical Significance....................... 3
Definition, Characteristics, and Uses of Effect Sizes................... 5
Some Factors Influencing Effect Sizes...................................... 6
Controversy About Null-Hypothesis Significance Testing 9
Purpose of This Book.. 11
Power Analysis 12
Replication and Meta-Analysis 13
Assumptions of Test Statistics and Effect Sizes........................... 15
Violations of Assumptions Suggested by Real Data..................... 17
Exploring the Data for a Possible Effect of a Treatment
on Variability.. 20
Worked Examples of Measures of Variability 26
Summary 28
Questions... 28

Chapter 2   Confidence Intervals for Comparing the Averages
of Two Groups 31

Introduction 31
Ratio-of-Means Effect Size... 31
Background 32
Confidence Intervals for $\mu_a - \mu_b$: Independent Groups 33
Frequentist and Bayesian Perspectives...................................... 38
Equivalence Testing, Non-Inferiority, and Superiority 40
Worked Example for Independent Groups................................. 42
Further Discussions and Methods... 44
Solutions to Violations of Assumptions: Welch's
Approximate Method 45
Worked Example of the Welch Method 47
Yuen's Confidence Interval for the Difference Between Two
Trimmed Means 47
Other Methods for Independent Groups 51

Criteria for Methods for Constructing a Confidence Interval....... 54
Dependent Groups... 55
Summary 58
Questions.. 59

Chapter 3   The Standardized Difference Between Means 61

Introduction 61
Standardized Difference Between Treatment
and Comparison Means Assuming Normality............................. 62
Uses and Limitations of a Standardized Difference 66
Equal or Unequal Variances.. 68
Outliers and Standardized-Difference Effect Sizes 72
Tentative Recommendations 73
Additional Standardized-Difference Effect Sizes
When There Are Outliers... 74
Confidence Intervals for Standardized-Difference Effect Sizes 75
Counternull Effect Size 83
Extreme Groups 85
Percent of Maximum Possible Score... 86
Dependent Groups... 87
Effect Sizes for Pretest–Posttest Control-Group Designs 90
Summary 92
Questions.. 94

Chapter 4   Correlational Effect Sizes and Related Topics 97

Introduction 97
Dichotomizing and Correlation.. 97
Point-Biserial Correlation.. 99
Unequal Base Rates in Nonexperimental Research.................... 102
Correcting for Bias 106
Confidence Intervals for r_{pop}.. 107
Null–Counternull Interval for r_{pop}... 108
Assumptions of Correlation and Point-Biserial Correlation 109
Unequal Sample Sizes in Experimental Research 115
Unreliability 116
Adjusting Effect Sizes for Unreliability 120
Restricted Range 123
Scale Coarseness 126
Small, Medium, and Large Effect Size Values 127
Binomial Effect Size Display 132
Coefficient of Determination.. 135
Criticisms of the Coefficient of Determination.......................... 140
Slopes as Effect Sizes... 142

Effect Sizes for Mediating and Moderating Variables 144
Summary 145
Questions 146

Chapter 5   Effect Size Measures That Go Beyond Comparing
Two Averages 149

Introduction 149
Probability of Superiority: Independent Groups 149
Introduction to Overlap and Related Measures 166
Dominance Measure 166
Cohen's Measures of Nonoverlap 167
Relationships Among Measures of Effect Size 169
Estimating Effect Sizes Throughout a Distribution 170
Other Graphical Estimators of Effect Sizes 172
Dependent Groups 172
Summary 174
Questions 175

Chapter 6   Effect Sizes for One-Way ANOVA and Nonparametric
Approaches 177

Introduction 177
Assumptions 178
ANOVA Results for This Chapter 178
Standardized-Difference Measure of Overall Effect Size 178
Standardized Overall Effect Size Using All Means 179
Strength of Association 181
Evaluation of Criticisms of Strength of Association 185
Standardized-Difference Effect Sizes for Contrasts 188
Worked Examples 189
Unstandardized Differences Between Means 191
More on Standardized Differences Between Means 194
Intransitivity and the *PS* Effect Size 196
Within-Groups Designs 196
Summary 201
Questions 202

Chapter 7   Effect Sizes for Factorial Designs 205

Introduction 205
Assumptions and Handling Violations 205
Discretizing Continuous Independent Variables 205
Factors: Targeted, Peripheral, Extrinsic, Intrinsic 206
Strength of Association: Proportion of Variance Explained 207

Designs and Results for This Chapter 211
Manipulated Factors Only 211
Manipulated Targeted Factor and Intrinsic Peripheral Factor 215
Illustrative Worked Examples 217
Comparisons of Levels of a Manipulated Factor at One
Level of a Peripheral Factor 220
Targeted Classificatory Factor and Extrinsic Peripheral Factor 223
Classificatory Factors Only 224
Statistical Inference and Further Reading 227
Within-Groups Factorial Designs 230
Additional Designs, Measures, and Discussion 233
Summary 235
Questions 237

Chapter 8   Effect Sizes for Categorical Variables 241

Introduction 241
Unreliability of Categorization 243
Dichotomizing a Continuous Variable 246
Chi-Square Test and Phi 247
Confidence Intervals and Null–Counternull Intervals for phi_{pop} 251
Difference Between Two Proportions 251
Relative Risk 259
Propensity-Score Analysis 263
Relative Risk Reduction 264
Number Needed to Treat 265
Relationships Among Measures 268
Odds Ratio 269
Tables Larger Than 2×2 277
Multiway Tables 279
More on Testing and Effect Sizes for Related Proportions 279
Further Discussions 280
Summary 281
Questions 282

Chapter 9   Effect Sizes for Ordinal Categorical Dependent Variables
(Rating Scales) 285

Introduction 285
Point-Biserial r Applied to Ordinal Categorical Data 288
Probability of Superiority Applied to Ordinal Data 292
Dominance Measure 298
Somers' D, the Risk Difference, and the NNT 299
Worked Example of the Dominance Statistic and NNT_{est} 300
Generalized Odds Ratio 301

Cumulative Odds Ratios...302
Phi Coefficient..304
Further Reading 304
Summary 305
Questions 305

Chapter 10 Effect Sizes for Multiple Regression/Correlation 307

Introduction 307
Multiple Coefficient of Determination 308
Semipartial Correlation 313
Partial Correlation 315
Statistical Control of Unwanted Effects............................317
Higher-Order Correlation Coefficients..............................318
More Statistical Significance Testing and Confidence Intervals 319
Sets of Included and Excluded X Variables.......................321
Multiple Regression and ANOVA: Dummy Coding..................323
Worked Example of Multiple Regression/Correlation 328
Nonlinear Regression 332
Hierarchical Linear Modeling (Multilevel Modeling)...............334
Path Analysis and Structural Equation Modeling...................335
Effect Size for Ordinal Multiple Regression 337
Additional Topics and Reading 337
Summary 339
Questions 341

Chapter 11 Effect Sizes for Analysis of Covariance....................................343

Introduction 343
ANCOVA in Nonexperimental Research............................344
Proportion of Variance Explained Overall.........................347
Proportion of Variance Explained by a Contrast 348
Standardized Difference Between Means............................348
Unstandardized Difference Between Means.........................350
Worked Examples of Effect Sizes 351
Summary 355
Questions 356

Chapter 12 Effect Sizes for Multivariate Analysis of Variance....................357

Introduction 357
Assumptions of MANOVA 358
Statistical Tests...358
Effect Sizes for One-Way MANOVA................................360
MANCOVA...371

Factorial Between-Groups MANOVA 373
One-Way Within-Groups MANOVA 378
Effect Sizes for Mixed MANOVA Designs 382
Effect Sizes for Within-Groups MANOVA Factorial Designs 387
Additional Analyses 388
Summary 388
Questions 389

References 391

Author Index 421

Subject Index 429

Preface

Emphasis on effect sizes is rapidly rising as at least 24 journals in various fields require that authors of research reports provide estimates of effect size. For certain kinds of applied research, it is no longer considered acceptable only to report that results were statistically significant. Statistically significant results indicate that a researcher has discovered some evidence of, say, a real difference between parameters or a real association between variables, but one of unknown size. Especially in applied research, such statements often need to be augmented with estimates of how different the average results for studied groups are or how strong the association between variables is. Those who apply the results of research often need to know more, for example, than that one therapy, one teaching method, one marketing campaign, or one medication appears to be better than another; they often need evidence of how much better it is (i.e., the estimated effect size). Chapter 1 provides a more detailed definition of effect size and discussion of those circumstances in which estimation of effect sizes is especially important.

The purpose of this book is to inform a broad readership (broad with respect to fields of research and extent of knowledge of general statistics) about a variety of measures and estimators of effect sizes for analysis of univariate and multivariate data, their proper applications and interpretations, and their limitations. Thus, this book focuses on analyzing the results of a study in terms of the size of the obtained effects.

CONTENTS

The book discusses a broad variety of measures and estimators of effect sizes for different kinds of variables (nominal, ordinal, continuous), and different circumstances and purposes. It provides detailed discussions of standardized and unstandardized differences between means (Chapters 2, 3, 6, 7, and 11), many of the correlational measures (Chapters 4 and 10), strength of association (Chapters 6, 7, and 10 through 12), association in contingency tables (Chapters 8 and 9), confidence intervals (Chapter 2 and thereafter for many measures), and some important less-known measures that are simple and more robust when assumptions are violated (Chapters 5 and 9). In the interest of fairness and completeness, for cases in which experts disagree about the appropriate measure of effect size, this book cites alternative viewpoints.

NEW TO THIS EDITION

This second edition
- Provides updated and more detailed discussions of the univariate effect size measures that were discussed in the first edition
- Adds univariate effect size measures that were not discussed in the first edition

- Adds figures and tables to demonstrate some important concepts graphically
- Adds three chapters on measures of effect sizes in multiple regression, analysis of covariance, and multivariate analysis of variance and other multivariate methods
- Expands coverage of effect size measures for dependent groups
- Expands the discussions of confidence intervals for effect sizes
- Discusses newer robust methods
- Expands the discussions of commercial software and cites more free software
- Adds pedagogical aids to all chapters: introductions, summaries, tips and pitfalls sections, and additional problems
- Adds sections on recommendations where helpful
- Adds a website with data sets, http://www.psypress.com/9780415877695

The usefulness of an estimate of effect size depends on the soundness of the underlying research method and, many believe, also on the features of the underlying statistical analysis; thus, this book discusses many issues involving methodology, psychometrics, and modern data analysis.

INTENDED AUDIENCE

The level and content of this book make it appropriate for use as a supplement for graduate courses in statistics in such fields as psychology, education, the social sciences, business, management, and medicine. The book is also appropriate for use as the text for a graduate course on effect sizes, or a special-topics seminar or independent-reading course in those fields. Because of its broad content and extensive references, the book is also intended to be a valuable resource for professional researchers and data analysts, graduate students who are analyzing data for theses, and advanced undergraduates who are doing research.

To enhance its use as a resource, the book briefly mentions, and provides references for, some topics for which constraint on length does not permit detailed discussion. Some instructors may choose to omit such material.

With regard to the first nine chapters of the book (univariate effect sizes), readers are expected to have knowledge of parametric statistics through factorial analysis of variance as well as some knowledge of chi-squared analysis of contingency tables. Some knowledge of nonparametric analysis in the case of two independent groups (i.e., the Mann–Whitney U test or the equivalent Wilcoxon W_m test) would be helpful, but not essential.

With regard to the final three chapters (multivariate effect sizes), we assume that some readers have only scant familiarity with the elements of multiple regression, analysis of covariance, and multivariate analysis of variance; thus, a brief conceptual overview is provided before discussing effect sizes. Where graduate students are sufficiently prepared in univariate and multivariate statistics, this book can be used as the textbook in an advanced statistics course. Although the book is not introductory with regard to statistics in general, we assume that many readers have little or no prior knowledge of measures of effect size and their estimation.

Chapter 1 includes a brief discussion, with many references, of the controversy about null-hypothesis significance testing. However, the use of appropriate effect sizes and confidence intervals for effect sizes is generally approved by those on either side of this controversy, either for replacing or augmenting testing for statistical significance. We note that the first edition of this book was favorably reviewed by those on either side of this controversy.

Readers should be able to find in this book many kinds of effect sizes that they can knowledgeably apply to many of their sets of data. We attempt to enhance the practicality of the book by the use of worked examples that often involve real data, for which the book provides calculations of estimates of effect sizes that had not previously been made by the original researchers. Finally, in addition to standard commercial software, we often cite free statistical software for special calculations of effect sizes and confidence intervals for them.

Acknowledgments

We are grateful for many insightful recommendations made by the following reviewers: Danica G. Hays, Old Dominion University; Shlomo Sawilowsky, Wayne State University; Aman Yadar, Purdue University; and two anonymous reviewers. Failure to implement any of their recommendations correctly is our fault. We also thank those who advised us on certain topics: Stephan Arndt, Thomas Baguley, Rex B. Kline, Helena C. Kraemer, Scott E. Maxwell, Robert E. McGrath, Robert G. Newcombe, Stephen F. Olejnik, John Ruscio, and Ted Steiner. Julie A. Robbins provided data and a figure. Robert J. McCoy provided assistance with word processing and graphics. Our editor, Debra Riegert, and editorial assistant, Andrea Zekus, provided generous, prompt, and highly professional assistance.

1 Introduction

INTRODUCTION

Simply defined for now, an effect size usually quantifies the degree of difference between or among groups or the strength of association between variables such as a *group-membership* variable and an *outcome* variable. This chapter introduces the general concept of effect sizes in the contexts of null-hypothesis significance testing (NHST), power analysis, and meta-analysis. The main focus of the rest of this book is on effect sizes for the purpose of analyzing the data from a single piece of research. For this purpose, this chapter discusses some assumptions of effect sizes and of the test statistics to which they often relate.

NULL-HYPOTHESIS SIGNIFICANCE TESTING

Much applied research begins with a research hypothesis that states that there is a relationship between two variables or a difference between two parameters, such as means. (In later chapters, we discuss research involving more than two variables or more than two parameters.) One typical form of the research hypothesis is that there is a nonzero correlation between the two variables in the population. Often one variable is a categorical independent variable involving group membership (a *grouping variable*), such as male versus female or Treatment *a* versus Treatment *b*, and the other variable is a continuous dependent variable, such as blood pressure, or score on an attitude scale or on a test of mental health or achievement.

In the case of a grouping variable, there are two customary forms of research hypothesis. The hypothesis may again be stated correlationally, positing a nonzero correlation between group membership and the dependent variable, as is discussed in Chapter 4. More often in this case of a grouping variable, the research hypothesis posits that there is a difference between means in the two populations. Although a researcher may prefer one approach, some readers of a research report may prefer the other. Therefore, a researcher should consider reporting effect sizes from both approaches.

The usual statistical analysis of the results from the kinds of research at hand involves testing a *null hypothesis* (H_0) that conflicts with the research hypothesis typically either by positing that the correlation between the two variables is zero in the population or by positing that there is no difference between the means of the two populations. (Strictly, a null hypothesis may posit any value for a parameter. When the null-hypothesized value corresponds to no effect, such as no difference between population means or zero correlation in the population, the null hypothesis is sometimes called a *nil hypothesis*, about which more is discussed later.)

The t statistic is usually used to test the H_0 against the research hypothesis regarding a difference between the means of two populations. The *significance level* (*p level*) that is attained by a test statistic such as t represents the probability that a result at least as extreme as the obtained result would occur if the H_0 were true. It is very important for applied researchers to recognize that this attained p value is not the probability that the H_0 is wrong, and it does not indicate how wrong H_0 is, the latter goal being a purpose of an effect size. Also, the p value traditionally informs a decision about whether or not to reject H_0, but it does not guide a decision about what further inference to make after rejecting a H_0.

Observe in Equation 1.1 for t for independent groups that the part of the formula that is usually of greatest interest in applied research that uses a familiar scale for the measure of the dependent variable is the numerator, the difference between means. (This difference is a major component of a common estimator of effect size that is discussed in Chapter 3.) However, Equation 1.1 reveals that whether or not t is large enough to attain statistical significance is not merely a function of how large this numerator is, but depends on how large this numerator is relative to the denominator. Equation 1.1 and the nature of division reveal that for any given difference between means an increase in sample sizes will increase the absolute value of t and, thus, decrease the magnitude of p. Therefore, a statistically significant t may indicate a large difference between means or perhaps a less important small difference that has been elevated to the status of statistical significance because the researcher had the resources to use relatively large samples.

Tips and Pitfalls

The lesson here is that the outcome of a t test, or an outcome using another test statistic, that indicates by, say, $p < .05$ that one treatment's result is statistically significantly different from another treatment's result, or that the treatment variable is statistically significantly related to the outcome variable, does not sufficiently indicate how much the groups differ or how strongly the variables are related. The degree of difference between groups and the strength of relationship between variables are matters of effect size. Attaining statistical significance depends on effect size, sample sizes, variances, choice of one-tailed or two-tailed testing, the adopted significance level, and the degree to which assumptions are satisfied.

In applied research it is often very important to estimate how much better a statistically significantly better treatment is. It is not enough to know merely that there is supposedly evidence (e.g., $p < .05$), or supposedly even stronger evidence (e.g., $p < .01$), that there is some unknown degree of difference in mean performance of the two groups. If the difference between two population means is not 0 it can be anywhere from nearly 0 to far from 0. If two treatments are not equally efficacious, the better of the two can be anywhere from slightly better to very much better than the other.

For an example involving the t test, suppose that a researcher were to compare the mean weights of two groups of overweight diabetic people who have undergone random assignment to either weight-reduction program a or b. Often the difference in mean postprogram weights would be tested using the t test of a H_0 that posits that there is no difference in mean weights, μ_a and μ_b, of populations who undertake program *a* or *b* (H_0: $\mu_a - \mu_b = 0$). The independent-groups *t* statistic in this nil-hypothesis case is

$$t = \frac{\bar{Y}_a - \bar{Y}_b}{\left[\dfrac{s_a^2}{n_a} + \dfrac{s_b^2}{n_b}\right]^{1/2}},\tag{1.1}$$

where $\bar{Y}$ values, s^2 values, and *n*s are sample means, variances, and sizes, respectively. Again, if the value of *t* is great enough (positive or negative) to place *t* in the extreme range of values that are improbable to occur if H_0 were true, the researcher will reject H_0 and conclude that it is plausible that there is a difference between the mean weights in the populations.

Tips and Pitfalls
Consider a possible limitation of the aforementioned interpretation of the statistically significant result. What the researcher has apparently discovered is that there is evidence that the difference between mean weights in the populations is not zero. Such information may be of use, especially if the overall costs of the two treatments are the same, but it would often be more informative to have an estimate of what the amount of difference is (an effect size) than merely learning that there is evidence of what it is not (i.e., not 0).

STATISTICALLY SIGNIFYING AND PRACTICAL SIGNIFICANCE

The phrase "statistically significant" can be misleading because synonyms of "significant" in the English language, but not in the language of statistics, are "important" and "large," and we have just observed with the *t* test, and could illustrate with other statistics such as *F* and χ^2, that a statistically significant result may not be a large or important result. "Statistically significant" is best thought of as meaning "statistically signifying." A statistically significant result is signifying that the result is sufficient, by the researcher's adopted standard of required evidence against H_0 (say, adopted significance level $\alpha < .05$), to justify rejecting H_0. There are possible substitutes for the phrase "statistically significant," such as "result (or difference) not likely attributable to chance," "difference beyond a reasonable doubt," "apparently truly (or really or convincingly) different," and "apparently real difference of as yet unknown magnitude."

A medical example of a statistically significant result that would not be practically significant in the sense of *clinical significance* would be a statistically significant lowering of weight or blood pressure that is too small to lower risk of disease importantly. Also, a statistically significant difference between a standard treatment and a placebo is less clinically significant than one of the same magnitude between a standard treatment and a new treatment. A psychotherapeutic example would be a statistically significant lowering of scores on a test of depression that is insufficient to be reflected in the clients' behaviors or self-reports of well-being. Another example would be a statistically significant difference between schoolgirls and schoolboys that is not large enough to justify a change in educational practice (*educational insignificance*). Thus, a result that attains a researcher's standard for "significance" may not attain a practitioner's standard of significance.

Bloom, Hill, Black, and Lipsey (2008) and Hill, Bloom, Black, and Lipsey (2008) discussed the use of benchmarks that proceed from effect sizes to assess the practical significance of educational interventions. Their approach emphasizes that it is not the mere numerical value of an effect size that is of importance but how such a value compares to important benchmarks in a field. In clinical research, one definition of a practically significant difference is the smallest amount of benefit that a treatment would have to provide to justify all costs, including risks, of the treatment, the benefit being determined by the patient. Matsumoto, Grissom, and Dinnel (2001) reported on the *cultural significance* of differences between Japan and the United States in terms of effect sizes involving mean differences.

Onwuegbuzie, Levin, and Leech (2003) recommended, where appropriate, that practical significance be conveyed in terms of *economic significance*. For example, when reporting the results of a successful treatment for improving the reading level of learning-disabled children, in addition to a p level and an estimate of a traditional effect size the researcher should report the estimated annual monetary savings per treated child with respect to reduced cost of special education and other costs of remedial instruction. Another example is a report stating that for every dollar a state spends on education (education being a "treatment" or "intervention") in a state university, the state's return benefit is eventually Y dollars ($Y > 1$). Harris (2009) proposed as a measure of educational significance the ratio of an effect size and the monetary cost of the intervention that brings about that effect size. In this proposal, to be considered large such a ratio must be at least as large as the largest such ratio for a competing intervention.

In clinical research the focus is often on the effect size for a treatment that is intended to reduce a risk factor for disease, such as lowering blood pressure or lowering cholesterol levels. However, the relative effect sizes of competing treatments with regard to a risk factor for a disease may not predict the treatments' relative effects on the ultimate outcomes, such as rate of mortality, because of possibly different side effects associated with the competing treatments. This is a matter of *net clinical benefit*. Similarly, in psychotherapeutic research the focus of estimation of effect size may be on competing treatments to reduce a risk factor such as suicidal thoughts, whereas the ultimate interest should be elsewhere, that is, effect sizes of competing treatments with regard to suicide itself in this case.

More is written about practical significance throughout this book, including the fact that the extent of practical significance is not always reflected by the magnitude of an effect size. The quality of a judgment about the practical significance of a result is enhanced by expertise in the area of research. Although effect size, a broad definition of which is discussed in the next section, is not synonymous with practical significance, knowledge of a result's effect size can inform a subjective judgment about practical significance.

DEFINITION, CHARACTERISTICS, AND USES OF EFFECT SIZES

We assume for now the case of the typical null hypothesis that implies that there is no effect or no relationship between variables; for example, a null hypothesis that states that there is no difference between means of populations or that the correlation between variables in the population is zero. Whereas a test of statistical significance is traditionally used to provide evidence (attained p level) that a null hypothesis is wrong, an effect size (ES) measures the degree to which such a null hypothesis is wrong (if it is wrong). Because of its pervasive use and usefulness, we use the name *effect size* for all such measures that are discussed in this book. Many effect size measures involve some form of correlation (Chapters 4 and 10) or its square (Chapters 4, 6, 7, 10, and 12), some form of standardized difference between means (Chapters 3, 6, 7, 11, and 12), or the degree of overlap of distributions (Chapter 5), but many measures that will be discussed do not fit into these categories. Again, we use the label effect size for measures of the degree to which results differ from what is implied for them by a typical null hypothesis.

Often the relationship between the numerical value of a test statistic (TS) and an estimator of ES is $ES_{est} = TS/f(N)$, where f(N) is some function of total sample size, such as degrees of freedom. Specific forms of this equation are available for many test statistics, including t, F, and χ^2, so that reported test statistics can be approximately converted to indirect estimates of effect size by a reader of a research report or a meta-analyst without access to the raw data that would be required to estimate an effect size directly. However, researchers who work with their own raw data (called *primary researchers*) and who use this book can estimate effect sizes directly so they do not need to use an approximate conversion equation to convert a value of the test statistic to an estimate of effect size.

Although some function of sample size typically appears in equations for estimators of effect sizes (explicitly, or implicitly in their denominators), these functions of sample sizes merely serve to compensate for the effect of sample size elsewhere in the equation, typically the numerator. However, sample sizes can influence the bias (often slight) of estimators in some cases. (Also, smaller sample size results in greater sampling variability of an estimator of effect size, which can increase the difference between the estimated effect size and the actual effect size in the population.) In various published literatures, studies with larger sample sizes tend to be associated with lower estimated effect sizes because attaining a statistically significant result is often a prerequisite for publication and the smaller a sample's effect size the larger the sample that is needed to attain statistical significance (Slavin & Smith, 2009).

Merely reporting an effect size without properly interpreting it adds little to a report of research. In their study of articles that appeared in 10 journals that publish educational research, Alhija and Levy (2009) reported that different conclusions could often be reached if reported effect sizes had been interpreted. The American Educational Research Association recommends including an estimate and interpretation of effect size for each important inferential statistic that is reported.

SOME FACTORS INFLUENCING EFFECT SIZES

Some important factors that influence estimates of effect size are (a) the research design, (b) which of a variety of possibly conflicting effect sizes a researcher chooses to report, (c) violations of assumptions such as equal variances and normality, and (d) the reliability of the scores on the dependent variable. Other influential factors include the nature of the participants and their variability (e.g., effect size might be larger when participants come from populations that are homogeneous with regard to background variables), the choice of measure of the dependent variable (alternative measures may differ in their reliability [Chapter 4] and in their sensitivity to the effect of the independent variable), and the amount of time between administration of a treatment and the collection of the data from which an effect size is calculated. The magnitudes of effect sizes for gender differences in mathematics vary depending on the domain of mathematics that is being tested and the form of the test (e.g., multiple-choice or open-ended; Liu & Wilson, 2009).

Sometimes a clinical study is stopped ahead of schedule because the results appear to be obviously favorable for a new treatment for a serious disease. In this case an estimate of effect size at that point is likely to be greater than it would have been if the study had proceeded to its scheduled end.

Some estimators of effect size are biased to an extent that depends on sample size, as is observed throughout this book. Also, in some areas of research effect sizes tend to be smaller in later research than in earlier research (*effect size decline*). Some of the possible reasons for such a decline relate to sample size and *publication bias* and *outcome reporting bias*, which are, respectively, the disinclination of many editors of journals to publish, and the disinclination of many researchers to submit, reports of research whose results do not attain statistical significance. Larger estimates of effect size in the distribution of possible sample effect sizes will be required to attain statistical significance in an earlier study than in a later study if the former uses smaller samples. In this case earlier published effect size estimates will be relatively large for a particular area of research whereas later published studies will be more likely to include relatively small estimates of effect size.

Another possible related reason for effect size decline over time is the statistical phenomenon called "regression to the mean," whereby an extreme sample value of a variable is likely to be followed by a less extreme sample value. The possible sequence of events is as follows. Because of sampling variability (greater with a smaller sample) a given sample is likely to produce an estimate of effect size that is greater or smaller than the population effect size. Assume the case in which it is a greater sample effect size that is obtained (an overestimate). The greater a sample effect size the more likely that the researcher will submit, and the editor will accept, for publication a report of that effect size. The greater the sample effect size the more likely that it is overestimating the population effect size and the more likely that a second independent sample will yield a less extreme estimate.

Staines and Cleland (2007) discussed additional factors that can possibly influence the size of effect, including partial-sample bias, researcher-allegiance bias, and wait-list-control-group bias. Such biases are especially plausible in clinical research.

A *partial-sample bias* (or bias from *differential attrition*) occurs when participants who drop out of a study would have contributed results that are different from the results from remaining participants. *Researcher-allegiance bias* occurs when a researcher favors one of the treatments that are being compared and the favoritism results in the preferred treatment being given an unintended advantage in the conduct of the study. For example, compared to the not-favored treatment, a favored treatment may be administered more effectively by more experienced and more motivated practitioners of that treatment.

A *wait-list-control-group bias* can occur in comparative psychotherapeutic studies in which those of the volunteers who are randomly assigned to treatment receive treatment promptly whereas those who are randomly assigned to be controls have to wait before being treated so that nontreatment data can be collected from them for the purpose of comparison with data from those who have already been treated. Patients who are treated promptly have an opportunity to improve not only from any direct benefits of treatment but also from any *placebo effect* that they gain from their expectation that they will get better because they are receiving professional help. On the other hand, members of the waiting control group not only receive no treatment prior to the collection of outcome data but they may well have a negative expectancy about their condition because they are disappointed by this fact, perhaps to the point of being demoralized and having their condition deteriorate. Negative expectancy and anxiety about possible risks from treatment, such as drugs or surgery, can cause some people to experience adverse effects. Such an experience is called a *nocebo effect*.

Effect sizes for treatments versus control comparison groups may be reduced to the extent that receipt of treatment is perceived as probable by participants in control groups. Particularly, signing an informed-consent form can enhance the perceived probability of treatment and, therefore, enhance a placebo effect in such comparison groups. Lipman (2008a) provided a concise discussion of factors that can influence the extent of a medical placebo effect. In any study that estimates an effect size for treatment versus control, or compares two or more such effect sizes, the strength of the placebo(s) must be considered when interpreting the effect size(s). Also, a nocebo effect can influence an effect size in a study in which a nocebo effect is greater for one treatment than another.

In applied experimental research the usefulness of an estimate of effect size depends on the *external validity* of the results, which is the generalizability of the results to the kind of population to which the researcher intended to apply the results. For example, in *randomized clinical trials* (*RCTs*, more generally *randomized controlled trials* or *experimental designs*), research reports should clearly describe such factors as the research setting, criteria for inclusion and exclusion for forming the pool of prospective participants from which random assignment was made, demographics and clinically relevant baseline characteristics of the participants, nature of any background treatment other than the treatment on which the experiment is based, strength and duration of the treatment, timing of the measurement of the outcome (follow-up?), attrition or removal of participants, adverse effects, reliability of the scores (Chapter 4), and clinical relevance of the measure of the dependent variable in cases in which they are indirect measures of the patient's problem. Also relevant are the levels of expertise of those who are administering the treatment(s). (In RCTs, in contrast with *observational studies* that are discussed in Chapter 8, participants are randomly assigned to conditions [e.g., treatment, control, placebo] to reduce the chance that groups will differ at baseline with respect to variables that might influence the results [*confounding variables*, e.g., gender, age] other than the variable(s) that the researcher intends to vary [*independent variables*].)

There may be important differences between characteristics of the participants in research and the people to whom the results of research are to be applied later (e.g., health and age in clinical research). Therefore, even the results of research that used random assignment should be said to provide evidence of the *efficacy* of treatments, not direct evidence of the *effectiveness* of treatments. Efficacy is the potential for effectiveness of a treatment in the realm of clinical practice because of promising results for that treatment in earlier clinical research. The effectiveness of a treatment is a matter of its success in actual applied settings (e.g., clinical settings). For example, many medical journals endorse a common set of standards of quality for RCTs known by the acronym *CONSORT* (*Consolidated Standards of Reporting Trials*). These standards emphasize the *internal validity* of a clinical trial, which addresses the issue of whether the results are correctly attributable to the treatment variable because of control of extraneous variables that could have influenced the results. The greatest benefit of random assignment is to bolster internal validity. Also, nonrandom attrition of participants can undo the initial equality of samples with respect to relevant variables in research with random assignment.

Tips and Pitfalls
Methods sections of reports of experimental studies should go beyond merely stating that participants were randomly assigned to groups because what happens to participants between the time of their random assignment and the collection of data can greatly influence the effect sizes and conclusions from the study. Medical researchers are setting a good example of becoming very much aware of this issue. Reports of RCTs increasingly have come to distinguish among three criteria for the inclusion or exclusion of data. First, there is the controversial *intent-to-treat* (or *intention-to-treat*), in which the data from all those were assigned to a condition are to be included in the analysis whether or not they received full treatment or any treatment. Second, there is the *per-protocol* criterion, in which only data from those who participated fully are included. Third, there is *modified intent-to-treat*, in which data from all patients assigned to a condition are to be considered for inclusion, whether or not the patients received treatment, but some data are to be excluded based on a predetermined criterion such as postrandomization discovery of a preexisting disease in a patient other than the disease targeted by the treatment. Fidler, Faulkner, and Cumming (2008) discussed estimation of effect sizes and construction of confidence intervals for effect sizes for intention-to-treat and per-protocol analyses.

The best way to compare treatments is in a head-to-head comparison in an experiment. However, in some areas of research, such as those that study the efficacy of a drug for attention-deficit hyperactivity disorder, direct comparison of alternative treatments is infrequent. Instead the typical study compares a drug with a placebo. In such cases one can compare the (a) effect sizes from experiments that involved drug *a* and a placebo and (b) effect sizes from experiments that involved drug *b* and a placebo. Such is one of the uses of effect sizes, but the usefulness of these comparisons depends on the essential features of the studies of drug *a* and drug *b* being comparable. The comparison of effect sizes can be undertaken using meta-analysis, which is discussed later in this chapter. To make an inference about the optimal or sufficient magnitude of a treatment, such as duration of therapy or dose of a drug, primary researchers can compare the estimates of effect size at each level of magnitude of the treatment.

Any effect size that is chosen from possible alternatives should be technically appropriate while being comprehensible to policy makers, such as educational or health officials who want to apply the results to some practical problem, and be minimally influenced by factors other than the studied independent variables. Such an ideal should be sought, but, as can be learned from the interpretations of various effect sizes in this book, very difficult to realize fully. For a review of the history of effect sizes refer to Huberty (2002).

CONTROVERSY ABOUT NULL-HYPOTHESIS SIGNIFICANCE TESTING

It can be argued that readers of a report of applied research that involves control or placebo groups, or that involves treatments whose costs are different, have a right to be informed of estimates of effect sizes. Some may even argue that not reporting such estimates in an understandable manner to those who apply the results of research in such cases (e.g., educators, health officials, managers of trainee programs, clinicians, governmental officials) is a kind of withholding of evidence. Indeed, the reporting of effect sizes has been likened to telling "the truth, the whole truth, and nothing but the truth" (Zakzanis, 2001). Increasingly, editors of journals that publish research are recommending, or requiring (but not necessarily enforcing), the reporting of estimates of effect sizes. For example, the American Psychological Association and the American Educational Research Association recommend, and the *Journal of Educational and Psychological Measurement* and at least 22 other journals as of the time of this writing require, the reporting of such estimates.

Tips and Pitfalls

There is disagreement regarding when estimates of effect sizes should be reported. On the one hand is the view that traditional NHST is meaningless because no nil hypothesis (i.e., no difference or zero correlation) can be literally true (at least for populations of infinite size measured on continuous variables). For example, according to this view no two or more population means can be exactly equal to all decimal places. (Consult Mulaik, Raju, & Harshman, 1997, for an opposing view.) Therefore, from this point of view that implies that no effect size can be exactly zero, the task of a researcher is to estimate the size of this "obviously" nonzero effect. Those who are in this camp believe that not reporting an effect size when the researcher concludes that the results are statistically "insignificant" is equivalent to treating such effect sizes as if they were known to be equal to zero when in fact they are not known to be equal to zero. (From the review of the magnitudes of many obtained effect sizes by Lipsey and Wilson [1993], Hunter and Schmidt [2004] estimated that 99.3% of the null-hypothesized 0 differences from research on psychological treatments are wrong [although it is possible that this percentage is somewhat positively biased].) The opposite opinion is that significance testing is paramount and that effect sizes are to be reported only when results are found to be statistically significant. For further discussions relating to this debate consult Anderson, Burnham, and Thompson (2000), Barnette and McLean (1999), Browne (2010), Carver (1978), Cortina and Landis (in press), Fan (2001), Hedges and Olkin (1985), Howard et al., (2009a,b), Hunter and Schmidt (1990), Knapp (2003), Knapp and Sawilowsky (2001), Levin and Robinson (2003), Onwuegbuzie and Levin (2003, 2005), Roberts and Henson (2003), Robinson and Levin (1997), Rosenthal, Rosnow, and Rubin (2000), Rosnow and Rosenthal (1989), Sawilowsky (2003a, 2003b, 2007a), Sawilowsky and Yoon (2002), Snyder and Lawson (1993), Staines and Cleland (2007), Thompson (1996, 2007), Vacha-Haase and Thompson (2004), and the articles in volume 33 (2004) of the *Journal of Economics*.

As we discuss in Chapters 3 and 6, many estimators of effect size tend to overestimate effect sizes in the population, overestimation that is called *positive* or *upward bias*. A major question that is debated is whether or not this upward bias of estimators of effect size is large enough (it is often very small except when sample sizes are very small) so that the reporting of a bias-based nonzero estimate of effect size will seriously inflate the overall estimate of effect size in a field of study when the null hypothesis is true (i.e., there is actually zero effect in the population) and the results are statistically insignificant. Those who are not concerned about such bias urge the reporting of all effect sizes, statistically significant or not significant, to improve the accuracy of meta-analyses. Their reasoning is that such reporting will avoid the problem of inflating overall estimates of effect size in the literature that would result from not including the smaller effect sizes that arise from primary studies whose results did not attain statistical significance.

Some are of the opinion that effect sizes are more important in applied research, in which one may be interested in whether or not the effect size is estimated to be large enough to be of practical use. In contrast, in theoretical research one may only be interested in whether or not results support a theory's prediction, say, for example, that mean a will be greater than mean b. In cases in which it is obvious that a traditional null hypothesis that posits a value of 0 for a parameter is wrong the research should address the question of how far from 0 the parameter is by estimating an effect size. For example, it is obvious that in the general population the size of children's vocabularies is positively correlated with their age ($r_{pop} > 0$), so research in that area would most usefully focus on constructing a confidence interval for the effect size, r_{pop}, as is discussed in Chapter 4. In cases in which a parameter is obviously not zero, one can also test a null hypothesis that posits that the parameter is equal to some specified nonzero value or conduct equivalence testing as is discussed in Chapters 2, 5, and 8.

PURPOSE OF THIS BOOK

It is not necessary for this book to discuss the controversy about NHST further because the purpose of this book is to inform readers about a variety of measures of effect size and their proper applications and limitations. Regardless of one's position about NHST, most researchers agree that estimates of effect size are often important for interpreting and reporting results. One reason that a variety of effect size measures is needed is that different kinds of measures are appropriate depending on whether variables are scaled categorically, ordinally, or continuously (and also sometimes depending on certain characteristics of the sampling method, and the research design and purpose, that are discussed where pertinent in later chapters). The results from a given study often lend themselves to more than one type of measure of effect size. These different measures can sometimes provide very different, even conflicting, perspectives on the results. Consumers of the results of research, including editors of journals, those in the news media who convey results to the public, and patients who are giving supposedly informed consent to treatment, often need to be made aware of the results in terms of alternative measures of effect sizes to guard against the possibility that biased or unwitting researchers have used a measure that makes a treatment appear to be more effective than another measure would have done. Some of the topics in Chapter 8 exemplify this issue particularly well. Also, alternative measures should be considered when the statistical assumptions of traditional measures are not satisfied.

Data sets can have complex characteristics. For example, traditionally researchers have focused on the effects of independent variables on just one characteristic of distributions of data, their centers, such as their means or medians, representing the effect on the typical (average) participant. However, a treatment can also have an effect on aspects of a distribution other than its center, such as its tails (Chapter 5). Treatment can have an effect on the center of a distribution and/or the variability around that center. For example, consider a treatment that increases the scores of some experimental-group participants and decreases the scores of others in that group, a *treatment × subject interaction*. The result is that the variability of the experimental group's distribution will be larger or smaller (may be greatly so) than the variability of the control or comparison group's distribution. Whether there is an increase or decrease in variability of the experimental group's distribution depends on whether it is the higher- or lower-performing participants who are improved or worsened by the treatment. In such cases the centers of the two distributions may be nearly the same whereas the treatment in fact has had an effect on the tails of a distribution. However, it is quite likely that a treatment will have an effect on both the center and the variability of a distribution because it is common to find that distributions that have higher means than other distributions also have the greater variabilities.

As is demonstrated in later examples in this book, by applying a variety of appropriate estimates of measures of effect size to the same set of data, researchers and readers of their reports can gain a broader perspective on the effects of an independent variable. In some later examples we observe that examination of estimates of different kinds of measures of effect size can greatly alter one's interpretation of results and of their importance. Also, any appropriate estimate of effect size that a researcher has calculated must be reported in order to guard against a biased interpretation of the results. However, we acknowledge, as will be observed from time to time in this book, that there can be disagreement among experts about the appropriate measure of effect size for certain kinds of data.

There are several excellent books that discuss effect sizes. Although this book cites this work when relevant, most of these books treat the topic in a different context (power analysis or meta-analysis) and for a purpose that is different from the purpose of this book, as we briefly discuss in the next two sections of this chapter.

POWER ANALYSIS

Some books consider effect sizes in the context of estimation of statistical power for determining needed sample sizes for planned research (Cohen, 1988; Kraemer & Thiemann, 1987; Murphy & Myors, 2008). The *power* of a statistical test is the probability that use of the test will lead to rejection of a false H_0. Statistical power decreases as population effect size decreases and increases as sample size increases, so deciding the minimum effect size that one is interested in having one's research detect is very important for researchers who are planning research. Books on power analysis are very useful for planning research, as they take into account power-determining factors such as the magnitude of effect that the research is intended to detect, the researcher's adopted alpha level, likely variances (influenced by factors that are discussed in this book such as the research design and the reliability of the scores), and maximum available sample sizes. (The use of such factors, including expected effect size, to estimate needed sample sizes is an example of what is called a *frequentist* approach. Discussion of an alternative *Bayesian* approach to estimating needed sample size can be found in Pezeshk, Maroufy, and Gittens [2009].)

The report by the American Psychological Association's Task Force on Statistical Inference urged researchers to report obtained estimates of effect sizes to facilitate future power analyses in a researcher's field of interest (Wilkinson & APA Task Force on Statistical Inference, 1999). (However, an appropriate kind of effect size for power analysis may sometimes not be an appropriate kind of effect size for data analysis [Feingold, 2009; Raudenbush & Liu, 2001].) Free applets for calculating power and estimating needed sample sizes for planned research are available, courtesy of Russell Lenth (2006), at http://www.stat.iowa.edu/~rlenth/Power/.

REPLICATION AND META-ANALYSIS

A single study is rarely definitive. Several books cover estimation of effect sizes in the context of *meta-analysis*. Meta-analytic methods are procedures for quantitatively summarizing the effect sizes from a set of related research studies in a specific area of research (replicated, i.e., repeated, studies). "Meta" in this context means "beyond" or "more comprehensive." Synonyms for meta-analyzing such sets of effect sizes include *quantitatively integrating, combining, synthesizing*, or *cumulating* them. Again, each individual study in the set of meta-analyzed studies is called primary research. In many applied areas, such as medical practice, effect sizes from meta-analyses are becoming major determinants of the treatments that are considered to constitute the *best evidence-based practice*.

Replicating *studies* means replicating methods, but does not necessarily mean obtaining replicated *results*, as we discuss later with regard to what are called moderator variables. Ioannidis (2005) discussed many factors that can influence the probability that a finding from a single study is true (critique by Goodman & Greenland, 2007). Vickers' (2006, 2008a) discussions of errors in recording and entering data further support the need for replication of important studies. Schmidt (2009) discussed different meanings and implementations of replication and offered recommendations.

Among other procedures, an early form of meta-analysis includes testing for homogeneity (i.e., equality) of the estimates of effect size from each primary study using the Q statistic or more recently proposed alternatives, such as I^2 (Borenstein et al., 2009). In the traditional meta-analytic method, if the estimated effect sizes from the primary (i.e., underlying) studies are declared to be homogeneous, they are averaged (weighting each primary estimate by the inverse of its sampling variance) to make the best estimate of the effect size in the population. If the primary estimates are declared to be heterogeneous (unequal), the meta-analyst in this type of meta-analysis then tests for *moderator variables* that may be responsible for the varying effect sizes. Moderator variables may be found to be varying characteristics of the participants across the primary studies (e.g., gender, age, ethnicity, educational level, or severity of illness) or varying kinds of designs across the primary studies (e.g., experimental versus nonexperimental designs or between-groups versus within-groups designs). Hunter and Schmidt (2004) generally opposed testing for homogeneity of effect sizes (also consult Schmidt, Oh, and Hayes, 2009). Construction of confidence intervals for the population effect size estimated from a meta-analysis can also be very informative, but problematic methods of meta-analysis may result in greatly overstated confidence levels (Bonett, 2009a; Schmidt et al., 2009). The construction of confidence intervals from primary research is discussed in Chapter 2 and thereafter throughout this book.

Among other factors, the accuracy of a meta-analysis depends on the representativeness of the primary studies on which it is based. Meta-analyses in many areas may overestimate effect size because some studies with effect sizes that are truly nonzero, but still too small to attain statistical significance, will have been excluded from the literature because of publication bias (Ferguson & Brannick, in press) and outcome reporting bias. Consult Borenstein et al. (2009) for further discussion.

Tips and Pitfalls

To accommodate readers of reports of primary research, especially readers who are meta-analysts, authors of such reports should not only include an estimate of effect size but also provide all of the summary statistics (e.g., means and variances in many cases) that readers may need to be able to calculate their preferred estimators of effect size, which may not be the type that was reported. Reporting effect sizes enables more informative comparison of results with earlier reported results and facilitates any later meta-analysis of such results. Meta-analyses that use previously reported effect sizes that had been directly calculated by primary researchers on their raw data will be more accurate than those that are based on effect sizes that had to be retrospectively estimated by meta-analysts using approximately accurate equations to convert the primary studies' reported test statistics to estimates of effect size. Effect sizes are often not reported in older articles or in articles that are published in journals that do not strictly require such reporting, nor are raw data typically conveniently available to meta-analysts. Therefore, as previously mentioned, books on meta-analytic methods include equations for converting previously reported test statistics into individual estimates of effect size that meta-analysts can then average.

For those who do not have access to the raw data, Walker (2005) provided IBM SPSS syntax for calculating many estimates of effect sizes for the univariate and multivariate cases of two independent groups either from test statistics (e.g., t) or from descriptive statistics. Again, when raw data are available, more accurate estimation of effect sizes can be made using the equations in this book.

Consider a set of primary studies in each one of which the dependent variable is some measure of mental health and the independent variable is membership in either a treated group or a control group. Most such studies yield a moderate value for estimated effect size (i.e., therapy usually seems to help, at least moderately), some yield a high or low positive value (i.e., therapy seems to help very much or very little), and a very small number of studies yield a negative value for the effect size, indicating possible harm from the therapy. Again, no one piece of primary research is necessarily definitive in its findings because of sampling variability and the previously discussed possibly moderating variables that vary among the individual studies, factors such as the nature of the therapy, diagnostic and demographic characteristics of the participants across the studies, kind of test of mental health, and characteristics of the therapists. An early example of a meta-analysis is the averaging of the effect size estimates from many such studies by Smith and Glass (1977). Consult Staines and Cleland (2007) for a discussion of possible biases of underestimation and overestimation of effect sizes in primary and meta-analytic studies.

Because the focus of this book is on direct estimation of effect sizes from the raw data of a primary research study, there will only be occasional mention of meta-analysis in later chapters. There are several approaches to meta-analytic methods.

Books that cover these methods include those by Borenstein et al. (2009) and Hunter and Schmidt (2004). The journal *Research Synthesis Methods* is devoted to methodology in meta-analysis and related topics.

ASSUMPTIONS OF TEST STATISTICS AND EFFECT SIZES

When statisticians create a new test statistic or measure of effect size they often do so for populations that have certain characteristics, which are called *assumptions*. For the *t* test, *F* test, and some common examples of effect sizes, two of these assumptions are that the populations from which the samples are drawn are normally distributed and have equal variances. The latter assumption is called *homogeneity of variance* or *homoscedasticity* (the latter from Greek words for "same" and "scattered"). When data come from populations with unequal variances this violation of homoscedasticity is called *heterogeneity of variance* or *heteroscedasticity*. When researchers use statistical tests whose developers assumed homoscedasticity, the researchers are likely not strictly holding this assumption but are assuming that the populations do not differ enough in their variances to invalidate the results of the test. However, many statistical tests may be more sensitive to seemingly small violations of assumptions than researchers realize. Throughout this book we observe how violation of assumptions can affect estimation and interpretation of effect sizes, and we discuss some alternative methods that accommodate such violations. There is a trend toward the use of modern methods that are more *robust* against violation of assumptions. (However, we observe later in this book that interpretation of inferential statistics that involve robust alternatives to the mean and variance can sometimes be problematic.)

Tips and Pitfalls

Often a researcher asserts that an effect size that involves the degree of difference between two means (Chapter 3) is significantly different from zero because significance was attained when comparing the two means by a *t* test. However, sufficient nonnormality and heteroscedasticity can result in the shape of the actual sampling distribution of the test statistic departing sufficiently from the theoretical sampling distribution of *t* (or *F*) so that, unbeknownst to the researcher, the actual *p* value for the result is importantly different from the *p* value that is observed in a printout. Even slight nonnormality can lower statistical power greatly (e.g., Wilcox, 2008a), and nonnormality can also inflate the probability of rejecting a true null hypothesis (Type I error) (Keselman, Algina, Lix, Wilcox, & Deering, 2008). Also, we observe in Chapter 3 that the usual interpretation of a widely used effect size involving the difference between two means is invalid under nonnormality.

It is well known that the rate of Type I error for the *t* test and *F* test is increased in the case of unequal sample sizes if sample sizes and variances of populations are negatively related, regardless of normality and sample sizes (e.g., Keselman et al., 2008). Also, even if sample sizes are equal and there is normality, when samples are small enough (maybe each $n \leq 7$), heteroscedasticity can inflate the rate of Type I error for the independent-groups t test beyond what is indicated by the observed p value (Ramsey, 1980; also consult Algina, Oshima, & Lin, 1994).

Tips and Pitfalls

Traditionally, many researchers have not been concerned about heteroscedasticity unless ratios of *sample* variances exceeded 3, but even under slight nonnormality a ratio of variances in the *population* as low as 1.5 can cause the t test to begin to falter. In this case a ratio of variances in the population that is equal to 1.5 can result in an apparent $p < .05$ masking an actual $p = .075$ for the t test (Reed & Stark, 2004). Considering the relatively low power of traditional tests of homoscedasticity (Grissom, 2000), a ratio of variances in the population that is equal to 1.5 would likely be very difficult to detect.

For references and further discussions of the consequences of, and solutions to, violation of assumptions on t testing and F testing, consult Sawilowsky (2002), Wilcox (2005a), and Wilcox and Keselman (2003). When incorrect conclusions from research jeopardize public health and safety, a data analyst has a special responsibility to deal with statistical assumptions correctly. Ramsey and Ramsey (2007) discussed the relative conservativeness of robust tests of equality of two variances.

Christensen (2005) noted that if results lead to rejection of a nil hypothesis it could be that the nil hypothesis is indeed false or it could mean only that one or more assumptions have been violated. If the latter were the case some would argue that there would thereby be insufficient evidence that an effect size involving the difference between two means is different from zero. Christensen also discussed how in the analysis of variance very small values of F, which are usually ignored by researchers, or large values of F, sometimes can be attributed to heteroscedasticity or other problems with the data.

Huberty's (2002) article on the history of effect sizes noted that heteroscedasticity is common but has been given insufficient attention in discussions of effect sizes. This book attempts to redress this shortcoming. The fact that nonnormality and heteroscedasticity can affect estimation and interpretation of effect sizes is of concern and discussed throughout this book because real data often exhibit such characteristics, as is documented in the next section.

Independence of scores is the very important assumption that the probability of each score in a group is not conditional on any other score in the group. For example, in research that compares the effectiveness of methods of teaching in elementary school, a disruptive child in a classroom will likely have a low score on the test of achievement that is the measure of the dependent variable and will also likely cause a lowering of scores of some other children in the classroom. In general, individual scores are less likely to be independent when treatment is administered to a group jointly instead of individually. Examples of the use of such jointly treated groups include research on group therapy, social interaction, classrooms or sets of two or more learners, and groups of job trainees. Stevens (2009) provided extensive discussion of the seriousness of violation of this assumption, including the facts that random sampling and random assignment do not eliminate the problem. In the case of tests for differences between or among independent groups, such as the between-groups t or F tests, it is also assumed that the scores in one group are independent of (i.e., not conditional on) the scores in any other group, as is discussed in Chapter 2. Violation of independence of scores can greatly inflate the rate of Type I error (e.g., consult Table 6.1 on p. 220 in Stevens) and distort estimates of effect sizes by influencing variances.

VIOLATIONS OF ASSUMPTIONS SUGGESTED BY REAL DATA

Unfortunately, violations of assumptions are commonly suggested by real data and often in combinations of violations. Micceri (1989) presented many examples of nonnormal data, reporting that only approximately 3% of data in educational and psychological research have the appearance of near-symmetry and light tails as in a normal distribution. Wilcox (1996) illustrated how two distributions can appear to be normal and appear to have very similar variances when in fact they have very different variances, even a ratio of variances greater than 10 to 1. Distributions of biomedical and ecological data have often been described as lumpy, irregular, skewed, and heavy-tailed. Because many measures of dependent variables in behavioral and biomedical research allow only positive values, positive skew, which is discussed later, is likely.

Tests of normality differ in various ways, including the characteristics of normality that they address and the manner in which they measure these characteristics. Seir (2002) evaluated the performances of 10 tests of normality with respect to their power and rate of Type I error for a wide range of sample sizes and distributions. Thadewald and Büning (2007) reported comparisons of power of various tests of normality depending on the nature of the departure from normality. Coin (2007) reported that many tests of normality were insensitive to nonnormal symmetrical distributions.

In a review of the literature Grissom (2000) noted that there are theoretical reasons to expect, and empirical results to document, likely heteroscedasticity throughout various areas of research. When raw data that are amounts or counts have some zeros (such as the number of alcoholic drinks consumed by some patients during an alcoholism rehabilitation program) group means and variances are often positively related (e.g., Sawilowsky, 2002). Therefore, distributions for samples with larger means often have larger variances than those for samples with smaller means, resulting in the possibility of heteroscedasticity. Again, homoscedasticity and heteroscedasticity are characteristics of populations, not samples, but these characteristics may not be accurately reflected by comparison of variances of samples taken from those populations because the sampling variability of variances is high. Refer to Sawilowsky for a discussion of the implications of the relationship between means and variances, including citations of an opposing view.

Sample distributions with greater *positive skew* tend to have the larger means and variances, again suggesting possible heteroscedasticity. Positive skew roughly means that a distribution is not symmetrically shaped because its right tail is more extensive than its left tail, the opposite being true for *negative skew*. Examples of positive skew include distributions of data from studies of difference thresholds (sensitivity to a change in a stimulus), reaction time, latency of response, time to complete a task, income, length of hospital stay, and galvanic skin response (emotional palm sweating). Malgady (2007) proposed an effect size for skew that is based on the value of skew relative to its maximum possible value, so this effect size ranges from 0 to 1.

Tips and Pitfalls
The problem of heteroscedasticity is often addressed by transforming the data to logarithms in an attempt to reduce the relationship between the means and variances. It would be beyond the scope of this book to discuss the possible failure of results from transformed data to apply to the original data; results such as p levels, confidence levels, effect sizes (Ruscio, 2008a), and inferences about main effects and interaction effects.

There are reasons for expecting heteroscedasticity in data from research on the efficacy of a treatment. First, a treatment may be more beneficial for some participants than for others, or even harmful for others. If this variability of responsiveness to treatment differs from treatment group a to treatment group b because of the natures of the treatments that are being compared, heteroscedasticity may result. For example, Lambert and Bergin (1994) found that there is deterioration in some patients in psychotherapy, usually more so in treated groups than in control groups. Mohr (1995) cited negative outcomes from therapy for some adults with psychosis. Also, some therapies may increase the violence of certain kinds of offenders (Rice, 1997).

Second, suppose that the measure of the dependent variable does not sufficiently cover the range of the underlying variable that it is supposed to be measuring (the *latent variable*). For example, a paper-and-pencil test of depression may not be covering the full range of depression that can actually occur in depressives. In this case a ceiling or floor effect can produce a greater reduction of variabilities within those groups whose treatments most greatly decrease or increase their scores.

A *ceiling effect* occurs when the highest score obtainable on a measure of the dependent variable does not represent the highest possible standing with respect to the latent (underlying) variable. For example, a classroom test is supposed to measure the latent variable of students' knowledge, but if the test is too easy a student who scores 100% may not have as much knowledge of the material as is possible, and another student who scores 100% may have even greater knowledge that the easy test does not enable that student to demonstrate. A *floor effect* occurs when the lowest score obtainable on a measure of the dependent variable does not represent the lowest possible standing with respect to the latent variable. For example, a screening test for memory disorder may be so difficult for the participants that among those memory-impaired patients who score 0 on the test there may be some who actually have even a poorer memory than the others who scored 0, but who cannot exhibit their poorer memory because scores below 0 are not possible. In addition to lowering an estimate of effect size, a ceiling effect can inflate the rate of Type I error.

Heteroscedasticity can also result from *outliers*, which are typically defined roughly as extremely atypically high or low scores. Outliers may merely reflect recording errors or another kind of research error, but they are common and should be reported as possibly reflecting an important effect of a treatment on a small minority of participants, or an indication of an important characteristic of a small minority of the participants. (Consult Vickers, 2006, for a checklist for avoiding recording errors and errors in data entry, data analysis, and manuscript preparation.) Outliers may arise from a small sub-population that differs from a larger sub-population from which most of the scores come.

Wilcox (2001, 2003) discussed a simple method for detecting outliers and also provided S-PLUS and R software functions for such detection (Wilcox, 2003, 2005a). This method is based on the *median absolute deviation (MAD)*. The *MAD* is defined and discussed as one of the alternative measures of variability in the last two sections of this chapter. Wilcox and Keselman (2003) further discussed detection and treatment of outliers and their effect on statistical power. Wilcox's code for R software for detecting outliers is freely downloadable from http://www-rcf.usc.edu/~rwilcox. Researchers should reflect on the possible reasons for any outliers and about what, if anything, to do about them in the analysis of their data. It is unlikely that a single definition or rule for dealing with outliers will be applicable to all data.

An overview of major developments in the detection of outliers was provided by Hadi, Imon, and Werner (2009). Again, we are concerned about outliers here because of the possibility that they may result in heteroscedasticity that can make the use of statistical tests and certain measures of effect size problematic.

The assumption of homoscedasticity amounts to an assumption that a ratio of variances in populations equals 1. Data support the theoretical expectation that heteroscedasticity is common. Wilcox (1987) found that ratios of largest to smallest sample variances, called maximum sample variance ratios (*VR*s), exceeding 16 are not uncommon, and there are reports of sample *VR*s above 566 (Keselman et al., 1998). Because of the great sampling variability of variances one can expect to find some sample *VR*s that greatly exceed the population *VR*s, especially when sample sizes are small. However, in a study of gender differences using $ns > 100$, a sample *VR* was approximately 18,000 (Pedersen, Miller, Putcha-Bhagavatula, & Yang, 2002). Grissom (2000) found that research reports in a single issue of the *Journal of Consulting and Clinical Psychology* contained sample *VR* values of 3.24, 4.00 (several), 6.48, 6.67, 7.32, 7.84, 25.00, and 281.79.

Groups that are formed by random assignment are expected to represent, by virtue of truly random assignment, populations with equal variances prior to treatment. However, preexisting groups often seem to represent populations with different variances. Humphreys (1988) discussed why gender differences in variability may be more important than gender differences in means.

Tips and Pitfalls
Because treatment can affect the variabilities as well as the centers of distributions, and because changes in variances can be of as much practical significance as are changes in means, researchers should think of variances not just with regard to whether or not their data satisfy the assumption of homoscedasticity, but as informative aspects of treatment effect. For example, Skinner (1958) predicted that programmed instruction, contrasted with traditional instruction, would result in lower variances in achievement scores. Similarly, in research on the outcome of therapy more support would be given for the efficacy of a therapy if it were found that the therapy not only results in a "healthier" mean on a test of mental health, but also in less variability on the test when contrasted with a control group or alternative therapy group. Also, a remedial program that is intended to raise all participants' competence levels to a minimally acceptable level could be considered to be a failure or a limited success if it brought the group mean up to that level but also greatly increased variability in part by lowering the performance of some participants. For example, a remedial program increased mean scholastic performance but also increased variability (Bryk, 1977; Raudenbush & Bryk, 1987). Keppel (1991) presented additional examples of treatments affecting variances. Bryk and Raudenbush (1988) presented methods in clinical outcome research for identifying the patient characteristics that result in heteroscedasticity and for separately estimating treatment effects for the identified types of patients. Consult Wilcox (2003) and Singh, Goyal, and Gil (2010) for discussions of comparing variances.

EXPLORING THE DATA FOR A POSSIBLE EFFECT OF A TREATMENT ON VARIABILITY

Because treatment often has an effect on variability, and unequal variances can influence the choice of a measure of effect size, it is worthwhile to consider the topic of exploring the data for a possible effect of treatment on variability. Also, as we soon observe, there sometimes are limitations to the use of the standard deviation as a measure of variability, and many common measures of effect size involve a standard deviation in their denominators. Therefore, in this section we also consider the use of alternative measures of variability.

Tips and Pitfalls
An obvious approach to determining whether or not a treatment has had an effect on variability would be to apply one of the common tests of homoscedasticity (typically outputted by statistical software) to determine if there is a statistically significant difference between the variances of the two samples. This approach is problematic because the traditional tests of homoscedasticity often produce inaccurate p values when sample sizes are small (say, each sample $n < 11$) or unequal, or distributions are not normal, and have low power even under normality. However, Wilcox (2003, 2005a) provided an S-PLUS software function for a bootstrap method for comparing two variances, a method that appears to produce accurate p values and acceptable power. A basic bootstrap method is

briefly described in Chapter 2. Bonett (2006) proposed a method for constructing a confidence interval for the ratio of two standard deviations (or two variances) for the case of dependent groups under nonnormality. For references and more details about traditional tests of homoscedasticity consult Grissom (2000).

SEQUENTIAL TESTING

It is common, and facilitated by major statistical software packages, to test for homoscedasticity and then conduct or report a conventional t test that assumes homoscedasticity if the difference in variances is not statistically significant. Some of those who require statistically significant results to justify reporting effect sizes for such results might be inclined to adopt such a sequence of testing. (The same sequential method is also common prior to conducting a conventional F test in the case of two or more means.) If the difference in variances is significant, the researcher forgoes the traditional t test for the Welch t test that does not assume homoscedasticity, as is discussed in Chapter 2. However, this sequential procedure is problematic not only because of likely low power for the test of homoscedasticity but because of the resulting increase in rate of Type I error for the test on means. A Type I error defeats the goal of many researchers of reporting an effect size only for statistically significant results. For discussions of the problem of sequential testing consult Sawilowsky and Spence (2007) and Serlin (2002). As Serlin noted, such inflation of Type I error can also result from the use of a test of symmetry to decide if a subsequent comparison of groups is to be made using a normality-assuming statistical test or a nonparametric test. Recently, some statisticians have come to recommend foregoing testing of assumptions and instead using a robust test, especially when the robust test has statistical power that is competitive with the power of the nonrobust test when assumptions are satisfied.

Although traditional inferential methods may often not be powerful enough to detect heteroscedasticity or yield accurate p values, researchers should at least report s^2 for each sample for informally comparing sample variabilities, and perhaps report other measures of the samples' variabilities, to which we now turn our attention. These measures of variability are less sensitive to outliers and skew than are the traditional variance and standard deviation, and they can provide better measures of the typical deviation from average scores under those conditions. Again, heteroscedasticity can invalidate some measures of effect size, as will be observed throughout this book. Also, we note in Chapter 3 and thereafter that these alternative measures of variability can also be of use in estimating an effect size.

VARIANCE AND RANGE

Recall that the variance of a sample, s^2, is the mean of squared deviations of raw scores from the mean:

$$s^2 = \frac{\sum (Y - \bar{Y})^2}{n} \qquad (1.2)$$

or, when the variance of a sample is used as an unbiased estimator of a population variance:

$$s^2 = \frac{\sum (Y - \bar{Y})^2}{n - 1}. \tag{1.3}$$

The variance and standard deviation will be observed in later chapters to be involved in various kinds of effect sizes. Unless otherwise noted in this book, s^2 will denote an unbiased estimate of population variance. Observe in Equations 1.2 and 1.3 that one or a few extremely outlying low or extremely outlying high scores can have a great effect on the variance. An outlying score contributes (adds) 1 to the denominator while contributing a large amount to the numerator because of its large squared deviation from the mean, whereas each small or moderate score contributes 1 to the denominator while contributing only a small or moderate amount to the numerator.

A statistic or a parameter is said to be *nonresistant* if only one or a few outliers can have a relatively large effect on it. Thus, the variance and standard deviation are nonresistant. Therefore, although presenting the sample variances or standard deviations for comparison across groups can be of use in a research report, researchers should consider additionally presenting an alternative measure of variability that is more resistant to outliers than the variance or standard deviation is.

Also, the median is a more outlier-resistant measure of a distribution's location (center) than is the arithmetic mean because the median, as the middle-ranked score, is influenced by the ranking, not the magnitude, of scores. The mean of raw scores, as we noted is true of the variance, has a numerator that can be greatly influenced by each extreme score, whereas each extreme score only adds 1 to the denominator. Consult Wilcox (2005a) for a discussion of resistance and different kinds of robustness, and for S-PLUS and R software functions for robust comparison of two variances and for constructing a confidence interval for $\sigma_1^2 - \sigma_2^2$, the difference between two populations' variances. (Unfortunately, the terminology and connotations for "robustness" are used inconsistently in the literature.) We previously cited in this chapter free access to Wilcox's code for R.

The range is not very useful as a measure of variability because it is extremely nonresistant. The range, by definition, is only sensitive to the most extremely high score and the most extremely low score, so the magnitude of either one of these scores can have a great effect on the range. However, researchers should report the lowest and highest score within each group because it can be informative to compare the lowest scores across the groups and to compare the highest scores across the groups. Also, the range can provide information about possible floor or ceiling effects.

WINSORIZED VARIANCE

Among the measures of variability within a sample that are more resistant to outliers than are the variance, standard deviation, and range, we consider the

Winsorized variance, the MAD, and the interquartile range, each of which will be observed in later chapters to be applicable, but not widely used, for conceptualizing an effect size. Calculation of one or more of these measures for each sample should also be considered for an informal exploration of a possible effect of an independent variable on variability. However, again we note that if groups have not been randomly formed, a posttreatment difference in variabilities of the samples may not necessarily be attributable, or entirely attributable, to an effect of treatment. Although the measures of variability that we consider here are not new to statisticians, they are only recently becoming widely known to researchers through the writings, frequently cited here, of Rand R. Wilcox.

The steps that follow for calculating a *Winsorized variance*, which is named for the statistician Charles Winsor, are clarified by the worked example in the next section. To calculate the Winsorized variance of a sample:

1. Order the scores in the sample from the lowest to the highest.
2. Remove the most extreme *.cn* of the lowest scores and remove the same *.cn* of the most extreme of the highest scores of that sample, where *.c* is a proportion (often .2) and *n* is the total sample size. If *.cn* is not an integer round it down to the nearest integer.
3. Call the lowest remaining score Y_L and the highest remaining score Y_H.
4. Replace each of the removed lowest scores with *.cn* repetitions of Y_L and replace each of the removed highest scores with *.cn* repetitions of Y_H, so that the total size of this reconstituted sample returns to its original size.
5. The Winsorized variance, s_w^2, is simply the unbiased variance (i.e., $n - 1$ in the denominator) of the reconstituted scores. The deviation scores whose squares are averaged in the Winsorized variance are the deviations of the reconstituted scores around the arithmetic mean of these reconstituted scores (i.e., the *Winsorized mean*), not around the original mean.

Depending on various factors, the amount of Winsorizing (i.e., removing and replacing) that is typically recommended is $.c = .10, .20$, or $.25$. The greater the value of c that is used the more the researcher is focusing on the variability of the more central subset of data. For example, when $.c = .20$, more than 20% of the scores would have to be outliers before the Winsorized variance would be influenced by outliers. Wilcox (1996, 2003) provided further discussion, references, and an S-PLUS software function (Wilcox, 2003) for calculating a Winsorized variance. However, of the alternatives to the nonresistant s^2 that we discuss here, we believe that s_w^2 may be the most grudgingly adopted by researchers for two reasons. First, many researchers may balk at the uncertainty regarding the choice of a value for c. Second, although Winsorizing is actually a decades-old procedure that has been used and recommended by respected statisticians, the procedure may seem to some researchers (excluding the present authors) to be "hocus-pocus." For similar reasons some instructors may refrain from teaching this method to students because of concern that it would encourage them to devise their own less justifiable methods for altering data. For a method that is perhaps less psychologically and pedagogically problematic than Winsorizing, but, as we exemplify in later chapters, also less wide-ranging in its possible applications to effect sizes, we turn now to the *MAD*.

MEDIAN ABSOLUTE DEVIATION

The *MAD* for a sample is calculated as follows:

1. Order the sample's scores from the lowest to the highest.
2. Find the median score, *Mdn*. If there is an even number of scores in a sample there will be two middle-ranked scores tied for the median. In this case calculate *Mdn* as the mid-point (arithmetic mean) of these two scores.
3. For each score in the sample find its absolute deviation from the sample's median by successively subtracting *Mdn* from each Y_i score, ignoring whether each such difference is positive or negative, to produce the set of deviations $|Y_1 - Mdn|, ..., |Y_n - Mdn|$.
4. Order the absolute deviations, $|Y_i - Mdn|$, from the lowest to the highest, to produce a series of increasing absolute numbers.
5. Obtain the *MAD* by finding the median of these absolute deviations.

The *MAD* is conceptually more similar to the traditional s than to s^2 because the latter involves squaring deviation scores whereas the *MAD* does not square deviations. The *MAD* is much more resistant to outliers than is the standard deviation. Under normality the $MAD = .6745s$. Wilcox (2003) provided an S-PLUS software function for calculating the *MAD*. Calculation by hand is demonstrated in the next section. Bonett and Seier (2003) proposed a method for constructing a confidence interval for the ratio of two *mean* absolute deviations from the median, and they discussed other robust methods that are applicable when distributions are extremely nonnormal.

QUANTILES

The final measure of variability that is discussed here is the interquartile range, which is based on *quantiles*. A *quantile* is roughly defined here as a score that is equal to or greater than a specified proportion of the scores in a distribution. Common examples of quantiles are quartiles, which divide the data into successive fourths of the data: .25, .50, .75, and 1.00. The second quartile, Q_2 (.50 quantile), is the overall median (*Mdn*) of the scores in the distribution, that is, the score that has .50 of the scores ranked below it. The first quartile, Q_1 (.25 quantile), is the median of the scores that rank below the overall *Mdn*, that is, the score that outranks 25% of the scores. The third quartile, Q_3 (.75 quantile), is the median of the scores that rank above the overall *Mdn*, that is, the score that outranks 75% of the scores. The more variable a distribution is the greater the difference there should be between the scores at Q_3 and Q_1, at least with respect to variability of the middle bulk of the data. A measure of such variability is the *interquartile range*, R_{iq}, which is defined as

$$R_{iq} = Q_3 - Q_1. \tag{1.4}$$

For normal distributions the approximate relationship between the ordinary s and R_{iq} is $s = .75R_{iq}$. When using statistical software packages researchers should try to ascertain how the software is defining quantiles because only a rough definition has been given here for our purposes and definitions vary. For example, consider the following small set of data that was presented for illustration of the problem to a statistical listserve by Dennis M. Roberts: 25, 30, 33, 39, 39, 40, 59, 67, 69, 94, 130. For these data, most software algorithms that were tested yield $Q_1 = 33$ and $Q_3 = 69$, but some yield $Q_1 = 36$ and $Q_3 = 68$, and another yields $Q_1 = 32.25$ and $Q_3 = 67.5$. Some software provide options for the algorithms that are to be used for the calculation.

There are additional measures that are more resistant to outliers than are s^2 and s, but discussion of these would be beyond the scope of this book. Note that what we loosely call a measure of variability in this book is technically called a measure of a distribution's *dispersion* or *scale*.

GRAPHICAL METHODS

Graphical methods for exploring differences between distributions in addition to differences between their means will be cited in Chapter 5. One such graphic depiction of data that is relevant to the present discussion and which researchers are urged to present for each sample is a *boxplot* (see Figure 1.2). Statistical software packages vary in the details of the boxplots that they present, but generally included are the range, median, first and third quartiles so that the interquartile range can be calculated, and outliers that can also give an indication of skew. Unfortunately, an outlier that is not detected using a boxplot may still importantly distort results of data analysis. Many statistical software packages produce two or more boxplots in the same figure for direct comparison. Trenkler (2002) provided software for a more detailed comparison of two or more boxplots. Boxplot methods should detect outliers while avoiding misclassifying a non-outlier as an outlier. One method may be better at detection whereas another method may be better at avoiding such misclassification (Carter, Schwertman, & Kiser, 2009).

A change or changes in location, variability, and/or shape of a distribution after treatment can be depicted graphically by a *bihistogram*. A bihistogram can be produced using the Dataplot free software, which is available at the time of this writing at http://www.itl.nist.gov/div898/handbook/eda/section3/bihistog. htm. Informative discussions of a variety of ways to convey results graphically can be found in Cleveland (1994) and Lane and Sándor (2009).

WORKED EXAMPLES OF MEASURES OF VARIABILITY

Consider the following real data that represent partial data from research on mothers of schizophrenic children (one of the two groups in research that will be discussed in detail where needed in Chapter 3): 1, 1, 1, 1, 2, 2, 2, 3, 3, 7. The possible scores ranged from 0 to 10. Observe in Figure 1.1 that the data are positively skewed.

Standard software output, or simple inspection of the data, yields for the median of the raw scores $Mdn = 2$. As should be expected, because positive skew pulls the very nonresistant mean to a value that is greater than the median, $\bar{Y} > Mdn$ in the present case; specifically, $\bar{Y} = 2.3$. Observe that although 9 of the 10 scores range from 1 to 3, the outlying score, 7, causes the range to be 6. Software output yields for the unbiased estimate of population variance for these data $s^2 = 3.34$. Although the present small set of data is not ideal for justifying the application of the alternative measures of variability, it serves to demonstrate the calculation of the Winsorized variance and the MAD. Again, many statistical software packages calculate R_{iq}. For this example, the calculation yields $R_{iq} = 2$.

We presented a value for R_{iq} for the current data only for completeness. Recall that there is a variety of algorithms used by software packages to calculate quartiles and that results such as the current $R_{iq} = 2$ may differ across different packages. Moreover, knowledge of the R_{iq} is of little value in the present case of a very small set of data with many ties.

Step 1 for calculating the Winsorized variance $\left(s_w^2\right)$, ordering the scores from the lowest to the highest, has already been done. For step 2, we use $c = 20$, so $.cn = .2(10) = 2$. Therefore, we remove the 2 lowest scores and the 2 highest scores, which leaves 6 of the original 10 scores remaining. Applying step 3, $Y_L = 1$ and $Y_H = 3$. Applying step 4, we replace the two lowest removed scores with two repetitions of $Y_L = 1$, and we replace the two highest removed scores with two repetitions of $Y_H = 3$, so that the reconstituted sample of $n = 10$ is 1, 1, 1, 1, 2, 2, 2, 3, 3, 3. Although steps 1 through 4 have not changed the left side of the distribution, the reconstituted data clearly are more symmetrical than before because of the removal and replacement of the outlying score, 7. For step 5, we use any statistical

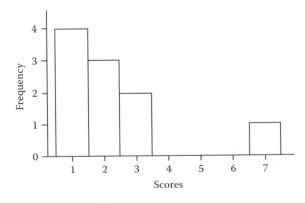

FIGURE 1.1   Skewed data ($n = 10$).

software to calculate, for the reconstituted data, the unbiased s^2 of Equation 1.3 to find that $s_w^2 = .767$. Observe that because of the removal and replacement of the outlier ($Y_i = 7$), as expected, $s_w^2 < s^2$; that is, $.767 < 3.34$. Also the mean of the reconstituted data, $\overline{Y}_w = 1.9$ is closer to the median, $Mdn = 2$, than was the original mean, $\overline{Y} = 2.3$. The range had been 6 but it is now 2, which well describes the reconstituted data in which every score is between 1 and 3, inclusive.

To calculate the MAD for the original data, we proceed to step 3 of that method because for step 1, ordering the scores from the lowest to the highest was previously done, and for step 2, we have already found that $Mdn = 2$. For step 3, we now find that the absolute deviation between each original score and the median is $|1 - 2| = 1$, $|1 - 2| = 1$, $|1 - 2| = 1$, $|1 - 2| = 1$, $|2 - 2| = 0$, $|2 - 2| = 0$, $|2 - 2| = 0$, $|3 - 2| = 1$, $|3 - 2| = 1$, and $|7 - 2| = 5$. For step 4, we order these absolute deviations from the lowest to the highest: 0, 0, 0, 1, 1, 1, 1, 1, 1, 5. For step 5, we find by inspection that the median of these absolute deviations is 1; that is, the $MAD = 1$.

With regard to the usual intention that the standard deviation measure within what distance from the mean the typical below-average and typical above-average scores lie, consider the following facts about the present data. Nine of the 10 original scores ($Y_i = 7$ being the exception) are within approximately 1 point of the mean ($\overline{Y} = 2.3$) but the standard deviation of these skewed data is $s = (s^2)^{1/2} = (3.34)^{1/2} = 1.83$, a value that is nearly twice as large as the typical distance (deviation) of the scores from the mean. In contrast the Winsorized standard deviation, which is $s_w = \left(s_w^2 \right)^{1/2} = (.767)^{1/2} = .876$, is close to the typical deviation of approximately 1 point for the Winsorized data and for the original data. Note that the MAD too is more representative of the typical amount of deviation from the original mean than the standard deviation is; that is, $MAD = 1$. However, the mere demonstration of the methods in this section with a single small set of data does not rise to the level of mathematical proof or even strong empirical evidence of their merits. Interested readers should refer to Wilcox (1996, 1997, 2003) and the references therein.

In the boxplots in Figure 1.2 for the current data, the asterisk indicates the outlier, the middle horizontal line within each box indicates the median, the black

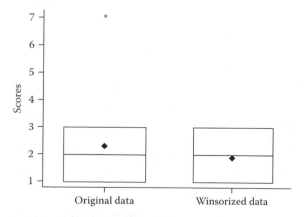

FIGURE 1.2   Boxplots of original and Winsorized data.

diamond within each box indicates the mean, and the lines that form the bottom and top of each box indicate the first and third quartiles, respectively. Because of the idiosyncratic nature of the current data set (many repeated values), the interquartile range for the Winsorized data (2) happens to be equal to the range of the Winsorized data.

SUMMARY

The result of a test of statistical significance does not directly estimate how much different a study's groups are or how strongly related variables are. For these purposes an estimate of effect size is required. Whereas a statistical test provides evidence regarding the possible falseness of a null hypothesis, an estimate of effect size provides evidence of the degree of such falseness. A "statistically significant" difference between groups or relationship between variables does not necessarily mean a large difference or strong relationship, but merely a degree of difference or relationship that is in the range of values that are unlikely to be attributable to chance.

Many factors can influence an effect size, including the research design, kind of effect size, reliability of the scores, nature of the participants, type of measure of the independent variable, time between treatment and data collection, various biases, and violation of assumptions. Research reports should include information about such factors and, even if reporting an estimate of effect size, to accommodate readers who might want to calculate another kind of estimator, provide all of the summary statistics (e.g., means and variances) that might be needed.

Statistical tests (e.g., t or F) that might be used to support a statement that an estimate of effect size is significantly greater than, say, zero can yield erroneous results when an assumption such as normality or equal variances is violated. There are theoretical reasons and empirical evidence to indicate that outliers and violations of assumptions, even extreme violations, are common. Therefore, researchers should consider using statistics that are more resistant to outliers than are the mean and variance, and robust statistical tests that are insensitive or less sensitive to violation of assumptions than are the t and F tests. Also, because treatments can affect variability as well as means, and preexisting groups (e.g., females and males) may differ in variability, researchers should explore their data for differences in variability between groups. There are arguments against sequentially testing for violation of equal variances and then testing for difference in means.

QUESTIONS

1.1 List six factors that influence the statistical significance of t.

1.2 What is the meaning of *statistical significance*, and what do the authors mean by *statistically signifying*?

1.3 Define *effect size* in general terms.

1.4 In what circumstances would the reporting of effect sizes be most useful?

1.5 What is the major issue in the debate regarding the reporting of effect sizes when results do not attain statistical significance?

1.6 Why should a researcher consider reporting more than one kind of effect size for a set of data?

1.7 What is often the relationship between a treatment's effect on means and variances?

1.8 Define (a) heteroscedasticity, (b) power analysis, (c) meta-analysis, (d) MAD, (e) interquartile range, (f) researcher-allegiance bias, (g) wait-list-control bias, (h) internal validity, (i) external validity, (j) randomized clinical trial, (k) ceiling and floor effects, (l) nonresistance and robustness, (m) quantile and quartile, (n) nil hypothesis, (o) differential attrition, (p) efficacy and effectiveness, (q) intent-to-treat, modified intent-to-treat, and per protocol criteria.

1.9 Is heteroscedasticity a practical concern for data analysts, or is it merely of theoretical interest? Explain briefly.

1.10 Define *outliers* and provide two possible causes of them.

1.11 Discuss whether or not the use of preexisting groups or randomly formed groups differently impacts the possibility of heteroscedasticity.

1.12 Discuss the usefulness of tests of homoscedasticity in general.

1.13 What effect can one or a few outliers have on the variance?

1.14 How resistant to outliers is the variance? In general terms, compare its resistance with that of four other measures of variability.

1.15 Which characteristics of data do boxplots usually depict?

1.16 What is often the relationship between the value of a test statistic and an estimate of effect size?

1.17 List 11 factors that can influence the value of an effect size.

1.18 Define and briefly discuss the problem of *publication bias* and define *outcome reporting bias*.

1.19 For the following real data (a) calculate the sample variance, Winsorized variance, MAD, and interquartile range; (b) construct a boxplot; (c) in light of the boxplot and the discussions in the text, discuss the differences in the numerical results and the appropriateness of each of these measures of variability: 2, 1, 1, 3, 2, 7, 2, 1, 3, 1, 0, 2, 4, 2, 3, 3, 0, 1, 2, 2.

2 Confidence Intervals for Comparing the Averages of Two Groups

INTRODUCTION

Recall that the *location* of a population is a parameter that is usually defined as a measure of its "average," commonly its mean or median. Recall also that the *t* test for the statistical significance of the difference between two sample means provides no direct estimation of the magnitude of the difference between the two population means. The difference between the two population means is another example of a parameter, and the difference between the two sample means is an example of a *point estimate* of a parameter. The *t* test and other statistical tests provide no information about the degree of precision with which a point estimate is estimating a parameter (i.e., the extent to which the point estimate is overestimating or underestimating the parameter because of sampling variability). Confidence intervals address the latter problem while also often providing the same information as would be provided by a statistical test.

The confidence intervals that are discussed in this chapter and the effect sizes in Chapter 3 all provide information that relates to the amount of difference between two populations' locations, including means. When the dependent variable is scaled in familiar units, and is of interest itself, instead of representing a latent (underlying) variable, a confidence interval for the mean difference can provide useful information about the results. Such a confidence interval, which is discussed in the next section, can be considered to be a confidence interval for an effect size that we later call an "unstandardized difference between means."

Examples of familiar scales include weight (in research on programs for weight loss), ounces of alcohol consumed, milligrams of drugs consumed, and counts of such things as family size, cigarettes smoked, acts of misbehavior (defined), days absent, days abstinent, dollars earned or spent, days of hospital stay, nervous tics, panic attacks, and relapses. Because a familiar scale is often also what is called a ratio scale we digress in the next section to discuss a simple effect size for such scales that is especially useful when data are not skewed.

RATIO-OF-MEANS EFFECT SIZE

A *ratio scale* is one that has a true zero instead of an arbitrary zero. Examples of ratio scales include the Kelvin scale of temperature (K) but neither the Fahrenheit (F) nor the Celsius (centigrade, C) scales. A true zero, which is also called an *absolute zero*, gives a scale the property that a ratio of values on the scale corresponds to the meaningful actual ratio of the attribute that is being scaled. For example, if one object has a length or weight (both being ratio scales) that is twice that of another object, then the first object truly possesses twice as much of the attribute that is being measured (length or weight) than is possessed by the second object. Therefore, 100°K is twice the temperature that is measured at 50°K, but 100°F (or °C) is not twice the temperature that is measured at 50°F (or °C). Similarly, persons who have twice the scores of other persons on tests of such attributes as depression, attitude, aptitude, and achievement (tests without true zeros) do not possess twice the amount of what such tests are measuring. An IQ of 120 does not reflect twice the intelligence (or whatever an IQ test is measuring) of an IQ of 60.

Values below 0 are only possible on a scale that is not a ratio scale. Temperatures below 0°F or 0°C are possible. Zero degrees Celsius is merely an arbitrary but reasonable choice for a starting point for a scale of temperature because it is the temperature at which water freezes at normal atmospheric pressure. Just as 0°F or 0°C does not represent an absence of temperature, a person who scores 0 on a scale that is not a ratio scale does not necessarily fail to possess any amount of the attribute that is being scaled.

When the dependent variable in an experiment is continuous with a true zero (i.e., a ratio scale), as is the case in our earlier examples of familiar scales but is often not the case in psychological and educational research, an alternative meaningful effect size is the ratio of two groups' means. For example, if the mean weight of a group of anorectic (i.e., self-starving) girls is 120 lb after their treatment and the mean weight of a second group of anorectic girls is 100 lb after another treatment, the estimated *ratio-of-means effect size* of the first treatment in relation to the second treatment is 120/100 = 1.2. Friedrich, Adhikari, and Beyene (2008) reported simulations that indicated that the ratio of means (also called *response ratio*) exhibits statistical performances (e.g., power) that are comparable to those of the difference between means, which is the major topic of this chapter, and the widely used standardized difference between means, which is the topic of the next chapter. Those authors also demonstrated the construction of a confidence interval for the ratio of means. Zheng, Shi, and Ma (2010) reported simulations that supported their proposed methods for testing and constructing confidence intervals for a difference between means and for a ratio of means under heteroscedasticity with normality. (When data are skewed the ratio of the two group's geometric means can be used as the effect size, provided that no $Y \leq 0$.)

BACKGROUND

The approach to confidence intervals in this book is the traditional frequentist approach. Lecoutre (2007) discussed the relationship between the frequentist approach and the increasingly used alternative, Bayesian approach, the latter yielding what are called *credible intervals*. (Thomas Bayes was an eighteenth century minister and mathematician.) Some distinctions between the two approaches are mentioned later in this chapter. By being introduced to the concept of confidence intervals in this chapter, those readers who are not very familiar with the topic should better understand the topics of confidence intervals for effect sizes that are presented in Chapter 3 and thereafter.

The American Psychological Association's Task Force on Statistical Inference (Wilkinson & APA Task Force on Statistical Inference, 1999) called for the greater use of confidence intervals, effect sizes, and confidence intervals for effect sizes, and the sixth edition of the *Publication Manual of the American Psychological Association* strongly recommended the use of confidence intervals (American Psychological Association, 2010). Sawilowsky (2003b) discussed philosophical debates about the concept of confidence intervals and their early history. As we note later in this chapter and thereafter, with regard to confidence intervals in general or specific kinds of confidence intervals, the method can sometimes have limitations and interpretive problems. Confidence intervals share some of the issues and limitations of testing of statistical significance, such as choice of an alpha level (confidence level) and robustness to violation of parametric assumptions.

CONFIDENCE INTERVALS FOR $\mu_a - \mu_b$: INDEPENDENT GROUPS

Especially for an applied researcher, the practically most important part of the equation for the t statistic that tests the usual null hypothesis about two population means is the numerator, $\overline{Y}_a - \overline{Y}_b$. Using sample $\overline{Y}_a - \overline{Y}_b$ to estimate the size of the difference between population μ_a and μ_b, which is an effect size that is called an *unstandardized difference between means*, can provide a very informative kind of result, again, especially when the dependent variable is a commonly understood variable. Recall the example from Chapter 1 in which we were interested in comparing the mean weights of diabetic participants in weight-reduction programs *a* and *b*. It would be of great practical interest in this case to acquire information about the amount of difference in mean population weights after treatment. The procedure for constructing a confidence interval uses the data from samples *a* and *b* to estimate a range of values that is likely to contain the value of $\mu_a - \mu_b$ within them, with a specifiable degree of confidence in this estimate. For example, a confidence interval for the difference in weight gain between two populations of anorectic girls who are represented by two samples who have received either Treatment *a* or Treatment *b* may lead to a reported result such as: "One can be approximately 95% confident that the interval between 10 and 20 lb contains the difference in mean gain of weight in the two populations."

Theoretically, although any given population of scores has a constant mean, equal-sized random samples from a population have varying means (sampling variability). Therefore, $\overline{Y}_a$ and $\overline{Y}_b$ may each be either overestimating or underestimating their respective population means. Thus, $\overline{Y}_a - \overline{Y}_b$ may well be larger or smaller than $\mu_a - \mu_b$ in any one sampling. In other words, there is a *margin of error* when using $\overline{Y}_a - \overline{Y}_b$ to estimate $\mu_a - \mu_b$. If there is such a margin of error it may be positive $(\overline{Y}_a - \overline{Y}_b) > (\mu_a - \mu_b)$, or negative $(\overline{Y}_a - \overline{Y}_b) < (\mu_a - \mu_b)$.

(The difference between the means of the samples is an unbiased estimator of the difference between the means of the populations.) The larger the sample sizes and the less variable the populations of raw scores, the smaller the absolute value of the margin of error will be. That is, as is reflected later in Equation 2.1, the margin of error is a function of the standard error. In the present case the standard error is the standard deviation of the distribution of differences between two populations' sample means. (This standard error is also the denominator of the equation for the t statistic for the difference between the means of two independent groups.)

Another factor that influences the margin of error is the level of confidence that one wants to have in one's estimate of a range of values that is likely to contain $\mu_a - \mu_b$. Although it may seem counterintuitive to some readers at first, we soon observe that the more confident one wants to be in this estimate the greater the margin of error will have to be. For a very simple example, it is safe to say that one can be 100% confident that the difference in mean annual incomes of the population of high-school dropouts and the population of college graduates would be found within the interval between $0 and $1 million, but our 100% confidence in this estimate is of no benefit because it involves an unacceptably large margin of error (i.e., an interval that is so wide that it provides an uninformative result). The actual difference between these two population means of annual income is obviously not near $0 or $1 million. (For the purpose of this section we used mean income as a dependent variable in our example despite the fact that income data are usually skewed and are typified by medians instead of means.)

A procedure that greatly decreases the margin of error without excessively reducing the level of confidence in the truth of the result would be useful. The tradition is to adopt what is called the 95% (or .95) confidence level that leads to an estimate of a range of values that will have a .95 probability of containing the value of $\mu_a - \mu_b$. When expressed as a decimal value (e.g., .95) the true *confidence level* of a confidence interval is also called the *probability coverage* of a confidence interval. To the extent that a method for constructing a confidence interval is inaccurate the actual probability coverage will depart from what it was intended to be and appears to be (e.g., depart from the nominal .95). Although 95% confidence may seem to some readers to be only slightly less confidence than 100% confidence, such a procedure typically results in a very much narrower, more informative, interval than in our example that compared incomes. For simplicity, the first procedure that we discuss assumes normality, homoscedasticity, and independent groups. (Generally, the accuracy of nominal confidence levels for the difference between means can be increased under nonnormality by increasing sample sizes.) The procedure is easily generalized to confidence levels other than the 95% level. First we consider the assumption of random sampling and consider further the assumption of independent groups.

In much research there is violation of the assumption of random sampling. Some finesse this problem (unsatisfactorily in the view of many) by concluding that research results apply to theoretical populations from which the samples would have constituted a random sample. It has been argued that such reasoning can be justified if the samples that were used seem to be reasonably representative of the kinds of people to whom one wants to generalize the results. In the case of experimental research, random assignment to treatments satisfies the assumption (in terms of the statistical validity of the results if not necessarily in terms of the generalizability of the results).

Independent groups can be roughly defined for our purposes as groups within which no individual's score is related to or predictable from the scores of any individual in another group. Groups are independent if the probability that an individual in a group will produce a certain score remains the same regardless of what score is produced by an individual in another group. Research with dependent groups requires methods for construction of confidence intervals that are different from methods used for research with independent groups, as we discuss in the penultimate section of this chapter.

Assuming, for simplicity, for now that the assumptions of independence, homoscedasticity, and normality have been satisfied, it can be shown that for constructing a confidence interval for $\mu_a - \mu_b$ the margin of error (*ME*) is given by

$$ME = t^* \left[s_p^2 \left(\frac{1}{n_a} + \frac{1}{n_b} \right) \right]^{1/2}. \tag{2.1}$$

The part of Equation 2.1 after t^* is the standard error of the difference between two sample means. (Again s_p^2 is the pooled variance on the assumption of homoscedasticity.) A standard error indicates the precision with which a statistic (e.g., $\bar{Y}_a - \bar{Y}_b$) is estimating a parameter (e.g., $\mu_a - \mu_b$), as does a confidence interval itself according to common interpretation. When Equation 2.1 is used to construct a 95% confidence interval, t^* is the absolute value of t that a table of critical values of t, or a density function for t in software such as TDIST, indicates is required to attain statistical significance at the .05 two-tailed level (or .025 one-tailed level) in a t test. (Yalta, 2008, reported on the accuracy of software for statistical distributions such as t.) For the 95% or any other level of confidence, s_p^2 is the pooled estimate of the assumed common variance of the two populations, σ^2. Use for the degrees-of-freedom for t, $df = n_a + n_b - 2$. Because for now we are assuming homoscedasticity, the best estimate of σ^2 is obtained by pooling the data from the two samples to calculate the usual weighted average of the two samples' estimates of σ^2 to produce (weighting by sample sizes via the separate sample's dfs)

$$s_p^2 = \frac{(n_a - 1)s_a^2 + (n_b - 1)s_b^2}{n_a + n_b - 2}. \tag{2.2}$$

(Note that some authors use s_p^2 to denote pooling variances by dividing the two groups' sums of squares by N instead of the currently more common $N - 2$, so our s_p^2 is synonymous with s_w^2, the pooled variance within groups.) Because approximately 95% of the time when such confidence intervals are constructed, in the current case, the value of $\bar{Y}_a - \bar{Y}_b$ may be overestimating or underestimating

$\mu_a - \mu_b$ by the $ME_{.95}$, one can conclude that approximately 95% of the time the following interval of values will contain the value of $\mu_a - \mu_b$:

$$(\overline{Y}_a - \overline{Y}_b) \pm ME_{.95}. \tag{2.3}$$

The value $(\overline{Y}_a - \overline{Y}_b) - ME_{.95}$ is called the *lower limit* (or lower bound) of the 95% confidence interval, and the value $(\overline{Y}_a - \overline{Y}_b) + ME_{.95}$ is called the *upper limit* (or upper bound) of the 95% confidence interval. A *confidence interval* is (for our present purpose) the interval of values between the lower limit and the upper limit. We often use *CI* for confidence interval, and to denote the 95% *CI* we also use .95 *CI* or $CI_{.95}$.

Again, confidence intervals for the difference between two locations can often provide useful information about the magnitude of the results. For example, in the case of comparing two weight-reduction programs for diabetics, suppose that, after 1 year in one or the other program, the lower and upper limits of a 95% confidence interval for $\mu_a - \mu_b$ were 1 and 2 lb, respectively. A between-program difference in mean population weights (a constant, but an unknown one) that we are 95% confident would be found in the interval between 1 and 2 lb after 1 year in the programs would seem to indicate that there is likely little practical difference in the effectiveness of the two programs, one of which seeming to be only negligibly better than the other at most. On the other hand, if the lower and upper limits were found to be, say, 20 and 30 lb, then one would be fairly confident that one has evidence (not proof) that the more effective program is substantially better.

Observe that in the two examples of outcomes that neither the interval from 1 to 2 nor the interval from 20 to 30 contains the value zero within it. It can be shown in the present case that if a 95% confidence interval does not contain the value zero the results imply that a two-tailed t test of H_0: $\mu_a - \mu_b = 0$ would have produced a statistically significant t at the .05 significance level. If the interval does contain the value zero, say, for example, limits of -10 and $+10$, we would conclude that the difference between $\overline{Y}_a$ and $\overline{Y}_b$ is not significant at the two-tailed .05 level of significance. In general, if one were to adopt a significance level α, when the $(1 - \alpha)$ confidence interval for the difference between two populations' means does not contain zero, this result is equivalent to having found a statistically significant difference between $\overline{Y}_a$ and $\overline{Y}_b$ at the two-tailed α significance level. Therefore, beyond the other information that it provides, such a confidence interval provides information that a t test of statistical significance would have provided. Also, when assumptions are satisfied the statistical power of a two-tailed t test, at level α, of a null hypothesis that specifies 0 difference between two populations' means equals the proportion of times that a confidence interval, at level $1 - \alpha$, for the difference between those means will contain the value 0 when the null hypothesis is false.

The concepts of Type I and Type II errors that are associated with statistical significance testing can be related to confidence intervals. In the case of confidence intervals, when the value of a parameter is truly as might be posited for it by a null hypothesis (e.g., 0) but the interval does not include that posited value, the equivalent of a Type I error has occurred. When the value of a parameter is not the same as a value that might be posited for it by a null hypothesis but the interval does include that posited value, the equivalent of a Type II error has occurred.

Suppose that a confidence interval contains 0 but is very wide. Some might interpret such a result as providing relatively weak evidence that the effect size is 0. Alternatively, suppose that the interval does not contain 0, but that the confidence limit that is farthest from 0 is still very close to 0. Some might interpret such a result as providing relatively strong evidence that the effect size is small. These possible interpretations are extensions from Bonett (2009b). Consult Knapp (2002) and Reichardt and Gollob (1997) for an argument justifying the use of confidence intervals in some cases and tests of statistical significance in other cases.

Tips and Pitfalls

A confidence interval should not be constructed contingent on first obtaining a statistically significant result because the *nominal* (i.e., supposed) *confidence level* will thereby become greater than the true confidence level (called *liberal probability coverage*). Also consult Serlin (2002). Knapp (2002) argued that researchers should plan either to construct a confidence interval or to test for statistical significance, depending on the purpose of the research.

A common procedure when a researcher plans to report a confidence interval for the difference between two populations' means is to construct a confidence interval first and then address the presence or absence of 0 (or other null-hypothesized value of the parameter) in the interval from the perspective of statistical significance testing. (This procedure is not appropriate or straightforward in cases in which confidence intervals and tests of statistical significance may produce inconsistent results, as is discussed in Chapter 8.)

One point of view is that testing statistical significance is appropriate as part of the gathering of evidence about a model to which the null hypothesis relates, whereas constructing a confidence interval is appropriate when evidence is sought about the precision of an estimate of a parameter such as $\mu_a - \mu_b$. In some simple cases in which assumptions are satisfied a reader of a report who so wishes can construct an approximate confidence interval if a report includes the values of the sample sizes, means, and variances.

To construct a confidence interval other than the .95 *CI*, in general the $(1 - \alpha)$ *CI*, the value of t^* that is used in Equation 2.1 is the absolute value of t that is required for two-tailed statistical significance at the chosen α significance level (the same t as for $\alpha/2$, one-tailed). For examples, for a .90 *CI* use the critical t required at $\alpha = .10$ two-tailed or $\alpha = .05$ one-tailed, and for a .99 *CI* use $\alpha = .01$ two-tailed or $\alpha = .005$ one-tailed. However, one would likely find that a .99 *CI* results in a very wide, less informative, interval, as was suggested in our example of comparison of incomes. For a given set of data, the lower the confidence level, the narrower the interval.

Tips and Pitfalls

Krantz (1999) maintained that the varying costs of a Type I error in different circumstances of research can justify the use of confidence levels that are far from .95 in either direction depending on what kind of practical application is to be made of the results. For example, research on an extremely costly (monetarily or otherwise) treatment may justify the adoption of a confidence level that is much higher than .95. In psychological research D. H. Krantz (personal communication, June 27, 2005) prefers .90 as a compromise between the .68 confidence level that is typically used in physics and the traditional .95 level that is typically used in behavioral science. In this view, on the other hand, in life-and-death areas such as toxicology research the social costs of not detecting that a toxic substance is toxic (a Type II error) may be great enough to justify the adoption of an alpha level that is greater than .05 and a confidence level that is less than .95.

For an analogy, consider the difference between a criminal trial and a civil trial, the defendant on trial being considered to be analogous to a null hypothesis whose fate awaits the presentation of the evidence against it. In a criminal trial, the cost of wrongly convicting an innocent defendant (a kind of Type I error) is often very great (imprisonment or death) so a high standard is set for conviction, that is, "guilt beyond a reasonable doubt" (analogous to $\alpha < .05, .01, ...?$). However, in a civil trial the cost when the jury or judge wrongly finds against the defendant is not death or even imprisonment, but monetary compensation that is to be paid by the defendant to the plaintiff. Because the cost of wrongly finding against the defendant in a civil case is much less than in a criminal case the standard of evidence (implicit "alpha level") that must be met to find against defendants is that the "preponderance of the evidence" (alpha merely $<.50?$) must be against them.

FREQUENTIST AND BAYESIAN PERSPECTIVES

Recall that the 95% *CI* is also called the .95 *CI*. Such a confidence interval is often interpreted to mean that there is a .95 probability that $\mu_a - \mu_b$ is within the calculated interval, as if $\mu_a - \mu_b$ were a random variable. This is a *Bayesian perspective* (Lecoutre, 2007). However, it is argued from a *frequentist perspective* (Lecoutre) that $\mu_a - \mu_b$ is actually a (unknown) constant in any specific pair of populations, and it is each confidence limit that is actually a variable. From a frequentist perspective, because of sampling variability, repeating a specific example of research by repeatedly randomly sampling equal-sized samples from two populations will produce varying values of $\overline{Y}_a - \overline{Y}_b$, whereas the actual value of $\mu_a - \mu_b$ remains constant for the specific pair of populations that are being repeatedly compared via their sample means. In other words, although a researcher actually samples from populations *a* and *b* only once each, varying results are possible for $\overline{Y}_a, \overline{Y}_b$, and, thereby, for $\overline{Y}_a - \overline{Y}_b$ across each of the theoretically possible instances of research. Similarly, variances of the samples from a given population will vary from instance to instance of research, so the margin of error is also a variable. Therefore, from this frequentist perspective, instead of saying that there is, say, a .95

probability that $\mu_a - \mu_b$ *is* a value within the calculated interval, one would say that there is a .95 probability that the calculated interval *will* contain the value of $\mu_a - \mu_b$. For example, if the actual difference between μ_a and μ_b were, say, exactly 10 lb, when constructing an accurate .95 *CI* there would be a .95 probability that the calculated interval will contain the value 10. According to the traditional frequentist approach, if this specific research were repeated an indefinitely large number of times, approaching infinity, the percentage of times that the calculated .95 confidence intervals would contain the value 10 would approach 95% if assumptions are satisfied (but consider the results from Cumming and colleagues at the end of this section). It is in this sense that a frequentist would interpret any statement that is made about the results from construction of confidence intervals in examples in this book. Christensen (2005) discussed criticisms and misunderstandings of confidence intervals.

The game of horseshoe tossing provides a rough analogy of a frequentist interpretation of a confidence interval that has been constructed using samples of a given size. In this analogy the targeted spike fixed in the ground represents a constant parameter (such as the difference between two populations' means), the left and right sides of the tossed horseshoe represent the limits of the interval, and an expert player who can surround the spike with the horseshoe in 95% of the tosses represents a researcher who has actually attained a .95 confidence level. What varies in the sample of tosses is not the location of the spike, but whether or not the tossed horseshoe surrounds it. For a listing of the common and the precise varying definitions of confidence intervals refer to Fidler and Thompson (2001). Also consult Thompson (2007) for further discussions.

Cumming and Finch (2005) and Cumming (2007, 2009) considered the use of figures to depict and interpret confidence intervals, in the case of normality and independent samples, including interpretation of the degree of overlap between a confidence interval for μ_a and a confidence interval for μ_b. Those authors provided a detailed discussion of the relationship between confidence intervals and *p* levels in the case of independent samples. For a somewhat different point of view consult Rouder and Morey (2005), and for a reply consult Fidler, Thomason, Cumming, Finch, and Leeman (2005). Consult Maghsoodloo and Huang (2010) for further discussion.

Tips and Pitfalls
Belia, Fidler, Williams, and Cumming (2005) discussed the misuse and proper interpretation of graphs that depict some sort of "interval" line vertically around the mean of each sample in a study that compares two means. Such lines, called *error bars*, sometimes are presented confusingly in research reports without a clear indication of what the error bars represent. Such a graph should be clearly identified as representing a confidence interval, standard deviation of the raw scores, or the standard deviation of the distribution of sample means (i.e., the standard error of the mean). Consult Wilcox (2009a) for related discussion.

Belia et al. (2005) also discussed the very different interpretations of such a graph when the groups are independent or dependent. They further discussed the apparently widely held beliefs in the case of independent groups that (a) when the two .95 confidence intervals around the separate population means do not *quite* overlap the difference between the two sample means will be *barely* statistically significant at the .05 level, and (b) when there is *any* overlap between the two .95 confidence intervals statistical significance at the .05 level will not be attained. The second belief is not true. The first belief is correct about declaring statistical significance in the case of confidence intervals that fall just slightly short of overlapping, but in the current example of .95 confidence intervals the *p* level would likely not be barely .05 but be very much below .05. In an example of just barely nonoverlapping .95 confidence intervals that Belia et al. provided, when using sample sizes that were similar and not small, $p \approx .006$.

Cumming, Williams, and Fidler (2004) reported that when assumptions are satisfied the first constructed .95 confidence interval for a population mean will, theoretically, *capture* (i.e., contain) the next found sample mean upon a replication 83.4%, not 95%, of the time. However, in real-world replications of a study the average *capture percentage* should be expected to be lower than 83.4% because of at least some variation between studies in methodological details and characteristics of the participants. Their results for the capture percentage for a confidence interval for a single mean may generalize to the present case of the difference between two independent means. Moreover, the capture percentages associated with confidence intervals for the various effect sizes that are discussed throughout this book may be lower than the confidence levels. The relationship between *p* values and overlap between confidence intervals for independent means can be explored using interactive software ("ESCI Inference by eye") that can be freely downloaded, courtesy of Geoff Cumming, from www.latrobe.edu.au/psy/esci. Woolfe and Cumming (2004) discussed the relationship between confidence intervals and the uncertainty of results. Finally, it is incorrect to interpret a confidence interval as providing equal support for all of the values within that interval (Louis & Zeger, 2007).

EQUIVALENCE TESTING, NON-INFERIORITY, AND SUPERIORITY

EQUIVALENCE

Whereas statistical significance testing in the case of two means addresses the equality or inequality of the means, *equivalence testing* addresses the *essentially equal* or *essentially unequal* efficacy of two treatments. In the case of means, two treatments are considered to be essentially equally efficacious if their means differ by no more than a pre-specified amount, which we label *min* for minimum, in either direction. The *min* in the present case is the difference between means that just falls short of what the researcher (or an administrative agency such as the Food and Drug Administration) considers to be practically important (e.g., clinically significant). A *min* is commonly called an *equivalence bound*. Therefore, a *min* is a pre-specified difference-between-means effect size that almost attains a magnitude that would be of interest.

A common procedure for equivalence testing involves conducting two one-sided tests (TOST being the acronym) at level α (say, .025), one testing for a positive difference and one testing for a negative difference between the means. Equivalence is established if the results of a t test of the null hypothesis H_1: $\mu_a - \mu_b \geq min$ and a t test of the null hypothesis H_2: $\mu_a - \mu_b \leq -min$ are both statistically significant (i.e., both hypotheses are rejected), where, again, the value of min has been pre-specified. Rejection of H_1 implies that μ_a is not greater than μ_b by an amount that is equal to or greater than min. Rejection of H_2 implies that μ_a is not less than μ_b by an amount that is equal to or greater than min. More elegantly, the two null hypotheses can be combined into H_3: $|\mu_a - \mu_b| \geq min$, rejection of which implies that the two treatments are equivalent because their absolute difference apparently does not attain the minimum required for a practically significant amount of difference. Such t testing can be undertaken with various commercial software, such as STATA and S-PLUS. A search of the internet reveals several sources for code to conduct equivalence testing using major software. Equivalence testing for the difference between two means can also be conducted using applets that are provided free courtesy of Russell Lenth (2006). These applets can be accessed using a Java-capable web browser to connect to http//:www.stat.uiowa.edu/~rlenth/Power

A confidence interval for equivalence can also be constructed to determine if the lower limit of the interval is within $-min$ and the upper limit of the interval is within min. Such limits within $-min$ and min, respectively, are taken as evidence of equivalence because $-min$ and min are outside the confidence interval. Suppose in this case of evidence for equivalence that the value 0 is not in the confidence interval. The fact that 0 is not in the interval provides evidence of a statistically significant difference between means, but the values of the limits indicate that the effects of the two treatments are *essentially* (not literally) equivalent. This is a case in which an effect size is apparently not zero, but still judged to be of no practical significance. One is reminded of the philosophical principle "A difference, in order to be a difference, must make a difference."

A .95 confidence interval in the present case corresponds to the use of $\alpha = .025$ for the alternative procedure of one-tailed testing of H_1 and H_2 and to the use of $\alpha = .05$ for the two-tailed test of H_3. For further discussions of testing equivalence using confidence intervals consult Steiger (2004).

Tips and Pitfalls

A major determinant of the results and usefulness of equivalence testing is the choice of an appropriate value for the minimum difference that constitutes equivalence. This issue is of concern in areas of research in which, unlike drug research, there is no standard for the min that is established by a governmental agency or in some other conventional way. However, in areas of research in which there is no conventional value for min some may argue that choosing a value for it is no more challenging than choosing an estimated effect size in order to estimate needed sample size in pre-research power analysis, or deciding whether or not an obtained difference between means or other obtained estimate of effect size is of practical significance when interpreting results. When a reasonable value is used for the *min* a statistically significant difference between means that does not exceed the *min* can be said to represent a practically insignificant effect size. For further discussion consult Lenth (2001). In his review of the topic Serlin (2002) called the values between −*min* and *min good-enough values*, and the range from −*min* to *min* the *good-enough belt*, because such values, although not equal to 0, are good enough to declare the means to be essentially equivalent. Serlin also called the previously discussed null hypotheses *range null hypotheses* because, unlike a traditional null hypothesis that posits a single value for a parameter, they posit a range of values that are within the −*min* or *min*. Refer to Steiger (2004) for related discussions. Consult Morey and Rouder (in press) for a Bayesian approach.

Consult Tryon and Lewis (2008) for discussion of construction of *inferential confidence intervals* that go beyond confidence intervals for equivalence by testing for three possibilities. The method tests for (a) equivalence, (b) difference, and (c) neither equivalence nor difference. The latter situation is called *indeterminancy*.

Non-Inferiority and Superiority

There is a procedure for testing simultaneously for *non-inferiority* and *superiority*, assuming normality and homoscedasticity, while controlling rates of Type I and Type II errors. In the present case of comparison of two means a treatment is said to be essentially non-inferior to another treatment if the difference between means indicates that its mean is not inferior to the other mean by more than a pre-specified amount in a one-tailed test. This pre-specified maximum acceptable difference is the maximum effect size that satisfies the given criterion of non-inferiority. A treatment is said to be essentially superior to another treatment if its mean is superior to the other mean by at least a pre-specified amount in a one-tailed test. This pre-specified minimum acceptable difference is the minimum effect size that satisfies the given criterion of superiority. Consult Koyama, Sampson, and Gleser (2005) for details.

WORKED EXAMPLE FOR INDEPENDENT GROUPS

The following example illustrates the traditional method for constructing a .95 *CI* for $\mu_a - \mu_b$, assuming normality and homoscedasticity, before we proceed to methods that are more robust.

In an unpublished study (Everitt; raw data published by Hand, Daly, Lunn, McConway, & Ostrowski, 1994) that compared Treatment *a* and Treatment *b* for young girls with anorexia nervosa (again, self-starvation) and used weight as the dependent variable the data yielded the following statistics: $\bar{Y}_a = 85.697$, $\bar{Y}_b = 81.108$, $s_a^2 = 69.755$, and $s_b^2 = 22.508$. The sample sizes were $n_a = 29$ and $n_b = 26$, so $df = 29 + 26 - 2 = 53$. Many statistical software packages will construct a confidence interval for the present case, but we illustrate calculation by hand to facilitate understanding the present procedure and those to come. We are assuming homoscedasticity for these data until later in this chapter for the purpose of demonstrating the calculations most simply. Using software for a density function for the t distribution (e.g., TDIST) one finds the critical value of t at $\alpha = .05$ (i.e., confidence level $1 - .05 = .95$) and $df = 53$. Such software indicates that $t^* = 2.006$. (Again, Yalta, 2008, reported on the accuracy of software for statistical distributions.)

Applying the required values that were reported earlier to Equation 2.2 yields

$$s_p^2 = \frac{[(29-1)69.755 + (26-1)22.508]}{29+26-2} = 47.469.$$

Applying the needed values now to Equation 2.1 yields

$$ME_{.95} = 2.006 \left[47.469 \left(\frac{1}{29} + \frac{1}{26} \right) \right]^{1/2} = 3.733.$$

Therefore, the limits of the .95 CI given by expression (2.3) are $CI_{.95}$: (85.697 − 81.108) ± 3.733.

The difference between 85.687 and 81.108 is 4.589, which is the point estimate of $\mu_a - \mu_b$. The interval is thus bounded by the lower limit of $4.589 - 3.733 = .856$ lb and the upper limit of $4.589 + 3.733 = 8.322$ lb. The interval from .856 to 8.322 does not include the value 0, so this confidence interval also indicates that the difference between $\overline{Y}_a$ and $\overline{Y}_b$ is statistically significant at the two-tailed .05 level. One can conclude that there is statistically significantly greater weight in the girls who underwent Treatment a compared to the girls who underwent Treatment b. One is also approximately 95% confident that the interval between .856 and 8.322 lb contains the difference in weight between the two treatment populations. That the sample sizes are not equal ($n_a = 29$, $n_b = 26$) is not necessarily problematic. However, if the smaller size of sample b resulted from participants dropping out for a reason that was related to the degree of effectiveness of a treatment (*nonrandom attrition*) then the confidence interval, and a test of significance, would not be valid. The point estimate and the limits of the interval are depicted in Figure 2.1.

Tips and Pitfalls

Again, the practical significance of the aforementioned result would be a matter for expert opinion in the field of study (medical opinion in this case), not a matter of

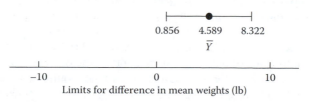

FIGURE 2.1 Limits for the 95% confidence interval for the difference in mean weights of anorectic girls who had been given either Treatment a or Treatment b.

statistical opinion. Similarly, suppose that the current confidence limits, .856 and 8.322, had resulted not from two treatments for anorexia nervosa but from two programs intended to raise the IQs of children who are about average in IQ. The practical significance of such limits (rounded to 1 and 8 IQ points) would be a matter about which educators or developmental psychologists should opine. In different fields of research the same numerical results may well have different degrees of practical significance.

Observe that there is approximately a 3:1 ratio of s_a^2 and s_b^2 in the present example ($69.755/22.508 \approx 3.1$). This ratio suggests possible heteroscedasticity although it could also be plausibly attributable to sampling variability of variances, which can be great. The possibility of heteroscedasticity suggests that one of the more robust methods that is discussed in later sections of this chapter may be more appropriate for the data at hand.

FURTHER DISCUSSIONS AND METHODS

For further discussions of methods for constructing more accurate confidence intervals when assumptions are satisfied consult Bird (2002), Cumming and Finch (2001), Lecoutre (2007), and Smithson (2001, 2003). Refer to Fidler and Thompson (2001) for an illustration of the use of IBM SPSS software for the construction of a confidence interval for $\mu_a - \mu_b$. For negative or moderated views of confidence intervals consult Feinstein (1998), Frick (1995), Parker (1995), and Knapp and Sawilowsky (2001). The latter reference argues that either testing statistical significance or constructing a confidence interval might be preferable in a given case of drawing an inference from data.

This chapter only considers the case in which the sampling distribution of the point estimate on which a confidence interval is based is symmetrically distributed. In such cases the resulting confidence interval is said to be symmetric because the value of the *ME* that is subtracted from the point estimate to find the lower limit of the interval is the same as the value that is added to the estimate to find the upper limit. Therefore, in such cases the upper and lower limits are equidistant from the estimate. However, when the sampling distribution of the point estimate is skewed (e.g., the sampling distribution of a proportion in a sample, such as the proportion of treated patients whose health improves), it is possible to construct an *asymmetric confidence interval*. An asymmetric confidence interval is one in which the value that is subtracted from the point estimate is not the same as the value that is added to the estimate to find, respectively, the lower and upper limits. In such cases the limits are calculated separately as values that cut off approximately $\alpha/2$ of the area of the sampling distribution at either end. Thus, with regard to an asymmetric confidence interval, the lower limit is the value that has $\alpha/2$ of the area of the sampling distribution below it and the upper limit is the value that has $\alpha/2$ of the area beyond it, with no requirement that these two values be equidistant from the estimate. With regard to an asymmetrical confidence interval, the distance between the point estimate and the lower limit and the distance between the point estimate and the upper limit are called the *lower width* and the *upper width*, respectively. (Asymmetric confidence intervals may arise more commonly in behavioral and social research than is generally acknowledged.) Discussions of other intervals, such as tolerance intervals and prediction intervals, would be beyond the scope of this book.

SOLUTIONS TO VIOLATIONS OF ASSUMPTIONS: WELCH'S APPROXIMATE METHOD

If the assumption of homoscedasticity is violated the use of the previously discussed t-based procedure can produce a misleading confidence level, unless perhaps $n_a = n_b \geq 15$ (Ramsey, 1980; Wilcox, 1997). May (2003) reported that violations of assumptions that cause inaccurate p levels also cause inaccuracy of apparent confidence levels. The effect of skew on the rate of Type II error of the t test was discussed by Vickers (2008b). Wilcox (2008a) described a situation in which skew surprisingly causes the power of the t test to *decrease* the more false the null hypothesis is.

Wilcox (2003, 2005a) discussed the influence of heavy-tailed distributions on confidence intervals even when samples are very large. In the case of heteroscedasticity, if $n_a \neq n_b$ the actual confidence level can be lower than the nominal one. For example, a supposed .95 CI may in fact be an interval that has much less than a .95 probability of containing the value of $\mu_a - \mu_b$. The least that a researcher should do about possible heteroscedasticity when constructing a confidence interval for $\mu_a - \mu_b$ under the assumption of normality would be to use samples as close to equal size as is possible and consisting of at least 15 participants each. However, an often more accurate, approximate procedure for constructing a confidence interval for $\mu_a - \mu_b$ in this case is Welch's (1938) *approximate solution*. The Welch method is often also called the Welch–James method (James, 1951) and sometimes called the Satterthwaite (1946) procedure, although the former involves slightly greater degrees of freedom. The methods involve approximate, not exact, degrees of freedom.

The Welch procedure accommodates heteroscedasticity in two ways. First, Equation 2.1 is modified so as to use estimates of σ_a^2 and σ_b^2 (population variances that are believed to be different) from s_a^2 and s_b^2 separately instead of pooling s_a^2 and s_b^2 to estimate a common population variance. Second, the equation for df is also modified (an example of an *approximate-degrees-of-freedom* or *adjusted-degrees-of-freedom* method) to take into account the inequality of σ_a^2 and σ_b^2. Thus, using a .95 CI again for our example, in this method,

$$ME_w = t^* \left[\frac{s_a^2}{n_a} + \frac{s_b^2}{n_b} \right]^{1/2}, \tag{2.4}$$

where
  w stands for Welch
  t^* is the absolute critical value of the t statistic that a t table or a density function for t in software indicates is required to attain significance at the two-tailed .05 level

The heteroscedasticity-adjusted degrees of freedom for the Welch procedure, df_w, is given by

$$df_w = \frac{\left[s_a^2/n_a + s_b^2/n_b \right]^2}{\left(s_a^2/n_a\right)^2/(n_a - 1) + \left(s_b^2/n_b\right)^2/(n_b - 1)}. \tag{2.5}$$

To find t^* enter a t table or use any software, such as TDIST, that provides a density function for t, at the df that results from Equation 2.5. The limits of the confidence interval are then found using expression (2.3), now with ME_w replacing ME.

The Welch method often results in a smaller margin of error than the usual, previously demonstrated, method that pools the two values of s^2 and leaves df unadjusted. (A smaller margin of error results in a narrower, more informative, confidence interval.) However, although the Welch method appears to counter heteroscedasticity well enough, it may not provide accurate confidence levels when at least one of the population distributions is not normal, especially (but not exclusively) when $n_a \neq n_b$.

According to the review by Wilcox (1996) the Welch method may perform at its worst when the two populations are skewed differently and sample sizes are small and unequal. Bonett and Price (2002) confirmed that the method is problematic when sample sizes are small and the two population distributions are grossly and very differently nonnormal. Again, at the very least researchers who are planning to construct confidence intervals for $\mu_a - \mu_b$ should try to use samples that are as large and as close to equal in size as is possible. Using equal or nearly equal-sized samples, ranging from $n = 10$ to 30 each, may result in sufficiently accurate confidence levels under some of types of nonnormality, but a researcher cannot be certain if the kind and degree of nonnormality in given populations represent an exception to this conclusion (Bonett & Price), perhaps especially when distributions have very heavy tails. Researchers should consider using one of the robust methods that deal simultaneously with heteroscedasticity and nonnormality when constructing a confidence interval to compare the locations of two groups. (Such methods are discussed later in this chapter.)

Tips and Pitfalls
The prevalence of disappointingly wide confidence intervals in the literature (including the confidence intervals that are based on real data in the present book) may be partly responsible for their infrequent use in behavioral research in the past. Also, the wider the confidence interval the less likely it becomes that the point estimate of the parameter will be closely replicated in other studies of that parameter. The application of methods that are more robust may result in narrower confidence intervals that inspire researchers to report confidence intervals routinely, where appropriate, as many methodologists have urged. A decision about reporting a confidence interval must be made a priori, not based on how pleasing its width is to the researcher.

WORKED EXAMPLE OF THE WELCH METHOD

The following hand-calculated example of the Welch method constructs a .95 *CI* for $\mu_a - \mu_b$ from the same data on weight gain in anorexia nervosa as in the previous example. Calculation by hand here should provide enhanced understanding of the method for those who are unfamiliar with it. Common commercial statistical software provides the Welch method as the alternative for the case of two independent groups with unequal variances.

One first finds df_w in order to determine the value of t^* to use in Equation 2.4 to obtain ME_w. Applying the previously stated values to Equation 2.5 yields

$$df_w = \frac{[69.755/29 + 22.508/26]^2}{(69.755/29)^2/(29-1) + (22.508/26)^2/(26-1)} = 45.221.$$

Rounded to the nearest integer, $df_w = 45$. Using any accurate software for a density function for t one finds that for $df = 45$ the critical value of $t = 2.014$. Applying this value of t^* and the other previously stated required values to Equation 2.4 yields $ME_w = 2.014[69.755/29 + 22.508/26]^{1/2} = 3.643$. Therefore, the limits of the .95 *CI* are, using expression (2.3) with *ME* replaced by ME_w, $CI_{.95}$: $(85.697 - 81.108) \pm$ 3.643; that is, $CI_{.95}$: 4.589 ± 3.643.

We previously found that the point estimate of $\mu_a - \mu_b$ is 4.589 lb for the present data. Now using the Welch method one finds that the margin of error associated with this point estimate is not ±3.733 lb, as before, but ±3.643 lb.

Observe that, as is often the case, $|ME_w| < |ME|$, 3.643 < 3.733, but the Welch-based interval, bounded by $4.589 - 3.643 = .946$ and $4.589 + 3.643 = 8.232$, is only slightly narrower than the previously constructed interval from .856 to 8.322. Provided that a researcher has used the more nearly accurate method, it is good to narrow the confidence interval without lowering the confidence level. As before, the interval does not contain the value 0, so this interval implies that $\overline{Y}_a$ is statistically significantly greater than $\overline{Y}_b$ at the .05 level, two-tailed.

Recall that the Welch method may not yield accurate confidence intervals when $n_a \neq n_b$. However, in the present example the samples sizes are not very unequal and not very small. In the next section we consider a method that addresses the problems of heteroscedasticity and skew at the same time.

YUEN'S CONFIDENCE INTERVAL FOR THE DIFFERENCE BETWEEN TWO TRIMMED MEANS

Yuen's (1974) method constructs a confidence interval for $\mu_{ta} - \mu_{tb}$, where each μ_t is a trimmed population mean. A *trimmed mean* of a sample ($\overline{Y}_t$) is the usual arithmetic mean calculated after removing (trimming) the c lowest and the same c highest scores, without replacing them. For our purpose we roughly define, say, the commonly recommended 20% μ_t as the arithmetic mean of those scores in the population that fall within the .20 and .80 quantiles of that population.

Thus, with 20% trimming in each tail a total of 40% of the data is trimmed. Choice of the optimum amount of trimming depends on several factors, the detailed discussion of which would be beyond the scope of this book. Trimming of $c\%$ of the scores has been reported to generally work well if fewer than $2c\%$ of the scores are outliers (Keselman et al., 2008).

Trimming has been recommended and is being increasingly studied by respected statistical methodologists, but the practice is not common. Many researchers and instructors of statistics are likely leery of any method that alters or discards data. This issue is discussed at greater length at the end of this section.

The optimum amount of trimming has appeared to range from 0% to slightly over 25%. The greater the number of outliers the greater the justification may be for, say, 25%, trimming. For a discussion of trimming less than 20% refer to Kowalchuk, Keselman, Wilcox, and Algina (2006). Consult Wilcox (2008a), Wilcox and Keselman (2002a), and Keselman et al. (2008) for detailed discussions and references on the optimum amount of trimming.

When population distributions are normal, which is not the assumption of this section, for simplicity one would use the usual arithmetic means, which is equivalent to 0% trimming. However, in this case of normality, or any other form of symmetry, the trimmed arithmetic mean is equal to the traditional arithmetic mean. Also, even 20% trimming does not greatly lower power under normality (Wilcox, 2008a). If one trimmed all but the middle-ranked score the trimmed mean would be the same as the median. Thus, a trimmed mean is conceptually and numerically between the traditional arithmetic mean (0% trimming) and the median (maximum trimming).

If one or more outliers are causing the departure from normality, then by eliminating the outlier(s) trimming brings the focus to the middle group of scores. Methods involving *adaptive trimming* empirically determine if trimming is warranted and, if so, how much trimming is optimal (Keselman, Wilcox, Lix, Algina, & Fradette, 2007).

Because it has traditionally been considered to be often optimum or close to optimum, 20% (.2) trimming is the method that we demonstrate. In this case $c = .2n$ for each sample. If c is not a whole number, then round c down to the nearest whole number. For example, if $n = 29$, $.2n = .2(29) = 5.8$, and, rounding down, $c = 5$. The number of remaining scores, n_r, in the group is equal to $n - 2c$. In the previous example of the anorectic sample that received Treatment a, $n_r = n_a - 2c = 29 - 2(5) = 19$. For the sample that received Treatment b, $c = .2n_b = .2(26) = 5.2$, which rounds to 5. For this group $n_r = n_b - .2c = 26 - 2(5) = 16$. We provide references for software after the labor-intensive manual calculation is demonstrated for the purpose of providing a greater understanding of the method.

The first step in the Yuen method is to arrange the scores for each group separately in order. Then, for each group separately, eliminate the $c = .2n$ most extreme low scores and eliminate the same number of the most extreme high scores. The procedure does not require that $n_a = n_b$. If $n_a \neq n_b$, it may or may not turn out that a different number of scores is trimmed from groups a and b depending on the results of rounding the values of c. Next, calculate the trimmed mean, $\overline{Y}_r$, for each group by applying the usual equation for the arithmetic mean using the remaining sample size, n_r, in the denominator: $\overline{Y}_t = (\Sigma Y)/n_r$. Continuing in this section with the previous data on weight gain in treated anorexia, one removes the five highest and five lowest scores from each sample to find the trimmed means of the remaining scores, $\overline{Y}_{ta} = 85.294$ and $\overline{Y}_{tb} = 81.031$.

The next step is to calculate the numerator of the Winsorized variance, SS_w, for each group by applying steps 3 through 5 for calculating a Winsorized variance that were presented in the section entitled "Worked examples of measures of variability" in Chapter 1. (Steps 1 and 2 of that procedure will already have been completed by this stage of the method.) Applying steps 3 through 5 to calculate the numerator of a Winsorized variance one replaces, in each sample, the trimmed five lowest original scores with five repetitions of the lowest remaining score, and one replaces the five trimmed highest original scores with five repetitions of the highest remaining score. Because $s^2 = SS/(n-1)$, $SS = s^2(n-1)$. Using any statistical software one finds that for the reconstituted samples (original remaining scores plus the scores that replaced the trimmed scores) $s^2_{wa} = 30.206$ and $s^2_{wb} = 12.718$. Therefore, $SS_{wa} = 30.206(29-1) = 845.768$ and $SS_{wb} = 12.718(26-1) = 317.950$.

Next, calculate a needed statistic, w_y, separately for each group, to find w_{ya} and w_{yb}, where again the subscript y stands for Yuen. The value of w_y is found separately for each sample by calculating

$$w_y = \frac{SS_w}{n_r(n_r - 1)}. \tag{2.6}$$

The ME_y for the confidence interval for $\mu_{ta} - \mu_{tb}$ is

$$ME_y = t^*(w_{ya} + w_{yb})^{1/2}, \tag{2.7}$$

and the confidence limits for $\mu_{ta} - \mu_{tb}$ become

$$(\overline{Y}_{ta} - \overline{Y}_{tb}) \pm ME_y \tag{2.8}$$

The df to be used to find the value of t^* in Yuen's procedure, df_y, is

$$df_y = \frac{(w_{ya} + w_{yb})^2}{\left(w_{ya}^2/(n_{ra} - 1)\right) + \left(w_{yb}^2/(n_{rb} - 1)\right)}. \tag{2.9}$$

Applying the previously reported required values to Equation 2.6 yields $w_{ya} = 845.768/19(19-1) = 2.473$, and $w_{yb} = 317.950/16(16-1) = 1.325$. Now applying the required values to Equation 2.9 yields

$$df_y = \frac{(2.473 + 1.325)^2}{2.473^2/(19-1) + 1.325^2/(16-1)} = 32.$$

Using any accurate software for the density function of t indicates that the critical value of t at $df = 32$ is 2.037. Now applying the obtained required values to Equation 2.7 yields, regarding the .95 CI, $ME_{y.95} = 2.037(2.473 + 1.325)^{1/2} = 3.970$. Finally, applying the required values to expression (2.8) one finds that the .95 CI is bounded by the limits $(85.294 - 81.031 = 4.263) \pm 3.970$. Thus, the point estimate of $\mu_{ta} - \mu_{tb}$ is 4.263 lb, and the .95 CI ranges from $4.263 - 3.970 = .293$ lb to $4.263 + 3.970 = 8.233$ lb.

Although this is not the case with regard to the present data, the Yuen method usually results in narrower confidence intervals than the Welch method (Wilcox, 1996). The present Yuen-based interval from .293 to 8.233 lb is wider than the previously calculated Welch-based interval from .946 to 8.232 lb. However, it is likely that the use of an alternative to s_w in the Yuen procedure would narrow the interval that it produced (Bunner & Sawilowsky, 2002).

All three of the methods that were applied to the data on anorexia lead to the same general conclusions. All three methods resulted in confidence intervals that did not contain the value 0, so one can conclude that the mean (or trimmed mean) weight of girls in sample a is statistically significantly greater than the mean (or trimmed mean) weight of girls in sample b at the two-tailed .05 level. Also, all three methods yielded a lower limit of mean (or trimmed mean) weight difference that is under 1 lb and an upper limit of mean (or trimmed mean) weight difference that is slightly over 8 lb. Again, a conclusion about the clinical significance of such results would be for specialists in the field of anorexia nervosa to consider.

Observe in Equations 2.7 and 2.9 that the Yuen method is a hybrid procedure of countering nonnormality by trimming, and countering heteroscedasticity (i.e., accommodating unequal Winsorized variances) by using the Welch method of adjusting degrees of freedom and treating sample variabilities separately instead of pooling them. Wilcox (2005a) aptly called the Yuen method the "Yuen–Welch" method and provided S-PLUS and R software functions for constructing a .95 CI using this method. Wilcox (1996) also provided Minitab macros for constructing the interval at the .95 or at other levels of confidence. Reed (2003) provided executable FORTRAN code for Yuen's method. Consult Keselman et al. (2008) for further discussion.

The Yuen method has competition such as bootstrapping methods that are discussed in the next section. Moreover, as was mentioned earlier, there may also be discomfort on the part of many researchers about trimming data in general and about lack of certainty about the optimum amount of trimming to be done for any particular set of data. However, there may be an irony here. It could be argued that some researchers would accept the use of medians, which amounts, in effect, to the maximum amount of trimming ("trimming" all but middle-ranked scores) but would be leery of the more modest amount of trimming (20%) that was discussed in this section. Also, as Wilcox (2001) pointed out, trimming is common in certain kinds of judging in athletic competition, such as removing the highest and lowest ratings before calculating the mean of the judges' ratings of a performance.

We have only discussed *symmetrical trimming*, which is trimming the same percentage of scores in each tail. However, to improve the rate of Type I error it may sometimes be better to use *asymmetrical trimming*, which is the trimming of different percentages of scores in each tail in order better to correct nonnormality and heteroscedasticity (Keselman, Algina, & Fradette, 2005).

Although by using the Yuen method one is not constructing a confidence interval for the traditional $\mu_a - \mu_b$, but for the much less familiar $\mu_{ta} - \mu_{tb}$, the researcher who is interested in constructing a confidence interval for the difference between the outcomes for the average (typical) members of population *a* and population *b* should recognize that, when there is skew, μ_t may better represent the score of the typical person in a population than would a skew-distorted traditional μ. For a negative view of trimming refer to Bonett and Price (2002).

OTHER METHODS FOR INDEPENDENT GROUPS

DIFFERENCE BETWEEN MEDIANS

There are other methods for constructing a confidence interval for the difference between two populations' locations as an effect size. Some such methods involve the difference between two medians (Bonett & Price, 2002; Wilcox, 1996, 2003a, 2005b, 2009a). Wilcox (2005b) conducted simulations that indicated that the Harrell–Davis method for medians provides good control of Type I error even when very small samples are drawn from heavy-tailed distributions. Roughly defined, a *heavy-tailed distribution* is one in which there are exceptionally many very small or very large values. Shulkin and Sawilowsky (2009) reported on methods for medians that appear to be superior to the Harrell–Davis method. Simulating various violations of normality, Mends-Cole (2008) reported the probability coverage and interval widths for methods for constructing a confidence interval for the difference between two independent medians, and also for the Welch and Yuen methods.

DIFFERENCE BETWEEN M-ESTIMATORS

The *one-step M-estimator method* is mentioned here because it is among the methods that appear to be often (but not always) better than the traditional method. The one-step M-estimator method is based on a refinement of the trimming procedure. (The letter M stands for maximum-likelihood-like.) There are two related issues when calculating trimmed means. We have already discussed the first issue, choosing how much trimming to do. Second, as we have also discussed, traditional trimming trims equally on both sides of a distribution. However, in the case of skew, traditional trimming results in trimming as many scores on the side of the distribution opposite to the skew, where trimming is not needed, or less needed, as on the skewed side of the distribution, where trimming is needed, or needed more. A measure of location whose value is minimally changed by outliers is called a *resistant measure of location*. M-estimators of location are resistant measures that can be based on determining how much, if any, trimming should be done separately for each side of a distribution.

The arithmetic mean gives equal weight to all scores (no trimming) when averaging scores. However, when calculating a trimmed mean traditional trimming in effect gives no weight to the trimmed scores and equal weight to each of the remaining scores and the scores that have replaced the trimmed scores. Using M-estimators is less drastic than using trimmed means because M-estimators are based on weighting scores with weights other than 0 (i.e., discarding) or 1 (i.e., keeping and treating equally) when calculating location by giving progressively more weight to the scores closer to the center of the distribution. Different M-estimators use different weighting schemes.

The simplest M-estimation procedure is called one-step M-estimation. A Minitab macro (Wilcox, 1996) and S-PLUS and R software functions (Wilcox, 2003, 2005a) are available for constructing a confidence interval for the difference between the locations of two populations using one-step M-estimation. When heteroscedasticity is caused by skew, using traditionally trimmed means may be better than using one-step M-estimators (Bickel & Lehmann, 1975), but both methods may yield inaccurate confidence levels when ns are below 20.

In general, because of the possibility of excessively inaccurate confidence levels, the original methods using one-step M-estimators are not recommended when both sample sizes are below 20. However, a modified version of such estimators may prove to be applicable to small samples (Wilcox, 2005a, with S-PLUS and R software functions). Accessible introductions to M-estimation can be found in Wilcox (2003), and Wilcox and Keselman (2003). Wilcox's code for the R software function is freely downloadable from http://www-rcf.usc.edu/~rwilcox.

BOOTSTRAPPING

With regard to the construction of confidence intervals for the difference between two populations' locations (again, such a difference being an effect size), the goal is to develop methods that are more accurate under a wider range of violations of assumptions and conditions, such as small sample sizes, than the methods that have been discussed in this and the preceding sections. One such robust method is the percentile t bootstrap method (also known as the bootstrap-t method) applied to one-step M-estimators (Wilcox, 2003, 2009a). There are various bootstrapping methods. We provide only a brief conceptual introduction to the simplest method of bootstrapping and references for detailed discussions.

A *bootstrap sample* can be obtained by randomly sampling n scores one at a time, *with replacement* one at a time, from the originally obtained sample of N scores, where $n < N$. Numerous such bootstrap samples are obtained (say, 600) using special software for the purpose. A targeted statistic of interest (e.g., the mean) is calculated for each bootstrap sample. Then a sampling distribution of all of these bootstrap-based values of the targeted statistic is generated. This sampling distribution is intended to approximate more accurately the actual sampling distribution of the targeted statistic when assumptions are not satisfied, as contrasted with its supposed theoretical distribution (e.g., the t distribution) when assumptions are satisfied.

The goal of *bootstrapping* in the present context is to base the construction of confidence intervals and significance testing on a bootstrap-based sampling distribution that more accurately approximates the *actual* sampling distribution of the statistic than does the traditional *supposed* sampling distribution that would be inapplicable when assumptions are violated. Recall that what we have called the margin of error is a function of the standard error of the relevant sampling distribution. Bootstrapping provides an empirical estimate of this standard error that can be used in place of what its theoretical value would be if assumptions were satisfied.

The statistical term "bootstrapping" originated from the phrase for the impossible task of "lifting oneself up by one's bootstraps," which originated from the fact that some boots include straps on the left and on the right top of each boot to facilitate pulling the boots on. The expectation that one can use such bootstraps to pull oneself up from the floor would be counterintuitive, a violation of the laws of physics. Similarly, to some non-statisticians the use of bootstrapping to approximate an actual complete sampling distribution (ideally based on an infinite number of values) may seem to be a vain attempt to gain such information from apparently merely repeatedly recycling the original data. (Recall, however, that each datum is replaced before the next datum is randomly drawn from the original sample.)

In a very simple bootstrapping method for constructing a 95% confidence interval, the lower and upper limits are the values that cut off the lower 2.5% and the upper 2.5%, respectively, of the values of the bootstrapped distribution. Specifically, the lower and upper limits of such a $(1 - \alpha)100\%$ confidence interval are the $\alpha/2$ and $1 - (\alpha/2)$ quantiles, respectively, of the *bootstrapped distribution*.

Wilcox (2003, 2005a) provided software functions for bootstrapping to construct confidence intervals. In the case of confidence intervals for the difference between two populations' locations (e.g., means, trimmed means, medians) bootstrap samples are taken from the two original samples that represent the two populations, and the difference between the two locations is calculated for each of the hundreds of pairs of bootstrapped samples. Refer to Wilcox (2003, 2005a, 2005b) and Keselman et al. (2008) for detailed descriptions of the applications of various bootstrap methods to attempt to improve the other methods that we have discussed. For criticisms of bootstrap methods for constructing confidence intervals refer to Gleser (1996). For a relatively non-technical discussions of bootstrap methods consult Thompson (1993, 1999) and Wood (2005), who discussed and provided simple programs for constructing confidence intervals for many common parameters.

This book only discusses confidence intervals that have a lower and an upper limit (*two-sided confidence intervals*). However, there are *one-sided confidence intervals* that involve only a lower limit or only an upper limit. For example, a researcher may be interested in acquiring evidence that a parameter, such as the difference between two populations' means, exceeds a certain minimum value. In such a case the lower limit for, say, a one-sided .95 *CI* is found by calculating the lower limit of a two-sided .90 *CI*. Consult Smithson (2003) for further discussion.

CRITERIA FOR METHODS FOR CONSTRUCTING A CONFIDENCE INTERVAL

There are various criteria for evaluating the performance of a method for constructing a confidence interval using computerized simulations, there being two that are the most widely used and likely sufficient for choosing between competing methods unless those methods perform equally with respect to those two criteria. First, one can calculate some sort of average of the probability coverages over repeated simulations for a given method. Ideally a method should produce intervals that on average include the targeted parameter (e.g., $\mu_a - \mu_b$) very close to $(1 - \alpha)100\%$ of the time or, better, a *minimum* at or very close to $(1 - \alpha)100\%$ of the time. An *exact confidence interval* is often defined as one that includes the parameter exactly $(1 - \alpha)100\%$ of the time. If the coverage probability is actually less than the nominal $(1 - \alpha)$, coverage is said to be *liberal*. If coverage is greater than $(1 - \alpha)$, coverage is said to be *conservative* (although some authors include the case of conservative coverage in their definition of an exact confidence interval).

Second, one compares the average widths of the confidence intervals over repeated simulations. Ideally a method should produce a narrow confidence interval while maintaining probability coverage at or above $1 - \alpha$. There is often a trade-off between probability coverage and narrowness of a confidence interval.

If the first two criteria do not distinguish between competing methods one should consider application of one or more of six additional criteria, for discussions of which consult Brown and Li (2005), Lawson (2004), and Smithson (2003). One sense in which a method may said to be "best" is if it yields confidence intervals that are found to have the lowest probability of containing values other than the true parameter at a given level of confidence. A method that satisfies this criterion is said to produce confidence intervals that are *uniformly most accurate* (Smithson). It is also desirable that the probability coverage get closer to $1 - \alpha$ rapidly and evenly as sample sizes increase and that a method produce *unbiased confidence intervals*, one definition of which is that when an interval does not contain the parameter the interval should be equally likely to be above or below the parameter.

Kelley, Maxwell, and Rausch (2003) recommended their method for constructing confidence intervals and calculating needed sample sizes when (a) desired widths are pre-specified or (b) the probability of attaining a stated desired width is pre-specified. This method is called the *accuracy in parameter estimation method (AIPE)* and was discussed further by Kelley and Maxwell (2003) and Maxwell, Kelley, and Rausch (2008). The AIPE method supplements a traditional pre-research power calculation for determining needed sample size. The purpose of such a method is to estimate the sample size that would be needed in order to construct a confidence interval that excludes a null-hypothesized value of the parameter when the null hypothesis is false. Kelley and Maxwell argued that the ideal sample size would be one that (a) yields enough power to be able to detect the minimum effect that the researcher considers to be important and (b) results in a reasonably accurate estimate (i.e., a narrow confidence interval) of the size of the effect. The researcher then chooses the larger of two estimates of needed sample sizes as estimated by application of the power-calculation approach and by application of the AIPE approach, that is, the sample size that is estimated to be needed to attain the desired accuracy and the desired statistical power. A problem arises if the estimated needed sample size greatly exceeds the researcher's resources.

We have been using the term "accuracy" of a confidence interval somewhat loosely. The *accuracy* of a method for constructing a confidence interval is related to, but not strictly synonymous with, the *narrowness* of the intervals. Consult Kelley and Maxwell (2008) for further discussions of accuracy and precision. Kelley and Maxwell and Maxwell, Kelley, and Rausch (2008) defined accuracy in estimating a parameter as a function of *precision*, which is the variance of the sampling distribution of the estimates of the parameter, and *bias*, which is a systematic tendency either to overestimate or underestimate the parameter when the parameter is not in the interval. For example, suppose that the correlation in a population, r_{pop}, is equal to .5. Suppose further that one method tends to produce .95 confidence intervals for $r_{pop} = .5$ with intervals from .6 to .7, whereas another method tends to produce .95 confidence intervals with intervals from .4 to .6. Although the first method tends to produce the narrower intervals, it is so positively biased it rarely will contain the true parameter, $r_{pop} = .5$. Thus, the accuracy of a method for constructing a confidence interval is a function of the narrowness and bias of the intervals that it produces.

DEPENDENT GROUPS

Construction of confidence intervals when using dependent groups requires modification of methods that are applicable to independent groups. *Dependent-groups designs* include *repeated-measures* (*within-groups, pretest–posttest*) and *matched-groups designs*. It is well known that interpreting results from a pretest–posttest design can be problematic, especially if the design does not involve a control or other comparison group and random assignment to each group. In a single-group pretest–posttest design for the study of the efficacy of a psychotherapy there is no control for such confounding factors as placebo effects, additional interventions that are not known to the researcher, and spontaneous changes in patients over time. Such factors can inflate estimates of effect size. (Consult Hunter & Schmidt, 2004, for a favorable view of the pretest–posttest design.) Also, the customary counterbalancing in repeated-measures designs does not protect against the possibility that a lingering effect of Treatment *a* when Treatment *b* is next applied may not be the same as the lingering effect of Treatment *b* when Treatment *a* is next applied (called *asymmetrical transfer of effect* or *differential carryover*). We now use real data from a pretest–posttest design to illustrate traditional construction of a confidence interval for dependent groups. Table 2.1 depicts the weights (pounds) of 17 anorectic girls before and after treatment (Everitt; raw data presented in Hand et al., 1994).

Assuming normality, we construct a .95 *CI* for the mean difference between posttreatment and pretreatment scores in the population, $\mu_a - \mu_b$. We begin by defining a difference score, $D_i = Y_a - Y_b$, where Y_a and Y_b are the scores

TABLE 2.1

Differences between Anorectics' Weights (in lb) Posttreatment and Pretreatment

Participant	Posttreatment	Pretreatment	Difference (D)
1	95.2	83.8	11.4
2	94.3	83.3	11.0
3	91.5	86.0	5.5
4	91.9	82.5	9.4
5	100.3	86.7	13.6
6	76.7	79.6	−2.9
7	76.8	76.9	−0.1
8	101.6	94.2	7.4
9	94.9	73.4	21.5
10	75.2	80.5	−5.3
11	77.8	81.6	−3.8
12	95.5	82.1	13.4
13	90.7	77.6	13.1
14	92.5	83.5	9.0
15	93.8	89.9	3.9
16	91.7	86.0	5.7
17	98.0	87.3	11.5

Source: Data from Everitt, B.S. *A Handbook of Small Data Sets*, D.J. Hand et al. (Eds.), Chapman & Hall, London, 1994.

(weights in the present example) of the same participants under, respectively, condition a (posttreatment weight) and condition b (pretreatment weight). Thus, for participant number 1 in Table 2.1 $D_1 = 95.2 - 83.8 = 11.4$. Because $\overline{Y}_a - \overline{Y}_b$ estimates $\mu_a - \mu_b$, and because it can easily be shown that the mean of such a set of D_i values, $\overline{D} = (\Sigma D)/n$, is also equal to $\overline{Y}_a - \overline{Y}_b$ (i.e., the mean difference score is equal to the difference between means), $\overline{D}$ too estimates $\mu_a - \mu_b$. Therefore, because $\overline{D}$ is a point estimate of $\mu_a - \mu_b$, a confidence interval for $\mu_a - \mu_b$ can be constructed around the value of $\overline{D}$.

Recall from expression (2.3) that the limits of the confidence intervals that are discussed in this chapter are given by the point estimate ± the margin of error (*ME*). In the case of two dependent groups the limits are thus

$$\overline{D} \pm ME_{\text{dep}}, \tag{2.10}$$

where "dep" stands for dependent, and

$$ME_{\text{dep}} = t^* \left(\frac{s_D}{n^{1/2}} \right). \tag{2.11}$$

The symbol s_D in Equation 2.11 represents the standard deviation of the values of D, and $s_D/n^{1/2}$ is the standard error of the mean of the values of D. The s_D is calculated as an unbiased estimate of σ_D in the population, so first $n - 1$ is used in the denominator of s_D whereas $n^{1/2}$, not $(n - 1)^{1/2}$, is then used in the denominator of the standard error of the mean, as shown in Equation 2.11, so as not to correct for bias twice. The n that is used in Equation 2.11 is the number of paired observations (i.e., the number of D_i values).

For a .95 CI one needs to find the value of t^* that is required for statistical significance at the two-tailed .05 level. The df for t^* for the case of dependent groups is given by $n - 1$. In the current example $df = n - 1 = 17 - 1 = 16$. The critical value of t^* will be found, in a t table or any accurate software for a density function for t, to be 2.120.

Using any statistical software to calculate the needed sample statistics one finds that $\bar{D} = 7.265$ and $s_D = 7.157$. Applying the required values to Equation 2.11 yields $ME_{dep} = 2.120(7.157/17^{1/2}) = 3.680$.

Finally, applying the required values to expression (2.10) yields the following lower and upper limits for the .95 CI for $\mu_a - \mu_b$: $\bar{D} \pm ME_{dep} = 7.265 - 3.680 = 3.6$ lb and $7.265 + 3.680 = 10.9$ lb, respectively. One is approximately 95% confident (again, assuming normality) that the interval between 3.6 and 10.9 contains the mean weight gain in the population. Because this interval does not contain the value 0, the gain in weight can be considered to be statistically significant at the .05 level, two-tailed. Again, in general we cannot nearly definitively attribute statistically significant gains or losses from pretreatment to posttreatment to the effect of a treatment unless there is random assignment to the treatment and to a control or comparison group. In the present example of treatments for anorexia, a control group was included by the researcher, but it would be beyond the scope of this chapter to discuss a further analysis of these data (e.g., analysis of covariance, as is discussed in Chapter 11).

Afshartous and Preston (2010) proposed and provided R software code for a method for constructing a confidence interval for the difference between two dependent means under heteroscedasticity. For dependent data in which the distribution of the D_i values is skewed, there is a Minitab macro (Wilcox, 1996) and there are S-PLUS and R software functions (Wilcox, 2005a) for constructing an approximate confidence interval for the difference between two quantiles. (Quantiles are defined in Chapter 1 and are discussed further in Chapter 5. Also, skew in distributions of raw scores is diminished by the use of difference scores.) For the case of two dependent groups Wilcox (2005a) also discussed and provided S-PLUS and R functions for constructing a confidence interval for the difference between two trimmed means and for differences between other measures of two distribution's locations. Wilcox (2005b) discussed methods for comparing the medians of two dependent groups. However, in the case of a confidence interval for the difference between means of dependent groups, for much real data skew may not greatly distort probability coverage. Skew does not cause a problem for Type I error (or probability coverage) if skew is identical in each dependent population (Wilcox, 2009a).

Cumming and Finch (2005) demonstrated that, in the case of two dependent groups, comparison of separate confidence intervals for each population's mean is not useful for making inferences about the difference between the two populations' means. Also consult Afshartous and Preston (2010) and Belia et al. (2005) about this topic. Fidler, Faulkner, and Cumming (2008) discussed the construction of confidence intervals for effect sizes for change in response over time in the context of their discussion of intention-to-treat and per-protocol analyses. (The latter two topics were discussed in Chapter 1.)

SUMMARY

This chapter adopted what is called a frequentist view of confidence intervals. A confidence interval provides information about the extent to which an estimate may be overestimating or underestimating a parameter such as (a) the difference between two population means or (b) a population effect size. Such information addresses the precision of an estimate. When the measure of a dependent variable is in familiar units (e.g., human weight or ounces of alcohol consumed) the difference between two population means itself can be considered to be an effect size. A confidence interval is bounded by a lower limit and an upper limit. The true confidence that one can have that such an interval has succeeded in containing the value of the targeted parameter is called the true confidence level or probability coverage, often desired to be .95.

For many parameters (e.g., the difference between two population means) finding that the confidence interval does not have a certain pre-specified value within it implies that if that value had been null hypothesized for the parameter the null hypothesis could have been rejected at the (1 − adopted confidence level) significance level in a statistical test of that hypothesis. For example, if assumptions are satisfied finding that a .95 confidence interval for the difference between two population means does not contain the value 0 implies that a two-tailed test of H_0: $\mu_a - \mu_b = 0$ would have resulted in a value of the t statistic that is statistically significant at the 1 − .95 = .05 level.

Problems can arise if assumptions are violated or if one only constructs a confidence interval contingent on first obtaining a statistically significant result. Before collecting data one should generally preplan to construct a confidence interval and adopt a desired confidence level, or test for statistical significance and adopt a significance level.

There are alternative methods for constructing a confidence interval for the difference between two population means, including the Welch method to counter violation of the assumption of unequal variances and the Yuen method to counter that violation as well as to counter nonnormal distributions using trimming. There are several criteria for choosing between competing methods. The most common goals are to use a method that results in the narrowest possible interval and that has actual probability coverage that is as close as possible to the adopted confidence level (or higher).

Methods for constructing confidence intervals for the difference between two population averages besides means (e.g., medians) are available. Also, alternative approaches to traditional testing for statistical significance or traditional construction of confidence intervals include testing for what are called equivalence of groups, non-inferiority of one specified group, or superiority of one specified group.

QUESTIONS

(You may answer questions about confidence intervals from a frequentist perspective.)

2.1   In what circumstance is a confidence interval most useful?

2.2   Provide a valid definition of a *confidence interval*.

2.3   Define (a) *lower and upper confidence limits*, (b) *confidence level*, (c) *liberal* and *conservative probability coverage*, (d) *independent groups*, (e) *bootstrap sample*, (f) *location* of a distribution, (g) *equivalence, non-inferiority*, and *superiority testing*, (h) *asymmetrical (differential) carryover of effect*, (i) *margin of error*, (j) *location*, (k) *heavy-tailed distribution*.

2.4   What is a common misinterpretation of, say, a 95% confidence interval?

2.5   To what does .95 refer in a 95% confidence interval?

2.6   In the concept of confidence intervals what is constant and what is a random variable?

2.7   List three factors that influence the magnitude of the margin of error, and what effect does each factor have?

2.8   What is the trade-off between using a 95% or a 99% confidence interval?

2.9   What assumption is being made when a pooled estimate is made of population variance?

2.10 For tests and confidence intervals involving the difference between two means what is the relationship between the confidence level and a significance level?

2.11 What factors influence the width of a confidence interval, and in what way for each?

2.12 In what specific ways is the game of horseshoe tossing analogous to the construction of confidence intervals?

2.13 Define and briefly discuss the purpose of *asymmetric confidence intervals*.

2.14 What is the purpose of Welch's approximate method for constructing confidence intervals, and when might a researcher consider using it?

2.15 What are the two differences between the Welch method and the traditional method for constructing confidence intervals?

2.16 What is the effect of skew on the Welch method?

2.17 Define *trimming* and discuss its purpose.

2.18 What factors might influence the optimal amount of trimming?

2.19 What is the purpose of Yuen's method, and in what ways is it a hybrid method?

2.20 What is the irony if a researcher would never consider using trimmed means but would consider using medians?

2.21 In the context of this chapter, what is the general purpose of bootstrapping?

2.22 Define and state the purpose of *one-sided confidence intervals.*

2.23 Define *difference-scores* and describe the role that they play in the construction of confidence intervals in the case of two dependent groups.

2.24 Describe two major criteria for evaluating the performance of a method for constructing a confidence interval.

2.25 What are the two major properties of a ratio scale?

2.26 Regarding most psychological and educational tests what does it mean (and *not* mean) if you score twice as many points on the test as someone else does?

2.27 How are error bars used inconsistently in reports of research?

2.28 Define and discuss *capture percentage* regarding a confidence interval for the mean of a population.

2.29 Describe the TOST procedure.

2.30 For the following real data construct a boxplot (and optionally other diagnostics of assumptions that your software may provide) for the data of each group. On the basis of the two boxplots (and other diagnostics, if any) and the discussions in the text speculate about the appropriateness of constructing a confidence interval for the mean difference using (a) the traditional method that assumes (rightly or wrongly) normality and equal variances, (b) the Welch method, (c) the Yuen method (trimmed means) using 20% trimming. Regardless of your speculation about their appropriateness, as an informative exercise proceed to construct 95% confidence intervals for the mean difference using methods (a), (b), and (c). Optionally, compare the results from application of the Yuen method using other reasonable trimming in addition to 20% trimming. Interpret each confidence interval from parts (a), (b), and (c), and discuss the differences in results in light of the discussions in the text.

Control group: 80.2, 80.1, 86.4, 86.3, 76.1, 78.1, 75.1, 86.7, 73.5, 84.6, 77.4, 79.5, 89.6, 81.4, 81.8, 77.3, 84.2.

Treated group: 95.2, 94.3, 91.5, 91.9, 100.3, 76.7, 76.8, 101.6, 94.9, 75.2, 77.8, 95.5, 90.7, 92.5, 93.8, 91.7, 98.0.

3 The Standardized Difference Between Means

INTRODUCTION

This chapter discusses estimation of the most widely used effect sizes for measuring the extent of difference between two population means for the case of comparing two groups, which either have been randomly formed or are pre-existing, such as women and men.

As was discussed in Chapter 2, confidence interval for the difference between two populations' means (or other measure of location) can be especially informative when the observed dependent variable is measured on a familiar scale that is of interest itself. However, often dependent variables are abstract unobserved variables that are measured indirectly using relatively unfamiliar measures. For example, consider research that compares Treatment *a* and Treatment *b* for depression, a variable that is more abstract and more problematic to measure directly than would be the case with the familiar dependent variable measures that were listed in Chapter 2 (e.g., human weight). Although depression is very real to the person who suffers from it, there is no single, direct way for a researcher to define and measure it as one can do for the familiar scales. There are several tests of depression that are used by researchers, as is true for many other variables outside of the physical sciences. Again, in such cases the presumed underlying variable is called the latent variable, and the score on the test that is believed to be measuring this dependent variable validly is called the measure of the dependent variable, or the observed or manifest variable. Yuan and Bentler (2006) discussed methods for comparing means of latent variables versus comparing means of manifest variables.

Suppose that confidence limits of 5 and 10 points mean difference in Beck Depression Inventory (BDI) scores of depressed groups that were given Treatment *a* or Treatment *b* are reported. Such a finding would be less familiar and less informative (except to specialists) than would be a report of confidence limits of 5 and 10 lb difference in mean weights in our earlier example of research on weight gain from treatments for anorexia. Furthermore, suppose that a researcher conducted a study that compared the efficacy of Treatment *a* and Treatment *b* for depression and that another researcher conducted another study that also compared these two treatments. Suppose also that the first researcher used the BDI as the measure of the dependent variable, whereas the second researcher used, for a conceptual replication of the first study, a different measure, say, the Hamilton Rating Scale for Depression. It would seem to be difficult to compare precisely or combine the results of these two studies because the two scales of depression are not the same. One would not know the relationship between the numerical scores on the two measures. An interval of, say, 5–10 points with respect to the difference between group means on one measure of depression would not necessarily represent the same degree of difference in underlying depression as would an interval of 5–10 points with respect to another measure of depression. What is needed is a measure of effect size that places different dependent variable measures on the same scale so that results from studies that use different measures can be compared or combined. (However, consult Baguley, 2009, 2010, for a somewhat moderated view.) One such measure of effect size is the standardized difference between means (SDM), a frequently used effect size to which we next turn our attention.

STANDARDIZED DIFFERENCE BETWEEN TREATMENT AND COMPARISON MEANS ASSUMING NORMALITY

An *SDM* is like a z score, $z_y = (Y - \mu_y)/\sigma_y$, that standardizes a difference in the sense that it divides it by a standard deviation, which becomes the unit of the z-score scale. A z score indicates how many standard deviations above or below μ_y a Y raw score is, and it can indicate more. For example, assume a normal distribution of raw scores so that z too will be normally distributed. In this case, inspecting a table of the standardized normal curve in any introductory statistics textbook, or a density function for a normal curve in software such as NORMDIST, one finds that approximately 84% of z scores fall below $z = +1.00$ (also inspect Figure 3.1 that is discussed later). (Again, Yalta, 2008, reported on the accuracy of statistical distributions in software.) Therefore, a z score can provide a very informative result, such as indicating that a score at $z = +1.00$ is outscoring approximately 84% of the other scores. Recall that in a normal curve approximately 34% of the scores lie between $z = 0$ and $z = +1.00$, approximately 14% of the scores lie between $z = +1.00$ and $z = +2.00$, and approximately 2% of the scores exceed $z = +2.00$. Because of symmetry these same percentages apply if one substitutes minus signs for the plus signs in the previous sentence. Thus, under normality,

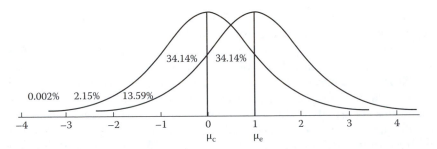

FIGURE 3.1 Assuming normality, when $d_{pop} = +1$ the mean score in the treated population will exceed approximately 84% of the scores in the control population.

a score at $z = +1.00$ is exceeding approximately $2\% + 14\% + 34\% + 34\% = 84\%$ of the scores.

Using z scores, or z-like measures, one can also compare results obtained from different scales, results that would not be comparable if one used raw scores. For example, one cannot directly compare a university student's grade-point average (GPA) with that student's Scholastic Aptitude Test (SAT) scores; they are on very different scales. The range of GPA scores is usually from 0 to 4.00, whereas it is safe to assume that any graduate of a university in the United States who had taken the SAT tests scored very much above 4 on them. In this example it would be meaningless to say that such a person scored "higher" on the SAT than on GPA. Similarly, it would be meaningless to conclude that most people are heavier than they are tall when one finds that most people have more pounds of weight than they have inches of height. However, one can meaningfully compare the otherwise incomparable by using z scores instead of raw scores in such examples. If one's z score on GPA was higher than one's z score on the SAT, relative to the same comparison group, then in fact that person did perform better in GPA than on the SAT (an overachiever). By using estimates of z-like measures of effect size researchers can compare or meta-analyze results from studies that use different dependent variable measures of the same underlying variable.

Assuming normality, one can obtain the same kind of information from an estimate of a z-like measure of effect size as one can obtain from a z score. Suppose that one divides the difference between a treated sample's mean, $\overline{Y}_e$ ("e" stands for an experimental or treated group), and a control sample's mean (or any comparison sample's mean), $\overline{Y}_c$, by the standard deviation of the control sample's scores, s_c. One then has for one possible estimator of an effect size an SDM,

$$d_G = \frac{\overline{Y}_e - \overline{Y}_c}{s_c}. \tag{3.1}$$

Equation 3.1 estimates the parameter

$$\Delta_G = \frac{\mu_e - \mu_c}{\sigma_c}. \tag{3.2}$$

Popularizing of the version of the effect-size estimator in Equation 3.1 is attributable to Gene V. Glass, whose name we denote by the subscript in d_G (e.g., Glass et al., 1981). In Equation 3.1 the standard deviation has $n - 1$ in its denominator. Statistical software typically uses $n - 1$ when calculating an estimate of the standard deviation in a population. (Glass et al. used $\hat{\Delta}$ for what we label d_G.) Later we observe in Equations 3.3 and 3.4, which are more generally stated versions of Glass's Equations 3.1 and 3.2, that the two groups that are being compared need not be experimental and control groups, but any two groups, such as women and men.

Similar to a z score, d_G estimates how many σ_c units above or below μ_c the value of μ_e is. Again if, say, $d_G = +1.00$, one is estimating that the average (mean) scoring members of the treated population score one σ_c unit above the scores of the average-scoring members of the control population. Also, if normality is correctly assumed in this example the average-scoring members of the treated population are estimated to be outscoring approximately 84% of the members of the control population. If, say, $d_G = -1.00$, one would estimate that the average-scoring members of the treated population are outscoring only approximately 16% of the members of the control population.

Of course, numerical results other than $d_G = +1.00$ or -1.00 are likely to occur, including results with decimal values, and they are similarly interpretable from a table of the normal curve or density function in software if one assumes normality. Figure 3.1 illustrates the example of $\Delta_G = +1.00$. To use Figure 3.1 to reflect on the implication of values of d_G that lead to an estimate other than $\Delta_G = +1.00$ the reader can imagine shifting the distribution of the treated population's scores to the right or to the left so that μ_e falls elsewhere on the control group's distribution. (Alternatively, for this purpose, inspect the first and last columns of Table 5.1.)

Recall that the mean of z scores is always 0, so the mean of the z scores of the control population is equal to 0. The mean of the z scores of the experimental (treated) population is also equal to 0 with respect to the distribution of z scores of its own population. However, in the example depicted in Figure 3.1 the mean of the raw scores of the experimental population correspond to $z = +1.00$ with respect to the distribution of z scores of the control population.

The d_G estimator of Δ_G has been widely used since the 1970s. Grissom (1996) provided many references for examples of values of d_G in research on psychotherapy outcome, and he also provided examples of averaged values of d_G from many meta-analyses on the efficacy of psychotherapy. These examples illustrate the use of Δ_G and d_G, so we consider them briefly here. Note first that when comparing various therapy groups (with the same disorder) with control groups one should not expect to obtain the same values of d_G from study to study because of sampling variability even if the therapies do not vary in efficacy.

Grissom (1996) found that in meta-analyses of studies that had compared psychotherapy groups and control groups the median value of d_G was +0.75, with values of d_G ranging from -0.35 to $+2.47$. Therefore, on the whole, therapies appear to be efficacious (median $d_G = +0.75$), with some therapies in some circumstances extremely so ($d_G = +2.47$), and very few possibly harmful (the rare negative values of d_G, such as -0.35). (Consult Staines & Cleland, 2007, for a discussion of biases of overestimation and underestimation that can influence estimation of effect size for the efficacy of psychotherapy.)

There is a minority opinion that psychotherapies have no specific benefits, only a placebo effect wherein any improvement in peoples' mental health is merely attributable to their expectation of therapeutic success, a kind of self-healing by a self-fulfilling prophecy. To explore this possibility Grissom (1996) also averaged d_G values that compared treated groups with placebo (i.e., "phony" or minimum-treatment) groups, and averaged d_G values that compared placebo and control (no-treatment) groups. (One can use the adaptable Equations 3.1 and 3.2 to compare two groups that undergo any two different conditions. The conditions do not have to be strictly treatment versus control.) When comparing treatment with placebo the median value of d_G was +0.58, suggesting that therapy provides more than a mere expectation of improvement (more than a placebo effect). However, when comparing placebo with control (placebo replaces treatment in Equation 3.1) the median value of d_G was +0.44. Together, all of these results suggest that there are placebo effects, but that there is more to the efficacy of therapy than just such placebo effects.

Tips and Pitfalls

Because of the possibility of a placebo effect, in many areas of research it would not be appropriate to compare the efficacies of two treatments using their effect sizes if one treatment's effect size is based on its difference from a control group and the other treatment's effect size is based on the more stringent criterion of its difference from a placebo group. For example, one should not compare the effect size for an antidepressant drug that is based on its group's difference from a placebo group with the effect size for a psychotherapy that is based on its group's difference from a control group.

(What we call a standardized-difference effect size or standardized-mean-difference effect size in this book is only one example of what are sometimes called *standardized effect sizes* in the literature. Standardized effect sizes are those that do not depend on the particular scale on which a variable is measured. Therefore, standardized effect sizes include d_{pop}, r_{pop} [Chapter 4], r^2_{pop} [Chapter 4], R^2_{pop} [Chapter 10], and the difference between proportions [Chapter 8]. Although we discuss such effect sizes in this book, to avoid confusion we do not use the general label standardized effect sizes. However, the distinction between standardized effect sizes and unstandardized effect sizes has important implications for the construction of confidence intervals; Kelley, 2007.)

In non-experimental research without a treated group (e.g., women's scores compared to men's scores) an experimental group's mean in Equations 3.1 and 3.2 is replaced by the mean of any kind of group whose performance one wants to evaluate with regard to the mean and standard deviation of the distribution of some baseline-comparison group. Therefore, more general forms of Equations 3.1 and 3.2 are, respectively,

$$d_G = \frac{\overline{Y}_a - \overline{Y}_b}{s_b} \tag{3.3}$$

and

$$\Delta_G = \frac{\mu_a - \mu_b}{\sigma_b}. \tag{3.4}$$

For a real example of such an application of d_G we use a study in which the psychologically healthy parent–child relationship scores of mothers of disturbed (schizophrenic) children (mother group *a*) were compared to those of mothers of normal children (mother group b), who served as the control or comparison group (Werner, Stabenau, & Pollin, 1970). In this example $\overline{Y}_a = 2.10$, $\overline{Y}_b = 3.55$, and $s_b = 1.88$. Therefore, $d_G = (2.10 - 3.55)/1.88 = -0.77$. Thus, the mothers of the disturbed children scored on average about three quarters of a standard deviation unit below the mean of the scores of the comparison mothers. Assuming normality for an illustrative purpose only, inspecting a table of the normal curve one estimates at $z = -0.77$ that the average-scoring mothers of the disturbed children would be outscored by approximately 78% of the comparison mothers. A two-tailed t test yields a statistically significant difference between the two means at the $p < .05$ level.

The results are consistent with three possible interpretations: (a) disturbance in parents genetically and/or experientially causes disturbance in their children, (b) disturbance in children causes disturbance in their parents, or (c) some combination of the first two interpretations can explain the results. We have assumed for simplicity in this example that the observed measure of the underlying dependent variable was valid and that the assumptions of normality and homoscedasticity were satisfied. However, the reliability of the scores in the present example is not likely to be among the highest. The effect of unreliability of the scores on estimation of effect sizes is discussed in detail in Chapter 4.

NONNORMALITY

When the distribution of scores of a comparison population is not normal the usual interpretation of a d_G or d in terms of estimating the percentile standing of the average-scoring members of another group with respect to the supposed normal distribution of the comparison group's scores would be invalid. Also, because standard deviations can be very sensitive to a distribution's shape, as was compellingly illustrated by Wilcox and Muska (1999), nonnormality can greatly influence the value of a standardized-mean-difference effect size and its estimate. The problem of normality has led many to prefer measures of effect size that do not require normality (Chapter 5).

USES AND LIMITATIONS OF A STANDARDIZED DIFFERENCE

In research other than physiological and biomedical research outcome variables are typically not the dependent variables of interest (e.g., depression) but are measures (e.g., the BDI) that are believed to be monotonically related to an underlying dependent variable. (In a monotonic relationship between variables each increase or decrease in one variable is accompanied by a change in the same direction by the other variable, but not necessarily to the same extent.) In such cases a standardized-difference effect size that is calculated on the *measure* of the latent dependent variable may not closely correspond to what the standardized difference would be if one could calculate it with respect to the targeted latent variable *itself*. This fact serves as another illustration that effect size is not necessarily equated with practical significance, and that when the dependent variable is a directly observable outcome on a familiar concrete scale (e.g., human weight) unstandardized differences and confidence intervals for them can be most informative. In clinical outcome research if an apparently large effect size does not correspond to a large enough difference in the underlying dependent variable to make an improvement in the lives of patients that is discernable to them or to others who observe them the result is not practically significant. Consult Maxwell and Delaney (1985) for further discussion of the relationship between results for observed scores and results for an underlying variable.

Another possible application of effect sizes such as the SDM is to acquire evidence about the relative sensitivity to treatment of alternative measures of outcome. The measure that yields a statistically significantly greater effect size would be considered by some to provide evidence that it is more sensitive to the treatment than is the other measure. Among other possible methods, the statistical significance of the difference between effect sizes may be tested using the Q statistic (Hedges & Olkin, 1985). Such a test is called a test of *homogeneity of effect sizes*. The Q test will not be powerful when there are only two effect sizes. Consult Hedges and Pigott (2001) for further discussion of the power of tests for homogeneity of effect sizes. Al-Kandari, Buhamra, and Ahmed (2007) proposed and evaluated a large-sample test for the equality of two effect sizes.

The Q test, as a test of statistical significance, only tests a null hypothesis that effect sizes are equal. Therefore, the Q test shares the characteristic of statistical tests of not directly indicating the degree to which a false null hypothesis is wrong. Thus, a statistically significant value of Q does not indicate how different the effect sizes are. However, a rival or complement to the Q statistic, the I^2 index, estimates the degree of inequality among effect sizes (Borenstein et al., 2009, who also discuss other measures). The I^2 index is intended to reflect the proportion of the total variability of the set of effect sizes, that is, variability between the effect sizes, which excludes within-study variability (i.e., excludes sampling variability).

Hedges (2011) defined and presented estimators of five standardized-mean-difference effect sizes for application to data from studies that involve multiple sites of research (*multisite research*). Sampling distributions and standard errors were also presented so that confidence intervals can be constructed.

With regard to effect sizes involving two groups' means, although we generally recommend the use of unstandardized differences when the measured dependent variable is of interest in its own right, such as weight, and standardized differences when the measured dependent variable represents an underlying variable, such as depression, there are possible exceptions. For example, suppose that a treated group of children exhibited a higher mean score on an IQ test than a control group, intelligence being the supposed latent variable. In this case it is unclear whether the more informative effect-size estimate would be, say, $d = .33$ or $\overline{X}_T - \overline{X}_C = 5$ IQ points (Baguley, 2009, 2010). Both results should be reported.

Limitations of sample standardized differences between means include the great sampling variability of standard deviations, which renders confidence intervals for such effect sizes often very wide. Also, as is discussed in Chapter 4, factors such as unreliability and range restriction can influence sample standardized differences by influencing a sample's standard deviation.

Tips and Pitfalls

Finally, a treatment may have importantly different effects on different dependent variables. For example, a treatment for an addiction may have effects that are different, or even opposite, on two addictions in multiply addicted persons. Therefore, one should not generalize about the magnitude or even the direction of an effect size from one dependent variable to a supposedly related dependent variable. For example, it would be very important to know if a treatment that had "successfully" targeted alcoholism or drug addiction had resulted in an increase in smoking.

EQUAL OR UNEQUAL VARIANCES

Glass et al. (1981) suggested the use of Equations 3.1 and 3.2 because treatment can affect variances and, therefore, cause heteroscedasticity. However, if the two populations that are being compared are assumed to have equal variances, then a better estimate of the denominator of a standardized difference between population means can be made if one pools the data from both samples to estimate the common σ instead of using s_b that is based on the data of only one sample. The pooled estimator, s_p, is based on a larger total sample ($N = n_a + n_b$ and $df = n_1 - 1 + n_2 - 1 = N - 2$) and is a less biased and less variable estimator of σ than s_b would be. To calculate s_p take the square root of the value of s_p^2 that is obtained from a printout or from Equation 2.2 that uses $n_i - 1$ in the denominator of each of the variances that is being pooled. The estimator of effect size in the present case is then

$$d = \frac{\overline{Y}_a - \overline{Y}_b}{s_p}, \tag{3.5}$$

which is currently commonly labeled *Cohen's d* by researchers (but originally was Cohen's d_s as we discuss later), and sometimes also correctly labeled *Hedges' g* (Hedges & Olkin, 1985) by many writers about effect sizes. This d estimates

$$d_{\text{pop}} = \frac{\mu_a - \mu_b}{\sigma}. \tag{3.6}$$

We define Cohen's d (i.e., also Hedges' g) in Equation 3.5 to agree with common, but not historically correct, practice. That is, for simplicity, when using d for power analysis (not data analysis), originally Cohen (1988) used n_a and n_b instead of $n_a - 1$ and $n_b - 1$ in the formula for s_p. However, Hedges and Olkin (1985) used $n_a - 1$ and $n_b - 1$ to estimate s_p for data analysis, as we do in Equation 2.2.

Recall from Chapter 1 that in general $ES = TS/f(N)$, where ES is some effect size and TS is a test statistic that is associated with that effect size. In the case of d of Equation 3.5, this relationship is satisfied by the *conversion* of t to $d = 2t/(N)^{1/2}$

when sample sizes are equal. When sample sizes are unequal one of the equations for conversion from the independent-groups t (not the paired-groups t) to d is $d = t[(n_a + n_b)/n_a n_b]^{1/2}$. Again, some writers about effect size, such as Rosnow and Rosenthal (2008), use g instead of d in the conversion formulas in this paragraph, such use of g being correct historically, but many research reports have come to use d for g. (Also, for the case of equal-sized samples, some writers use $df = N - 2$ instead of N in the aforementioned formula that converts t to d, but there will be little difference in the results when N is large.) We next clarify the notational inconsistencies in the literature for the interested reader, although we attempt to be clear about which estimator of effect size we are using throughout this book.

Note first that for an effect size for the purpose of data analysis, which is our purpose (contrasted with the purpose of pre-research power calculations to estimate needed sample size), Cohen (1988, pp. 66–67) used the notation d_s (currently rarely used) where we use d in Equation 3.5. Also, Cohen used simply d, without the subscript, to denote the targeted population effect size (a parameter) in the context of pre-research power calculations for estimating needed sample sizes, which was the main purpose of his book. However, for many years, since 1988, many researchers and some writers about effect sizes have come to use simply d to denote Cohen's variance-pooling standardized-difference estimator of effect size for data analysis. Therefore, in Equation 3.5 and throughout this book, we now also adopt the d notation to simplify what otherwise might be unnecessarily confusing to readers.

Also, to avoid confusing Cohen's d (i.e., formerly d_s) with what was denoted Glass' d (no pooling) originally in the literature, we adopt the notation d_G (again, G for Gene Glass) in Equations 3.1 and 3.3. Regarding historical precedence, Cohen's d notation dates to 1962, Glass' d dates to 1976, and Hedges' g dates to 1981.

Throughout this book we distinguish between situations in which Cohen's d (pooling variances on the assumption of homoscedasticity) or Glass' d_G (standardizing the mean difference using the s of one of the groups) may be preferred. For justifiable simplification for their purposes some authors (e.g., McGrath & Meyer, 2006, who were clear about their usage) define g as we have, but use d to denote standardizing the difference between two means using an s_{pooled}, the denominator of which involves $n_a + n_b = N$ instead of the $n_a - 1 + n_b - 1 = N - 2$ that we use. Also, it is likely that many authors of research reports who write that they are reporting "d" as an SDM that involves pooling for the standardizer are actually reporting the estimate of effect size that is represented by Equation 3.5 because they use major software that automatically uses $n_a - 1 + n_b - 1$ (i.e., $N - 2$) in the denominator to calculate an unbiased pooled estimate of σ^2. Such usage further justifies our use of the d notation for what was originally denoted d_s or g decades ago.

Tips and Pitfalls
Authors should make clear which standardizer they are using. McGrath and Meyer (2006, Table 1, p. 388) provided a summary of various writers' differing notations and definitions for standardized-mean-difference effect-size parameters and estimators.

Also consult Keselman et al. (2008, Table 4, p. 117). Again, we sympathize with readers who find the notational inconsistency confusing, and we attempt to be clear throughout this book about the precise kind of effect size that is being denoted.

Of course, when $\sigma_a = \sigma_b = \sigma$, d and d_G are estimating the same $d_{pop} = \Delta_G$. However, in this case it will still be very unlikely that $s_a = s_b = s_p$ because of the great variability of standard deviations from different samples drawn from the same population (sampling variability), so it will be very unlikely that $d = d_G$. Similarly, differing estimates of the parameter will likely result from using s_a instead of s_b in the denominator of the estimator even when $\sigma_a = \sigma_b = \sigma$ because sampling variability can cause s_a to differ from s_b, the more so the smaller the sample sizes. Research reports should clearly state which effect-size parameter is being estimated and which s has been used in the denominator of the estimator.

Both Cohen's d and Glass' d_G have some *positive bias* (i.e., tending to overestimate their respective parameters), the more so the smaller the sample sizes and the larger the effect size in the population. When the standardized-mean-difference parameter equals zero there is no bias. Although d is less biased than d_G, its bias can be reduced by using Hedges' approximately unbiased adjusted d_{adj} given by

$$d_{adj} = d\left[1 - \frac{3}{4df - 1}\right], \tag{3.7}$$

where $df = n_a + n_b - 2$ (Hedges & Olkin, 1985). Glass' d_G can also have its bias reduced by substituting d_G for d in Equation 3.7 and using $df = n_c - 1$, where n_c is the n for the sample whose s is used in the denominator.

Tips and Pitfalls
The two adjusted estimators are seldom used because bias and bias reduction have traditionally been considered to be slight unless sample sizes are very small. However, as was discussed in the section entitled "Controversy about null-hypothesis significance testing" in Chapter 1 regarding the debate about whether or not effect sizes should be reported when results are statistically insignificant, some believe that the bias is sufficient to cause concern. Consult the references that we provided in that section of Chapter 1 for discussions of this issue. Also, some experts are concerned about the biased estimation (prediction) of an effect size in a future replication from an effect size in a current study (Thompson, 1993). Vacha-Haase and Thompson (2004) recommended the use of bias-corrected estimators of effect size because they are likely to yield estimates that will be closer to the estimates that are found in future replications of the study.

Recall that if population means differ it is also likely that population standard deviations differ. This heteroscedasticity can cause problems. First, because $\sigma_a \neq \sigma_b$, $(\mu_a - \mu_b)/\sigma_b \neq (\mu_a - \mu_b)/\sigma_a$. In this case the Δ_G parameter that is being estimated using one of the samples as the control or baseline group that provides the estimate of the standardizer will not be the same as the Δ_G that is being estimated if one uses the other sample as the baseline group that provides the estimate of the standardizer. Also, the equations provided by Hedges and Olkin (1985) for constructing confidence intervals for d_{pop} assume homoscedasticity. Hogarty and Kromrey (2001) demonstrated the influence of heteroscedasticity and nonnormality on d. Even slight nonnormality can greatly lower d_{pop} (Wilcox, 2008a).

UNEQUAL BASE RATES AND OTHER ISSUES

One should be cautious about interpreting a difference between two values of a standardized-mean-difference effect size from two experimental studies that did not use the same kinds of participants (e.g., females in one study and males in the other study). A difference between the two values of d_G, or between the two values of d, may reflect a difference between means or a difference in standard deviations in the two demographic groups (Baguley, 2009, 2010). Again, reporting all relevant information (ns, means, standard deviations) enables readers of research reports to compare standard deviations (at least informally) and enables readers who prefer an unstandardized difference between means, where appropriate, to calculate an estimate when an SDM has been reported.

Tips and Pitfalls

Ruscio (2008a) demonstrated the extent of sensitivity of d to a difference in sample sizes when population variances are unequal, and, in research on pre-existing groups, the extent of sensitivity of d_{pop} to unequal *population base rates* when population variances are unequal. Base rates are the proportions of each of the two kinds of studied groups in the sample or population of interest in the research, such as the proportions of schizophrenics and "normals" or college educated and not college educated. In this book we note situations in which difference in base rates in the population, or difference between sample base rates and population base rates, can be problematic for estimation of some kinds of effect sizes, which are called *base-rate-sensitive effect sizes*.

Recall that pooling sample variances (under the assumption of homoscedasticity) to calculate s_p for Equation 3.5 requires weighting each sample variance by its sample size (or by $n - 1$). If the sample with the larger sample size has the larger variance, s_p will be increased and d, thereby, will be decreased, and vice versa if the sample with the larger sample size has the smaller variance. Similarly, Ruscio (2008a) demonstrated the extent to which d_{pop} decreases when the population with the larger variance has the larger base rate (greater proportion of members), the more so the greater the variance ratio. These facts support the use of Glass' d_G (Equation 3.1 or 3.3) to estimate Glass' Δ_G (Equation 3.2), if one of the groups is a meaningful comparison group such as a control group or a standard-treatment group that is being contrasted with a group that is receiving a new treatment. (Some authors prefer d_{pop} to Δ_G because of the greater sampling variability of the latter.) The sensitivity of d to unequal sample sizes and the sensitivity of d_{pop} to unequal base rates under heteroscedasticity support the use of the probabilistic measures of effect size that are discussed in Chapter 5. These measures and their estimators are not sensitive to heteroscedasticity, or unequal base rates or sample sizes. There is an extensive discussion of unequal base rates in Chapter 4.

To counter heteroscedasticity, Cohen (1988) suggested using for the standardizer in the population d the square root of the mean of σ_a^2 and σ_b^2, estimated by

$$s' = \left[\frac{s_a^2 + s_b^2}{2}\right]^{1/2}. \tag{3.8}$$

Researchers who use the s' (our notation, not Cohen's) as the estimator of a population standardizer instead of the previously discussed estimators of σ_a or σ_b should recognize that they are estimating the σ of a hypothetical population whose σ is between σ_a and σ_b (which is a concern for some experts but not others). In this case, therefore, such researchers are estimating a d_{pop} in a hypothetical population, an effect size that we label here d'_{pop}.

In their discussions of methods for constructing confidence intervals for an SDM, Bonett (2008) recommended this d'_{pop} effect size for data analysis but Keselman et al. (2008) did not recommend it for this purpose. Acknowledging that this effect size would not be meaningful when heteroscedasticity is more than slight, Bonett argued for its use instead of the effect size that pools variances because of the poor performance of the latter even under slight heteroscedasticity when sample sizes are unequal.

Keselman et al. (2008) disapproved of the standardizer in Equation 3.8 because it estimates a population standardizer that pools unequal variances. (Pooling of sample variances is often done in t testing and in calculating the traditional d to obtain a better estimate of what is assumed to be the same variance in two populations. However, the pooling that is undertaken in the context of Equation 3.8 pools variances for the denominator of the population d as well as the sample d for the purpose of using a compromise standardizer when population variances are assumed to be unequal.)

Tips and Pitfalls

Authors of research reports often seem to confuse the various standardized-mean-difference effect sizes. Indeed, even decades ago when there were fewer choices for a standardizer Glass et al. (1981) acknowledged that the choice was perplexing. The reader should take comfort in the fact that we attempt to simplify the choice later in the section entitled "Tentative recommendations".

OUTLIERS AND STANDARDIZED-DIFFERENCE EFFECT SIZES

There are factors that can cause standardized mean differences to appear misleadingly large or small. For example, suppose that one or more outliers cause positive skew in the group that does *not* provide the standardizer when calculating d_G. Such outliers will increase the mean of that group. Therefore, the difference between means will have been increased, but not the standardizer, resulting in an inflated d_G. Alternatively, positive skew that is caused by outliers only in the group that provides the s standardizer, or positive skew that is caused by outliers in both groups when s_p is the standardizer, will likely result in a lowering of d_G or d, respectively. Such lowering is likely because a given increase in the denominator (standardizer) can have a greater impact on the estimate of the standardized difference than an increase in the numerator.

Wilcox (2006a) illustrated a situation in which visually the overlap of a pair of normal-looking distributions appeared to be identical to the overlap of another pair of normal-looking distributions. In fact, although the difference between the means is the same for both pairs of distributions, $d_{pop} = .8$ for one pair and $d_{pop} = .24$ for the other pair. The explanation is that the distributions in the first pair are normal and the distributions in the second pair are actually contaminated normal distributions with a much larger, but not discernibly so, standard deviation that greatly lowers d_{pop}. A *contaminated normal distribution* (also known as a mixed normal distribution) is a superficially normal-looking distribution that results when two subpopulations that constitute the population are each normally distributed and have the same mean, but have different variances. As Wilcox (2006a) noted, the broader issue is not the question of how common contaminated normal distributions are, but the fact that outliers are common (Wilcox, 2003).

TENTATIVE RECOMMENDATIONS

When homoscedasticity is correctly assumed the best estimator of the common σ is s_p, resulting in the d or d_{adj} estimator of effect size. If homoscedasticity is not assumed use the s of whichever sample is the reasonable baseline-comparison group. For example, use the s of the control or placebo group as the standardizer or, if a new treatment is being compared with a standard treatment, use the s of the sample that is receiving the standard treatment. It may sometimes be informative to calculate and report estimates of two kinds of Δ_G, one based on s_a and the other based on s_b. For example, in studies that compare genders one can estimate a Δ_G to estimate where the mean female score stands in relation to the population distribution of males' scores (i.e., s_{males} is the standardizer), and estimate another Δ_G to estimate where the mean male score stands in relation to the population distribution of females' scores (i.e., $s_{females}$ is the standardizer). A modest additional suggestion is to use $ns > 10$ and as close to equal as possible. (However, much larger ns are likely required to construct informatively narrow confidence intervals.) When homoscedasticity is not assumed one may also use as an estimate of the standardizer the square root of the mean of the two sample variances as in Equation 3.8, recognizing that such a choice is not universally accepted, and will be unwise if there is reason to expect a large difference in population variances.

Tips and Pitfalls
Again we state that if more than one estimator is calculated the researcher should report all such calculated estimators. It would be unacceptable to report only the effect size, the magnitude of which is most supportive of the case that the researcher is trying to make. Again, at the time of this writing editors of journals that recommend or require the reporting of effect sizes do not specify which

kinds of effect size are to be reported. The important point is that at least one appropriate estimate of effect size should be reported whenever such reporting would be informative.

NORMED DEPENDENT VARIABLES

In areas of research in which the measure of the dependent variable is a common test that has been normed on a vast sample, such as has been done for many major clinical and educational tests, there is another solution to heteroscedasticity. (A *normed test* is one whose distribution's shape, mean, and standard deviation have already been determined separately for certain demographic groups by applying the test to, say, many thousands of people [the normative groups]. For example, there are norms for the scales of the MMPI personality inventory and for various IQ and academic admissions tests, such as the SAT and Graduate Record Examination.) In this case, for an estimator of Δ_G one can divide $\overline{Y}_a - \overline{Y}_n$ by s_n, where n stands for the normative group. The use of such a constant s_n by all researchers who are working in the same field of research decreases uncertainty about the value of Δ_G. This is so because when not using the common s_n different researchers will find greatly varying estimates of Δ_G, even if their values of $\overline{Y}_a - \overline{Y}_b$ do not differ very much, simply because of the varying values of s from study to study.

For an example of the method, suppose that for a normative group of babies $\overline{Y}_n = 100$ and $s_n = 15$ on a test of their developmental quotient, a test whose population of scores we will consider to be normally distributed. Suppose further that a special diet or treatment that is given to an experimental group of babies results in their $\overline{Y}_a = 110$. In this case we estimate that $d_{pop} = (110 - 100)/15 = +0.67$, the average treated babies scoring $0.67s_n$ units above the average of the normative babies. Inspection of a table of the normal curve indicates that a z of $+0.67$ is a result that outscores approximately 75% of the normative babies.

To determine whether such an effect size that is standardized by s_n is statistically significantly different from 0 one would be inclined to compare the means using a t test. However, in the present case one group (the normative group) is assumed to have a known variance, whereas the treated group has an unknown variance. In such a situation one should consider using the t test for the case of one assumed known variance and one unknown variance that was proposed by Maity and Sherman (2006). An alternative to the use of published norms for the control-group mean is the use of the average mean of control groups from an available meta-analysis. Nasiakos, Cribbie, and Arpin-Cribbie (2010) discussed such methods and the different conclusions to which alternative approaches might lead.

ADDITIONAL STANDARDIZED-DIFFERENCE EFFECT SIZES WHEN THERE ARE OUTLIERS

The previous section was entitled "Tentative recommendations" because other types of estimators have been proposed for use when there are outliers that can influence the means and standard deviations. A simple suggestion by Hedges and

Olkin (1985) for a somewhat outlier-resistant estimator is to trim the highest and lowest scores from each group, replace $\bar{Y}_a - \bar{Y}_b$ with $Mdn_a - Mdn_b$, and use as the standardizer in place of the standard deviation the range of the trimmed data or some other measure of variability that is more outlier resistant than is the standard deviation. One such alternative to the standard deviation is the median absolute deviation from the median. Another alternative standardizer is $.75R_{iq}$, as proposed by Laird and Mosteller (1990) to provide some resistance to outliers while using a denominator that approximates the standard deviation. The R_{iq} was discussed in Chapter 1, from which recall that $.75R_{iq}$ approximates s when there is normality.

As Wilcox (1996) pointed out, the use of one of the relatively outlier-resistant measures of variability instead of the standard deviation does not assure that the variabilities of the two populations will be equal when their means are not equal. Also, although at the current stage of development of methodology for effect sizes it is appropriate in this book to present a great variety of measures, eventually the field should settle on the use of a reduced number of appropriate measures. A more consistent use of measures of effect size by primary researchers would facilitate the comparison of results from study to study.

Kromrey and Coughlin (2007) provided a SAS/IML macro for a trimmed d, which is the difference between two sample trimmed means (as defined in Chapter 2) divided by the square root of the Winsorized variance (as defined in Chapter 1).

It can be argued that replacing the standard deviation as the standardizer with a "better" measure of variability sacrifices the kind of simple interpretation of a standardized-mean-difference effect size that we discussed in relation to Figure 3.1. However, under nonnormality such an interpretation is lost regardless of the choice of standardizer. Also, to be appealing a new standardizer would have to result in an effect-size measure for which a well-behaved confidence interval can be constructed.

CONFIDENCE INTERVALS FOR STANDARDIZED-DIFFERENCE EFFECT SIZES

Again, when the measure of the dependent variable is of direct interest instead of representing an underlying variable that is of interest, a confidence interval for the unstandardized difference between means, $\mu_a - \mu_b$, may be preferable to a confidence interval for the standardized difference. Also, estimation of $\mu_a - \mu_b$ may be simpler and more resistant to skew than estimation of an effect size with the additional parameter, σ, in the denominator; that is, $(\mu_a - \mu_b)/\sigma$. However, if normality is assumed correctly, use of the standardized difference permits estimation of the percentile placement of the average member of one population with respect to the distribution of scores of the other population (as was discussed with regard to Figure 3.1). In some cases in which an observed dependent variable that is of direct interest is used, a researcher should consider reporting both a standardized and an unstandardized difference between means, for the different information that each can provide, and confidence intervals for them. We turn our attention now to construction of confidence intervals for the standardized difference between two means.

The smaller the sample size the greater the variability of the sampling distribution of an estimator. Thus, the smaller the sample size the more likely it is that there will be a large discrepancy between a value of d or d_G and the value of d_{pop} or Δ_G that it is estimating. (Consult Bradley, Smith, & Stoica, 2002, for discussions of consequences of this fact.) Therefore, a sufficiently narrow confidence interval for a standardized-difference effect size can be very informative. Often the greater the difference between the two sample sizes the wider the confidence interval.

More accurate, but more complex, methods for constructing confidence intervals for a standardized-difference effect size are discussed later. First a simple approximate method for manual calculation is demonstrated. This method becomes less accurate to the extent that the assumptions of homoscedasticity and normality are not met, the smaller the sample sizes (say, $n_a < 10$ and $n_b < 10$), and the more that the parameter departs from 0.

An approximate 95% CI for d_{pop} is given by

$$.95 \; CI \; d_{pop} : d \pm z_{.025}s_d, \tag{3.9}$$

where

$z_{.025}$ is the positive value of z that has 2.5% of the area of the normal curve beyond it, namely, $z = +1.96$

s_d is the estimated standard deviation of the theoretical sampling distribution of d

To calculate s_d, following Hedges and Olkin (1985), take the square root of

$$s_d^2 = \frac{n_a + n_b}{n_a n_b} + \frac{d^2}{2(n_a + n_b)}. \tag{3.10}$$

For example, suppose that one wants to construct a 95% CI for d_{pop} when $d = +0.70$, $n_a = n_b = 20$, and one is not adjusting d for bias because bias is likely very slight when each $n = 20$. In this case $s_d^2 = [(20 + 20)/(20 \times 20)] + [.70^2/(2(20 + 20))] = 0.106$, so $s_d = (0.106)^{1/2} = 0.326$. Therefore, the limits of the .95 CI are $0.70 \pm 1.96(0.326)$. The lower limit for this confidence interval is 0.06 and the upper limit is 1.34, which is a disappointingly wide interval. Thus, one estimates that the interval from .06 to 1.34 would contain the value of d_{pop} approximately 95% of the time. Hedges and Olkin (1985) applied the methods of Equations 3.9 and 3.10 not to d but to d adjusted for bias, which is the d_{adj} of our Equation 3.7.

Recall from Chapter 1 that there are opposing views regarding the relevance of null-hypothesis significance testing. Therefore, authors (and readers) of a research report may have varying reactions to the fact that the confidence interval from .06 to 1.34 does not contain 0, a result that also provides evidence at the two-tailed .05 level of statistical significance that d_{pop} does not equal 0. The fact that this result attains statistical significance would be considered to be important by someone who is interested in evidence regarding a theory that predicts a difference between the two groups. This significance-testing perspective would also be important if the research were comparing two treatments of equal overall cost, so the main issue would then be if one of the two treatments were more efficacious.

On the other hand, suppose that there are two competing treatments and that the prior literature includes an estimate of effect size when comparing one of those treatments to a control condition. Suppose further that the present research is estimating an effect size when comparing the other competing treatment to a control condition. In this case the interest would be in the magnitude of the currently obtained effect-size estimate and of the confidence limits, and in comparing the present effect-size estimate and confidence limits with the prior results as evidence regarding the competition between the two treatments.

Tips and Pitfalls
If sample size is small enough and/or d_{pop} is large enough, the approximate confidence interval may be so inaccurate as to render rejecting or failing to reject H_0: $d_{pop} = 0$ on the basis of the absence or presence of 0 in the interval questionable.

NARROWING THE CONFIDENCE INTERVAL

Returning to our numerical example, observe that the obtained confidence interval is not as informative as one would want it to be because the interval ranges from a value that would generally be considered to be a very small effect size (0.06) to a value that would generally be considered to be a large effect size (1.34). One would like to have obtained a narrower confidence interval. Recall from Chapter 2 that in order to attempt to narrow a confidence interval some have suggested that researchers consider adopting a level of confidence lower than .95. The reader can try this as an exercise by constructing a $(1 - \alpha)$ CI, where $\alpha > .05$ in order to narrow the confidence interval by paying the price of having the confidence level below .95. In this case the only element in Equation 3.9 that changes is that $z_{.025}$ is replaced by $z_{\alpha/2}$. This $z_{\alpha/2}$ applies because the middle $100(1 - \alpha)\%$ of the normal curve has one half of the remaining area of the curve above it, that is, $100(\alpha/2)\%$ above it. However, a .95 CI is traditional and the editors and manuscript reviewers of some journals, and some professors who are supervising student research, may be uncomfortable with a result reported with less than 95% confidence.

As a further exercise in narrowing confidence intervals (before the research is begun) by increasing ns while still striving for 95% confidence we change our example by now supposing that we had originally used $n_a = n_b = 50$ instead of 20, while $d = +0.70$ again. Using $n_a = n_b = 50$ in Equation 3.10 and then taking the square root of the obtained s_d^2 one finds that now $s_d = 0.206$. The limits for the 95% CI for d_{pop} then become $0.70 \pm 1.96(0.206)$, yielding lower and upper limits of 0.30 and 1.10, respectively. This is still not a very narrow confidence interval, but it is narrower than the original confidence interval that was constructed using smaller ns. The approach of Kelley et al. (2003) and Kelley and Rausch (2006) involves estimating the sample size needed to construct a confidence interval (a) whose expected width will be no greater than a specified width or (b) with a specified probability of having a width that is no greater than is specified. Unfortunately, confidence intervals for d_{pop} tend to be very wide, and very large samples may often be required to narrow them satisfactorily.

As d_{pop} increases the sample size needed to shorten a confidence interval does not necessarily decrease (Algina, Keselman, & Penfield, 2005a). Also, although confidence intervals for d_{pop} become wider the larger the value of d, this effect is slight except for relatively large values of d.

COMBINING CONFIDENCE INTERVALS FOR d_{pop} AND ALSO FOR $\mu_a - \mu_b$

When assumptions are satisfied, for a more accurate method for constructing a confidence interval for d_{pop} using IBM SPSS or other software refer to Fidler and Thompson (2001) and Smithson (2001, 2003). Some rationale for this method is discussed in the next section on noncentral distributions. Additional such software for constructing confidence intervals, combining them, and better understanding their meaning is Cumming's (Cumming & Finch, 2001) "Exploratory Software for Confidence Intervals (ESCI)." For an example of output from ESCI inspect Figure 3.2 that will be discussed shortly. ESCI runs under Excel and can, as of the time of this writing, be downloaded from http://www.latrobe.edu.au/psy/esci. This site also has useful links.

Satisfactorily narrow confidence intervals may often require impractically large sample sizes (Kelley & Rausch, 2006) so that a single study often cannot yield a nearly definitive result. However, using software such as ESCI, combining a set of confidence intervals from related studies (i.e., studies with the same variation of the independent variable, and same dependent variable or same latent variable) may home in on a more accurate estimate of an effect size (Cumming & Finch, 2001). In this case of related studies the Results section of a report of a later study can include a single figure that depicts a confidence interval from its study together with the confidence intervals from all of the previous studies. Such a figure places the current results in a broader context and can greatly facilitate interpretation of the current results as integrated with the previous results. The ESCI software can produce such a figure, as is illustrated by Thompson (2002) and by Figure 3.2. Such a figure turns a primary study into a more informative meta-analysis. Figures that depict point estimates and the confidence intervals associated with them for a set of related studies are called *forest plots*. Forest plots for many kinds of effect size are illustrated in Borenstein et al. (2009) and can be constructed using the commercial software Comprehensive Meta-Analysis Version 2 (consult www.Meta-Analysis.com).

For further discussion of confidence intervals for standardized-difference effect sizes consult Cumming and Finch (2001), Hedges and Olkin (1985), and

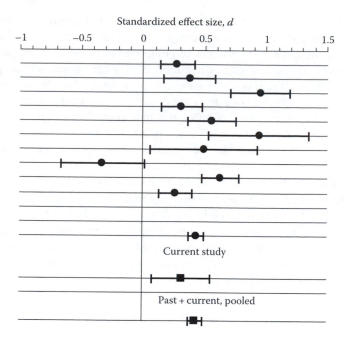

FIGURE 3.2 The 95% confidence intervals, produced by ESCI, for placebo versus drug for depression. (Data from Gorecki, J.A. (now J. A. Robbins), *A Meta-Analysis of the Effectiveness of Antidepressants Compared to Placebo*, unpublished master's thesis, San Francisco State University, San Francisco, CA, 2002.) (British spelling per ESCI output.)

Thompson (2002). Hedges and Olkin provided monographs (charts) for approximate confidence limits for d_{pop} when $0 \leq d \leq 1.5$ and $n_a = n_b = 2$–10.

Figure 3.2 depicts 95% *CI*s for d_{pop} that were produced by the ESCI software option called "MA [Meta-Analytic] Thinking." The *d* values, calculated on real data (Gorecki, 2002), were defined as $d = (\bar{Y}_{placebo} - \bar{Y}_{drug})/s_p$ in studies of depression. The figure is only intended to illustrate an ESCI result because there were actually 11 prior studies to be compared with the latest study but ESCI permitted depiction of confidence intervals for up to 10 prior studies, a pooled (averaged) confidence interval for those studies, a confidence interval from the current primary researcher's latest study, and a confidence interval based on a final pooling of the 10 prior studies and the latest study. The pooled confidence intervals represent a kind of meta-analysis undertaken by a primary researcher whose study has predecessors. The more that the *CI*s in a figure such as Figure 3.2 overlap the more replicable the results appear to be.

For the case in which the scale of the dependent variable is of direct interest so that the difference between unstandardized means is an informative effect size, Bonett (2009a) recommended a similar approach for integrating the effect size from a current primary study with the effect sizes from previous studies whose results the current study is attempting to replicate. For example, suppose that a current study repeats the same treatment-versus-control conditions that had been used in three previous studies. The researcher can first construct a confidence interval for the difference between the current control-group mean and the overall mean of the three previous control-group means (a complex comparison or linear contrast as is discussed in Chapter 6). Such a confidence interval provides evidence of the replicability of the four control-group results. The researcher can then construct a confidence interval for the difference between the current treatment-group mean and the overall mean of the four control-group means, which is another linear contrast. This confidence interval provides evidence of a treatment effect. Confidence intervals for linear contrasts can be constructed under heteroscedasticity using a Satterthwaite (Welch-like) method that is described in various sources including Maxwell and Delaney (2004). Wilcox (2003) discussed and provided S-PLUS software functions for robust methods.

Bonett (2009a) also discussed how a new study can extend previous findings about effect size that arose from one-way designs by conducting research in which a possible modifier of the effect size is studied by including it in a second stratum in a factorial design. For example, if the earlier studies had all used men, the new study can add women to create gender as a second factor.

CONFIDENCE INTERVALS USING NONCENTRAL DISTRIBUTIONS

If normality and homoscedasticity are satisfied, an *exact* (in terms of probability coverage) confidence interval for d_{pop} can be constructed using the noncentral t distribution and software as is discussed in this section. Under nonnormality the probability coverage when using this method will not exactly equal the nominal $100(1 - \alpha)\%$ (Algina & Keselman, 2003). A relatively brief account of this method is given here. The interested reader should consult the provided references.

The t distribution that is used to test the usual null hypothesis (that the difference between the means of two populations is 0) is centered symmetrically about the value 0 because the initial presumption in research that uses hypothesis testing is that H_0 is true. Such a t distribution that is centered symmetrically about 0 is called a *central t distribution*. (Not all central distributions are symmetrical.) However, when one constructs a confidence interval for d_{pop} there is no null hypothesis being tested at that time, so the relevant sampling distribution is a t distribution that may not be centered at 0 and may not be symmetrical. Assuming normality for the populations of scores, such a t distribution is called a *noncentral t distribution*.

The noncentral t distribution differs more from the central t distribution with respect to its center and degree of skew the more d_{pop} departs from 0 and the smaller the sample sizes (or, precisely, the degrees of freedom). Therefore, if assumptions are satisfied, the more d_{pop} departs from 0, and the smaller the sample sizes, the more improvement there will be in the performance of confidence intervals that are based on the noncentral t distribution instead of the central t distribution. The ESCI software that was cited in the previous section and some other software for the construction of such confidence intervals are based on the noncentral t distribution.

Constructing a confidence interval for d_{pop} using a noncentral t distribution requires a procedure in which the lower limit and the upper limit of the interval have to be estimated separately because they are not equidistant from the point estimate. Thus, such a confidence interval is not necessarily a symmetrical one bounded by the point estimate plus or minus a constant margin of error. The procedure is an *iterative* (i.e., repetitive) one in which successive approximations of each confidence limit are made until a value is found that has .025 (in the case of a 95% *CI*) of the noncentral t distribution in the tail beyond it. Therefore, software is required for the otherwise prohibitively laborious construction of confidence intervals using noncentral distributions. (Lecoutre, 2007, warned about the inaccuracy of some computer programs for the noncentral t distribution when sample sizes or effect sizes are large.)

The shape of the noncentral t distribution depends not only on sample sizes but also on the value of what is called the noncentrality parameter. The *noncentrality parameter*, which is often represented by the Greek letters λ (*lambda*) or Δ (not to be confused with Glass' effect-size parameter, Δ_G), reflects the degree of departure of a noncentral distribution from a central distribution (also the degree of falseness of the H_0). Therefore, for example, for a given df the value of t that has 2.5% of the area of its distribution beyond it in a tail will not be the same within the central and noncentral t distributions if H_0 is false. The noncentrality parameter depends on the difference between 0 and the true value of d_{pop}. Specifically, $\lambda = d_{pop}[(n_a n_b)/(n_a + n_b)]^{1/2}$. The confidence limits for λ are found first using the described iterative procedure and then those two limits are divided by the quantity in the brackets in the preceding formula to find the limits for d_{pop}.

For detailed discussions of the construction of confidence intervals that are based on noncentral distributions consult Cumming and Finch (2001), Kelley (2007), Smithson (2001, 2003), Steiger and Fouladi (1997), and Thompson (2002). Kelley's procedure uses a function for R software. Smithson's (2001) procedure uses IBM SPSS scripts. For application of SAS consult Odgaard and Fowler (2010). When homoscedasticity and normality are satisfied the p value and sample sizes from a t test can be converted into an estimate of d_{pop} and an exact confidence interval for it (Browne, 2010). For a given p value, as total sample size increases the lower and upper limits of the confidence interval decrease.

ROBUST CONFIDENCE INTERVALS FOR THE STANDARDIZED DIFFERENCE

Hogarty and Kromrey (2004) found that when primary studies exhibit nonnormality and heteroscedasticity none of the methods involving means that they simulated satisfactorily estimated d_{pop}. Negative bias and probability coverage for confidence intervals that was lower than nominal resulted under some conditions. Similarly, Hess, Kromrey, Ferron, Hogarty, and Hines (2005) found in simulations that probability coverage for confidence intervals for d_{pop}, with or without adjustment of each d for bias, was inaccurate under nonnormality and heteroscedasticity. Kelley's (2005) simulations of nonnormality indicated that a bias-corrected bootstrap method is preferable for constructing a confidence interval for d_{pop}. Algina, Keselman, and Penfield (2006a) confirmed Kelley's results to some extent, but they found that, unlike a method that we discuss later in this section (Algina, Keselman, & Penfield, 2006b) under some additional conditions of nonnormality the method does not maintain satisfactory probability coverage. Hess and Kromrey (2004) further discussed the use of bootstrapping to construct a confidence interval for d_{pop} under nonnormality and heteroscedasticity.

Keselman, Algina, and Fradette (2005) addressed nonnormality by simulating the performances of methods for a priori symmetrical trimming (i.e., deciding the amount of equal trimming in each tail before data are collected) and asymmetrical trimming in which the different amount of trimming in each tail (as needed to reduce or eliminate outliers) is decided by inspection of the data. In cases of trimming, the numerator of the robust standardized-difference parameter for which a confidence interval is constructed is the difference between two trimmed means, and the denominator is the square root of the pooled Winsorized variances (as defined in Chapter 1). Probability coverage was found to be generally satisfactorily accurate using a priori symmetrical trimming or post hoc asymmetrical trimming, especially when using sample sizes greater than 20 each. (Also consult Algina et al., 2006b, and the next paragraph, for further developments.) Similarly, Algina, Keselman, and Penfield (2005a) studied and recommended the use of 20% trimming together with the Winsorized standardizer to form the robust effect size. As a refinement, such an effect size can be multiplied by .642 to render it comparable to the traditional effect size in the case in which normality and homoscedasticity are satisfied.

Algina et al. (2005a) also simulated the performances of confidence intervals for the robust standardized (Winsorized) difference between trimmed means using methods based on either the noncentral t distribution or on a procedure called the *percentile bootstrap*. In a percentile bootstrap method the confidence limits are given by the $\alpha/2$ and the $1 - (\alpha/2)$ quantiles of the empirical distribution that emerges from the bootstrapping (as previously defined). The normal distribution and six nonnormal distributions were simulated. Both methods appeared to be generally satisfactory under the conditions that were studied, especially when d_{pop} was not large and sample sizes were not small. The method that was based on the noncentral t distribution yielded better probability coverage, but the percentile bootstrap method yielded the narrower intervals. Findings reported by Algina et al. (2006b) supported the use of the percentile bootstrap method to construct a confidence interval for the population standardized (Winsorized) difference between trimmed means under nonnormality. In this case probability coverage was close to the nominal .95.

Algina et al. (2005a) provided an example in which the difference between the means of two populations is the same in two pairs of distributions, one pair consisting of two normal distributions and the other pair consisting of two very normal-looking distributions that were actually nonnormal because of heavy tails. Although the separations within the two pairs of distributions look similar, leading one to expect similar values of d_{pop}, the values of the traditional nonrobust d_{pop} were 1.00 and .30. A Visual Basic program to construct a confidence interval for the robust effect size (i.e., trimming and Winsorizing) is available, courtesy of James Algina, at http://plaza.ufl.edu/algina/index.programs.html. (Bonett, 2008, questioned the interpretability of the difference between two trimmed means standardized by a Winsorized standard deviation in terms of visualizing the degree of separation between distributions.)

With regard to constructing a CI for Glass' Δ_G, consider group a or group b to be the jth group whose population standard deviation, σ_j, serves as the standardizer so that the effect size is denoted by Δ_j. An approximate CI can be constructed for Δ_j using the noncentral t distribution if normality is assumed. An alternative under nonnormality is to construct the confidence interval for Δ_j using a method based on percentile bootstrapping, as we previously described. Consult Algina et al. (2006b) and Keselman et al. (2008) for details.

Bonett (2008) discussed a relatively simple method for constructing an approximate confidence interval for an SDM. Simulations that were based on sampling from normal distributions indicated that a slight increase in needed sample size might be a price for relaxing the assumption of homoscedasticity, but increasing sample size will not improve poor coverage probabilities that arise from excessive nonnormality. The standardizer in Bonett's method is estimated by Equation 3.8.

Bonett's (2008) method might fail if there is more than a slight departure from normality and homoscedasticity. With regard to the requirement of at least approximate normality, Bonett suggested the use of a *normalizing transformation* (a *logarithmic transformation* being a common example). Bonett argued that the difficulty in interpreting a mean and a difference between means when the dependent variable has been transformed in the case of an unstandardized difference need not be a concern in the case of a standardized difference because the focus is then on standard deviation units of difference and not on the unit of measurement of the dependent variable. However, some researchers may be concerned about the possibility that a nonlinear transformation might reverse the original order of the magnitudes of the means. Perhaps, counterintuitively, if a nonlinear transformation results in a monotonic relationship between original scores and transformed scores, it may not also result in a monotonic relationship between means of original scores and means of transformed scores (e.g., Kruskal, 1978).

COUNTERNULL EFFECT SIZE

Recall that a typical null hypothesis about μ_a and μ_b is that their difference equals 0 (a nil hypothesis). This H_0 implies another; namely, H_0: $d_{pop} = 0$. In traditional significance testing if the obtained value of t is not far enough away from 0, given the degrees of freedom, one decides not to reject H_0, and, by implication, one concludes that the result of the t test provides insufficient evidence that d_{pop} is other than 0. However, Robert Rosenthal and his colleagues considered such reasoning to be incomplete. For example, suppose that the sample d is above 0, but insufficiently so to attain statistical significance. This result can be explained, as is traditional, by the population d_{pop} actually being 0 whereas the sample d happened by chance (sampling variability) to overestimate d_{pop} in this instance of research.

However, another plausible explanation of the result is that d_{pop} is actually above 0, and more above 0 than d is, so d happened by chance to underestimate d_{pop} this time. Therefore, according to this reasoning a value of d that is above or below 0 by a certain amount is providing just as much evidence that $d_{pop} = 2d$ as it is providing evidence that $d_{pop} = 0$ because d is no closer to 0 (1 d distance away from 0) than d is to $2d_{pop}$ (1 d distance away from $2d_{pop}$). For example, if d is, say, +0.60, this result is just as consistent with $d_{pop} = +1.20$ as with $d_{pop} = 0$ because +0.60 is just as close to +1.20 as it is to 0. The sample d is just as likely to be underestimating d_{pop} by a certain amount as it is to be overestimating d_{pop} by that amount (except for some positive bias as is discussed next).

In the current example, assuming that a t test results in t and, by implication, d being statistically insignificantly different from 0, it would thus seem to be as justifiable to conclude that d is insignificantly different from +1.20 as it would be to conclude that d is insignificantly different from 0. (However, the reasoning in this section is only approximately true because of the slight bias that standardized-difference estimators have toward overestimating effect size. The reasoning is more accurate the larger the ns or if a bias-adjusted estimator, as was previously discussed, is used.) The reasoning in this section is entirely based on the results at hand, there being no other considerations. However, with regard to research that is conducted in the context of well-grounded theory or well-replicated prior results a value of $d_{pop} = 2d$ may be more or less plausible than a value of $d_{pop} = 0$.

The current reasoning leads to a measure of effect size called the *counternull value of an effect size* (Rosnow & Rosenthal, 2008; also consult Lecoutre, 2007). Here we simply call this measure the *counternull effect size, ES_{cn}*. In the case of standardized-difference effect sizes, if one is, by implication of t testing H_0: $\mu_a - \mu_b = 0$, indirectly testing H_0: $ES_{pop} = 0$, then

$$ES_{cn} = 2ES. \tag{3.11}$$

When null-hypothesizing a value of ES_{pop} other than 0, the more general equation is

$$ES_{cn} = 2ES - ES_{null}, \tag{3.12}$$

where ES_{null} is the null-hypothesized value of ES_{pop}. Equations 3.11 and 3.12 will be observed to apply to some (not all) other kinds of effect sizes throughout this book.

In our present example, in which the estimate of effect size (i.e., d) = +0.60, application of Equation 3.11 yields the estimate $ES_{cn} = 2(+0.60) = +1.20$. Therefore, the *null–counternull interval* ranges from 0 to +1.20. In other words, the results are approximately as consistent with $d_{pop} = +1.20$ as they are with $d_{pop} = 0$. Also, if the counternull value had been selected to be the null-hypothesized value of d_{pop} (i.e., H_0: $d_{pop} = 1.20$ in the present example), the p level attained by the results at hand would have been the same as it is when H_0: $d_{pop} = 0$ is tested. This statement applies to any kind of effect size.

Equations 3.11 and 3.12 are applicable only to estimators that have a symmetrical sampling distribution, such as d. For equations for application to estimators that have asymmetrical distributions, such as the correlation coefficient r (discussed in the next chapter), refer to Rosenthal et al. (2000), who also discussed a kind of confidence level for a null–counternull interval. To understand such a confidence level, recall the hypothetical example in which $n_a = n_b = 20$ and $d = +0.70$. In that example the estimate of ES was $d = +0.70$ and, assuming the usual $ES_{null} = 0$ in this example, by Equation 3.11 $ES_{cn} = 2ES = 2(+0.70) = +1.40$. Suppose further that the two-tailed p level for the obtained t in this example had been found to be, say, $p = .04$. Recall also that a t test conducted at the two-tailed α level is associated with a confidence interval for the difference between the two involved population means in which one is approximately $100(1 - \alpha)\%$ confident. Similarly, in the present example one can be approximately $100(1 - p)\% = 100(1 - .04)\% = 96\%$ confident in the null–counternull interval of 0 to +1.40, where p is the obtained two-tailed significance level. However, the confidence level for a traditional confidence interval is based on a fixed probability $(1 - \alpha)$ that is set in advance by the researcher, typically .95, whereas the confidence level for a null–counternull interval is based on a result-determined probability, the two-tailed p level attained by a test statistic such as t.

A null–counternull interval can provide information that is only slightly conceptually similar to, and not likely nearly numerically the same as, the information that is provided by a confidence interval. Both intervals bracket the obtained estimate of effect size, but, unlike the lower limit of a confidence interval, when $ES_{null} = 0$, the lower limit of the null–counternull interval will always be 0. Confidence intervals and null–counternull intervals cannot be directly compared or combined.

Some researchers who are conducting studies in which their focus is not on significance testing may also be inclined to avoid the null–counternull approach because, like significance testing, this approach typically focuses on the value 0, although, unlike significance testing, it also focuses on a value at some distance from 0 (the counternull value). A confidence interval also calls one's attention to a set of plausible values for the unknown parameter that are somewhat consistent with the data (although less likely to be equal to the parameter than the point estimate is).

EXTREME GROUPS

A method that is often problematic for effect sizes is the *extreme-groups method*, in which data analysis is applied only to the data from individuals who score at the extreme low and extreme high ends of the distribution of the scores on the independent variable. Often the approximate lower and upper quartiles (or tertiles, i.e., 33%) are used as the *cut points* to form the two groups. Results from such studies may not generalize to the full range of the "split" variable when such generalization is of interest to the researcher. The extreme-groups method will typically result in overestimation of d_{pop} and many other measures of effect size that are discussed later in this book. However, an extreme-group method is valid if the research is actually focused only on extreme groups, the cut points are determined prior to collecting data (i.e., the criteria for defining "extreme" are predetermined), and the results are not generalized to a full range of the data. For example, research can validly focus on the difference in risk for acquiring a disease in groups that have been exposed to very low or very high levels of something that may be harmful (e.g., microwaves?) or beneficial (antioxidants in the diet). Also, a tertile or quartile split avoids the misclassification problem of the traditional split at the median score. It is more likely that there will be measurement error (Chapter 4) from misclassifying observed scores near the median into the upper or lower 50% with respect to the underlying variable than misclassifying high scorers as low scorers or low scorers as high scorers.

Preacher, Rucker, MacCallum, and Nicewander (2005) provided extensive discussion and references on the topic of extreme groups. Consult DeCoster, Iselin, and Gallucci (2009) for a more favorable view.

PERCENT OF MAXIMUM POSSIBLE SCORE

We have previously discussed some implications of the fact that measures of dependent variables in the behavioral sciences are often based on scales that are often not comparable unit for unit from measure to alternative measure of the same (presumably) underlying variable (e.g., depression). However, one of the possible linear transformations of the scores from such more-or-less arbitrary scales can add meaning to the scores if the maximum and minimum possible scores are known. This linear transformation of a score is the *percent of maximum possible score* (*POMP*) given by

$$POMP = 100\% \left[\frac{(Score_{obs} - Min)}{(Max - Min)} \right], \tag{3.13}$$

where obs = observed, *Min* = the minimum possible score, and *Max* = the maximum possible score. Such a transformation produces a scale that ranges from 0% to 100%. In cases in which *Min* = 0 Equation 3.15 simplifies to the form that is commonly used in scholastic grading on examinations, *grade* = (*Score*$_{obs}$/*Max*)100% (e.g., grade = (80/100)100% = 80%). Cohen, Cohen, Aiken, and West (1999) concluded that the use of the *POMP* was superior to traditional scoring with respect to their seven criteria for the information value of scales. Those authors compared the *POMP* to the traditional scoring of an individual's performance: the simple sum of item scores, the mean of the item scores, and the *z* score.

Where applicable, authors of reports of research should consider reporting the mean *POMP* for each group, the difference between the two mean *POMPs* constituting another estimator of effect size that can be reported together with any other relevant estimator of effect size. Because the *POMP* is a linear transformation of the original scores, if the original mean scores are statistically significantly different at level *p*, the means of the two groups' *POMPs* will be statistically significantly different at the same level of *p*. Also, standardized-difference effect sizes, correlations, and statistical power are unchanged when original scores are transformed to *POMP* scores. Furthermore, because a confidence interval for an unstandardized difference between two means is less informative when the measure of the dependent variable is a scale with more-or-less arbitrary units, a more informative confidence interval can be had in this case by converting the limits of the confidence interval to their equivalent *POMP* values. However, authors of reports should make clear to their readers that the *POMP*-based confidence interval relates to a difference between mean percentages, not a difference that has been converted to a percentage.

Tips and Pitfalls

POMP scoring is not always advisable and it is not a cure-all. *POMP* should not replace scoring that is on a scale that is already meaningful, and it does not resolve the usual possible problems such as unsatisfactory reliability or validity of the original scores. Also, as is the case with any kind of scoring or effect size the *POMP* must be interpreted in context. For example, a grade of 85% on an examination in high school would be interpreted differently from a grade of 85% on an examination in graduate school. Furthermore, the rankings underlying such *POMP*s should be taken into account. For example, a *POMP* = 85% might rank a student anywhere from last to first among the examinees.

DEPENDENT GROUPS

CHOICE OF STANDARDIZER

Equations 3.3 through 3.6 are also applicable to dependent-groups designs, the latter two equations being applicable when homoscedasticity is assumed. In the case of a pretest–posttest design the means in the numerators of these four equations become the pretest and posttest means (e.g., $\overline{Y}_{pre}$ and $\overline{Y}_{post}$ when using Equation 3.3 or 3.5). In this case the standardizer in Equation 3.3 can be s_{pre}. If homoscedasticity is assumed the pooled standard deviation, s_p, can also be used to produce instead of the d of Equation 3.5. Because $n_a = n_b$ in the present case, s_p is merely the square root of the mean of s_{pre}^2 and s_{post}^2; $s_p = \left[\left(s_{pre}^2 + s_{post}^2\right)/2\right]^{1/2}$. Some methodologists would advise that s_{post} generally not be used for the standardizer because, as was discussed in Chapter 1, treatment can increase variability of posttest scores, which, in turn, decreases the estimate of effect size. Similarly, to the extent that treatment increases variability of posttest scores an estimate of effect size that uses the pooled s as the standardizer will also be reduced. On the other hand, Keselman et al. (2008) noted that some researchers may prefer that pretest scores be used as a covariate instead of being used as a level of the independent variable, so that one is left with s_{post} as the standardizer. (Analysis of covariance is the topic of Chapter 11.)

The choice of a standardizer for the estimation of a standardized-difference effect size should be based on the nature of the population of scores to which one wants to generalize the results in the sample. Therefore, in the case of a pretest–posttest design some have argued that the standardizer for an estimator of d_{pop}

should not be based on a standard deviation of raw scores as in the previous paragraph, but instead should be the standard deviation of the difference scores (e.g., the standard deviation, s_D, of the data in column D in Table 2.1). The rationale of those who take this position is that in this design one should be interested in generalizing to the mean posttreatment–pretreatment differences in individuals relative to the population of such difference scores.

Each standardizer has its purpose. For example, in areas of research that consist of a mix of between-group and within-group studies of the same variables, greater comparability with results from the between-groups studies can be attained if the within-group studies use a standardizer that is based on the s of the raw scores. Consult the references that were cited by Morris and DeShon (2002) for discussions supporting either the standard deviation of raw scores or the standard deviation of the posttreatment–pretreatment difference scores as the standardizer.

The kind of dependent-groups d_{pop} parameter that is being estimated differs depending on the kind of standardizer that is used in the estimator, so one should consider which parameter one wishes to estimate when choosing a standardizer; for example, $(\mu_{pre} - \mu_{post})/\sigma_d$ or $(\mu_{pre} - \mu_{post})/\sigma_Y$. One should also realize that because of the correlation between pretest and posttest scores the standard deviation of the difference scores will be smaller than the standard deviation of the raw scores and, thereby, yield a larger estimate of effect size. Researchers should consider reporting multiple estimates of effect size that are based on the competing standardizers and providing at least brief discussions of the implications of the various reported estimates.

CONFIDENCE INTERVALS

In the pretest–posttest design if one uses σ_d as the standardizer then the noncentral methods that we previously discussed for independent groups can be used to construct an "exact" confidence interval in the dependent-groups case (Cumming & Finch, 2001). Again, "exact" assumes that normality is satisfied. However, in the case of nonnormality one approach is to use *large-sample theory* (whereby an otherwise nonnormal sampling distribution converges toward normality as sample size increases) to construct a confidence interval for the population difference between two dependent means, standardized by the standard deviation of the difference scores (Al-Kandari, Buhamra, & Ahmed, 2005). Bonett (2008) presented a modification of his method, which we previously discussed, for the case in which the interest is in pretest–posttest difference scores. As was previously mentioned, Bonett's methods may fail under more than slight departures from normality and homoscedasticity.

CORRECTION FOR BIAS

Recall that a correction for the bias in d for independent samples when samples are very small was given in Equation 3.7. We are not aware of a well-established correction for d in the case of very small dependent samples. However, after preliminary study Bonett (2009b) tentatively proposed such a correction for bias for very small paired samples in primary studies when using his preferred d that standardizes using Equation 3.8. The bias-reducing factor that multiplies Bonett's d for dependent samples is given by $[(n - 2)/n - 1)]^{1/2}$, where n is the number of pairs. Bonett recommended that meta-analysts use this correction for every value of his dependent-samples d, regardless of sample size, because of accumulation of negligible bias from primary-study d values into important bias for the meta-analytic average d.

HOMOSCEDASTICITY NOT ASSUMED

When homoscedasticity is not assumed Equations 3.3 and 3.4 appear to be appropriate for a dependent-groups design, especially when the group that provides the standardizer is a control group or standard-treatment group that is being compared to a new treatment. Also applicable to this case is the robust modification of these equations that was previously discussed in the context of the independent-groups design. As before, the modification consists of the use of trimmed means, Winsorized variances, and multiplying the resulting effect size by .642. Keselman et al. (2008) discussed the construction of a robust CI for such a modified effect size.

TESTING STATISTICAL SIGNIFICANCE

For testing the statistical significance of the difference between the two dependent means that are involved in a standardized-difference effect size researchers typically use the one-sample t test that is applied to the difference scores. The previously cited large-sample method by Al-Kandari et al. (2005) can also be used to test one-tailed and two-tailed hypotheses in the nonnormal case of the difference between two dependent means.

MORE ON CONFIDENCE INTERVALS AND OTHER MEASURES

Consult Algina and Keselman (2003b) for a method for constructing an approximate confidence interval for a standardized difference effect size for the case of dependent groups with equal or unequal variances. Their method appears to provide satisfactorily accurate confidence levels under the conditions they simulated for the true values of d_{pop} and for the strengths of correlation between the two populations of scores. For a nominal .95 confidence level their slightly conservative method resulted in actual coverage probabilities that ranged from .951 to .972. The degree of correlation between the two populations of scores seemed to have little effect on the coverage probabilities. (However, the power of a large-sample hypothesis test in the dependent-group case can increase greatly as correlation increases [Al-Kandari et al., 2005].) Also, as the true value of d_{pop} increased the coverage probabilities became slightly more conservative. Specifically, when the true values of d_{pop} ranged from 0 to 1.6 the probability coverage ranged from .951 to .971, values that are extremely close or satisfactorily close to the nominal confidence level of .95 in the simulations. The method can be undertaken using any software package that provides noncentrality parameters for noncentral

t distributions, such as SAS (the SAS function TNONCT), that Algina and Keselman (2003b) recommended as being particularly useful for this purpose.

The method used by Algina and Keselman (2003b) assumes normality (bivariate normality as defined in Chapter 4) but was extended by Algina, Keselman, and Penfield (2005b) to the nonnormal case. Simulations in the latter study indicated that probability coverage can generally be maintained between .925 and .975 (for the nominal .95 level) by using, instead of the noncentral t distribution, trimmed means, Winsorized variances, and bootstrapping. A free Windows-based program that is written in Visual Basic 6.0 is available, courtesy of James Algina, for constructing percentile bootstrap confidence intervals for the cases in which the standard deviation is based on the variance of one group or the two pooled variances. The address for the software is http://plaza.ufl.edu/algina/index.programs.html.

For nonparametric estimation of standardized-difference effect sizes for pretest–posttest designs consult Hedges and Olkin (1985), Kraemer and Andrews (1982), and Krauth (1983). Consult Wilcox (2003) for other approaches to effect sizes when comparing two dependent groups.

As was mentioned in the section entitled "Exploring the data for a possible effect of treatment on variability" in Chapter 1, with citation of free Dataplot software, a change or changes in location, variability, and/or shape between pretest and posttest can be depicted graphically using a bihistogram. Finally, consider the case in which not only are two groups related (e.g., repeated measures or matched pairs) but also within each group there are multiple data from the same individuals. Nakagawa and Cuthill (2007) provided an example and a formula for a d value for this complex case.

EFFECT SIZES FOR PRETEST–POSTTEST CONTROL-GROUP DESIGNS

Consider a design that extends the pretest–posttest design by adding a comparison group (typically a no-treatment control group) that also is pretested and posttested. Such a design is called the *pretest–posttest control-group design*, and is intended to control for variables, such as maturation between pretesting and posttesting, which would otherwise be confounded with treatment in the pretest–posttest design. An independent-groups t test is often used to compare the mean difference scores for the two groups (although other analyses are possible, such as an analysis of covariance, as in Chapter 11).

Suppose that the researcher is interested in estimating an effect size that takes into account all four pretest and posttest means and uses for the standardizer a standard deviation that is assumed to be equal in the treated and control populations. Such an effect-size parameter is the difference between the standardized mean change for the treated and control groups, d_{diffpop}, which simplifies to

$$d_{\text{diffpop}} = \left[\frac{(\mu_{\text{tpost}} - \mu_{\text{tpre}}) - (\mu_{\text{cpost}} - \mu_{\text{cpre}})}{\sigma} \right], \tag{3.14}$$

where t and c represent treatment and control, respectively. We consider three estimators of d_{diffpop} based on three possible standardizers.

First, after Becker (1988) one can use

$$d_1 = \left[\frac{(\overline{Y}_{\text{tpost}} - \overline{Y}_{\text{tpre}})}{s_{\text{tpre}}} - \frac{(\overline{Y}_{\text{cpost}} - \overline{Y}_{\text{cpre}})}{s_{\text{cpre}}} \right]. \tag{3.15}$$

The positive bias in d_1 can be approximately corrected by applying Equation 3.7 to each of the separate standardized differences on the right side of Equation 3.15 using $df = n_j - 1$ in Equation 3.7 for each group but, as usual, the bias is slight except for very small samples.

Second, because we are thus far assuming homoscedasticity whereas Equation 3.15 uses separate estimates of standard deviation, one can instead attempt to achieve a better estimate of the assumed common σ by pooling the two pretest variances and estimating d_{diffpop} using, after Carlson and Schmidt (1999),

$$d_2 = \left[\frac{(\overline{Y}_{\text{tpost}} - \overline{Y}_{\text{tpre}}) - (\overline{Y}_{\text{cpost}} - \overline{Y}_{\text{cpre}})}{s_{\text{poolpre}}} \right], \tag{3.16}$$

where s_{poolpre} is the square root of the two pooled variances, obtained in the usual manner. Again, if one wishes to reduce the usually slight positive bias one can multiply d_2 by the correction factor given by Equation 3.7. In this case the degrees of freedom called for by Equation 3.7 is $df = n_t + n_c - 2$.

Third, again based on the assumption of homoscedasticity one can attempt to achieve an even better estimate of σ by pooling all four available sample variances: treatment pretest and posttest, and control pretest and posttest. The numerator of this pooled variance is the usual sum of weighted separate variances (four variances in this case), the four weights being $n_j - 1$, and the denominator is $2(n_t + n_c - 2)$.

The resulting estimator of d_{diffpop} is, after Taylor and White (1992),

$$d_3 = \frac{\left[(\overline{Y}_{\text{tpost}} - \overline{Y}_{\text{tpre}}) - (\overline{Y}_{\text{cpost}} - \overline{Y}_{\text{cpre}}) \right]}{s_{\text{poolprepost}}}. \tag{3.17}$$

Again, one can attempt to reduce the usually slight positive bias of d_3 by multiplying d_3 by the correction factor given by Equation 3.7, with the degrees of freedom in Equation 3.7 now being $df = 2n_t + 2n_c - 4$. However, especially when pretest scores and posttest scores are highly correlated, the bias correction may insufficiently reduce the positive bias in d_3 (Morris, 2008).

Although estimates from d_1, d_2, and d_3 often vary little, large differences are possible. Therefore, we now discuss the comparison of the three estimators that was provided by Morris (2008) and make a recommendation. One criterion for a better estimator is lower sampling variability. However, although d_3 uses twice the data that d_2 uses, simulations by Morris revealed that d_3 has only slightly lower sampling variability than does d_2. Further, recall from the discussion of Equation 3.14 that thus far equality of variances of the treated and control groups has been assumed. However, as was discussed in Chapter 1, it is quite possible that treatment increases variability. Therefore, we prefer d_2 to d_3 because inflated posttest variance from treatment will result in underestimation of d_{diffpop} by inflating the denominator of d_3. Also, as Morris noted, unlike d_1 and d_2, d_3 has a currently unknown and complex sampling variance. The sampling variance of d_2 is smaller than that of d_1, so we generally also prefer d_2 to d_1. Furthermore, the standardizer in d_2 is not altered if treatment has an effect on variability. Consult Feingold (2009) for additional discussion of standardized-difference effect sizes for this design.

EFFECT SIZES FOR PRETEST–POSTTEST CONTROL-GROUP DESIGNS WITH MULTIPLE OBSERVATIONS (GROWTH)

Often there are additional observations on the treated and control groups along the timeline between the pretest and the posttest, giving rise to additional possible effect sizes. From a *growth-modeling* perspective the additional observations provide information about the between-groups difference in rate of change (growth rates) in the scores across all observations over the course of the timeline. For example, the number of new words acquired per week over a school term (growth in vocabulary) by two groups of pupils who are given different teaching methods for acquisition of vocabulary can be compared. The difference in change (growth) between two groups can yield an effect size. Consult Feingold (2009) and Raudenbush and Liu (2001) for details on this topic, which is discussed further in Chapter 4. Also consult Nakagawa and Cuthill (2007).

Liu, Lu, Mogg, Mallick, and Mehrotra (2009) discussed construction of confidence intervals for the case in which an unstandardized within-group difference between the mean at baseline and the mean at the last observation for each group, and for the between-group differences in such change, are of interest. Those authors also discussed the alternative of using the baseline scores as a covariate in an analysis of covariance (Chapter 11).

SUMMARY

When an observed dependent variable is on a more or less arbitrary scale that is intended to measure a presumed latent variable (i.e., an unobserved underlying variable), an SDM instead of an unstandardized difference can serve as an informative effect size. An example is the use of psychological tests that are intended to measure underlying psychological dimensions. An SDM effect size places different observed dependent variable measures on the same scale (i.e., the scale of standard deviation units) so that results from different studies that use the same independent variables but different measures of the *same* underlying dependent variables can be compared or combined.

An SDM has some properties of a z score (i.e., unbounded negative and positive values, and a value of 0 when there is no effect), as it divides a difference by a standard deviation, a procedure that is called standardizing. In this case it is the difference between two groups' means that is being standardized. For example, suppose that there are two groups, such as a treated group and a control group. Dividing the difference between the two samples' means by the standard deviation of the control sample provides an estimate of how many standard deviation units apart the two population means are. Also, assuming population normality, this effect-size estimator estimates the percentage of members of one population who outscore the mean of the other population.

Besides a treated group and a control (or placebo) group the two compared groups can be two treated groups or two pre-existing groups, such as females and males. If equal population variances is correctly assumed a pooled estimate of the assumed common population standard deviation provides a standardizer that is a better estimate of the population standard deviation than the standard deviation of one of the groups would be. Population nonnormality or unequal variances can be problematic for the SDM.

The traditional effect-size estimator, d, that standardizes by first pooling the two samples variances is sensitive to unequal population variances combined with unequal sample sizes. Additional standardizers, some not widely known, are available to counter outliers and unequal variances. A common simple solution when population variances are not assumed to be equal, a new treatment is being studied, and one of the groups can serve as a reasonable comparison group (e.g., a control group or a standard-treatment group) is the use of the standard deviation of that comparison group as a defensible standardizer. A group for which there are available norms can also serve as a comparison group. Also, in research on pre-existing groups the population effect size, d_{pop}, is sensitive to unequal proportions of the two kinds of groups in the population (e.g., depressives and non-depressives).

Effect size can be informative regarding the practical significance of results, but effect size is not synonymous with practical significance. For example, an effect size that is based on an observed measure of a targeted latent variable (e.g., depression) may not correspond to what the effect size would be if it could be based on the latent variable itself. Also, effect-size estimates can differ for (a) different measures of a latent variable that is wrongly believed to be the same in each study, (b) groups that are of different demographics, and (c) biased or bias-adjusted estimates. Although some make a case for its regular use, the sample standardized difference that is adjusted for positive bias (i.e., tendency to overestimate) is seldom used because the bias is considered to be slight for reasonably sized samples. We generally disapprove of the use of extreme groups to increase statistical power because this method typically results in overestimation of d_{pop}.

There are different standardizers possible for the pretest–posttest design. Each has its purpose. The choice should be based on the nature of the population of scores to which one wants to generalize the results. For the pretest–posttest control-group design we generally prefer the estimator d_2 in Equation 3.16.

Researchers should be clear about which kind of standardized difference effect size they are reporting and should consider reporting multiple effect sizes when the alternative standardizers are equally defensible. All calculated estimates should be reported, not just the most impressive one. Very importantly, a confidence interval should be reported for any kind of d_{pop} that has been estimated. Also, a research report should include all relevant summary statistics and sample sizes as a courtesy to readers who may want to calculate an effect-size estimate other than any that is reported.

QUESTIONS

3.1 In which circumstance can an SDM be more informative than a simple difference between means?

3.2 Define (a) *latent variable*, (b) *counternull effect size* and *counternull interval*, (c) *base-rate-sensitive effect size*.

3.3 Assuming normality, interpret $d = +1.00$ when using Equation 3.1, and explain the interpretation.

3.4 If population variances are equal, what are the two advantages of pooling sample variances to estimate the common population variance?

3.5 Distinguish between Glass's d_G and Cohen's d.

3.6 Why is it unlikely that Glass' d_G will equal Cohen's d even if population variances are equal?

3.7 What is the direction of bias of Cohen's d and Glass' d_G, what two factors influence this bias, and in what ways do these two factors influence the bias?

3.8 Why is Hedges' bias-adjusted version of g or d seldom used by researchers?

3.9 In what ways does heteroscedasticity cause problems for the use of standardized differences between means?

3.10 Which standardized-difference effect size is recommended when homoscedasticity is assumed, and why?

3.11 Discuss two approaches to estimating effect size that should be considered when homoscedasticity is not assumed.

3.12 What might be a solution to the problem of estimating effect size in the face of heteroscedasticity in areas of research that use a normed test for the measure of the dependent variable, and why is this so?

3.13 Why is nonnormality problematic for the usual interpretation of d?

3.14 In what way may a large effect size for a treatment for an addiction be too optimistically interpreted?

3.15 Describe two alternative standardized-difference estimators of effect size when there are outliers.

3.16 In which research context is the magnitude of the effect size of greatest interest?

3.17 Besides .95, which part of Expression 3.9 changes if one adopts a confidence level other than .95, and why?

3.18 Identify two ways in which a plan for data analysis can narrow the eventual confidence interval.

3.19 Contrast the central t distribution and a noncentral t distribution.

3.20 Which two factors influence the difference between the central and noncentral t distributions, and in what ways?

3.21 What is the rationale for a counternull effect size?

3.22 When should a researcher consider using a null–counternull interval?

3.23 Contrast a null–counternull interval and a confidence interval.

3.24 How can Equations 3.3 through 3.6 be applied to the case of dependent groups?

3.25 What is the effect of nonnormality on the value of d?

3.26 Discuss the base-rate sensitivity of d_{pop} under heteroscedasticity.

3.27 Why should it be expected that d would be sensitive to a difference between sizes of samples under heteroscedasticity?

3.28 Briefly define *percentile bootstrapping*.

3.29 Why is the use of extreme groups problematic?

3.30 Discuss the *POMP* method and its limitations.

3.31 Briefly define *large-sample theory*.

3.32 Which equation do the authors prefer for estimating a standardized-difference effect size for the pretest–posttest control-group design, and why do they prefer it?

3.33 For the following real data involving mothers of schizophrenics (Group a) and mothers of normals (Group b) (a) provide a boxplot (and optionally any other diagnostics for satisfaction of assumptions that may be outputted by your software) for each group; (b) in light of the discussions in the text and the diagnostic evidence from part (a) discuss the appropriateness of estimating an SDM using each of the standardizers in Equations 3.1, 3.3, 3.5, and 3.8; (c) regardless of the evidence of their appropriateness, as an informative exercise estimate an SDM using each of these standardizers (in the case of Equation 3.3 calculate an estimate using s_b and another using s_a); (d) interpret each of the five obtained estimates and discuss their differences; (e) apply the adjustment in Equation 3.7 to the result from Equation 3.5 and discuss any difference between the two results.

Group a: 2, 1, 1, 3, 2, 7, 2, 1, 3, 1, 0, 2, 4, 2, 3, 3, 0, 1, 2, 2
Group b: 8, 4, 6, 3, 1, 4, 4, 6, 4, 2, 2, 1, 1, 4, 3, 3, 2, 6, 3, 4

3.34 Regarding the data in Question 3.33, and considering the results of the boxplots and of any other diagnostics regarding assumptions obtained in Question 33, (a) construct the most appropriate confidence interval for a standardized-mean-difference effect size that software available to you provides and (b) discuss that confidence interval and the appropriateness of competing methods for constructing a confidence interval for those data.

3.35 Assuming now that the data from Groups a and b in Question 3.33 represent pretest and posttest scores, respectively, (a) estimate an appropriate standardized-mean-difference effect size, (b) construct a confidence interval for it, and (c) discuss your choice of method in light of competing methods.

4 Correlational Effect Sizes and Related Topics

INTRODUCTION

When X and Y are continuous random variables the familiar sample *Pearson correlation coefficient*, r, is commonly considered to be an estimator of effect size in terms of the size (magnitude of r) and direction (sign of r) of a linear relationship between X and Y. Although the Y variable has been continuous thus far in this book, the independent variable (X) has been a fixed dichotomous variable such as membership in group a or group b, but a correlational effect size is available for this case. A fixed variable is one whose values have been chosen by the researcher as being of particular interest; that is, the values of the X variable were not obtained randomly. Computational formulas and software for r require both X and Y to be quantitative variables, but we soon observe that calculating an r between a truly dichotomous categorical X variable and a quantitative Y variable as an effect size does not present a problem.

A *truly dichotomous variable* means a naturally dichotomous (or nearly so) variable, such as gender, or an independent variable that is created by assigning participants into two different treatment groups to conduct an experiment. We are excluding the usually problematic procedure of creating a dichotomous variable by arbitrarily dichotomizing originally continuous scores into two groups, say, those above the median versus those below the median (a *median split*).

DICHOTOMIZING AND CORRELATION

When an originally continuous variable is dichotomized, it will nearly always correlate lower with another variable than if it had not been dichotomized, and it cannot attain the usual maximum absolute value of correlation with a continuous variable; i.e., $r = |1|$. (Dichotomizing should not be confused with the use of extreme groups because in the former all data are divided into two sets whereas in the latter the middle bulk of data is discarded.) Also, squeezing a continuous variable into $c > 2$ finite categories (e.g., categories low, medium, and high, quantitatively coded as, say, values 1, 2, and 3) will usually lower r.

Hunter and Schmidt (2004) discussed the method for correcting the reduction of r that results when continuous variable X or Y, or both, have been artificially dichotomized using a median split or any other kind of split into two categories. For example, for the common case in which X is a continuous variable that has been dichotomized at the median the corrected value of r is $r/.80$.

Conflicting estimates of other measures of effect size can emerge depending on the cutoff point used to divide a continuous variable into two categories. Meehl (1992) discussed circumstances that may justify dichotomizing.

DIFFERENT KINDS OF CORRELATIONAL EFFECT SIZES

If it is assumed that the continuous variable underlying the dichotomous X has a bivariate normal distribution with the continuous Y the correlation is properly called a *biserial correlation*. The dichotomizing split in this case need not be at the median. Bivariate normality is discussed in a later section of this chapter. Further discussion of rendering an r that is based on dichotomizing a continuous independent variable approximately comparable to an r that is based on the original continuous independent variable was provided by DeCoster et al. (2009).

If both continuous X and Y have been split at the median (the correlation between two dichotomous variables being an example of a *phi coefficient*) the doubly corrected correlation is $r/(.80)(.80) = r/.64$. Ruscio (2008a) discussed the fact that d is not a valid estimator of d_{pop} when it is based on dichotomizing a continuous independent variable.

The correlation between two dichotomous variables that are assumed to represent two linearly related, normally distributed underlying variables that are split at any point is called a *tetrachoric* correlation, r_t. The division of each continuous variable into two groups of data in this case is an assumption of the researcher, not a dichotomizing that has been undertaken by the researcher. For example, if patients are categorized as Anxious versus Not Anxious on the basis of subjective judgment, some researchers might assume that the underlying anxiety is a normally distributed variable. This is different from the problematic case in which instead of basing statistical analysis on available scores on a test of anxiety the researcher uses a split of those scores into two categories. When each of the continuous variables that are assumed to underlie the dichotomous variables is distributed normally, whether or not they are jointly normal, the tetrachoric correlation may satisfactorily estimate the common Pearson correlation coefficient under certain conditions (Genest & Lévesque, 2009).

Although by definition the division of each of the continuous variables into two groupings may exist anywhere along the continua, the sampling variability of r_t is increased the greater the differences between the proportions of cases in each grouping and the smaller the total sample size. For example, if unbeknownst to the researcher there is, say, a 95% versus 5% split of the cases in the two groups that are assumed to represent an underlying continuous variable, the sampling error of r_t will likely be unacceptably large and a confidence interval for the Pearson r_{pop} based on r_t will be unacceptably wide. A 50% versus 50% split would be preferable. We generally do not recommend use of the r_t in applied research because of its dependence on its assumptions and the great influence of the nature of the supposed split. However, the r_t can be of use in theoretical research. Consult Kraemer (2006) for further discussion of the r_t.

POINT-BISERIAL CORRELATION

The common procedure for calculating an r effect size between a truly dichotomous qualitative grouping variable (e.g., female and male, Treatment a and Treatment b) and a quantitative variable from raw data is to code membership in group a or group b numerically using any pair of different numbers. For example, membership in group a can be coded, say, "1," and membership in group b can be coded, say, "2." Thus, in a data file each member of group a would be represented by entering a 1 in the X column and each member of group b would be represented by entering a 2 in the X column. (Often 0 and 1 are used instead of 1 and 2, but the numerical coding only requires that the two numbers be different.) Each participant's score on the measure of the dependent variable is entered in the Y column of the data file. The magnitude of r will remain the same regardless of which two different numbers are chosen for the coding. The only aspect of the coding that the researcher must keep in mind when interpreting the obtained sample r is which group was assigned the higher number. If r is found to be positive, that means that the sample that had been assigned the higher number on X (say 2, instead of 1) tended to score higher than the other sample on the Y variable. If r is negative then the sample that had been assigned the higher number on X tended to score lower than the other sample on the Y variable.

The correlation between a dichotomous variable, say X, and a continuous variable, say Y, is generally called a *point-biserial correlation*, r_{pb}, the sample value of which is a commonly used estimator of effect size in the two-group case. (Strictly, a point-biserial r actually involves two *random* variables, so when the values of X are not random but are purposely chosen by the researcher [the *fixed* model], the correlation might better be given a different name [Kraemer, 2005]. However, for practical purposes this distinction is typically ignored so we will not make this distinction in this book.)

The point-biserial correlation coefficient is the familiar Pearson correlation coefficient for the case in which one variable is truly dichotomous and the other variable is continuous. Therefore, for some purposes that are discussed later, when using r_{pb} one does not have to look for statistical software that includes r_{pb}. One simply uses any software for the usual r and enters the numerical codes in the X column according to each participant's group membership. For the case of a truly dichotomous independent variable in which the two population sizes are conceptually equal (e.g., most experiments) or factually essentially equal (e.g., gender), the point-biserial r ranges from -1 to $+1$, assuming equal sample sizes or adjustment for unequal sample sizes (Hunter & Schmidt, 2004; discussed later). When only a t statistic and degrees of freedom ($df = n_1 + n_2 - 2$) have been reported for the case of a naturally dichotomous independent variable and a continuous dependent variable a value of r_{pb} can be approximately estimated using $r_{pb} = [t^2/(t^2 + df)]^{1/2}$.

Pearson correlations are not ratio scaled. For example, an $r_{pb} = .4$ does *not* represent twice the strength of relationship (i.e., twice the effect size) of $r_{pb} = .2$. (By the concept of coefficient of determination that is discussed later in this chapter the former value represents a fourfold increase in strength of relationship compared to the later value.)

When one is interested in estimating the correlation between two variables and there are two or more sets of data available, say, from different studies or multiple centers of research (e.g., hospitals or schools) in one large study, the manner of estimating the correlation can profoundly influence the result. The estimate of correlation that is obtained by averaging r from each study can be extremely different or opposite from the single r that is obtained by pooling the separate data into one set. The separate sets of data may each yield $r = 0$, whereas the combined set yields $r > 0$ (*Yule's paradox*). Alternatively, the separate sets may each yield small values of r, whereas the combined set yields $r = 0$. If a researcher has good reason to combine such multiple sets of data the research report should also present the separate values of r.

Observe in Equation 4.1 that r_{pop}, which is the population r or population r_{pb}, is a type of standardized effect size when it is expressed as

$$r_{pop} = \frac{\sum [(X - \mu_X)(Y - \mu_Y)]}{N \sigma_X \sigma_Y}, \tag{4.1}$$

which is a definitional equation for r_{pop} from which computational equations for r derive. In this version of the equation for r_{pop} observe that what is called the *covariance* of X and Y (i.e., the numerator) is "standardized" by a function of the standard deviations (i.e., the denominator).

Suppose that one's purpose is to use r_{pb} inferentially to predict values of one variable from the other in the population, and the two sample sizes of the dichotomous variable are unequal and are at least approximately in the same proportion as the two population sizes. In this case one should not use the previously discussed procedure of applying numerically coded values for the levels of the dichotomous variable to software for the ordinary r to render the result an r_{pb}. (The rationale is discussed later.) Instead, for this case one can use an approximate conversion formula (after Kraemer, 2006; equivalent to Eq. 21 in Rosnow & Rosenthal, 2008, and the equation in footnote 4 on p. 389 in McGrath & Meyer, 2006),

$$r_{pb} = \frac{d}{[d^2 + ((N-2)/Np_1p_2)]^{1/2}}, \tag{4.2}$$

where
N is the total sample size, $n_1 + n_2$
each $p_j = n_j/N$, the proportion of the total sample that is in a given sample

Equation 4.2 looks different from slightly less accurate conversion equations often seen in other writing because some authors define d with the standardizer based on the use of N instead of $N - 2$ in the denominator of the pooled variances (e.g., McGrath & Meyer, 2006), as was discussed in Chapter 3, which properly simplifies the equation for certain purposes. Also, some conversion equations assume equal sample sizes, which also simplifies the equation. Further, some equations use a function of p_1 and p_2 (also denoted p and q) instead of a function of n_1 and n_2; that is, $p_1p_2 = n_1n_2/N^2$. Except for the case of small sample sizes the various approximate conversion formulas yield very similar results. Indeed, for small to moderate values of d (say, $-.4 < d < +.4$) and equal sample sizes, the simplification $r_{pb} = d/2$ yields a fairly good approximation (but not recommended for research reports). For additional discussions of alternative conversion formulas, consult Hunter and Schmidt (2004), McGrath and Meyer (2006), and Rosnow and Rosenthal (2008).

Tips and Pitfalls

As McGrath and Meyer (2006) noted, even estimators of different kinds of effect size measures that can be converted to each other might yield very different conclusions about the results, as is observed throughout this book. McGrath and Meyer provided an extensive discussion of the sensitivity of r_{pb} to the difference between the two populations' base rates (i.e., population proportions p_1 and p_2), an important topic that is discussed further in later sections in this chapter. Consult Kraemer (2006) for formulas that modify r_{pb} for the case of a dichotomized independent variable.

CORRELATION AND POINT-BISERIAL CORRELATION IN EXTREME GROUPS

Recall from Chapter 3 that the method of extreme groups often inflates estimates of effect size. Such inflation includes r_{pb}. Research reports should not compare, and meta-analyses should not combine, estimates of r_{pop} that are based on a mixture of extreme-group and full-range studies. Also, the use of the data only from the two extreme subgroups eliminates one's ability to detect the form of the overall relationship between two full-range continuous variables.

OTHER VIEWS OF CORRELATION AND POINT-BISERIAL CORRELATION

Fine-Grained Correlation

It is worthwhile to note other views of the correlation coefficient to broaden one's perspective on this effect size. Levine (2005) argued that Pearson's r, as a summary statistic, too coarsely relates X and Y and is outdated in the era of powerful computing that can provide much finer-grained estimates of the relationship between the variables. Such finer-grained analyses may reveal nontrivial exceptions to the *global* (i.e., overall) relationship between X and Y in smaller regions of the relationship (i.e., *local* effect size). The point is that within certain limited ranges of values of X the relationships between X and Y might be different from the overall relationship between X and Y over the full range of values of X. Hufthammer (2005) discussed local and global measures of relationship, an effect size that captures both kinds of relationship, and two kinds of graphical displays that may indicate a relationship and distinguish between the two types. Wilcox (2007b) proposed a local measure of relationship that allows heteroscedasticity and nonlinearity.

Spurious Correlation

Consider three variables (X, Y, and Z) involved in a correlational effect size. The correlation between two variables will be influenced if they share a common term in their numerators or denominators, such as correlating variable X/Z with variable Y/Z, variable Z/X, or variable Z. The resulting correlation is said to be a kind of *spurious correlation*. Consider the example of correlating cities' felony crime rates with cities' population sizes. This example uses as an effect size the correlation between (a) the number of felonies (X) divided by the size of cities' populations (Z) (i.e., the dependent variable is X/Z = crime rate) and (b) population sizes of cities (i.e., the independent variable is Z). In this example the shared quantity in the independent and dependent variables is Z. Because Z is obviously correlated with Z one would be correlating independent variable Z with a dependent variable that also reflects Z; that is, X/Z; Consult Cohen et al. (2004) and McNemar (1962) for further discussions. Note that one might argue that it is an interpretation of a correlation that might be spurious, not the correlation.

UNEQUAL BASE RATES IN NONEXPERIMENTAL RESEARCH

To illustrate the application and sometimes misapplication of r_{pb} we again use the research that was discussed in Chapter 3 in which the "healthy" parent–child relationship scores of mothers with normal children (group b) were compared with those from mothers of disturbed children (group a). In that example, $d_G = -.77$, indicating that, in the samples, mothers of normal children tended to outscore mothers of disturbed children by about .77 of a standard deviation unit. (In that example the standardizer was the s of the scores of the normals' mothers, not the s_p based on pooling variances, so the estimator was d_G, not d.) If the mothers of the schizophrenic children are numerically coded with $X = 1$ and the mothers of the normal children are coded $X = 2$, using any software that calculates r one finds that $r_{pb} = .396 \approx .40$. The positive correlation indicates that the sample that was coded 2 (normals) tended to outscore the sample that was coded 1 (schizophrenic). This is a finding that d_G already indicated in its own way in Chapter 3 by being negative when in its numerator the higher-scoring mothers' mean (normals) was subtracted from the lower-scoring mothers' mean (schizophrenic).

An r of approximately .4 would be considered to be moderately large in comparison with typical values of r in many areas of behavioral and biomedical research, as we discuss later in this chapter. Thus, finding that $d_G = -.77$ and $r_{pb} = .40$ seems to indicate in two different ways that there is what would usually be considered to be a moderately strong relationship between the independent and dependent variables in this example. However, the calculation of r_{pb} using the ordinary Pearson r in software ignored the fact, which can sometimes be critically important for making inferences to populations, that the proportion of mothers of schizophrenics, say, p_s, and the proportion of mothers of normals, say, p_n, in the total population of mothers are very different. To begin to clarify this issue, which is discussed in detail in the next section, we calculate here an estimate of r_{pb} by converting a known value of d to r_{pb} using Equation 4.2.

Equation 4.2 involves d, in which the standardizer, s_p, is based on pooling variances on the assumption of homoscedasticity and the goal of reducing sampling variability, not on d_G, which does not assume homoscedasticity. If we calculate d instead of d_G for the mothers' data the numerator remains $2.10 - 3.55 = -1.45$, from Chapter 3, but the standardizer in the denominator becomes $s_p = 1.7225272$ by taking the square root of the value obtained by application of Equation 2.2 for the pooled variance in Chapter 2. Therefore, $d = -1.45/1.7225272 \approx -.84$. Converting d to r_{pb} using Equation 4.2 yields

$$r_{pb} = \frac{d}{[d^2 + ((N-2)/Np_1p_2)]^{1/2}}$$

$$= \frac{-.84}{[(-.84)^2 + ((40-2)/(40)(.5)(.5))]^{1/2}}$$

$$= .396 \text{ or } -.396.$$

The numerical result is either $+.396$ or $-.396$ because the denominator of Equation 4.2 is a square root. However, recall that it was the mothers of the normal children who constituted the group that was coded "2" to calculate r_{pb} directly using software, and we know from Chapter 3 that those mothers had the higher mean score (also reflected by d_G and d being negative when the means of those mothers was subtracted from the means of the schizophrenics' mothers). Therefore, r_{pb} must be positive, $r_{pb} = .396$, which is the same value that was obtained when using software to calculate r_{pb} directly from raw data.

PREDICTABILITY AND UNEQUAL BASE RATES

Thus far we have been interested in r_{pb} to estimate an effect size in terms of the *magnitude of relationship* between the type of mother and the scores on the dependent variable, an effect size estimator that serves a purpose that is somewhat similar to d or d_G, which estimates the *magnitude of a mean difference* in standard deviation units. However, if one is interested in the *predictability* of one variable from the other, because of unequal base rates (p_1 and p_2) of schizophrenia and "normality" in the population, the two values of r_{pb} that were calculated thus far are merely descriptive correlations that are applicable only to the sample under the conditions of the current example. By predictability, in the current example, we mean predicting scores, Y, on the continuous variable from knowledge of the grouping variable (normal versus schizophrenic), X (or predicting X from Y). The explanation is straightforward. First, the standard deviation of a set of the same two consecutive numbers, such as the current 1s and 2s, or the frequently used 0s and 1s, is given by $(p_1p_2)^{1/2}$, so the standard deviation of the dichotomous variable is $(p_1p_2)^{1/2}$. Second, inspection of Equation 4.2 reveals that as p_1p_2 decreases r_{pb} decreases. Third, p_1p_2 is at its maximum when $p_1 = p_2$. Therefore, the conversion from d to r_{pb} is at its maximum when sample p_1 and p_2 are equal (i.e., equal sample sizes), and similarly the conversion of d_{pop} to r_{pb} in the population is at its maximum when population $p_1 = p_2$. We turn now to the implications of this reasoning for our present example and similar examples that researchers may encounter in research that is nonexperimental and in which the proportions of the two groups are not the same in the population.

Recall that in the current example $n_1 = n_2$, so the conversion of d to r_{pb} yielded a maximum value of r_{pb} for the data in the samples at hand. However, it is reasonable to assume that the proportion of schizophrenics is roughly .02 or lower in the population, so the proportion of non-schizophrenics is roughly .98. Therefore, instead of $p_1 = p_2$ in the population, in our current example, $p_1 = .01$ or .02 and $p_2 = .99$ or .98 would be much closer to the truth. (Similarly, highly discrepant values of population p_1 and p_2 appear to be common with regard to many psychological, behavioral, psychiatric, and medical disorders; McGrath & Meyer, 2006.) Therefore, if n_1 and n_2 had not been chosen to be equal, unlike the present real example, but instead one sample had been, say, approximately 49 times larger than the other (admittedly impractical) to be consistent with $p_1 = .02$ and $p_2 = .98$, the calculated r_{pb} would have been very much smaller than the current .396.

Tips and Pitfalls

We now illustrate how greatly a calculated r_{pb} is diminished when sample p_1 and p_2 are very different and are taken into account. Suppose that, in order to have the sample p_1 and p_2 match an estimated $p_1 = .02$ and $p_2 = .98$ in the population, the researchers in our current example had used $n_1 = 20$ and $n_2 = 980$ (again, admittedly very unlikely, but illustrative). If one estimates r_{pb} from $d = -.84$ using Equation 4.2 again, but this time with $N = 1000$, $p_1 = .02$, and $p_2 = .98$, one finds that the estimate is greatly reduced from .396 to .117. The latter small value of r_{pb} indicates poor predictability of one variable from another in the sense that it is difficult to make accurate predictions when phenomena are rare (e.g., rate of schizophrenia $\approx .02$). McGrath and Meyer (2006, Table 2, p. 390, and Table 3, p. 392) provide additional real examples of the effect of unequal base rates. We next elaborate and provide recommendations.

CHOICE BETWEEN d_{pop} AND r_{pop}

Whichever kind of effect size is used we again urge the reporting of a confidence interval. The problems of unequal base rates and unequal variances are avoided if one uses the unstandardized difference between means as an effect size instead of d_{pop} or r_{pop}. This is the approach that we favor when the observed dependent variable is of interest in its own right (e.g., weight in a study of weight-loss programs) instead of representing a supposed underlying variable.

Alternatively, as discussed in Chapter 3, if the dependent variable has been normed (e.g., a scale, say, depression, of a widely used inventory of personality) so that the population standard deviation is believed to be known to a satisfactory degree of accuracy, a reasonable estimator of effect size is a d that is standardized with that standard deviation.

If neither of the preceding alternatives apply, one may be confused by the discrepancy between the implications of estimates of effect sizes such as the present $d = -.84$, which is often a moderately large effect size in many areas of research, and an estimated $r_{pb} = .117$ for the same data, which is often a small effect size. Therefore, regarding the choice of estimating and reporting d_{pop} versus r_{pop}, first, when a researcher is interested in estimating the degree of difference between two populations we recommend the use of d (if its assumptions are accepted). However, the value of d is sensitive to a difference in sample sizes if there is heteroscedasticity, so the use of one of the alternative measures of a standardized mean difference under heteroscedasticity (Chapter 3) or the robust probability-of-superiority measure of effect size (Chapter 5) should be considered in this case.

Second, if a researcher is interested in estimating the predictability of one variable from the other variable in the population (not a major purpose of this book), one should consider, where practical, using sample sizes that are consistent with the estimated population p_1 and p_2 (if known, at least approximately) or reporting r_{pb} using an approximate conversion formula such as Equation 4.2 that reflects the two base rates. (If applicable, reports should include a brief explanation to the reader about the attenuating effect of unequal base rates on r_{pb}.)

Third, the r_{pb} with equal sample sizes is also applicable without taking into account population p_1 and p_2 (e.g., using standard software for r to calculate r_{pb}) if a researcher is interested in estimating the strength of association between the two variables (not in the previously discussed sense of predictability). (It is possible that some may disagree with this statement except when the sample p_1 and p_2 match the population p_1 and p_2.)

Fourth, when population $p_1 = p_2$ and sample sizes are equal r_{pb} may always be calculated using software for the ordinary r. Fifth, when the different perspectives on the results that are provided by d and r_{pb} are both relevant to the researcher's purposes, the researcher should consider reporting both kinds of estimates with an appropriate explanation if population base rates differ.

The value of sample r_{pb} is always sensitive to sample p_1 and p_2 (i.e., relative sample sizes). The relevant issue is whether such sensitivity to p_1 and p_2 is or is not relevant to a given researcher's purpose in estimating and reporting a particular kind of effect size. However, a reader of a research report may have an interest in the relationship between the two variables that is different from the researcher's interest. Therefore, researchers who are going to provide an r_{pb} in their reports should consider providing, when applicable, an r_{pb} that is calculated using an equation such as Equation 4.2 that takes base rates into account and an r_{pb} that does not take base rates into account together with an explanation of the different information that each provides.

Finally, one might prefer a base-rate insensitive measure of effect size if one wants to make inferences from a study to a broad range of populations with varying base rates. However, if one does not generalize results beyond the population that was studied then a base-rate sensitive measure of effect size might be preferred. Consult McGrath and Meyer (2006) for a further recommendation, further discussion of the relative merits of r_{pb} and d, and important implications of base rates for power analysis (also consult Ruscio, 2008a) and meta-analysis.

In an attempt to maximize statistical power researchers often equalize sample sizes (Rosnow & Rosenthal, 2008; Ruscio, 2008a), although this is not always optimal for increasing power. However, if $p_1 \neq p_2$ in the population, using $n_1 = n_2$ for sample sizes can render the sample r_{pb} unrepresentative of r_{pop} if the purpose of the research is to estimate predictability and population base rates are unknown and cannot be credibly estimated. If population p_1 and p_2 are known or are credibly estimated the problem can be resolved by using an equation that takes p_1 and p_2 into account, such as Equation 4.2, to calculate the estimate of r_{pop}.

Ruscio (2008a) noted that when variances of the continuous variable are unequal for the two populations the maximum value of r_{pop} occurs when population base rates are unequal, so he argued that maximum power can be achieved by appropriate selection of unequal sample sizes in this case. However, such heteroscedasticity can be very problematic for the inferential use of correlation and point-biserial correlation coefficients, as is discussed later in the section on assumptions.

Finally, common software that calculates an r (r_{pb} in the present case) also tests H_0: $r_{pop} = 0$ and provides a p level for the result of that test. There is an equation that relates r_{pb} to t (Equation 4.10), and the p level attained by r when conducting a two-tailed test of H_0: $r_{pop} = 0$ will be the same as the p level attained by t when conducting a two-tailed test of H_0: $\mu_a - \mu_b = 0$ if assumptions are satisfied.

CORRECTING FOR BIAS

Values of r and r_{pb} are negatively biased (i.e., tending to underestimate r_{pop}), usually slightly so. Bias is greater the closer r_{pop} is to ±.577, and for small samples, but still not generally considered to be of importance if the total sample size is greater than, say, 15. Hedges and Olkin (1985) provided the following equation for an approximately unbiased estimator:

$$r_{approx} = r + \frac{r(1-r^2)}{2(N-3)}.$$

(4.3)

Other approximate bias-correcting equations are available but a correction is rarely used because the bias is generally considered to be negligible. It is possible that bias will be less than rounding error when the total sample size is greater than 20.

CONFIDENCE INTERVALS FOR r_{pop}

Construction of a confidence interval for r_{pop} can be complex, and there may be no entirely satisfactory method. One valid method for constructing a confidence interval for r_{pop} that is based on r_{pb}, when assumptions are satisfied, involves the parameter η_{pop} (i.e., eta) that is discussed in Chapter 6 as a measure of association in analysis of variance. The population r_{pb} is the limiting case of η_{pop} when there are just two levels (group membership) of the independent variable. The method, using the noncentral F distribution, was discussed by Fidler and Thompson (2001) and Smithson (2001, 2003). A confidence interval for r_{pop} can also be constructed using the STATISTICA Power Analysis software.

Wilcox (2003) presented an S-PLUS software function for a modified bootstrap method for a .95 *CI* that appears to have fairly accurate probability coverage (i.e., actual confidence level close to .95) provided that the absolute value of r in the population is not extremely large, say, below .8 (but not 0). Such values for r_{pop} would be the case in most research in the behavioral sciences. (A basic bootstrap method was briefly introduced in Chapter 2.) Wilcox's method seems to perform well when assumptions are violated, even with sample sizes as small as 20. These assumptions are discussed later in this chapter.

CONFIDENCE INTERVAL USING FISHER'S Z_r TRANSFORMATION

Although we prefer methods that are based on robust methods, for completeness and pedagogical value we illustrate the manual construction of a widely used approximate 95% confidence interval for r_{pop} that uses Fisher's Z_r transformation from r. The approximation is less accurate the smaller the sample size, especially the larger the value of r_{pop}, and the method may be unsatisfactory under bivariate nonnormality. Fisher's Z_r is approximately normally distributed given by

$$Z_r = .5ln\left[\frac{1+r}{1-r}\right], \tag{4.4}$$

where *ln* is the natural logarithm. The margin of error, ME_Z, is given by

$$ME_{Z_r} = z_{\alpha/2}S_{Z_r}, \tag{4.5}$$

where
  z is the conventional standard score, $z_{\alpha/2} = 1.96$ in the case of a .95 *CI* under the assumption of normality
  S_{Z_r} is the standard deviation of the distribution of Z_r given by

$$S_{Z_r} = \frac{1}{(N-3)^{1/2}}. \tag{4.6}$$

The confidence limits are thus given by

$$Z_r \pm 1.96 \left[\frac{1}{N-3} \right]^{1/2}. \tag{4.7}$$

The confidence limits from expression (4.7) are then transformed back to confidence limits for r_{pop} by applying the following conversion to each limit:

$$r_{\text{pop}} = \frac{e^{2Z_r} - 1}{e^{2Z_r} + 1}, \tag{4.8}$$

where e = 2.71828… (the base of the natural logarithm).

We construct a 95% CI for r_{pop} for an example in which r_{pb} = .40 and N = 40, using the Z_r method. Such a confidence interval is not expected to be symmetrical around r_{pb}. Applying r_{pb} = .400 to Equation 4.4, Z_r = .5ln[(1 + .400)/(1 − .400)] = .4236. Applying N = 40 to Equation 4.6 yields S_{Z_r} = 1/(40 − 3)$^{1/2}$ = .1644. Applying the obtained values to expression (4.7) results in the limits .4236 ± 1.96(.1644). Therefore, the lower and upper confidence limits for Z_r are .101 and .746, respectively. Using Equation 4.8 to transform these limits to lower and upper limits, respectively, for r_{pop} yields [2.7183$^{2(.101)}$ − 1]/[2.7183$^{2(.101)}$ + 1] = .101 and [2.7183$^{2(.746)}$ − 1]/[2.7183$^{2(.746)}$ + 1] = .633. Therefore, the .95 approximate confidence interval for r_{pop} spans .101 and .633. The absence of the value 0 in the .95 confidence interval is consistent with finding a statistically significant difference between the mean scores of the two samples at the p = .05 level (approximately), two-tailed. Observe also that, as expected, the confidence interval is not symmetrical around the point estimate r_{pb} = .40. That is, .101 and .633 are not equidistant from .400. Also, as is often the case unless samples are very large, the confidence interval is very wide. Calculation of Equations 4.4 and 4.8 can be done using software such as SAS and IBM SPSS.

Fouladi and Steiger (2008) extended results on the distribution of Z_r and discussed implications of those results for the construction of confidence intervals and performance of statistical tests when sample sizes are small. Hafdahl and Williams (2009) reported simulations and concluded that many criticisms of the use of Fisher's Z_r transformation may be unfounded, especially with a modified transformation of Z_r to r.

NULL–COUNTERNULL INTERVAL FOR r_{pop}

A null–counternull interval (discussed in Chapter 3) can also be constructed for r_{pop}. If the null hypothesis is the usual H_0: r_{pop} = 0, the null value of such an interval is 0. When r_{pop} is estimated by r_{pb}, Rosenthal et al. (2000) have shown that the counternull value of an r_{pop}, denoted r_{cn} here, is estimated by

$$r_{cn} = \frac{2r_{\text{pb}}}{(1 + 3r_{\text{pb}}^2)^{1/2}}. \tag{4.9}$$

In the present example $r_{pb} = .40$, so $r_{cn} = 2(.40)/[1 + 3(.40^2)]^{1/2} = .66$. Therefore, the interval runs from 0 to .66. Thus, the results would provide about as much support for the proposition that r_{pop} is .66 as they would for the proposition that $r_{pop} = 0$. Perhaps a null–counternull interval for r_{pop} would be of greatest relevance to researchers who focus on the null-hypothesized value of 0 for r_{pop}. The counternull value brings attention also to an equally plausible value based on the data. A counternull value of an r_{pop} that is well above 0 illustrates that r_{pop} might not be 0 even when the evidence is insufficient to reject the null hypothesis. However, such a counternull value, no matter how great, does not prove that r_{pop} is not 0 or not close to 0.

In Chapter 3, we observed that the level of confidence in a null–counternull interval is given by $100(1 - p)$, where p is the two-tailed probability obtained in a t test for the statistical significance of the difference between two sample means. In the present case the t test is testing for the statistical significance of r_{pb}. We also observed that Equations 3.11 and 3.12 for counternull values applied only to effect sizes that have a symmetrical sampling distribution, such as d_{pop}. Therefore, when an r_{pop} is based not on r_{pb} but on an r for two continuous variables, the manner in which the asymmetrical sampling distribution of r_{pop} is generally handled is first to convert the sample r to Z_r using Equation 4.4 because, as was discussed in the preceding section, the sampling distribution of Z_r is approximately normal. Next the counternull value of Z_r is $2Z_r$ because the distribution of Z_r is symmetrical, and, as was discussed in Chapter 3 with regard to Equation 3.11, when a sampling distribution is symmetrical a counternull effect size is twice the value of the effect size. Finally, the counternull value for Z_r is converted to a counternull value for r_{pop} using Equation 4.8.

ASSUMPTIONS OF CORRELATION AND POINT-BISERIAL CORRELATION

Traditional correlational analysis of data requires independence of the X scores and independence of the Y scores within a group (i.e., each participant contributes only one X value and only one Y value). No further assumptions are required if correlation is to be used solely as a statistic that is descriptive of a sample. However, assumptions are relevant if correlation is to be used inferentially to generalize to a population, as it is in this chapter. The nature of the assumptions depends on the use to which correlational analysis is to be put.

HOMOSCEDASTICITY

Note first regarding assumptions that in the case of r_{pb} there are three distributions of Y to consider: the distribution of Y for group a, the distribution of Y for group b, and the overall distribution of Y for the combined data for the two groups. The first two distributions are called the *conditional distributions* of Y (conditional on whether one is considering the distribution of Y values at $X = a$ or at $X = b$), and the overall distribution of Y is called the *marginal distribution* of Y. The three distributions are

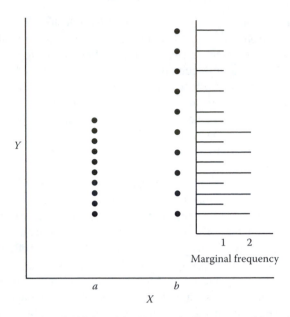

FIGURE 4.1   Unequal variabilities of the Y scores in Groups a and b result in skew in the marginal frequency distribution of Y.

depicted in Figure 4.1. In the case of two continuous (more or less) variables there is an indefinitely large number of conditional distributions of X and of Y.

Recall that the t test assumes normality and homoscedasticity. Also, if a bivariate normal distribution is assumed in the population then there is a statistic, which involves only the sample r (or r_{pb}) and N, that follows a t distribution and permits a t test to test H_0: $r_{pop} = 0$, that is, Equation 4.10. (Bivariate normality is defined in the next section.) Therefore, if it is using the usual Student's t test to test H_0: $r_{pop} = 0$, the software is assuming homoscedasticity; that is, it is assuming equal variances of the populations' conditional distributions of Y. If there is heteroscedasticity the denominator of t (standard error of the difference between two means) will be incorrect, possibly resulting in lower statistical power and less accurate confidence intervals. Even under normality, heteroscedasticity can cause probability coverage for confidence intervals for r_{pop} to be lower than nominal (Wilcox, 2005a). Also, if the conventional t test is used and the printed out p and the actual (unknown) p are below .05, this result may not in fact be signaling a nonzero correlation, but instead merely signaling heteroscedasticity. Heteroscedasticity is actually another kind of dependency between X and Y, a dependency between the variability of Y and the value of X. Wilcox (2005c) discussed estimation of the conditional variance of Y.

Note that in the case of an independent variable, X, whose values are fixed by the researcher instead of being random, a t test for r (e.g., r_{pb} when there are only two such fixed values) does not assume bivariate normality, but just that the conditional distributions of Y be normal with equal variances.

Wilcox and Keselman (2006) discussed methods for detecting heteroscedasticity in simple regression, many of which yielded high rates of Type I error. However, those authors recommended use of one of the methods that was found to reject a false null hypothesis, which posited homoscedasticity, at the $\alpha < .01$ level under a condition in which a competing method could not even reject this false null hypothesis at the $\alpha < .05$ level. For our present purpose simple regression can be defined as the nature of the relationship between one Y variable and one X variable. Equations 4.19 and 4.20 are examples of simple regression. When values of Y are to be predicted from values of X from such a regression equation the process is called "the regression of Y on X."

A general nonparametric approach to linear regression (i.e., a straight-line relationship between X and Y) under heteroscedasticity was presented by Leslie, Kohn, and Nott (2007). Davies, Gather, and Weinert (2008) simulated the performance of various methods of nonparametric regression. Nonparametric regression requires few assumptions about the nature of a nonlinear relationship when estimating that relationship.

BIVARIATE NORMALITY

The inferential use of the Pearson product-moment correlation coefficient was developed on the assumption of *bivariate normality*. Bivariate normality exists when the joint distribution of the (X,Y) paired variables has the shape of a three-dimensional bell. Any vertical (i.e., perpendicular to the X,Y plane) slice through the bell will yield a normal curve at the intersection. Bivariate normality requires that several criteria be satisfied. First, all conditional distributions of Y must be normal. Second, all conditional distributions of X (i.e., conditional on the value of Y) must be normal. (Normality of the marginal distributions of X and of Y does not indicate bivariate normality.) Third, homoscedasticity is assumed; that is, the conditional variances of Y must be equal at each value of X, and the conditional variances of X must be equal at each value of Y. Fourth, the conditional means of Y must be linearly or at least monitonically related to X, and the conditional means of X must be linearly or at least monitonically related to Y.

It would seem to be impossible for all aspects of the assumption of bivariate normality to be exactly satisfied. Thus, as we soon discuss, the issue becomes one of how robust the inferential use of the Pearson correlation coefficient is to the perhaps inevitable violation of assumptions.

MAXIMUM VALUE OF THE PEARSON CORRELATION COEFFICIENT

First we consider the role that is played by marginal distributions in the negative and positive bounds of a correlation coefficient, which are not always -1 and 1. Skew in the opposite direction for the marginal distributions of variables X and Y lowers the maximum value of r (Carroll, 1961). Further, as was discussed in Chapter 1, skew from outliers can increase variability, and in Equation 4.1 standard deviations are observed in the denominator of r_{pop}, so skew can increase the denominator of r_{pop}. Therefore, skew in either X or Y can decrease r_{pop} (and sample r).

Tips and Pitfalls

In general the maximum value for a Pearson correlation coefficient depends on the shapes of the two marginal distributions. Given the shapes of the two marginal distributions it is possible for the maximum Pearson correlation to be nearly 0.

MORE ON ROBUSTNESS

An assumption of normality of the conditional distribution of X at each level of Y cannot and need not be satisfied by the dichotomous X variable in the case of inferential use of r_{pb} under the fixed-effects model (known as the standard or fixed regression model), but skew in the X variable can be avoided by the use of equal sample sizes. The distribution of the X variable in the point-biserial case is merely a stack of, say, 1s and a stack of, say, 2s, or of 0s and 1s. Although normality of X is not assumed for the inferential use of r_{pb}, normality and homoscedasticity of the two conditional distributions of Y are assumed. We next turn our attention to studies of the robustness of the correlation coefficient in the case of continuous (more or less) X and Y variables. Such results may generally apply to the point-biserial correlation because in that case Y is continuous and X is subject to skew (i.e., $n_1 \neq n_2$).

Mathematical and simulation studies over the past 100 years have produced incomplete and sometimes inconsistent results about the robustness of the correlation coefficient. The extensive review of these studies by King (2003) found that it is most reasonable to conclude that when $r_{pop} = 0$ robustness is often adequate if violation of assumptions is not great. However, because researchers typically choose X and Y variables for which r_{pop} is not likely to be 0 and because real data often violate assumptions, the inferential use of the Pearson correlation coefficient may often be suspect.

Tips and Pitfalls

Outliers (even one outlier) and distributions with thicker tails ("heavy-tailed distributions") than those of the normal curve can affect r, and r_{pop} and a confidence interval for it (Wilcox, 2005a). The use of large sample sizes may help in this situation somewhat, but not under all conditions. Even slight changes in the shape of a marginal distribution in the population can greatly alter the value of r_{pop}, including reversing its sign (Wilcox). For example, outliers can cause $r_{pop} > 0$ even when the general trend is for Y to decrease as X increases.

For the case of a point-biserial correlation there is a distinction between a difference in the shapes of the conditional distributions of Y for an (a) *underlying* construct in the two populations and (b) observed *measure* of that construct in the two samples (Cohen et al., 2003). In the case of different distributional shapes for the construct in the two populations, the resulting reduction in an upper limit below |1| for r_{pop} is not a problem; it is a natural phenomenon, a reflection of the real world. However, there is a problem of r_{pb} underestimating r_{pop}

if the two sample distributions differ in shape when the two populations do not, or if the two sample distributions differ more in shape than the two population distributions do.

In reports of research that uses r or r_{pb} authors should include *scatterplots* (e.g., Figure 4.1 and figures that appear later in this chapter) and cautionary remarks about the possible effects of outliers, heavy tails, and heteroscedasticity. In the case of r_{pb} a scatterplot may well imply heteroscedasticity with respect to the two conditional distributions of Y, and skew in the marginal distribution of Y, or neither, because such skew and heteroscedasticity are often associated. Such is the case in the example in Figure 4.1. In the case of r a scatterplot that suggests skew in the marginal distribution of X and/or Y may also indicate curvilinearity, heteroscedasticity, and nonnormal conditional distributions.

Tips and Pitfalls

Recall that the correlation coefficient reflects only a linear component of a relationship between two variables. Curvilinearity reduces the absolute value of a correlation coefficient. For example, if $Y = X^2$, Y is perfectly predictable from X, but it is possible that $r_{pop} = 0$ in this case when X can have negative and positive values.

Refer to Wilcox (2005a) for additional discussions of assumptions underlying the use of r_{pop} and for alternatives to r_{pop} for measuring the relationship between two variables.

MORE ON OUTLIERS

When one is studying the regression of variable Y on variable X (i.e., Y is a predicted variable and X is the predictor variable) a *regression outlier* is a value of Y that is distant from the majority of the other values of Y at a given value of X. There are varying definitions of such a distance. Wilcox (2003) provided S-PLUS software functions for detecting outliers according to his definition of that distance.

Outliers are not always problematic. For example, an X_i and Y_i pair of scores in which X_i and Y_i are equally outlying might not importantly influence the value of a correlation coefficient. Thus, a person who is 7 ft tall (outlier) and weighs 275 lb (outlier in the same direction) will not likely influence the value of the correlation between height and weight as much as a person who is an outlier with respect to just one of the variables (e.g., 6 ft 3 in. tall and 150 lb). The most *influential case* for, say, an otherwise positive correlation would be one in which a person is an outlier in the opposite direction with respect to X and Y, which lowers the correlation. Recall in this regard the lowering of the absolute value of a correlation when the skew in X is in the opposite direction from the skew in Y.

A common method for studying the influence of an outlier is to remove the outlier temporarily to observe the effect of its removal on important quantities such as estimates of r_{pop} and confidence levels for r_{pop}. Wilcox (2005a) provided S-PLUS and R software functions for detecting outliers and leverage points (soon defined) in regression. Free access to Wilcox's code for R was previously cited in Chapters 1 and 2.

Considering again the regression of Y on X, an extreme value of X is called a *leverage point*. A *good leverage point* is an extreme value that does not run counter to the overall relationship between X and Y; it has negligible or no influence. The extremely tall but equally extremely heavy person in our example of correlating height and weight provides an example of a good leverage point. A *bad leverage point* runs counter to the overall relationship (e.g., an extremely tall person who is very underweight); it has *influence*. It is the latter that can distort estimates of parameters. Simply permanently removing outliers and then proceeding with traditional nonrobust methods would be very unsatisfactory. Better methods are discussed in the next section.

NONPARAMETRIC ALTERNATIVES TO THE PEARSON CORRELATION COEFFICIENT

Two well-known nonparametric alternatives to the Pearson correlation are *Kendall's tau* (τ) and *Spearman's rho* (ρ), the latter being Pearson's correlation applied to the ranks of the scores instead of the raw scores. If scores are tied equal ranks can be assigned, but there are other methods. Rho and tau are not affected as much by a few discrepant values as is r, but they are affected. The original Kendall's tau is properly labeled tau_a because a later version, tau_b, was introduced to correct for ties. (A third version was studied by Woods, 2007.) A large difference between rho and the Pearson r is an indication that the assumptions underlying the Pearson r are importantly violated.

One of several ways to describe tau is in terms of the degree of consistency of the increase or decrease in Y as X increases, regardless of linearity or nonlinearity of the relationship. The more consistent the increase or decrease the closer tau approaches $+1$ or -1, respectively (and the fewer the changes of the sign of the slopes along the line that relates X and Y). The line is straight or smoothly curved upward or downward in the case of a perfect relationship, which is said to be a *monotonic* one. Consult Kraemer (2006) for a discussion of differences between tau and rho. Gilpin (1993) reviewed formulas and provided a table for converting tau_a to rho, r, r^2, Fisher's Z_r, and d. Woods (2007) discussed construction of confidence intervals for tau_a, tau_b, and rho. Rupinsky and Dunlap (1996) discussed and provided tables converting tau_b and rho to r, and reported good accuracy of Kendall's conversion formulas.

Much software reports tau and rho, and their p values, including the S-PLUS and R functions that were provided by Wilcox (2005a). (The accuracy of the p value that is reported for rho by some major software may be questionable if the p value is based on the t distribution, especially if samples are small.) Although tau and rho are resistant to outliers in the marginal distributions of X and Y, outliers in the conditional distributions can greatly influence their values. Also, heteroscedasticity in the conditional distributions can increase the rate of Type I error when testing H_0: rho $= 0$ or H_0: tau $= 0$. As we previously discussed in the case with Pearson's correlation, rejecting such a null hypothesis may in some instances be more of a reflection of heteroscedasticity than any other characteristic of the data. However, apparently rho and tau can be rendered resistant to heteroscedasticity by applying a percentile bootstrapping method to them. Wilcox (2005a) provided S-PLUS and R software functions for this method and reported that it maintains good control of the rate of Type I error. Nonetheless, as few as two outliers in the wrong place can greatly influence the values of rho and tau. When the data are originally ordinal a bootstrap method for constructing a confidence interval for rho has been recommended (Ruscio, 2008b).

Wilcox (2005a) also discussed and provided S-PLUS and R software functions for eliminating outliers or giving them less weight in the calculations. Wilcox provided additional S-PLUS and R functions for testing for independence of variables that can either be linearly or curvilinearly related. The method makes use of 20% trimming and bootstrapping. We cited free access to Wilcox's code for R in Chapters 1 and 2.

Wilcox (2006b, 2007a) discussed methods for testing for homoscedasticity in simple nonparametric regression. His simulations indicated that an improved method also results in a test of independence that is sensitive to a greater variety of associations between two variables than is Pearson's r and controls Type I error well. Because measures of dependent variables are often actually ordinal, despite a superficial numerical appearance of being interval, Long, Feng, and Cliff (2003) recommended the use of nonparametric (i.e., ordinal) measures of correlation as an alternative to Pearson's correlation.

Finally, if assumptions have been sufficiently satisfied so that t testing and the use of a Pearson r are appropriate, and one wants to determine the p level for an r_{pb} (or r) that has been reported in the literature without p but with sample size, convert r_{pb} (or r) to t using

$$t = r_{pb}\left[\frac{N-2}{1-r_{pb}^2}\right]^{1/2}, \tag{4.10}$$

where N is the total number of participants. Then use software for the density function of t, or a t table at the $df = N - 2$ row, to ascertain the statistical significance of this value of t, which will also be the statistical significance of r_{pb}.

UNEQUAL SAMPLE SIZES IN EXPERIMENTAL RESEARCH

If $n_a \neq n_b$ in experimental research the resulting *attenuation* (reduction) of r_{pb} from unequal sample sizes will generally cause an underestimation of r_{pop}. The degree of such attenuation of r_{pb} increases the more disproportional n_a and n_b are in this case. As was discussed previously, unequal sample sizes reduces the variance of the dichotomous variable, which causes a reduction in r_{pb}. Again, in experimental research it is generally the case that the compared populations are of equal size. When $n_a \neq n_b$ in experimental research one can calculate an attenuation-corrected r_{pb}, which we denote r_c, using

$$r_c = \frac{ar_{pb}}{[r_{pb}^2(a^2-1)+1]^{1/2}}, \tag{4.11}$$

where $a = [.25/p_1 p_2]^{1/2}$, and p_1 and p_2, as before, are the proportions of total sample size in each group. It does not matter which of n_a or n_b is associated with p_1 or p_2. In areas of experimental research in which the ratio n_1/n_2 does not equal 1 in all studies, the different studies of the same X variable and the same Y variable may obtain different values of uncorrected r_{pb} partly because of different values of n_a/n_b from study to study. Therefore, values of r_{pb} should not be compared or meta-analyzed in such cases unless the values of r_{pb} have been corrected for unequal sample sizes as needed. However, the correction will have little effect when sample sizes are only slightly disproportional. (Consult McGrath & Meyer, 2006, for an exception to the correction for unequal sample size in an experiment that involves manipulation of a variable that simulates a situation that less than 50% of the population experience in everyday life.)

UNRELIABILITY

Unreliability of the scores on the measure of the dependent variable or unreliability of the measurement or manipulation of the independent variable is an additional factor that can attenuate an estimate of r_{pop} and standardized-difference estimators of effect sizes. Roughly for our purpose here, *unreliability of scores* means the extent to which scores are reflecting *measurement error*, that is, something other than the true value of what is being measured. Measurement error causes scores from measurement instance to measurement instance to be inconsistent (i.e., unrepeatable, unreliable) in the sense that one cannot rely on getting consistent observed scores (say, over time) for an individual from the test or measure even when the magnitude of the underlying attribute that one is attempting to measure has not changed.

According to *classical measurement theory*, in which error of measurement is assumed to be random, an observed score, say, Y, is assumed partly to reflect the true score on Y and partly to reflect the amount of error in measuring Y:

$$Y = Y_{true} + error \tag{4.12}$$

and

$$\sigma_{tot}^2 = \sigma_{true}^2 + \sigma_{error}^2, \tag{4.13}$$

where
σ_{tot}^2 is the total variance of the observed Y scores
σ_{true}^2 is the portion of the total variance that is true variance
σ_{error}^2 is the variance that is attributable to random error

For an example of Equation 4.12, if an object truly weighs 100 lb ($Y_{true} = 100$) but is observed to weigh 105 lb on a defective scale (observed $Y = 105$ lb), the amount of measurement error in that instance of weighing is +5 lb. (According to the simplifying theory an error of overestimation by a certain amount is as likely as an error of underestimation by that amount; i.e., there is *random error.*) The σ^2_{true} is the variance that would remain if there were no random measurement error, in which case σ^2_{tot} would equal σ^2_{true}. One can then define

$$reliability = \frac{\sigma^2_{true}}{\sigma^2_{tot}}. \tag{4.14}$$

That is, reliability is the proportion of the total variance of scores that is true variance, and, as a proportion, reliability ranges from 0 to 1. Observe in Equation 4.13 that measurement error inflates total variance and, therefore, inflates standard deviations. In so doing, measurement error lowers power of statistical tests, lowers estimates of effect size, and widens confidence intervals. Estimates of measurement error are called *reliability coefficients*, of which there are several with different purposes. Observe in Equations 4.13 and 4.14 that if there is no measurement error all of σ^2_{tot} is true variance, in which case *reliability* $= \sigma^2_{true}/\sigma^2_{true} = 1$. At the other extreme, if measurements were completely random there would be no true variance and *reliability* $= 0/\sigma^2_{tot} = 0$, so, again, reliability ranges from 0 to 1.

RELIABILITY AND VALIDITY

High estimated reliability provides evidence that a measure is measuring whatever it is measuring consistently in the setting in which it is being applied. However, it is possible that what is being reliably measured is something other than what the researcher is intending to measure (i.e., the intended latent variable). For a hypothetical example, suppose that an instructor offered to grade students' essay examinations not on the basis of the content of the essays but instead entirely on the basis of very carefully measuring the students' heights. Because students' heights can likely be measured more reliably than their performances on an essay examination, the students should not object to the proposed method of grading on the basis of unreliability, but on the basis of no validity for height as a measure of knowledge of course material.

TEST–RETEST RELIABILITY

One of the common ways to estimate the reliability of scores is to administer the measure to a large sample and then re-administer the same measure to the same sample within a short enough period of time so that there is minimum opportunity for the sample's true scores to change. In this case measurement error would be reflected by inconsistency in the observed scores. If one calls the scores from the first administration of the measure Y_1 values and calls the scores from the second administration of the measure Y_2 values, and then calculates the r between these Y_1 values and Y_2 values, one will have an estimate of the reliability of the measure's scores. Such a procedure is called *test–retest reliability*, and the resulting r

is one example of a reliability coefficient, denoted r_{yy}. (Where needed for clarity, hereafter, we sometimes use r_{xy} in place of what was previously simply denoted r, and we use r_{xx} to represent the reliability coefficient for the X variable. The subscripts xx and yy indicate that one is correlating a variable with itself.) Because r theoretically ranges from -1 to $+1$, ideally one would want r_{yy} and r_{xx} to be as close to $+1$ as possible, indicating perfect reliability. Unfortunately, some tests in behavioral science (and perhaps some medical tests) have only modest values of r_{yy}. For example, the least reliable of the tests of personality may have r_{yy} values that are approximately equal to .3 or .4. At the other extreme, one expects a modern digital scale to measure weight with r_{yy} very close to 1. Reliability will often be decreased if the previously discussed method of extreme-groups data analysis is used instead of using the full range of scores. A more stringent conceptualization of test-retest reliability considers the means and variances of Y_1 scores and Y_2 scores, and addresses the extent to which Y_2 scores equal Y_1 scores (Barchard, in press).

ATTENUATION OF CORRELATION

Because r_{pb}, as an r, is intended to reflect the covariation of X and Y, that is, the extent to which true variation in Y is related to true variation in X, unreliability results in an attenuation of r. The r is attenuated because the measurement error that underlies the unreliability of Y adds variability to Y (increases s_y), but this additional variability is an unsystematic variability that is not related to variation in the X variable. (One might recall from introductory statistics that r is the mean product of z scores, $r = \Sigma(z_x z_y)/N$, and that a z score has s in its denominator.) Because the t statistic and standardized-difference estimators of effect sizes have s values in their denominators, and because unreliability increases s, unreliability reduces the value of t and also a standardized-difference estimator of effect size. Credé (2010) discussed the attenuation of r caused by even low rates of random responding when dependent variables are measured by psychological inventories.

PURSUIT OF RELIABILITY

To avoid underestimating effect sizes the most reliable valid measures of the involved variables should be sought. Information about the reliability (and validity) of many published tests can be found in the regularly updated book called the *Mental Measurements Yearbook* (as of the time of this writing, *The Sixteenth Mental Measurements Yearbook*; Spies & Plake, 2005). An index of the tests and measurements that have been reviewed there can currently be found at http://www.unl.edu/buros/indexbimm.html. The American Psychological Association's Task Force on Statistical Inference (Wilkinson & APA Task Force on Statistical Inference, 1999) noted that an assessment of reliability is required in order to interpret estimates of effect size. Consult Vacha-Haase, Kogan, and Thompson (2000a) for further discussion. A confidence interval for r_{yy} in the population can be constructed as was discussed in this chapter for an r_{pop} in general.

DEMOGRAPHICS AND RELIABILITY OF SCORES

It may be the case that the reliability of the scores is greater when using participants with certain demographics than when using other participants with different demographics. Groups that differ in s_y may also differ in r_{yy}. (For a debate on whether reliability is a characteristic of the measuring instrument [e.g., a psychological test] or a characteristic of the scores that result from application of the measure, and the consequences of the use of one or the other conceptualization of reliability, consult Sawilowsky, 2003b, 2003c, Thompson, 2003, and Thompson & Vacha-Haase, 2003.)

The most relevant r_{yy} that a prospective researcher should seek in the literature is a r_{yy} that has been obtained when using participants who are as similar as possible to the participants in the pending research. If a relevant r_{yy} cannot be found in a search of the literature, a researcher who is using a measure of questionable reliability should consider conducting a reliability study on a similar sample prior to the main research. Also, the reliabilities of the scores across studies of the same underlying outcome variable may vary either because of relevant differences between the participants across studies or because of the use of different measures of the outcome variable. Therefore, one should not compare effect sizes without considering the possible influence of such *differential reliability*.

Researchers should consider reporting separate reliability coefficients for each kind of group in any study without random assignment because of the previously discussed possibility of demographic influences on reliability. Differential reliability across groups complicates the adjustment of estimates of effect size for attenuation attributable to unreliability. Such adjustment is discussed in a later section.

RELIABILITY OF THE INDEPENDENT VARIABLE AND TREATMENT INTEGRITY

Researchers should also be concerned about the reliability with which the X variable is being measured or administered because the previous discussion about the consequences of unreliability of the Y variable also applies to the X variable. Even in the case of r_{pb}, in which X has only two values, membership in group a or group b, unreliability of the X variable can occur, along with its attenuating effects. For example, consider the case of research with pre-existing groups, such as the comparison of the mothers of schizophrenic children and normal children that we discussed in Chapter 3 and earlier in this chapter. In such cases r_{pb} and d would be lowered to the extent that the diagnoses of schizophrenia and normality were made unreliably.

In experimental research the reliability of administration of the dichotomous X variable is maintained to the extent that all members of group a are in fact treated in the same way (the "a" way) and all members of group b are treated in the same way (the "b" way) as planned, and that all members of a group follow their instructions in the same way.

In areas of research in which the treatment is complex, such as comparing two psychotherapies or two teaching methods, it may be more difficult to administer treatment reliably than in other areas of research. The extent to which a treatment is administered according to the research plan, and, therefore, administered consistently across all of the members of a particular treatment group, is called *treatment integrity*.

When treatment integrity has not been at the highest level, again the values of the estimator of effect size, the value of *t*, and the power of the *t* test may have been seriously reduced by such unreliability. In such cases a research report should comment about the level of treatment integrity. A more general name for treatment integrity in experimental research is *experimental control*. Researchers should control all extraneous variables to maximize the extent to which variation of the independent variable itself is responsible for variation of the values of the dependent variable from group *a* to group *b*. To the extent that extraneous variables are not controlled they will inflate *s* values with unsystematic variability, resulting in the previously discussed consequences for statistical testing and estimation of effect sizes.

ADJUSTING EFFECT SIZES FOR UNRELIABILITY

There is an equation for correcting for the attenuation in r, r_{pb}, or other estimator of effect size, that has been caused by unreliable measurement of the scores on the dependent variable. The equation for correcting for attenuation results in an estimate of an adjusted effect size that would be expected to occur if Y could be measured perfectly reliably. In general an estimator of effect size that is adjusted for unreliability of the scores on the dependent variable, denoted here ES_{adj}, is given by

$$ES_{adj} = \frac{ES}{r_{yy}^{1/2}}. \qquad (4.15)$$

In the case of nonexperimental studies, an adjustment for unreliability of the X variable can be made by substituting r_{xx} for r_{yy} in Equation 4.15. Alternatively, $(r_{xx}r_{yy})^{1/2}$ can be used instead for the denominator there to adjust for both sources of unreliability at once (Equation 4.16). For the more complicated case of adjusting estimators of effect size for unreliability of the X variable in experimental studies, and for other discussion, consult Hunter and Schmidt (2004). For additional discussion of correction of effect sizes for unreliability consult Baugh (2002a,b).

The adjustment of an estimate of effect size for the unreliability of both X and Y is based on Spearman's equation for doubly adjusting an r_{xy} for the two possible manifestations of unreliability:

$$r_{adj} = \frac{r_{xy}}{(r_{xx}r_{yy})^{1/2}}. \qquad (4.16)$$

(Spearman's adjusted r [not to be confused with Spearman's *rho*] assumes that the error components [$error_y$ and $error_x$] in $Y = Y_{true} + error_y$ and $X = X_{true} + error_x$ are independent, which appears to be a reasonable assumption in experimental research but questionable in nonexperimental research.)

RESISTANCE TO ADJUSTING FOR UNRELIABILITY

Despite the decrease in effect size caused by unreliability, an adjustment for unreliability is rarely used, apparently for one or more reasons other than the fact that, unfortunately, psychometrics is apparently decreasingly a part of undergraduate and graduate curricula. (*Psychometrics*, defined minimally here, is the study of proper methods for constructing tests, scales, and measurements in general, and assessing the various forms of their reliability and validity.) The first possible reason for not making the adjustment is simply that r_{yy} may not be known in the literature and the researcher does not want to delay the research by preceding it by one's own in-house reliability check. Second, some researchers use variables whose scores are known to be, or are believed to be, generally very reliable. Third, some researchers may be satisfied merely to have their results attain statistical significance, believing that unreliability was not a problem if it was not extreme enough to have caused a statistically insignificant result. However, even if results do attain statistical significance, reliability may still have been low enough to result in a substantial underestimation of effect size and a substantial widening of a confidence interval for it. Fourth, some researchers may be concerned that their unreliability-corrected estimates of effect size will be less accurate to the extent that their estimation of reliability is inaccurate. Fifth, it is possible that some researchers may be forgoing the correction for unreliability because they believe that underestimation of effect size is acceptable and only overestimation is unacceptable. (Consult Hunter & Schmidt, 2004, for a contrary opinion.) The reader is encouraged to reflect on the merits of all of these possible reasons for not calculating and reporting a corrected estimate of effect size.

There is also a philosophical objection to the adjustment on the part of some researchers who believe that it is not worthwhile to calculate an estimate of an effect size that is only theoretically possible in an ideal world in which the actually less than perfectly reliable measure of the dependent variable could be measured perfectly reliably, an ideal that is not currently realizable for the measures of their dependent variables. (Hunter & Schmidt, 2004, represent the opposing view with regard to correcting for unreliability and other artifacts.) To accommodate this objection we recommend that researchers consider reporting adjusted estimates of effect size and the original unadjusted estimates, recognizing that some readers of their reports might be more, or less, interested in the reporting of corrected estimates of effect sizes than the researchers are.

CONSTRUCTING A CONFIDENCE INTERVAL CORRECTED FOR UNRELIABILITY

To construct a confidence interval for any effect size, ES_{pop} (including r_{pop}), in which the limits of the interval are those that are adjusted for unreliability, one first constructs the confidence interval using one of the previously discussed methods that is applied to the unadjusted sample *ES*. Then, the adjustment in Equation 4.15 or 4.16 is applied to the lower limit and the upper limit of the interval. One should still strive to use the most reliable measures even when planning to use the correction for unreliability.

OTHER ARTIFACTS

Hunter and Schmidt (2004) provided extensive and authoritative discussions of *artifacts*, such as unreliability, that can cause underestimation of effect sizes and provided corrections for them. Additional artifacts include sampling error, imperfect construct validity of the independent and dependent variables, computational and other errors, extraneous factors introduced by aspects of a study's procedures, and restricted range. It would be beyond the scope of this book to discuss this list of topics. It will have to suffice for us to discuss only the artifact of restricted range, to which we turn later in this chapter.

At the time of this writing, Windows-based commercial software is available, called "Hunter-Schmidt Meta-Analysis Programs Package" for calculating artifact-adjusted estimates of correlation and the standardized difference between means, including programs for correcting individual correlations and standardized differences between means for primary researchers. Currently, the package can be ordered from frank-schmidt@uiowa.edu, flschmidt@mchsi.com, or huy-le@uiowa.edu. Hunter and Schmidt (2004) discussed other software for similar purposes.

RELIABILITY, CONSTRUCT VALIDITY INVARIANCE, AND COMPARABILITY OF EFFECT SIZES

Construct validity invariance (measurement invariance, measurement equivalence) is satisfied when across studies different measures of supposedly the same underlying construct are truly measuring the same construct, an assumption that must be made when primary researchers or meta-analysts compare or combine effect sizes from different studies. When an item or scale does not measure the same thing in different kinds of samples there is said to be *differential item* (or *scale*) *functioning*. Nugent (2009) reported results of simulations of the effects of violation of construct validity invariance on standardized-mean-difference and correlational effect sizes. The results indicated that violation of the invariance assumption can cause great inconsistency in estimates of effect size. Meade (2010a; correction 2010b) discussed various effect sizes for quantifying the extent of differential item or scale functioning. Also consult DeMars (2011).

Measurement equivalence is required for the validity of comparisons between non-randomly-formed groups. Estimates of effect size can be decreased, increased, or changed in direction compared to the population effect size when measurement equivalence is violated (Sharma, Durvasola, & Ployhart, in press). Nye and Drasgow (2011) proposed an effect size for measurement equivalence.

One type of reliability is *internal-consistency reliability*, which reflects the extent to which the items on a given test or measure are measuring the same construct. Construct validity invariance is more likely to the extent that different measures each have internal-consistency reliability, a traditional but often problematic index of which is *Cronbach's coefficient alpha*. Issue number 1, volume 74, 2009, of the journal *Psychometrika* included many articles on the use and misuse of Cronbach's alpha.

RESTRICTED RANGE

Another possible attenuator of r or r_{pb} is called *restricted* (or *truncated*) *range*, which usually means using samples whose extent of variation on the independent variable is less than the extent of variation of that variable in the population to which the results are to be generalized. An example of the effect of restricted range is the lower r between Scholastic Aptitude Test (SAT) scores and grade-point averages at U.S. universities with the most demanding standards for admission (restricting most admissions to those ranging from high to very high SAT scores) compared to the r between SAT scores and grade-point averages at less restrictive universities (accepting students across a wider range of SAT scores). There is no problem of restricted range if it is the specific purpose of a researcher to study, say, a shorter than normal duration of therapy or a lower than normal dose of a drug, without generalizing the results to longer durations or higher doses.

Recall that the sample or population point-biserial correlation is sensitive to the difference between the proportions p_1 and p_2 of the total sample or population, respectively, in the two groups, and recall that group membership (i.e., the dichotomous independent variable) is coded numerically, say "1" and "2." The variance of a dichotomous variable is a function of $p_1 p_2$ in the sample or population such that the greater the difference between p_1 and p_2 the smaller the variance. Specifically, the value of population σ_x in Equation 4.1, or s_x in a sample, is given by the population or sample $[p_1 p_2]^{1/2}$, respectively. Therefore, stating that the sample r_{pb} is sensitive to base rates is equivalent to stating that the sample r_{pb} is sensitive to the variance of the grouping variable (i.e., the variance of the independent variable consisting, say, of 1s and 2s). Thus, the lowering of the variance of the independent variable in the sample because of unequal base rates, and the resulting lowering of sample r_{pb}, provide an example of lowering of a sample correlation coefficient resulting from range restriction (i.e., restriction of score variance). Consult McGrath and Meyer (2006) for further discussion.

DIRECT AND INDIRECT RANGE RESTRICTION

Direct range restriction occurs when the researcher knows in advance that the range of the independent variable is restricted. Instances in which the range is restricted because the available participants merely happen to be, instead if being selected to be, less variable than the population are examples of *indirect range restriction*. Suppose that an organizational researcher studies as an effect size the correlation between (a) a cognitive ability (Y) that is related to job performance and measured by the job application test, and (b) holding a 2-year or 4-year college degree (X). If the study is undertaken using job applicants there is no range restriction in variable Y. However, if the study is undertaken retrospectively to validate the test using long-term employees who have been doing the job in question, there may well be an indirect range restriction because such employees presumably exclude those whose level of performance with respect to the cognitive ability in question was not high enough to (a) have passed the job application test and be hired and (b) continue being employed at the particular job.

Hunter and Schmidt (2004) and Hunter, Schmidt, and Le (2006) discussed methods for correcting for direct and indirect range restrictions. However, again, as should be the case within a fixed-effects approach, when generalizations of results are confined to populations of whom the samples are representative in their range of the independent variable, instead of more general populations, no such correction need be made. Preacher et al. (2005) discussed the use of the traditional equation for correcting r for restricted range for the additional purpose of correcting r from bias arising from the use of extreme groups. The correction for indirect range restriction proposed by Hunter et al. shows evidence of providing a satisfactory estimate of r_{pop} (Le & Schmidt, 2006).

By lowering r restricted range also lowers the power of a test of H_0: r_{pop} = 0. Restricted range can also occur in the measure of the *dependent* variable if would-be high-scoring and/or would-be low-scoring participants drop out of the research before their data are obtained. Hunter and Schmidt (2004) provided a statistical correction for the case in which restriction of the range of the dependent variable is not accompanied by restriction of the range of the independent variable. Figure 4.2 depicts the great lowering of the value of r, compared to r_{pop},

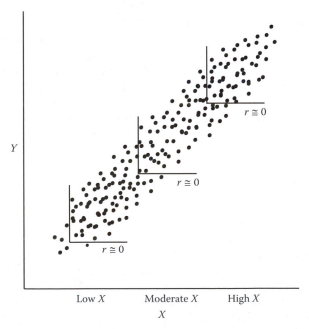

FIGURE 4.2   A case in which the overall correlation between X and Y (r_{pop}) is much higher than it would be estimated to be if the range of X in the sample were restricted to only low values, only moderate values, or only high values.

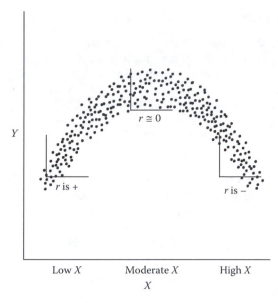

Y

$r \cong 0$

r is +

r is −

Low *X*   Moderate *X*   High *X*

X

FIGURE 4.3   If the overall relationship between *X* and *Y* is curvilinear in the population, restricting the range of *X* in the sample to only low, only moderate, or only high values can affect the size and sign of *r* in the sample.

in samples in which *X* varies much less than it does in the population. Note in Figure 4.2 that over a restricted range of *X* the range of *Y* becomes restricted. Such double restriction of range can occur if $0 < |r| < 1$ (Baguley, 2009).

Although typically not the case, restricted range can cause an increase in *r* (Wilcox, 2001). Suppose also, for example, that a relationship between two variables is curvilinear in the population and the sample is one in which the range of *X* is restricted. In this case the magnitude and sign of *r* in the sample may depend on whether the range is restricted to low, moderate, or high values of *X*. This case is depicted in Figure 4.3.

$r_{pop} = 0$ Does Not Necessarily Mean Independence

Recall that *r* reflects only a linear component of a relationship between two variables. One implication of this fact is that $r_{pop} = 0$ does not necessarily imply independence (i.e., no effect) as is illustrated in Figure 4.3 in which r_{pop} may be equal to zero but there is obviously a degree of curvilinear dependence of *Y* on *X*. Further, consider the complete dependence of *Y* on *X* when $Y = X^{C > 0}$. In this case of complete dependence, $r_{pop} = 0$ over an entire negative and positive range of *X* because the negative association between *X* and *Y* for negative values of *X* is canceled by the equally positive association between *X* and *Y* for positive values of *X*. This example and Figure 4.3 provide one kind of example of different values of local versus global associations between variables.

RESTRICTED RANGE, STRENGTH OF MANIPULATION, AND POWER

In the case of standardized-difference estimators of effect size, not letting Treatment *a* and Treatment *b* differ as much in the research as they do or may do in real-world application of these two treatments is also a restriction of range that lowers the value of the estimator. In experimental research the extent of difference between two treatments or among multiple treatments is called the *strength of manipulation*. A weaker manipulation of the independent variable in the research setting than occurs in the world of practice would be a case of restricted range.

Tips and Pitfalls

Restricted range is not only likely to lower the value of any kind of estimator of effect size, it can also lower the value of test statistics, such as *t*, thereby lowering statistical power. Therefore, in applied areas researchers should use ranges of the independent variable that are as similar as possible to those that would be found in the population to which the results are to be generalized.

Consult Abelson (1995) for a discussion of the *causal efficacy ratio* that he proposed as an effect size that is relative to the *cause size* (i.e., an effect size that is relative to the strength of the manipulation). An example is provided later in this chapter. Also consult Tryon's (2001) discussion of such an effect size.

CORRECTING FOR RESTRICTED RANGE

Chan and Chan (2004) discussed results of Monte Carlo simulations of a bootstrap method for estimating the standard error and constructing a confidence interval for an r_{pop}, the estimate of which has been corrected for restricted range. Raju, Lezotte, Fearing, and Oshima (2006) discussed correction of an *r* for direct range restriction in *X* and unreliability in both *X* and *Y*. Wilcox (2005a) discussed additional factors than can affect the Pearson *r*.

SCALE COARSENESS

A scale of measurement is said to have *scale coarseness* when it uses a limited number of categories to represent a continuous underlying construct. For example, if attitude is assumed to be continuous, ranging from the most extremely unfavorable to the most extremely favorable, but attitude is observed (recorded) using a Likert scale (e.g., Disagree Strongly, Disagree, Agree, Agree Strongly), the scaling is said to be coarse. In such cases information is lost because persons with somewhat, but not greatly, different underlying true scores are necessarily placed in the same category. Such coarseness in one or both of the two variables reduces their correlation. For example, in such a case if the point-biserial correlation between gender and attitude (numerically scaled; e.g., 1, 2, 3, 4) is used as an effect size, the latter will be underestimated.

The artifact of scale coarseness relates only to the case in which an unmeasured assumed underlying continuous variable is indirectly measured on an ordinal scale that has a limited number of categories. As such, scale coarseness is distinct from random measurement error and also distinct from the artifact in which a variable is first measured continuously and thereafter is compressed into a limited number of ordinal categories by the researcher using cutoff points such as the median or quartiles. Aguinis, Pierce, and Culpepper (2009) described and extended the long-known but apparently rarely used Peters–van Voorhis method for correcting the artifactual reduction of r by scale coarseness and discussed a method for constructing a confidence interval for r_{pop} that applies the corrected rs to the limits.

The correction assumes a linear relationship between X and Y, equal-interval scoring for the categories (e.g., 1, 2, 3...), and finite underlying continua for coarse scales. There are separate correction factors for underlying variables that are assumed to be normally distributed or uniformly (i.e., rectangularly) distributed. The method for normal distributions has been found to be accurate when both X and Y are severely skewed unless X and/or Y are dichotomies (Wylie, 1976). Simulations by Aguinis et al. (2009) indicated that the method is accurate across the range of r_{pop} and for scales comprised of 2–20 points. Courtesy of Herman Aguinis and his coworkers, a program for the calculation of the corrected r and construction of the confidence interval is freely downloadable from http://carbon.cudenver.edu/~haguinis/. Click on the link "Scale Coarseness Program."

Using our notation the correction equation is $r_{csc} = r/c_X c_Y$, where r_{csc} is the r corrected for scale coarseness, and c_X and c_Y are the correction divisors for scales X and Y. The correction divisors depend on the number of scale points (categories). The greater the number of scale points the smaller the required correction because the less coarse the scale. If only one of the scales is coarse (e.g., the other scale is continuous or a natural dichotomy such as gender or treatment category) the correction divisor for the variable that is not coarse is 1 (i.e., no correction). An example of the use of the correction is provided in Chapter 9.

As is the case with regard to corrections for other artifactual reductions of r, a confidence interval for r_{pop} that is based on a coarseness-corrected r will be wider than one that is based entirely on an uncorrected r (Aguinis et al., 2009). The confidence interval is most easily constructed simply by applying the correction to the lower and upper limits of a confidence interval that had been constructed using the uncorrected r. A larger sample size and the use of more points on the scale can reduce the width. Aguinis et al. also discussed eliminating or reducing scale coarseness methodologically, where practical, by the use of a line segment, without scale points, on which a respondent responds by marking the line at a chosen distance from its origin. The distance of the mark from the origin of the line provides the score for that respondent.

SMALL, MEDIUM, AND LARGE EFFECT SIZE VALUES

In behavioral, psychological, and educational research standardized-difference estimates are rarely more extreme than (ignoring sign) 2.00 and r_{pb} estimates are rarely beyond .70, with both kinds of estimates typically being very much less extreme than these values. However, categorizing values of estimates of effect size as small, medium, or large (Cohen, 1988) is necessarily somewhat arbitrary. Such categories are relative to such factors as the particular area of research and that area's degree of experimental control of extraneous variables and the reliabilities of the scores on its measures of dependent variables. For example, an effect size of a certain magnitude may be relatively large if it occurs in some area of research in social psychology whereas that same value may not be relatively large if it occurs in some possibly more controlled area of research such as neuropsychology. Also, even in the same field of study two observers of a given value of effect size may rate the practical importance of that value differently, and such ratings may change over time. For example, in educational research a minimum standard for practical significance has been considered by some to be estimated $d_{pop} = 0.33$ (Gall, Borg, & Gall, 1996), with a range of approximately 0.25–0.50 for the minimum standard. Cohen did not intend that his labels small, medium, and large be used rigidly out of the context of a particular area of research and its stage of development.

Tips and Pitfalls

Although it is commonly done, the effect size from a study should not be compared to Cohen's general standards for small, medium, and large effect sizes that are discussed in the following. Instead an effect size should be compared to other effect sizes in the same specific area of research. Also, it is possible for effect sizes to be smaller later in a large-sample randomized clinical trial than earlier in that same trial. For example, patients who volunteer later in a large clinical trial may be more variable with respect to the severity of the targeted disease than are patients who volunteer earlier. Greater variance results in a smaller standardized difference between means.

With appropriate tentativeness and a disclaimer Cohen (1988) offered admittedly rough criteria for small, medium, and large effect sizes, and examples within each category. (We ignore the sign of the effect sizes, which is not relevant here.) We will relate Cohen's criteria to the distribution of standardized-difference estimates of effect sizes that have been reported in various areas of research. It is very important to note that the values that we cite in the following for Cohen's criteria for small, medium, and large effect sizes are based on the population values of point-biserial correlations (when base rates are equal) and their equivalent values of d_{pop} (Cohen, p. 82), so these values will not agree with some of those that appear elsewhere in the literature and that are not based on the point-biserial correlation.

SMALL EFFECT SIZES

Cohen (1988) categorized as small $d_{pop} \leq .20$ and $r_{pop} \leq .10$, with regard to the point-biserial correlation. Cohen's examples of sample values of effect size that fall into this category include (a) the slight superiority of mean IQ in non-twins compared to twins, (b) the slightly greater mean height of 16-year-old girls compared to 15-year-old girls, and (c) some differences between women and men on some scales of the Wechsler Adult Intelligence Test. Lipsey and Wilson (1993) found that the lowest 25% of the distribution of psychological, behavioral, and educational examples of standardized-difference estimates of effect size were on the order of $d \leq .30$, which is equivalent to $r_{pb} \leq .15$, and somewhat supports Cohen's criteria. (Also, there is apparently little basis for a proposed criterion of $d_{pop} \geq .25$ as a benchmark for an educational intervention having attained practical significance [Bloom et al., 2008]). Similarly, approximately one-third of point-biserial correlation coefficients were found to be below .17 (Hemphill, 2003).

MEDIUM EFFECT SIZES

Cohen (1988) categorized as medium, $d_{pop} = .5$ and $r_{pop} = .243$. Consistent with these criteria for a medium effect size Lipsey and Wilson (1993) found that the median $d = .5$ and Hemphill (2003) reported that the middle third of point-biserial correlation coefficients fell between .17 and .28. Cohen's criterion is also consistent with typical effect sizes in counseling psychology and social psychology. Cohen's approximate examples include the greater mean height of 18-year-old women compared to 14-year-old girls, and the greater mean IQ of (a) clerical compared to semi-skilled workers and (b) professional compared to managerial workers. Recall from Chapter 3 that Grissom (1996) found when comparing placebo groups to control groups in psychotherapy research the median $d = .44$ and when comparing treated groups to placebo groups the median $d = .58$, which are roughly equivalent to $r_{pb} = .22$ and .27, respectively. However, with regard to research on treatments to improve academic achievement, although the mean estimated effect size for interventions at the middle-school level, $d = .51$, corresponds to Cohen's standard for a medium effect size, the mean estimated effect sizes for interventions at the elementary-school and high-school levels are much below that standard, $d = .33$ and $d = .27$, respectively (Hill et al., 2008).

LARGE EFFECT SIZES

Cohen (1988) categorized as large $d_{pop} \geq .8$ and $r_{pop} \geq .371$. His examples include the greater mean height of 18-year-old women compared to 13-year-old girls, and the higher mean IQ of holders of PhD degrees compared to first-year college students. Somewhat consistent with Cohen's criteria, Lipsey and Wilson (1993) found that the top 25% of values of d were $d \geq .67$, roughly corresponding to $r_{pb} \geq .32$, and Hemphill (2003) reported that the upper third of point-biserial correlation coefficients ranged from .29 to .60. Recall from Chapter 3 that Grissom (1996) found that the most efficacious psychotherapy produced a (very rare) median $d = 2.47$, roughly corresponding to $r_{pb} = .78$.

Cohen's (1988) lower bound for a medium d_{pop} (i.e., .5) is equidistant from his upper bound for a small effect size ($d_{pop} = .2$) and his lower bound for a large effect size ($d_{pop} = .8$). (The relationship between Cohen's standards for small, medium, and large effect sizes and the amount of overlap between the two groups' distributions can be observed in Table 5.1; also observe Figure 3.1.)

There can be great variation around the mean effect size in a given area of research depending on specific details of the research. For example, in experiments to improve scholastic achievement in elementary-school pupils the mean $d = .44$ for specialized tests, mean $d = .23$ for narrowly focused standardized tests, and mean $d = .07$ for broad standardized tests (Hill et al., 2008).

CONVERTING r_{pb} TO d

If r_{pb} is reported as an estimate of effect size and a reader of the report is interested in d, the r_{pb} can be converted to d if homoscedasticity is assumed using

$$d = 2r_{pb} \left[\frac{[(N-2)/N]^{1/2}}{\left(1 - r_{pb}^2\right)^{1/2}} \right], \qquad (4.17)$$

where N is the total sample size. Except for very small sample sizes a reasonably accurate simpler equation is the commonly used

$$d = \frac{2r_{pb}}{(1 - r_{pb}^2)^{1/2}}. \qquad (4.18)$$

We demonstrate Equation 4.17 using the real data from Chapter 3 that compared (a) mothers of schizophrenics (group a when a d was calculated directly in Chapter 3 and coded 1 when r_{pb} was calculated earlier in the present chapter) and (b) mothers of normals (group b and coded 2). Total sample size was 40 and r_{pb} was found earlier to be .3957336 (undoing the previous rounding) so

$$d = 2(.3957336) \left[\frac{((40-2)/40)^{1/2}}{(1 - .3957336^2)^{1/2}} \right] \approx .84 \text{ or } -.84$$

Again, the mean for the normals' mothers was reported in Chapter 3 to be higher than the mean for the schizophrenics' mothers, so whether a d is positive or negative is merely a matter of whether the mean for the normals' mothers would be placed at the left or the right of the numerator when calculating d directly using Equation 3.3. Placing the mean for the normals' mothers at the right of the numerator in Chapter 3, d was found to be $-.84$, which equals the value of d that has now been calculated using Equation 4.17 for a conversion from r_{pb}.

SIZE OF EFFECT VERSUS MAGNITUDE OF IMPORTANCE

The designations small, medium, and large effect sizes do not necessarily correspond to the degree of practical significance or theoretical significance of an effect. For example, when a theory predicts no effect, studies consistently finding little or no effect can be interpreted as being highly theoretically significant in the sense that the theory is being confirmed to a high degree of approximation. Consult Krantz (1999) for an example.

Tips and Pitfalls

As we previously noted, judgment about the practical significance of an effect depends on the context of the research, and the specific expertise and the values of the person who is judging the practical significance. For example, finding a small lowering of death rate from a new therapy for a widespread and likely fatal disease would be of greater practical significance than finding a large improvement in cure rate for a new drug for athlete's foot. Also, consider a disease that is rare and very serious or fatal, and for which there is an effective childhood vaccine. Because the disease is rare even without vaccination, the estimate of effect size for such a vaccination may be very small, but the practical significance can be very great if the vaccine is inexpensive and generally risk-free, as well as being very effective.

Critiques of Designations as Small, Medium, and Large Effect Sizes

Refer to Glass et al. (1981) for opposition to the designations small, medium, and large effect sizes. Cynics have called such designations, when used too generally, *T-shirt effect sizes*: small, medium, and large (leaving out petite and extra large). Hill and Thompson (2004) discussed the fact that even in the same general area of research two equal values of an effect size in two studies might not have the same clinical significance.

Sometimes the practical significance of an effect can be measured tangibly. For example, Breaugh (2003) reviewed cases of utility analyses in which estimates were made of the amount of money that employers could save by subjecting job applicants to realistic job previews (RJPs). Although the point-biserial correlation between the independent variable of RJP versus no RJP and the dependent variable of employee turnover was very small, $r_{pb} = .09$, employers could judge the practical significance of the results by evaluating the amount of money that a utility analysis estimated would be saved by the small reduction in employee turnover that was associated with the RJP program.

Breaugh (2003) also cited an example in which small but consistent bias effects in ratings of the performance of female employees can result over the years in a large number of women unfairly denied promotion. Consult Prentice and Miller (1992) for additional examples of apparently small effect sizes that can be practically important. Cortina and Landis (2009) discussed important small effect sizes and less important large effect sizes. For discussions of paradoxes involving miniscule effect sizes that can represent very important effects consult Abelson (1985) and Sawilowsky (2005).

Tips and Pitfalls

When interpreting an estimate of effect size one should not be prematurely impressed with a reported non-zero value of r or d when there is no rational explanation for the supposed relationship and the result has not been replicated by other studies. Such findings, especially when based on small samples, may be just chance findings, which are often called *nonsense correlations*. Also, when assumptions are satisfied even an $|r|$ as great as approximately $|.631|$ or $|.876|$ fails to attain statistical significance at the .05 level when $N = 10$ or $N = 5$, respectively. Both of these values of sample r are much higher than Cohen's criterion for a large r_{pop} ($\geq .371$), but they do not attain statistical significance when sample size is small.

SOME EMPIRICAL BENCHMARKS FOR JUDGING PRACTICAL SIGNIFICANCE

Three empirical benchmarks for judging the practical significance of standard-ized mean difference effect sizes were proposed by Hill et al. (2008). These benchmarks especially, but not exclusively, relate to educational interventions that are intended to improve student achievement. The benchmarks reflect the kind of treatment, sample, and outcome variable that were used.

The first such benchmark compares a treatment's effect size to the baseline effect size that is found based merely on a year of growth in academic achieve-ment, for which there are ample records for nationally normed tests for grades 1 through 12. This baseline effect size is the standardized difference between mean score from one grade to the next grade (e.g., sophomore year to junior year in high school). The second benchmark relates a treatment's effect size to existing differ-ences between subgroups of students. For example, a treatment's effect size can be compared to the known standardized mean difference in reading or mathematics between two ethnic groups, two income-level groups, or male and female students. Third, an effect size for a treatment can be compared to previously reported effect sizes involving similar interventions, grade levels, subpopulations, and outcome measures. Researchers who use benchmarks similar to those that have been men-tioned in this section should make sure that the standardizer that they use for the treatment effect is comparable to the standardizer that was used for the benchmark effect. Consult Hill et al. (2008) and Bloom et al. (2008) for detailed discussion of the implications and limitations of their proposed benchmarks.

BINOMIAL EFFECT SIZE DISPLAY

Rosenthal and Rubin (1982) presented a tabular illustration to aid in the inter-pretation of any kind of r, including the point-biserial r. The table is called the *binomial effect size display*, *BESD*, and was intended especially to illustrate the possibly great practical importance of a supposedly small value for any type of r. The BESD, as we soon discuss, is not itself an estimator of effect size but is intended instead to be a hypothetical illustration of what can be inferred about effect size from the size of any r. We discuss its limitations in the next section.

The BESD develops from the fact that r can also be applied to data in which both the X and Y variables are dichotomies. In the case of dichotomous X and Y variables the name for such a correlation is the *phi coefficient*, phi being the Greek letter ϕ. For example, X could be Treatment a versus Treatment b, and

Y could be the categories *Patient Better after Treatment* and *Patient Not Better after Treatment*. One codes X values, say, "1" for Treatment a and, say, "2" for Treatment b, as one would if one were calculating r_{pb}, but now for calculating phi, Y is also coded numerically, say, "1" for *Better* and, say, "2" for *Not Better*. Phi is the r between the X variable's set of 1s and 2s and the Y variable's set of 1s and 2s. Even if software does not seem to indicate that it can calculate phi, when calculating the usual r for the data in a file with two values, such as 1 and 2, in the X column and two values, such as 1 and 2, in the Y column, the software is in fact calculating phi. (In Chapter 8, we discuss another context for phi as an estimator of effect size and another way to calculate it.)

By supposing that $n_a = n_b$, and by treating a value of an r for the moment as if it had been a value of phi, we now observe that one can construct a hypothetical table (the BESD) that illustrates another kind of interpretation or implication of the value of an r. For example, suppose that an obtained value of an r is a "modest" .20. Although the r is based on a continuous Y variable, to obtain a different perspective on this result the BESD pretends for the moment that X and Y had both been dichotomous variables and that the $r = .20$ had, therefore, instead been a phi = .20. Table 4.1 depicts what results would look like if phi = .20 and, for example, $n_a = n_b = 100$. An r equal to .20 may not seem to some to represent an effect size that would be of great practical importance. However, observe in Table 4.1 that if the r of .20 had instead been a phi = .20 (the basis of Table 4.1) such results would have indicated that 20% more participants improve under Treatment a than improve under Treatment b (i.e., 60% – 40% = 20%).

Observe in Table 4.1 that 60 of a total of 100 participants (60%) in Treatment a are classified as being *Better* after treatment than they had been before treatment and 40 of a total of 100 participants in Treatment b are classified as being *Better* after treatment than they had been before treatment. These percentages are called the *success percentages* for the two treatments or, when expressed as rates (e.g., .60), *success rates*. The result appears now, in terms of the BESD-produced success percentages, to be more impressive. For example, if many thousands or millions of patients in actual clinical practice were going to be given Treatment a instead of the old Treatment b because of the results in Table 4.1 (assuming for the moment that the sample phi of .20 is reflecting a population phi of .20), then one would be improving the health of an additional 20% of

---

TABLE 4.1

A Binomial Effect Size Display

	Participant Better (Y = 1)	Participant Not Better (Y = 2)	Totals
Treatment a (X = 1)	60	40	100
Treatment b (X = 2)	40		100

many thousands or millions of people beyond the number that would have been improved by the use of Treatment b.

The more serious the type of illness the greater would be the medical and social significance of the present numerical result (assuming also that Treatment a were not prohibitively expensive or risky). The most extreme example would be the case of any fairly common and possibly fatal disease of which 20% more of hundreds of thousands or millions of patients worldwide would be cured by using Treatment a instead of Treatment b. Again, such results are more impressive than an $r = .20$ would seem to indicate at first glance. However, the 20% increase in success percentage for Treatment a versus Treatment b does not apply directly to the original raw data because the BESD table is hypothetical. The BESD is simply a hypothetical way to interpret an r (or r_{pb}) by addressing the following question: "What if both X and Y had been dichotomous variables, and, therefore, the r had been a phi coefficient, and the resulting 2×2 table had uniform margin totals (explained later), what would the increase in success percentage have been by using Treatment a instead of Treatment b"? In many instances of research the original data will already have arisen from a 2×2 table, but not always one that satisfies the specific criteria for a BESD table that will be discussed in the next section.

In general for any r, to find the success percentage (*Better*) for the treatment coded $X = 1$ in a BESD use $100[.50 + (r/2)]\%$. Because the two percentages in a row of a BESD must add to 100%, the failure percentage for the row $X = 1$ is 100% minus the row's success percentage. The success percentage for the row $X = 2$ in a BESD is given by $100[.50 - (r/2)]\%$, and its failure percentage is 100% minus the success percentage for that row. In the example of Table 4.1, $r = $ phi $= .20$, so the success percentage for Treatment a is $100[.50 + (.20/2)]\% = 60\%$ and its failure percentage is $100\% - 60\% = 40\%$. The greater the value of r the greater the difference will be between the success percentages of the two treatments. Specifically, the difference between these two success percentages will be given by $(100r)\%$. Therefore, even before constructing the BESD one knows that when $r = .20$ the difference in success percentages will be $[100(.20)]\% = 20\%$ if the original data are recast into an appropriate BESD.

LIMITATIONS OF THE BESD

There are limitations of the BESD and its resulting estimation of the difference between the success percentages of two treatments. First, the difference in the success percentages from the BESD is only equal to phi if the overall success percentage = overall failure percentage = 50%, and if the two groups are of the same size (Strahan, 1991). The result is a table that is said to have *uniform margins*. Observe that Table 4.1 satisfies these criteria because the two samples are of the same size, the overall (i.e., marginal) success percentage equals $(60 + 40)/200 = 50\%$, and the overall failure percentage equals $[(40 + 60)/200] = 50\%$. However, it can be argued that this first criticism is actually not a limitation but merely part of the definition of a BESD, but some may counter that this is a distinction without a difference.

When the criteria for a BESD are satisfied the resulting difference in success percentages is relevant to the hypothetical population whose data are represented by the BESD. However, are the results relevant to the population that gave rise to the original real data that were recast into the BESD table, or relevant to any real population (Hsu, 2004)? The population for which the BESD-generated difference in success percentages in a table such as Table 4.1 is most relevant is a population each half of which received either Treatment a or Treatment b, and half of which improved and half did not. Again, this limitation may be considered by some to be merely an inherent aspect of the definition of the BESD.

Cases in which the original data are available are the cases that are most relevant to this book because it is addressed to those who produce data (primary researchers). It makes more sense in such cases of original 2 × 2 tables to compare the two treatments based on the actual data instead of the hypothetical BESD. For example, in such cases one may use the relative risk or other effect sizes for data in a 2 × 2 table, as is discussed in Chapter 8. Also, suppose that the success percentage and failure percentage in the real population to which the sample results are to be generalized are not each equal to 50%. In this case a BESD-based difference between success percentages in the sample will be biased toward overestimating the difference between success percentages for the two treatments in that population.

Additional problems can arise when the original measure of the dependent variable is continuous instead of dichotomous. In this case researchers often split scores of each of the two samples at the overall median of the scores in order to form equal-sized overall "successful" and "failing" categories, thereby satisfying the criteria for the hypothetical BESD table. However, defining success or failure in terms of scoring below or above the overall median score often may not be realistic. For example, not every treated depressed patient who scores below the median on a test of depression can be considered to be cured or much of a therapeutic success.

For a response to some of the criticisms of the BESD method refer to Rosenthal (1991a). Consult Rosenthal (2000) and Rosnow and Rosenthal (2003) for further discussions of the BESD. Consult Hsu (2004) for an extensive critique of the BESD.

COEFFICIENT OF DETERMINATION

We assume in this section that for cases involving r_{pb} sample sizes are equal and that difference in population base rates is not an issue, as was discussed previously in this chapter. The square of the sample correlation coefficient, r^2 (or r_{pb}^2), that is called the sample *coefficient of determination*, has been widely used as an estimator of r_{pop}^2, an effect size that is called the population coefficient of determination. (We use the notation r^2 for the coefficient of determination generally, and r_{pb}^2 when the discussion is restricted to the case of a truly dichotomous X variable.) There are several phrases that are typically used (accurately or inaccurately, depending on the context) to define or interpret a coefficient of determination. The usual interpretation of r_{pop}^2 is that r_{pop}^2 indicates the proportion of the variance of Y (i.e., a proportion of σ_y^2) that is *predictable from, explained by, shared by, related to, associated with,* or *determined by* its linear association with X or variation in X. The adjective "linear" is crucial in the case of the r between two continuous variables (but not in the case of r_{pb}, in which one variable is dichotomous) because, as was previously discussed, r only reflects the linear part of a relationship between continuous X and Y variables. Also, the applicability of one or more of the preceding italicized phrases depends on to which of its variety of uses r is being applied and on models of the X and Y variables (Beatty, 2002; Ozer, 1985). For example, Ozer argued that when the same latent variable underlies the observed variables X and Y, r itself, not r^2, estimates the proportion of variance that is shared by X and Y. Thus, in the application of r to reliability it is assumed that X_1 and Y (i.e., X_2) are measuring the same latent variable, so r itself estimates the proportion of shared variance in that case. Also consult Beatty.

INTERPRETING THE COEFFICIENT OF DETERMINATION

There are various interpretations of the coefficient of determination (Rovine & von Eye, 1997; Wilcox, 2007b). Regarding the most common interpretation, it can be shown mathematically that, under certain conditions and assumptions (Ozer, 1985), but not others, r_{pop}^2 is the ratio of (a) the part of the variance of the scores on the dependent variable that is related to variation of the independent variable (*explained variance*) and (b) the *total variance* of the scores (related and not related to the independent variable). For the first of the two most extreme examples, if $r_{pop} = 0$, $r_{pop}^2 = 0$ and none of the variation of the scores is explained by variation of the independent variable. On the other hand, if $r_{pop} = 1$, $r_{pop}^2 = 1$ and all of the variation of the scores is related to the variation of the independent variable. In other words, when the coefficient of determination is 0, by knowing the values of the independent variable one knows 0% of what one needs to know in order to predict the scores on the measure of the dependent variable, but, when this coefficient is 1, one knows 100% of what one needs to know in order to predict the scores. In this latter case all of the points in the scatterplot that relates variables X and Y fall on the straight *line of best fit* through the points (a *regression line* or *prediction line* of perfect fit in this case) so that there is no variation of Y at a given value of X, rendering Y values perfectly predictable from knowledge of X. The previously discussed limitations of r when assumptions are violated apply to r^2. For the approximate median r_{pb} found in behavioral and educational research, $r_{pb} = .24$, $r_{pb}^2 = .24^2 = .0576$; therefore, independent variables in these areas of research on average are estimated to account for about 6% of the variance of scores on the measures of dependent variables.

CONFIDENCE INTERVALS AND FURTHER DISCUSSIONS

A confidence interval for r_{pop}^2 can be constructed using one of the previously discussed methods for constructing a confidence interval for r_{pop}. For the present purpose the lower and upper limits of the confidence interval for r_{pop} are squared to obtain the limits for r_{pop}^2. Wang and Thompson (2007) discussed the fact that r^2 is slightly biased when samples are small, and they found that two of the various methods for correcting for bias work well, including Ezekiel's traditional method. Wilcox (2008b) reported small-sample performances of robust nonparametric estimators of an analog of r_{pop}^2.

Tips and Pitfalls

The words "determined" and "explained" can be misleading when used in the context of nonexperimental research. To speak of the independent variable determining variation of the dependent variable in the context of nonexperimental research might imply to some a causal connection between variation of the independent variable and the magnitudes of the scores. In this nonexperimental case a correlation coefficient is reflecting covariation between X and Y, not necessarily causality of the magnitudes of the scores. In this case if, for example, the coefficient of determination in the sample is equal to .49, it is estimated that 49% of the variance of the scores is explained by variation in the X variable. Accounting for the degree of variation of scores is not the same as accounting for the magnitudes of the scores.

Only in research in which participants have been randomly assigned to treatments (experiments) and, therefore, there has been control of extraneous variables can one reasonably speak of variation (manipulation) of the independent variable causing or determining the scores. Therefore, in nonexperimental research perhaps one should consider foregoing the use of the word "determination" and instead refer to r^2 as the proportion of variance of the scores that is associated with or related to variation of the independent variable. However, it has been argued that squaring r (or r_{pb}) to obtain a coefficient of determination is not appropriate in the case of experimental research, and that r itself is the appropriate estimator of an effect size in the experimental case. Consult Ozer (1985) and Beatty (2002) for this argument. A reader of a research report can readily calculate r^2 if only r is reported, or calculate r (at least its magnitude if not its sign in all cases) if only r^2 is reported.

Causality

Not only does the word *determination* in the label "coefficient of determination" perhaps imply causality when in the case of nonexperimental research it should not, the same incorrect implication obtains for the word *effect* in the label "effect size" in the nonexperimental case. A fact that everyone who has had a course in statistics should recall is that if X is found to be related to Y it may mean that X causes Y or Y causes X, but it could also mean that one or more Z variables (i.e., *confounding variables*) are responsible for the result. More complex causal paths are also possible. Approaches to causal inference from nonexperimental data focus on problematic statistical adjustments (Chapters 10 and 11) or improved designs to eliminate or reduce factors that threaten the validity of causal inferences.

WHEN TO USE r_{pop} VERSUS r_{pop}^2

It should be clear that r and r^2 generally serve different purposes. For another example consider the following form of the equation for the linear *regression* of Y on X (i.e., the equation for predicting Y from a given value of X, based on the correlation between X and Y):

$$Y' = \bar{Y} + r\left(\frac{s_y}{s_x}\right)(X - \bar{X}), \tag{4.19}$$

where Y' is the predicted value of Y. It can be shown that the correlation between X and Y also equals the correlation between Y' and Y. (The equality of these two correlations makes sense intuitively because the stronger the correlation between X and Y, the greater the accuracy in predicting Y from X; i.e., the *observed* values of Y will be found to be closer to the values of Y'.) Therefore, it can be argued that if one is interested in the extent to which the observed data correspond to the predicted data then r_{pop} is the parameter to be estimated, whereas if one is interested in the extent to which variation in Y is associated with variation in X then r^2 in the population is often the parameter to be estimated (but, again, consult Beatty, 2002, and Ozer, 1985). The assumptions of the inferential use of the linear regression model are that the conditional distributions of Y are normal, of equal variance, and with means that lie on a straight line. The marginal distribution of Y need not be normal, and the distribution of the selected values of X that were used in the research cannot be normal because their number is quite finite. Equation 4.19 and the statements made hereafter in this chapter are based on *least-squares regression*, which means that the traditional (but not necessarily always optimal) criterion that is used for determining the line (equation) of best fit is that it is the line that minimizes the squared deviations from it, that is, minimizes the squared errors of prediction.

Observe in Equation 4.19 that if $r = 0$ all terms to the right of $\bar{Y}$ drop out and $Y' = \bar{Y}$. Further observe in Equation 4.19 that the larger the absolute value of r the more Y' departs from $\bar{Y}$. Therefore, it may be said that the smaller the value of r the more the predicted value of Y *falls back to* (i.e., *regresses* to) merely the overall mean of the Y values. (Note also that Equation 4.19 satisfies a verbal definition of a straight line: a variable $[Y']$ equals a constant $[\bar{Y}]$ plus the product of another constant $[r(s_y/s_x)]$ and a variable $[X - \bar{X}]$.)

PICTURING THE COEFFICIENT OF DETERMINATION

Figure 4.4 illustrates the concept of the sample coefficient of determination by considering just one of the points of data. The other scatter points are assumed but not shown and the solid line represents the line of best fit that would be described by Equation 4.19. Consider the actual data point that is at X_i, Y_i, and

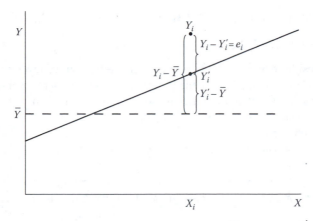

FIGURE 4.4   The deviation of a score, Y_i, from the mean, $\bar{Y}$, consists of $Y_i' - \bar{Y}$, which is not 0 when $r \neq 0$, and $Y_i - Y_i'$, which is an error of prediction.

also consider the Y score that is predicted at that same X_i (i.e., Y_i') by the prediction line (prediction equation). Observe in Figure 4.4 that the deviation of Y_i from $\bar{Y}$ consists of two parts: (a) $Y_i' - \bar{Y}$, which is explained by the fact that there is a nonzero correlation between X and Y, and (b) $Y_i - Y_i'$, which is not explained by the correlation and is an error of prediction (e).

Now recall that the numerator of a variance is a sum of squared deviations (SS). Therefore, the sum of all of the squared values of $Y_i - \bar{Y}$ across the entire set of data is called the total sum of squares (SS_{tot}), the sum of all of the squared values of $Y_i' - \bar{Y}$ is called the predictable or explained sum of squares (SS_{exp}), and the sum of all of the squared values of $Y_i - Y_i'$ can be called the *residual sum of squares*, the *error sum of squares*, or the *unexplained sum of squares* (SS_{unexp}). The coefficient of determination in the sample, r^2, is equal to SS_{exp}/SS_{tot}, which is also *the proportion of total variance in Y that is explained by its correlation with X.* (Alternatively, r^2 can be defined as $s_{Y'}^2/s_Y^2$, and also as $(SS_{tot} - SS_{unexp})/SS_{tot}$; i.e., the latter is the relative reduction of error of prediction by using values of Y' instead of values of $\bar{Y}$ as predicted values.) The relationship between the coefficient of determination and the standardized difference between means, d, when there are two groups is obtained by squaring both sides of Equation 4.2.

Tips and Pitfalls
To say that a portion of variance is "unexplained" is not equivalent to saying that all of that portion is immutably "unexplainable," just as a currently unidentified flying object will not necessarily forever be unidentified. The error in predicting Y can often be reduced (i.e., a lessening of unexplained variance) by the use of additional relevant predictors in combination with X, a topic of multiple regression that is discussed in Chapter 10.

CRITICISMS OF THE COEFFICIENT OF DETERMINATION

MISLEADINGLY SMALL VALUES

We now consider reasons why the use of r^2 has fallen out of favor recently with some researchers. First, squaring the typically small or moderate values of r (i.e., r typically closer to 0 than to 1) that are found in psychological, behavioral, and educational research results in yet smaller numerical values of r^2 such as the typical $r^2 = .06$ compared to the underlying $r = .24$. Some have argued that such small values for an estimator can lead to underestimation of the practical importance of the effect size. However, this is a less compelling reason for discarding r^2 when the readership of a report of research has sufficient familiarity with statistics and when the author of the report has provided the readers with discussion of the implications and limitations of the r^2, and also provided them with other perspectives on the data. Also, the typically low or moderate values of r^2 can often be informative in some contexts. For example, some reports of research make very much of, say, an obtained $r = .7$. The resulting $r^2 = .7^2 = .49$ informs one that the X variable is estimated to explain less than half (49%) of the variance of the Y variable. Such a result alerts one to the need to search for one or more additional X variables (multiple correlation) to explain a greater percentage of the variance of Y, as is discussed in Chapter 10. Note, however, the importance of sample size in the interpretation. If $N \leq 8$, $r^2 = .49$ will not attain statistical significance at the $p = .05$ level, two-tailed.

Breaugh (2003) reviewed an example in which the dichotomous independent variable was which of two hospitals conducted a given coronary bypass operation, and the dichotomous dependent variable was surviving versus not surviving the surgery. In this example it was found that $r = .07$, so the coefficient of determination is .0049. Therefore, because choice of hospital "only" related to less than one-half of 1% of the variance (.0049) in the survivability variable some may conclude that choosing between the two hospitals would be of little effect and of little practical importance. However, looking at the data from another perspective one learns that the mortality rate for the surgery at one of the hospitals was 1.40% whereas the mortality rate at the other hospital was 3.60%—a mortality rate that is 2.57 times greater. Again we observe that it can be very instructive to analyze a set of data from different perspectives. The kind of r that was applied to the data in the example of the two hospitals is the phi coefficient, which, as is discussed in Chapter 8, is only appropriate for such data when sampling is naturalistic (cross-sectional) as is discussed in the same chapter as are other measures of effect size for such data.

Recall that Rosenthal and Rubin (1982) intended the previously discussed BESD to rectify the perceived problem of the use of r^2 causing an undervaluing of effect size. In the BESD example we discussed a way (however problematic) to interpret an r_{pb} of .20 that increased the apparent practical importance of the finding (Table 4.1). On the other hand, r^2 in that example is $(.20)^2 = .04$, indicating that only 4% of the variance of the dependent variable is related to varying treatment from a to b. (If 4% of the variability in the dependent variable is determined by variation of the independent variable, then $1 - r^2 = 1 - 4\% = 96\%$ of the variability of the dependent variable is not determined by variation of the independent variable. The quantity $1 - r^2$ is called the *coefficient of nondetermination*.) Even Cohen's (1988) "large" effect size of $r_{pop} \geq .371$ results in $r_{pop}^2 \geq .138$, that is, less than 14% of the variance of the dependent variable being associated with variation of the independent variable when the effect size has attained Cohen's minimum standard for large.

Breaugh (2003) provided examples of the underestimation of the practical importance of an effect size that can be caused by incautious or incomplete interpretation of the coefficient of determination. Even modest values of the coefficient of determination can be of practical significance. Recall that a numerically small effect size can have great practical significance when it involves a very important dependent variable and is applicable to a vast number of people.

Consider the correlation between scores on a personnel-selection test and performance on the job (a *predictive validity coefficient*, r_{pv}). A typical validity coefficient of $r_{pv} = .4$ results in a coefficient of determination of "only" .16. However, a validity coefficient of .4 indicates that for each one-standard-deviation-unit increase in mean test score that an employer sets as a minimum criterion for hiring, there is an estimated .40 standard-deviation-unit increase in job performance. Such an increase may well be of substantial economic significance to an employer (Hunter & Schmidt, 2004).

The fact that each one-standard-deviation-unit increase in the mean value of X results in an estimated r-standard-deviation-unit increase in Y (e.g., increase by $.4s$ units when $r = .4$) can be explained by recourse to the z-score form of the equation for a prediction line:

$$z_y' = r z_x, \qquad (4.20)$$

where z_y' is the predicted z score on the Y variable. Because z scores are deviation scores in standard deviation units one observes in Equation 4.20 that the value of r determines by how many standard deviation units of Y the value of Y is predicted to increase for individuals for each standard-deviation-unit increase in their scores on X (i.e., r is the multiplier). We observe later that a change in Y per unit change in X can be a very informative effect size. (Observe that Equation 4.20 also satisfies a verbal equation for a straight line: a variable $[z_y']$ equals a constant $[0$, and therefore omitted from the equation$]$ plus the product of a constant $[r]$ and a variable $[z_x]$.)

DIRECTIONLESS EFFECT SIZE

A second reason for the decreasing use of r^2 as an estimator of an effect size by some researchers is that, unlike a d or r (or r_{pb}), it is directionless; it cannot be negative. For example, if in gender research males had been assigned the lower of the two numerical codes (e.g., $X = 1$ for males and $X = 2$ for females), when r_{pb}

is positive one knows that males produced the lower mean score on the dependent variable, and when r_{pb} is negative one knows that males produced the higher mean. However, of course, the square of a positive r and the square of a negative r of the same magnitude are the same value. Therefore, meta-analysts cannot meaningfully average the values of r_{pb}^2 from a set of studies in which some yielded negative and some yielded positive values of r_{pb}. Primary researchers who report r^2 should always report it together with r or r_{pb}, either of which can be averaged by meta-analysts.

FURTHER DISCUSSIONS

A third reason for the current disfavor of r^2 among some researchers is the availability of alternative kinds of measures of effect size that did not exist or were not widely known when r^2 became popular many decades ago. Fourth, those who advocate the use of methods that are more robust than Pearson's correlation coefficient to measure the relationship between variables would also argue that another reason to avoid the use of the coefficient of determination is that its magnitude can be affected by the previously discussed conditions that can affect the correlation coefficient, such as curvilinearity (not relevant to r_{pb}) and outliers.

Tips and Pitfalls

Regarding the typically small values of r^2 outside of the physical sciences, human behavior is *multiply determined*; that is, there are many genetic and experiential differences among people. Therefore, pre-existing genetic and experiential differences among individuals likely often determine much of the variability in the dependent variables that are used in behavioral science and in other "people sciences," often leaving little opportunity for a researcher's single independent variable to contribute a relatively large proportion of the total variability. In more informative factorial designs (Chapters 7 and 10 through 12) one can vary multiple independent variables to estimate their combined and individual relationships with the scores on the dependent variable. Also, unless one is very unwise in one's choice of independent variables, the *multiple correlation*, R, between a set of independent variables and a dependent variable will be greater than any of the separate values of r, and the resulting *multiple coefficient of determination*, R^2, will be greater than any of the separate values of r^2. Multiple correlation and R^2 are main topics of Chapter 10, and other measures of the proportion of explained variance are discussed in Chapter 6 and thereafter.

SLOPES AS EFFECT SIZES

Recall from Equation 4.20 that the z-score form of the prediction (regression) equation is $z_y' = rz_x$. The slope (called the *standardized beta regression coefficient or standardized beta weight*, β) of the line simply equals r in *this* form of the equation. The *raw-score form* of this equation is given by Equation 4.19, where the slope of the line, ($\Delta Y'/\Delta X = B$), is given by $r(s_y/s_x)$, which is called an *unstandardized regression weight* or *unstandardized regression coefficient (B)*. (The term "weight" relates to the fact that β and B determine how much weight z_x or X is given when using them to predict z_y or Y, respectively.) The β and B coefficients are examples of correlational effect sizes because the stronger the relationship between X and Y the larger these coefficients.

When Y is an observed variable of practical importance the unstandardized slope of the prediction line in raw-score form estimates a very informative effect size. For an example of the usefulness of the slope, the estimated increase in fuel mileage ($\Delta Y'$) for each 1 lb reduction in vehicular weight ($\Delta X = 1$) is an effect size of great practical importance. We are assuming the case of a linear relationship between X and Y over the range of X that is of interest because $\Delta Y'/\Delta X = r(s_y/s_x)$ only for linear relationships.

GROWTH MODELING

In *growth-modeling designs* that compare the changes in a series of observations over time for two groups (Chapter 3), the difference between the slopes for the two groups is often used for the effect size (Feingold, 2009; Raudenbush & Liu, 2001). Also consult Nakagawa and Cuthill (2007) and Kuljanin, Braun, and DeShon (in press). For a set of articles on measuring change in individuals longitudinally using different models of growth consult the special issue on this topic in the journal *Educational Research and Evaluation*, 2008, volume 14, issue 4.

FURTHER DISCUSSIONS

The raw-score form of the equation for the regression line and for the slope (effect size) are more appropriate than the standardized form (i.e., z-score form) when the independent and dependent variables are familiar variables that are of interest themselves, not merely measures of underlying constructs. For example, consider the dependent variable personal income and the independent variable years of college attended. An effect size is easier to understand if a researcher reports that there is a specified dollar amount of increased personal future income per each additional year of college attended (i.e., effect size = slope= [income increase/each year of attendance]) than if it were instead reported that there is, say, a 0.3 standard-deviation-unit increase in income per each standard-deviation-unit increase in years of college attended. (Also, income data are skewed so the standard deviation is a problematic measure of variability in this case.)

Abelson (1997) considered the unstandardized slope to be superior to r as an effect size because, unlike r, (a) meaningful units are possible with the slope as in the previous examples (i.e., vehicular weight, fuel mileage, income, years), and (b) the slope of a straight line is not influenced by restricted range (i.e., the slope of a straight line is constant throughout the range of the variables). Consult Cohen et al. (2003) and Smithson (2003) for discussions of constructing a confidence interval for the slope.

Methods that are likely more robust for testing hypotheses or constructing a .95 confidence interval for a slope in least-squares regression are incorporated in the R software functions olshc4 and lsfitci, which were discussed, along with alternative estimators of slope, by Wilcox (2005a). The R software is freely downloadable at http://cran.R-project.org. The R functions that are cited in this book are generally in the files Rallfunv1-v7 and Rallfunv2-v7, which are freely downloadable, courtesy of Rand Wilcox, at www-rcf.usc.edu/~rwilcox/. The R functions are also available as S-PLUS functions in the commercial software S-PLUS in the files allfunv1-v7 and allfunv2-v7, these latter files also being freely downloadable at the Wilcox site. Smithson (2003) discussed a *d*-like estimator of effect size relating to a regression coefficient.

EFFECT SIZES FOR MEDIATING AND MODERATING VARIABLES

A *mediating variable* (*mediator*) is one which intervenes between the predictor X and the predicted Y and is responsible for all or part of the relationship between X and Y. In nonexperimental research, when there is a relationship between a classificatory X variable (e.g., gender, ethnicity, political or religious affiliation) and a Y variable there is often a mediating variable (e.g., biological or socioeconomic) that is posited to underlie all or part of the relationship. Preacher (2008) critiqued existing measures of effect size for mediating variables (such measures also being called *indirect effects*) and proposed effect size measures involving slopes or the proportion of variance explained by a mediating variable. For a brief account consult Preacher, who also proposed graphical methods for complementing effect sizes for mediation. For more detailed accounts consult Preacher and Hayes (2008) and Preacher and Kelley (2011).

Simulations by Cheung (2009) on the performances of 11 methods for constructing a confidence interval for a standardized measure of indirect effect size in a mediation analysis indicated that some methods maintained coverage probability best, including two bootstrap methods. Fairchild, MacKinnon, Taborga, and Taylor (2009) simulated the performances of their proposed proportion-of-variance-accounted-for measures of effect size for mediating variables that appeared to have acceptably small bias. However, de Hues (in press) reported that this method can be problematic.

Mediating variables should not be confused with *moderating variables* (*moderators*) that modify the relationship between X and Y. When the relationship between X and Y is modified at different levels of a third variable, such a third variable is called a moderator and such modification is called an *interaction* between X and the moderating variable. An example of gender as a moderating variable would be a case in which the relationship between the duration of a treatment (X) and the amount of benefit (Y) from the treatment is different for women and men. Effect sizes for interaction are discussed in Chapters 7, 10, and 12. Mediating and moderating variables are more likely to be detected if continuous variables are treated as such instead of being dichotomized. Dichotomizing lowers effect sizes for mediating and moderating variables.

SUMMARY

When X and Y are continuous random variables the sample Pearson correlation coefficient, r, is commonly used as an estimator of effect size in terms of the size (magnitude of r) and direction (sign of r) of a linear relationship between X and Y. When one of the variables is *truly* dichotomous, such as female and male or Treatment a and Treatment b, the correlation is commonly called a point-biserial correlation, r_{pb}. If the dichotomy is an arbitrary slicing of a continuous variable into two numerically coded categories, or if a continuous variable is sliced into several numerically coded ordered categories (e.g., 1 = "low," 2 = "medium," 3 = "high,"), r_{pb} or r, respectively, will usually be reduced. However, if an r_{pb} is based on extreme groups that are selected only from the low and high ends of a continuous variable r_{pb} will be inflated.

Sample r and r_{pb} are negatively biased (i.e., tending to underestimate) estimators of r_{pop}, but the bias is generally slight for samples at least of moderate size, so an approximately unbiased adjusted version of sample r or r_{pb} is rarely used. Also, assumptions of bivariate normality and homoscedasticity are relevant if a sample r is to be used to make inferences to a population. For example, the nonnormal shapes of the population distributions of X and Y can lower the maximum value of r_{pop} below |1|, such as skew of X and Y in opposite directions lowering the maximum value. Inferential use of r_{pb} does not and cannot require normality of the dichotomous X grouping variable. However, using equal sample sizes for the two groups avoids skew of that variable that can lower r_{pb}, causing it further to underestimate r_{pop} as a measure of effect size. Outliers can affect correlation coefficients and confidence intervals, so the reporting of scatterplots is strongly recommended. A scatterplot can also suggest heteroscedasticity and curvilinearity, the latter of which lowers the value r_{pop} because, again, this correlation only reflects the degree of the linear relationship between X and Y.

Construction of confidence intervals for r_{pop} is strongly recommended. A widely used method is based on Fisher's conversion of r to Z_r, but researchers should consider using methods that are apparently more robust. Among more robust measures of correlation there are nonparametric (e.g., rho and tau) and modern parametric methods. A null–counternull interval can also be constructed, but such an interval provides information that is different from the kind of information that is provided by a confidence interval.

As was observed in Equation 4.2, the value of r_{pb} is sensitive to the base rates (relative sample sizes) of the two samples (e.g., proportions of schizophrenics and non-schizophrenics). If the base rates of the two samples are different from the base rates in the two populations, and one is interested in r_{pb} for the purpose of predicting Y from X or X from Y, the r_{pb} as often calculated (i.e., not taking base rates into account) is only descriptive of the sample; it is not generalizable to the population. If r_{pb} is not being used for prediction, but instead it is being used to estimate r_{pop} as a measure of effect size in the population in terms of the magnitude of the relationship between the grouping variable X and the dependent variable Y, unequal base rates in the population need not be taken into account.

A researcher's purpose in calculating r_{pb} (either prediction or estimation of effect size) may not be the same as the interest that some readers of the report have in r_{pb}, so researchers should consider reporting the versions of r_{pb} that do and do not take the base rates into account, with an interpretation of each. In the case of experimental research the two populations are generally conceptualized as being of equal size, so it is again recommended that the two sample sizes be equal, or that the equation for correcting r_{pb} for unequal sample sizes be used, to avoid underestimating r_{pop} by r_{pb}. Also, in this chapter we made recommendations regarding the choice of r_{pop} or d_{pop} as the effect size that should be estimated.

The values of sample correlation coefficients and other estimators of effect size can also be attenuated by unreliability of scores on the dependent variable, unreliability of measurement or of administration of the independent variable, and restricted range. There are equations for correcting estimates of effect size for unreliability or restricted range.

Cohen's criteria for small, medium, and large effect sizes provide an indication of the magnitudes of effects generally found across wide areas of behavioral research, but those criteria do not necessarily apply to a given effect size from a specific area of research. What may be a large effect size in one area of research may be a small effect size in another area. Also, an effect of a given size may be of greater practical significance in one area of research than in another.

The BESD has assumptions and limitations that are important. It should be considered to be an alternative hypothetical way to interpret a correlation coefficient. The sample coefficient of determination effect size interprets a sample correlation coefficient in terms of its square, which in many cases estimates the population proportion of variance in the dependent variable that is attributable to that variable's linear relationship with the independent variable. In nonexperimental research the word "determination" should not imply a causal connection between the two variables. The slope of a straight regression line of best fit that relates X and Y can be a very informative effect size. Also, there are effect sizes for mediating and moderating variables.

Because of the many factors that can influence a correlation coefficient, researchers should report and discuss, when available and applicable, sample sizes, estimates of population base rates, ranges of X and Y in the sample relative to what they might be in the population, relevant demographics, and reliability coefficients. Correction for scale coarseness should also be considered where relevant.

QUESTIONS

4.1 Define (a) a *truly dichotomous* variable, (b) *BESD*, (c) *coefficients* of *determination* and *nondetermination*, (d) *bivariate normality*, (e) *reliability coefficient*, (f) *Yule's paradox*, (g) *influence*, (h) *good and bad leverage points*, (i) *construct validity*, (j) *internal-consistency reliability*, (k) *direct and indirect range restriction*, (l) *residual sum of squares*, (m) *regression coefficient*, (n) *biserial correlation*, (o) *spurious correlation*, (p) *mediating and moderating variables*.

4.2 State two possible consequences of dichotomizing a continuous variable.

4.3 Describe the simple procedure for coding a qualitative dichotomous variable for calculating its correlation with a continuous variable (assume equal samples sizes and equal population sizes).

4.4 Define point-biserial r as it is commonly used, and what is its interpretation in the sample when it is negative and when it is positive?

4.5 What is the relationship between a two-tailed test of the null hypothesis that the point-biserial r in the population is 0 and a two-tailed test of the null hypothesis that the two population means are equal?

4.6 What is the direction of bias of the sample r and r_{pb}, and which two factors influence the magnitude of this bias and in what way does each exert its influence?

4.7 What is the focus of researchers who are interested in a null–counternull interval for r_{pop}?

4.8 In what circumstance might skew be especially problematic for r, and in what way?

4.9 What is the effect of curvilinearity on r or r_{pop}?

4.10 Describe a circumstance (other than sample size) in which an outlier of a given degree of extremeness would have greater influence on the value of r than that same outlier would have in another circumstance.

4.11 How does the possible reduction of the value of r_{pb} by unequal sample size relate to Question 4.8?

4.12 Why might it be problematic to compare values of r_{pb} from different experiments that used unequal sample sizes, and what can resolve this problem?

4.13 Define *test–retest unreliability*, and what is its effect on a correlation coefficient and on statistical power?

4.14 What is the difference between the information that is provided by confidence intervals and null–counternull intervals?

4.15 Name and describe three distributions that are relevant regarding assumptions in the case of r_{pb}.

4.16 State three possible consequences, if there is heteroscedasticity, of using software that assumes homoscedasticity when testing the null hypothesis that r_{pop} equals 0.

4.17 What is the relevance of possible differences in the reliabilities of different measures of the dependent variable for comparisons of effect sizes across studies?

4.18 How can unreliability of the independent variable come about?

4.19 Define and discuss how *treatment integrity* relates to this chapter.

4.20 List five reasons why the adjustment for unreliability is rarely used.

4.21 Discuss what the text calls a "philosophical objection" that some researchers have regarding the use of an adjustment for unreliability.

4.22 Define *restricted range* and state how it typically (not always) influences r.

4.23 How can restricted range occur in a dependent variable?

4.24 What is the justification for, and the possible problem with, the labels small, medium, and large effect sizes?

4.25 Why should one not be overly impressed with a reported large estimated effect size of which there has not yet been an attempt at replication?

4.26 How does one find the difference between the two success percentages in a BESD?

4.27 Discuss three possible limitations of the BESD.

4.28 How might the word *determination* be misinterpreted in the label *coefficient of determination*?

4.29 What is the usual effect of restricted range on statistical power?

4.30 Define *strength of manipulation* and what is its effect on effect size?

4.31 Describe and discuss three reasons for the reduced use of the coefficient of determination in recent years.

4.32 Discuss why it should not be surprising that coefficients of determination are typically not very large in research involving human behavior (ignoring the issue of squaring for the purpose of this question).

4.33 Regarding Equations 4.19 and 4.20, explain why one follows from the other.

4.34 Explain why Equations 4.19 and 4.20 satisfy equations for straight lines.

4.35 Using Equation 4.19, what is the predicted value of Y when there is no correlation between X and Y, and in what way is the correct answer consistent with Equation 4.20?

4.36 When are unequal base rates problematic in nonexperimental research?

4.37 What are the considerations when one is deciding whether to estimate r_{pop} or d_{pop} when planning research?

4.38 What is the relationship between Pearson's r and Spearman's *rho*?

4.39 What is the relationship among reliability, true variance, and total variance?

4.40 In what way might the label "unexplained variance" be misinterpreted?

4.41 With regard to making predictions, what is the practical implication of the z-score form of the regression equation?

4.42 Discuss the unstandardized slope as an effect size.

4.43 Discuss the tetrachoric correlation: its purpose, assumptions, and factors that influence its value.

4.44 Use Equation 4.18 to convert $r_{pb} = .3957336$ to d. Why is it not surprising that the result is not the same as was found in the text when using Equation 4.17 to make the conversion?

4.45 Use available software to (a) confirm the value of r_{pb} that was reported in this chapter *as an estimator of effect size*, not for the purpose of prediction (i.e., ignore base rates), for the data that compared the two groups of mothers and (b) construct a 95% confidence interval for the r_{pop} for these data using the conversion of r to Z_r and a confidence interval using any other method available to you, and discuss any difference between the two confidence intervals. The data are in Question 3.33.

5 Effect Size Measures That Go Beyond Comparing Two Averages

INTRODUCTION

The unstandardized and standardized difference between means and the point-biserial correlation are not the only effect sizes that reflect a difference between two groups with respect to a continuous dependent variable. This chapter considers effect sizes that can reflect important differences between two groups other than differences in their *locations* (e.g., other than their means).

PROBABILITY OF SUPERIORITY: INDEPENDENT GROUPS

Consider estimating an effect size that would reflect what would happen if one were able to take each score from population *a* and compare it with each score from population *b*, one at a time, to see which of the two scores is larger, such comparisons being repeated until every score from population *a* had been compared to every score from population *b*. If most of the time in these pairings of a score from population *a* and a score from population *b* the score from population *a* is the higher of the two this would indicate a tendency for superior performance in population *a*, and vice versa if most of the time the higher score in the pair is the one from population *b*. (We are assuming for the moment that higher scoring is desirable, but the methods that we discuss do not depend on such an assumption.) The result of such a method for comparing two populations is a measure of effect size that does not involve comparing the locations, such as means or medians, of the two distributions. This effect size is defined as "the probability that a randomly sampled member of population *a* will have a score (Y_a) that is higher than the score (Y_b) attained by a randomly sampled member of population *b*." This definition should become much clearer in the examples that follow.

The notation that is used here for the current effect size is $\Pr(Y_a > Y_b)$, where Pr stands for probability. This $\Pr(Y_a > Y_b)$ measure has no widely used name, although names have been given to its estimators (Grissom, 1994a, 1994b, 1996; Grissom & Kim, 2001; McGraw & Wong, 1992). In the references that were just cited Grissom named an estimator of $\Pr(Y_a > Y_b)$ the *probability of superiority* (PS).

In this book we instead use the name probability of superiority to label the parameter $\Pr(Y_a > Y_b)$ itself (not an estimator of it), so that we now define

$$PS = \Pr(Y_a > Y_b).\qquad(5.1)$$

(Temporarily we are assuming no tied scores between groups.) The *PS* measures the *stochastic* (i.e., *probabilistic*) *superiority* of one group's scores over another group's scores. Because the *PS* is a probability and probabilities range from 0 to 1, the *PS* ranges from 0 to 1. Therefore, the two most extreme results when comparing populations *a* and *b* are (a) *PS* = 0, in which every member of population *a* is outscored by every member of population *b*, and (b) *PS* = 1, in which every member of population *a* outscores every member of population *b*. The least extreme overall result (no effect of group membership one way or the other) would be *PS* = .5, in which members of populations *a* and *b* outscore each other equally often.

A proportion in a sample estimates a probability in a population. For example, if one counts, say, 52 heads results in a sample of 100 (random) tosses of a coin, the proportion of heads in that sample's results is 52/100 = .52, and the estimate of the probability of heads for a population of random tosses of that coin would be .52. Similarly, the *PS* can be estimated from the proportion of times that the n_a participants in sample *a* outscore the n_b participants in sample *b* in head-to-head comparisons of scores within all possible pairings of the score of a member of one sample with the score of a member of the other sample. The total number of possible such comparisons is given by the product of the two sample sizes, $n_a n_b$. Therefore, if, say, $n_a = n_b = 10$ (sample sizes do not have to be equal), and in 70 of the $n_a n_b = 100$ comparisons the score from the member of sample *a* is greater than the score from the member of sample *b*, then the estimate of the *PS* is 70/100 = .70.

SIMPLE EXAMPLE OF THE PROBABILITY OF SUPERIORITY

For a simple example, suppose that sample *a* has three members, persons A, B, and C; and sample *b* has three members, persons D, E, and F. There are $n_a n_b$ = 3 × 3 = 9 total possible pairings of scores from a member of each sample to be used in order to observe who has the higher score: pairings of persons A versus D, A versus E, A versus F, B versus D, B versus E, B versus F, C versus D, C versus E, and C versus F. Suppose that in five of these nine pairings of scores the scores of persons A, B, and C (sample *a*) are greater than the scores of persons D, E, and F (sample *b*), and in the other four pairings sample *b* "wins." In this example the estimate of the *PS* is 5/9 = .56. (In actual research one would not want to base the estimate on such small samples.)

The estimate of *PS* will be greater than .5 when members of sample *a* outscore members of sample *b* in more than one-half of the pairings, and the estimate will be less than .5 when members of sample *a* are outscored by members of sample *b* in more than one-half of the pairings. When there are ties the simplest solution is to allocate one-half of the ties to each group. Thus, in the aforementioned example if members of sample a had outscored members of sample b not five but four times in the nine pairings, with one tie, one-half of the tie would be awarded as a superior outcome (a win) to each sample. Therefore, there would be 4.5 superior outcomes for each sample in the nine pairings of its members with the members of the other sample, and the estimate of the PS would therefore be 4.5/9 = .5.

ESTIMATION USING THE MANN–WHITNEY U STATISTIC

The number of times that a randomly selected score from one specified sample is higher than the randomly selected score from the other sample to which it is compared (i.e., the number of wins for, say, sample a) is called the Mann–Whitney U statistic. Recalling that the total number of possible comparisons (pairings) is $n_a n_b$, and now using $\hat{p}_{a>b}$ to denote the sample proportion that estimates the PS we define

$$\hat{p}_{a>b} = \frac{U}{n_a n_b}. \tag{5.2}$$

In other words, in Equation 5.2 the numerator is the number of wins for a specified sample and the denominator is the number of opportunities to win in head-to-head comparisons of each of its member's scores with each of the scores of the other sample's members. Again, if there are ties, one of the solutions is to add one-half of the number of ties to U in Equation 5.2. The value of U can be calculated manually but it can be laborious to do so except for very small samples. Although currently major statistical software packages do not calculate $\hat{p}_{a>b}$ many do calculate the U statistic (or the equivalent Wilcoxon W_m statistic). If the value of U is obtained through the use of software one then divides this outputted U by $n_a n_b$ to find the estimator, $\hat{p}_{a>b}$. Currently, U can be calculated using the NPAR1WAY procedure in SAS, and using the sequence Analyze, Nonparametric Tests, and Two Independent Samples in IBM SPSS. If software provides the equivalent Wilcoxon W_m rank-sum statistic instead of the U statistic, and if there are no ties, find U by calculating $U = W_m - [n_s(n_s + 1)]/2$, where n_s is the smaller sample size or, if sample sizes are equal, the size of one sample. Observe that Equation 5.2 satisfies the general equation, which was shown in Chapter 1, for the relationship between an estimate of effect size (ES_{est}) and a test statistic (TS): $ES_{est} = TS/[f(N)]$. In the case of Equation 5.2, $ES_{est} = \hat{p}_{a>b}$, $TS = U$, and $f(N) = n_a n_b$.

CHOOSING BETWEEN THE PROBABILITY OF SUPERIORITY AND d_{pop}

Researchers who focus on means and assume normality may prefer to use the t test to compare the means and use the d_{pop} of Chapter 3 for an effect size. Researchers who do not assume normality and who are interested in a measure of the extent to which the scores in one group are probabilistically superior to those in another group will prefer to use the PS or a similar measure that is discussed later. Also, under nonnormality and small samples, the U test appears to be more powerful than the t test for detecting a shift in location (Weber & Sawilowsky, 2009).

(Shift is discussed later in this chapter.) As is true of d_{pop}, the *PS* is an especially useful measure of effect size when the units of the measure of the dependent variable are not familiar (e.g., points on a test of depression).

As is discussed in Chapter 8, some measures of effect size for contingency tables can be converted to the *PS*, and, as is discussed in Chapter 9, the *PS* is applicable to ordinal measures of dependent variables. Therefore, the *PS* might be considered to be a unifying effect size. However, because many readers of research reports are accustomed to the comparison of means, authors who provide estimates of the *PS* should consider also providing Cohen's *d* or Glass' d_G.

TESTING SIGNIFICANCE AND CONSTRUCTING CONFIDENCE INTERVALS

Under homoscedasticity one may use the original *U* test to test H_0: *PS* = .5 against H_{alt}: *PS* ≠ .5. However, the original *U* test that is usually provided by software is not robust against heteroscedasticity because the test assumes that the two distributions have identical shapes.

Reiczigel, Zakariás, and Rózsa (2005) reported good control of Type I error by their proposed bootstrap rank-based two-tailed Welch *t* test to test H_0: *PS* = .5 under nonnormality. Brunner, Domhof, and Langer (2002), Brunner and Munzel (2000), and Cliff (1996b) discussed inference making for the *PS* and related measures that overcome the shortcomings of the *U* test. Consult Wilcox (1996, 2005a), Vargha and Delaney (2000), and Delaney and Vargha (2002) for extensive discussions of robust methods for testing H_0: *PS* = .5.

Arguments in support of the use of the *PS* and discussions of its relationships with other measures of effect size were provided by Acion, Peterson, Temple, and Arndt (2006a; also consult their authors' reply, 2006b, and their correction, 2007), Kraemer and Kupfer (2006), Newcombe (2006b), and Ruscio (2008a). The *PS* can also be used to compare a group of interest to a normative group (Newcombe).

Wilcox presented a Minitab macro (Wilcox, 1996) and S-PLUS and R software functions (Wilcox, 2005a) for constructing a confidence interval for the *PS* that is based on Fligner and Policello's (1981) heteroscedasticity-adjusted *U* statistic (U'), and one based on a method by Mee (1990). Newcombe (2006b, 2006c) developed methods for constructing approximate confidence intervals for the *PS* and compared them to earlier methods. When sample sizes and $\hat{p}_{a>b}$ were moderate there was not much difference among the confidence intervals constructed by all of the methods studied.

FURTHER DISCUSSIONS

Refer to Vargha and Delaney (2000) for further critiques of alternative methods for constructing a confidence interval for the *PS*, equations for manual calculation, and for extension of the *PS* to comparisons of multiple groups. Also refer to Brunner and Puri (2001) for extensions of the *PS* to multiple groups and to factorial designs. Brunner and Munzel (2000) and Cliff (1996b) presented further robust methods that can be used to test the null hypothesis that *PS* = .5, and to provide an estimate of the *PS* and construct a confidence interval for it. These methods seem to be applicable when there are ties, heteroscedasticity, or both. Mee's (1990) method assumes that there are no ties. Wilcox (2003, 2005a) provided accessible discussions of the Brunner–Munzel and Cliff methods and S-PLUS and R software functions for the calculations for the current case of only two groups and for extension to the case in which groups are compared two at a time from multiple groups. (Wilcox called the *PS p* or *P*, and Vargha and Delaney called it *A*.) For further favorable evaluation of the Brunner–Munzel method consult Reiczigel et al. (2005), but also consult Cliff (1996b), Fagerland and Sandvik (2009), and Wilcox (2009a). Cliff's (1996b) method may better control Type I error when sample sizes are very small (Neuhäuser, Lösch, & Jöckel, 2007).

Recall the concept of equivalence testing from Chapter 2. A method for equivalence testing when using the *PS* was provided by Wellek and Hampel (1999). Finally, if the grouping variable represents a true dichotomy instead of an artificial dichotomization, $p_{a>b}$ is not influenced by a difference in sample sizes (Ruscio, 2008a).

TIES

Theoretically, if a dependent variable is continuous, as is assumed by the Mann–Whitney–Wilcoxon test, there can be no tied scores. However, in practice dependent variables are inherently discrete (discontinuous), or continuous latent variables are measured coarsely, either case resulting in possible ties between groups. Fay (2006) studied the consequences for Type I error, robustness, and statistical power for nine methods of resolving ties between groups when using the Mann–Whitney–Wilcoxon test or five other nonparametric tests.

Tips and Pitfalls

The simple method of dropping ties and reducing sample size performed very poorly under all conditions that Fay (2006) simulated. (This method should not be confused with acceptable methods that ignore ties but do not reduce sample size.) The method of randomly resolving each tie in favor of one or the other group performed best in terms of controlling Type I error while maintaining power under most of the simulated conditions. Fay acknowledged the objection to this random-resolution method on the grounds that it renders the outcome of a statistical test dependent on a secondary random event. Objections likely can be made to any other tie-resolving method. For further discussions of ties consult Brunner and Munzel (2000), Fay (2003), and Randles (2001).

WORKED EXAMPLE OF THE PROBABILITY OF SUPERIORITY

Recall from Chapter 3 the example in which the scores of the mothers of schizophrenic children (sample *a*) were compared to those of the mothers of normal children (sample *b*). We observed in Chapter 3 that there is a moderately large estimated effect size involving the type of mother and the score on a measure of

healthy parent–child relationship, as was indicated by $d_G = -.77$. We now estimate the *PS* for the data of this example. Because $n_a = n_b = 20$ in this example,
$n_a n_b = 20 \times 20 = 400$. Four hundred is too many pairings for calculating U
manually conveniently. Therefore, one uses software (many kinds of common
statistical software can do this) to find that for these data $U = 103$. Then, calculating the estimate of the *PS* using Equation 5.2, $\hat{p}_{a>b} = U/n_a n_b = 103/400 = .26$. This
result estimates that in the populations there is a .26 probability that a randomly
sampled mother of a schizophrenic child will outscore a randomly sampled
mother of a normal child.

Under the assumption of homoscedasticity one can test H_0: $PS = .5$ using the
ordinary U test or equivalent W_m test, one of which is often provided by statistical software packages. Because such software reveals a statistically significant
U at $p < .05$ two-tailed for the present data one can in this case conclude that
$\hat{p}_{a>b} = .26$ indicates that the $PS \neq .5$. Specifically, assuming homoscedasticity,
one concludes that the population of schizophrenics' mothers tend to score lower
(as defined by the *PS*) when compared to the population of the normals' mothers
(i.e., $PS < .5$). A researcher who does not assume homoscedasticity should test for
statistical significance and construct a confidence interval for the *PS* using one of
the alternative robust methods that can be found in the sources that were cited in
the previous section.

LARGE-SAMPLE APPROXIMATION: MANN–WHITNEY U OR WILCOXON W_m

We reported $p < .05$ for the present result instead of reporting a specific value for
p because we are not confident in specific outputted p values beyond the .05 level
for the sample sizes in the present example, as is discussed next.

As sample sizes increase the sampling distributions of values of U or W_m
approach normality. Therefore, some software that includes the Mann–Whitney
U test or the equivalent Wilcoxon W_m test may be basing the critical values
needed for statistical significance on what is called a *large-sample approximation* of these critical values. Because some textbooks do not have tables of critical
values for these two statistics, or may have tables that lack critical values for the
particular sample sizes or for the alpha levels of interest in a particular instance
of research, recourse to a table of the normal curve or normal density function
in software is convenient. Unfortunately, the literature is inconsistent in its recommendations about how large samples should be before the convenient normal
curve provides a satisfactory approximation to the sampling distributions of these
statistics. However, computer simulations by Fahoome (2002) indicated that, if
sample sizes are equal, each $n = 15$ is a satisfactory minimum when testing at
the .05 alpha level and each $n = 29$ is a satisfactory minimum when testing
at the .01 level. Fay (2002) provided Fortran 90 programs for use by researchers
who need exact critical values for W_m for a wide range of sample sizes and for a
wide range of alpha levels.

Fagerland and Sandvik (2009) conducted extensive simulations that
indicated that the rate of Type I error of the large-sample approximate

Mann–Whitney–Wilcoxon test can be greatly influenced by moderate differences in variances and moderate skew, the more so when the two distributions have different degrees of skew. Similar problems were found by those authors for the Fligner–Policello and the Brunner–Munzel tests, with the latter generally performing better.

AREA UNDER THE CURVE

Many authors in medical statistics and other fields write about $\Pr(Y_a > Y_b)$ in terms of what is called the area under the *receiver operating characteristic*, using the acronyms *ROC* or *AUC* (*area under the curve*; Kraemer, 2008). This is an elegant and useful approach when writing for statisticians. However, we believe that the verbal definition of the *PS* and the common notation $\Pr(Y_a > Y_b)$ that we and some other authors use are more understandable for many consumers of statistical results. Kraemer proposed methods based on the *AUC* for determining (a) on what kind of person a treatment or a health-risk factor has an effect (i.e., determining dichotomous moderating variables), (b) how such an effect comes about (i.e., determining dichotomous mediating variables), and (c) how clinically significant the effect sizes of such moderators and mediators are.

GENERALIZED ODDS RATIO

Because the maximum probability or proportion equals 1, the sum of the probabilities or proportions of occurrences of all of the possible outcomes of an event must sum to 1. (For the simplest example, the probability that a toss of an unbiased coin will produce either a head or a tail equals .5 + .5 = 1.) Therefore, if there are no ties then $\Pr(Y_a > Y_b) + \Pr(Y_a < Y_b) = 1$, $\hat{p}_{a>b} + \hat{p}_{a<b} = 1$, and $\hat{p}_{a<b} = 1 - \hat{p}_{a>b}$. Thus, when there are no ties, an approximate estimator of another kind of effect size, namely, Agresti's (1980, 2010) *generalized odds ratio* (OR_{gpop}) parameter, arises by calculating the ratio

$$OR_g = \frac{\hat{p}_{a>b}}{\hat{p}_{b>a}}. \tag{5.3}$$

The inverse of this ratio can also be used with the appropriate reversal of the interpretation of the result. The current estimated parameter (also known as *Agresti's alpha*) is

$$OR_{gpop} = \frac{\Pr(Y_a > Y_b)}{\Pr(Y_b > Y_a)}. \tag{5.4}$$

The OR_{gpop} measures the odds (not the probability) that a randomly drawn outcome from one population will be superior to a randomly drawn outcome from the other population. Consult Browne (2010) for discussion of construction of a confidence interval for such odds from a known p level and N from a t test, when assumptions are satisfied.

Tips and Pitfalls

Because it ignores ties the original OR_{gpop} can give the impression that an effect is larger than would be the case if ties were taken into account. If there are ties, then one-half of the ties can be added to the value of U that is used to calculate the estimator in the numerator of Equation 5.3 and one-half of the ties can be added to the value of U that is used to calculate the estimator in the denominator of Equation 5.3. Such equal allocation of ties results in estimation of a modified version of OR_g (O'Brien & Castelloe, 2007). (A tie-breaking method that does not change the value of the modified OR_{gpop} and renders Agresti's OR_{gpop} identical to the modified OR_{gpop} is discussed in Chapter 9 where ties are of greater concern.) When there is no relationship between the independent variable of membership in either sample a or sample b and the overall ranking of the scores on the measure of the dependent variable, $\hat{p}_{a>b} = \hat{p}_{a<b} = .5$ and $\hat{p}_{a>b}/\hat{p}_{a<b} = .5/.5 = 1$. The greater the relationship between group membership and the overall ranking of the scores in the samples the more the estimate of the generalized odds ratio moves above 1 when sample a generally has the higher-scoring member (more "wins" in the head-to-head comparisons) or away from 1 toward 0 when sample b generally has the higher-scoring member. This ratio also estimates an answer to the following question about the two populations. For all pairings of a member of population a with a member of population b, how many times more pairings would there be in which a member of population a scores higher than in which a member of population b scores higher? When using instead the ratio $\hat{p}_{b>a}/\hat{p}_{b<a}$ as an estimator (the inverse of the previous ratio) replace the word *higher* with the word *lower* in the preceding question. Unlike the *PS* and r_{pop} and their estimates, but like d_{pop}, d, and d_G, the sample and population generalized odds ratios are unbounded (i.e., ranging to infinity).

For an example consider again the data involving the two samples of mothers. Recall from a previous calculation that in this example $\hat{p}_{a>b} = .26$, so one finds now that $\hat{p}_{a<b} = 1 - \hat{p}_{a>b} = 1 - .26 = .74$, and $\hat{p}_{a<b}/\hat{p}_{a>b} = .74/.26 = 2.8$. One thus estimates, excluding ties, that in the populations there would be 2.8 times more pairings in which the schizophrenics' mothers are outscored by the normals' mothers than in which the schizophrenics' mothers outscore the normals' mothers. Alternatively worded, one estimates that the odds are nearly 3:1 that a randomly drawn mother of a normal child will outscore a randomly drawn mother of a schizophrenic child.

ASSUMPTIONS AND PROPERTIES OF THE *PS*

The original purpose of the U test was to test if scores in one population are *stochastically larger* (i.e., likely to be larger) than scores in another population, assuming that both populations have the same, but not necessarily normal, shape. (This test was later observed to be equivalent to an earlier test by Wilcoxon, the W_m rank-sum test.) In other words, the purpose of the U test was to test if there is a tendency for the score at the ith percentile of population a to be larger than the score at that same ith percentile in population b. A percentile that is frequently of interest is the 50th percentile, which is the median (*Mdn*) in general and also the mean in the case of symmetrical distributions.

Shift Model

When using the U test to test the sometimes inappropriate and uninformative (as is demonstrated later) H_0: $Mdn_{popa} = Mdn_{popb}$ against the alternative H_{alt}: $Mdn_{popa} \neq Mdn_{popb}$, one is in effect assuming that if treatment or group membership has an effect it will be always to add or always to subtract a certain constant number of points, say, k points, to each score in a group's distribution. Adding a constant k or subtracting a constant k to each score in a group shifts its distribution to the right or to the left, respectively, by k points without changing its shape.

The concept of an additive effect of treatment is called a *shift model*, in which a treatment merely always adds or always subtracts a constant number of points to what the score of each participant in a group would have been if each of those participants had been in the other group. (We consider testing the difference between two medians sometimes to be not very informative because even when two populations' medians are equal it can still be the case that $PS \neq .5$, as we soon discuss.) The t test for the difference between two means also assumes a shift model.

Tips and Pitfalls

The shift model may often not be the most realistic model of the effect of treatments (or group membership) in behavioral, psychological, educational, or medical research. It seems reasonable to assume instead that treatment may often have a varying effect on the individuals in a treated group. In this case a treatment may perhaps increase the scores of all participants by varying amounts, decrease scores of all participants by varying amounts, or increase the scores of some while decreasing the scores of others by varying amounts. In such cases scores are moved to the right and/or to the left by *varying* amounts. The well-known name for the varying effect of treatment on different individuals is *treatment × subject interaction*. Consult Howard, Kraus, and Vessey (1994) for discussion of treatment × subject interaction in relation to the *PS* and the overlap between the two group's distributions.

Chen and Luo (2004) proposed a modification of the small-sample U test (n_a, $n_b \leq 20$) to construct a confidence interval for the amount of shift (*shift parameter*) in the presence of ties. Tasdan and Sievers (2009) proposed procedures for estimating, testing, and constructing a confidence interval for a shift parameter using what is called a smoothed Mann–Whitney–Wilcoxon method.

As Delaney and Vargha (2002) pointed out with examples, the shift model, with its usual resulting comparison of means (or medians), is appropriate when one is interested in information about which treatment produces the lower or higher average score, but the *PS* is appropriate when one is interested in information about which treatment is likely to help the greater number of people. For example, a therapist may well be more interested in the latter, whereas a medical insurance company may well be more interested in information about which treatment on average results in the lower cost.

Tips and Pitfalls

The shift model is often not plausible in cases in which the researcher's hypothesis is that a treatment will *decrease* the counts of adverse events (e.g., number of cigarettes smoked, alcoholic drinks consumed, or days hospitalized). Such numbers cannot be negative. Therefore, in many such cases the treatment cannot cause a *constant* shift downward because some patients' baseline counts may be so low (e.g., infrequent smokers) that for the treatment to shift their counts as far downward as it does for patients with higher baseline counts (e.g., heavy smokers), their counts would have to be negative after treatment. Similarly, the shift model also does not apply if, prior to onset of a treatment that increases scoring, some participants already perform at or very near the highest possible score. In such cases a *constant* shift upward in the scores of all treated participants would be unlikely or impossible. Consult Callaert (1999) for further discussion of the implications of the shift model.

TECHNICAL NOTE 5.1: RELATIONSHIP BETWEEN THE *PS* AND MEDIANS

The U test and its extensions are generally best *not* considered to be tests of H_0: $Mdn_{popa} = Mdn_{popb}$ but to be tests of H_0: $Mdn_{diff} = 0$ (when there are no ties), where "diff" is the difference between a score from population a and a score from population b. This generally true statement may seem to be counterintuitive because a comparable statement about the means of two populations would not be true. That is, the difference between the means of two populations equals the mean of the differences between the scores of the two populations (i.e., the mean difference score of two equal-sized columns of data equals the difference between column means). However, it can be shown that the difference between medians is *not* equal to the median of differences (e.g., Wilcox, 2006c). Moreover, a two-tailed test of H_0: $Mdn_{diff} = 0$ is equivalent to a two-tailed test of H_0: $Pr(Y_a > Y_b) = .5$, which is the overall effect size in which we are interested here (Wilcox, 2006c). Therefore, evidence that the $PS \neq .5$ is equivalent to evidence that the typical (i.e., median) pair-wise difference between scores in population a and scores in population b is not 0. Wilcox (2006a) discussed a graphical effect size that is based on the foregoing concepts. There are robust methods for testing and constructing a confidence interval for the difference between two medians for the cases of independent groups and dependent groups (Wilcox, 2005b, 2009a).

HETEROSCEDASTICITY

The PS used as a measure of effect size is insensitive to heteroscedasticity (and outliers and population base rate difference). However, in the case of the U test of a null hypothesis about the PS that uses for the critical values the actual probability distribution of U instead of the normal approximation, heteroscedasticity can influence the result of the test because the critical values of the test were derived assuming equal shapes of the two populations, an assumption that can be violated by heteroscedasticity. Also, when instead using the normal approximation for the

U test, heteroscedasticity may result in an incorrect estimation of the standard error of U. This problem for the normal approximation can cause an increase in rate of Type I error if there is a negative relationship between the variances of the populations and the sample sizes. If instead there is a positive relationship between the variances and the sample sizes, heteroscedasticity may cause a decrease in the power of the test. For further discussions consult Delaney and Vargha (2002), Vargha and Delaney (2000), and Wilcox (2003, 2005a). Regarding precedence, because the earlier Wilcoxon W_m test is equivalent to the Mann–Whitney U test, the U test is often called the Wilcoxon–Mann–Whitney U test.

COMMON LANGUAGE EFFECT SIZE STATISTIC

When raw data are not available the PS can be estimated from sample means and variances, assuming normality and homoscedasticity, using an estimator that McGraw and Wong (1992) called the *common language effect size statistic*, denoted CL. Also consult Simonoff, Hochberg, and Reiser (1986). The CL is based on a z score, Z_{CL},

$$Z_{CL} = \frac{\overline{Y}_a - \overline{Y}_b}{\left(s_a^2 + s_b^2\right)^{1/2}}. \tag{5.5}$$

The proportion of the area under the normal curve that is below Z_{CL} is the CL statistic that estimates the PS. For example, if a $Z_{CL} = +1.00$ or -1.00 inspection of a table of the normal curve, or a normal density function in software, reveals that the PS would be estimated to be .84 or .16, respectively. For the ongoing example that compares the two groups of mothers, using Equation 5.5 and the means and variances that were presented for this study in Chapter 3, $Z_{CL} = (2.10 - 3.55)/(2.41 + 3.52)^{1/2} = -.60$. Inspecting a table of the normal curve one finds that approximately .27 of the area of the normal curve is below $z = -.60$, so the estimate of PS is .27 when the schizophrenics' mothers are group a. Observe that this estimate of .27 for the PS using the CL is very close to the estimate .26 that we previously obtained when using the raw data and $\hat{p}_{a>b}$ as the estimator. Consult Grissom and Kim (2001) for comparisons of the values of estimates using $\hat{p}_{a>b}$ and estimates using the CL when both are applied to sets of real data, and for the results of some simulations of the effect of heteroscedasticity on the two estimators. For further results of simulations of the robustness of various methods for testing H_0: $PS = .5$, consult Vargha and Delaney (2000) and Delaney and Vargha (2002). Kromrey and Coughlin (2007) provided SAS/IML macros for calculating the CL and $\hat{p}_{a>b}$, which they called $\hat{A}$ after Vargha and Delaney. Dunlop (1999) provided software to calculate the CL.

RELATIONSHIP BETWEEN THE PS AND d_{pop}

It is useful to know the relationship between the PS and d_{pop} because the two measures can provide different perspectives on the results. Also, when assumptions are satisfied, by converting an estimate of PS to estimated d_{pop} one can use tables that are based on d_{pop} (e.g., Cohen & Cohen, 1988) for estimating needed sample sizes when planning a study that will estimate PS as the effect size. Kraemer and Kupfer (2006) provided a table for estimating needed sample sizes to attain statistical power = .80 for various expected values of PS from 0 to 1.

Under normality and homoscedasticity

$$Z_{CL} = \frac{d_{pop}}{(2)^{1/2}} \approx .707 d_{pop}. \qquad (5.6)$$

That is, in this case

$$PS = \Phi\left(\frac{d_{pop}}{(2)^{1/2}}\right) \approx \Phi(.707 d_{pop}), \qquad (5.7)$$

where $\Phi()$ is commonly known as the *cumulative density function*, or *cumulative probability function*, of the standard normal curve (although mathematicians typically delete the word *cumulative* as redundant). The notation $\Phi()$ denotes the proportion of the area of the normal curve that is below the value of the z score that is given by the value in the parentheses. For example, if $d_{pop} = 1$ then the value in the parentheses on the far right side of Equation 5.7 is approximately $.707 \times 1 = .707 \approx .71$, and a table of the normal curve (or software) reveals that the proportion of the normal curve that is below $z = .71$ is approximately .760, so estimated $PS = .76$.

Under normality and homoscedasticity the estimate of the PS is approximately given by substituting d for d_{pop} in Equation 5.7. In the running example in which two samples of mothers were compared, it was estimated in Chapter 3, assuming homoscedasticity and pooling variances to calculate the standardizer, that $d_{pop} = -.84$, approximately. Applying this value to Equation 5.7 one finds that the proportion of the area under the normal curve below $z = .707(-.84) = -.59388$ is approximately .28. This value is satisfactorily close to the two previous estimates of the PS for the example that indicated that the probability that a schizophrenic's mother outscores a normal's mother is estimated to be .26 or .27. Estimates of the PS will be slightly more accurate if $1/(2)^{1/2}$ carried to more decimal places is used instead of .707 in Equation 5.7.

If one wants to convert PS to d_{pop} approximately then the procedure relating to Equation 5.7 is reversed by recourse to the *inverse cumulative density function*, again using a table or any software that provides this information (e.g., NORMSINV). (Yalta, 2008, reported on the accuracy of software for statistical distributions, including the inverse standard normal distribution.) Specifically, from Equation 5.7 it is observed that d_{pop} is equal to the number that when multiplied by .707 (or, more accurately, multiplied by $1/[2]^{1/2}$) yields a z value that has p proportion of the area of the standard normal curve below it, where $p = PS$. For example when $p = PS = .5$, $z = 0$ in the normal curve. The number that when multiplied by .707 yields 0 is, of course, also 0. Therefore, when $PS = .5$, $d_{pop} = 0$ when assumptions are satisfied. For another example, when $p = PS = .760$, one observes in a table of the normal curve or software output that $z \approx .7$. The number that when multiplied by .707 yields approximately .7 is 1. Therefore, when $PS = .760$, $d_{pop} \approx 1$, as was previously shown.

Consider again the example of the comparison of the two groups of mothers for which we estimated $PS = .28$ using Equation 5.7. Suppose that knowing the estimate $PS = .28$ we did not yet know the estimated value of d_{pop}. Inspection of a table of the normal curve indicates that approximately .28 of its area lies below $z \approx -.59$. Solving Equation 5.6 for d_{pop} yields $d_{pop} \approx Z_{CL}/.707$. However, for a more accurate result we carry Z_{CL} and $1/(2)^{1/2}$ to more decimal places than before to find that $d_{pop} \approx -.59388/.7071068 \approx -.84$, which equals the previously obtained estimate.

Consult Grissom (1994a) for equations that relate t, r_{pb}, and Z_{CL}, and consult Ruscio (2008a) for equations for approximately converting to and from d, r_{pb}, and the CL. Note that the d that was used by Ruscio was Cohen's (1988) original simplified d that was based on assuming homoscedasticity and pooling variances using N instead of degrees of freedom in the denominator. Ruscio also provided a table that compares the features of d, r_{pb}, and $\hat{p}_{a>b}$ (the latter being labeled A in Ruscio). Browne (2010) discussed the estimation of the PS from known values of the attained p level (i.e., significance level) and N from a t test when assumptions are satisfied.

TECHNICAL NOTE 5.2: THE *PS* AND ITS ESTIMATORS

The PS measures the overall tendency of scores from group a to outrank the scores from group b across all pairings of the scores of the members of each group. Therefore, the PS is an ordinal measure of effect size, reflecting not the absolute magnitudes of the paired scores but the rank order of these paired scores. Although, outside of the physical sciences, one often treats scores as if they were on an interval scale, many of the measures of dependent variables are likely monotonically, but not necessarily linearly, related to the latent variables that they are measuring. In other words, the scores presumably increase and decrease along with the latent variables (i.e., have the same rank order as the latent variables) but not necessarily to the same degree. Monotonic transformations of the data leave the ordinally oriented PS invariant. Therefore, different measures of the same dependent variable should leave the PS invariant. (Standardized-mean-difference effect sizes are invariant only under linear transformations of the measure of the dependent variable; Ruscio, 2008a.)

Theoretically, $\hat{p}_{a>b}$ is a consistent and unbiased estimator of the PS for measures of the dependent variable that are at least ordinal. A *consistent estimator* is one whose difference from the parameter that it is estimating approaches 0 as sample size increases. Also, using $\hat{p}_{a>b}$ to test H_0: $PS = .5$ against H_{alt}: $PS \neq .5$, or against a one-tailed alternative, is a *consistent test* in the sense that the power of such a test approaches 1 as sample sizes approach infinity. It can be shown that the CL strictly only estimates the PS under normality and homoscedasticity. For more discussion of the PS and its estimators consult Vargha and Delaney (2000).

EFFECT SIZES CAN MISLEAD ABOUT THE RELATIONSHIP BETWEEN DISTRIBUTIONS

A *cumulative proportion* is the proportion of the total scores that are equal to or lower than a given value of Y. For example, in a normal distribution the cumulative proportion at the mean, which is equal to the median in this case, is .5. A graph whose vertical axis depicts the values of the cumulative proportions across the values of Y is called a *cumulative distribution function* (*cdf*).

In the present case of comparing two populations or two samples the two *cdf*s may be denoted $F(Y)$ and $G(Y)$, which are read "F of Y" (meaning a function of Y) and "G of Y" (also meaning a function of Y), respectively. At each value of Y the height of the $F(Y)$ or $G(Y)$ represents the proportion of the scores in the given population or sample that are at or below that value of Y (i.e., a cumulative proportion), Y increasing from left to right on the horizontal axis of the graph. Therefore, if, say, the members of population a tend to outscore the members of population b the *cdf* for population a will tend to be *lower* than the *cdf* for population b because the proportion of the scores that are at or *below* a given value of Y will tend to be *lower* for a population whose members tend to score *higher* than the members of another population.

Consider the *cdf*s for the Y_b and Y_a scores from populations a and b, which we denote $F_b(Y)$ and $G_a(Y)$, respectively. In the sense of the *PS*, maximum probabilistic superiority of population a over population b (i.e., $\Pr(Y_a > Y_b) = 1$) corresponds to $F_b(Y) > G_a(Y)$ throughout the entire range of Y in the population (i.e., the *cdf* for population a would be lower than the *cdf* for population b throughout the range of Y). The case in which $F_b(Y) = G_a(Y)$ throughout the entire range of Y in the population corresponds to $\Pr(Y_a > Y_b) = .5$ (i.e., the two *cdf*s entirely overlap).

As is true of other effect sizes, the $\Pr(Y_a > Y_b)$ provides only a single number that cannot encapsulate possibly complex differences between two populations. A comparison of the two *cdf*s in figures such as Figures 5.1 through 5.4 demonstrates the variety of possible differences between two populations throughout the entire range of the dependent variable. Using the current notation there are two possible one-tailed alternatives to H_0: $F_b(Y) = G_a(Y)$. The first such alternative is H_{alt}: $G_a(Y) \leq F_b(Y)$, with $G_a(Y) < F_b(Y)$ at least at one value of Y. The second possible alternative to the null hypothesis is H_{alt}: $G_a(Y) \geq F_b(Y)$, with $G_a(Y_a) > F_b(Y)$ at least at one value of Y. The two-tailed alternative to H_0: $F_b(Y) = G_a(Y)$ is that $G_a(Y) \neq F_b(Y)$ at least at one value of Y and either $G_a(Y) \leq F_b(Y)$ or $G_a(Y) \geq F_b(Y)$. Testing such hypotheses is discussed in several texts on nonparametric statistics including that by Gibbons (1985). Consult Callaert (1999) for further discussion. Also consult the references that were cited earlier in this chapter for testing H_0: $PS = .5$ robustly.

Observe in Figures 5.1 through 5.4 that Callaert (1999) graphically illustrated important facts about the relationships among two *cdf*s, two medians, and the *PS*. (In these figures the vertical axes, which are $F_b(Y)$ and $G_a(Y)$, are simply labeled "Cumulative proportions.") First, Treatment a can be better or worse than

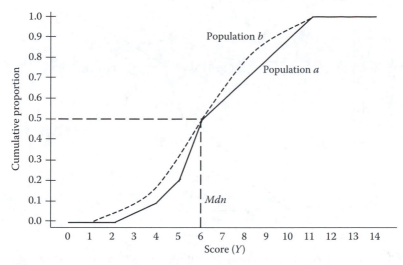

FIGURE 5.1   Although $Mdn_a = Mdn_b$, population a scores superiorly to population b nearly everywhere throughout the range of Y. (Adapted from Callaert, H., *J. Stat. Educ.*, 7, 6, 1999. Copyright 2000 by Herman Callaert. With permission.)

FIGURE 5.2   Although $Mdn_a > Mdn_b$, population b scores superiorly to population a in the regions of the left and right tails. (Adapted from Callaert, H., *J. Stat. Educ.*, 7, 7, 1999. Copyright 2000 by Herman Callaert. With permission.)

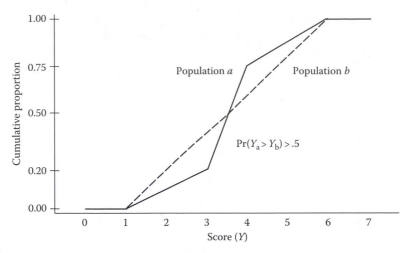

FIGURE 5.3 Although $\Pr(Y_a > Y_b) > .5$ (slightly), population b scores superiorly to population a in almost half of the range of Y. (Adapted from Callaert, H., *J. Stat. Educ.*, 7, 7, 1999. Copyright 2000 by Herman Callaert. With permission.)

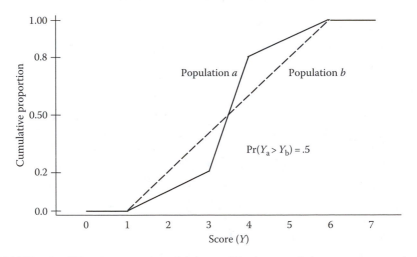

FIGURE 5.4 When $\Pr(Y_a > Y_b) = .5$ it is possible that population a scores superiorly to population b in one region of the range of Y and inferiorly to population b in another region. (Adapted from Callaert, H., *J. Stat. Educ.*, 7, 7, 1999. Copyright 2000 by Herman Callaert. With permission.)

Treatment b overall, as indicated by comparing the two *cdf*s, even when $Mdn_{popa} = Mdn_{popb}$, as is depicted in Figure 5.1. Second, Mdn_{popa} can be larger or smaller than Mdn_{popb} even when, as depicted in the *cdf*s, Treatment b is better or worse, respectively, than Treatment a in the tail regions of the range of Y. This situation is depicted in Figure 5.2. Third, when the $PS > .5$ the treatment that is thereby said to be probabilistically *inferior* can still be the *superior* treatment in terms of the relative heights of the *cdf*s in nearly half of the range of *Y*. This situation is depicted in Figure 5.3. Fourth, when the *PS* = .5 it is possible that $F_b(Y)$ is higher than $G_a(Y)$ in one tail whereas $G_a(Y)$ is higher than $F_b(Y)$ in the other tail, as is depicted in Figure 5.4, whose scores were contrived so that *PS* equals exactly .5. (The very slight difference between Figures 5.3 and 5.4 is not readily discernable.)

An important lesson from the foregoing discussion and figures is that there is a variety of relationships between the population distributions of Y_a and Y_b that can result in a given value of the *PS* that is not exactly equal to .5. Similarly, when the *PS* = .5 it is not necessarily true that the distributions of Y_a and Y_b are identical because, for example, *PS* = .5 can occur when $F_b(Y) > G_a(Y)$ for half of the overall distribution of *Y* and $G_a(Y) > F_b(Y)$ for the other half of the distribution. Again, no one measure of effect size reflects all of the useful information in data.

Vargha and Delaney (1998) provided examples, necessarily involving skewed data, in which a sample that is superior to another sample in terms of its estimated *PS* actually has a mean that is lower than the mean of the otherwise inferior sample (where a higher mean represented better performance). Also consult Howard et al. (1994). We recommend the reporting of figures such as Figures 5.1 through 5.4 for one's data, together with estimates of effect size.

Figure 5.5 depicts the *cdf*s for the previously discussed data that compared the mothers of schizophrenic children (sample *s* here) to the mothers of normal children (sample *n* here). In this case, consistent with our previous estimation that $Pr(Y_s > Y_n) = .26$, observe in Figure 5.5 that the *cdf* for the mothers of the schizophrenics is nearly everywhere higher than the *cdf* for the mothers of the normal children. (Recall that a *higher cdf* at a given value of *Y* indicates a tendency to be *lower* scoring than the other group up to and including that value of *Y*.) Consult Callaert (1999) for further discussion of the limitations of testing for the differences between two medians.

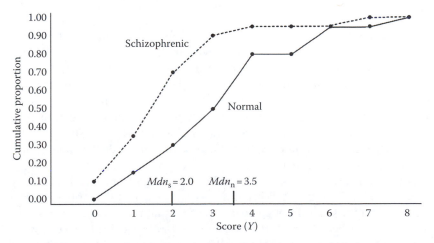

FIGURE 5.5 Mothers of schizophrenic children (sample *s*) score inferiorly to mothers of normal children (sample *n*) nearly everywhere across the range of *Y*, $Mdn_s < Mdn_n$, and estimated $Pr(Y_s > Y_n) = .26$.

INTRODUCTION TO OVERLAP AND RELATED MEASURES

Measures of effect size can be related to the relative positions of the distributions of scores from populations a and b. When there is no effect, $d_{pop} = 0$, $r_{pop} = 0$, and $PS = .5$. In this case, if assumptions are satisfied, probability distributions a and b completely overlap. (We refer here to the *normal probability distributions*, not the *cdfs*.) When there is a maximum effect, d_{pop} is at its maximum negative or positive value for the data, $r_{pop} = +1$ or -1, and $PS = 0$ or 1 depending on whether it is population b or population a that is superior in all of the head-to-head comparisons between scores. In this case of maximum effect there is no overlap of the two distributions; even the lowest score in the higher-scoring group is higher than the highest score in the lower-scoring group. Intermediate values of effect size result in less extreme amounts of overlap than in the two previous cases. Consult Howard et al. (1994) for discussion of the implications of overlap. Nonoverlap is discussed later in this chapter.

DOMINANCE MEASURE

Cliff (1993) discussed a variation on the *PS* concept that avoids dealing directly with ties by considering only those pairings in which $Y_a > Y_b$ or $Y_b > Y_a$. We call this measure the *dominance measure* of effect size, *DM*, here because Cliff called its estimator the *dominance statistic* (also known as the *delta statistic*), which we denote *ds*. This measure is defined as

$$DM = \Pr(Y_a > Y_b) - \Pr(Y_b > Y_a) \tag{5.8}$$

and its estimator, *ds*, is given by

$$ds = \hat{p}_{a>b} - \hat{p}_{b>a}. \tag{5.9}$$

Here the $\hat{p}$ values are, as before, given by $U/n_a n_b$ for each group, except for including in each group's U only the number of wins in the $n_a n_b$ pairings of scores from groups a and b, with no allocation of any ties. For example, suppose that $n_a = n_b = 10$, and of the $10 \times 10 = 100$ pairings group a has the higher of the two paired scores 50 times, group b has the higher score 40 times, and there are 10 ties within the paired scores. In this case, $\hat{p}_{a>b} = 50/100 = .5$, $\hat{p}_{b>a} = 40/100 = .4$, and, therefore, the estimate of the *DM* using Equation 5.9 is $.5 - .4 = +.1$, suggesting a slight or moderate superiority of group a. Note that one does not reduce n_a and n_b by the number of ties when calculating $n_a n_b$.

Because, as probabilities, both Pr values can range from 0 to 1, *DM* ranges from $0 - 1 = -1$ to $1 - 0 = +1$. When $DM = -1$ the populations' distributions do not overlap, all of the scores from group a being below all of the scores from group b, and vice versa when $DM = +1$. For values of the *DM* between the two extremes of -1 and $+1$ there is intermediate overlap. When there is an equal number of wins for groups a and b in their pairings, $\hat{p}_{a>b} = \hat{p}_{b>a} = .5$ and the estimate of the *DM* using Equation 5.9 is $ds = .5 - .5 = 0$. In this case there is no effect and complete overlap.

Kromrey and Coughlin (2007) provided an SAS/IML macro for calculating the *DS*, which they called the delta statistic. Refer to Cliff (1993) and Long et al. (2003) for discussions of significance testing and construction of confidence intervals for the *DM* for the independent-groups and the dependent-groups cases and for software to undertake the calculations. The *ds* is used to test H_0: $DM = 0$ against H_{alt}: $DM \neq 0$ without assuming identical distributions. The *DM* is a linear function of the *PS* and, if there are no ties,

$$DM = 2PS - 1. \tag{5.10}$$

Any valid method of point estimation, hypothesis testing, or construction of confidence intervals for the *PS* is applicable to the *DM*. For the confidence limits for the *DM* multiply the lower and upper confidence limits for the *PS* by 2 and subtract 1. Cliff and his colleagues prefer ordinal measures of effect size, such as the *PS* and *DM*, for behavioral research because (a) they believe that most measures of dependent variables in behavioral sciences are ordinal and means of essentially ordinal scales are of little meaning, and (b) ordinal measures are resistant to outliers. For example, no matter how far apart the first-ranked and second-ranked scores are they are still ranked first and second; distance does not matter as it does when scales are interval.

As was previously discussed with regard to the *PS*, ordinal measures of effect size such as the *DM* theoretically apply not only to the measures of the dependent variables but also to the latent variables to which the dependent variables are monitonically, but not necessarily linearly, related. Similarly, as is the case with the *PS*, a monotonic transformation of the data, or a change to another measure of the dependent variable that is monitonically related to a previous measure of the dependent variable, will not change the value of the previous *DM*.

Hess et al. (2005) reported simulations that indicated that under nonnormality and heteroscedasticity, bootstrap-based confidence intervals yielded better probability coverage for confidence intervals for the *DM* than for the standardized difference between means.

Wilcox (2003) provided S-PLUS software functions for Cliff's (1996a) robust method for constructing a confidence interval for the *DM* for the case of only two groups and for the case of groups taken two at a time from multiple groups. Preliminary findings by Wilcox (2003) indicated that Cliff's (1993) method provides good control of Type I error even when there are many tied values, a situation that may be problematic for competing methods. An example of the *DM* is presented in Chapter 9 along with more discussion.

COHEN'S MEASURES OF NONOVERLAP

If assumptions of normality and homoscedasticity are satisfied, and if populations are of equal size (as the hypothetical populations always are in experimental research), one can estimate the *percentage of nonoverlap* of the normal distributions of populations *a* and *b* as a measure of effect size. One of the methods uses as an estimate of nonoverlap the percentage of the members of the higher-scoring sample who score above the median (same as the mean when normality is satisfied) of the lower-scoring sample. We observed with regard to Figure 3.1 that when $d_{pop} = 1$ the mean of the higher-scoring population lies $1\sigma_y$ unit above the mean of the lower-scoring population. Because, under normality, 50% of the scores are at or above the median and approximately 34% of the scores lie between the mean and $1\sigma_y$ unit above the median (i.e., $z = 1$), when $d_{pop} = 1$ one infers that approximately 50% + 34% = 84% of the scores of the superior group exceed the median of the comparison group. Cohen (1988) denoted this percentage as a nonoverlap measure of effect size, U_3, to contrast it with his related measures, U_1 and U_2, which require the same assumptions and which we discuss briefly later.

When there is no effect we previously observed that $d_{pop} = 0$, $r_{pop} = 0$, and the $PS = .5$, and now we add that $U_3 = 50\%$. In this case 50% of the scores from population a are at or above the median of the scores from population b, but so too are 50% of the scores from population b at or above its own median, so there is complete overlap (0% nonoverlap). As d_{pop} increases above 0, U_3 approaches 100%. For example, if $d_{pop} = 3.4$ then $U_3 > 99.95\%$, nearly all of the scores from population a being above the median of population b, as is shown in Table 5.1. U_3 can also be defined as the probability that the score of a randomly sampled member of one population will exceed the median score of the members of the other population.

TABLE 5.1
Approximate Relationships among Some Measures of Effect Size

d_{pop}	r_{pop}^a	PS^a	$U_3(\%)$
0	.000	.500	50.0
.1	.050	.528	54.0
.2	.100	.556	57.9
.3	.148	.584	61.8
.4	.196	.611	65.5
.5	.243	.638	69.1
.6	.287	.664	72.6
.7	.330	.690	75.8
.8	.371	.714	78.8
.9	.410	.738	81.6
1.0	.447	.760	84.1
1.5	.600	.856	93.3
2.0	.707	.921	97.7
2.5	.781	.962	99.4
3.0	.832	.983	99.9
3.4	.862	.992	>99.95

Note: [a]When converting from the positive values of r_{pop} in this table to the PS the PS must be defined as $Pr (Y_1 < Y_2)$ instead of $Pr (Y_1 > Y_2)$. When converting from negative values of r_{pop} to the PS the PS is defined as $Pr (Y_1 > Y_2)$.

In research that is intended to improve scores compared to a control, placebo, or standard-treatment group, a case of successful treatment is sometimes defined (but not always justifiably so) as any score that exceeds the median of the comparison group. Then, the percentage of the scores from the treated group that exceed the median score of the comparison group is called the *success percentage* of the treatment. When assumptions are satisfied the success percentage is, by definition, U_3. For further discussions consult Lipsey (2000) and Lipsey and Wilson (2001). For more complex but robust approaches to overlap measures of effect size, called I-index effect sizes, which do not assume normality or homoscedasticity, refer to Hess, Olejnik, and Huberty (2001). Natesan and Thompson (2007) extended simulation studies of the robustness of such group overlap indices of effect size to cases of small samples. Browne (2010) related the maximum and minimum separation of two normal distributions to the values of p and N from a t test when assumptions are satisfied. Senn (2011) discussed the problem of generalizing overlap (or nonoverlap) from a given study to a future study in which the distribution of scores may vary from what it had been.

Cohen's (1988) U_1 measure is the percentage of scores that do not overlap in the two distributions, another measure that increases as d_{pop} increases. For examples, when $d_{\text{pop}} = 0$, $U_1 = 0\%$, and when $d_{\text{pop}} = 4.0$, $U_1 = 97.7\%$. Cohen's other measure of nonoverlap, U_2, is the percentage of scores in one population that exceed the same percentage in another population, which also increases as d_{pop} increases. U_2 ranges from 50% to 100%. For example, when $d_{\text{pop}} = 0$, $U_2 = 50.0\%$, and when $d_{\text{pop}} = 4.0$, $U_2 = 97.7\%$.

Kraemer and Andrews (1982) proposed a nonparametric index of overlap between two distributions based on the proportion of scores in one group that are below the median of the other group. Kromrey and Coughlin (2007) provided an SAS/IML macro for calculating this index of overlap. Wilcox and Muska (1999) proposed a nonparametric estimator of an effect size that measures the extent of evidence that a score came from one population instead of a second population. This effect size, which is called W, is the probability that a score will be correctly classified as coming from one of two groups. Kromrey and Coughlin also provided SAS/IML macros for calculating two estimators of W.

RELATIONSHIPS AMONG MEASURES OF EFFECT SIZE

Although Cohen's (1988) use of the letter U was apparently merely coincidental to the Wilcoxon–Mann–Whitney U statistic, there is a relationship, when assumptions are met, between U_3 and the *PS*. Indeed, many of the measures of effect size that are discussed in this book are related when assumptions are met. Numerous approximately equivalent values among many measures can be found in tables provided by Howard et al. (1994, p. 305), Kraemer and Kupfer (2006, p. 992), Rosenthal et al. (2000, pp. 16–21), Lipsey and Wilson (2001, p. 153), Cohen (1988,

p. 22), and Grissom (1994a, p. 315). Table 5.1 presents an abbreviated set of approximate relationships among some measures of effect size.

The values of r_{pop} and U_3 in Table 5.1 assume that the two populations are of equal size, which is true for experiments in principle and sufficiently satisfied for comparisons of gender. The values in Table 5.1 are more accurate the more nearly normality and homoscedasticity are satisfied. The larger the sample sizes that are used to estimate a measure of effect size the more accurate such a table will be in using that measure to convert to another measure in the table. Using conversion formulas in Chapter 8 one can approximately convert many effect sizes there for contingency tables to the effect sizes that appear in Table 5.1.

The relationship between Kendall's tau_{pop} nonparametric measure of correlation, which was discussed in Chapter 4, and the *PS* was discussed by Acion et al. (2006a). A program using IBM SPSS is available to convert Kendall's tau_{pop} to various other effect sizes (Walker, 2003).

The first two columns of Table 5.1 are based on the following relationship between d_{pop} and r_{pop} when variances are equal:

$$r_{\text{pop}} = \frac{d_{\text{pop}}}{\left(d_{\text{pop}}^2 + 4\right)^{1/2}}. \tag{5.11}$$

Again, the r_{pop} is the point-biserial correlation in the population. It can be shown that when *N*s are indefinitely large and equal, as they are in populations in experiments and in some other studies such as gender comparisons, Equation 5.11 is equivalent to Equation 4.2.

ESTIMATING EFFECT SIZES THROUGHOUT A DISTRIBUTION

Tips and Pitfalls

Traditional measures of effect size may be insufficiently informative or even misleading when there is heteroscedasticity or inequality of shapes of the distributions. For example, suppose that a treatment causes some participants to score higher and some to score lower than they would have scored if they had been in the comparison group. In this case the treated group's variability will increase or decrease depending on whether it was the higher- or lower-scoring participants whose scores were increased or decreased by the treatment. However, although variability has been changed by the treatment in this example, the two groups' means and/or medians may remain nearly the same (possible, but less likely than the example that is presented in the next paragraph). In this case, if one estimates an effect size with $\bar{Y}_a - \bar{Y}_b$ or $Mdn_a - Mdn_b$ in the numerator, the estimate may be a value that is not far from zero, although the treatment may have had a moderate or large effect on the tails if not much effect on the center of the treated group's distribution. The effect on variability may have resulted from the treatment having "pulled" tails outward or having "pushed" tails inward. Wilcox (2006a) discussed an example in which gender difference was slight in the center but great in the tails of the distribution.

In another case, the treatment may have an effect throughout a distribution, changing both the center and the tails of the treated group's distribution. Recall that it is common for the group with the higher mean also to have the greater variability. In this case, if one now considers a combined distribution that contains all of the scores of the treated and comparison groups, the proportions of the treated group's scores among the overall high scores and among the overall low scores can be different from what would be implied by an estimate of d_{pop} or U_3. Hedges and Nowell (1995) provided a specific example. In this example, if $d_{pop} = +.3$, distributions are normal, and the variance of the treated population's scores is only 15% greater than the variance of the comparison population's scores, one would find approximately 2.5 times more treated participants' scores than comparison participants' scores in the top 5% of the combined distribution. For more discussion and examples consult Feingold (1992, 1995) and O'Brien (1988). The kinds of results that have just been discussed may occur even under homoscedasticity if the two groups' distributions have different shapes. To accommodate the possibility of treatment effects that are not restricted to the centers of distributions other measures of effect size have been proposed, such as the measures that are briefly discussed in the next two sections.

Tail-Based Method and Shift-Function Methods

Informative methods have been proposed for measuring effect size at places along a distribution in addition to its center. Such methods are necessarily more complex than the usual methods so they have not been widely used. Hedges and Friedman (1993) and Gao, Wan, Zhang, Redden, and Allison (2008) proposed measures of effect size that compare groups at specified points in the tail of a distribution that are of particular interest to the researcher.

Doksum (1977) presented a graphical method for comparing two groups not only at the centers of their distributions but, more informatively, at various other quantiles. Recall from Chapter 1 that a quantile can be roughly defined as a score that is equal to or greater than a specified proportion of the scores in a distribution. Wilcox (2005a) illustrated how distributions a and b can have equal means and equal variances but $Y_a > Y_b$ at some quantile of the overall distribution and $Y_a < Y_b$ at another quantile. Again, such a result is evidence against a shift model, wherein Y_a would either be greater than Y_b by a constant amount or lower than Y_b by a constant amount at all quantiles of the overall distribution. Wilcox (2006d, 2006f) discussed advantages of comparing quantiles.

For more detailed discussions consult Doksum (1977) and Wilcox (2003, 2005a). For a Minitab macro for the method consult Wilcox (1996) and for S-PLUS R software functions consult Wilcox (2005a).

OTHER GRAPHICAL ESTIMATORS OF EFFECT SIZES

Additional graphical methods for estimating effect sizes at various points along a distribution include the Wilk and Gnanadesikan percentile comparison graph and the Tukey sum-difference graph (Cleveland, 1988, 1994). The percentile comparison graph plots percentiles from one group's distribution against the same percentiles from the other group's distribution. Cleveland (1994) demonstrated the use of the percentile comparison graph for the cases of unequal and equal sample sizes. A linear relationship between the two sets of percentiles would be consistent with the shift model that we previously discussed and would thus help to justify the use of effect sizes that compare means (or medians). On the other hand, a nonlinear relationship would further justify use of the *PS*.

Darlington (1973) presented an ordinal dominance curve for depicting the ordinal relationship between two sets of data, a graph that is similar to the percentile comparison graph. The proportion of the total area under the ordinal dominance curve corresponds to an estimate of the *PS*. This estimate can readily be made by inspection of the ordinal dominance curve as described by Darlington, who also demonstrated other uses of the curve for comparing two groups. For related discussion consult Brownie (1988). Comparison of distributions using boxplots was discussed in Chapter 1. Lane and Sándor (2009) provided recommendations for improving graphs for conveying distributional differences between groups.

DEPENDENT GROUPS

The probability of superiority, *PS*, as previously defined and estimated in this chapter is not applicable to the dependent-groups design without modification. For the case of dependent groups, if there are no ties, one can define and estimate an effect size that we label PS_{dep} as

$$PS_{\text{dep}} = \Pr\left(Y_{ib} > Y_{ia}\right), \qquad (5.12)$$

where

Y_{ib} is the score of an individual under condition b

Y_{ia} is the score of that same (or a related or matched) individual under condition a

We use the repeated-measures (i.e., same individual in each condition) case for the remainder of this section.

The PS_{dep} as defined in Equation 5.12 is the probability that within a randomly sampled pair of dependent scores (e.g., two scores from the same participant under two different conditions) the score obtained under condition b will be greater than the score obtained under condition a. Note the difference between the previously presented definition of the *PS* and the definition of the PS_{dep}. In the case of the PS_{dep} one is estimating an effect size that would arise if, for each member of the sampled population, one could compare a member's score under condition b to that *same member's* score under condition a to observe which is greater.

One begins estimating PS_{dep} by comparing each person's score under condition a with the same person's score under condition b. The estimate of PS_{dep} is the proportion of all such within-participant comparisons in which a participant's score under condition b is greater than that participant's score under condition a. Ties are ignored in the present method. For example, if there are $n = 100$ participants of whom 60 score higher under condition b than they do under condition a, the estimate of PS_{dep} is $\hat{p}_{dep} = 60/100 = .60$. In the example that follows we define as a *win* for condition b each instance in which a participant scores higher under condition b than under condition a. We use the letter w for the total number of such wins for condition b throughout the n comparisons. Therefore,

$$\hat{p}_{dep} = \frac{w}{n}. \tag{5.13}$$

When there are ties one can add one-half of the ties to the numerator of the estimator in Equation 5.13, or discard ties in both the numerator and the denominator. We recommend that researchers provide both results, so that their results can be compared, or meta-analyzed, with either kind of previously reported results.

An example should make estimation of PS_{dep} very clear. Recall the example in Table 2.1 in which the weights of $n = 17$ anorectic girls are shown posttreatment (Y_{ib}) and pretreatment (Y_{ia}). In that table 13 of the 17 girls weighed more posttreatment than they did pretreatment, so the number of wins for posttreatment weight is $w = 13$. (The four exceptions to weight gain were girls # 6, 7, 10, and 11; there were no tied posttreatment and pretreatment weights.) Therefore, $\hat{p}_{dep} = w/n = 13/17 = .76$. One thus estimates that for a randomly sampled member of a population of anorectic girls, of whom these 17 girls would be representative, there is a .76 probability of weight gain from pretreatment to posttreatment.

Manual calculation of a confidence interval for PS_{dep} is easiest in the extreme cases in which $w = 0, 1, n,$ or $n - 1$ (Wilcox, 2005a). Somewhat more laborious manual calculation is also possible for all other values of w by following the steps provided by Wilcox for Pratt's method. Wilcox, who called the PS_{dep} simply p, also provided an S-PLUS and R software function for computing a confidence interval for PS_{dep} for any value of w. Wilcox (2009a) related $\hat{p}_{dep}$ to the classical *sign test* that can be used to test H_0: $PS_{dep} = .5$ (i.e., no effect).

Hand (1992) discussed how in some circumstances the PS may not in fact be the best measure of the probability that a certain treatment will be better than another treatment for a future treated individual, but that the PS_{dep} can be ideal for this purpose. Refer to Vargha and Delaney (2000) for further discussion of application of probabilistic superiority to the case of two dependent groups, and consult Brunner and Puri (2001) for extension to multiple groups and factorial designs. Again, Hand and others do not use our PS and PS_{dep} notations. Authors vary in their notation for these probabilities.

Long et al. (2003) and Feng (2007) extended estimation of the previously discussed dominance measure, and testing and construction of confidence intervals for it, to the case of dependent groups. This apparently robust measure is called *ordinal d for paired data.* Wilcox (2006e, 2006f) discussed an extension of the shift-function method to the case of dependent groups and an apparently superior method when there are ties.

SUMMARY

For continuous dependent variables there are informative measures of effect size that do not involve correlations or differences between means. For example, the *PS* (probability of superiority), which is best estimated using a function of the *U* statistic, is the probability that a randomly sampled member of a given population will have a score that is higher than the score of a randomly sampled member of another given population. The application can be experimental (e.g., groups given treatment *a* or treatment *b*) or nonexperimental (e.g., females and males). There is also a version of the *PS* for dependent groups. Researchers who do not focus on means and who do not assume normality should consider report-ing an estimate of the *PS*. Assuming normality and equal variances, when only means and variances are available from someone else's report, one can estimate the *PS* from those statistics using what is called the common language effect size statistic.

The *PS* ranges from 0 to 1, with .5 representing no superiority of either group. The traditional *U* test of the null hypothesis that *PS* = .5 is sensitive to unequal variances, but there are modifications of the *U* test to counter this violation. Construction of a confidence interval for the *PS* is recommended using one of the apparently robust methods. There are also methods that accommodate tied scores between the two groups. A simple method assigns half of the ties as a "win" (i.e., a superior score) for each group.

There are measures of effect size that are related to the *PS*. The generalized odds ratio measures the odds (not the probability) that a randomly drawn member of a given population will outscore a randomly drawn member of the other population. The dominance measure, estimated by the dominance statistic, accommodates ties and ranges from -1 to 1, with 0 representing dominance by neither group.

Often an implicit assumption in data analysis is the shift model, which assumes that if there is an effect of group membership (e.g., receiving treatment *a* or *b*) the effect is one in which membership in a given group always adds or always sub-tracts a constant number of points to what the score of each participant in that group would have been if each of those participants had been in the other group. This assumption may not be realistic in most research because a given treatment may result in an increase, decrease, or neither in various members in the given treatment group even if *on average* there is shift in a particular direction for that group. Use of the *PS* does not depend on the correctness of the shift model.

It is important to note that the *PS* and a standardized difference between means provide only a single value that cannot encapsulate possibly complex differences between two populations. Figures were provided in this chapter to illustrate that underlying a given value of the *PS*, or a given difference between two medians, there is a variety of possible differences between two populations throughout the entire range of the dependent variable. Several other graphical descriptions of effect sizes in samples were mentioned as were measures of overlap of distributions and measures of effect size at locations in the tails of distributions.

QUESTIONS

5.1 Define (a) *probability of superiority* for independent groups, (b) *consistent estimator*, (c) *consistent test*, (d) *cumulative proportion*, (e) *cumulative distribution function*, (f) Cohen's U_1 and U_2.

5.2 Interpret $PS = 0$, $PS = .5$, and $PS = 1$.

5.3 What is the focus of researchers who prefer to use a t test and to estimate a standardized difference between means and what is the focus of researchers who prefers to use the U test and estimate a PS?

5.4 What is a shift model and why might this model be unrealistic in many cases of behavioral research?

5.5 In which circumstance might a shift model be more appropriate and in which circumstance might the PS be more appropriate?

5.6 What is the effect of heteroscedasticity on the original U test and on the usual normal approximation for the U test?

5.7 What is the common language effect size statistic?

5.8 What is a major implication of the existence of a monotonic relationship between a measure of a dependent variable and a latent variable that it is measuring in behavioral science?

5.9 Identify two assumptions of the common language effect size statistic.

5.10 If assumptions are satisfied, describe the extent of overlap between the two distributions when $PS = 0$, $PS = .5$, and $PS = 1$.

5.11 Define and discuss the purpose of the *dominance measure* of effect size.

5.12 Define Cohen's U_3 and list three requirements for its appropriate use.

5.13 Discuss the relationship between U_3 and the success percentage.

5.14 Define the *probability of superiority* for the case of dependent groups, and describe the procedure for estimating it.

5.15 Discuss the relationship between the difference between medians and $Pr(Y_a > Y_b)$.

5.16 Discuss the problem of handling ties when using nonparametric methods.

5.17 Define and discuss the use of a *generalized odds ratio*.

5.18 Briefly discuss how effect sizes can mislead regarding the relationship between distributions.

5.19 Why do Cliff and his colleagues prefer ordinal measures of effect size for most measures of dependent variables in behavioral research?

5.20 For the data of Question 2.30 calculate and interpret (a) a nonparametric estimate of the PS, (b) an estimate of the generalized odds ratio, and (c) an estimate of the dominance measure.

5.21 Calculate a nonparametric estimate and a parametric estimate of the PS for the real data of Question 3.33 to confirm the results reported for those data in the present chapter.

6 Effect Sizes for One-Way ANOVA and Nonparametric Approaches

INTRODUCTION

The F test of the null hypothesis that a set of population means is equal provides no direct information about the extent to which two or more of those means are not equal. For this purpose an estimation of effect size is needed. This chapter addresses overall effect sizes and effect sizes for contrasts between means when three or more groups are being compared with respect to a continuous dependent variable. The discussions in this and in the next chapter assume the *fixed-effects model*, in which the levels of the independent variable that are being compared are all of the possible variations of the independent variable, or have been specifically chosen by the researcher to represent only those variations to which the results are to be generalized (e.g., Treatments a, b, and c). (In the alternative random-effects model the levels of the independent variable have been randomly selected to represent all levels. For example, a researcher might randomly select a sample of teachers to study whether different teachers teaching the same subject yield different mean test scores that generalize to the population of teachers of that subject. Each teacher is a level of the independent variable.) We begin with methods for independent groups. Methods for dependent groups are discussed later in this chapter.

For the purposes of this chapter the levels of the independent variable should be truly categorical (e.g., Treatments a, b, and c, or Democrat, Republican, Independent, and Other). The levels should not be more-or-less arbitrary categorizations of an originally continuous independent variable (e.g., low, medium, and high dose of a drug). An ANOVA (analysis of variance) does not take into account the ordinal nature of such categories, and categorizing an originally continuous independent variable may lower the reliability of the variable, statistical power, and estimates of effect sizes. Also, different cutoff criteria for the categorizations from study to study may contribute to artifactual inconsistency of the results across studies. However, we are *not* cautioning against the use of particular levels of a continuous independent variable in ANOVA when those levels are the ones that are of special interest to the researcher—levels with regard to which generalization is to be made to a population (i.e., the fixed-effects model).

ASSUMPTIONS

The ANOVA F test assumes homoscedasticity and normality, and its statistical power, accuracy of estimation of its associated effect sizes, and the accuracy of its obtained p levels can be reduced importantly by sufficient violation of these assumptions. (The critically important assumption of independence of scores within a group was discussed in Chapter 2 and is not revisited here.) Wilcox (2007a) summarized some of the effects of violation of assumptions. Consult Grissom (2000) and Wilcox (2003, 2005a) for further discussions.

ANOVA RESULTS FOR THIS CHAPTER

For worked examples of the estimators of effect sizes that are presented in this chapter for between-groups designs, we use ANOVA results from an unpublished study in which the levels of the independent variable were five methods of presentation of material to be learned and the dependent variable was the recall scores for that material (Wright, 1946; cited by McNemar, 1962). This study preceded the time when it was common for researchers to estimate effect size. Non-statistical details about this research do not concern us here. What one needs to know for the calculations in this chapter is presented in Table 6.1.

STANDARDIZED-DIFFERENCE MEASURE OF OVERALL EFFECT SIZE

The simplest measure of an overall standardized-difference effect size is given by

$$d_{\text{mmpop}} = \frac{\mu_{\text{max}} - \mu_{\text{min}}}{\sigma}, \tag{6.1}$$

TABLE 6.1
Information Needed for the Calculations in Chapter 6

$k = 5$:	Group 1 ($n = 16$)	Group 2 ($n = 16$)	Group 3 ($n = 16$)	Group 4 ($n = 16$)	Group 5 ($n = 16$)	Totals ($N = 80$)
Sample mean ($\overline{Y}_i$)	3.56	6.38	9.13	10.75	13.44	$\overline{Y}_{\text{all}} = 8.65$
Sample standard deviation (s_i)	2.25	2.79	3.82	2.98	3.36	

Source: The data are from Wright, S.T., Spacing of practice in verbal learning and the maturation hypothesis, unpublished master's thesis, Stanford University, Stanford, CA, 1946.

Notes: $SS_b = 937.82$, $SS_w = 714.38$, $SS_{\text{tot}} = 1652.20$; $MS_b = 234.46$, $MS_w = 9.53$; $F(4,75) = 24.60$, $p < .001$.

---

where

μ_{max} and μ_{min} represent, respectively, the highest and the lowest population means from the sampled populations

σ is the assumed common standard deviation within the populations, which is estimated by $MS_w^{1/2}$

The value of MS_w is obtained from the software output for the F test or calculated using an equation for pooling separate variances:

$$MS_w = \frac{(n_1 - 1)s_1^2 + \cdots + (n_k - 1)s_k^2}{N - k}. \tag{6.2}$$

The estimator of the effect size that is given by Equation 6.1 is

$$d_{mm} = \frac{\overline{Y}_{max} - \overline{Y}_{min}}{MS_w^{1/2}}. \tag{6.3}$$

Applying the values from the current set of ANOVA results in Table 6.1 to Equation 6.3 yields $d_{mm} = (13.44 - 3.56)/9.53^{1/2} = 3.20$. Thus, the highest and lowest population means are estimated to be 3.20 standard deviation units apart, where the standard deviation is assumed to be the same for each population that is represented in the study.

Tips and Pitfalls

It is not always true that when the overall F is statistically significant a test of $\overline{Y}_{max} - \overline{Y}_{min}$ will also yield statistical significance. Discussions of testing the statistical significance of $\overline{Y}_{max} - \overline{Y}_{min}$ and testing differences within other pairs of means among the k means are presented later in this chapter. Also, the measure d_{mmpop} should only be estimated if the researcher justifies a genuine interest in it as a measure of overall effect size. The motivation for its use should not be merely to present the obviously highest value of a d possible. Not surprisingly for standardized-difference estimators of effect size, d_{mm} tends to overestimate d_{mmpop}.

STANDARDIZED OVERALL EFFECT SIZE USING ALL MEANS

The d_{mmpop} and d_{mm} of Equations 6.1 and 6.3 ignore all of the means except the two most extreme means. There is a measure of overall standardized effect size in one-way ANOVA that uses all of the means. This effect size, which assumes homoscedasticity, is f (Cohen, 1988; Fleishman, 1980), a measure of a kind of standardized typical effect in the population across all of the levels of the independent variable. The value of f is given by

$$f = \frac{\sigma_\mu}{\sigma}, \tag{6.4}$$

where

σ_μ is the standard deviation of all of the means of the populations that are represented by the samples (based on the deviation of each mean from the mean of all of the means)

σ is the common (assumed) standard deviation within each population

Thus, σ_μ is the typical effect and σ standardizes it. When there is no effect $f = 0$. Theoretically, the upper bound of f is infinity. Even slight departures from normality can greatly lower f (Wilcox, 2008a). An estimator of f is given by

$$\hat{f} = \frac{s_{\bar{Y}}}{MS_w^{1/2}}, \qquad (6.5)$$

where $s_{\bar{Y}}$ is the standard deviation of the set of all of the values of $\bar{Y}$ from $\bar{Y}_1$ to $\bar{Y}_k$. Thus, for equal sample sizes,

$$s_{\bar{Y}} = \left[\frac{\Sigma(\bar{Y}_i - \bar{Y}_{all})^2}{k-1} \right]^{1/2}, \qquad (6.6)$$

where, as previously defined, $\bar{Y}_{all}$ is the mean of all sample means. In Equation 6.6 each $\bar{Y}_i - \bar{Y}_{all}$ reflects the effect of the ith level of the independent variable, so $s_{\bar{Y}}$ reflects a kind of average effect in the sample across the levels of the independent variable. Therefore, $\hat{f}$ estimates the standardized typical effect. Consult Cohen for the case of $\hat{f}$ with unequal sample sizes. Applying the results from the present recall study to Equation 6.6 yields

$$s_{\bar{Y}} = \left[\frac{\begin{array}{c}(3.56-8.65)^2 + (6.38-8.65)^2 + (9.13-8.65)^2 \\ + (10.75-8.65)^2 + (13.44-8.65)^2\end{array}}{5-1} \right]^{1/2} = 3.829.$$

Therefore, using Equation 6.5, $\hat{f} = 3.83/9.53^{1/2} = 1.24$. The average effect across the samples is 1.24 standard deviation units.

Although they have the same denominator, d_{mm} should be expected to be greater than $\hat{f}$ because of the difference between their numerators. The numerator of d_{mm} is the range of the means whereas the numerator of $\hat{f}$ is the standard deviation of that same set of means, which is obviously a smaller number. In fact d_{mm} is often two to four times larger than $\hat{f}$. Consistent with this typical result, for the present data on recall, d_{mm} is more than 2.5 times greater than $\hat{f}$: $d_{mm}/\hat{f} = 3.20/1.24 = 2.58$.

The estimator in Equation 6.5 is positively (i.e., upwardly) biased because the sample means in the numerator are likely to vary more than do the population means. An unbiased estimator of f is

$$\hat{f}_{\text{unbiased}} = \left[\frac{(k-1)(F-1)}{N} \right]^{1/2}. \qquad (6.7)$$

Refer to Maxwell and Delaney (2004) for further discussion of such bias. Applying the data in Table 6.1 to Equation 6.7 yields $f_{\text{unbiased}} = [(5 - 1)(24.60 - 1)/80]^{1/2} = 1.09$. Observe that this estimate for f is lower than the positively biased one produced by Equation 6.5 (i.e., $1.09 < 1.24$), as it should be.

RELATED MEASURES

Kelley (2007) provided functions for R software for constructing a confidence interval for a measure of the *signal-to-noise ratio* effect size (or its square root), which is the population variance of the *standardized means* and is estimated by $n\hat{f}^2$, where n is the common sample size for each group. A population standardized mean is defined as μ/σ. The greater the effect of an independent variable, the greater the variance and standard deviation of μ/σ. By the *transformation principle of confidence intervals* if one has constructed a confidence interval for a parameter, the square root of which is of interest, one can find the limits of a confidence interval for this latter parameter by taking the square roots of the lower and upper limits of the confidence interval for the original parameter. Kelley's functions are applicable to any fixed-effects factor in one-way or factorial ANOVA. Kulinskaya and Staudte (2006) recommended using a weighted modification of f^2 as an effect size when population variances are not assumed to be equal. There is a variant of f, denoted *RMSSE* (root mean square standardized effect), which was proposed by Steiger and Fouladi (1997). The *RMSSE* is the square root of the average squared standardized effect (averaged by the $k - 1$ independent effects that are possible in one-way fixed-effects ANOVA).

STRENGTH OF ASSOCIATION

Recall from the section entitled "The coefficient of determination" in Chapter 4 that in the two-group case r_{pb}^2 has traditionally been used to estimate the proportion of the total variance in the dependent variable that is associated with variation in the independent variable. Similar estimators of effect size have traditionally been used for one-way ANOVA designs in which $k > 2$. These estimators are intended to reflect *strength of association* on a scale ranging from 0 (no association) to 1 (maximum association).

ETA SQUARED (η^2)

In this book we generally denote the parameter that measures the *proportion of the variance* in the population's scores that is accounted for by variation in the independent variable POV_{pop} (sometimes called elsewhere *proportional reduction in error in the population, PRE_{pop}*). A traditional but especially problematic estimator of this strength-of-association parameter is η^2 (lowercase Greek letter eta), which is given by

$$\eta^2 = \frac{SS_b}{SS_{tot}}. \tag{6.8}$$

The numerator of Equation 6.8 reflects the part of total variability that is attributable to variation in the independent variable and the denominator reflects total variability. Often the POV_{pop} parameter is denoted η^2, which, for clarity, we instead denote η_{pop}^2 for now, and its estimator in Equation 6.8 is often denoted $\hat{\eta}^2$, whereas we use η^2. Furthering the confusion in the literature, the original name for η was the *correlation ratio*, but this name has since come to be used by some for η^2. When the independent variable is quantitative η_{pop} represents a correlation between the independent variable and the dependent variable, but, unlike r_{pop}, η_{pop} reflects curvilinear as well as linear relationship in that case. When there are two groups η_{pop} has the same absolute magnitude as r_{pop}. Also, the previously discussed f is related to η_{pop}^2 by $f = \left[\eta_{pop}^2 / \left(1 - \eta_{pop}^2\right) \right]^{1/2}$.

Tips and Pitfalls

A major flaw of η^2 as an estimator of strength of association is that it is more positively biased than are its competitors. This estimator tends to overestimate η_{pop}^2 because its numerator, SS_b, is inflated by some error variability. Even if an independent variable accounted for none of the variance in the population of scores, sampling variability would be expected to result in $SS_b > 0$. Bias is less for larger sample sizes and for larger effects in the population. For further discussions of such bias, consult Carroll and Nordholm (1975) and Maxwell and Delaney (2004). Because, as is discussed in the next section, we prefer a less biased estimator than η^2, and because some readers might otherwise wrongly assume hereafter in this chapter and in later chapters that the notation η_{pop}^2 refers to a parameter that is necessarily estimated by η^2 of Equation 6.8, we now use POV_{pop} (proportion of variance explained in the population) instead of η_{pop}^2 to denote the estimated parameter.

Epsilon Squared (ε^2) and Omega Squared (ω^2)

A somewhat less biased alternative estimator of POV_{pop} is ε^2 (lowercase Greek letter epsilon), which is often denoted $\hat{\varepsilon}^2$, and a more nearly unbiased estimator is ω^2 (lowercase Greek letter omega), which is often denoted $\hat{\omega}^2$; consult Keselman (1975). The bias of ω^2 is minimal (Carroll & Nordholm, 1975). The equations are

$$\varepsilon^2 = \frac{SS_b - (k-1)MS_w}{SS_{tot}} \tag{6.9}$$

and (Hays, 1994)

$$\omega^2 = \frac{SS_b - (k-1)MS_w}{SS_{tot} + MS_w}.$$ (6.10)

Equal sample sizes and homoscedasticity are assumed for the moment. Software output for the ANOVA F test typically includes one or more estimators of POV_{pop}. However, manual calculation is easy (demonstrated later) because the needed SS and MS_w values are available from ANOVA output. We encourage the use of the minimally biased ω^2 for those who are interested in estimating strength of association. (Analogous to the use of ω^2 as an estimator of effect size for the fixed-effects model, the sample *intraclass correlation* is used in the random-effects model. For discussion consult Maxwell & Delaney, 2004.)

Tips and Pitfalls

A statistically significant overall F can be taken as evidence that ω^2 is significantly greater than 0. However, confidence intervals are especially important here because of the high sampling variability of the estimators (Maxwell, Camp, & Arvey, 1981). For example, Carroll and Nordholm (1975) found great sampling variability even when $N = 90$ and $k = 3$. High sampling variability results in estimates often being far from the effect size that is being estimated.

CONFIDENCE INTERVALS FOR POV_{pop}

For rough purposes approximate confidence limits for POV_{pop} based on ω^2 can be obtained using graphs (called nomographs) that can be found in Abu Libdeh (1984). Assuming normality and, especially, homoscedasticity, noncentral distributions provide one of the methods that can be used to construct such confidence intervals. As was discussed in the section on noncentral distributions in Chapter 3, software is required for their construction, so no example of manual calculation is presented here. Refer to Fidler and Thompson (2001) for a demonstration of the use of IBM SPSS to construct a confidence interval for POV_{pop} that is based on a noncentral distribution. Also consult Smithson (2003) and Steiger (2004) for this purpose. At the time of this writing Michael Smithson provides IBM SPSS, SAS, S-PLUS, and R scripts for constructing such a confidence interval. These scripts can be accessed at http://psychology.anu.edu.au/people/smithson/details/CIstuff/CI.html. STATISTICA software can also produce such a confidence interval, as can R functions provided by Kelley (2007).

Unfortunately, confidence intervals for POV_{pop} can be very wide. Finch and French (in press) found that sample size and population effect size influence the width and probability coverage of three compared methods for constructing a confidence interval for POV_{pop} based on omega squared.

REPORTING POV: ASSUMPTIONS AND AN EXAMPLE

As a measure of a proportion (of total variance of the dependent variable that is associated with variation of the independent variable) the value of POV_{pop} cannot be below 0, but inspection of Equations 6.9 and 6.10 reveals that the values of the estimators can be below 0. Also, there are alternative equations for estimating

POV_{pop} that have a factor of $F - 1$ in the numerator, with a multiplier $(k - 1)$ that must be positive. For example, when ns are equal in each group, $\omega^2 = (k - 1)(F - 1)/[(k - 1)(F - 1) + kn]$ (Keppel & Wickens, 2004). Therefore, if F is between 0 and 1 the estimate of POV_{pop} will be negative.

The expected value of F for fixed-effects ANOVA with equal sample sizes when the H_0 is true is $(N - k)/(N - k - 2)$, which approaches 1 for a fixed value of k as total sample size, N, increases. Voelkle, Ackerman, and Wittman (2007) discussed how the use of adjusted ε^2 and adjusted ω^2 solves the problem of unadjusted estimates of effect size sometimes being above, or well above, zero when $F < 1$, which is always a statistically insignificant value of F. When $F < 1$ a bias-adjusted estimate will be negative when H_0 is true, and the best estimate of POV_{pop} is zero.

Hays (1994) recommended that when the value of ω^2 is below 0 the value should be reported as 0. However, some meta-analysts are concerned that replacing negative estimates with zeros may cause an additional positive bias in an estimate that is based on averaging estimates in a meta-analysis. Similarly, Fidler and Thompson (2001) argued that any obtained negative value should be reported as such instead of converting it to 0 so that the full width of a confidence interval can be reported. However, when a negative value is reported, a reader of a research report has an opportunity to interpret it as 0. Consult Vaughan and Corballis (1969) for additional discussions of this issue.

For an example of ω^2 we apply the results from the study of recall (Table 6.1) to Equation 6.10 to find that $\omega^2 = (937.82 - (5 - 1)9.53)/(1652.20 + 9.53) = .541$. Therefore, one estimates that 54% of the variance of the recall scores is attributable to varying the method of presentation of the material that is to be learned. This estimation is subject to the limitations that are discussed later in the section entitled "Evaluation of criticisms of strength of association". The value of ω^2 can be declared to be statistically significantly different from 0 at the $p < .001$ level because the omnibus $F = 24.6$ (4,75) was statistically significant ($p < .001$).

Estimation of POV_{pop} is sensitive to heteroscedasticity and nonnormality, and interpretation is especially problematic under heteroscedasticity. Kulinskaya and Staudte (2006) reported simulations of the performance of their proposed strength-of association effect size for one-way ANOVA under the conditions of outliers and heteroscedasticity. Those authors reported accurate probability coverage of nominal .95 confidence intervals for their proposed effect size under a broad range of values for the parameters.

STRENGTH OF ASSOCIATION FOR SPECIFIC COMPARISONS

Estimation of the strength of association within just two of the $k > 2$ groups at a time may be called estimation of a *specific* or *focused strength of association*. Such an estimation provides more detailed information than do the previously discussed estimators of overall strength of association. To make such a focused estimate one can use

$$\omega_{comp}^2 = \frac{SS_{comp} - MS_w}{SS_{tot} + MS_w}, \qquad (6.11)$$

where the subscript comp represents comparison (between two groups). The symbol $SS_{contrast}$ is sometimes used instead of SS_{comp}. (Often *comparison* refers to two means whereas *contrast* refers to more than two means, as in the next paragraph.) Observe the similarity between Equations 6.10 and 6.11. In Equation 6.11 SS_{comp} replaces the SS_b of Equation 6.10, and the $(k - 1)$ of Equation 6.10 is now $2 - 1 = 1$ in Equation 6.11 because only two groups are involved now. To find SS_{comp} in the present case of making a simple comparison involving two of the k means, $\bar{Y}_i$ and $\bar{Y}_j$, use

$$SS_{comp} = \frac{(\bar{Y}_i - \bar{Y}_j)^2}{(1/n_i) + (1/n_j)}. \qquad (6.12)$$

Consult Olejnik and Algina (2000) for a more general formulation and a worked example of Equation 6.12 that involves the case of a complex comparison (often simply called a contrast), such as comparing the mean of a control group with the overall mean of two or more combined treatment groups.

   In the research on recall two of the five group means were $\bar{Y}_i = 10.75$ and $\bar{Y}_j = 6.38$. Using these two means for an example and using that study's ANOVA results that are presented in Table 6.1, we apply Equation 6.12 to find that in this example $SS_{comp} = (10.75 - 6.38)^2/(1/16 + 1/16) = 152.78$. Now applying Equation 6.11, $\omega^2_{comp} = (152.78 - 9.53)/(1652.20 + 9.53) = .09$. Therefore, one estimates (subject to the limitations that are discussed in the next section) that 9% of the variability of the recall scores is attributable to whether presentation method i or presentation method j is used for learning the material that is to be recalled. Consult Keppel and Wickens (2004), Maxwell et al. (1981), Olejnik and Algina (2000), and Vaughan and Corballis (1969) for further discussions of estimating strength of association for specific comparisons. Furr (2004) discussed squared and unsquared effect sizes for specific contrasts.

EVALUATION OF CRITICISMS OF STRENGTH OF ASSOCIATION

When $k = 2$ the estimators of POV_{pop} are conceptually similar to, but not identical to, r^2_{pb}, the sample point-biserial coefficient of determination that was discussed in Chapter 4. Such estimators and the POV_{pop} that they estimate share some of the criticisms of r^2_{pb} and r^2_{pop} that have appeared in the literature and that were discussed in Chapter 4. We briefly review and evaluate these criticisms and evaluate some others. We repeatedly state in this book that no effect size or estimator is without one or more limitations. Furthermore, some of the limitations of POV_{pop} and its estimators are also applicable to measures of the standardized difference between means and their estimators. Also, some of the limitations are more of a problem for meta-analysis than for the underlying primary research that is the focus of this book. (For an argument that these estimators may not actually estimate POV_{pop} consult Murray & Dosser, 1987.)

MISLEADINGLY LOW VALUES

Recall first from the section entitled "The coefficient of determination" in Chapter 4 that effect sizes that involve squaring values that are below 1 yield values that are often closer to zero than to 1 in the human sciences. A consequence of this that is sometimes pointed out in the literature is a possible undervaluing of the importance of the result. A statistically inexperienced reader of a research report or summary, one who is familiar with little more than the 0%–100% scale of percentages, will not likely be familiar with the range of typical values of estimates of a standardized-difference effect size or POV_{pop} effect size. Therefore, if, say, the estimate from an obtained d is that $d_{pop} = .5$, a value that is approximately equivalent to $POV_{pop} = .05$, then such a statistically inexperienced reader may be more impressed by the effect of the independent variable if an estimated $d_{pop} = .5$ is reported than if an estimated $POV_{pop} = .05$ is reported.

The aforementioned criticism of the POV_{pop} approach to effect size is less applicable the more statistical knowledge that the intended readership of a research report has and the more that the author of a report does to disabuse readers of incorrect interpretation of the results. Indeed, the more warnings about this limitation that appear in the literature the less susceptibility there will be to such undervaluing. On the other hand, a low value for an estimate of POV_{pop} can be informative in alerting one to the need to (a) search for additional independent variables that might contribute further to determining variation in the dependent variable and/or (b) improve control of extraneous variables that contribute to error variability in the research and that thereby lower an estimate of the POV_{pop}.

CRITICISM OF A DIRECTIONLESS MEASURE

Also recall from Chapter 4 and from earlier in this chapter that estimators of effect size that involve squaring become directionless; they cannot be negative, rendering them typically useless for averaging in meta-analysis. The inappropriateness of averaging estimates of POV_{pop} across studies can be readily seen by recognizing that the same value for the estimate would be obtained in two studies if all of the values of the terms in Equation 6.8, 6.9, or 6.10 were the same in both studies even if the rank order of the k means were opposite in the two studies. An example of this situation would be one in which the most, intermediate, and least efficacious treatments in Study 1 were, respectively, Treatments a, b, and c, whereas the ranking of efficacy in Study 2 was Treatments c, b, and a. The two estimates of POV_{pop} would be the same although the two studies produced opposite results. This is more of a problem for a meta-analyst than for a primary researcher. However, this limitation reminds once again that research reports should include means for all samples, rendering it easier to interpret the results in the context of the results from other related studies.

CRITICISM OF LACK OF SPECIFICITY OF POV_{pop}

A third criticism that is sometimes raised is easy to accommodate. Namely, unlike a typical standardized-difference effect size for $k = 2$, the most commonly used

POV_{pop} effect size for $k > 2$ designs (estimated by Equation 6.8, 6.9, or 6.10) is *global*; that is, it provides information about the overall association between the independent and dependent variables but does not provide details about specific comparisons within the k levels of the independent variable. This limitation can be avoided by applying Equation 6.11 to two samples at a time from the k samples.

MULTIPLE DETERMINATION

A fourth criticism is related to the first criticism. Recall from the section entitled "The coefficient of determination" in Chapter 4 that human behavior (e.g., the measure of the dependent variable) is *multiply determined*; that is, it is influenced by a variety of genetic and background experiential variables (both kinds being extraneous variables in much research). Therefore, it is usually unreasonable to expect that any single independent variable is going to contribute a very large proportion of what determines variability of the dependent variable. More statistically experienced consumers of research reports will take multiple determinations and typical sizes of estimates of a POV_{pop} into account when interpreting an estimate of a POV_{pop}. However, those readers of reports who are inexperienced in statistics might merely note that an estimated POV_{pop} is not very far above 0% and mistakenly conclude that the effect, therefore, must be of little practical importance. In fact, a small-appearing estimate of POV_{pop} may actually be practically important and may also be typical, or larger than typical, of the effect of independent variables in a given area of the human sciences. A report of research can deal with this possible problem by tailoring the Discussion section to the expected level of statistical knowledge of the readership.

DEPENDENCE ON THE CHOICE OF LEVELS

The literature includes a fifth criticism of the POV_{pop} measure that is applied under the fixed-effects model; namely, that its magnitude depends on which of the possible levels of the independent variable are selected by the researcher for the study. For example, including an extreme level, such as a no-treatment control group (i.e., a *strong manipulation*), can increase the estimate. (In a strong manipulation there is a large difference in magnitudes of the lowest and highest values of the quantitative independent variable.) However, standardized-difference effect sizes are similarly dependent on the range of difference between the two levels of the independent variable that are being compared. For example, one is likely to obtain a larger value of an estimate of a POV_{pop} or standardized-difference effect size if one compares a high dose of a drug with a zero dose (placebo) than if one compares two intermediate doses. This criticism can be countered if the researcher chooses the levels of the independent variable sensibly and limits the interpretation of the results to those levels only, as is required under the fixed-effects model. In applied research a researcher's "sensible" choice of levels of the independent variable would be those that are comparable to the levels that are currently used, or are likely to be adopted, in practice. Observe by inspecting the numerators of Equations 6.9 and 6.10 that an estimate of overall POV_{pop} is also affected by the number of levels of the independent variable, k; also consult Barnette and McLean (1999).

INFLUENCE OF UNRELIABILITY

As is the case for other kinds of effect size, estimates of POV_{pop} will be reduced by unreliable measurement of the dependent variable; or by unreliable measurement, unreliable recording, or unreliable manipulation of the independent variable, all of which was discussed in Chapter 4. The estimate of the POV_{pop} can be no greater than, and likely is often much less than, the product of r_{xx} and r_{yy}, which are the reliability coefficients (Chapter 4) of the independent variable and the measure of the dependent variable, respectively. In many cases the reliability of the independent variable will not be known. However, if one assumes that for a manipulated independent variable (i.e., an experiment) $r_{xx} = 1$, or nearly so, then the estimate of the POV_{pop} will have an upper limit at or slightly below the value of r_{yy}.

The lower the reliabilities, the greater the contribution of error variance to the total variance of the data, and, therefore, the lower the proportion of total variance of the data that is associated with variation of the independent variable. (Observe that the denominators of Equations 6.9 through 6.11 become greater the greater the error variability.) Also, as was previously stated, estimators of POV_{pop} assume homoscedasticity, and they can especially overestimate POV_{pop} when there is heteroscedasticity and unequal ns (Carroll & Nordholm, 1975).

INFLUENCE OF DESIGN CHARACTERISTICS AND FURTHER READING

Analysis of data occurs in a context of design characteristics that can influence the results (Wilson & Lipsey, 2001). Therefore, when interpreting results and when comparing them with those from other studies one should be cognizant of the research design and context that gave rise to those results. Thus, a researcher should report, subject to the other limitations that have been discussed, that it is estimated that $P\%$ of the variance of the measure of the dependent variable is accounted for when the kind of participants who were used are assigned to each of the k levels of the independent variable that were used. Further, one should be cautions about comparing estimates of POV_{pop} from studies with different sample sizes (Murray & Dosser, 1987).

Olejnik and Algina (2003) provided measures of *generalized* POV_{pop} that are applicable to between-group and repeated-measures designs (provided that a univariate approach to repeated-measures designs is taken), so that POV effect size estimates from different designs can be compared. Also consult Bakeman (2005), who discussed some limitations and easy calculation using output from common statistical packages.

STANDARDIZED-DIFFERENCE EFFECT SIZES FOR CONTRASTS

When an estimator of a standardized-difference effect size involves the mean ($\overline{Y}_c$) of a control, placebo, or standard-treatment comparison group, and the mean of any one of the other groups ($\overline{Y}_i$), and homoscedasticity is not assumed, it is sensible to use the standard deviation of such a comparison group, s_c, for estimating the standardized mean difference to obtain

$$d_{comp} = \frac{\bar{Y}_i - \bar{Y}_c}{s_c}.$$ (6.13)

Alternatively, if one assumes homoscedasticity of the two populations whose samples are involved in the comparison, the pooled standard deviation from these two samples, s_p, may be used instead to find as the estimator

$$d_p = \frac{\bar{Y}_i - \bar{Y}_j}{s_p},$$ (6.14)

where j represents a control or any other kind of group. If one assumes homoscedasticity of all of the k populations (more questionable) the best standard deviation by which to divide the difference between any two of the means, including $\bar{Y}_i - \bar{Y}_c$, is the standard deviation that is based on pooling the within-group variances of all k groups, $MS_w^{1/2}$, producing as the estimator

$$d_{msw} = \frac{\bar{Y}_i - \bar{Y}_j}{MS_w^{1/2}}.$$ (6.15)

As is discussed in the next section, the estimators in Equations 6.13 through 6.15 have a somewhat different interpretation. Also, under homoscedasticity, using the $MS_w^{1/2}$ as the standardizer as in Equation 6.15 results in a better estimate of the effect size in the population, a more powerful test of the comparison between μ_i and μ_j, and a more accurate confidence interval for the standardized or unstandardized $\mu_i - \mu_j$. However, the greater the number of groups, the greater the chance of heteroscedasticity.

Tips and Pitfalls
A problem may occur when applying Equation 6.14 to more than one of the possible pairs of the k means. To some extent differences among the two or more values of d_p may arise merely from varying values of s_i from comparison to comparison, even if the same, $\bar{Y}_j$ say, $\bar{Y}_c$, is used for each d_p. Even when there is homoscedasticity, sampling variability of values of s_i^2 can cause great variation in the different values of s_i^2 that contribute to the pooling of an s_i^2 and an s_j^2 for each d_p. Such sampling variability should be taken into account when interpreting differences among the values of d_p.

WORKED EXAMPLES

We use the results in Table 6.1 from the research on recall to demonstrate calculation and interpretation of all of the estimators that were presented previously. For examples of calculation of Equations 6.13 and 6.14 we use $\bar{Y}_2 = 6.38$ for $\bar{Y}_i$, and $\bar{Y}_5 = 13.44$ for $\bar{Y}_c$ and $\bar{Y}_j$. Therefore, s_c is $s_5 = 3.36$ and s_p is based on pooling the variances of samples 2 and 5, in which $s_2^2 = 2.79^2 = 7.78$ and $s_5^2 = 3.36^2 = 11.29$. Values of s^2 for each sample can be obtained from software output or from an equation for manual calculation: $s^2 = [(\Sigma Y^2) - n(\bar{Y}^2)]/(n - 1)$. We previously reported that $MS_w = 9.53$ for the current data on recall.

One pools the variances $s_2^2 = 7.78$ and $s_5^2 = 11.29$ to find s_p^2 using Equation 6.16:

$$s_p^2 = \frac{(n_i - 1)s_i^2 + (n_j - 1)s_j^2}{n_i + n_j - 2}. \tag{6.16}$$

Using Equation 6.16, $s_p^2 = [(16 - 1)7.78 + (16 - 1)11.29]/(16 + 16 - 2) = 9.54$ and $s_p = 9.54^{1/2} = 3.09$.

Applying the needed values mentioned earlier to Equations 6.13 through 6.15, respectively, yields $d_{comp} = (6.38 - 13.44)/3.36 = -2.10$, $d_p = (6.38 - 13.44)/3.09 = -2.28$, and $d_{msw} = (6.38 - 13.44)/9.53^{1/2} = -2.29$. From the value of d_{comp} one estimates that, with regard to the comparison population's distribution and standard deviation, the mean of population i is 2.10 standard deviation units below the mean of the comparison population. From the value of d_p one estimates that, with regard to the distribution of population j and a common standard deviation for populations i and j, the mean of population i is 2.28 standard deviation units below the mean of population j. Finally, from the value of d_{msw} one estimates that, with regard to the distribution of population j and a common standard deviation for all five of the involved populations, the mean of population i is 2.29 standard deviation units below the mean of population j.

If one assumes normality for the two compared populations, one can interpret the results in terms of an estimation of what percentage of the members of one population score higher or lower than the average-scoring members of the other population. (If needed, refer to Chapter 3 for a refresher on this topic.) A researcher should decide a priori which pair or pairs of means are of interest and then choose among Equations 6.13 through 6.15 based on whether or not homoscedasticity is to be assumed. Any estimate that is calculated must then be reported.

It can be shown that when participants have been randomly assigned to the levels of the independent variable a pooled or unpooled standardizer will reflect the full range of variability in the entire sampled population. However, when the independent variable is classificatory (e.g., gender, ethnicity, political affiliation) and has an effect, the pooled standardizer under homoscedasticity will reflect the range of variability in only one of the sampled populations. Olejnik and Algina (2000) discussed this problem and provided a corrected standardizer, but admit that it would not be a good idea to adopt this standardizer because it would result in estimates that could not be compared with estimates that have resulted from decades of research that used the standardizers in Equations 6.13 through 6.15.

UNSTANDARDIZED DIFFERENCES BETWEEN MEANS

Before considering standardized differences between means further we discuss methods for unstandardized differences between means as effect sizes. There is a vast literature on this topic, which warrants extensive discussion here. Recall from the opening sections of Chapters 2 and 3 that unstandardized differences between means can be especially informative effect sizes when the dependent variable is scaled in familiar units such as weight lost or gained, ounces of alcohol or number of cigarettes consumed, days abstinent or absent, or dollars spent. Such dependent variables are of intrinsic interest and are not merely representing underlying variables. (Also, when a measure of a dependent variable that is used to represent a latent variable [e.g., depression] is not linearly related to it, an effect size calculated on the former will not correspond to an effect size for the latter.) Bond, Wiitala, and Richard (2003) argued for routine use of unstandardized differences in such cases (also Baguley, 2009, 2010) and demonstrated a method for their use in meta-analysis.

When different researchers use different measures of the presumed same latent variable (e.g., depression) standardizing a mean difference places the mean differences that emerge from the different studies on the same scale and thereby renders them comparable. (Consult Baguley, 2010, for a moderated view.) However, when the dependent variable is of interest in its own right different researchers use the same dependent variable (e.g., weight in comparative studies of weight-loss programs), so there is no need for further standardization, and unstandardized mean differences are recommended.

Tukey HSD Method and Some Competitors

Tests of the statistical significance of all of the $\overline{Y}_i - \overline{Y}_j$ pairings, including $\overline{Y}_{max} - \overline{Y}_{min}$, and construction of confidence intervals that are based on all such unstandardized effect sizes ("simultaneous confidence intervals") are often conducted using John Tukey's HSD (*honestly statistically different*) test of pair-wise comparisons. (Whereas an *individual confidence level* gives the probability, say, .95, that a confidence interval contains the targeted parameter, a *simultaneous confidence level* gives the probability that each of the entire set of constructed confidence intervals, taken together, contains its targeted parameter.) This method is widely available in software packages.

Tips and Pitfalls

When using some methods of pair-wise comparisons as unstandardized effect sizes, such as the Tukey method, it is customary, but unwise in terms of loss of statistical power, to have conducted a previous omnibus (overall) F test. Tukey's HSD method should be a substitute for, not a follow-up to, an omnibus test. (The well-known Scheffé method, that is not discussed here, and Dayton's, 2003, method, that is discussed here, are exceptions.) Consult Sawilowsky and Spence (2007) and Wilcox (2009a) for elaboration of this issue of problematic prior omnibus F testing. Further, the results of an omnibus F test may not be consistent with those of the Tukey test. The omnibus F may be significant even when none of the pair-wise comparisons is significant, and vice versa. The researcher's initial research hypothesis or hypotheses should determine whether to use an omnibus F test and omnibus estimator of effect size or pair-wise comparisons of means and their related specific (focused) effect sizes. Also, an advantage of pair-wise effect sizes for comparisons across studies is that omnibus effect sizes can be similar or identical in different studies even if the pattern of pair-wise effect sizes is very different.

The original Tukey HSD method assumes homoscedasticity and normality. The procedures for the Tukey HSD method for pair-wise significance testing and construction of confidence intervals, including modifications for unequal n and heteroscedasticity, are explained in detail in Maxwell and Delaney (2004). For more robust methods consult Cribbie and Keselman (2003a), Cribbie, Wilcox, Bewell, and Keselman (2007), Keselman et al. (2008), Keselman et al. (2007), Kowalchuk et al. (2006), Kulinskaya, Dollinger, Knight, and Gao (2004), and Wilcox (2006d). Wilcox (2003, 2005a) provided various S-PLUS and R software functions for robust methods of pair-wise comparisons.

Comparison of Each Group with a Baseline Group

In the case of planned comparisons between each mean and the mean of a single baseline group (i.e., a control, placebo, or standard-treatment group as in the numerator of Equation 6.13), the Dunnett *many-one method* may be used for significance testing and construction of simultaneous confidence intervals for all of the values of $\mu_i - \mu_c$ as unstandardized effect sizes. The procedure, which assumes homoscedasticity, can be found in Maxwell and Delaney (2004). (The Dunnett many-one method is not the same and is not for the same purpose as the Dunnett T3 method.)

Tips and Pitfalls

Multiple pair-wise comparisons of means effect sizes can produce contradictory results that are difficult to interpret. Consider an example in which the mean of each treatment group is compared to the mean of the same baseline group (a "many-one" set of pair-wise comparisons) and only some of the treatment groups' means are found to be statistically significantly different from the baseline group's mean. Suppose further that the researcher then conducts pair-wise comparisons among all of the means of the treatment groups. Interpretation regarding these latter comparisons is problematic regarding comparisons involving a mean that was statistically significantly superior to the mean of the baseline group (i.e., an efficacious treatment) and a mean that was not statistically superior to the mean of the baseline group (i.e., a not efficacious treatment) if the difference between these latter two means does not attain statistical significance. In this case of *intransitivity* there is a contradictory result that an efficacious treatment appears to be no better than a treatment that is not efficacious. Intransitive results are discussed further later.

Maxwell (2004) discussed power implications for methods of multiple comparisons, distinguishing among *power for a specific comparison*, *any-pair power* to detect at least one pair-wise difference, and *all-pairs power* to detect all differences within pairs of means. Low power for a specific comparison can result in inconsistent results across studies even when any-pair power is adequate.

Comparisons involving the mean of two or more means are called *complex comparisons*, *complex contrasts*, or, more generally, linear contrasts as effect sizes. An example would be the difference between the mean of a control group and the overall mean of two or more treatment groups. Construction of confidence intervals for such complex contrasts was discussed by Maxwell and Delaney (2004). Robust methods using S-PLUS software functions were discussed by Wilcox (2003).

INTRANSITIVE RESULTS

Methods of pair-wise comparisons, such as Tukey's method, can produce *intransitive* (i.e., contradictory) *results* as effect sizes. For example, suppose that there are three groups, so that one can test H_0: $\mu_1 = \mu_2$, H_0: $\mu_2 = \mu_3$, and H_0: $\mu_1 = \mu_3$. Unfortunately, it is possible for a method of pair-wise comparisons to produce intransitive results, such as seeming to indicate that $\mu_1 = \mu_2$, $\mu_2 = \mu_3$, and, contradictorily, $\mu_1 > \mu_3$. It is not known how common this problem of intransitivity is in real data.

When there is intransitivity the true pattern (i.e., order) of the magnitudes of the population means is unclear, so the estimation of effect sizes that are based on those means is problematic. Dayton (2003) proposed making inferences about the true pattern of the means of the involved populations. The method is intended to be applicable to the case of homoscedasticity or the case in which the pattern of the magnitudes of the variances in the populations is the same as the pattern of the means in the populations. The method generally appears to be robust to nonnormality and to heteroscedasticity in most cases, generally providing good control of Type I error and good power (Cribbie & Keselman, 2003a, 2003b; Dayton). Computations can be implemented using Excel (Dayton) or a SAS program (Dayton & Pan, 2005).

EXPERIMENT-WISE ERROR RATE AND FALSE DISCOVERY RATE

Pan and Dayton (2005) discussed additional problems arising from traditional methods for making all pair-wise comparisons for independent groups as effect sizes. These problems are the control of the *experiment-wise error rate* (α_{EW}, i.e., the probability that at least one of the comparisons will result in a Type I error) and choosing from the resulting variety of competing methods that differ in their approach to controlling such error and differ in power. Those authors argued that such problems can be avoided and the interpretation of results enhanced by considering the previously discussed patterns of the magnitudes of the means instead of pair-wise differences. Researchers with limited resources may be disheartened to observe in a table that Pan and Dayton provided that, with only three groups with different means and effect size magnitude $f = .40$ (large, by Cohen's, 1988, general criteria), the Tukey HSD test is estimated to require total $N = 360$ to attain power $= .80$ to reject all three H_0: $\mu_i = \mu_j$ at $\alpha < .05$. (The effect size $f = .40$ is approximately equivalent to $POV_{pop} = .14$.)

Authors such as Keppel and Zedeck (1989) and Thompson (1991) have argued that correcting for inflation of experiment-wise error rate when conducting multiple comparisons can needlessly lower power in the case in which the specific comparisons were pre-planned on the basis of theory. However, those authors also suggested one or another criterion for upper limits for the number of planned comparisons beyond which researchers should consider correcting for experiment-wise error rate. Also, the Dunn–Šidák multiple-comparison procedure for any set of a priori comparisons between means or confidence intervals is slightly more powerful than the traditional Dunn–Bonferroni procedure that specifies a desired experiment-wise error rate (e.g., .05) across the set of comparisons. There are methods of multiple comparisons that are intended to control the *false discovery rate* (*FDR*, also known as the *false discovery proportion*), which is the expected ratio of the number of falsely rejected null hypotheses to the number of rejected null hypotheses (Benjamini, 2010). The 2010, volume 2, issue 6, of *Biometrical Journal* is devoted to the topic of multiple comparisons.

MORE ON STANDARDIZED DIFFERENCES BETWEEN MEANS

CONFIDENCE INTERVALS

Approximate confidence intervals for each d_{pop}, the standardized difference between population means, can be obtained, assuming homoscedasticity, by dividing the lower and upper limits of the confidence interval for each unstandardized pair-wise difference between population means by $MS_w^{1/2}$. Refer to Steiger (1999) for software for constructing exact confidence intervals for a standardized-difference effect size (as estimated by our Equation 6.14) that arises from planned contrasts when sample sizes are equal. The exact confidence intervals use noncentral distributions. Steiger and Fouladi (1997) and Smithson (2003) illustrated the method.

Bird (2002) presented an approximate method for the construction of a confidence interval for d_{pop} that is based on the usual (i.e., central) t distribution. (Assuming normality, an exact confidence interval would require the use of the noncentral t distribution that was discussed in Chapter 3.) This method also assumes homoscedasticity by using the square root of MS_w from the ANOVA results to standardize the difference between the two means of interest. For further discussion consult Lecoutre (2007). Consult Algina and Keselman (2003b) for a method and a SAS/IML program for constructing an exact confidence interval for each d_{pop}, assuming homoscedasticity. This method provides the option to obtain the standardizer by pooling all variances in the design or just the variances of the two groups that are involved in the effect size.

Robust Methods

Keselman et al. (2008) discussed the use of percentile bootstrapping and robust estimation of means and variances to construct a robust *CI* for a pair-wise standardized-difference effect size. The method is also applicable to standardized complex contrasts. Free SAS/IML software for implementation, courtesy of Keselman et al. and the American Psychological Association, is available from http://dx.doi.org/1037/1082-989X/13.2.110.supp.

Bonett (2008) reported simulations that indicated good probability coverage for his method for constructing a confidence interval for a standardized contrast of means under slight heteroscedasticity (population variance ratio = 1.5) in the cases of $k = 3$ and $k = 4$. His method assumes normality. His preferred estimator of the standardizer, unless there is reason to expect more than slight heteroscedasticity, is the square root of the mean of the unbiased estimates of the variances of the populations. This estimator is the same as $MS_w^{1/2}$ when sample sizes are equal. Bonett's method is also applicable to the use of the standard deviation of a given group, such as a control group, as the standardizer, or the square root of the mean of the variances of only those groups that are involved in the contrast of means. As previously mentioned, Bonett's methods might fail under more than slight departures from homoscedasticity and normality. Bonett (2009b) further provided formulas for estimating needed sample sizes for standardized linear contrasts of $k \geq 2$ means.

For a measure of effect size for two or more groups in a randomized longitudinal design consult Maxwell (1998). Rosenthal et al. (2000) provided an alternative treatment of effect sizes in terms of correlational contrasts for one-way and factorial designs. Timm (2004) proposed the *ubiquitous effect size index* for exploratory experiments. Timm's method is applicable to omnibus *F* tests or tests of contrasts. This descriptive effect size reduces to *d* in the case of two samples of equal size.

Nonparametric Approaches

Serlin, Carr, and Marascuilo (1982) proposed a strength-of-association (i.e., POV_{pop}) analog effect size for the Kruskal–Wallis nonparametric alternative to parametric ANOVA. For the case in which two groups at a time from multiple groups are compared, Wilcox (2003, 2005a) discussed and provided S-PLUS and R software functions for the estimation of the nonparametric $Pr(Y_i > Y_j)$ and dominance measures of effect size that were discussed in Chapter 5. Consult Long et al. (2003) for further discussions of multiple comparisons involving the dominance measure for one-way and factorial designs. Consult Vargha and Delaney (2000) and Brunner and Puri (2001) for extensions of $Pr(Y_i > Y_j)$ to multiple-group and factorial designs.

INTRANSITIVITY AND THE *PS* EFFECT SIZE

We previously noted that it is possible for methods of pair-wise comparisons as unstandardized effect sizes, such as Tukey's HSD method, to yield intransitive results. Intransitivity is also possible when pair-wise estimates of the probability-of-superiority effect size (*PS*), $\Pr(Y_i > Y_j)$, of Chapter 5 are made in the $k > 2$ case. Newcombe (2006b) illustrated how such intransitivity can happen. Consult Vargha (2005) for further discussion.

One approach to avoiding intransitivity in the application of the probability of superiority to the case of $k > 2$ groups involves all of the $\Pr(Y_i > Y_u)$ as effect sizes, where i represents any one of the populations and u represents the union (i.e., the combination) of all of the other groups. The $\Pr(Y_i > Y_u)$ is the probability that a randomly sampled member of population i will have a score that is higher than the score from a randomly sampled member of a combined population that consists of members of all populations that are represented in the study with the exception of population i (Vargha & Delaney, 2000).

Contrasting with the approach of Vargha and Delaney (2000), which can be called the *one-against-the-others approach*, Brunner and Puri (2001) proposed what can be called the *one-against-all approach*. Unlike Vargha–Delaney, in the Brunner–Puri approach each individual group i is compared to the grand combined group that now *includes* group i. Thus, in this approach, unlike the previous approach, each group is compared to a constant comparison group in each estimation of $\Pr(Y_i > Y_{all})$ as an effect size. Details are in Brunner and Puri and Vargha and Delaney (2004). Wilcox (2003) provided S-PLUS functions for the calculations.

WITHIN-GROUPS DESIGNS

In the case of within-groups designs meta-analysts must avoid inflating estimates of standardized-difference effect sizes by the use of invalid conversion formulas from reported values of t or F. Valid formulas for approximately converting values of t or F from earlier primary research to an estimate of effect size are available (cf. Cortina & Nouri, 2000). However, this section discusses estimation of effect sizes from raw data so conversion formulas are not needed here.

For one-way ANOVA within-groups designs (e.g., repeated-measures designs) primary researchers can use the same equations that were presented in this chapter for the independent-groups design to calculate estimates of standardized-difference effect sizes. If a repeated-measures design has involved a pretest, the pretest mean ($\overline{Y}_{pre}$) can be one of any two compared means, and the standard deviation may be s_{pre}, s_p, or $MS_w^{1/2}$. The latter two standardizers assume homoscedasticity with regard either to the two compared groups or all of the groups, respectively. (Statistical software may not automatically generate s_{pre}, s_p, or $MS_w^{1/2}$ when it computes a within-groups ANOVA. However, such software does allow one to compute the variance of data within a single condition of the design. Therefore, one may use the variances so generated to calculate $MS_w^{1/2}$ and s_p using Equations 6.2 and 6.16, respectively.)

CONFIDENCE INTERVALS

Consult Algina and Keselman (2003b) for a method and a SAS/IML program for constructing an approximate confidence interval for a standardized-difference effect size under homoscedasticity or heteroscedasticity in a within-groups design. Bonett (2008) reported simulations that indicated good probability coverage for his proposed method for constructing a confidence interval for a standardized contrast of means for within-groups designs under normality, slight heteroscedasticity, and a range of correlations among the groups. We discussed this method earlier in this chapter in the context of between-groups designs. Bonett (2009) further provided formulas for estimating needed sample sizes for standardized linear contrasts of $k \geq 2$ means for the within-groups case.

Again, when dependent variables are measured on scales that are of direct interest (e.g., dieters' weights, daily ounces of alcohol consumed by alcoholics) instead of scales that stand-in for latent variables of interest, an unstandardized difference between means (or medians) is an appropriate effect size. Blouin and Riopelle (2005) discussed the problem of confidence intervals for mean differences yielding results that are inconsistent with the results from statistical significance testing in within-groups ANOVA when studying the pattern of the means. Wilcox (2006g) discussed a small-sample method and a large-sample method for making pair-wise comparisons of medians of dependent groups in one-way ANOVA. Nashimoto and Wright (2007) reported simulations that indicated that their proposed procedures for multiple comparisons of medians perform much better than traditional methods for means when distributions are heavy tailed.

PAIR-WISE COMPARISONS AND SPHERICITY

For methods for making all pair-wise comparisons (planned or unplanned) of the $\overline{Y}_i - \overline{Y}_j$ differences as unstandardized effect sizes for dependent data, including the construction of simultaneous confidence intervals, refer to Maxwell and Delaney's (2004) and Wilcox's (2003) discussions of the Bonferroni–Dunn method. Consult Wilcox (2005a) for robust methods and R and S-PLUS functions for constructing confidence intervals for pair-wise comparisons of dependent means using trimmed means or M-estimators of location.

The Tukey HSD method is not recommended for significance testing and the construction of confidence intervals in the case of dependent data because, as is not the case for the Bonferroni–Dunn method, the Tukey method may not maintain experiment-wise error rate at the desired level (e.g., $\alpha_{EW} < .05$) unless the *sphericity assumption* is satisfied. (Of the several ways to define sphericity the simplest focuses on the variance of the difference scores ($Y_i - Y_j$) with respect to compared levels i and j. Sphericity is satisfied when the population variances of such difference scores are the same for all such pairs of levels.) When sphericity is violated the rate of Type I error departs from the nominal rate. Because tests of sphericity may not have sufficient power to detect its violation it is best to use methods that do not assume sphericity (e.g., better to use a multivariate than a univariate approach to designs with dependent groups, as is discussed in Chapter 12).

Refer to Wilcox and Keselman (2002) for simulations of the effectiveness of methods to deal with the problem of outliers when conducting all comparisons of the locations (e.g., trimmed means) of one specific condition and each of the other conditions (another many-one procedure) in the case of unstandardized effect sizes for dependent data. Dayton's (2003; Dayton & Pan, 2005) previously discussed method and suggested software for detecting the pattern of relationships among the means of the populations are also applicable to the case of dependent groups.

PROPORTION OF VARIANCE EXPLAINED

To estimate overall POV_{pop} in a one-way ANOVA design with repeated measures one can use

$$\omega^2 = \frac{(k-1)(MS_{effect} - MS_{t \times s})}{SS_{tot} + MS_{sub}},$$

(6.17)

where
  k is the number of levels of the factor of interest
  MS_{effect} is the mean square for the main effect of that factor
  $MS_{t \times s}$ is the mean square for the interaction between that factor and the subject factor
  SS_{tot} is the total sum of squares
  MS_{sub} is the mean square for subjects

If software does not produce this estimate directly, calculation can be done manually by obtaining the needed values from output. At the time of this writing in order to find SS_{tot} for Equation 6.17 using IBM SPSS, or to find SS_{tot} and MS_{sub} using SAS, data must be entered as if the within-subjects factor were a between-subjects factor, so that it appears that there is no within-subjects factor. The approach underlying Equation 6.17 addresses a one-way dependent-groups ANOVA as if it were a two-way design in which the main factor is Treatment or some classificatory factor of interest, the other factor is Subjects, and the error term is the mean square for interaction. Recall from earlier in this chapter that Olejnik and Algina (2003) and Bakeman (2005) discussed the use (with some limitations) of generalized POV_{pop} to render estimates of this effect size comparable for between-groups and repeated-measures designs.

MORE ON CHOICE OF STANDARDIZER

Tips and Pitfalls
It would be inappropriate to use the current $MS^{1/2}$ for interaction as a standardizer for a standardized-difference effect size because this choice would render such an effect size not comparable with effect sizes from between-groups studies of

the same levels of the same independent variable. The standardizer in between-groups designs includes subject variability, whereas the $MS^{1/2}$ for interaction in within-groups designs does not, rendering $MS^{1/2}$ smaller and, therefore, rendering the d for which such an $MS^{1/2}$ is used as the standardizer an unrealistically large estimator. One should use a reasonable standardizer that reflects subject variability in the within-groups case so that the estimator will reflect variability that the effect size in the population reflects. Following Maxwell and Delaney (2004), this goal results in the use of an MS that has a numerator that sums the SS for subjects and the SS for interaction, and a denominator that sums the df for subjects $(n - 1)$ and the df for interaction $[(k - 1)(n - 1)]$. This sum is $(n - 1) + [(k - 1)(n - 1)] = k(n - 1)$. We denote the resulting standardizer s_{wg} (i.e., standard deviation for the within-groups case):

$$ s_{wg} = \left[\frac{SS_{sub} + SS_{txs}}{k(n-1)} \right]^{1/2}. \tag{6.18} $$

The advantage of using the standardizer in Equation 6.18 is that it is comparable to $MS_w^{1/2}$ from a between-groups design. Both standardizers assume homoscedasticity across all of the populations that are represented in the study, not just the two populations that are involved in the effect size. For this reason those whose research questions are consistent with the use of a standardizer that is based on a group's pretest scores or scores from a control or standard-treatment condition should consider using the standard deviation from such a single group of scores as a standardizer that does not assume homoscedasticity.

PARTIAL POV_{pop} VERSUS POV_{pop}

It has been argued that a *partial* POV_{pop} should be estimated for within-groups designs instead of the kind of *whole* POV_{pop} that appears in Equation 6.17 (Keppel & Wickens, 2004) because estimation of partial POV_{pop} excludes subject variability and excluding subject variability to increase statistical power is a major reason for adopting a within-groups design. Olejnik and Algina (2000) and Keppel and Wickens provided relevant equations (e.g., Equations 6.19 and 12.9). For a contrary view consult Maxwell and Delaney (2004), who recommended the estimation of whole POV_{pop} for within-subjects designs because doing so estimates the proportional role of the independent variable in accounting for total variability that *includes subject variability,* as is also the case in between-groups designs. We discuss estimation of partial and whole POV_{pop} further in Chapters 7 and 12.

We demonstrate the application of Equation 6.17 using data that preceded the introduction of ω^2 as an estimate of POV_{pop}. The dependent variable was visual acuity and the treatments were three distances at which the target was viewed by four participants (Walker, 1947; cited by McNemar, 1962). Substantive details of the research and possible alternative analyses of the data do not concern us here. The values that are required for Equation 6.17 (directly or indirectly) and later are

$k = 3$, $SS_{effect} = 1095.50$, $SS_{t \times s} = 596.50$, $n = 4$, $SS_{tot} = 2290.25$, and $SS_{sub} = 598.25$. The effect of treatment is statistically significant, $F(2, 6) = 5.51$, $p < .05$. Dividing the values of SS by the appropriate degrees of freedom to obtain the required values of MS yields

$$\omega^2 = \frac{(3-1)[(1095.50/(3-1)) - (596.50/(3-1)(4-1))]}{2290.25 + (598.25/(4-1))} = .36.$$

Therefore, one estimates that the varying distances at which the target is viewed account for 36% of the variance in acuity scores, under the conditions in which the research was conducted.

One version of the equations for an estimated partial ω^2 is

$$\omega^2_{partial} = \left[\frac{(k-1)(MS_{effect} - MS_{t \times s})}{(k-1)(MS_{effect}) + (kn - k + 1)(MS_{t \times s})} \right]. \tag{6.19}$$

Applying the values from the present example to Equation 6.19 yields

$$\omega^2_{partial} = \frac{(3-1)[(1095.50/(3-1)) - (596.50/(3-1)(4-1))]}{(3-1)[1095.50/(3-1)] + [(3 \times 4) - 3 + 1][596.50/(3-1)(4-1)]} = .43.$$

Therefore, it would be concluded by those who favor the approach of estimating partial POV_{pop} that is represented by Equation 6.19 that it is estimated that varying viewing distances accounts for approximately 43% of the variance in visual acuity. Observe that the estimate of partial POV_{pop}, 43%, is greater than the previously obtained estimate of whole POV_{pop}, 36%. Such a difference should be expected because estimates of partial POV_{pop} exclude subject variance from total variance, so the independent variable has less total variance to account for when estimating partial POV_{pop} instead of whole POV_{pop}. A researcher would use whole POV_{pop} for within-groups designs if interested in POV_{pop} with regard to total variability (as reflected by the denominator in Equation 6.17) or use partial POV_{pop} if interested in POV_{pop} with regard to the variability in the data excluding subject variability (as reflected by the denominator of Equation 6.19).

Tips and Pitfalls
Research reports should be clear about which kind of estimated POV_{pop} is being reported so that readers will not be misled into comparing the particular reported estimate with the other, incomparable, kind of estimate that readers may find elsewhere in the literature. Researchers should also consider, as a courtesy to a wider range of readers, reporting and interpreting both kinds of estimates because some readers may have an opinion about which kind of estimate is appropriate that is different from the opinion of the researcher. Finally, reports should also include

the equation that is used to estimate partial ω^2 because it possible that equations that are provided by different statistical authors for the within-groups case will yield somewhat different results.

WORKED EXAMPLE OF ESTIMATION OF WITHIN-GROUPS d_{pop}

To calculate estimates of a within-groups standardized-difference effect size, which we denote d_{wg}, using Equation 6.18 for the denominator of the estimator, one also needs for the current real example the information that, for the numerators of the three possible pair-wise estimates, $\overline{Y}_1 = 8.5$, $\overline{Y}_2 = 23.7$, and $\overline{Y}_3 = 31.5$. For example, to estimate a standardized pair-wise effect size for populations 1 and 2 one finds that, $d_{wg} = (8.5 - 23.7)/[(598.25 + 596.50)/3(4 - 1)]^{1/2} = -1.32$. Thus, the mean of population 1 is estimated to be approximately 1.32 standard deviation units lower than the mean of population 2, assuming homoscedasticity and using the standardizer defined by Equation 6.18.

MORE METHODS AND ADDITIONAL READING

Rosenthal et al. (2000) presented an alternative treatment of effect sizes for one-way and factorial-dependent group designs in terms of correlational types of contrasts (also discussed by Furr, 2004). Keppel and Wickens (2004) provided additional equations for whole and partial ω^2 for the case of dependent groups using values of F instead of values of SS and MS.

For extensions of the nonparametric approach that we call the probability-of-superiority effect size to dependent multiple groups in one-way and factorial designs consult Vargha and Delaney (2000) and Brunner and Puri (2001). Similarly, Newcombe (2007) recommended methods for nonparametric estimation and construction of confidence intervals for an effect size for pair-wise comparisons from $k \geq 2$ dependent groups. The methods are based on the Wilcoxon matched-pairs signed-ranks test statistic.

Serlin et al. (1982) proposed an analog of the POV_{pop} effect size for the nonparametric Friedman test alternative to the one-way ANOVA F test for dependent groups. Lecoutre and Derzko (2001) discussed equivalence testing (defined in Chapter 2) for the case of one-way fixed-effects independent groups and repeated-measures ANOVA.

SUMMARY

The F test in the ANOVA provides no direct information about effect sizes, but there are many effect sizes that can be estimated that focus on the overall effect of the independent variable or focus on the effects of its paired levels.

Under homoscedasticity, when the F test is used the f measure as estimated by the unbiased estimator is applicable as a standardized overall effect size that involves all of the group means. The standardized-difference effect size, d_{mmpop}, which uses only the largest and smallest means should not be used merely to report the largest kind of d effect size. To estimate proportion of variance explained (POV_{pop}) overall or pair-wise we recommend the use of ω^2 as the least biased estimator, and we recommend constructing a confidence interval for POV_{pop}. Criticisms of POV_{pop} were reviewed.

For standardized pair-wise comparisons, basing the standardizer on the standard deviation of a comparison group or on pooling variances depends on whether or not homoscedasticity is assumed. However, when means are of interest and the observed dependent variable is on a meaningful (familiar) scale that is of interest in its own right the use of unstandardized mean differences is preferable to standardized mean differences as effect sizes. Tukey HSD multiple-comparison testing of the statistical significance of the unstandardized pair-wise differences should not be preceded by an omnibus F test and lends itself to construction of confidence intervals, but it has alternatives that are apparently more robust.

Construction of confidence intervals is recommended when undertaking pair-wise comparisons or complex contrasts involving unstandardized differences between means. There are also methods for controlling the experiment-wise error rate when making pair-wise comparisons, and there is debate about loss of power when doing so. A related issue is the control of the FDR. Methods of pair-wise comparisons of unstandardized differences between means (e.g., Tukey HSD testing) are subject to intransitive results (i.e., contradictory differences between paired means), but there are methods that avoid intransitivity. Construction of confidence intervals is also recommended when using pair-wise standardized differences between means. There are also omnibus and pair-wise nonparametric methods available for that case.

The same equations that were presented in this chapter for standardized mean differences for independent groups are applicable to the within-groups case. For this case the choice of standardizer depends on the nature of the population to which the results are to be generalized. The $MS^{1/2}$ for interaction should generally not be used as a standardizer. Again, construction of confidence intervals is recommended, as is the use of the more robust methods when assumptions may be violated. The Tukey HSD method is not recommended for the within-groups case because of possible violation of an assumption that is called sphericity.

The debate about whether whole POV_{pop} or partial POV_{pop} should be estimated in the within-groups case was discussed. Estimates of partial POV_{pop} should not be reported instead of whole POV_{pop} merely for the invalid purpose of reporting a higher value. Researchers should consider reporting both kinds of estimate with an explanation of each. At the very least, reports should be clear about which kind of estimate of POV_{pop} is being reported.

QUESTIONS

6.1 Why test for the significance of the difference between the greatest and the smallest of the sample means if the overall F test has already been found to be significant, provided that one has a legitimate reason for wanting to compare these two means?

6.2 Define f conceptually, stating why it is an effect size.

6.3 In which direction is the estimator in Equation 6.5 biased, and why?

6.4 Why is the sample eta squared a problematic estimator of POV_{pop}?

6.5 How do the sample epsilon squared and omega squared attempt to reduce biased estimation, and which is less biased?

6.6 How does one determine if omega squared is statistically significantly greater than 0?

6.7 Why are confidence intervals especially important for estimators of POV_{pop}?

6.8 Discuss the rationale that some methodologists use for reporting negative estimates of POV_{pop} as such, instead of reporting them as 0.

6.9 List those limitations or criticisms of POV_{pop} and its estimators that may apply, and those that would not apply, to standardized differences between means.

6.10 How and why does unreliability of scores affect estimates of POV_{pop}?

6.11 What would be more accurate wording in a "Results" section of a research report than merely stating that the independent variable accounted for an estimated $P\%$ of the variance of the dependent variable?

6.12 Name three choices for the standardizer of a standardized difference between two of k means, and when would each choice be appropriate?

6.13 Why should one be cautious when interpreting differences among the values of the estimator in Equation 6.14?

6.14 In which circumstance are statistical inferences and confidence intervals about an unstandardized difference between two means especially informative?

6.15 Would the results of an omnibus F test and applications of the Tukey HSD test always be consistent? Explain.

6.16 What assumption is being made if one constructs a confidence interval for the standardized difference between two of k population means by dividing the upper and lower limits of the confidence interval for the unstandardized pair-wise difference by $MS_w^{1/2}$? Answer using more than one word.

6.17 List the numbers of the equations in this chapter for between-groups standardized mean differences that would also be applicable to within-groups designs.

6.18 Define (a) *intransitivity* when comparing means, (b) the *transformation principle of confidence intervals*, (c) *experiment-wise error rate*, (d) *FDR*, (e) *power for a specific comparison*, (f) *any-pair power*, (g) *all-pairs power*, and (h) *fixed-effects model*.

6.19 Briefly discuss the arguments regarding estimating partial or whole POV_{pop}.

6.20 For the three columns of posttest data in Table 11.1 calculate and interpret an estimate of (a) d_{mmpop}, (b) f (using the unbiased estimator), (c) POV_{pop} (least biased), (d) POV_{pop} for the specific comparison between the control group and Therapy b, and (e) standardized mean difference between the control group and Therapy b, justifying your choice of standardizer.

7 Effect Sizes for Factorial Designs

INTRODUCTION

Again, F tests for the equality of population means for main effects of factors and F tests for interactions provide no direct information about the size of such effects. In this chapter we discuss a variety of estimators of standardized-difference and strength-of-association (population proportion-of variance-explained, POV_{pop}) effect sizes for factorial designs with fixed-effects factors. Effect sizes for each factor, interaction, and simple effects are considered. Prior to the section on within-groups designs the discussion and examples involve between-groups factors.

We focus on assumptions, the nature of the populations to which results are to be generalized, and pair-wise comparisons as unstandardized and standardized effect sizes.

ASSUMPTIONS AND HANDLING VIOLATIONS

The usual assumptions of independence, homoscedasticity, and normality apply. (It can also be argued that an additional important assumption involves the nature of an interaction among the factors; Sawilowsky, 1985.) The previously discussed problems of increased rate of Type I error and lowered power that can arise from violations of assumptions in one-way ANOVA (Chapter 6) apply to factorial ANOVA. Under nonnormality and heteroscedasticity, transforming the data to ranks and applying the Welch test may satisfactorily control Type I error while maintaining power when analyzing data from 2 × 2 designs (Mills, Cribbie, & Luh, 2009). The use of ranks raises the issue of whether parametric or nonparametric effect sizes (both being discussed later in this chapter) would be appropriate. Wilcox (2009a) provided concise discussion of the rationale, computational examples, and a table of critical values for a method that controls family-wise error (i.e., an overall error defined later) when making pair-wise comparisons as unstandardized effect sizes using the Welch test. To counter violation of assumptions Wilcox (2005a) discussed and provided R and S-PLUS functions for (a) two-way and three-way designs using trimmed means and (b) two-way designs using medians.

DISCRETIZING CONTINUOUS INDEPENDENT VARIABLES

In Chapter 6 we cautioned against *discretizing* (i.e., categorizing) continuous independent variables (e.g., high, medium, low) when data have been collected from a continuous range of values of the measure of the independent variable.

An ANOVA ignores the ordinal nature of such categorization, and such categorization can lower reliability, statistical power, and estimates of effect size. Additionally, in the current case of factorial designs, the loss of variance that results from categorizing such continuous independent variables can reduce the detectability of interactions. Note that here we are *not* cautioning against the use of particular levels of an underlying continuous independent variable when those levels are the only ones of interest to the researcher (i.e., a fixed-effects model). The extreme case of discretizing is to dichotomize continuous independent variables. Consult DeCoster et al. (2009) and the references therein for problems, including lowering of estimates of effect size, that can arise from that method.

FACTORS: TARGETED, PERIPHERAL, EXTRINSIC, INTRINSIC

We call the factor with respect to which one estimates an effect size the *targeted factor*. Any other factor in the design we call a *peripheral factor*. If later in the analysis of the same set of data a researcher estimates an effect size with respect to a factor that had previously been a peripheral factor, the roles and labels for this factor and the previously targeted factor are reversed. A peripheral factor is also called an *off factor*.

The appropriate procedures for estimating an effect size from a factorial design depend in part on whether targeted and peripheral factors are *extrinsic* or *intrinsic*. *Extrinsic factors* are factors that do not ordinarily or naturally vary in the population to which the results are to be generalized. Extrinsic factors are often manipulated factors that are treatment variables that are imposed on the participants. *Intrinsic factors* are those that do naturally vary in the population to which the results are to be generalized—factors such as gender, ethnicity, or occupational or educational level. Intrinsic factors are typically *classificatory factors* (the label that we use in this chapter), which are also called in the literature *subject factors*, *grouping factors*, *stratified factors*, *organismic factors*, or *individual-difference factors*. A factor that is currently correctly considered to be extrinsic may become intrinsic in a population of interest in the future. For example, an experimental treatment would be an extrinsic factor currently but it may be widely adopted in the future, rendering it intrinsic at that time.

Tips and Pitfalls

An extremely important consideration when choosing a method for estimating a standardized-difference effect size or POV_{pop} effect size with regard to a targeted factor is whether the peripheral factor is extrinsic or intrinsic. As we soon explain, when a peripheral factor is extrinsic one should generally choose a method in which variance in the data that is attributable to that factor is held constant, making no contribution to the standardizer or to the total variance that is to be accounted for by the targeted factor. When a peripheral factor is intrinsic one should generally choose a method in which variance that is attributable to the peripheral factor is permitted to contribute to the magnitude of the standardizer or to the total variance that is to be accounted for by the targeted factor.

Therefore, when deciding the role that a peripheral factor is to play the researcher must consider the nature of the population with respect to which the estimate of effect size is to be made. If a peripheral factor does not typically vary in the population that is of interest (usually a variable that is manipulated in research, but not in nature), one will choose a method that ignores variability in the data that is attributable to that peripheral factor. If a peripheral factor does typically vary in the population that is of interest (often a classificatory factor such as gender), one will choose a method in which variability that is attributable to such a peripheral factor is permitted to contribute to the standardizer or to total variability.

STRENGTH OF ASSOCIATION: PROPORTION OF VARIANCE EXPLAINED

Estimation of POV_{pop}, which, again, is the proportion of variance of the scores on the dependent variable that is related to variation of the independent variable, is more complicated with regard to factorial designs than is the case with the one-way design, even in the simplest case, which we consider here, in which all sample sizes are equal. In general for the effect of some factor, or the effect of interaction, when the peripheral factors are intrinsic one can estimate POV_{pop} using the sample omega squared:

$$\omega^2 = \frac{SS_{effect} - (df_{effect}MS_w)}{SS_{tot} + MS_w}. \tag{7.1}$$

All MS, SS, and df values are available from, or can be calculated from, the output from the software for the ANOVA F test. With regard to the main effect of Factor A, $SS_{effect} = SS_A$ and $df_{effect} = a - 1$, where a is the number of levels of Factor A. With regard to the main effect of Factor B, substitute B and b (i.e., the number of levels of Factor B) for A and a in the previous sentence, and so forth for the main effect of any other factor in the design. With regard to the interaction effect in a two-way design $SS_{effect} = SS_{AB}$ and $df_{effect} = (a - 1)(b - 1)$. In the section entitled "Illustrative worked examples", we apply Equation 7.1 using an example that is integrated with examples of estimating standardized differences between means for the same data.

Equation 7.1 provides an estimate of the proportion of the total variance of the measure of the dependent variable that is accounted for by an independent variable (or by interaction in the factorial case), as does Equation 6.10 for the one-way design. However, in the present case of factorial designs there can be more sources of variance than in the one-way case because of the contributions made to total variance by one or more additional factors and interactions. An effect of, say, Factor A may yield a different value of ω^2 if it is researched in the context of a one-way design instead of a factorial design, in which there will be more sources of variance that account for the total variance. As was stated previously, estimates of effect size must be interpreted in the context of the design whose results produced the estimate. A method that is intended to render estimates of POV_{pop} from factorial designs comparable to those from one-way designs is discussed in the next section.

The designs in this chapter are *crossed designs*, in which each level of a factor is combined with each level of another factor. For a method for correcting for overestimation of POV_{pop} by omega squared in *nested designs*, in which each level of a factor is combined with only one level of another factor, consult Wampold and Serlin (2000). Also consult the series of articles that debate the matter (Crits-Christoph, Tu, & Gallop, 2003; Serlin, Wampold, & Levin, 2003; Siemer & Joormann, 2003a, 2003b).

PARTIAL ω^2

An alternative conceptualization of estimation of POV_{pop} from factorial designs with extrinsic factors modifies Equation 7.1 so as to attempt to eliminate the contribution that any extrinsic peripheral factor might make to total variance. The resulting measure is called a *partial* POV_{pop}. Whereas a *whole* POV_{pop} measures the strength of an effect relative to the total variance from error and from all effects, a partial POV_{pop} measures the strength of an effect relative to variance that is not attributable to other effects (i.e., not attributable to variability of other factors). The excluded effects are those that would not be present if the levels of the targeted factor had been researched in a one-way design. For this purpose partial eta squared and partial omega squared, the latter being a less biased estimator (Chapter 6), have been traditionally used. Partial POV_{pop} is valid for the present purpose, subject to the limitations of measures of POV_{pop} that were discussed in Chapter 6. Partial POV will always be larger than whole POV unless none of the *partialed* (i.e., excluded) *effects* is contributing systematic variance to total variance. Partial omega squared, $\omega_{partial}^2$, for any effect is given by

$$\omega_{partial}^2 = \frac{SS_{effect} - (df_{effect}MS_w)}{SS_{effect} + (N - df_{effect})MS_w},$$ (7.2)

where N is the total sample size and, if output does not include the partial omega squared, calculation is again simple because all of the needed values are available from the output from the ANOVA F test. Again we defer a worked example until later the section entitled "Illustrative worked examples" so that discussion of the example can be integrated with discussions of worked examples of other estimators of effect size for the same set of data.

A research report must make clear whether a reported estimate of POV_{pop} is based on the whole ω^2 or $\omega_{partial}^2$. Unfortunately, because values of estimates of whole POV_{pop} and of partial POV_{pop} can be very different, the more so the more complex a design, some writing and some software may be unclear or incorrect about which of the two estimators it is discussing or outputting. One serious consequence of such confusion would be misleading meta-analyses in which the meta-analysts are unknowingly integrating sets of two different kinds of estimates of POV_{pop}.

Tips and Pitfalls

If a report of primary research provides an equation for its estimator of POV_{pop} readers should examine the denominator to observe if Equation 7.1 or 7.2 is being used if the report is otherwise unclear about which kind of estimator has been used. Surveys have indicated that many reports of research are unclear about whether whole or partial POV is being reported (Kieffer, Reese, & Thompson, 2001; Vacha-Haase, Nilsson, Reetz, Lance, & Thompson, 2000b). Pierce, Block, and Aguinis (2004) provided examples of misreporting estimates of partial eta squared as whole eta squared, and they discussed the adverse effects of such error for theory, application, and meta-analysis. One indication that a report has mistakenly represented estimated partial POV_{pop} as estimated whole POV_{pop} occurs when more than one estimated POV_{pop} is reported for the same dependent variable and these estimates of POV_{pop} sum to more than 1. Such a sum is possible only for estimates of partial POV_{pop} because each estimate of partial POV_{pop} is calculated using a different denominator, whereas each estimate of whole POV_{pop} is calculated using the same denominator. Consult Pierce et al. for further details. Those authors found in a sample of studies that estimates of partial POV_{pop} can be greater than .5 when estimates of whole POV_{pop} for the same data are less than .2.

Partial POV_{pop} will often be inappropriate in designs with *blocking factors*, such as *randomized block designs*, which reduce MS_w. The use of blocking to reduce MS_w for the purpose of increasing statistical power is commendable, but the reduction of MS_w inflates an estimate of partial POV_{pop}, rendering the estimate not comparable to those from studies without blocking. Recent versions of some commercial software that previously outputted only partial η^2 (again, eta squared) also output whole η^2.

COMPARING VALUES OF ω^2

It is not necessarily true that a value of ω^2_{effect} whose corresponding F is statistically significant is estimating a greater POV_{pop} than one whose corresponding F is not statistically significant. The two F tests may have simply differed in statistical power. Also, a larger significant F does not necessarily indicate that its corresponding POV_{pop} is greater than the POV_{pop} that relates to a smaller significant F for another factor. Estimates of POV_{pop} have great sampling variability, so they are quite imprecise.

In the case of comparison of effect sizes of continuous independent variables (e.g., a levels of medication dosage and b levels of treatment duration), any difference in estimated values of POV_{pop} (or d_{pop}) for the factors may merely reflect a difference in the *strength of manipulation* of the factors. Moreover, in many cases it may not be possible to compare two strengths of manipulation; this would be an "apples versus oranges" comparison. For example, suppose that Factor B is duration of psychotherapy and Factor A is dose of anti-depressive drug. What range of levels of weeks of therapy would represent a manipulation whose strength is comparable to a certain range of levels of milligrams of the drug? On the other hand, it could be argued that if the levels of each of the two compared factors represent standard levels of these factors in clinical practice it may be justifiable to interpret a comparison of the two estimates of POV_{pop} or of d_{pop} in this context. Furthermore, because estimates of POV_{pop} have great sampling variability, even if two strengths of manipulation were comparable it would be difficult to generalize about the difference between two values of POV_{pop} merely by comparing the two estimates.

Tips and Pitfalls

The great sampling variability of estimates of POV_{pop} argues for the use of confidence intervals for a POV_{pop}. Also, one should not compare estimates of partial POV_{pop} for two factors in the same study because, as can be observed in Equation 7.2, the denominator of an estimate of partial POV_{pop} can have a different value for each factor (different sources of variability). For a similar reason one should not ordinarily compare estimates of POV_{pop} for the effect of a given factor from two studies that do not use the same peripheral factors and the same levels of those peripheral factors.

Ronis' (1981) method for comparing values of estimated POV_{pop} across studies applies only to factorial designs with two levels per factor. Fowler (1987) provided a method that can be applied to larger designs, and is applicable to within-groups designs and between-groups designs, but it is very complicated.

Cohen (1973) recommended that one estimate partial POV_{pop} if one wants to compare the estimates of POV_{pop} that are obtained by different studies of the same number of levels of the same targeted factor when that factor has been combined with peripheral factors that differ across the studies. Keppel and Wickens (2004) recommended the use of partial omega squared instead of whole omega squared for specific comparisons. In this case only variability that arises from the comparison and from error are involved in the effect size. For further discussions consult Levine and Hullett (2002), Maxwell and Delaney (2004), Maxwell et al. (1981), and Olejnik and Algina (2003).

Different research designs can produce greatly varying estimates of POV_{pop}, rendering comparisons or meta-analyses of estimates of POV_{pop} problematic if they do not take the different research features into account. Because such comparisons across different designs can be misleading, Olejnik and Algina (2003) provided many formulas for estimated *generalized eta squared* and *generalized omega squared* that are intended to provide comparable estimators across a great variety of research designs. Similarly, Gillett (2003) provided formulas for rendering standardized-difference estimators of effect size from factorial designs comparable to those from single-factor designs.

RATIOS OF ESTIMATES OF EFFECT SIZE

One should be very cautious about deciding on the relative importance of two factors by inspecting the ratio of their estimates of effect size because of the great sampling variability of such estimates and because the strengths of manipulation of the two factors might differ. Also, the ratio of values of ω^2 for two factors can be very different from the ratio of two estimates of standardized-difference effect size for those two factors. Therefore, these two kinds of estimators would generally result in different conclusions about the relative effect sizes of the two factors.

DESIGNS AND RESULTS FOR THIS CHAPTER

Tables 7.1 through 7.5 depict three of the designs and the results that are discussed in the remainder of the between-groups part of this chapter. It is important to note that we have placed subscripts denoting column factors ahead of subscripts denoting row factors, whereas the more common notation in factorial ANOVA reverses this sequence. However, in this chapter we are beginning with the case in which the targeted factor for estimation of effect size is a column factor, and we want to be consistent with the notation that was used by two of the major sources on effect sizes to which we refer readers. These sources place the subscript for a targeted factor first. The meaning of the superscript asterisks in the notation for the column variances in Table 7.3 will be explained where these variances are relevant in the later section entitled "Manipulated targeted factor and intrinsic peripheral factor".

MANIPULATED FACTORS ONLY

The appropriate procedure for calculating an estimate of a standardized-difference effect size that involves two means at a time in a factorial design depends in part on whether the targeted factor is manipulated or classificatory and whether

TABLE 7.1

A 2 × 2 Design with Two Extrinsic Factors

		Factor A	
		Therapy 1	Therapy 2
Factor B	Drug	Cell 1	Cell 2
	No drug	Cell 3	Cell 4
		$\overline{Y}_{1.}$	$\overline{Y}_{2.}$

TABLE 7.2

A 3 × 2 Design with an Extrinsic and an Intrinsic Factor

		Factor A		
		Treatment 1	Treatment 2	Treatment 3
Factor B	Female	Cell 1	Cell 2	Cell 3
	Male	Cell 4	Cell 5	Cell 6

TABLE 7.3

Hypothetical Results from a 2 × 2 Design with One Extrinsic and One Intrinsic Factor

		Factor A		
		Treatment 1	**Treatment 2**	
Factor B	Female	1, 1, 1, 1, 2, 2, 2, 2, 3, 4	2, 2, 3, 3, 3, 3, 3, 4, 4, 4	
		$\overline{Y}_{11} = 1.9$	$\overline{Y}_{21} = 3.1$	$\overline{Y}_{.1} = 2.5$
		$s_{11}^2 = .989$	$s_{21}^2 = .544$	$s_{.1}^2 = 1.105$
	Male	1, 1, 2, 2, 2, 2, 2, 2, 3, 4	1, 2, 2, 3, 3, 3, 3, 4, 4, 4	
		$\overline{Y}_{12} = 2.1$	$\overline{Y}_{22} = 2.9$	$\overline{Y}_{.2} = 2.5$
		$s_{12}^2 = .767$	$s_{22}^2 = .989$	$s_{.2}^2 = 1.000$
		$\overline{Y}_{1.} = 2.0$	$\overline{Y}_{2.} = 3.0$	
		$s_{1.}^{*2} = .842$	$s_{2.}^{*2} = .737$	

TABLE 7.4

ANOVA Output for the Data in Table 7.3

Source	SS	Df	MS	F	P
A	10.000	1	10.000	12.16	0.002
B	0.000	1	0.000	0.00	1.000
A × B	0.400	1	0.400	0.049	0.497
Within	29.600	36	0.822		

TABLE 7.5

A 3 × 2 × 2 Design with One Extrinsic and Two Intrinsic Factors

			Factor A		
			Treatment 1	**Treatment 2**	**Treatment 3**
Factor B	Female	White	Cell 1	Cell 2	Cell 3
		Non-white	Cell 4	Cell 5	Cell 6
	Male	White	Cell 7	Cell 8	Cell 9
		Non-white	Cell 10	Cell 11	Cell 12

the peripheral factor is extrinsic or intrinsic. To focus on the main ideas we first and mostly consider the two-way design. Suppose first that each factor is a manipulated factor, as in Table 7.1, so that the peripheral factor is extrinsic. Suppose further that one wants to compare Psychotherapies 1 and 2 overall, so the numerator of the standardized difference is $\overline{Y}_{1.} - \overline{Y}_{2.}$, where 1 and 2 represent columns 1 and 2 and the dot reminds us that we are considering column 1 or 2 period, over all rows, not just a part of column 1 or a part of column 2 in combination with any particular row (i.e., not a cell of the table). These two means are thus column marginal means. Therefore, in the present example Factor A is the targeted factor and Factor B is the peripheral factor. As in Chapter 3, in this chapter we use d_G (again, G for Gene Glass) to denote estimators whose standardizers are based on taking the square root of the variance of one group, and we use d to denote estimators whose standardizers are based on taking the square root of two or more pooled variances (i.e., the pooling-based standardizers s_p and $MS_w^{1/2}$ of Chapter 6).

Tips and Pitfalls
Recall that the choice of a standardizer by which to divide the difference between samples' means to calculate a d or d_G from a factorial design depends on one's conception of the population to which one wants to generalize the results. Suppose that one wants to generalize the results to a population that does not naturally vary with respect to the peripheral factor. Such will often (not always) be the case when each factor is a manipulated factor. In this case the peripheral factor would not contribute to variability in the measure of the dependent variable in the population so one should not let it contribute to the magnitude of the standardizer that is used to calculate the estimate of effect size. Such additional variability in sample data from a peripheral factor that is assumed not to vary in the population would lower the value of the estimate of effect size by inflating the standardizer in its denominator. There are options for choice of standardizer in this case. (In the case of clinical problems for which the psychotherapy and the drug therapy at hand are combined in practice, Table 7.1 and the present example do not provide an example of a peripheral factor that does not vary in the population of interest to the researcher. In this case the discussion and methods in this section do not apply.)

CHOICE OF STANDARDIZER

First, suppose that both factors in a two-way design have a combined control group (e.g., cell 3 in Table 7.1 if Therapy 1 were actually No Therapy), and that homoscedasticity of the variances across the margins of the peripheral factor is not assumed. By homoscedasticity across the margins of the peripheral factor we mean equality of the variances of the populations that are represented by each level of the peripheral factor over all of the levels of the targeted factor. In Table 7.1, the example of such homoscedasticity would be equality of variances of a population that receives the drug (represented by the combined participants in cells 1 and 2) and a population that does not receive the drug (represented by the combined participants in cells 3 and 4), that is, homoscedasticity of the population row margin variances in the present case. (Although the factors in Table 7.3 do not represent the current example of estimation of effect size, $s_{.1}^2$ and $s_{.2}^2$ in that table exemplify row marginal sample variances that estimate the population variances to whose homoscedasticity we are now referring.) We will not interrupt the development of the discussion here by demonstrating estimation of effect size when such marginal homoscedasticity of the peripheral factor is assumed because the method is the same as the one that we demonstrate later using Equation 7.20 in the section entitled "Within-groups factorial designs".

When such marginal homoscedasticity of the peripheral factor is not assumed one may want to use the standard deviation of the group that is a control group with respect to both factors as the standardizer, s_c. For example, in Table 7.1 if Therapy 1 were in fact No Therapy (control or placebo) one may want to use the standard deviation of cell 3 (a No-Therapy No-Drug cell in this case) as the standardizer. This method would also be applicable if, instead of a control-group cell, the design included a cell that represented a standard (in practice) combination of a level of Factor A and a level of Factor B, that is, a standard-treatment comparison group. In either of these cases we label the estimate of effect size d_{comp} (*comp* for comparison group) and use for the estimator

$$d_{comp} = \frac{\bar{Y}_{1.} - \bar{Y}_{2.}}{s_c}. \tag{7.3}$$

If instead one assumes homoscedasticity for all of the populations that are represented by all of the cells in the design (perhaps unlikely because there are four or more populations involved) an option for a standardizer in the present case would be to use the pooled standard deviation, $MS_w^{1/2}$, of all of the groups, resulting in the estimator

$$d_{msw} = \frac{\bar{Y}_{1.} - \bar{Y}_{2.}}{MS_w^{1/2}}. \tag{7.4}$$

The discussion of the benefits and risks when using Equation 6.15 is applicable to the use of the similar Equation 7.4. The method of Equation 7.4 does not deflate d_{msw} by inflating the standardizer because MS_w is based on pooling the within-cell SS values, and within each cell no factor in the design is varying, including the peripheral factor. Therefore, the peripheral factor is not contributing to the magnitude of the standardizer, just as we are assuming in this section that it does not contribute to variability in the population of interest. Versions of Equations 7.3 and 7.4 with appropriately changed subscripts can also be used to compare the means of two levels of the manipulated factor that had previously been designated as a peripheral factor but thereafter became a newly targeted factor, using the same reasoning as before. In this case the previously targeted factor now becomes the peripheral factor.

Keselman et al. (2008) discussed the use of the standardizer in Equation 7.3 in conjunction with their adjusted-degrees-of-freedom method applied to trimmed means and Winsorized variance to construct a robust CI around a standardized-difference effect size. The method also applies to construction of a robust *CI* around an interaction contrast. The free Keselman et al. SAS/IML software that was cited in Chapter 6 is applicable to factorial designs. Worked examples using Equations 7.3 and 7.4 are presented later in the section entitled "Within-groups factorial designs", where their application is also appropriate.

MANIPULATED TARGETED FACTOR AND INTRINSIC PERIPHERAL FACTOR

Suppose now the case of Table 7.2, in which there is a manipulated factor and an intrinsic classificatory factor, and that one wants to calculate an estimate of effect size for two levels of the manipulated factor. Unlike the previous case of Table 7.1, in the present case the intrinsic factor, gender, does vary in the population so one may now want to let the part of the variance in the measure of the dependent variable that is attributable to the intrinsic factor also contribute to the standardizer. Such an effect size would be comparable to one from a one-way design involving the same two levels of the manipulated factor because any gender-related variance in the dependent variable would contribute to the standardizer in the one-way design as it does to the factorial design. Consult Olejnik and Algina (2000) for a detailed discussion of the justification for the alternative standardizers for the present case.

CHOICE OF STANDARDIZER

First, in the present case there is an option for choice of a standardizer if there is a control condition (or standard-treatment comparison condition), say Treatment 1 in Table 7.2 if Treatment 1 were actually, say, a No-Treatment control. In this case one may want to use for the standardizer the overall *s* of the control groups across the levels of the peripheral factor (overall *s* of cells 1 and 4 combined). In our present example in which Treatment 1 of Table 7.2 is the control condition, this standardizer would be $s_{1.}$, the marginal *s* of column 1. Using this method one is collapsing (combining) the levels of the peripheral factor so that for the moment the design is equivalent to a one-way design in which the targeted treatment factor is the only factor. This method does not assume homoscedasticity because it does not pool variances (i.e., cells 1 and 4 are considered to represent one group). Also, because the standardizer is based on a now combined group of women and men it reflects any gender-based variability of the measure of the dependent variable in the population. The present method yields as an estimator of effect size

$$d_{\text{comp}*} = \frac{\bar{Y}_{1.} - \bar{Y}_{2.}}{s_{1.}}. \tag{7.5}$$

When there are more than two levels of the targeted manipulated factor, as is the case in Table 7.2, the numerical subscripts in Equation 7.5 vary depending on which column represents the control (or standard-treatment) condition and which column contains the groups (level) with which it is being compared.

If the targeted factor is represented by the rows instead of the columns of a table, the dots in Equation 7.5 precede the numerical subscripts (e.g., $s_{1.}$ becomes $s_{.1}$) and *row* replaces *column* in the previous discussion. A definitional equation, Equation 7.15, for $s_{.1}$ (the row case) is provided later in the section entitled "Classificatory factors only", using notation that is not yet needed. Computational formulas and some worked examples are also provided there.

Whether or not there is a control or standard-treatment level there is an alternative more complex standardizer for the present design and purpose. This standardizer, which assumes homoscedasticity of all of the populations that are involved in the estimate, was discussed by Cortina and Nouri (2000). The method involves a special kind of pooling from cells that is consistent with the goal of this section to let variance in the measure of the dependent variable that is attributable to the peripheral factor contribute to the magnitude of the standardizer. One first calculates, separately for each of the two variances that are later going to be entered into a modified version of the formula for pooling,

$$s_{t.}^{*2} = \frac{\Sigma(n_{tp} - 1)s_{tp}^2 + \Sigma n_{tp}(\overline{Y}_{tp} - \overline{Y}_{t.})^2}{n_{t.} - 1}, \tag{7.6}$$

where
  t stands for targeted
  p stands for peripheral
  tp stands for a cell at the tth level of the targeted factor and the pth level of the peripheral factor
  $t.$ stands for a level of the targeted factor over the levels of the peripheral factor, which is at a margin of a table (e.g., the margin of column 1 or column 2 in Table 7.2)

The asterisk indicates a special kind of variance that has had variance that is attributable to the peripheral factor "added back" to it. The summation in Equation 7.6 is undertaken over the levels of the peripheral factor, there being two such levels in the present case of Table 7.2. Observe that Equation 7.6 begins, before the plus sign, as if it were going to be the usual formula for pooling variances (i.e., MS_w), but the expression in the numerator after the plus sign adds the now appropriate portion of variability that is attributable to the peripheral factor. Therefore, we denote the resulting standardizer that is presented in Equation 7.7, s_{msw+}.

Equation 7.6 yields the overall variance of all participants who were subjected to a level within the targeted factor for the purpose of estimating an effect size that involves that level. This variance is the variance of all such participants as if they were combined into one larger group at that level of the targeted factor, ignoring the sub-groupings that are based on the peripheral factor. This variance serves the purpose of being comparable to the variance that would be obtained if that level of the targeted factor had been studied in a one-way design. The estimate of effect size that results from this approach will thus be comparable to an estimate that would arise from such a one-way design.

Again, Equation 7.6 is calculated twice, once each for the two compared levels of the targeted factor, to find the special kind of $s_{1.}^2$ and $s_{2.}^2$ (in the present example), $s_{1.}^{*2}$ and $s_{2.}^{*2}$, to enter into the pooling Equation 7.7 for the standardizer:

$$s_{msw+} = \left[\frac{(n_{1.} - 1)s_{1.}^{*2} + (n_{2.} - 1)s_{2.}^{*2}}{n_{1.} + n_{2.} - 2} \right]^{1/2}. \tag{7.7}$$

The resulting estimator is then given by

$$d_{msw+} = \frac{\bar{Y}_{1.} - \bar{Y}_{2.}}{s_{msw+}}. \tag{7.8}$$

As was previously stated, the numerical subscripts and the sequence of the numerical and dot parts of a subscript depend, respectively, on which two levels of a multi-leveled targeted factor are being compared (e.g., columns 1 and 2, 1 and 3, or 2 and 3), and on whether the targeted factor is represented by the rows or columns of the table. We discuss another approach to this case in the next section.

Consider the case in which there is a great difference in within-group variability between the blocks (i.e., rows) in block × treatment designs such as the designs depicted in Tables 7.2 and 7.3. In this case Bonett (2008) recommended that the most meaningful *standardized interaction effect* would use only the within-block variances to determine the standardizer for effect sizes involving a difference between means in a given block. For example, if there were a very great difference in variances between the Female (F) and Male (M) rows in Table 7.3 the standardized effect size for interaction would be given by $(\mu_{11} - \mu_{21})/\sigma_F - (\mu_{12} - \mu_{22})/\sigma_M$. Bonett discussed such an effect size and a method for constructing a confidence interval for it under normality and moderate heteroscedasticity across the involved columns. A later section in this chapter is devoted to effect sizes for interaction.

ILLUSTRATIVE WORKED EXAMPLES

Table 7.3 depicts hypothetical data in a simplified version of Table 7.2 in which there are now only two levels of the targeted manipulated factor that is represented by the columns. The cells' raw scores are degrees of respondents' endorsements of an attitudinal statement with respect to a 4-point rating scale ranging from *strongly disagree* to *strongly agree*. The treatments represent alternative wording for the attitudinal statement. It is supposed that 20 women and 20 men were randomly assigned, 10 each to each treatment. The table includes cell and marginal values of $\bar{Y}$ and s^2. Because the contrived data are presented only for the purpose of illustrating calculations and interpretations homoscedasticity is assumed as needed.

Before we begin estimating effect sizes some comments are in order about the example at hand. First, although rating-scale items are typically used in combination with other such items on the same topic to form *summated rating scales*, our example that uses just one rating-scale item (a *Likert scale*) is nonetheless relevant because a rating-scale item is sometimes used alone to address a specific research question. (However, because of measurement error multi-item scales are generally preferable to single-item scales because multiple items provide an opportunity for positive and negative measurement error to cancel.) Also, although some (e.g., Cliff, 1993) have recommended using ordinal measures, such as the probability of superiority and the dominance measure that are discussed in Chapters 5 and 9, to analyze data from rating scales many researchers still use parametric methods involving means for such ordinal data. However, violation of the assumption of normality in the case of data from rating scales may be especially problematic the fewer the number of categories, the smaller the sample size, and the more extreme the mean rating in the population. Thus, we use hypothetical data from a rating scale here only because they provide a simple example for our purpose of illustrating effect sizes. We further discuss the controversial application of parametric methods to ordinal data in Chapter 9.

PRESENCE OF A CONTROL OR STANDARD-TREATMENT GROUP

Suppose first that Treatment 1 in Table 7.3 is a control (or standard-treatment) level and, as was discussed in the previous section, one wants to estimate an effect size from a standardized $\bar{Y}_1 - \bar{Y}_2$ that would be comparable to an estimate that would arise from a design in which treatment were the only factor. For this case one can standardize using the overall s of the control group in Table 7.3: $(s_{1.}^{*2})^{1/2} = (.842)^{1/2} = .918$. The overall s of a column is the s of a group consisting of all of the participants in all of the cells of that column (column data across rows treated as one set of data). As should be clear from our previous explanation of the variance that Equation 7.6 yields, this overall s is not the square root of the mean of the variances of cells 1 and 3 in the current example that involves Table 7.3. That is, this overall s is not $[(.989 + .767)/2]^{1/2}$. Applying Equation 7.3, which is applicable in the present case, one finds $d_{comp} = (2.0 - 3.0)/.918 = -1.09$.

Therefore, one estimates that, with respect to the control population's distribution and σ, the mean of the control population is estimated to be 1.09 standard deviations below the mean of the population that receives Treatment 2.

ASSUMING HOMOSCEDASTICITY

Regardless of the existence of a control level, if one assumes homoscedasticity of all of the involved populations the special pooling method of Equations 7.6 and 7.7 can be used as the first step toward standardizing the difference between $\bar{Y}_1$ and $\bar{Y}_2$ in Table 7.3 with the method of Equation 7.8 (Cortina & Nouri, 2000). First, one applies the results of column 1 to Equation 7.6 to find

$$s_{1.}^{*2} = \frac{[(10-1).989] + [(10-1).767] + [10(1.9-2.0)^2 + [10(2.1-2.0)^2]}{20-1} = .842.$$

One then applies the results of column 2 to Equation 7.6 to find

$$s_{2.}^{*2} = \frac{[(10-1.544)]+[(10-1).989]+[10(3.1-3.0)^2]+[10(2.9-3.0)^2]}{20-1} = .737.$$

Applying the two preceding results to Equation 7.7 one finds the standardizer

$$s_{msw+} = \left[\frac{(20-1).842+(20-1).737}{20+20-2}\right]^{1/2} = .889.$$

Applying the difference between the two targeted column means, 2.0 and 3.0, and the standardizer, .889, to Equation 7.8 one finds $d_{msw+} = (2.0 - 3.0)/.889 = -1.12$.

Therefore, the mean of the population that receives Treatment 1 is estimated to be 1.12 standard deviations below the mean of the population that receives Treatment 2, where the standard deviation is assumed to be a value common to the populations. Observe that the present result, $d_{msw+} = -1.12$, is close to the previous result, $d_{comp} = -1.09$. Such similarity of results is attributable to the fact that the sample variances in the cells happen not to be as different in the case of the contrived data of Table 7.4 as they might well be in the case of real data.

The output from any ANOVA software, such as what is presented in Table 7.4, provides needed information to proceed with some additional estimation and interpretation of effect sizes for the data of Table 7.3. However, output did not provide the total SS directly, so one calculates that $SS_{tot} = SS_A + SS_B + SS_{AB} + SS_w = 10 + 0 + .400 + 29.600 = 40.000$. Observe in Table 7.3 that the marginal means of the Female and Male rows happen to be equal (both 2.5) so obviously d or $d_G = 0$ in such a case regardless of which standardizer is used. For the targeted Treatment factor, A, observe in Table 7.4 that $F(1,36) = 12.16$ and $p = .002$, so one has evidence of a statistically significant difference between the marginal means (a main effect) of Treatments 1 and 2.

METHOD WHEN THERE IS LIMITED ACCESS TO ANOTHER'S RESULTS

The foregoing method is feasible for primary researchers because they have access to the required descriptive statistics. There is an alternative approach in which a classificatory peripheral factor varies in the population (intrinsic factor) and a researcher wants to compare one's estimate of effect size with a previously reported estimate but there is limited access to the required descriptive statistics for conversion to such an estimate. Suppose that a primary researcher wants to compare one's obtained d in this case with a d that this researcher wants to calculate from an earlier comparable study authored by another researcher who did not report a d. Typically the needed descriptive statistics from the earlier study will not be available for undertaking our previously discussed calculation of such a d. The standardizer in this case can be obtained from the previous study's ANOVA summary table by calculating the square root of the variance that results from adding the SS values from all sources other than the targeted manipulated factor and then dividing by the degrees of freedom that are associated with these included sources. For example, suppose that one wants a standardizer for the difference between the two treatment means in Table 7.3 (marginal column means) and that the variance that is attributable to the peripheral factor of gender is to contribute to the standardizer. Using all of the values of SS and df for the data in Table 7.3 that are presented in Table 7.4, except for those for the targeted factor of treatment (Factor A), the standardizer is given by $([SS_B + SS_{AB} + SS_w]/[df_B + df_{AB} + df_w])^{1/2} = ([.000 + .400 + 29.600]/[1 + 1 + 36])^{1/2} = .889$, which, as it should be, is the same as the previously obtained standardizer using Equation 7.7.

Another approach for the present case is applicable when one does not have access to the means and standard deviations, but has access to values of degrees of freedom, F, and sample sizes. The method that yields the same result as the previous two methods is attributable to Morris and DeShon (1997); also consult Cortina and Nouri (2000).

ESTIMATION OF POV_{pop} AND PARTIAL POV_{pop}

Applying the ANOVA results from Table 7.4 to Equation 7.1 yields $\omega^2 = [10 - 1(.822)]/(40 + .822) = .22$, and applying the outputted results to Equation 7.2 yields $\omega^2_{partial} = [10 - 1(.822)]/[10 + (40 - 1).822] = .22$. Recalling the discussion of the difference between ω^2 and $\omega^2_{partial}$ early in this chapter, one should expect the two estimates to be very similar in the case of the hypothetical data of Table 7.4 because Factor B happened to contribute no variability to these data (output $SS_B = 0$). Interaction (statistically insignificant in this example) contributed just enough variability to the data (outputted $SS_{AB} = .400$) to cause a very slight difference in the magnitudes of the two kinds of estimates of a POV_{pop}, but rounding to two decimal places renders ω^2 equal to $\omega^2_{partial}$ in this example. We conclude, subject to the previously discussed limitations of POV_{pop} in Chapter 6, that the Treatment factor is estimated to account for 22% of the variance in the scores under the specific conditions of the research.

COMPARISONS OF LEVELS OF A MANIPULATED FACTOR AT ONE LEVEL OF A PERIPHERAL FACTOR

Suppose now that one wants a standardized comparison of two levels of a manipulated factor at one level of a peripheral factor at a time. For example, with regard to Table 7.2, suppose that one wants to compare Treatment 1 and Treatment 2 separately for women only, or for men only. (These two effect sizes may well be different because of a gender-related difference in means and/or standard deviations.) Thus, one would be interested in an estimate of effect size involving two values of $\overline{Y}_{tp}$ (i.e., two cells, such as cells 1 and 2) where, again, t stands for a level of the targeted factor and p stands for a level of the peripheral factor. Such separate comparisons are especially appropriate if there is an interaction between the targeted manipulated and peripheral factors. (Again, there may really be an interaction regardless of the result of a possibly low-powered F test for interaction.)

If, say, one wants to standardize the difference between the means of cells 1 and 2 in Table 7.2 ($\overline{Y}_{11}$ and $\overline{Y}_{21}$, respectively) and Treatment 1 is a control level or standard-treatment comparison level, one can standardize the mean difference using the standard deviation of cell 1, namely s_{cell}, if one is not assuming homoscedasticity. In this case the estimator is

$$d_{level} = \frac{\overline{Y}_{11} - \overline{Y}_{21}}{s_{cell}}. \tag{7.9}$$

The subscripts for the two values of $\overline{Y}$ in Equation 7.9 change depending on which two levels of the targeted manipulated factor are involved in the comparison, and at which level of the peripheral factor the comparison takes place. (We previously explained why we adopted notation in which the subscript for a column precedes the subscript for a row.)

For a numerical example for the present case suppose that one wants to make a standardized comparison of the means of Treatments 1 and 2 in Table 7.3 separately for men and women, and suppose further that Treatment 1 is a control level. We demonstrate the method by applying the results in the Male row of Table 7.3 to Equation 7.9. In this case the numerator of Equation 7.9 becomes ($\overline{Y}_{12} - \overline{Y}_{22}$) and, because Table 7.3 shows that the sample variance in the cell for Male-Treatment 1 is .767, $d_{level} = (2.1 - 2.9)/.767^{1/2} = -.91$. Therefore, with respect to the Male-Control population's distribution and σ, it is estimated that the mean of the Male-Treatment 2 population is approximately nine-tenths of a standard deviation above the mean of the Male-Control population. If these are the kinds of populations that the researcher is seeking to address, then the method of Equation 7.9 is an appropriate one. Again, the method of estimation that is chosen must be consistent with the kind of effect-size parameter that the researcher wishes to estimate and the assumptions (e.g., homoscedasticity) that are made about the involved populations.

ASSUMING HOMOSCEDASTICITY

There are alternatives to the foregoing procedure. If one assumes homoscedasticity with regard to the two populations whose sample (cell) means are being compared one can calculate the standardizer by pooling the two involved values of s^2_{cell}. For an example now involving cells 1 and 2 of Table 7.3, the standardizer, namely s_{pcells} (p denotes pooling), is given by a common version of the general Equation 6.16 for pooling two variances:

$$s_{pcells} = \left[\frac{(n_{11} - 1)s^2_{11} + (n_{21} - 1)s^2_{21}}{n_{11} + n_{21} - 2} \right]^{1/2}. \tag{7.10}$$

Equation 7.10 results in the estimator

$$d_{\text{level}} = \frac{\overline{Y}_{11} - \overline{Y}_{21}}{s_{\text{pcells}}}. \tag{7.11}$$

Now applying the results in the Female row of Table 7.3 to Equation 7.10 one finds that

$$s_{\text{pcells}} = \left[\frac{(10-1).989 + (10-1).544}{10+10-2} \right]^{1/2} = .875.$$

Therefore, Equation 7.11 yields $d_{\text{level}} = (1.9 - 3.1)/.875 = -1.37$. One estimates that, with regard to the Female-Treatment 2 population's distribution and σ, which is assumed to be the same as the σ of the Female-Treatment 1 population's σ, the mean of the latter population is 1.37 σ units below the mean of the former population.

If there is only one manipulated factor, as is the case in Table 7.3, and if one assumes homoscedasticity with regard to all of the populations that are represented by the cells in the design, one can use $MS_{\text{w}}^{1/2}$ as the standardizer for the present purpose. The resulting estimator when interest is in $\overline{Y}_{11} - \overline{Y}_{21}$ is then given by

$$d_{\text{levelmsw}} = \frac{\overline{Y}_{11} - \overline{Y}_{21}}{MS_{\text{w}}^{1/2}}. \tag{7.12}$$

Using MS_{w} from the ANOVA output that was reported in Table 7.4, applying the results in the Female row of Table 7.3 to Equation 7.12 yields $d_{\text{levelmsw}} = (1.9 - 3.1)/.822^{1/2} = -1.32$. The mean of the Female-Treatment 1 population is estimated to be 1.32 σ units lower than the mean of the Female-Treatment 2 population, where σ is assumed to be common for all of the populations that are represented in the design.

Tips and Pitfalls

Under homoscedasticity of all represented populations $MS_{\text{w}}^{1/2}$ provides a better estimate of the common σ within all of these populations than does s_{pcells}, resulting in a d that is a better estimator of a d_{pop}. However, again, there is greater risk that the assumption of homoscedasticity is wrong, and perhaps importantly so, when one assumes that four or more populations that involve combined levels of manipulated and classificatory factors are homoscedastic (as could be the case in Table 7.2 or 7.3) than when one assumes that two populations at the same level of a classificatory factor are homoscedastic. Equation 7.12 is not applicable when there is more than one manipulated factor. Olejnik and Algina (2000) provided discussion of this somewhat more complicated case.

TARGETED CLASSIFICATORY FACTOR AND EXTRINSIC PERIPHERAL FACTOR

Suppose now that one wants to standardize a comparison between two levels of an intrinsic factor (a classificatory factor here) when there are one or more extrinsic peripheral factors and there are no or any number of additional intrinsic factors. When gender is the targeted classificatory factor Tables 7.2, 7.3, and 7.5 illustrate such designs. We consider the case that is represented by Tables 7.2 and 7.3, in which the numerator of the estimator is $(\bar{Y}_{.1} - \bar{Y}_{.2})$, which is the difference between the marginal means of the Female row and Male row in the present example. The difference between these two means happens to be 0 in the case of Table 7.3, so we focus on calculation of an appropriate standardizer for illustrative purposes.

Suppose further that one wants to examine the mean for one gender in relation to the mean and distribution of scores of the other gender. For example, suppose that one wants to calculate by how many standard deviation units the marginal sample mean of the Males $(\bar{Y}_{.2})$ is below or above the marginal sample mean of the Females $(\bar{Y}_{.1})$, where the standard deviation unit is the s for the distribution of scores for the Females. If the peripheral factor (treatment in the present case) does not ordinarily vary in the population it is an extrinsic factor. In this case one should not use for the standardizer the square root of the variance of the row for the Females, $s_{.1}^2$ in Table 7.2 or 7.3, which would reflect variance that is attributable to treatment. Instead one can standardize using the square root of the variance obtained from pooling the variances of all of the cells for the Females (cells 1, 2, and 3 in Table 7.2 or cells 1 and 2 in Table 7.3) to find s_{pcells}, where again p stands for pooled. Within these cells treatment does not vary so variance within a cell is not influenced by varying the extrinsic peripheral factor across cells. The following version of the pooling formula may be used to pool the cell variances:

$$s_{\text{pcells}} = \left[\frac{\Sigma[(n_{\text{cell}} - 1)s_{\text{cell}}^2]}{\Sigma(n_{\text{cell}} - 1)} \right]^{1/2}. \tag{7.13}$$

The summation in Equation 7.13 is conducted over the levels of the peripheral factor. If an example involves a table such as Table 7.2 the summation would be over cells 1, 2, and 3. The resulting estimator is

$$d_{\text{classp}} = \frac{\bar{Y}_{.1} - \bar{Y}_{.2}}{s_{\text{pcells}}}, \tag{7.14}$$

where again class stands for classificatory. This method assumes homoscedasticity of the populations whose samples' cell variances are being pooled.

For simplicity we again use the data of Table 7.3 for the current case and purpose that we have been discussing, and we suppose that one wants to standardize the difference between the marginal means of the rows for the Females and Males in such a table. In such a case of a 2×2 table, Equation 7.13 reduces to Equation 7.10, and yields, just as was found previously when the data of Table 7.3 were applied to Equation 7.10,

$$s_{\text{pcells}} = \left[\frac{(10-1).989 + (10-1).544}{(10-1) + (10-1)} \right]^{1/2} = .875.$$

In the current case of a two-way design, if one assumes homoscedasticity of all of the populations that are represented by the cells in the table one can use $MS_{\text{w}}^{1/2}$ as the standardizer to find an estimator for a comparison of the marginal means of two levels of a classificatory factor. We would label such an estimator d_{classmsw}. If there are one or more classificatory factors in addition to the targeted classificatory factor, as in Table 7.5, consult Olejnik and Algina (2000) for a modification of the standardizer.

CLASSIFICATORY FACTORS ONLY

Suppose now that the column factor in Table 7.2 were not treatment (manipulated) but ethnicity, so that the design now consisted only of the classificatory factors gender and ethnicity. Suppose also that one wants to standardize the overall mean difference between females and males (gender targeted, ethnicity peripheral, for the moment)—that is, the difference between the means of the rows for females and males, $\bar{Y}_{.1} - \bar{Y}_{.2}$, in the now revised Table 7.2. Again there are alternative standardizers for this purpose.

Consider first the case in which one wants to calculate by how many standard deviation units the marginal mean for the males $(\bar{Y}_{.2})$ is below or above the females' marginal mean $(\bar{Y}_{.1})$, with regard to the overall distribution of the females' scores. In this case, unlike the case in the previous section, in many instances the current peripheral factor, ethnicity, does naturally vary in the population that is of interest (an intrinsic factor). Therefore, one should now want the standardizer to reflect variance that is attributable to ethnicity.

CHOICE OF STANDARDIZER

For the present purpose the overall s of all of the females' scores can be used for the standardizer. In the case of the now modified version of Table 7.2, this standardizer is the square root of the marginal variance of row 1: $(s_{.1}^2)^{1/2}$. This standardizer is defined by (but conveniently calculated using Equation 7.17) an equation that is based on deviation scores:

$$s_{.1} = \left[\frac{\Sigma(Y_{itp} - \bar{Y}_{.1})^2}{n_{.1} - 1} \right]^{1/2}, \tag{7.15}$$

where, in the present example, Y_{itp} is an ith raw score in a cell of the row (or column in other examples) whose marginal s is to be the standardizer, the summation is over all such raw scores in this row, t is the level of the targeted factor on which the standardizer is based (female level here), and p is a level of the peripheral factor: $p = 1, 2$, and 3 in Table 7.2. The resulting estimator is then

$$d_{\text{class}} = \frac{\bar{Y}_{.1} - \bar{Y}_{.2}}{s_{.1}}. \tag{7.16}$$

The method that underlies Equation 7.16 does not assume homoscedasticity with regard to the two populations that are being compared. However, because the subpopulations (i.e., the ethnic subpopulations in the present example) may have unequal variances, a more accurate estimation of the overall population's standard deviation that the standardizer is estimating may be had if the proportions of the participants in each subsample correspond to their proportions in the overall population. For example, if ethnic Subpopulation a constitutes, say, 13% of the population, then ideally 13% of the participants should be from ethnic group a. If the subpopulations also differ in their means (often the case when variances differ), then choosing subsample sizes to match the proportions in the subpopulations will also likely make the mean of each of the two targeted levels that are being compared (e.g., male and female) a more accurate estimate of the mean of its population. A subsample should not have more or less influence on the standard deviation or mean of the overall sample than it has in the overall population. Thus, appropriate sampling will improve the numerator and denominator of Equation 7.16 as estimators. Similarly, one should also be concerned about the appropriateness of estimating POV_{pop} in a population whose proportions of subpopulations do not correspond closely to the proportions of participants in the various levels of the categorical factor (e.g., ethnicity or gender) that represent those subpopulations in the research. Consult the section entitled "Unequal base rates in nonexperimental research" in Chapter 4 for related discussion.

EASIER CALCULATION OF THE STANDARDIZER

One easy way to calculate the standardizer that is defined by Equation 7.15 for the present case would be to use any statistical software to create a data file consisting of all of the $n_{.t}$ (i.e., $n_{.1}$ in the present example) raw scores, as if all of the scores in the row that produce the standardizer constituted a single group. One would then compute the s for this group of scores. This $s_{.t}$ ($s_{.1}$ in the present example) should derive from the square root of the unbiased s^2 (i.e., using $n - 1$, not n, in the denominator). This $s_{.t}$ can also be calculated from another equation for the present case:

$$s_{.1} = \left[\frac{(\Sigma Y_{itp}^2) - n_{.i}\bar{Y}_{.1}^2}{n_{.1} - 1} \right]^{1/2}. \tag{7.17}$$

For simplicity we use the data of Table 7.3 to demonstrate the calculation of $s_{.1}$, pretending now, to fit the present case, that the columns there represent a peripheral classificatory factor, such as ethnicity, instead of a treatment factor. First, from the kind of data file that was just described for all of the scores in the standardizer's row, software output yielded $s_{.1}^2 = 1.105$, so $s_{.1} = 1.105^{1/2} = 1.051$. Using Equation 7.17 confirms the previous result that

$$
s_{.1} = \left[\frac{\begin{array}{l} 1^2 + 1^2 + 1^2 + 1^2 + 2^2 + 2^2 + 2^2 + 2^2 + 3^2 + 4^2 + 2^2 \\ 2^2 + 3^2 + 3^2 + 3^2 + 3^2 + 3^2 + 4^2 + 4^2 + 4^2 - 20(2.5^2) \end{array}}{20 - 1} \right]^{1/2} = 1.051.
$$

The d_{class} of Equation 7.16 is comparable to a d that would arise from a one-way design in which the targeted classificatory factor was the only independent variable in the design. To illustrate another standardizer that would accomplish this purpose we again use the example of gender as the targeted factor. In our present modified version of Table 7.2, in which ethnicity is a peripheral column factor replacing the treatment factor, one can base the standardizer on the pooled variances of the row margins, $s_{.1}^2$ and $s_{.2}^2$, each one of which reflects variability attributable to ethnicity as the population would. One pools using Equation 7.18 below that is another version of the general equation for pooling two variances. We denote the resulting standardizer s_{classp}, where again p denotes pooled. This method assumes homoscedasticity of the populations that are represented by the two compared levels of the targeted factor. Again, as was discussed regarding the method that underlies formula 7.16, ideally the proportions of the participants in each subsample (e.g., proportions of ethnic groups) should be equal to their proportions in the population. The current standardizer is

$$
s_{\text{classp}} = \left[\frac{(n_{.1} - 1)s_{.1}^2 + (n_{.2} - 1)s_{.2}^2}{n_{.1} + n_{.2} - 2} \right]^{1/2}. \tag{7.18}
$$

The resulting estimator is then given by

$$
d_{\text{classp}}^* = \frac{\bar{Y}_{.1} - \bar{Y}_{.2}}{s_{\text{classp}}}. \tag{7.19}
$$

The asterisk is applied to the d of Equation 7.19 to distinguish it from the d of Equation 7.14. Continuing to use the modified version of Table 7.2 in which the column factor is now a peripheral classificatory factor instead of a treatment factor, one already knows from the preceding calculation that $s_{.1}^2 = 1.105$. After creating a data file for the data of row 2 (Male row) as was previously described for the data of row 1, one finds that software output yields $s_{.2}^2 = 1.000$. Therefore, using Equation 7.18 to obtain the standardizer one finds that

$$
s_{\text{classp}} = \left[\frac{(20 - 1)1.105 + (20 - 1)1.00}{20 + 20 - 2} \right]^{1/2} = 1.026.
$$

Calculating the Standardizer When Cell Sizes Are Equal

There is an alternative method for calculating s_{classp} that is applicable when there is any number of levels of the targeted classificatory factor and all cell sample sizes are equal. In this case one can use output from ANOVA software to calculate, for entry into Equation 7.19,

$$s_{classp} = \left[\frac{SS_{tot} - SS_{tc}}{N - k_{tc}} \right]^{1/2}, \tag{7.20}$$

where

SS_{tc} is the SS for the targeted classificatory factor

N is the total sample size

k_{tc} is the number of levels of the targeted classificatory factor (Olejnik & Algina, 2000)

Observe in the numerator of Equation 7.20 that variability that is attributable to the targeted factor is subtracted from total variability leaving only variability that is attributable to the peripheral factor, which, as was previously discussed, is appropriate in the case that is considered in this section.

In the ANOVA summarizing Table 7.4, for the present example that uses the values in the revised Table 7.3, SS_{tc} is SS_B, $N = 40$, and $k_{tc} = 2$. Table 7.4 reveals for the data of Table 7.3 that, by summing all SS values, $SS_{tot} = 40.000$ and $SS_B = 0.000$. Applying Equation 7.20 one thus finds that $s_{classp} = [(40.000 - 0.000)/(40 - 2)]^{1/2} = 1.026$. This value agrees with the previous value for s_{classp} that was calculated from files for data from separate rows instead of ANOVA output.

We do not proceed to calculate an estimate of effect size that is based on the standardized difference between the row marginal means for the data of the modified Table 7.3 because $\overline{Y}_{.1} - \overline{Y}_{.2} = 0$ in that table. However, the method, and also the interpretation when the mean difference is not 0, should be clear from the previous worked examples and discussions. Again, when selecting from a variety of possible standardizers for an estimator one should make a choice that is based on one's decision regarding which version of the effect-size parameter the sample effect size is to be estimating. As we have noted, each standardizer and its resulting d or d_G have a somewhat different purpose and/or underlying assumption about homoscedasticity.

STATISTICAL INFERENCE AND FURTHER READING

Smithson (2001) discussed the use of IBM SPSS to construct a confidence interval for POV_{pop} (denoted η^2) and for a related effect size that is proportional to the f that we discuss in Chapter 6. Fidler and Thompson (2001) further illustrated application of Smithson's (2001) method to an $a \times b$ design. Smithson (2003) demonstrated the construction of confidence intervals for partial POV_{pop} and related measures. Estimation of POV_{pop} in complex designs was discussed by Vaughan and Corballis (1969). Olejnik and Algina (2000) discussed estimation of POV_{pop} in designs with covariates and split-plot designs (discussed later).

Bird (2002) discussed methods, under the assumptions of normality and homoscedasticity, for constructing individual and simultaneous confidence intervals for standardized differences between means, and the implementation of these methods using readily available software. Steiger and Fouladi (1997) discussed the construction of exact confidence intervals.

As was mentioned in Chapter 6, an approximate confidence interval for a standardized difference between means can be constructed by dividing the limits that are obtained for the unstandardized difference by $MS_w^{1/2}$. This method assumes homoscedasticity. Also, recall from our earlier discussion that when $MS_w^{1/2}$ is the standardizer in a factorial design, one is not permitting variability that is attributable to a peripheral factor to contribute to the standardizer. Therefore, the use of $MS_w^{1/2}$ would not be appropriate if the peripheral factor is a classificatory one that varies in the population that is of interest.

As discussed in earlier chapters, when the dependent variable is measured in familiar units that are of direct interest, effect sizes in terms of raw (i.e., unstandardized) differences between means can be very informative and readily interpreted. It is routine to conduct tests of significance and construct simultaneous confidence intervals involving comparisons within pairs of means whose differences are not standardized. Maxwell and Delaney (2004) discussed methods for the homoscedastic or heteroscedastic cases. The Bonferroni–Dunn method can be used to make planned pair-wise comparisons. (However, unless there is only a small number of comparisons, one may be concerned about the loss of statistical power for each comparison.) Alternatively, the Tukey HSD method is applicable. Wilcox (2003) discussed and provided S-PLUS software functions for less known robust methods for pair-wise comparisons (more generally, linear contrasts) and construction of simultaneous confidence intervals involving the pairs of means of interest.

Timm's (2004) ubiquitous effect size index, which, as we mention in Chapter 6, assumes homoscedasticity, is applicable to F tests and tests of contrasts in exploratory studies that use factorial designs. Brunner and Puri (2001) extended application of what we call the probability of superiority measure of effect size in Chapters 5 and 6 to factorial designs.

FAMILY-WISE ERROR

The tests involving interaction and each main effect are often considered to represent a different set or *family* of tests. This thinking gives rise to the concept of *family-wise error rate*, that is, the probability that at least one Type I error will be made in a specified family of tests. In an $a \times b$ design there will be three families of tests: those involving (a) the $a \times b$ interaction, (b) Factor A, and (c) Factor B. In the case of one-way ANOVA there is only one family of tests so there is no difference between the family-wise error rate and the experiment-wise error rate there. However, in a factorial design the latter will be greater than the former because across the entire experiment the separate error rates for each family cumulate. The total number of tests across the entire experiment is the sum of all of the tests in the separate families, so in a factorial design there are always more opportunities for per-comparison Type I errors in the entire experiment than in any one family. The issue of Type I errors is especially important for those who believe that effect sizes should only be reported for statistically significant results, as was discussed with many citations in Chapter 1.

Effect Sizes for Interaction

Abelson and Prentice (1997) and Olejnik and Algina (2000) presented methods for calculating an estimator of effect size for interaction. Maxwell and Delaney (2004) discussed methods for testing the statistical significance of the differences among the cell means that are involved in a factor that may or may not be interacting with another factor. Such cell-wise comparisons test for simple effects. A comparison of marginal means (testing main effects) when there is interaction merely provides an overall (i.e., an average) comparison of levels of the targeted factor. Such a comparison, or estimation of an effect size that is based on such a comparison, can be misleading because when there is an interaction a difference between targeted marginal means does not reflect a constant difference between cell means at levels of the targeted factor at each level of a peripheral factor. Estimation of standardized-difference effect sizes for the kind of cell-wise comparisons at hand was discussed in the section entitled "Comparisons of levels of a manipulated factor at one level of a peripheral factor". Aside from the statistical issues, in research that has theoretical implications explaining an interaction would be of great importance. For further discussion consult Sawilowsky and Fahoome (2003).

Maxwell and Delaney (2004) and the references therein provided detailed discussions of interaction including alternative approaches, confidence intervals for the standardized and unstandardized population differences between the cell means, and a measure of strength of association for interaction contrasts. Keppel and Wickens (2004) recommended and presented equations for estimating partial omega squared for simple effects, and any contrasts that are based on them, for the case of manipulated factors.

Nonparametric Approach

An alternative nonparametric approach to interaction makes use of the concept of probability of superiority (PS) that was discussed in Chapters 5 and 6: $\Pr(Y_i > Y_j)$. In the 2×2 factorial case one can test the null hypothesis that the probability of superiority of a randomly selected score from one level of a factor over a randomly selected score from the other level of a factor is the same at each of the two levels of the other factor (i.e., testing for no interaction). Wilcox (2005a) provided S-PLUS and R functions for conducting such a test for interaction for $a \times b$ designs. Each of the estimated PSs also serves as an effect size that may be of interest. Long, Feng, and Cliff (2003) extended the use of the previously discussed (Chapter 5) dominance measure of effect size to main effects and interaction effects in factorial designs.

RISK-STRATIFIED ANALYSIS

The topic of interaction is related to the topic of *risk-stratified analyses*, which is a set of *subgroup* × *treatment* methods for analyzing results separately for subgroups that are distinguished by differing characteristics on variables that are related to the dependent variable. Greater benefits, or greater harm, may occur in a subgroup (e.g., females or males) than in the overall sample.

WITHIN-GROUPS FACTORIAL DESIGNS

In the case of factorial designs with only within-groups factors primary researchers can usually conceptualize and estimate a standardized difference between means using the same reasoning and the same methods that were presented using Equations 7.3 and 7.4 from the earlier section entitled "Manipulated factors only". There is not literally an MS_w in designs with only within-group factors, but it is valid here to apply Equation 7.4 as if the data had come from a between-subjects design. There is variability within each cell of a within-groups design, as there is within each cell of a between-subjects design, and the subject variables that underlie population variability will be reflected by this variability in both types of design. (In the section entitled "Proportion of Variance Explained" in Chapter 6, we present instructions for using statistical software packages to calculate standardizers in the case of one-way within-groups designs. Those instructions are also applicable to the denominators of Equations 7.3 and 7.4.) Typically, a within-groups factor will be manipulated rather than classificatory because researchers often subject the same participant to different levels of treatment at different times, but they typically cannot vary the classification of a person (e.g., gender or ethnicity).

CHOICE OF STANDARDIZER

In the case of within-groups factorial designs variance in the measure of the dependent variable that is attributable to variation of the peripheral manipulated factor should not contribute to the variance that is reflected by the standardizer if the peripheral manipulated factor does not vary in the population of interest, as it typically does not. For an example, suppose now that in Table 7.3 Treatment 1 and Treatment 2 were, respectively, the absence and presence of a new drug for Alzheimer's disease, drug A, with Factor A being a within-groups factor. Suppose also that in Table 7.3 Factor B were not gender but instead the absence (row 1) or presence (row 2) of a very different kind of drug for Alzheimer's disease, drug B, Factor B also being a within-groups factor. The data in Table 7.3 might represent the patients' scores on a short test of recall memory, or the number of symptoms remaining, after treatment with one or the other drug, a combination of the two drugs, or neither drug. Because of our purpose here we do not discuss methodological issues (other than supposing counterbalancing) in the present hypothetical research, but instead proceed directly to demonstrating alternative estimators of a standardized difference between means for the case of within-groups factorial designs.

Using Factor A for the targeted factor and supposing now that cell 1 represents a control group (or standard-treatment comparison group) in the current example of the revised factor B in Table 7.3 one can first apply Equation 7.3 to the data to find that $d_{comp} = (2.00 - 3.00)/.989^{1/2} = -1.01$. If one assumes homoscedasticity of all four populations of scores that are represented in the design (cells 1 through 4), and recalling from Table 7.4 that we found that $MS_w = .822$ for the data of Table 7.3, one can alternatively apply Equation 7.4 to find that $d_{msw} = (2.00 - 3.00)/.822^{1/2} = -1.10$.

If homoscedasticity with regard to the marginal variances of peripheral Factor B is assumed, one can standardize using the square root of the pooled variances in the margins of rows 1 and 2: $s_{.1}^2 = 1.105$ and $s_{.2}^2 = 1.000$. Because the sample sizes for the two rows are the same, the pooled variance is merely the mean of the two variances; $s_{prm}^2 = (1.105 + 1.000)/2 = 1.053$, where p denotes pooled and rm denotes repeated measures. The standardizer is then $s_{prm} = 1.053^{1/2} = 1.026$. The estimator for the present purpose is given by

$$d_{prm} = \frac{\bar{Y}_{1.} - \bar{Y}_{2.}}{s_{prm}}. \tag{7.21}$$

For the data at hand $d_{prm} = (2.00 - 3.00)/1.026 = -.97$. The results from applying Equations 7.3, 7.4, and 7.21 are not very different in the artificial case of the data of Table 7.3 because the variances in that table are not as different as they are likely to be in the case of real data. Again, the choice of standardizer is based on the assumptions that the researcher makes about the variances of the involved populations. The interpretation of the estimates in terms of population parameters and distributions should be clear from the earlier discussions. For further discussions of Equations 7.3 and 7.4, and the basis for Equation 7.21, review the earlier section entitled "Manipulated factors only".

Unstandardized Differences and Confidence Intervals

Again, when one is interested in means we recommend unstandardized differences if the measure of the dependent variable is a scale that is of inherent interest. Maxwell and Delaney (2004) discussed construction of confidence intervals for the difference between marginal means and for the unstandardized difference between cell means within the framework of a multivariate approach to two-way within-groups designs. Consult Wilcox (2003) for discussions and S-PLUS functions for less known robust methods for unstandardized pair-wise comparisons for two-way within-groups designs. Wilcox (2005a) also provided S-PLUS and R functions (free access to which was cited in our Chapters 1 and 2) for robust methods for constructing simultaneous confidence intervals for pair-wise comparisons when using within-groups-by-between-groups designs.

Keselman et al. (2008) discussed construction of a *CI* for a robust modification of Glass' Δ_G effect size for a factorial repeated-measures design. This modified effect size should be multiplied by .642 to attempt to place it on a scale that is similar to the scale of Glass' effect size (Equations 3.1 and 3.2). We previously cited the free Keselman et al. software. We discuss effect sizes for designs with a mixture of between-groups and within-groups factors (*split-plot designs*) in the context of multivariate analyses in Chapter 12.

STANDARDIZED DIFFERENCES AND CONFIDENCE INTERVALS

Cortina and Nouri (2000) discussed Becker's (1988) equation for the sampling variance of a *d* from a within-groups factor, such an equation being required to construct a confidence interval for d_{pop}. Bird (2002) provided an example of the use of IBM SPSS to construct simultaneous confidence intervals for standardized-difference effect sizes, assuming homoscedasticity, from a split-plot design. Approximate individual and simultaneous confidence intervals can be constructed, again assuming homoscedasticity, using the downloadable free software PSY (from Kevin Bird and his colleagues), which we cited in Chapter 6.

NONPARAMETRIC APPROACHES

Brunner and Puri (2001) discussed extension of what we call the probability of superiority *PS* measure of effect size to within-groups factorial designs. Wilcox (2005a) discussed and provided S-PLUS and R software functions for extending the use of the *PS* to the case of split-plot designs.

Recall the discussion of the dominance measure of effect size, which is related to the probability of superiority, in Chapter 5. Cliff (1996b; also Long et al., 2003) extended the dominance measure to the case of factorial designs with repeated measures and designs with between-groups and within-groups factors. For example, consider the *pretest–posttest control-group design*, which has two independent groups, each with a pretest and a posttest. A null hypothesis can be tested and a confidence interval can be constructed for a dominance measure regarding a possible difference between the changes from pretest to posttest for the two groups. Also, if an additional between-groups factor is added the repeated-measures dominance method can be applied to main effects, interactions, and multiple pair-wise comparisons (Long et al.).

Finally, Wilcox (2005d) discussed robust methods for omnibus tests and linear contrasts involving medians (unstandardized effect sizes) in factorial within-groups designs. Access to S-PLUS and R software functions was also provided.

POV_{pop} AND PARTIAL POV_{pop}

Maxwell and Delaney (2004) presented one of the various formulas that estimate POV_{pop} for the main effect of the targeted factor in a within-groups factorial design.

Their version of such a formula is a partial omega squared that partials (excludes) variance of all non-targeted effects except subject variance from total variance. This approach renders the estimate comparable to what it would have been if the targeted factor had been manipulated in a one-way between-groups design (if this is the goal of the researcher) because in such a one-way design subject variance contributes to total variance.

Tips and Pitfalls

Authors of research reports should be clear about which of the conceptually different formulas has been used to estimate POV_{pop} for a targeted factor in a within-groups factorial design so that readers or later meta-analysts will not unwittingly compare or combine estimates of incomparable measures. For example, other possible approaches may partial out all effects, including the main effect of subjects, or partial out no effects (an estimation of whole POV_{pop}, not partial POV_{pop}). Reports should also provide a rationale for the researcher's choice of approach, not choose an approach merely because it yields a larger estimate, and include all estimates that were calculated. Consult Olejnik and Algina (2000, 2003) for further discussions.

Consult Maxwell and Delaney (2004) for detailed discussions of assumptions and analyses of marginal means and interactions in the case of within-groups factorial designs. With regard to split-plot designs, those authors again provided detailed discussions of the construction of confidence intervals for the variety of contrasts that are possible and formulas for partial omega squared for each kind of factor and for interaction. Again, those formulas for partial omega squared have a different conceptual basis and form from those that might be found elsewhere (cf. Olejnik & Algina, 2000). Keppel and Wickens (2004) discussed the difficulties in interpreting a partial POV in the case of factorial within-groups designs because of uncertainty about the error terms in this case.

ADDITIONAL DESIGNS, MEASURES, AND DISCUSSION

There are methods for calculating estimators of standardized mean differences available for various additional factorial designs. Constraints on length prohibit discussions of these methods but the basic concepts and worked examples that have been presented here should prepare the reader to understand such methods, which are well presented elsewhere. Cortina and Nouri (2000) and Olejnik and Algina (2000) discussed methods for $a \times b$ and $a \times b \times c$ designs. The latter authors, and Gillett (2003), discussed methods related to split-plot designs. Wilcox (2003) discussed and provided S-PLUS functions for robust linear contrasts for two-way split-plot designs.

The previously mentioned methods proposed by Bonett (2008) for constructing confidence intervals for standardized mean differences for between-groups and within-groups factorial designs under normality and slight heteroscedasticity are also applicable to split-plot designs. For example, suppose that in Table 7.3 the levels of the row variable were not Female and Male but Pretest and Posttest, rendering the row variable a within-groups variable with the column variable remaining as a between-groups variable. For this case an effect size can be based on the standardized difference between two differences between means—the difference between the pretest and posttest means under Treatment 1 minus the difference between the pretest and posttest means under Treatment 2. In the case of the currently revised rows of Table 7.3 Bonett's effect size is given by

$$d_{\text{pop}} = \frac{(\mu_{11} - \mu_{12}) - (\mu_{21} - \mu_{22})}{\sigma}, \tag{7.22}$$

where the standardizer is estimated using all four cell variances because heteroscedasticity among them is assumed to be no worse than slight.

Sometimes authors of research reports attempt to convey information about an unstandardized difference between cell means by presenting figures depicting *separate* confidence intervals or *separate* standard-error bars around *each* mean with the intention of interpreting them in terms of the *difference* between the two means. Cumming and Finch (2005) discussed serious interpretative problems when such figures are used in the case of within-group factors. For another point of view regarding confidence intervals for separate means versus confidence intervals for the difference between two means in the case of 2×2 within-groups designs consult Rouder and Morey (2005).

For discussions of estimation of POV_{pop} for designs with random factors or mixed random and fixed factors, consult Vaughan and Corballis (1969), Olejnik and Algina (2000), and Maxwell and Delaney (2004). The latter authors also discussed estimation of POV_{pop} and tests and construction of confidence intervals for differences between marginal means in the case of nested designs. Keppel and Wickens (2004) discussed estimation of whole and partial POV_{pop} for $a \times b \times c$ designs. They recommended estimation of whole POV_{pop} only when the two peripheral factors are blocking factors and partial POV_{pop} when the peripheral factors are manipulated factors. Keppel and Wickens also discussed estimation of what can be called semipartial POV_{pop} for the case in which one peripheral factor is manipulated and the other is a blocking factor. For an alternative correlational approach to effect sizes for between-groups and within-groups factorial designs consult Rosenthal et al. (2000).

Sawilowsky (2007a) presented both sides of the controversial issue of the sequence in which the various effects in a factorial design should be considered and tested. He argued that testing interactions is paramount. Interactions are *ordinal* or *disordinal*. In an ordinal interaction a factor is more efficacious under one or more levels of another factor than at one or more other levels of that latter factor. For example, a drug might be efficacious for women and men, but more so for one of the genders; that is, the order, but not the magnitude, of efficaciousness is the same for women and men. In a disordinal interaction a factor is efficacious at one or more levels of another factor, but not efficacious at one or more other levels of that latter factor. For example, a drug might be efficacious for men, but not efficacious for women. Sawilowsky further argued that in the presence of statistically significant ordinal interaction non-robustness is increased and analysis of main effects is unwarranted.

Tips and Pitfalls

Because methodological and design features can contribute much to the magnitude of an effect size research reports should include at least a brief comment about every characteristic of the study that could plausibly influence the effect size. Also, there can be conflicting results in between-groups and within-groups studies of the same variables. In their analysis of the effects of psychological, behavioral, and educational treatments Wilson and Lipsey (2001) estimated, as a first approximation, that the type of research design (randomized versus nonrandomized, between-groups versus within-groups) and choice of observed measure of a latent dependent variable are the methodological features (modifiers) that correlate highest with estimates of effect size, but many other methodological features correlate with these estimates. Also, estimates of effect size may also differ depending on the extent of variability of the participants. For example, for a given pair of levels of a factor and a given measure of a dependent variable, effect sizes may be different for a population of college students and the quite possibly more variable general population (an example of *external invalidity*). Therefore, one should be cautious about comparing estimates of effect sizes across studies that used samples from populations that may have different variabilities on the dependent variable.

Again, by being explicit about all plausibly relevant methodological features of their research authors of reports can facilitate interpretation of results and facilitate meta-analyses that can systematically study such methodological variables as possible moderators of the magnitudes of estimates of effect size across studies.

SUMMARY

For factorial designs there are various ways to conceptualize and estimate an effect size when faced with a given targeted factor and a given mix of manipulated and/or classificatory factors. Sometimes in the literature there is disagreement about the appropriate method for a given purpose. There may be disagreement about how to estimate d_{pop}, partial POV_{pop}, and whole POV_{pop}, and about whether d_{pop}, partial POV_{pop}, or whole POV_{pop} is the more useful measure for a given set of data. Researchers should think carefully about the purpose of their research and of the nature of the populations of interest before deciding on an appropriate measure and estimator. Also, continuous independent variables should not be discretized (e.g., categorized into high, medium, and low groupings) unless the focus of the research is just on those levels. Discretizing can lower reliability, statistical power, estimates of effect sizes, and the detectability of interactions.

Choice of appropriate effect sizes for various purposes depends in part on distinctions between factors that are targeted for calculation of an effect size versus those that are peripheral ("off factors" that are not targeted for the moment), and whether or not targeted and peripheral factors are extrinsic (often, manipulated factors that do not ordinarily vary in the population) or intrinsic (factors such as gender that ordinarily vary in the population). For example, when a peripheral factor is extrinsic researchers should generally choose a measure of effect size in which variance that is attributable to that factor is held constant so as not to contribute to the standardizer in a d type of effect size or to the total variance that is to be accounted for in a POV type of effect size. The choice of standardizer also depends on whether or not homoscedasticity is assumed, and whether or not the design includes a control or standard-treatment comparison group whose standard deviation provides a reasonable choice for the standardizer. Also, there is a greater risk that an assumption of homoscedasticity is wrong, and perhaps importantly so, when one assumes that all of the population variances are equal than when assumes that just those populations that are directly involved in the effect size have equal variances.

Whole ω^2 is applicable as the least biased estimator of whole POV_{pop}. However, for comparison with a *whole* POV_{pop} from a one-way between-groups design that studied the same levels of the same independent variable, *partial* ω^2 can be used to produce the least biased estimate of *partial* POV_{pop} from a within-groups factorial design. Researchers should be clear about which type of POV they are reporting, and they should consider reporting both with an interpretation of each. Because of great sampling variability construction of a confidence interval for a whole or partial POV_{pop} is especially important.

When the dependent variable is in familiar units (e.g., pounds of human weight) and is of interest in its own right instead of representing an underlying latent variable, unstandardized mean differences can be informative and readily interpreted. There are various multiple-comparison methods for testing for the statistical significance of such unstandardized differences and for constructing confidence intervals for their population values. Researchers should also consider the use of apparently more robust parametric methods and nonparametric methods that are available for between-groups and within-groups factorial design. The nonparametric methods relate to the probability of superiority and dominance measures of effect size that were discussed in Chapter 5.

Effect sizes and confidence intervals relating to interaction can be very informative. Related to interaction is risk-stratified analysis that analyzes results separately for subgroups that differ with respect to variables that are associated with the dependent variable.

When there are only within-groups factors a d type of effect size can usually be estimated using Equations 7.3 and 7.4. The choice of standardizer depends on whether or not homoscedasticity is assumed and whether or not there is a control or standard-treatment group whose standard deviation reasonably provides a standardizer. However, again when the dependent variable is of interest in its own right unstandardized differences between means are recommended as effect sizes. Whether standardized or unstandardized differences are used for the within-groups case we recommend the construction of confidence intervals and consideration of the use of apparently more robust methods. References and a standardized-difference effect size for split-plot designs were provided, as were references to discussions of d and POV types of effect sizes for additional factorial designs.

Because varying methods can result in apparently conflicting results of estimation of effect sizes in the literature it is imperative that researchers make clear in their reports all relevant aspects of the method that they have used. Authors of research reports should also consider reporting not just one kind of estimate of effect size but two or more defensible alternatively conceptualized estimates to provide themselves and their readers with alternative perspectives on the results.

QUESTIONS

7.1 Define (a) targeted and peripheral factors, (b) extrinsic and intrinsic factors.

7.2 How does the distinction between extrinsic and intrinsic factors influence the procedure one adopts for estimating an effect size?

7.3 Are intrinsic factors always classificatory factors? Explain.

7.4 Why is estimation of the POV_{pop} more complicated in the case of factorial designs than in the case of one-way designs?

7.5 What is the purpose of a partial POV_{pop}?

7.6 Discuss why it is problematic to compare two values of an estimated POV_{pop} based on the relative sizes of their values, of the values of their associated Fs, or of the values of significance levels attained by their Fs.

7.7 Why is it problematic to compare two estimates of partial POV_{pop} for two factors in the same study?

7.8 Which two conditions should ordinarily be met if one wants validly to compare estimates of a POV_{pop} for the same factor from different factorial studies?

7.9 Why is it problematic to interpret the relative importance of two factors by inspecting the ratio of their sample POVs?

7.10 How do the nature of the targeted factor and the nature of the peripheral factor influence the choice of a procedure for estimating a standardized effect size?

7.11 How do the nature of one's assumption about homoscedasticity and the presence of a control group or standard-treatment comparison group influence one's choice of a standardizer?

7.12 What assumption underlies the use of Equation 7.6, and in simplest terms, what is the nature of the variance that it produces?

7.13 Briefly describe three procedures for estimating a standardized difference between means at two levels of a manipulated factor at a given level of a peripheral factor, and how does one choose from among these three procedures?

7.14 Briefly describe how one estimates a standardized difference between means at two levels of an intrinsic factor when there is at least one extrinsic peripheral factor.

7.15 Discuss one procedure for estimating a standardized overall difference between means of a classificatory factor when the peripheral factor is intrinsic.

7.16 When would it be inappropriate to use the square root of MS_w as a standardizer even when homoscedasticity of all involved populations is assumed?

7.17 What effect might one's choice of a measure for the dependent variable (when there are alternative measures) have on the results of the various significance tests and estimates of effect size that emerge from a factorial ANOVA?

7.18 Why are Equations 7.3 and 7.4 typically applicable to within-groups designs?

7.19 Discuss the roles that methodological and design features may play in the magnitude of an estimated effect size.

7.20 Briefly explain why partial POV is expected to be greater than whole POV.

7.21 Discuss the consequences of mistakenly reporting a partial POV as a whole POV.

7.22 Consider the following between-groups data.

		Factor A	
Factor B	**Level 1**	**Level 2**	**Level 3**
	9	5	18
Level 1	7	1	17
	8	3	14
	10	11	8
Level 2	12	10	7
	9	10	10

Calculate and interpret (a) omega squared for manipulated Factor A if Factor B is intrinsic, (b) partial omega squared for Factor A if Factor B is extrinsic, (c) d_{comp} comparing levels 1 and 2 of Factor A if both factors are manipulated, marginal homoscedasticity of peripheral Factor B is not assumed, and the cell at Level 1 of both factors represents a standard-treatment comparison group, (d) d_{msw} as in part (c), but now assuming homoscedasticity for all six populations that are represented in the design, (e) d^*_{comp}, as in part (c), but now with peripheral Factor B being intrinsic, (f) d_{level}, as in part (e), but now the comparison is made only at Level 1 of peripheral Factor B, (g) $d_{levelmsw}$, as in part (f), but now assuming homoscedasticity for all six populations in the design.

7.23 With regard to the data of Question 7.22 calculate and interpret (a) d_{class} for Levels 1 and 2 of classificatory Factor B if peripheral Factor A is also classificatory and one wants to estimate by how many standard deviation units the marginal mean for participants at Level 2 of Factor B is above or below the marginal mean for participants at Level 1 of Factor B with regard to the overall distribution of scores for those at Level 1 (not assuming any homoscedasticity) and (b) d^*_{classp} as in part (a), but now assuming homoscedasticity with regard to the two compared populations.

7.24 Suppose now that Factors A and B in Question 7.22 are within-groups factors. Calculate and interpret d_{prm} involving Levels 1 and 2 of targeted Factor A assuming homoscedasticity with regard to the marginal variances of peripheral Factor B.

8 Effect Sizes for Categorical Variables

INTRODUCTION

The chi-square test for the *presence* of an association between categorical variables does not provide direct information about the *strength* of such an association. This chapter discusses many of the effect sizes (i.e., measures of strength of association) that are applicable to categorical variables.

An unordered categorical variable is also called a *nominal*, *discrete*, or *qualitative variable* because its variations (categories) are names for qualities (characteristics). Common examples of categorical variables include gender: female and male; political affiliation: Democrat, Republican, or other; treatment: therapy a, therapy b, therapy c, etc.; outcome: patient improved, patient unimproved. When a categorical variable has only two possible values it is called a *dichotomous*, *binomial*, or *binary variable*. When more than two categorical values are possible the variable is called *multinomial*.

CONTINGENCY TABLES

When each of the variables in the research is categorical the data are usually presented in a table such as Table 8.1. In the simplest case only two variables are being studied, one variable being represented by the rows and the other by the columns of the table. In this case the table is called a *two-way table*. The general designation of a two-way table is $r \times c$ table, in which r and c stand for rows and columns, respectively. For a specific $r \times c$ table the letters r and c are replaced by the number of rows and the number of columns in that table, respectively. The common 2×2 table is also called a *fourfold table* because the table contains four cells. Two-way tables or *multi-way tables* (i.e., more than two variables) are also called *cross-classification tables* or *contingency tables*. The cells of cross-classification tables classify each participant across two or more variables. Within each cell of the table is the number of participants that fall into the row category and the column category that the cell represents. Such data are called *cell counts* or *cell frequencies*.

The name "contingency" table refers to the fact that the traditional purpose of analyzing the table's data is to determine if there is a contingency (i.e., *association* or *dependence*) between the variables. In a common clinical example one may want to determine if participants' falling into the outcome categories

TABLE 8.1

Frequencies of Outcomes after Treatment

		Symptoms		
		Remain	Gone	Totals
Therapy	Psychotherapy	$f_{11} = 14$	$f_{12} = 22$	36
	Drug therapy	$f_{21} = 22$	$f_{22} = 10$	32
	Totals	36	32	68

patient improved or *patient unimproved* is contingent on which treatment category the patient was in. In this example there is an independent variable (the type of treatment given) and a dependent variable (the outcome of *improved* or *unimproved*), although the categorical variables need not be classifiable as independent variables or dependent variables. For example, in research that relates religious affiliation and political affiliation the researcher need not designate an independent variable and a dependent variable, although the researcher may have a theory about the relationship that does specify that, say, religious affiliation is the independent variable and political affiliation is the dependent variable.

The total count for each row across the columns is placed at the right margin of the table, and the total count for each column across the rows is placed at the lower margin of the table. The row totals and the column totals are each called *marginal totals*. The set of all row marginal totals and the set of all column marginal totals are each called *marginal distributions*.

Table 8.1 is a 2 × 2 contingency table that is based on actual data. The clinical details are not relevant to our discussion of estimating an effect size for such data. We now assume that the data in Table 8.1 represent the fourfold categorizations of 68 former pain patients whose files had been sampled from a clinic that had provided either psychotherapy or drug therapy for a certain kind of pain. Such a method of research is called a *naturalistic* or *cross-sectional study*. In this method the researcher decides only the total number of participants to be sampled, not the row or column totals. These latter totals emerge naturally when the total sample is categorized. A common clinical example of naturalistic sampling involves an attempt to relate a disease to a preceding exposure (e.g., smoking). For such a purpose it is necessary to be certain that the exposure actually preceded the disease. Naturalistic sampling is common in survey research.

In Table 8.1 the letter f stands for frequency of occurrence in a cell, and the two subscripts stand for the row and column, respectively, that the cell frequency represents. For example, f_{21} stands for the frequency with which participants are found in the cell representing the crossing of the second row and the first column, namely 22 of the 32 patients who received drug therapy. The early discussions in this chapter involve independent samples.

UNRELIABILITY OF CATEGORIZATION

Consult Fleiss, Levin, and Paik (2003) for discussions of cases in which there are missing data or in which some participants have been misclassified into the categories. Fleiss et al. also discussed measurement of what is often labeled *inter-rater agreement*. We prefer the more generally applicable label *inter-judge agreement* (or *inter-judge reliability*), especially when categories are nominal (i.e., unlike *ordered categories*, such as mild, moderate, or severe disease), because we prefer that the use of the word "rater" be restricted to the case of categorizing on an *ordinal scale* (i.e., rating the *extent* of some characteristic, not just naming it). We discuss inter-rater agreement further in Chapter 9 on effect sizes for ordinal scales.

KAPPA MEASURES OF INTER-JUDGE AGREEMENT AND EFFECT SIZE

When participants in research are subjectively categorized the strong possibility of unreliability of the categorization arises. As was discussed in Chapter 4 unreliability reduces the power of statistical tests and lowers estimates of effect size. The most widely used statistic for quantifying the extent of agreement of the categorization of participants or objects by two independent judges, such as clinicians judging whether treatment was a success or a failure for each patient is Cohen's (1960) kappa (κ). Kappa, as a measure of inter-judge agreement in the sample, provides the proportion of the categorizations in which the two judges placed a participant's result in the same category, such proportion being corrected for mere chance agreement. If the obtained proportion of cases for which the categorizations agree is equal to or greater than what would be expected by chance $\kappa \geq 0$, and if there is agreement for every categorization $\kappa = 1$. The minimum value of kappa when there is complete disagreement depends on the distribution of cases in the margins of the table, with the minimum value of kappa ranging from -1 to 0, inclusive.

Interpretation of the sign and magnitude of kappa can be complicated. Consult Heo (2008) for further discussion and references. Kappa can also importantly be interpreted as a sample strength-of-association effect size that is related to the phi coefficient and risk difference effect sizes that are discussed later in this chapter (Kraemer, Periyakoil, & Noda, 2004). In the present case kappa reflects the association between the categorizations by two judges.

There can be two or more categories. Each "judge" need not be a human being; for example, a judge can be a computerized diagnostic procedure or a team of experts who reach a consensus categorization for each patient. Kappa can estimate agreement between such a judge and another judge of the same kind or of a different kind.

For a sample, $\kappa = (Prop_{agree} - Prop_{expagree})/(Maxprop_{agree} - Prop_{expagree})$, where $Prop_{agree}$ is the observed proportion of categorizations on which the judges agree, $Prop_{expagree}$ is the proportion of categorizations for which agreement is expected by mere chance, and $Maxprop_{agree}$ is the maximum possible proportion of categorizations for which there can be agreement, the latter being equal to 1. For the

TABLE 8.2

Two Judges' Categorizations of Patients after Treatment

		Judge 1		
		Better	Not Better	Totals
	Better	45	15	60
Judge 2	Not better	6	20	26
	Totals	51	35	86

definition of population kappa, all proportions in the equation are replaced by probabilities. The assumptions for the Cohen's kappa that we discuss here are that the cases (e.g., patients or interviewees) that are being categorized are independent; the categories of the scale are independent, mutually exclusive, and exhaustive; and that the judges categorize independently.

For computation, sample $\kappa = (\Sigma f_o - \Sigma f_e)/(N - \Sigma f_e)$, where each relevant f_o is the observed frequency with which the judges agree in their categorizations of cases into a given cell, each f_e is the expected frequency of agreement in categorizations of cases into a given relevant cell by mere chance, and N is the total number of cases. The relevant cells are those in which the categorizations by the two judges agree. In Table 8.2 the relevant cells are the two cells in the diagonal from the upper left to the lower right of the table. The number of relevant cells equals the number of classifications into which judges are categorizing.

From the multiplication theorem of probability it can be shown that the value of each f_e is $(f_{row} \times f_{col})/N$, where each relevant f_{row} is the total number of cases in a table's row in which there is a cell that represents agreed categorizations, and each relevant f_{col} is the total number of cases in that same cell's column. As observed earlier in the computational equation for sample kappa, the values of f_e for such relevant cells that depict agreement in categorizations are summed.

When there are more than two categories and two categories are combined the value of kappa will be increased or decreased depending on which categories are combined (Warrens, 2010). It is invalid to combine categories after results are obtained for the purpose of reporting only the higher value.

Worked Example of Kappa

Consider the hypothetical data in Table 8.2, which depicts the categorizations of 86 treated patients into Patient Better or Patient Not Better by two judges. The total of the frequencies of the two cells in the diagonal of the table from upper left to lower right, which we call the first cell and fourth cell (i.e., the Better–Better cell and the Not Better–Not Better cell, respectively), provides the total number of categorizations for which there is agreement: $\Sigma f_o = 45 + 20 = 65$.

The f_e for the first cell equals $(f_{row} \times f_{col})/N = (60 \times 51)/86 = 35.581395$, and the f_e for the fourth cell equals $(26 \times 35)/86 = 10.581395$, so one sums these two values to find $\Sigma f_e = 46.16279$. (Observe that the two relevant cells [i.e., the cells in which there is agreement] each have a greater frequency of observed agreement than what would be expected by chance: $f_o = 45$ versus $f_e \approx 36$ and $f_o = 20$ versus $f_e \approx 11$.)

To calculate sample kappa one enters the previously calculated values into the computational equation to find that $\kappa = (65 - 46.16279)/(86 - 46.16279) \approx .473$. Therefore, in the sample the difference between the obtained agreement and agreement expected by mere chance is approximately 47% of the maximum possible difference. By some standards $\kappa = .47$ would be considered to be "fairly good" or "moderately good" agreement, but we generally disapprove of such out-of-context benchmarks, just as we do for evaluating effect sizes. The evaluation of a given value of kappa should depend on the expertise of the judges and the complexity of the characteristic that is being categorized.

Valid hypothesis testing is available for null-hypothesized values of κ_{pop} other than 0 (Fleiss et al., 2003). In most applications testing H_0: $\kappa_{pop} = 0$ would be of little value, as is generally true of measures of reliability, because one usually expects agreement to be better than chance, so it is highly unlikely that $\kappa_{pop} = 0$. Therefore, software output for a confidence interval for population kappa should be of greater interest than testing H_0: $\kappa_{pop} = 0$. For example, SAS currently outputs Cohen's kappa and confidence limits using the AGREE option in PROC FREQ. For the data of Table 8.2, the outputted kappa is .4729 and the lower and upper 95% confidence limits for κ_{pop} are .2842 and .6616, respectively.

Because the sampling distribution of kappa approaches normality as sample size increases, one can construct an approximate confidence interval for population kappa manually using a method that is analogous to the normality-assuming method that was discussed in Chapter 2 regarding Equations 2.1 and 2.3. That is, because the middle 95% of the values under the standard normal curve lie between −1.96 and +1.96, the 95% confidence limits for population kappa are given by sample $\kappa \pm 1.96 SE_k$, where SE_k is the standard deviation of the sampling distribution of kappa (standard error). Using the somewhat complex improved formula for SE_k that is in Fleiss et al. (2003), $SE_k = .0963$ for the current data. Therefore the confidence limits are estimated to be .4729 $\pm$ 1.96(.0963), which are .6616 and .2842, as before.

If the point estimate of kappa that is outputted by SAS is close enough to 1 the outputted value of the upper confidence limit might be greater than the maximum possible value for kappa, which, again, is 1. In this case the upper limit should be reported as 1. The population to which a confidence interval for population kappa might generalize is a population (e.g., patients) of which the sample is representative, classified into the particular categories used by the particular judges used. Because it is sensitive to the marginal distribution in the table, two or more values of Cohen's kappa should not be compared unless they arise from tables with identical marginal distributions.

INTRACLASS KAPPA

There are several variants of kappa and other measures of reliability of judges or raters. Restriction of space does not permit detailed discussion here. Kappa can be generalized to the case of more than two judges (Agresti, 2002; Fleiss et al., 2003) and can be applicable to situations other than inter-judge agreement (Fleiss et al.).

Kraemer (2006) argued for the use of *intraclass kappa* by applying the *intraclass correlation coefficient (ICC)* as a method for measuring agreement between or among two or more judges who are making dichotomous categorizations when inference is to be made to a population. Consult Maxwell and Delaney (2004) for details. It is relatively simple to construct a confidence interval for the population intraclass kappa when there are only two judges and the sample size is at least moderate (Kraemer et al., 2004). Rousson (2011) discussed interpretation of statistical models for the *ICC* that apply to the cases of either an infinite population of judges or the sample of judges constituting the population of interest.

The *ICC* method can be applied to more than two judges. Also, there can be more than two categories (the *multinomial* case). For details consult Fleiss et al. (2003) and Maxwell and Delaney (2004). However, Kraemer et al. (2004) argued against use of intraclass kappa when there are more than two categories. The population intraclass kappa can also be used as a measure of association in 2×2 tables (Kraemer, 2006), and the *ICC* can be used as an effect size (Maxwell & Delaney). Warrens (2008) discussed measures of inter-judge agreement besides kappa. Consult Hsu (2003) and von Eye and von Eye (2005) for critiques of Cohen's kappa and related measures. Bendermacher and Souren (2009) proposed an alternative measure.

DICHOTOMIZING A CONTINUOUS VARIABLE

The statistical and effect-size procedures that are discussed in this chapter for 2×2 tables are applied here only to originally discrete (i.e., truly, or originally dichotomous) variables, not arbitrarily dichotomized variables. The procedures are problematic when the row or the column variable has been dichotomized by the researcher into, say, *participant better* versus *participant not better* categories from an originally continuous variable. For example, suppose that two therapies are to be compared for their effect on anxiety. Suppose further that two categories of anxiety are formed by the researcher by categorizing as high or low anxiety those who score above or below the median (or some other cut-point), respectively, on a continuous scale of anxiety. Such arbitrary dichotomizing may render the procedures in this chapter questionable because the effect size may depend not only on the relative efficacy of the two therapies, as they should, but also on the arbitrary cut-point the researcher decided to use to lump everyone below the cut-point together as *low anxiety* and to lump everyone above the cut-point together as *high anxiety*. If some other arbitrary cut-points had been used, such as the lowest 25% of scores on the continuous anxiety test (*low anxiety*) and the highest 25% of scores (*high anxiety*), the results from statistical tests and estimation of effect size may differ from those arising from the equally arbitrary (although customary) use of the median as the cut-point. Methods that were presented earlier throughout this book are generally more appropriate than dichotomizing when the dependent variable is continuous. Recall also that dichotomizing can lower statistical power.

CHI-SQUARE TEST AND PHI

CHI-SQUARE (χ^2) TEST

The most common test of the statistical significance of the association between the row and column variables in a table such as Table 8.1 is the χ^2 *test of association*. The degrees of freedom for the common form of this test is given by $df = (r - 1)(c - 1)$, which in the case of a 2×2 table yields $df = (2 - 1)(2 - 1) = 1$. However, whereas the χ^2 test addresses the issue of whether or not there is an association, the emphasis in this book is on estimating the strength of this association with an appropriate estimator of effect size.

Tips and Pitfalls
The magnitude of χ^2 does not necessarily indicate the strength of the association between the row and column variables. The numerical value of χ^2 (Equation 8.1) depends not only on the strength of association but also on the total sample size. Thus, if in a contingency table the pattern of the cell data were to remain the same (i.e., the same strength of association) but the sample size were increased, χ^2 would increase. What is needed is a measure of the strength of the association between the row and column variables that is not affected, or less affected, by the total sample size. Kraemer (2006) discussed many measures of effect size for a 2×2 table. In this chapter we discuss the more widely used measures.

PHI$_{pop}$ EFFECT SIZE

One common, but often problematic, measure of effect size for a 2×2 table is the population correlation coefficient, r_{pop} (i.e., the common Pearson correlation between, in this case, a dichotomous X variable and a dichotomous Y variable). An r_{pop} arising from a 2×2 table is called a population *phi coefficient*, which is denoted phi$_{pop}$ here and estimated by the sample phi. In the statistical literature what we denote in this book as phi$_{pop}$ is usually denoted Φ and the estimator phi is usually denoted ϕ (Greek uppercase and lowercase letter phi, respectively). Note that χ^2 can be considered to be a sum of standardized effects:

$$\chi^2 = \Sigma \frac{(f_o - f_e)^2}{f_e},$$
(8.1)

where f_o and f_e are the observed frequencies and expected frequencies, respectively, in a cell, and the summation is over all four cells. (In this case the standardizer is f_e.) Therefore, as can be observed in Equation 8.2, phi$_{pop}$ can be considered to be a kind of average effect, namely, the square root of the mean of the standardized effects. For formal expression of this parameter and further discussions consult Hays (1994) and Kraemer (2006). It is not surprising that phi_{pop} is a kind of average because r_{pop}, of which phi_{pop} is a special case, is a mean, the mean of products of z scores in the population:

$$r_{pop} = \frac{\Sigma z_x z_y}{N}.$$

Phi can be calculated most simply by using

$$phi = \left[\frac{\chi^2}{N}\right]^{1/2}, \tag{8.2}$$

where N is the total sample size. Observe in Equation 8.2 how phi, as an estimator of effect size, compensates for the influence of sample size on χ^2 by dividing χ^2 by N.

MINIMUM SAMPLE SIZES

It is often recommended in the literature that chi square only be used when sample size is said to be "not small," so that the value of the expected frequency will not be "small" and the rate of Type I error not be inflated. Often it is specifically recommended that chi square not be used if $f_e < 5$, but this tradition began as an apparently arbitrary choice (Campbell, 2007). Also, such recommendations are inconsistent in the literature, widely ranging from, say, $f_e = .8$ to $f_e = 10$ as lower limits of appropriateness of chi square (von Eye & Mun, 2003). Campbell argued for the use of a modified formula for chi square that reduces Type I error and is applicable whenever each $f_e > 1$.

WORKED EXAMPLE

For the purpose of applying phi to data from naturalistic sampling one can also calculate, as equivalent to Equation 8.1, a χ^2 using

$$\chi^2 = \frac{N(f_{11}f_{22} - f_{12}f_{21})^2}{n_{r1}n_{r2}n_{c1}n_{c2}}, \tag{8.3}$$

where n_{r1}, n_{r2}, n_{c1}, and n_{c2}, represent the number of participants in row 1, row 2, column 1, and column 2, respectively.

For the data of Table 8.1 software or manual calculation yields $\chi^2 = 6.06$, $p = .013$ at $df = (r - 1)(c - 1) = (2 - 1)(2 - 1) = 1$, so application of Equation 8.2 yields phi = $(6.06/68)^{1/2} = .30$, a value that may be considered to be statistically significantly different from 0 at the same $p = .013$. Different software and different textbooks often use formulas for χ^2 that are different from Equation 8.3. Some superficially different looking formulas for χ^2 are actually functionally equivalent formulas that yield identical results. Another difference between formulas is a matter of adjusting or not adjusting the numerator of χ^2 for the fact that its continuous theoretical distribution (used to obtain the p value) is not perfectly represented by its actual discrete empirical sampling distribution. The adjustment is commonly called the *continuity correction* or *Yates' continuity correction*, but Campbell (2007) studied several versions of the chi-square test and concluded that Yates' correction is an overcorrection and that its use is inappropriate. Different versions of the chi-square test will yield results that are more similar the larger the sample sizes. To calculate phi the unadjusted χ^2 is used as in Equation 8.3.

SIGN OF PHI

The value of phi_{pop} theoretically ranges from -1 to $+1$. However, because Equation 8.2 produces a square root it may not be immediately clear whether phi is positive or negative. However, the sign of phi is a trivial result of the order in which the two columns or the two rows are arranged. For example, if Table 8.1 had drug therapy and its results in the first row, and psychotherapy and its results in the second row, the sign of phi, but not its size, would change. In order to interpret the current obtained phi (i.e., $+.30$ or $-.30$) note first that *symptoms gone* is the better of the two outcome categories. Observe also that $22/36 = .61$ of the total psychotherapy patients attained this good outcome, whereas $10/32 = .31$ of the total patients in drug therapy attained it. Therefore, one now has the proper interpretation of the obtained phi. Because χ^2 and, by implication, phi, are statistically significant, and a greater proportion of the psychotherapy patients than the drug patients are found in the better outcome category, one can conclude that psychotherapy is statistically significantly better than drug therapy in the particular clinical example of the data in Table 8.1.

Because one now has the proper interpretation of the results the question of the sign of phi is unimportant. However, using the reasoning of Chapter 4 regarding the sign of the point-biserial r, the reader should be able to recognize now that $r = phi$ is negative for the data of Table 8.1 using the usual kind of coding of the X and Y variables. If one were to code, say, row 1 as $X = 1$, row 2 as $X = 2$, column 1 as $Y = 1$, and column 2 as $Y = 2$, phi would be negative because there would be a tendency for those in the *lower* category of X (i.e., row 1) to be in the *higher* category of Y (i.e., column 2), and for those in the *higher* category of X (i.e., row 2) to be in the *lower* category of Y (i.e., column 1). This pattern of results defines a negative relationship between variables.

LIMITATIONS OF PHI

Unfortunately, the value of phi is not only influenced by the strength of association between the row and column variables, as it should be, but also by variation in the margin totals (references in Warrens, 2008), which was called sensitivity to sample base rates in the discussion of the point-biserial r in Chapter 4. Therefore, the use of phi is only recommended in naturalistic research, wherein the researcher has chosen only the total sample size, not the row or column sample sizes. In this case any variation between the two column totals or between the two row totals is natural rather than being based on the researcher's arbitrary choices of row or column sample sizes.

Tips and Pitfalls

A phi arising from another study of the same two dichotomous variables, but using a sampling method other than naturalistic sampling, would not be comparable to a phi based on naturalistic sampling; that is, the value of phi can vary across studies using different sampling methods to study the same pair of dichotomous variables. Also, phi can only attain the extreme values of −1 or +1 (perfect correlations) when both variables are truly dichotomous and when the proportion of the total participants found in either one of the row margins is the same as the proportion of the total participants who are found in either one of the column margins.

The requirement about the equality of a row proportion and a column proportion to maintain the possibility of phi = +1 or −1 as extreme limits is related to the problem of reduction of r by unequal skew of an X variable and a Y variable that was discussed in the section entitled "Assumptions of correlation and point-biserial correlation" in Chapter 4. In naturalistic sampling a reduction of the absolute upper limit for phi because of the failure of a row proportion to equal a column proportion may merely be reflecting a natural phenomenon in the two populations instead of reflecting the researcher's arbitrary choice of the two sample sizes. Consult the treatments of phi in Carroll (1961), Cohen et al. (2003), Haddock, Rindskopf, and Shadish (1998), and Kraemer (2006).

For the present example in Table 8.1 the proportions of the total 68 participants that are found in row 1, row 2, column 1, and column 2 are 36/68 = .53, 32/68 = .47, 36/68 = .53, and 32/68 = .47, respectively. The row and column marginal distributions of Table 8.1 happen to satisfy the proportionality criterion for a 2 × 2 table in which the possible absolute upper limit of phi is 1, although satisfying this criterion is not necessary in the case of naturalistic sampling. IBM SPSS is among the statistical packages that output phi. The phi coefficient and many less widely known measures of association for 2 × 2 tables that were discussed by Warrens (2008) can be implemented in the hierarchical cluster routine of IBM SPSS.

Further Discussions and Reading

The performances of chi-square and five other tests and measures for association in 2 × 2 tables were simulated by von Eye and Mun (2003), who noted that such tests and measures can be sensitive to different characteristics of the data and differ in ways other than power. This fact is especially important because major software packages offer a large number of choices for analysis of such tables. The discussions in this chapter, the concluding Table 8.5 at the end of this chapter, and the review by Kraemer (2006) should help in the choice of an analysis. Again, if more than one measure is estimated each must be reported and any discrepancies discussed.

von Eye and Mun reported generally (not always) comparable rates of Type I error for the competing tests, and von Weber, von Eye, and Lautsch (2004) reported generally comparable power for 11 tests for 2 × 2 tables. Agresti (2011) compared methods for constructing confidence intervals for different effect sizes for categorical data under different conditions.

CONFIDENCE INTERVALS AND NULL–COUNTERNULL INTERVALS FOR PHI$_{pop}$

Refer to Fleiss et al. (2003) for discussion of a method for constructing a large-sample approximate confidence interval for phi$_{pop}$. A confidence interval for phi$_{pop}$ (or phi$_{pop}^2$) can also be constructed using the noncentral χ^2 distribution. (Noncentrality was discussed in Chapter 3.) The method can be implemented using IBM SPSS, SAS, S-PLUS, or R software. Computing routines are currently available free courtesy of Michael Smithson at http://psychology.anu.edu.au/people/smithson/details/CIstuff/CI.html. The method, as discussed by Smithson (2003), actually constructs a confidence interval for Cramér's V_{pop}, which is discussed later in this chapter and is equivalent to phi$_{pop}$ in the case of 2 × 2 tables. A null–counternull interval can be constructed for phi$_{pop}$ using Equation 4.2 to find the counternull value.

DIFFERENCE BETWEEN TWO PROPORTIONS

One frequently important purpose of an effect size is to convey the meaning of research results in the most understandable form for persons who have little or no knowledge of statistics: persons such as clients, patients and patient's caregivers, and some educational, governmental, or health-insurance officials. For this purpose perhaps the simplest estimate of the association between the variables in a 2 × 2 table is the difference between two independent proportions, which estimates the difference between the probabilities of a given outcome in two independent populations (i.e., the *difference between two independent binomial probabilities*, $P_1 - P_2$). This measure of effect size is sensitive to population base rates. When statistical tests and construction of confidence intervals are conducted in the traditional ways this measure is only appropriate for studies that used random assignment, or the prospective or retrospective versions of purposive sampling. In *purposive sampling* for two groups the researcher samples a predetermined number of participants who are selected because they have a certain characteristic and a predetermined number of participants who are selected because they have an alternative characteristic (e.g., males and females, or past treatment with either Drug *a* or Drug *b*). The distinction between the prospective and retrospective versions of purposive sampling will be discussed later where needed in the section entitled "Relative risk".

The difference between two independent proportions is also appropriate under naturalistic sampling if statistical testing and the construction of confidence intervals are undertaken using the approach described by Martín Andrés,

Tapia García, and del Moral Ávila (2008), and available by their courtesy at http://www.ugr.es/local/bioest/EQUIV_ASO.EXE. Adjusting estimates and confidence intervals for $P_1 - P_2$ for confounding variables was discussed by Ukoumunne, Williamson, Forbes, Gulliford, and Carlin (2010).

WORKED EXAMPLE

For a worked example we again use the instructive real data of Table 8.1, but now we assume that the participants had been randomly assigned to their treatment groups. Note first that the sample sizes differ in Table 8.1 (36 and 32). All that is required for random assignment is that each of the N total participants be assigned to conditions without bias, and not that ns necessarily be equal.

The first step is to choose one of the two outcome categories to serve as what we call the *targeted category* or *targeted outcome*. In Table 8.1 one can use "Symptoms Gone" as the targeted category, but we observe later that it does not matter which category of outcome is chosen for this purpose. The next step is to calculate the proportion of the total participants in Sample 1 (Treatment 1) who have that targeted outcome and the proportion of the total participants in Sample 2 (Treatment 2) who have that targeted outcome. In the present example, .61 of the psychotherapy patients and .31 of the drug therapy patients became free of their symptoms. One then finds the difference between these two proportions, .61 − .31 = .30. This sample result estimates that the probability that a member of the population that receives psychotherapy will be relieved of symptoms is .61 and the probability that a member of the population that receives drug therapy will be relieved of symptoms is .31. Another interpretation is that the results lead to an estimate that of every 100 members of the population of those who are given psychotherapy for the symptoms at hand, 30 (i.e., 61 − 31 = 30) more patients will be relieved of these symptoms than would have been relieved of them had they been given the drug therapy instead.

We continue to use column 2 of Table 8.1 (Symptoms Gone) as the targeted category. Now call the proportion, p, of the total participants in row 1 who fall into column 2 p_1, and call the proportion of the total participants in row 2 who fall into column 2 p_2. Therefore, the previously found proportions are $p_1 = .61$ and $p_2 = .31$.

RELATIONSHIP TO PHI

The absolute difference between the two proportions is the same as the absolute value of phi for the 2 × 2 table, both being equal to .30 for the data of Table 8.1. Recall from the section on the BESD (binomial effect-size display) in Chapter 4 that, with regard to a table such as Table 8.1, p_1 and p_2 are often called the *success proportions*, and their difference will be equal to phi when the marginal totals in the table are uniform. (However, uniform marginal totals are less likely under random assignment or naturalistic sampling.)

Recall also that it is often the case that different kinds of measures of effect size can provide different perspectives on data. A phi = .30 may not seem to be very impressive to some, and the corresponding coefficient of determination (Chapter 4) of $r^2 = phi^2 = .30^2 = .09$ may seem to be even less impressive. However, a success proportion of .61 for one therapy that is nearly double the success proportion of .31 for another therapy seems to be very impressive. The difference between the *failure proportions* (e.g., the Symptoms Remain cells of Table 8.1) in clinical outcome research is commonly called the *risk difference* (*RD*), *risk reduction*, or *absolute risk reduction*. The label risk difference is also used in epidemiological research that compares the proportions of people who do and who do not develop a certain disease (e.g., lung cancer) when having or not having a preceding risk factor (e.g., smoking).

MORE ON COMPETING TESTS FOR 2 × 2 TABLES

Because the method in the present example involved random assignment to treatments instead of naturalistic sampling, there are more appropriate approaches to testing statistical significance and for estimating an effect size than an approach that is based on phi for the data of Table 8.1 (Fleiss et al., 2003; Wilcox, 1996). A recommended kind of approach for the present example of random assignment and an interest in a readily understood effect size is to focus directly on the difference between two proportions. Because a proportion, p, in a sample estimates a probability, P, in a population one may test H_0: $P_1 = P_2$ against H_{alt}: $P_1 \neq P_2$, two-tailed, where P_1 and P_2 are estimated by p_1 and p_2, respectively. In general P_i is the probability that a member of the population who has been assigned the treatment in row i will have the targeted outcome, and P_j is the probability that a member of the population that has been assigned the treatment in row j will have the targeted outcome. The estimator $p_1 - p_2$ is an unbiased estimator of $P_1 - P_2$.

Again, a researcher may choose to use the category that is represented by column 1 as the targeted category instead of using the category that is represented by column 2. The choice is of no statistical consequence because the same significance level will be attained when the difference between two proportions is based on column 1 as when it is based on column 2. Of course, finding that, say, the success rate (proportion) for Therapy i is statistically significantly higher than the success rate for Therapy j is equivalent to finding that the failure rate for Therapy i is statistically significantly lower than the failure rate for Therapy j.

There are competing methods for testing H_0: $P_1 = P_2$ (Agresti, 2002; Fleiss et al., 2003; Martín Andrés & Herranz Tejedor, 2004). Comparisons of the power of exact tests for 2 × 2 tables under various kinds of sampling were reported by Martín Andrés, Silva Mato, Tapia García, and Sánchez Quevedo (2004). Skipka, Munk, and Freitag (2004) also compared exact tests and found that there is a trade-off between the power and simplicity of a method. Wilcox (1996) provided a Minitab macro for one of the methods. Kang, Lee, and Park (2006) compared the rates of Type I error for three large-sample tests of $P_1 - P_2$.

UNCONDITIONAL AND EXACT TESTS

Digressing temporarily from the specific example of the data in Table 8.1, we discuss some preliminary considerations, beginning with the major controversy about whether tests for 2 × 2 tables should be *conditional* or *unconditional*. *Conditional* and *unconditional tests* are also known as *marginal-dependent* and *marginal-independent* (or *marginal-free*) tests, respectively. The issue is a matter of the extent to which margins in the contingency table are fixed and thereby constrain the possible values in the sampling distribution of the test statistic. For example, if each sample of a predetermined size is selected from one or the other of two populations and Sample *a* and Sample *b* are represented, say, in the rows (as in the examples involving naturalistic sampling in this book), then only the row margin totals are fixed and it has been argued that unconditional tests are applicable. The case in which all four marginal totals are fixed is rare, so it will not be discussed here. Consult Fleiss et al. (2003).

Fisher–Irwin "Exact" Test

Some general and specialized statistical packages (e.g., StatXact) provide a so-called *exact test* (but note our further discussion about the limitation of "exactness") that is based on the foregoing discussion and that is known as *Fisher's exact test* or the *Fisher–Irwin exact test*. Not all forms of an exact test are conditional tests (e.g., van der Meulen, 2008). Also, it is possible that an approximate test (i.e., a test using a large-sample-based approximation to the actual sampling distribution of the test statistic) will be more powerful than an exact test. A conditional and an unconditional exact test can be implemented in StatXact software.

Campbell (2007) discussed versions of the Fisher–Irwin test and argued that the test be used only when one or more expected frequencies are below 1. Campbell further argued that in all other cases power is increased by using his modified formula for chi square instead of the Fisher–Irwin test. Another more powerful version of the Fisher–Irwin test was discussed by van der Meulen (2008). Discussions about characteristics and relationships regarding chi-square and five other tests for 2 × 2 tables were provided by von Eye and Mun (2003). von Weber et al. (2004) critiqued chi-square and 10 other tests.

Regarding the adjective "exact" in exact tests, such tests use exact distributions instead of large-sample approximate distributions. However, the obtained *p* level is not exact; it is the upper limit of what the actual rate of Type I error might be. For this reason exact tests are generally said to be *conservative*. Consult Agresti (2002, 2007) for further explanation of the conservativeness of the Fisher–Irwin exact test compared to traditional unconditional tests. Further discussion of the controversy about conditional versus unconditional tests would be beyond the scope of this book. Antonio Martín Andrés and his colleagues provide free programs for analyzing the data in univariate and multivariate 2 × 2 tables at http://www.ugr.es/~bioest/software.htm.

MORE ON TESTING H_0: $P_1 = P_2$

Manual calculation is possible for the Storer–Kim method for testing H_0: $P_1 = P_2$ against H_{alt}: $P_1 \neq P_2$, but it is laborious (Wilcox, 1996). The calculation can be performed using a Minitab macro (Wilcox) or S-PLUS or R functions (Wilcox, 2005a). For pedagogical purposes we demonstrate a simpler traditional, but less accurate, manual method. The method is an example of what is called a *large-sample*, *approximate*, or *asymptotic method* because its accuracy increases as sample sizes n_1 and n_2 (e.g., the two row totals in Table 8.1) increase. We provide criteria for defining "large sample" in the current context later. After defining an additional concept we provide a detailed illustration of the method.

The mean proportion, $\bar{p}$, is the proportion of all participants (both samples) that are found in the targeted category. In the example of Table 8.1, in which column 2 represents the targeted category,

$$\bar{p} = \frac{f_{12} + f_{22}}{N}, \tag{8.4}$$

where N is the total sample size ($n_1 + n_2$). For Table 8.1 $\bar{p} = (22 + 10)/68 = .47$, a value that one needs for the test of the current H_0: $P_1 = P_2$. The mean proportion can also be called the pooled estimate of P, that is, the overall population proportion of those who would be found in the targeted category. Because one initially assumes that H_0 is true one assumes that $P_1 = P_2 = P$, and that, therefore, the best estimate of P is obtained by pooling (averaging) p_1 and p_2 as in Equation 8.4.

Recall that to convert a statistic to a z (i.e., a standardized value) one divides the difference between that statistic and its mean by the standard deviation of that statistic. The statistic of interest here is $p_1 - p_2$. The expected mean of this statistic upon repeated sampling of it, assuming that H_0 is true, is 0. The standard deviation of the sampling distribution of values of $p_1 - p_2$, again assuming that H_0 is true, is shown in the denominator of Equation 8.5:

$$z_{p_1 - p_2} = \frac{p_1 - p_2 - 0}{[(\bar{p}(1 - \bar{p}))/n_1 + (\bar{p}(1 - \bar{p}))/n_2]^{1/2}}. \tag{8.5}$$

(We retained the unnecessary value 0 in Equation 8.5 only to make clear that the equation represents a kind of z. The mean of a statistic that is being transformed to a z appears as the subtracted term on the right side of the numerator of an equation for a z.) The larger the sample sizes the closer the distribution of $z_{p_1 - p_2}$ will approximate the normal curve. Using the previous calculations of p_1, p_2, and $\bar{p}$, the application of the data of Table 8.1 to Equation 8.5 yields

$$z_{p_1 - p_2} = \frac{.61 - .31 - 0}{[(.47(1 - .47)/36) + (.47(1 - .47)/32)]^{1/2}} = 2.47.$$

Referring $z = 2.47$ to a table of the normal curve one finds that this z, and, therefore, $p_1 - p_2$, are statistically significantly different from 0 at an obtained significance level beyond .0136.

There is an adjustment of Equation 8.5 whereby 0 in the numerator is replaced by $.5(1/n_1 + 1/n_2)$ to attempt to produce a better approximation of the sampling distribution to the normal curve. Replacing 0 with this value in the present example yields $z = 2.23$, a value that is statistically significant at an obtained significance level beyond .0258. Alternatively, Campbell (2007) argued for multiplying the right side of Equation 8.5 by $[(N - 1)/N]^{1/2}$, where N is the total sample size.

FURTHER DISCUSSIONS AND INTRANSITIVITY

Refer to Fleiss et al. (2003) for a discussion of comparison of proportions from more than two independent samples. Recall from the discussion of multiple comparisons of means in the section on statistical significance in Chapter 6 that the methods (e.g., the Tukey HSD method) may result in contradictory evidence about the pair-wise differences among the means (intransitivity). The same problem of intransitive results can occur when making pair-wise comparisons from three or more proportions. For example, suppose that a third therapy were represented by a third row added to Table 8.1 (Therapy 3), so that one would now be interested in the proportion of patients whose symptoms are gone after Therapy 1, 2, or 3, that is P_1, P_2, and P_3. Suppose further that one tested H_0: $P_1 = P_2$, H_0: $P_1 = P_3$, and H_0: $P_2 = P_3$ simply by applying the current method in this section (or some traditional competing method) three times. Controlling for rate of experiment-wise error by using the Bonferroni–Dunn adjustment, say, by adopting the $.05/3 = .0167$ alpha level for each of the three tests would be commendable (although perhaps excessively conservative), but a problem of possible intransitivity remains.

An example of one of the possible sets of intransitive results from the three tests would be results that suggest the following contradictory relationships: $P_1 = P_2$, $P_2 = P_3$, and $P_1 > P_3$. Such a pattern of values cannot be true. A method for detecting the pattern of relationships among more than two proportions in independent populations was proposed by Dayton (2003). The method can be implemented using Microsoft Excel with or without additional software programs. For details consult Dayton, who did not recommend his method for researchers whose interest in pair-wise comparisons is greater than their interest in the overall pattern of the sizes of the proportions.

INFERIORITY, NON-INFERIORITY, AND EQUIVALENCE

Fleiss et al. (2003) discussed the comparison of two proportions in the case of experiments that are called non-inferiority trials, which seek evidence that a treatment (or control condition) is not worse than another treatment by a pre-specified amount, which may be called the non-inferiority margin (i.e., the minimum effect size that the researcher considers to be important). Those authors also discussed the comparison of proportions in the case of equivalence testing, which seeks evidence that a treatment is neither better nor worse than another treatment by a pre-specified amount (again, the minimum effect size that would be considered to be important). These methods are best used when the researcher can make an informed decision about what minimum difference between the two proportions can be reasonably judged to be of no practical importance in a particular instance of research. These alternatives to traditional null-hypothesis testing were discussed in Chapter 2.

Lloyd (2010) evaluated methods for testing whether the difference between two proportions exceeds the non-inferiority margin. Tryon (2005) and Tryon and Lewis (2007) proposed a method for testing for the equivalence and/or difference between two independent proportions using a confidence interval around each proportion (inferential confidence intervals as is briefly discussed in Chapter 2). Martín Andrés et al. (2008) also discussed testing equivalence and non-inferiority for two independent proportions. Cumming (2009) discussed the relationship between the amount of overlap between confidence intervals for each proportion and the p values when testing for the difference between the two proportions. StatXact software provides exact tests of equivalence, inferiority, and superiority when comparing two proportions in the independent-groups or dependent-groups cases.

CROSSOVER DESIGN

One repeated-measures version of experimental research is the sometimes-problematic *crossover design* (Fleiss et al., 2003). In this counterbalanced design each participant receives each of the two treatments *a* and *b*, one at a time, in either the sequence *ab* for a randomly chosen one-half of the participants or the sequence *ba* for the other half of the participants. The rows of a 2 × 2 table can then be labeled *ab* and *ba*, and the columns can be labeled *a Better* and *b Better*. The difference between the proportion of times that Treatment *a* is better and the proportion of times that Treatment *b* is better ($p_1 - p_2$) is an effect size that can be analyzed as discussed previously and further next.

CONFIDENCE INTERVALS FOR $P_1 - P_2$

Again, for our initial purpose of conveying a basic understanding we first demonstrate the simplest method for manual construction of an approximate confidence interval for the difference between proportions (probabilities) in two independent populations. We then provide references for methods that are more accurate but are also more complex. As is the case for approximate methods, the accuracy of the following large-sample method increases with increasing sample sizes. Also, the method performs better the farther P_1 and P_2 are from 0 and 1.

In general the simplest $(1 - \alpha)$ confidence interval (CI) for $P_1 - P_2$ can be approximated by the limits

$$CI_{P_1 - P_2} : (p_1 - p_2) \pm ME, \tag{8.6}$$

where ME is the margin of error in using $p_1 - p_2$ to estimate $P_1 - P_2$:

$$ME = z^* s_{p_1 - p_2},$$ (8.7)

where
  z^* is the positive value of z that has $\alpha/2$ of the area of the normal curve beyond it
  $s_{p_1 - p_2}$ is the approximate standard deviation of the sampling distribution of the
    difference between p_1 and p_2 (i.e., the standard error)

If one seeks the usual $.95CI$ (i.e., using $\alpha/2 = .05/2 = .025$) then one will recall or observe in a table of the normal curve that $z^* = +1.96$.

For the confidence interval one does not use the same formula for $s_{p_1 - p_2}$ that is used in the denominator of Equation 8.5 when one tests $H_0: P_1 = P_2$. For the confidence interval one no longer pools p_1 and p_2 to estimate the previously supposed common value of $P_1 = P_2 = P$ that we assumed before we rejected H_0. Instead, one now estimates the values of P_1 and P_2 separately using p_1 and p_2 in the equation for $s_{p_1 - p_2}$:

$$s_{p_1 - p_2} = \left[\frac{p_1(1 - p_1)}{n_1} + \frac{p_2(1 - p_2)}{n_2} \right]^{1/2}.$$ (8.8)

(One pools p_1 and p_2 for the test of statistical significance because one is then assuming the truth of H_0, but there is no such assumption when constructing a confidence interval.) The large-sample confidence interval at hand is called a *Wald confidence interval*.

For the data of Table 8.1, $p_1 - p_2 = .61 - .31 = .30$, $z^* = +1.96$ because one is seeking a $.95$ CI, $1 - p_1 = 1 - .61 = .39$, $n_1 = 36$, $1 - p_2 = 1 - .31 = .69$, and $n_2 = 32$. Therefore, applying the values to Equation 8.7, the ME that one subtracts from and adds to $p_1 - p_2$ is equal to $1.96[.61(1 - .61)/36 + .31(1 - .31)/32]^{1/2} = .23$. The limits of the confidence interval are thus $.30 \pm .23$. One is thus approximately 95% confident that the interval from $.30 - .23 = .07$ to $.30 + .23 = .53$ would capture the difference between P_1 and P_2. Unfortunately, as is often the case, the interval is rather wide. Nonetheless, the interval does not contain the value 0, a finding that is consistent with the result from testing $H_0: P_1 = P_2$. However, sometimes the result of a test of statistical significance at a specific α level and the $(1 - \alpha)$ CI for $P_1 - P_2$ do not produce consistent results. Consult Fleiss et al. (2003) for discussion and references regarding such inconsistent results.

More Accurate Confidence Intervals and Further Discussions

Efforts to construct a more accurate confidence interval for $P_1 - P_2$ have been ongoing for decades. The simple method of Expression 8.6 and Equation 8.7 can result in an interval that, broad as it can often be, actually tends to be inaccurately narrow. Beal (1987) compared various methods and recommended and described an improved method for which Wilcox (1996) described manual calculation and provided a Minitab macro and later (Wilcox, 2003a) provided an S-PLUS software function. (StatXact software constructs an exact confidence interval for the independent- and dependent-groups cases.) Consult the discussion and references in Agresti (2002) for both independent-groups and dependent-groups cases. Newcombe (1998a) compared 11 methods (also consult Newcombe & Nurminen, in press) and Martín Andrés and Herranz Tejedor (2003, 2004) discussed exact and approximate methods. Pradhan and Banerjee (2008) discussed and presented a SAS/IML program for the implementation of a method that appeared to compare well with the best of the methods that Newcombe had compared. Lin, Newcombe, Lipsitz, and Carter (2009) reported favorable performance of their method for estimating P_1 and P_2 and constructing a confidence for their difference. Kulinskaya, Morgenthaler, and Staudte (2010) proposed methods that appear to compare favorably with other methods and to be well suited for meta-analysis.

Consult Schaarschmidt, Sill, and Hothorn (2008) and Donner and Zou (2011) for the case of construction of confidence intervals for contrasts among multiple proportions. Fleiss et al. (2003) and Cohen (1988) discussed and presented tables for estimating needed sample sizes for detecting a specified difference between P_1 and P_2. Simulations by Tang, Ling, Ling, and Tian (2009) indicated good performance of their method for constructing an approximate confidence interval for the difference between two binomial proportions for paired data even for small sample sizes. Excel spreadsheets for construction of improved confidence intervals for $P_1 - P_2$ for the independent-groups and paired-groups cases currently can be freely downloaded courtesy of Robert G. Newcombe from http://www.cardiff. ac.uk/medicine/epidemiology_statistics/research/statistics/newcombe.

RELATIVE RISK

The data in Table 8.1 resulted from research in which participants had been randomly assigned to Therapy 1 or Therapy 2. In this experimental case (and some other cases as discussed later in this chapter) an effect size that is generally called *relative risk* is applicable. We now turn to the development of this measure.

A certain difference between P_1 and P_2 may have more practical importance when the estimated P values are both close to 0 or 1 than when they are both close to .5. For example, suppose that $P_1 = .010$ and $P_2 = .001$, or that $P_1 = .500$ and $P_2 = .491$. In both cases $P_1 - P_2 = .009$, but in the first case P_1 is 10 times greater than P_2, $(P_1/P_2 = .010/.001 = 10)$, and in the second case P_1 is only 1.018 times greater than P_2, $(P_1/P_2 = .500/.491 = 1.018)$. Thus, the ratio of the two probabilities can be very informative. For 2×2 tables the ratio of the two probabilities is the parameter denoted here RR (which is also called the *rate ratio* or *risk ratio*). The estimate of RR, rr (somewhat biased), is calculated using the two sample proportions:

$$rr = \frac{p_1}{p_2}. \qquad (8.9)$$

As before, p_1 and p_2 represent the proportion of those participants in Samples 1 and 2, respectively, who fall into the targeted category, which again can be represented either by column 1 or column 2 in a table such as Table 8.1. In Table 8.1, if column 1 represents the targeted category then $rr_1 = (14/36)(22/32) = .57$, and if column 2 represents the targeted category then $rr_2 = (22/36)(10/32) = 1.96$. In the latter case there is an estimated nearly 2 to 1 greater probability of therapeutic success for psychotherapy than for drug therapy for the clinical problem at hand. Kraemer (2006) provided various equivalent definitions of RR.

Jewell (1986) proposed the following unbiased estimator of RR, which we label rr_{unb} and write in terms of the four cell frequencies in the 2×2 table for the case in which column 1 is the targeted column:

$$rr_{unb} = \frac{f_{11}(f_{12} + f_{22} + 1)}{(f_{11} + f_{21})(f_{12} + 1)}. \qquad (8.10)$$

If the two terms of +1 are removed from Equation 8.10 this equation becomes equivalent to the biased estimator in Equation 8.9. Applying the data of Table 8.1 to Equation 8.10 for the case again in which column 1 is the targeted column, $rr_{unb} = 14(22 + 10 + 1)/(14 + 22)(22 + 1) = .56$, which is very close to the biased estimate.

The name relative risk relates to medical research, in which the targeted category is classification of people as having a disease versus the category of not having the disease (the binomial dependent variable). One sample has at least one presumed risk factor for the disease (e.g., smokers) and the other sample does not have this risk factor (the binomial independent variable). (In nonexperimental studies it is possible that the risk factor is not a cause of the disease, but merely a correlate of it, such as a case in which handedness is found to be associated with a disease.) However, because it seems strange to use the label "relative risk" when applying the ratio to a column such as column 2 in Table 8.1, which represents a successful outcome of therapy, in such cases one can simply refer to RR and rr as success rate ratios, or as the ratio of two independent probabilities or the ratio of two independent proportions, respectively. Fleiss (1994) discussed uses and limitations of RR in primary research and meta-analysis. Yelland, Salter, and Ryan (2011) evaluated the performances of 10 methods for estimating and constructing confidence intervals for an RR.

CONFIDENCE INTERVALS FOR RELATIVE RISK AND FURTHER DISCUSSIONS

Except for very large samples an expression for a confidence interval for a population relative risk (RR) can be complex because of the extreme skew of the sampling distribution. Major software constructs such confidence intervals. Also consult Smithson (2003).

Zou and Donner (2008) reported simulations that indicated good performance for their proposed method for constructing a confidence interval for RR for the case of small to moderate sample sizes, a case for which some other methods may not be applicable or may not perform well. The method is a general one with other applications, including estimating a difference between two effect sizes. Reiczigel, Abonyi-Tóth, and Singer (2008) proposed a method for deriving exact tests and confidence intervals for functions of two binomial parameters, such as the risk difference and the *RR*. Price and Bonett (2008) reported simulations that indicated good performance of a computationally simple approximate Bayesian method for construction of a confidence interval for *RR* for two independent binomial proportions. Those authors also provided formulas estimating needed sample sizes to attain a desired precision for the intervals. Klingenberg (2010) discussed methods for constructing simultaneous confidence intervals for *RR* when many treatment groups are to be compared with a control group.

INTERPRETATIONAL PROBLEMS

One of the limitations of the *RR* is that its different values when based on one or the other of the two outcome categories, and its different values depending on one's choice of numerator and denominator, can lead to different impressions of the result. (In a 2×2 table there are four possible values of *rr* that can be calculated.) A problem can arise because, as a ratio of two proportions, the *RR* or *rr* can range from 0 to 1 if the group with the smaller proportion (lower risk) happens to be represented in the numerator, but it can range from 1 to ∞ if the group with the smaller proportion is represented in the denominator. The problem can be partially resolved by reporting the common or natural logarithm (*ln*) of *rr* as an estimate (somewhat biased) of the *ln* of *RR*. When the smaller proportion is in the numerator *ln rr* ranges from 0 to $-\infty$, whereas when the larger proportion is in the numerator *ln rr* ranges from 0 to $+\infty$. The contingency table or the actual raw proportions should always be reported no matter how the *rr* is reported.

For an example of the issue that we have raised regarding the interpretation of a risk ratio, consider the case involving the two hospitals that provided coronary bypass surgery, an example that is discussed in the section entitled "Coefficient of determination" in Chapter 4. We observed previously that the relative risk, based on the *rr* defined as the ratio of the mortality percentages for the two hospitals (i.e., a ratio of *failure rates*), was 3.60%/1.40% = 2.57. On the other hand, if one reverses the choice of which hospital's percentage of mortality is placed in the numerator the *rr* now equals approximately .39, which is likely a much smaller-appearing effect for some non-statisticians. However, the two values of *rr* are merely reciprocal fractions that convey the same meaning (i.e., 1/2.57 ≈ .39). Furthermore, defining the *rr* as the ratio of the survivability percentages for the two hospitals (i.e., a ratio of *success rates*) Breaugh (2003) noted that if one reverses the choice of which hospital's percentages are to appear in the numerator of the ratio the *rr* for these data can be calculated as (100% − 1.40%)/(100% − 3.60%) = 1.02. This latter result conveys a much smaller apparent effect of choice of hospital than does the previously obtained *rr* = 2.57. This example provides a compelling reason to present the results both ways.

REPORT ACTUAL RISKS

Unless the actual risks are reported the rr can be misleading. For example, it has been estimated that very active persons are 2.4 times more likely to have a heart attack during exercise than when not exercising (i.e., $rr = 2.4$). However, the risk of having a heart attack while such persons are not exercising for the same period of time has been reported to be approximately only 1 in 4,800,000. Therefore, the increase in risk by the factor of 2.4 while exercising raises the risk to a still very low level of fewer than 3 in 4,800,000 (Consumers Union, 2005). In another example a drug was advertised as decreasing the risk of heart attack by 50% (i.e., $rr = .50$ when comparing treatment and placebo). However, the risks of heart attack during the 4 years of the study were 1% and 2% for treatment and placebo, respectively, so risk reduction was 2% − 1% = 1%, which is a less impressive-appearing result to a statistical layperson (Lipman, 2008b).

Whereas an estimate of RR is not likely to change for participants with different baseline rates for the presenting problem, an estimate of $P_1 - P_2$ will likely increase for participants with higher baseline rates. Bonett and Price (2006) discussed the construction of confidence intervals for an RR for paired data, and Newcombe (2007) and Nam (2008) commented on that paper.

PROSPECTIVE AND RETROSPECTIVE RESEARCH

The RR is applicable to data that arise from research that uses random assignment, or naturalistic or prospective research, but not from retrospective research, although it is often used in the latter. We have previously defined naturalistic research. In a common form of *prospective research* the researcher selects n_1 participants who have a suspected risk factor (e.g., children whose parents have abused drugs) and n_2 participants who do not have the suspected risk factor. The two samples are tracked for a predetermined period of time to determine the number from each sample who do and do not develop the targeted outcome (e.g., abuse drugs themselves). From the definition it should be clear why prospective research is also called *cohort, forward-going,* or *follow-up* research.

In *retrospective research* (also called *case–control research*) the researcher selects n_1 participants who already exhibit the targeted outcome (the cases) and n_2 participants who do not exhibit the targeted outcome (the controls). The backgrounds of the two samples are examined to observe how many in each sample had or did not have the suspected risk factor.

Often the participants are selected so that each individual in a group is matched (with respect to apparently relevant variables) with an individual in the other group. The matching is undertaken in an attempt to reduce variability or to control for confounding variables such as age or gender. In such a case the analysis of the data must take the matching into account (Agresti, 2002; Fleiss et al., 2003). Arceneaux, Gerber, and Green (2010) reported a case in which matching resulted in a large overestimation of effect size, and Rose and van der Laan (2008) argued that in most cases unmatched designs are preferable.

Prospective and retrospective research are examples of *observational research*, which is also called in clinical studies *population research* or *epidemiological research*. For practical or ethical reasons observational research is more applicable than experimental research for the study in human beings of (a) harmful exposures (e.g., smoking), (b) rare outcomes, and (c) outcomes that are long delayed after exposure to the risk factor (e.g., smoking and lung cancer, sunburns and skin cancer). Observational research is also useful for estimating the effectiveness of a treatment in practice after evidence of its efficacy has been provided by a randomized experiment. The matter of whether or not a design has yielded evidence of merely an association between variables or a causal connection between variables is crucial to interpreting a result as correlational (i.e., strictly, an *association* size, not an *effect* size) or causal (*effect* size). Austin and Laupacis (2011) discussed adjustments to observational-research-based estimates of some of the effect sizes in this chapter to attempt to counter the distorting effects of confounding variables. One of the methods is the topic of the next section.

PROPENSITY-SCORE ANALYSIS

A retrospective study can sometimes be upgraded somewhat by a propensity-score analysis, a major effect size for which is discussed in the next section. Each participant's *propensity score* is defined as the conditional probability that the participant, based on one or more characteristics, will belong to one or another group (e.g., Treatment 1 or Treatment 2) in the retrospective study. (The characteristics include covariates and possible outcomes.) For example, in an experiment that compares a drug therapy to a psychotherapy for depression one expects that random assignment to groups will on average balance relevant patient characteristics between the two groups. However, in a retrospective study it may be that those who had received the drug therapy differed in one or more relevant ways from those who had received the psychotherapy (e.g., a difference in initial severity of depression). Such confounding variables can result in very misleading results, including very distorted estimates of effect size.

Berk and Newton (1985) provided a real example of the use of propensity-score analysis in their retrospective study of the influence of prior arrest versus non-arrest for wife-beating on later wife-beating. The propensity score was the probability of having been arrested (versus not having been arrested) for the men's previous behavior of wife-beating. (Both groups of men had beaten their wives but, for whatever reason, not all had been arrested for it.) The probability of having been arrested was estimated using 14 covariates, which were characteristics either of the batterer or of the battery. Results suggested that men who had high propensity scores for being arrested but had not been arrested were the most likely to repeat battery on their wives. In such an example estimates of effect sizes for an oversimplified independent variable of prior arrest versus no prior arrest (i.e., ignoring propensity scores) would be misleading.

There are numerous methods for propensity-score analysis. In simulations Austin (2009) found that seven of the eight methods that were studied produced similar estimates of effect size. The measure of effect size that was used was the relative risk reduction, to which we turn our attention in the next section. Thoemmes and Kim (2011) suggested solutions to common errors in estimation and reporting in propensity-score analyses. The 2011, volume 46, issue 3 of the journal *Multivariate Behavioral* Research is devoted to propensity-score analysis.

RELATIVE RISK REDUCTION

The risk difference $(P_1 - P_2)$ relative to the baseline or control level of risk (P_1) can be used as a measure of effect size for data in 2 × 2 tables. This measure is called the *relative risk reduction, RRR* given by

$$RRR = \frac{P_1 - P_2}{P_1}. \qquad (8.11)$$

The *RRR* is estimated (with some bias) by

$$rrr = \frac{p_1 - p_2}{p_1}. \qquad (8.12)$$

The *RRR* is the complement of an *RR*; that is, $1 - (P_2/P_1) = (P_1 - P_2)/P_1$.

With regard to the *RRR* and all measures of effect size we maintain throughout this book that researchers should give much thought to their choice of a measure and consider reporting estimates of more than one measure when there are other applicable measures. This is especially important when different measures lead to different or even conflicting interpretations of the results. For example, consider an advertisement that stated that women who took a particular anti-osteoporosis drug experienced a 68% reduction in fractures of vertebrae. This assertion was based on the estimated *RRR* as follows. The rate of fracture in the placebo group was $p_1 = .00738$, and the rate in the treated group was $p_2 = .00238$. Therefore, $rrr = (p_1 - p_2)/p_1 = (.00738 - .00238)/.00738 = .68$. If one instead calculates estimates of the simple relative risk (of fracture) or the simple risk difference for these data one finds that $rr = p_1/p_2 = .00738/.00238 = 3.10$ and $p_1 - p_2 = .00738 - .00238 = .005$, respectively. The latter estimate means that the use of the drug is expected to result in 5 fewer fractures per 1000 women. Our point is not that the advertisement overstated the benefit of the drug but that for non-statisticians the $rrr = .668$ and $rr = 3.10$ would likely appear to be more impressive results than the risk difference of .005. (This example also illustrates the importance of reporting p_1 and p_2 regardless of the estimated effect size that is being reported.)

NUMBER NEEDED TO TREAT

Another measure of effect size for 2×2 tables in which one group is a treated group and the other is a control or otherwise treated group is the problematic *number needed to treat* (NNT_{pop}). The NNT_{pop} measures the number of people, on average, who would have to be given the experimental treatment (instead of being in the other group) per each such person who can be expected to benefit from it (or, if NNT_{pop} is negative, per each such person who can be expected to be harmed by it):

$$NNT_{pop} = \frac{1}{P_c - P_e},$$

(8.13)

where
    P_c is the probability that a member of the comparison group (e.g., control or standard-treatment group) will be found in the worse of the two categories of outcome (e.g., the no-benefit category)
    P_e is the probability that a member of the experimentally treated (e.g., new experimental-treatment group) group will be found in that worse category of outcome

In Equation 8.13 the NNT_{pop} is observed to be the reciprocal of the difference between the probability that a member of the comparison group (c) will show no benefit (e.g., symptoms remain) and the probability that a member of the new-treatment group (e) will show no benefit. Thus, the NNT_{pop} is the reciprocal of the previously discussed risk difference. The NNT_{pop} is estimated by

$$NNT_{est} = \frac{1}{p_c - p_e},$$

(8.14)

where p_c and p_e are the proportions in the samples that estimate their respective probabilities in Equation 8.13. (Sometimes the absolute values of the differences in Equations 8.13 and 8.14 are used for a reason to be discussed later.)

If there are N total patients and, say, $p_e > p_c$, then the experimental treatment will be successful with $N(p_e - p_c)$ more patients on average than the comparison treatment. For example, suppose that $N = 100$, $p_e = .55$, and $p_c = .45$, where N is the total number of participants. In this case, on average, if the 100 patients were all treated with the experimental treatment or all treated with the comparison treatment, $100(.55 - .45) = 10$ more patients can be expected to be treated successfully if given the experimental treatment than if given the comparison treatment. That is, $100(.55) = 55$ is 10 more than $100(.45) = 45$.

The more effective an experimental treatment is, relative to the control or competing treatment, the *smaller* the positive value of NNT_{pop}, with $NNT_{pop} = 1$ being the best result for the targeted treatment. (Values between -1 and $+1$, exclusive, are mathematically problematic; Duncan & Olkin, 2005.) When $NNT_{pop} = 1$ every person who is given the experimental treatment is expected to benefit. The number needed to treat is not intended for data arising from naturalistic sampling.

The use of the number needed to treat is demonstrated here by comparing a new psychotherapy as an experimental treatment and a drug therapy as a standard treatment in rows 1 and 2, respectively, of Table 8.1. (Although the data in Table 8.1 are real, the description of the nature of the research has been altered for our present illustrative purpose.) The required probabilities are estimated by the relevant proportions in the table. The NNT_{est} from the data in Table 8.1 is given by the reciprocal of the difference between the proportion of the participants in the standard-treatment group whose symptoms remain ($22/32 = .6875$) and the proportion of the participants in the treated group whose symptoms remain ($14/36 = .3889$). The difference between these two proportions is $.6875 - .3889 = .2986$. Thus, $NNT_{est} = 1/.2986 = 3.35$. Rounding up to $NNT_{est} = 4$ would often be done for a conservative estimate because in the case of the NNT the higher the number the lower the magnitude of the effect. If, say, one uses $NNT_{est} = 4$ one is estimating that, on average, for every four patients treated with the new psychotherapy instead of the standard drug therapy one patient will become free of symptoms who would not have otherwise become free of symptoms.

The NNT can be used as an effect size in areas besides clinical research. For example, the NNT can be used as part of a program in educational or organizational research to evaluate the costs and benefits of a remedial class for students or a training class for employees. In both kinds of research participants in the class and control participants would be classified in a 2×2 table as having attained or not having attained a targeted skill.

Those who support the use of the NNT consider it to be informative regarding the practical significance of results. Considering the estimated NNT in the context of the costs or risks of an experimental treatment and the seriousness of an illness, or the seriousness of the lack of mastery of a certain skill, can aid in the decision about whether a new treatment or program should be adopted. For example, one would not want to adopt a moderately expensive and somewhat risky medical treatment when the NNT_{est} is relatively large unless the disease were sufficiently serious.

The values of NNT_{pop} that may seem to some to be useful for such decision-making are the upper and lower limits of a confidence interval for it. Kraemer and Kupfer (2006) suggested that an estimated value of NNT_{pop} equal to, say, 100 or 1000 might serve as a threshold for clinically significant results in the case of a low-cost and low-risk treatment (e.g., vaccination) to prevent a disabling or fatal disease in a population at low risk for the disease. Alternatively, in the case of a high-risk treatment (e.g., radical surgery or very high dose of drug) in a population at high risk for the same disease an estimated NNT_{pop} equal to, say, 10 might serve as a threshold for clinical significance. According to such thinking, treatment that is intended to bring about an early cure for a disease would allow a higher estimated NNT_{pop} as a threshold for clinical significance than would treatment that is intended only to reduce symptoms somewhat. Again, unlike other effect sizes, the more efficacious a new treatment is relative to the comparison condition, the *smaller* the NNT_{pop}.

SIGNIFICANCE TESTING AND CONFIDENCE INTERVALS FOR NNT_{pop}

Detailed discussions of the complex and controversial topics of significance testing for NNT_{est} and construction of a confidence interval for NNT_{pop} would be beyond the scope of this book, so we only briefly comment on these and related issues. First, if one were testing a traditional null hypothesis about there being no effect of treatment, then one would be attempting a mathematically problematic test of H_0: $NNT_{pop} = \infty$ or a problematic indirect test of statistical significance by examining a confidence interval for NNT_{pop} to observe if the interval contains the value ∞.

The simplest approach to a confidence interval for NNT_{pop} would be first to construct a confidence interval for the difference between the two populations' probabilities (i.e., the population risk difference) that are involved in the NNT_{pop}, using one of the methods that was previously discussed in this chapter or discussed by Fleiss et al. (2003). Then, the reciprocals of the confidence limits satisfy the definition of NNT_{pop} and provide the limits for its confidence interval (e.g., Kraemer & Kupfer, 2006).

The *number needed to harm* (*NNH*) is the label for a negative value for what would otherwise be called the *NNT*, as defined by Equations 8.13 and 8.14. The theoretical range for the *NNH* is from $-\infty$ to -1, inclusive, whereas the useful lower bound for the *NNT* is 1. (The problematic value ∞ will be discussed further.) In research in which both a benefit and a risk of the treatment were found the *NNT* can be reported for the dependent variable for which a benefit was found (e.g., decreased alcohol consumption) and the *NNH* can be reported for the other dependent variable for which a risk was found (e.g., increased smoking).

Consult Duncan and Olkin (2005) for many references to discussions of the construction of a confidence interval for the NNT_{pop}. However, some statisticians reject attempts to construct a traditional confidence interval for the NNT_{pop} because of the problematic interpretation of values between -1 and $+1$, exclusive (Hutton, 2004). Also, the meaningless upper bound (∞) of an estimate of the NNT_{pop}, which occurs when $p_c = p_e$, (i.e., $1/(p_c - p_e) = 1/0 = \infty$) causes some statisticians to reject the NNT_{pop} entirely as an effect size (e.g., Hutton). This topic and various adjustments of the NNT_{est} for bias were discussed at length by Duncan and Olkin. Among statisticians who do not entirely reject the use of the *NNT* there seems to be some agreement that the estimated risk difference (i.e., the difference between probabilities) should be used to construct confidence intervals whereas its reciprocal, estimated NNT_{pop}, can be useful for communicating clinical significance, especially to laypeople. We believe additionally that an estimated difference in probabilities, when stated as proportions and when reported together with the two proportions, can also often communicate clinical significance well.

Tips and Pitfalls

Because the NNT_{pop} varies with the baseline risk a point estimate and confidence limits for the NNT_{pop} from prior research are most useful for a practitioner whose clients or patients are very similar to those who participated in the research from which the earlier NNT_{pop} had been estimated. The baseline risk is estimated from the proportion of the comparison participants who were classified as having had the "bad" event (e.g., $p_c = 22/32 \approx .69$ in Table 8.1). The lower the baseline risk the lower the justification may be for implementing the experimental treatment, depending again on the seriousness of the targeted problem and the overall cost of that treatment.

RELATIONSHIPS AMONG MEASURES

It is useful to know the relationships among measures of effect size because different measures can provide different perspectives on the results. First, Equation 8.13 shows the relationship between the risk difference (or failure-rate difference) in the population (RD) and NNT_{pop}. Solving for $P_c - P_e$ ($=RD$) in Equation 8.13 yields

$$RD = P_c - P_e = \frac{1}{NNT_{pop}}. \tag{8.15}$$

Also, RD can be converted to the probability of superiority (the PS of Chapters 5 and 9) for 2×2 tables using

$$PS = .5(RD + 1). \tag{8.16}$$

Furthermore, in the case of 2×2 tables RD is the same as the dominance measure (DM) that was discussed in Chapter 5 and defined in Equation 5.9.

$$RD = DM = \Pr(Y_e > Y_c) - \Pr(Y_c > Y_e) \tag{8.17}$$

(Hsu, 2004; Kraemer, 2006). For the case of 2×2 tables not only the RD but also the PS can be approximately converted to the standardized difference between means, d_{pop} (as defined by Equation 3.6). The PS can be approximately converted to d_{pop} using the method involving Equation 5.8. Using the same method the RD can be approximately transformed to d_{pop} after using Equation 8.16 to transform RD to the PS. Again using the same method NNT_{pop} can also be approximately converted to d_{pop} by first using Equation 8.18 to transform NNT_{pop} to the PS:

$$PS = .5\left[\frac{1}{NNT_{pop}} + 1\right]. \tag{8.18}$$

Some examples of relationships among measures are depicted in Table 1 in Kraemer and Kupfer (2006). (In that table what we call here the PS is labeled AUC [*area under the curve*] and what we call RD is labeled SRD [success rate difference].)

ODDS RATIO

The final measure of effect size for a 2 × 2 table that we discuss is the popular but problematic population *odds ratio*, OR_{pop}, which is a measure of how many times greater the odds are that a member of a certain population will fall into a certain category than the odds are that a member of another population will fall into that category. Although the odds ratio has several limitations we discuss this popular measure at length for those who will use it only for its intended limited purpose (based on its definition). Relatively insensitive to base rates, the odds ratio is applicable to research that uses random assignment, naturalistic research, prospective research, and retrospective research, but not generally as an approximation of the relative risk as some have used it. As the baseline rate of the outcome variable (e.g., disease) approaches zero the value of OR_{pop} approaches the value of the *RR*. However, the *RR* and the OR_{pop} are generally not equivalent and should not be treated as such. For example, the OR_{pop} is always farther from the typically null-hypothesized value of 1 than is the *RR*, so it may provide an inflated indication of an effect size. Also, when compared to the same comparison group, two treatments can have the same OR_{pop} but different relative risk reduction, or vice versa, or the two measures can order the efficacy of two treatments differently. Unlike the phi coefficient, the possible range of values of an odds ratio is not limited by the marginal distributions of the contingency table. However, an odds ratio can be transformed such that its values will be similar to those of phi and it will range from −1 to 1 (Bonett & Price, 2007).

A sample odds ratio provides an estimate of the ratio of (a) the odds that participants of a certain kind (e.g., females) attain a certain category (e.g., voting Democrat instead of voting Republican) and (b) those same odds for participants of another kind (e.g., males). An odds ratio can be calculated for any pair of categories of a variable (e.g., gender) that is being related to another pair of categories of another variable (e.g., political preference).

For a formal definition of OR_{pop}, consider the common case in which membership in a category with respect to one of the two variables can be said to precede categorization with respect to the other variable. For example, type of therapy precedes the symptoms-status outcome in Table 8.1, and being male or female precedes agreeing or disagreeing in Table 8.3. Now label a targeted outcome category T (e.g., agree), the alternative outcome category being labeled not T. Then label a temporally preceding category (e.g., man) pc. Where *P* stands for probability, a measure of the odds that T will occur conditional on pc occurring is given by $Odds_{pc} = P(\text{T}|\text{pc})/P(\text{not T}|\text{pc})$. Similarly, the odds that T will occur conditional on category pc not occurring (e.g., woman) is given by $Odds_{notpc} = P(\text{T}|\text{not pc})/P(\text{not T}|\text{not pc})$. The ratio of these two odds in the population is the odds ratio

$$OR_{pop} = \frac{Odds_{pc}}{Odds_{notpc}}. \tag{8.19}$$

TABLE 8.3

Gender Difference in Attitude toward a Controversial Statement

	Agree	Disagree	Totals
Men	$f_{11} = 10$	$f_{12} = 13$	23
Women	$f_{21} = 1$	$f_{22} = 23$	24
Totals	11	36	47

For the case in which an experimental group is compared to a control or comparison group, in terms of probabilities

$$OR_{pop} = \frac{P_e(1 - P_c)}{P_c(1 - P_e)}. \tag{8.20}$$

(The numerator and the denominator of Equation 8.20 each represent odds.) Again, the probabilities are estimated by the proportions in the involved cells of the table. Consult Kraemer (2006) for various equivalent ways to define OR_{pop}. Liberman (2005) discussed the relationship between OR_{pop} and probabilities.

WORKED EXAMPLE

In Table 8.3, as in Table 8.1, the values of cells f_{11}, f_{12}, f_{21}, and f_{22} represent the counts (frequencies) of participants in the first row and first column, first row and second column, second row and first column, and second row and second column, respectively. We now use the category that is represented by column 1 as the targeted category. The sample odds that a participant who is in row 1 will be in column 1 instead of column 2 are given by f_{11}/f_{12}, which are $10/13 \approx .77$ in the case of Table 8.3. In a study that is comparing two kinds of participants, who are represented by the two rows in the present example, one can evaluate these odds in relation to similarly calculated odds for participants who are in the second row. The odds that a participant in row 2 will be in column 1 instead of column 2 are given by f_{21}/f_{22}, which are $1/23 \approx .04$ in the case of Table 8.3. The ratio of the two sample odds (a biased estimator of OR_{pop}), denoted OR, is given by $(f_{11}/f_{12})/(f_{21}/f_{22})$, which, is equivalent to

$$OR = \frac{f_{11}f_{22}}{f_{12}f_{21}}. \tag{8.21}$$

In Equation 8.21 each cell frequency is being multiplied by the cell frequency that is diagonally across from it in a table such as Table 8.3. For this reason the odds ratio is also called a *cross-products ratio*. Also, odds are not the same as probabilities (although, as in Equation 8.20, they can be calculated using probabilities). For example, with regard to Table 8.3, the *odds* that a man will be in the *Agree* category instead of the *Disagree* category are given by $10/13 = .77$. However, the

probability that a man will be in the *agree* category is estimated by the proportion
10/23 = .43, where 23 is the total number of men in the sample.

The estimator of $Odds_{pop}$ given in Equation 8.21 is biased. Bias can be reduced
by using an adjusted sample odds ratio, OR_{adj}, as the estimator:

$$OR_{adj} = \frac{(f_{11} + .5)(f_{22} + .5)}{(f_{12} + .5)(f_{21} + .5)}. \qquad (8.22)$$

Later discussion shows further possible benefits of the addition of .5 to each cell
of the table. Consult Agresti (2002) and Duncan and Olkin (2005) for further
discussions.

Table 8.3 depicts actual data but the example should be considered to be hypothetical because the column labels, row labels, and the title have been changed to
suit the purpose of this section. A perspective on these data emerges if one calculates the *OR* that relates the odds that a man will *agree* instead of *disagree* to the
odds that a woman will *agree* instead of *disagree* with a controversial test statement
that was presented to all participants by the researcher. Applying Equation 8.21,
one finds that *OR* = 10(23)/13(1) = 17.69. (Equation 8.22 is applied later.) Thus, the
odds that a man will *agree* with the controversial statement are estimated to be
nearly 18 times greater than the odds that a woman will *agree* with it. However,
out of context this result can be somewhat misleading or incomplete. That is, if one
inspects Table 8.3, which the researcher would be obliged to include in a research
report, one also observes that in fact in the samples a majority of men (13 of 23) as
well as a (larger) majority of women (23 of 24) *disagree* with the statement.

PROBLEM OF EMPTY CELLS

Odds ratios range from zero to infinity, attaining either of these extreme values
when one of the cell frequencies is zero. A zero cell frequency in the population
is called a *structural zero*. (The OR_{pop} may be said to be undefined when P_e or
P_c in Equation 8.20 equals 0.) When there is no association between the row and
column variables OR_{pop} = 1. Although a zero in a sample cell (a *sampling zero*) is
not highly unlikely, a structural zero would be unlikely in many areas of research
because it would be unlikely that a researcher would include a variable into one
of whose categories no member of the population falls. Observe in the real data
of Table 8.3 that the table comes very close to having a zero in *sample* cell$_{21}$, in
which $f_{21} = 1$. In a research in which OR_{pop} would not likely be zero or infinity, a
value of zero or infinity for the sample *OR* would be unwelcome. Therefore, when
an empty cell in sample data does not reflect a zero population frequency for that
cell a solution for this problem is required. One of the possible solutions is to
increase one's chance of adding an entry or entries to the empty cell by increasing
total sample size by a fixed number. A common alternative solution is to adjust the
sample *OR* to an OR_{adj} by adding a very small constant to the frequency of each
cell, not just to the empty one, as in Equation 8.22. Recommended such constants
in the literature range from 10^{-8} to .5, inclusive.

Consult Agresti's (1990, 2002) discussions of the problem of the empty cell. Even when no cell frequency is zero, adding a constant, such as .5, has been recommended to attempt to improve OR as an estimator of OR_{pop}. If a constant has been added to each cell the researcher should report having done so and report OR and OR_{adj}. Adding .5 to each cell in Table 8.3 to apply Equation 8.22 changes the estimated odds ratio from 17.69 to 12.19. (The calculation is left as an exercise in the section entitled "Questions".) Unfortunately, adding a constant to each cell can sometimes actually cause OR_{adj} to provide a less accurate estimate of OR_{pop} and lower the power of a test of statistical significance of OR, facts that provide even more reason to report results with both OR and OR_{adj}. Consult Agresti (2002) for discussions of adjustment methods that are less arbitrary than adding constants to cells. Subbiah and Srinivasan (2008) discussed the possibly changed interpretation of an effect size such as the odds ratio that may arise by adding a constant. Greenland (2010) also discussed the problematic traditional use of constants and proposed a modification of the constants.

PRACTICAL SIGNIFICANCE, BASELINE RATE, AND FURTHER DISCUSSIONS

Again, no measure of effect size is without limitations. Although the numerical value of an odds ratio is relatively independent of the baseline rate, the practical significance of a given odds ratio depends greatly on the baseline rate. For example, suppose that the odds of getting a certain disease in a control sample are twice as great as those same odds in a sample that is given a preventative treatment ($OR = 2$). The practical significance of this $OR = 2$ is much greater if the baseline rate of this disease (i.e., the proportion of untreated individuals who get the disease) is, say, .01 than if it is, say, .000001. Halving one's odds of getting a common disease (high baseline rate) is more important than halving one's odds of getting an extremely rare disease (low baseline rate), assuming that the diseases are of equal seriousness.

Tchetgen Tchetgen and Rotnitzky (2011) proposed a method for improving estimation of OR_{pop} in nonexperimental research by adjusting for confounding variables. Consult Kraemer (2003), Kraemer and Kupfer (2006), and Rosenthal (2000) for illustrations of results for which the odds ratio can be misleading. For a review of criticisms and suggested modifications of odds ratios consult Fleiss et al. (2003), and for further discussions consult Agresti (2002), Fleiss (1994), Haddock et al. (1998), Newcombe (2006a), Rudas (1998), and Simon (2007).

Tips and Pitfalls

Brumback and Berg (2008) discussed the problem of possible inconsistent differences in results from odds ratios, risk differences, and relative risks from one population to another. An effect that appears to be stronger in one population than it is in another population using one of these measures may not appear to be stronger when using another of them. Also, Kraemer and Kupfer (2006) demonstrated that any value of $OR_{pop} > 1$ can correspond to a value of NNT_{pop} that is high enough to be clinically insignificant. The odds ratio can exaggerate the association between disease and a risk factor (Kraemer, 2010). Because of these and other limitations of the odds ratio some statisticians consider the odds ratio not to be an effect size, but instead merely a measure of whether or not there exists an association between the row and column variables (i.e., a statistically significant $OR > 1$). Again, researchers should consider reporting estimates of more than one measure.

CONVERTING ODDS RATIOS TO CORRELATION COEFFICIENTS AND STANDARDIZED DIFFERENCES

A primary researcher (or meta-analyst) who uses an odds ratio may want to compare or combine the results from 2×2 tables with those from one or more related studies that used instead some form of correlation coefficient or a standardized difference between means as the measure of effect size. An odds ratio (and a relative risk) can be approximately converted to the point-biserial correlation and phi coefficient (if the marginal proportions are equal or nearly so) using formulas provided by Bonett (2007). Consult Kraemer (2006) for related discussions. The three transformations of the odds ratio share the properties of values of 0, −1, and +1 under no association, maximum negative association, and maximum positive association, respectively, all independent of the marginal totals in the table.

To convert an odds ratio to a standardized difference between means, d, one can first use the methods in Bonett (2007) to convert an odds ratio approximately either to phi or r_{pb}, and then approximately convert that coefficient to d using an equation for that purpose that is also in Bonett. (The equation for approximately converting r_{pb} to d also appears as Equation 4.18.) However, the Hasselblad and Hedges (1995) direct method for approximately converting an odds ratio to d does so by multiplying $ln\ OR$ by $1/(1.81)$, or, more precisely, by $(3)^{1/2}/\pi$ where $ln\ OR$ is the natural logarithm of OR and $\pi = 3.14159$ (also consult Chinn, 2000, 2002). That is, $ln\ OR = d(\pi)/(3)^{1/2}$, so $d = (3)^{1/2}\ ln\ OR/\pi$. The unadjusted $OR = 17.69$ for the data of Table 8.3 converts to a d that is approximately equal to 1.6 or 1.7 using approximate conversions known as the Ulrich–Wirtz conversion or Yule's conversion, both of which can be found in Bonett. Using the Hasselblad–Hedges conversion to d, $ln\ OR/1.81 = 2.8729995/1.81 = 1.587 = d$ for the same unadjusted $OR = 17.69$, which essentially agrees with the two results of $d = 1.6$ or 1.7 from the other conversion formulas. (In a report of research one might additionally report a conversion from OR_{adj}.)

We applied the three conversion formulas to the data of Table 8.3 merely to observe how similar the three results might be for the data at hand, ignoring for the moment the degree to which these data satisfy the assumptions of the conversion formulas. Yule's method assumes equality of the marginal proportions in the table. The Ulrich–Wirtz method assumes that a normally distributed latent variable underlies the dichotomous observed outcome variable, which is attitude in the case of Table 8.3. (By "dichotomous" we do not mean the problematic *dichotomizing* of *available* continuous data. In the present case of Table 8.3 we are assuming that the data are known only dichotomously [Agree versus Disagree], which is a form of dichotomy that is less problematic for statistical analyses, as was discussed in Chapter 4 in the section on scale coarseness.) The Hasselblad–Hedges method assumes equal variances and a logistic distribution for the variable underlying the measure of the dependent variable. The latter assumption is not easily tested. (Roughly, a *logistic distribution* is a symmetrical bell-shaped probability distribution with somewhat heavier tails than a normal distribution.) For further discussion of estimating a standardized-mean-difference effect size from 2×2 tables consult Sánchez-Meca, Martin-Martinez, and Chacón-Moscoso (2003).

Testing H_0: $OR_{pop} = 1$

The null hypothesis H_0: $OR_{pop} = 1$ can be tested approximately against the alternative hypothesis H_{alt}: $OR_{pop} \neq 1$ using the common adjusted χ^2 test of association (i.e., subtracting .5 in the numerator before squaring for each cell). This method is more accurate the larger the expected frequencies in each cell, and it may be problematic when any expected frequency is small. The test statistic is

$$\chi^2 = \sum \frac{\left[| f_{rc} - (n_r n_c / N) | - .5 \right]^2}{n_r n_c / N},$$
(8.23)

where
   the summation is over the four cells of the table
   f_{rc} is the observed frequency in a cell
   n_r and n_c are the total frequency for the particular row and the total frequency
      for a particular column that a given cell is in, respectively

The value $n_r n_c / N$ is the expected frequency for a given cell under the null hypothesis.
   Applying the data of Table 8.3 to Equation 8.23 for manual calculation one finds that

$$\chi^2 = [|10 - (23 \times 11/47)| - .5]^2 / (23 \times 11/47) + [|13 - (23 \times 36/47)| - .5]^2 /$$

$$(23 \times 36/47) + [|1 - (24 \times 11/47)| - .5]^2 / (24 \times 11/47)$$

$$+ [|23 - (24 \times 36/47)| - .5]^2 / (24 \times 36/47) = 8.05.$$

Recall that the degrees of freedom for a chi-square test of association is given by $df = (r - 1)(c - 1)$, so $df = (2 - 1)(2 - 1) = 1$ for Table 8.3. When $df = 1$ the obtained value, 8.05, is statistically significant beyond the .005 level. One thus has sufficient evidence that OR_{pop} does not equal 1. Refer to Fleiss et al. (2003) for a detailed discussion of approximate and exact p values for the present case.
   Munk, Skipka, and Stratmann (2005) proposed a general exact method for testing hypotheses or demonstrating non-inferiority or superiority in the 2×2 case using OR_{pop}, risk difference, or relative risk. Lui and Chang (2011) proposed tests for non-inferiority and equivalence in crossover designs using

the odds ratio. (Non-inferiority, superiority, and equivalence were discussed in Chapter 2.)

Finally, data in 2 × 2 tables are often analyzed using *logistic regression*, in which group membership (X) is used to predict the natural logarithm of the odds (Y) that an individual will be in the outcome category of interest. The natural logarithm of an odds is called a *logit*.

CONSTRUCTION OF CONFIDENCE INTERVALS FOR OR_{pop}

Because an odds ratio can range from 0 to $+\infty$ it is bounded only at the lower end of its distribution, which causes the distribution of *OR* to be extremely skewed except when sample size is very large. However, the natural logarithm of an *OR*, *ln OR*, is not bounded on one side, so its distribution is not similarly skewed. Therefore, one of the simpler competing methods for constructing an approximate confidence interval for OR_{pop} is based on a normal distribution of *ln OR*. Again, the larger the sample, the better the approximation to normality. We present the simplest manual method for our purpose of illustration and then we cite references for methods that may perform better but are more complex.

First, a confidence interval for *ln* OR_{pop} is constructed. Then the antilogarithms of the limits of this interval provide the limits of the confidence interval for OR_{pop}. Adding the constant .5 to each cell frequency may reduce the bias in estimating *ln* OR_{pop} so we use this adjustment that has a long history. The limits of the $(1 - \alpha)$ CI for *ln* OR_{pop} are approximated by

$$\ln OR \pm z_{\alpha/2}S_{lnOR}, \tag{8.24}$$

where $z_{\alpha/2}$ is the value of z (the standard normal deviate) beyond which lies the upper $\alpha/2$ proportion of the area under the normal curve.

S_{lnOR} is the standard deviation of the sampling distribution of *ln OR* (i.e., the standard error) given by

$$S_{lnOR} = \left[\frac{1}{f_{11}+.5} + \frac{1}{f_{12}+.5} + \frac{1}{f_{21}+.5} + \frac{1}{f_{22}+.5} \right]^{1/2}. \tag{8.25}$$

For the data of Table 8.3,

$$S_{lnOR} = \left[\frac{1}{10+.5} + \frac{1}{13+.5} + \frac{1}{1+.5} + \frac{1}{23+.5} \right]^{1/2} = .937.$$

Again, if seeking the usual $(1 - \alpha) = (1 - .05) = .95$ CI, one uses $z_{\alpha/2} = 1.96$ because a total of $.025 + .025 = .05$ of the area of the normal curve lies in the tails beyond $z = \pm1.96$. Therefore, the .95 confidence limits for *ln* OR_{pop}, based on $OR_{adj} = 12.19$

from the previous section, are $ln\ 12.19 \pm 1.96(.937)$, which are .664 and 4.337. The antilogarithms of .664 and 4.337 yield, as the .95 confidence limits for OR_{pop}, 1.94 and 76.48. The interval does not contain the value 1, which provides evidence that there is a difference between the odds in each population (i.e., an association between the row and column variables). However, the interval is disappointingly wide, as is often the case with confidence intervals that are not based on very large samples.

The present method often is somewhat conservative in the sense of understating the actual probability coverage. Therefore, those who construct and report a nominal .90 confidence interval, in addition to their reported .95 confidence interval, for OR_{pop} may be able thereby to produce a somewhat narrower interval that actually has more than a .90 probability of containing OR_{pop}. A confidence interval of the type that has been demonstrated here is not defined when the sample $OR = 0$ or ∞.

The statistical packages SAS (i.e., PROC FREQ) and StatXact provide software for the construction of a confidence interval for OR_{pop} that relates to Fisher's exact test for 2×2 tables for small samples. If there were a given null-hypothesized value for OR_{pop} such a 95% confidence interval should contain all of the possible values of OR_{pop} that have $p > .05$ probability of occurring if that null hypothesis were true. However, again the actual probability coverage for such confidence intervals is likely to be greater than the nominal confidence level. Agresti (2007) discussed a method to reduce this conservativeness and to shorten the interval.

Simulating the performances of 10 methods for constructing a confidence interval for OR_{pop} for sample sizes up to 20 per group, Lawson (2004) found that a method by Cornfield performed best and that the simpler method that has been demonstrated here ranked a close second. Agresti, Bini, Bertacinni, and Ryu (2008) reported favorable results from simulations of the performance of their recommended method for constructing *simultaneous confidence intervals* (defined in Chapter 6) for odds ratios, relative risk, and the differences between proportions. Tryon and Lewis (2009) extended their method of inferential confidence intervals to the evaluation of *difference*, *trivial difference*, *equivalence*, and *indeterminacy* for the case of two independent proportions and odds ratios.

NULL–COUNTERNULL INTERVAL FOR OR_{pop}

If the null hypothesis that is being tested originally is H_0: $OR_{pop} = 1$ (i.e., no association) this is equivalent to testing H_0: $ln\ OR_{pop} = 0$. Therefore, because the distribution of $ln\ OR$ is symmetrical, one can also construct a null–counternull interval indirectly for OR_{pop} using Equation 3.12 by starting with such an interval for $ln\ OR_{pop}$. Recall from the discussion of Equation 3.12 that the null value of the interval is the null-hypothesized value of the effect size (ES_{null}), which in the present logarithmic case is 0, and the counternull value is $2ES$, which is 2 $ln(12.19) = 2(2.5) = 5$. Taking antilogarithms of 0 and 5, the null–counternull interval for OR_{pop} itself ranges from 1 to 148.41, again a disappointingly wide interval. Therefore, the statistically significant results provide as much evidence for the proposition that $OR_{pop} = 148.41$ as they do for the proposition that $OR_{pop} = 1$.

One may well be concerned about a null–counternull interval as wide as 1–148.41. In this regard note that it is intrinsic to the null–counternull interval to grow wider the larger the obtained estimate of the effect size because its starting point is always the null-hypothesized value of ES (usually the extreme value of ES that indicates no association), and its endpoint, which, in the case of symmetrical sampling distributions, is twice the obtained value of the estimate of ES. Also, unlike a confidence interval, a null–counternull interval cannot be made narrower by increasing sample size. Again, a null–counternull interval does not have the same purpose as a confidence interval and is not a substitute for a confidence interval.

TABLES LARGER THAN 2 × 2

It would be beyond the scope of this book to present a detailed discussion of measures of effect size for $r \times c$ tables that are larger than 2 × 2, which we call large $r \times c$ tables. For example, if Table 8.3 had an additional column for a *No Opinion* category it would be an example of a large $r \times c$ table (specifically, a 2 × 3 table). It will suffice to discuss two common methods in some detail, make some general comments, and provide references for detailed treatment of the possible methods.

One may begin analysis of data in a large $r \times c$ table with the usual χ^2 test of association between the row and column variables, again with $df = (r - 1)(c - 1)$. The traditional measures of the overall strength of association between the row and column variables, when sampling has been naturalistic, are *Pearson's contingency coefficient*, CC_{pop}, and *Cramér's* V_{pop}, which are estimated by

$$CC = \left[\frac{\chi^2}{\chi^2 + N} \right]^{1/2} \tag{8.26}$$

and

$$V = \left[\frac{\chi^2}{N \min(r-1, c-1)} \right]^{1/2}, \tag{8.27}$$

where $min(r - 1, c - 1)$ means the smaller of $r - 1$ and $c - 1$. Cramér's V_{pop} ranges from 0 (no association) to 1 (maximum association, but attainable only under certain conditions). However, the upper limits of the CC and CC_{pop} are less than 1. Also, unless $r = c$, V can equal 1 even when there is less than a maximum association between the row and column variables in the population. Consult Berry, Johnston, and Mielke (2006) and Siegel and Castellan (1988) for further discussions of limitations of V. Observe in Equation 8.27 that for 2 × c (or r × 2) tables $min(r - 1, c - 1) = 1$, and, therefore, $V = [\chi^2/N(1)]$ in this case, which is the phi coefficient. Thus, phi is the limiting case of V. As was noted with regard to phi$_{pop}$ in the section entitled "Chi-square test and phi", V_{pop} too is a kind of average effect, the square root of the mean of the squared standardized effects.

CC and V estimate CC_{pop} and V_{pop}, respectively, for further discussions of which consult Hays (1994) and Smithson (2003). Major software such as IBM SPSS outputs an estimate of V_{pop}. StatXact and IBM SPSS Exact calculate exact contingency coefficients. Computing routines for constructing an approximate confidence interval for V_{pop} using IBM SPSS, SAS, S-PLUS, or R are available free, courtesy of Michael Smithson, at http://psychology.anu.edu.au/people/smithson/ details/CIstuff/CI.html. The use of V^2, phi^2, and the square of the Goodman–Kruskal tau to attempt to estimate analogs of proportion of variance-explained effect size was discussed by Berry et al. (2006). Berry et al. further discussed interpretative difficulties of V^2.

Tips and Pitfalls

Two or more values of the CC should not be compared or averaged unless they arise from tables with the same dimensions, that is, the same number of rows and the same number of columns, but equal sample sizes is not required. The same is true of two or more values of V. There is no interpretation of an isolated value of V or V^2 in terms of odds or probabilities.

For large $r \times c$ tables Agresti (2002) discussed the *uncertainty coefficient* as another overall measure of association that ranges from 0 to 1. We do not discuss this measure because of its complexity, and it may not be understandable for many practitioners and their clients (Helena C. Kraemer, personal communication, August 2, 2009). The meaning of CC_{pop} and V_{pop} may also be difficult to communicate to non-statisticians.

Tests of association in $r \times c$ tables that are larger than 2×2 are provided by SAS PROC FREQ and StatXact. However, the CC_{pop} and V_{pop}, as measures of the overall association between the two variables, are not as informative as are finer-grained indices of strength of association in a large $r \times c$ table. There are methods that attempt to pinpoint the source or sources of association in the subparts of a large $r \times c$ table (Agresti, 1990, 2002; Fleiss et al., 2003). For two-way tables that are larger than 2×2 a recommended approach when assignment is random is to apply the method in Fleiss et al. for comparing multiple proportions.

Odds Ratios for Large $r \times c$ Tables

Recall that an odds ratio applies to a 2×2 table. However, a researcher should not divide a large $r \times c$ table, step by step, into all possible 2×2 sub-tables to calculate a separate OR for each of these sub-tables. In this inappropriate method each cell would be involved in more than one 2×2 sub-table and in more than one OR, resulting in much redundant information. The number of theoretically possible such 2×2 sub-tables is $[r(r - 1)/2][c(c - 1)/2]$. However, Agresti (1990, 2002) demonstrated that using only cells in adjacent rows and adjacent columns to form 2×2 sub-tables results in a minimum number of ORs that serve as a sufficient descriptive fine-grained analysis of the association between the row and column variables for the sample data. For a relatively simple procedure for constructing

TABLE 8.4

An Example of a Multi-Way Table

		Democrat	Republican	Other
White	Female			
	Male			
Non-white	Female			
	Male			

simultaneous confidence intervals for a limited set of population ORs from a large $r \times c$ table consult Wickens (1989).

MULTIWAY TABLES

Contingency tables that relate more than two categorical variables, each of which consists of two or more categories, are called *multiway tables* (e.g., $a \times b \times c$). An example would be a table that relates the independent variables' ethnicity and gender to the dependent variable political affiliation, although the variables do not have to be designated as independent variables or dependent variables. Table 8.4, a $2 \times 2 \times 3$ table, illustrates this hypothetical example.

Multiway tables may be used in nonexperimental research that relates an outcome variable to an explanatory variable. Because there is no random assignment one may attempt to control for possibly confounding variables by including such variables in the table and analyses. One can then study the association between the two variables of interest while holding one or more control variables constant. Agresti (2007) provided examples. Consult Wickens (1989) for an overview of effect sizes for multiway tables. Wickens called some measures of effect size *association coefficients*. Rudas (1998) discussed odds ratios for tables in which there are two categories for each of more than two variables (called 2^k tables).

MORE ON TESTING AND EFFECT SIZES FOR RELATED PROPORTIONS

Suppose that an outcome variable is dichotomous and one wants to test the equality of the proportions of matched individuals in each of two or more groups who are found in a specified outcome category. (We previously cited articles that found fault with matching.) The ultimate matching occurs when the same individuals are used in each group (repeated measures). A widely used test for the equality of two matched proportions is the McNemar (1947) test, which is extended for two or more matched groups by Cochran's Q test. (Both tests can be subsumed under a test by Mantel and Haenszel, as was discussed by Agresti, 2002. Berry, Johnston, & Mielke, 2010, discussed measures of effect size for the Mantel–Haenszel test.) Westfall, Troendle, and Pennello (2010) proposed methods for comparing two matched proportions at a time from multiple matched proportions using the McNemar test.

A conceptually simple estimator of an effect size for the present case is Q/Q_{max}, where Q_{max} is the maximum value that Cochran's Q statistic can attain for a given design. Serlin et al. (1982), who proposed Q/Q_{max} and a related estimator of effect size for the McNemar test as analogs to eta squared, provided a formula for Q_{max}. However, Berry et al. (2007) argued for an alternative formula for an effect size associated with Cochran's Q. Fleiss et al. (2003) discussed as *correlated binary data* the case of repeated measurements in longitudinal studies, in which each participant is categorized twice or more over time.

FURTHER DISCUSSIONS

Suppose that two 2×2 tables are available involving the same pairs of categorical variables (e.g., Treatment versus Control and Improved versus Unimproved), but each table involves a different level of a third variable (e.g., gender). Suppose further that the estimated association between the two main variables of interest is in the same direction in each table. It would be tempting to strive to increase statistical power by combining all of the data into one 2×2 table and also to estimate an effect size from that single table. However, it is possible that the aggregated single table will yield an estimated association between the two variables that is in the opposite direction from what it had been in each of the two original tables. Such a phenomenon of contradictory combined results is called *Simpson's paradox*. Even if a researcher has good reason to aggregate the data (perhaps for exploratory purposes) a report should include analyses of the data in the separate tables.

Rosenthal and Rosnow (2008) discussed results from three sets of data using the relative risk, odds ratio, risk difference, and phi. Unfortunately, the values of these estimators of effect size did not change consistently with each other as the data changed across the three sets. (Such a finding bolsters our recommendation that more than one appropriate effect size be reported for a given set of data from a 2×2 table.) Those authors proposed a solution to the problem using the BESD that we discussed in Chapter 4. So and Sham (2010) discussed the relationships among the odds ratio, relative risk, and the prediction of risk of disease in studies of genetic association.

There are many methods for analyzing data in contingency tables that are beyond the scope of discussion here. StatXact, IBM SPSS Exact, and LogXact are specialized statistical packages for such analyses. Alan Agresti currently provides a website with updated information for application of major software (SAS, IBM SPSS, S-Plus, R) to analyses of categorical data: www.stat.ufl.edu/~aa.cda/software.html. An appendix in Agresti (2007) focused on such applications using SAS. Agresti (2002) discussed a variety of software for analyzing contingency tables with ordered or unordered categories.

Biswas and Park (2008) reviewed existing measures of association between nominal categorical variables and they proposed new symmetrical measures. A *symmetrical measure* of association yields the same value regardless of which variable is considered to be the independent or dependent variable. An *asymmetrical measure* of association yields a different value depending on whether the row or column variable is designated as the dependent variable.

As is discussed in Chapter 7, methodological differences can result in differences in estimated effect sizes across studies. In the current case of categorical outcomes one such methodological factor in clinical outcome studies is the stringency of the researcher's standard for categorizing a patient as improved. One should expect smaller effect sizes in studies that used a more conservative standard for patient improvement. Finally, the topic of risk-stratified analysis that was defined in Chapter 7 is relevant to researchers who use the effect sizes in this chapter.

SUMMARY

In the case of naturalistic sampling, in which a given number of participants is categorized with respect to two truly dichotomous variables in a 2 × 2 table, possibly appropriate measures of effect size in the population are the phi coefficient, relative risk, and the odds ratio. However, those contemplating using the odds ratio should only do so after considering its limitations as discussed in this chapter and in detail by Kraemer (2004, 2006). The difference between two independent proportions (risk difference) would be appropriate under naturalistic sampling if the method discussed by Martín Andrés et al. (2008) is used for testing and for construction of confidence intervals.

When participants have been randomly assigned into two treatment groups that are to be classified into a 2 × 2 table, appropriate measures of effect size are the population risk difference, relative risk, and (possibly) odds ratio. The risk difference is also applicable when sampling is prospective or retrospective, whereas the relative risk is applicable to prospective sampling. The recommendations in this section are summarized in Table 8.5, but one must also take into account the previously discussed limitations of the measures. Recommendations were also made by Kraemer (2006), who showed that there are relationships among many measures of effect size for 2 × 2 tables.

TABLE 8.5
Effect Sizes for 2 × 2 Tables

Method of Grouping	Appropriate Effect Sizes			
	phi_{pop}	$P_1 - P_2$	RR_{pop}	OR_{pop}
Naturalistic	Yes	No [a]	Yes	Yes
Random assignment	No	Yes	Yes	Yes
Prospective	No	Yes	Yes	Yes
Retrospective	No	Yes	No	Yes

[a] $P_1 - P_2$ would be appropriate under naturalistic sampling if the method discussed by Martín Andrés et al. (2008) is used for testing and construction of confidence intervals.

Because very different perspectives on the results may be provided by different measures of effect sizes for contingency tables researchers should consider reporting an estimate of more than one appropriate measure. Reports should also include the contingency tables so that readers can calculate estimates of additional effect sizes and check the symmetry of the row and column marginal distributions when such symmetry is relevant.

For two-way tables that are larger than 2 × 2, if sampling is naturalistic Cramér's V can be reported with cautionary remarks about its limitations. When such a table has resulted from a study that used random assignment one can apply the method in Fleiss et al. (2003) for comparing multiple proportions. Methods are also available when participants are matched (matched proportions).

QUESTIONS

8.1 Distinguish between a nominal variable and an ordinal categorical variable, providing an example of each that is not in the text.

8.2 Define *naturalistic sampling* and state two other names for it.

8.3 *Misclassification* is related to what common problem of measurement?

8.4 Why might the application of the methods for 2 × 2 tables in this chapter be problematic if applied to *dichotomized* variables instead of originally dichotomous variables?

8.5 Why is the chi-square statistic not an example of an estimator of effect size?

8.6 In which way is a *phi* coefficient a special case of the common Pearson *r*?

8.7 How does phi_{pop}, as an effect size, compensate for the influence of sample size on chi square?

8.8 How does one interpret a positive or negative value for *phi* in terms of the relationship between the two rows and the two columns?

8.9 If rows 1 and 2 are switched, or if columns 1 and 2 are switched, what would be the effect on a nonzero value of *phi*?

8.10 Why is *phi* only applicable to data that arise from naturalistic sampling?

8.11 For which kinds of sampling or assignment of participants is the difference between two proportions an appropriate effect size?

8.12 What does a proportion in a representative sample estimate in a population?

8.13 When the difference between two proportions is transformed to a *z*, what influences how closely the distribution of such *z* values approximates the normal curve?

8.14 Provide a general kind of example of intransitive results when making pairwise comparisons from among $k > 2$ proportions. (A general answer stated symbolically suffices.)

8.15 What influences the accuracy of the normal-approximation procedure for constructing a confidence interval for the difference between two probabilities?

8.16 Explain why the interpretation of a given difference between two probabilities depends on whether both probabilities are close to 1 or 0 on the one hand, or both are close to .5.

8.17 Define *relative risk* and explain when it is most useful.

8.18 What may be a better name than relative risk when this measure is applied to a category that represents a successful outcome?

8.19 Discuss a limitation of relative risk as an effect size.

8.20 For which kinds of categorizing or assignment of participants is relative risk applicable?

8.21 Define *odds ratio* (a) in general terms, (b) formally.

8.22 To which kinds of categorization or assignment of participants is an odds ratio applicable?

8.23 Calculate and interpret an odds ratio for the data of Table 8.1, and construct a 95% confidence interval for it.

8.24 Why is an empty cell problematic for a sample odds ratio?

8.25 How does one test the null hypothesis that the population odds ratio is equal to 1 against the alternate hypothesis that it is not equal to 1?

8.26 Name two common measures of the overall association between row and column variables for tables larger than 2×2.

8.27 For which kind of sampling are the two measures in Question 8.26 applicable?

8.28 Two or more values of the CC should only be compared or averaged for tables that have what in common?

8.29 Two or more values of V should only be compared or averaged for tables that have what in common?

8.30 Why should a research report always present a contingency table on whose data an estimate of effect size is reported?

8.31 Define the NNT_{pop} and the NNH_{pop}, and discuss their meanings.

8.32 Apply Equation 8.22 to the data of Table 8.3 to verify that $OR_{adj} = 12.19$.

8.33 Give an example, which is not in this book, in which an estimate of NNT_{pop} might be used to indicate practical significance in an area other than clinical research.

8.34 Define (a) *binomial* and *multinomial variables*, (b) *marginal distribution* of a contingency table, (c) *asymptotic method*, (d) *conditional* and *unconditional tests*, (e) *cross-over design*, (f) *propensity-score analysis*, (g) *logit*, (h) *Simpson's paradox*, (i) *cross-classification table*, (j) *prospective* and *retrospective research*.

8.35 What is the relationship between the RD_{pop} and the NNT_{pop}?

8.36 What is the purpose of Cohen's kappa?

8.37 Assuming that row 1 of Table 8.3 represented a standard treatment, row 2 represented a new treatment, column 1 represented Symptoms Remain, and column 2 represented Symptoms Gone, calculate the (a) risk difference, (b) relative risk, (c) number needed to treat. Compare the interpretations of the three results in light of the odds ratio that was reported in the text for the data of Table 8.3.

8.38 Construct and interpret 95% confidence intervals for the population values of as many of the four effect sizes (include the odds ratio) in Question 8.37 as your available software provides.

9 Effect Sizes for Ordinal Categorical Dependent Variables (Rating Scales)

INTRODUCTION

Often one of the two categorical variables that are being related is an ordinal categorical variable, which is a set of categories that has a meaningful order. Examples of ordinal categorical variables include the set of rating-scale categories Worse, Unimproved, Moderately Improved, and Much Improved; the set of attitudinal-scale categories Strongly Agree, Agree, Disagree, and Strongly Disagree; and a scale from Severe Pain to No Pain. The technical name for such ordinal categorical variables is *ordered polytomy*. The focus of this chapter is on some relatively simple methods for estimation of an effect size in tables with two rows that represent two groups and three or more columns that represent ordinal categorical outcomes ($2 \times c$ tables). The methods also apply to the case of two ordinal categorical outcomes; $c = 2$. However, the fewer the outcome categories the more likely it would be that there will be an increase in the number of tied outcomes between the groups, a problem that is discussed later in this chapter.

Table 9.1 provides an example, involving real data, in which participants were randomly assigned to one or another treatment. The roles of the rows and columns can be reversed, so the methods also apply to comparable $r \times 2$ tables. The clinical details do not concern us here, but we do observe that the column that is labeled "Improved" suggests that neither therapy was very successful. The results were based on a 4-year follow-up after therapy and the presenting problem (marital problems) was likely deteriorating just prior to the start of therapy. The data are from Snyder, Wills, and Grady-Fletcher (1991).

SOME CAUTIONS AND CHOICE OF NUMBER OF CATEGORIES

The number of ordinal categories to be used should be the greatest number of categories into which the participants can be reliably placed. Again, if the data are originally continuous it is generally not appropriate to slice the continuous scores into ordinal categories because of the ensuing lowering of both statistical power and estimation of effect size. Also, one should be very cautious about comparing effect sizes across studies that involve attitudinal scales. Such effect sizes can vary if there are differences in the number of items, number of categories of response, or the proportion of positively and negatively worded items across studies.

TABLE 9.1

Ordinal Categorical Outcomes of Two Psychotherapies

	1 Worse	2 No Change	3 Improved	Total
Therapy 1	3	22	4	29
Therapy 2	12	13	1	26

Tips and Pitfalls

The optimal number of categories likely varies across situations. The use of even a few categories can be excessive with regard to test–retest reliability if some of the categories are insufficiently different to elicit a consistent choice by the respondent. Hairsplitting choices may annoy respondents enough to cause rushing and inattentiveness, which will decrease reliability. Hairsplitting choices may also promote excessive use of such choices as Neutral or Undecided (if either is available) that do not reflect a respondent's actual attitude. Even the common scale Strongly Agree, Agree, Disagree, Strongly Disagree may be problematic for some respondents who cannot discriminate between the first two, and/or between the last two, categories. There may also be a disinclination in some cultures to express an extreme attitude.

The number of categories that is optimal for a given purpose may not be optimal for another purpose. For example, the number of categories that is estimated to be optimal for, say, maximizing test–retest reliability may not be the same as the number of categories that is optimal for, say, justifying the use of a certain test statistic's distribution to analyze the data.

Association, Agreement, and Weighted Kappa

Depending on who is doing the categorizing, there may be variation in the data and, therefore, the statistical significance of the association between the row and column variables as well as the effect size that is used to measure the strength of that association. For example, there may not be high *inter-rater agreement* (*inter-rater reliability*) across categorizations done by a patient, a close relative of the patient, and/or a professional observer of the patient. Therefore, one should be appropriately cautious in interpreting such results. Also, agreement between ratings should be distinguished from association between ratings. If one's ratings *systematically* differ from another's ratings there is an association but not agreement.

In the case of Table 8.4, the categorizations by judges can be no further than one category apart, so the extent of possible disagreement about the categorization of a given person (or object) is limited. However, in the current case of placing a person into one of $c > 2$ ordinal categories more extensive disagreement in categorization is possible. The greater the separation of the categorizations of a given person by judges on an ordinal scale the more serious the disagreement in that case. For example, on the scale patient Worse, Unimproved, Better, or Cured after treatment, judging a given patient Worse versus judging that patient Better is a more serious disagreement than judging a patient Unimproved versus judging that patient Better.

Cohen's kappa of Chapter 8 can be modified to *weighted kappa* for such cases because the relative seriousness of a disagreement can be weighted by the extent of separation of categorizations. The weights range from 0 to 1, inclusive. Details can be found in Agresti (2002, 2010), Fleiss et al. (2003), Heo (2008), and Kraemer (2006). Weighted kappa is higher than kappa, and the decision to use weighted kappa instead of kappa should not be made only for the purpose of reporting a higher value for estimated agreement.

Internal-Consistency Reliability

Zumbo, Gadermann, and Zeisser (2007) discussed simulations that indicated the superiority of what they labeled *ordinal coefficient alpha* and *ordinal coefficient theta* compared to the traditional Cronbach's coefficient alpha as an estimate of the *internal consistency* of a scale such as a (Likert) summated rating scale. Internal consistency is the overall extent to which the items on a scale correlate with each other. A scale with little internal consistency cannot be said to be measuring any single underlying variable. Therefore, an effect size that compares groups with respect to scores on such an internally inconsistent measure would have little meaning. Also, major software does not take ordinality into account when using traditional coefficient alpha as a default for estimating internal consistency.

INSENSITIVITY OF CHI SQUARE TO ORDINALITY

Before discussing estimation of effect sizes for the kind of data at hand we caution about the manner of testing the statistical significance of the association between the row and column variables. Suppose that the researcher's hypothesis is that one specified treatment is better than the other, that is, a specified ordering of the efficacies of the two treatments. Such a research hypothesis leads to a one-tailed test. Alternatively, suppose that the researcher's hypothesis is that one treatment or the other (unspecified) is better—a prediction that there will be an unspecified ordering of the efficacies of the two treatments. This latter hypothesis leads to a two-tailed test. One or the other of these two *ordinal hypotheses* provides the alternative to the usual null hypothesis that posits no association between the row and column variables. An ordinal hypothesis is a hypothesis that predicts not just a difference between the two treatments in the distribution of their scores in the outcome categories, but predicts that there will be a superior outcome for one (specified if directional or unspecified if not directional) of the two treatments. Such ordinal researchers' hypotheses are of interest in this chapter.

A χ^2 test is inappropriate to test the null hypotheses at hand because the value of χ^2 is insensitive to the ordinal nature of ordinal categorical variables. In the current ordinal case a χ^2 test can only validly test a not-very-useful "nonordinal" researcher's hypothesis that the two groups are in some way not distributed the same in the various outcome categories (Grissom, 1994b). Also, recall from Chapter 8 that the magnitude of χ^2 is not an estimator of effect size because it is very sensitive to sample size, not just to the strength of association between the variables.

POINT-BISERIAL *r* APPLIED TO ORDINAL CATEGORICAL DATA

Although we soon observe that there are many limitations to this method some might consider calculating a point-biserial correlation, r_{pb}, (consult Chapter 4) as a simple estimate of an effect size for data such as those in Table 9.1, which depicts real experimental data. To calculate r_{pb} first the *c* column ordinal category labels are replaced by ordered numerical values, such as 1, 2, ..., *c*. For the column categories in Table 9.1 one might use 1, 2, and 3, and call these the *scores* on a *Y* variable. Next, the labels for the row categories are replaced with numerical values, say 1 and 2, and these are called the *scores* on an *X* variable. One then uses any statistical software to calculate the correlation coefficient for the now numerical *X* and *Y* variables.

Software output yields $r_{pb} = -.397$ for the data of Table 9.1. When the sample sizes are unequal, as they are in Table 9.1, one can correct for the attenuation of r_{pb} that results from such inequality by using Equation 4.6 for r_c, where c denotes corrected. Because sample sizes are reasonably large and not very different for the data of Table 9.1, not surprisingly, the correction makes little difference in this case: $r_c = -.398$. The output also indicates that $r_{pb} = -.397$ is statistically significantly different from 0 at the $p < .002$ level, two-tailed. The negative correlation indicates that Therapy 1 is inferred to be better than Therapy 2. One can now conclude, subject to the limitations that are discussed later, that Therapy 1 has a statistically significant and apparently moderately strong superiority over Therapy 2.

CONFIDENCE INTERVAL FOR r_{pop}

Recall from Chapter 4 that construction of an accurate confidence interval for r_{pop} can be complex, and that there may be no entirely satisfactory method. Also, the likely presence of many ties in the case of $2 \times c$ tables should be problematic for the distribution theory that underlies the construction of a confidence interval for r_{pop}, especially when $r_{pop} \neq 0$. Consult the section entitled "Confidence intervals for r_{pop}" in Chapter 4 for a brief discussion of the improved methods for construction of a confidence interval for r_{pop} by Smithson (2003) and Wilcox (2003). One might consider constructing an approximate confidence interval for r_{pop} using Fisher's Z_r transformation as was demonstrated in detail in Chapter 4. However, we suspect that for $2 \times c$ tables, where the *c* outcome categories are ordinal, this method would be unsatisfactory because of ties and bivariate nonnormality.

NULL–COUNTERNULL INTERVAL FOR r_{pop}

We now construct a null–counternull interval for r_{pop} for the data of Table 9.1 using Equation 4.9. As we discussed in Chapter 8, one knows in advance that the null–counternull interval will be wide when the rejected null hypothesis is

H_0: $r_{pop} = 0$ and the obtained estimate of effect size is at least relatively large, as is true with regard to the data in Table 9.1. Because our null-hypothesized value of r_{pop} is 0, the lower limit of the interval (null value) is 0. Applying the corrected $r_{pb} = -.398$ to Equation 4.9, $r_{cn} = 2r/(1 + 3r^2)^{1/2}$, one finds that the upper limit (counternull value) is $2(-.398)/[1 + 3(-.398^2)]^{1/2} = -.655$. Thus, the interval runs from 0 to $-.655$. Therefore, the statistically significant result provides as much support for the proposition that $r_{pop} = 0$ as it does for the proposition that $r_{pop} = -.655$. As was previously discussed, the information that would be provided by a confidence interval would be different.

ADDITIONAL LIMITATIONS OF r_{pop} FOR $2 \times c$ TABLES

For general discussion of limitations of r_{pb} consult the section entitled "Assumptions of Correlation and Point-Biserial Correlation" in Chapter 4. The limitations may be especially troublesome in cases, such as the present one, in which there are very few values of the X and Y variables (two and three values, respectively). Such data cause concerns such as the possibly inaccurate obtained p levels for the t test that is used to test for the statistical significance of r_{pb}. However, in the present ordinal example there are some seemingly favorable circumstances that possibly somewhat reduce the risk to the accuracy of the p level (but not other risks) when using r_{pb}. First, sample sizes are reasonably large. Second, the obtained p level is well beyond the customary minimum criterion of .05. Also, some studies have indicated that statistical power and accurate p levels can be maintained for the t test even when the Y variable is dichotomous (resulting in a 2×2 table) if sample sizes are greater than 20 each, as they are in our example (D'Agostino, 1971; Lunney, 1970). A dichotomy is a much coarser scaling of categorical outcome than the polytomy of tables such as Table 9.1. However, it may not be possible for r adequately to estimate an association between the dichotomous variable and a continuous variable underlying the ordinal outcome variable when there are very few ordinal categories. There is no rule of thumb for a sufficient number of categories in this regard, but recall from the section entitled "Scale coarseness" in Chapter 4 that the use of ordinal scales when the unmeasured underlying construct (e.g., attitude) is continuous artifactually reduces r or r_{pb}. Such negative bias is greater the fewer the number of scale points or ordinal categories.

One may choose to adopt the assumptions underlying the Peters–van Voorhis method for correcting r (or r_{pb}) for scale coarseness, a method that is discussed and extended by Aguinis et al. (2009) and summarized by us in the section entitled "Scale coarseness" in Chapter 4. Applying the method to the data of Table 9.1 we observe that the coarsely scaled outcome variable has three categories and recall that the r_{pb} corrected for unequal sample sizes was $-.398$ (uncorrected $r = -.397$). We use the equation from Chapter 4 for correcting for scale coarseness, $r_{csc} = r/(c_X c_Y)$, where the current r is $r_{pb} = -.398$ and the correction divisor for variable X (Therapy 1 versus Therapy 2) is $c_X = 1$ (i.e., no correction) because this is not a coarsely scaled variable but a true dichotomy. From Peters–van Voorhis tables in Aguinis et al. the correction divisor for a coarsely scaled variable with three categories is observed to be $c_Y = .859$. Therefore, the coarseness-corrected estimate of the point-biserial correlation is $r_{csc} = -.398/1(.859) = -.463$.

Tables of size 2×2 were discussed in Chapter 8. Unlike the case for polytomies (i.e., rows > 2 and/or columns > 2), if two dichotomous ordinal variables are coarsely scaled (e.g., patient Better/Not Better and patient Motivated/Not Motivated) the normality-assuming method for correcting correlation for coarse scaling may not yield accurate corrections when the underlying continuous variables are greatly skewed. The reduction in r by scale coarseness is greater the larger r_{pop} and the fewer the categories (Aguinis et al., 2009).

Regarding the t test of the statistical significance of r_{pb}, it has been reported that even when sample sizes are as small as 5 the p levels for the t test can be accurate when there are at least three ordinal categories (Bevan, Denton, & Meyers, 1974). Also, Nanna and Sawilowsky (1998) showed that the t test can be robust with respect to Type I error and can maintain power when applied to data from rating scales. However, Maxwell and Delaney (1985) showed that, under heteroscedasticity and equality of means of populations, parametric methods applied to ordinal data may result in misleading conclusions (although in experimental research it may not be common to find that treatments change variances without changing means). For references to many articles whose conclusions favor one or the other side of this longstanding controversy about the use of parametric methods for ordinal data consult Long (2005), Nanna (2002), and Maxwell and Delaney (2004).

Ordinal methods, such as those that are discussed in this chapter, do not assume equal intervals of difference between successive response categories. (Use of the polychoric correlation for $r \times c$ ordinal categorical contingency tables assumes an underlying bivariate normal distribution for the ordinal row and column variables. The same assumption is made by use of the tetrachoric correlation for 2×2 ordinal categorical tables.). For example, when using an ordinal measure it is not assumed that the difference between, say, Agree and Agree Strongly is the same as the difference between Disagree and Disagree Strongly, with respect to an underlying continuous variable of intensity of attitude. However, such is not true of the point-biserial r, which can be sensitive to the choice of numerical scores for the ordinal response categories because r_{pb} estimates the relationship between the dichotomous variable and the *magnitudes* of the scores on the response variable.

CHOICE OF SCORES FOR ORDINAL CATEGORIES

One may also be concerned about the arbitrary nature of our equal-interval scoring of the columns (1, 2, 3) in Table 9.1 because other sets of three increasing numbers could have been used. Snedecor and Cochran (1989) and Moses (1986) reported that *moderate* differences among ordered, but not necessarily equally spaced, numerical scores that replace ordinal categories do not result in important differences in the value of t. However, recall from Chapter 4 that the correction of correlation for scale coarseness assumes equally spaced scores. Also, assigning scores is more complicated when the outcome categories represent ordered intervals (groupings) of values of a quantitative variable. For example, Delaney and Vargha (2002) reported that there was a statistically significant difference between the means for two treatments for problem drinking when increasing levels of alcohol consumption were ordinally numerically scaled with equal spacing as 1 (abstinence), 2 (2–6 drinks per week), 3 (between 7 and 140 drinks per week), and 4 (more than 140 drinks per week). However, there was not a statistically significant difference when the same four levels of drinking were scaled with slightly unequal spacing as 0, 2, 3, 4. Consult Agresti (2002) for similar results.

For variables for which there is no obvious choice of score spacing, such as the dependent variable in Table 9.1, Agresti (2002) acknowledges that equal spacing of scores is often a reasonable choice (except when the categories have very different frequencies; Agresti, 2007), and he discussed *correspondence analysis*, which can be informative regarding the spacing of the scores. (Correspondence analysis depicts association in $r \times c$ tables graphically and can be undertaken currently using SAS with PROC CORRESP.) The topic was extensively reviewed in Fielding's (1997) article on scoring ordinal categories.

Agresti (2007) described another approach to assigning scores to categories that represent ordered intervals of values of a quantitative variable. In this method the *midpoints* of each category serves as the numerical score for that category. However, the method is problematic in cases, such as the present one, in which the final category has no upper bound (e.g., "more than" 140 drinks per week). (If, unbeknownst to the researcher, a continuous latent variable underlies the scale, one would want the spacing of scores to be consistent with the differences between the underlying values.) For such troublesome cases Agresti (2002) recommends the use of a type of *sensitivity analysis* in which the results from two or three sensible scoring schemes are compared. One can then only hope that the results will not be importantly different. In any event, the results from each of the scoring schemes must be presented. The discussion by Gautam and Ashikaga (2003) can help researchers determine if they will reach different conclusions by assigning different scores to an open-ended final category. However, researchers who want to avoid the complications of assigning scores should consider those methods forthcoming in this chapter that do not require assigning scores to categories.

FURTHER DISCUSSION OF r_{pb} FOR $2 \times c$ TABLES

Some researchers will remain concerned about the validity of r_{pb} and the accuracy of the p levels of the t test under the following combination of circumstances: small sample sizes, as few as three ordinal categories, possible skew or skew in different directions for the two groups, and possible heteroscedasticity. Because the lowest and/or highest extremes of the ordinal categories may not be as extreme as the actual most extreme standings of the participants with regard to the construct that underlies the rating scale, skew or differential skew may result. For example, suppose that there are respondents in one group who disagree *extremely* strongly with a presented attitudinal statement and respondents in the other group who agree *extremely* strongly with it. If the scale does not include these very extreme categories the responses of the two groups will "bunch up" with those in the less extreme strongly disagree or strongly agree categories, respectively. The consequence will be skew in different directions for the two groups as well as a restricted range of the measure of the dependent variable, which, as was discussed in Chapter 4, can be problematic for r_{pb} and a t test for its statistical significance.

Tips and Pitfalls

Cliff (1993, 1996a) argued that there is rarely empirical justification for treating the numbers that are assigned to ordinal categories as having other than ordinal properties. Those who share such views should consider using the rank-based measures that are to be discussed in this chapter. Also consult Long (2005) and Long et al. (2003).

Many alternatives to r_{pb} have been developed for the present case in which one variable is dichotomous and the other is ordinal categorical. One such method is logistic regression, which is mentioned in Chapter 8 with regard to odds ratios and is revisited briefly in Chapter 10. In logistic regression there are measures of effect size that are roughly analogous to the coefficient of determination, r^2, which is discussed in Chapter 4 and the coefficient of multiple determination, R^2, which is discussed in Chapter 10. For discussions of analogs to coefficients of determination when the dependent variable is ordinal, consult Borooah (2002), Huynh (2002), and Lacy (2006). We now turn to an effect size for ordinal categorical data that is less problematic than the point-biserial correlation and does not require the assigning of scores to the categories of outcome.

PROBABILITY OF SUPERIORITY APPLIED TO ORDINAL DATA

The part of the following material that is background information is explained in more detail in Chapter 5, where the effect size that we call the probability of superiority (*PS*) is introduced in the context of a continuous Y variable. Recall that the *PS* is defined as the probability that a randomly sampled member of Population a will have a score (Y_a) that is higher than the score (Y_b) attained by a randomly sampled member of Population b. Symbolically,

$$PS = \Pr(Y_a > Y_b) + .5\Pr(Y_a = Y_b). \tag{9.1}$$

Before the plus sign, Equation 9.1 is the same as Equation 5.1. In Chapter 5 we were focusing on continuous variables, with respect to which *theoretically* there can be no ties. However, in the present case of a small number of outcome categories, ties (i.e., pairings of a member from each population that result in $Y_a = Y_b$) are very likely and they must be accommodated in some way. Equation 9.1 accommodates ties by assuming that, with regard to an *underlying* variable that is theoretically continuous (i.e., no ties), one-half of the time the *observed* $Y_a = Y_b$ actually represents, *in the populations*, $Y_a > Y_b$ and one-half of the time such an apparent tie actually represents $Y_a < Y_b$. Thus, Equation 9.1 adds $.5\Pr(Y_a = Y_b)$ to the definition of the *PS* for greater generality than Equation 5.1. If there are no ties $.5\Pr(Y_a = Y_b) = .5(0) = 0$.

In the current example of Table 9.1 a represents Therapy 1 and b represents Therapy 2, so we now call these therapies Therapy a and Therapy b, respectively.

The *PS* is estimated by $\hat{p}_{a>b}$, which, as was discussed in Chapter 5, is the propor-tion of times that members of Sample *a* have a better outcome than members of Sample *b* when the outcome of each member of Sample *a* is compared to the outcome of each member of Sample *b*, one by one. In Table 9.1 we consider the outcome No Change ($Y = 2$) to be better than the outcome Worse ($Y = 1$), and the outcome Improved ($Y = 3$) to be better than the outcome No Change. The number of times that the outcome for a member of Sample *a* is better than the outcome for the compared member of Sample *b* in all of these head-to-head comparisons is called the *U* statistic. (We soon consider the computational han-dling of ties.) The total number of such head-to-head comparisons is given by the product of the two sample sizes, n_a and n_b. Therefore, an estimate of the *PS* is given by Equation 5.2; $\hat{p}_{a>b} = U/n_a n_b$. This estimator and the *PS* are not sensitive to the magnitudes of the scores that are being compared two at a time; they are only sensitive to which of the two scores is higher (better), that is, an ordering of the two scores. Therefore, the *PS* and its estimator are applicable to $2 \times c$ tables in which the *c* categories are ordinal categorical. Because, again, numerous ties are likely when comparing two scores at a time when outcomes are categorical, the more so the smaller the effect size and the fewer the categories (consult Fay, 2003), we pay particular attention to the handling of ties in the following sections.

WORKED EXAMPLE OF THE *PS* FOR ORDINAL CATEGORICAL DATA

Although a standard statistical software package may provide at least intermedi-ate values for the calculations, we describe calculation by hand to provide readers with a better understanding of the concept of the *PS* when applied to ordinal cat-egorical data. We estimate $PS = \Pr(Y_a > Y_b) + .5\Pr(Y_a = Y_b)$ using S_a to denote the number of times that a member of Sample *a* has an outcome that is superior to the outcome for the compared member of Sample *b*. We use *T* to denote the number of times that the two outcomes are tied. Again, a tie occurs whenever the two participants who are being compared have outcomes that are in the same outcome category (e.g., same column of Table 9.1). The number of ties arising from each column (outcome category) of the table is the product of the two cell frequencies in the column. Using the simple tie-handling method that was recommended by Moses, Emerson, and Hosseini (1984) and also adopted by Delaney and Vargha (2002) we allocate ties equally to each group by counting each tie as one-half of a *win* assigned to each of the two samples. For further discussions of ties consult the references in Chapter 5. Thus,

$$U = S_a + .5T, \tag{9.2}$$

where, again, *U* is the numerator of the estimator of the *PS* (i.e., $U/n_a n_b$).

Calculating S_a by beginning with the third outcome category (Improved) of Table 9.1, observe that the outcomes of the 4 patients in the first row (now called Therapy *a*) are superior to those of $13 + 12 = 25$ of the patients in row 2 (now called Therapy *b*). Therefore, thus far $4(13 + 12) = 100$ pairings of patients have been found in which Therapy a had the superior outcome. Similarly, moving now to the third column (No Change) of the table observe that the outcomes of 22 of the patients in Therapy a are superior to those of 12 of the patients in Therapy b. This latter result adds $22 \times 12 = 264$ to the previous subtotal of 100 pairings within which patients in Therapy a had the superior outcome. Therefore, $S_a = 100 + 264 = 364$. The number of ties arising from columns 1, 2, and 3 is $3 \times 12 = 36$, $22 \times 13 = 286$, and $4 \times 1 = 4$, respectively; so $T = 36 + 286 + 4 = 326$. Thus, $U = S_a + .5T = 364 + .5(326) = 527$. That is, the number of head-to-head comparisons in which a patient in Therapy a had a better outcome than a patient in Therapy b when one allocates ties equally is 527. There were $n_a n_b = 29 \times 26 = 754$ total comparisons made. Therefore, the proportion of times that a patient in Therapy a had an outcome that was superior to the outcome of a compared patient in Therapy b, $\hat{p}_{a>b}$ (with equal allocation of ties), is $527/754 = .699$. One thus estimates that there is nearly a .7 probability that a randomly sampled patient from a population that receives Therapy a will outperform a randomly sampled patient from a population that receives Therapy b.

Testing H_0: $PS = .5$

If type of therapy has no effect on outcome, $PS = .5$. Before citing methods that may be more robust we discuss traditional methods for testing $PS = .5$. As was discussed in Chapter 5, one may test H_0: $PS = .5$ against H_{alt}: $PS \neq .5$ using the Wilcoxon–Mann–Whitney U test. However, as was discussed in Chapter 5, heteroscedasticity can result in a loss of power, or inaccurate p levels and inaccurate confidence intervals for the PS.

   Some statistical software packages can be used to conduct a U test from ordinal categorical data if a data file is created in which the ordinal categories are replaced by a set of any increasing positive numbers, as we have already done for the columns of Table 9.1. Available software may instead provide an equivalent test using Wilcoxon's W_m statistic. Software may also use an approximating normal distribution instead of the exact distribution of the U statistic and use as the standard deviation of this distribution (the standard error) a value that has not been adjusted for ties. We adjust the test for the case of ties later in this section. (One should not use the equation for converting Wilcoxon's W_m statistic to U that was presented in Chapter 5 and assumes continuous data because the equation is not applicable when there are ties, as is very likely in the present ordinal categorical case.)

   A manually calculated U test is often conducted using a normal approximation. (When tests that were developed for continuous data are applied to discrete data, as the U test sometimes is, such tests are approximate and likely conservative.) For ordinal categorical data there is an old three-part rule of thumb (possible modification of which we suggest later) that has been used to justify use of the version of the U test that uses the normal approximation. The rule consists of (a) $n_a \geq 10$, (b) $n_b \geq 10$, and (c) no column total frequency (i.e., column ties) > $.5N$, where $N = n_a + n_b$ (Emerson & Moses, 1985; Moses et al., 1984). According to this rule, if all of these three criteria are satisfied the following transformation of U to z is made, and the obtained z, which we denote z_u, is referred to the normal curve to determine if it is at least as extreme as the critical value that is required for the adopted significance level (e.g., $z = \pm 1.96$ for the .05 level, two-tailed):

$$z_u = \frac{U - .5 n_a n_b}{s_u},$$ (9.3)

where s_u is the standard deviation of the distribution of U (standard error) given by

$$s_u = \left[\frac{n_a n_b (n_a + n_b + 1)}{12} \right]^{1/2}.$$ (9.4)

With regard to the minimum sample sizes that may justify use of the normal approximation, recall from Chapter 5 that Fahoome (2002) found that the minimum equal sample sizes that would justify the use of the normal approximation for the W_m test (again, equivalent to the U test), in terms of adequately controlling Type I error, were 15 for tests at the .05 level and 29 for tests at the .01 level. Therefore, until there is further evidence about minimum sample sizes for the case of using the normal approximation to test $PS = .5$ with ordinal categorical data, perhaps a better rule of thumb would be to substitute Fahoome's minimum sample sizes for those in criteria (a) and (b) in the previously described old rule.

Adjusting for Ties

A more accurate significance level can be attained by adjusting s_u for ties. Such an adjustment might be especially beneficial if any column total contains more than one-half of the total participants. This condition violates criterion (c) that was previously listed for justifying use of a normal approximation. Because some software may not make this adjustment we demonstrate the manual adjustment. Observe that column "2" of Table 9.1 contains $22 + 13 = 35$ of the $29 + 26 = 55$ of the total patients. Because $35/55 = .64$, which is greater than the adopted criterion maximum of .5 for the proportion of the total participants who may fall into any one column, we use the adjusted s_u, denoted s_{adj}, in the denominator of z_u for a more accurate test:

$$s_{adj} = s_u \left[1 - \frac{\sum (f_i^3 - f_i)}{N^3 - N} \right]^{1/2},$$ (9.5)

where f_i is a column total frequency (again, the column's number of ties) and the summation is over all columns.

Beginning the calculation with Equation 9.4 for s_u one finds for the data of Table 9.1 that $s_u = [29(26)(29 + 26 + 1)/12] = 59.318$. Next, one calculates $f_i^3 - f_i$

for each of the columns 1, 2, and 3 in that order. These results are $15^3 - 15 = 3,360$, $35^3 - 35 = 42,840$, and $5^3 - 5 = 120$, respectively. Summing these last three values yields $3,360 + 42,840 + 120 = 46,320$. Applying 46,320 to Equation 9.5 yields $s_{adj} = 59.318[1 - 46,320/(55^3 - 55)]^{1/2} = 50.385$. Applying Equation 9.3 with s_{adj} replacing s_u yields $z_u = [527 - .5(29)(26)]/50.385 = 2.98$. A z that is equal to 2.98 is statistically significant beyond the .0028 level, two-tailed. There is thus support for a researcher's hypothesis that one of the therapies is better than the other therapy, and we soon find that Therapy a is the better one.

Observe first that adjusting s_u for ties has resulted in a different obtained significance level from the value of .0114 that was previously obtained, although both levels represent statistical significance at $p < .02$. Because we defined the PS in terms of the probability that $Y_a > Y_b$, instead of defining it (equally validly) in terms of the probability that $Y_b > Y_b$, and because the estimate of the PS equals .699, which is a value that is *greater* than the null-hypothesized value of .5, the therapy for which there is the reported statistically significant evidence of superiority is Therapy a. Furthermore, because U is statistically significant beyond the .0028 (approximately) two-tailed level, the estimate .699 is also statistically significantly greater than .5 beyond the .0028 two-tailed level.

When both n_a and $n_b > 10$ the presence of many ties, as is the case with the data of Table 9.1, has been reported to result generally in the approximate p level being within 50% of the true p level (Emerson & Moses, 1985; but also consult Fay, 2003). In the present example the obtained p level, .0028, is so far from the usual criterion of .05 that perhaps one need not be very concerned about the exact p level attained by the results. However, especially when more than half of the participants fall in one outcome column (many ties) and the approximate obtained p level is close to .05, a researcher may prefer to report an exact obtained p level as is discussed later.

Again, the PS is applicable to tables that have as few as two ordinal outcome categories, although more ties are likely when there are only two outcome categories. Tables 4.1 and 8.1 provide examples because Participant Better versus Participant Not Better after treatment in Table 4.1 and Symptoms Remain versus Symptoms Gone after treatment in Table 8.1 represent in each case an ordering of outcomes.

One outcome is not just different from the other, as would be the case for a nominal scale, but in examples such as Tables 4.1 and 8.1 one outcome can be considered to be superior to the alternative outcome. However, using only two outcome categories when there are more than two usable outcomes needlessly increases ties (and decreases estimation of effect size).

Exact p Levels and Robustness

An exact p level for testing H_0: $PS = .5$ against H_{alt}: $PS \neq .5$ can be obtained using StatXact, IBM SPSS Exact, or SAS. For further discussions of the PS and U test in general, review the section entitled "The probability of superiority: Independent groups" in Chapter 5. Compared to the point-biserial correlation the PS is more robust to outliers, and its value is not influenced by a difference in the rates of occurrence of the two groups in the population (e.g., schizophrenic versus non-schizophrenic) or a difference in sample sizes.

Consult Delaney and Vargha (2002) for discussion of hypothesis testing for the current case of ordinal categorical dependent variables. However, such methods may inflate Type I error under some conditions of nonnormality. Delaney and Vargha demonstrated that these methods might not perform well when extreme skew is combined with one or both sample sizes being at or below 10. Minimum sample sizes between 20 and 30 each may be satisfactory.

CONFIDENCE INTERVALS FOR THE *PS*

Simulations by Newcombe (2006c) indicated that the approximate method for constructing confidence intervals for the *PS* for the case of a continuous dependent variable that was mentioned in Chapter 5 performs well when there are five ordinal outcome categories. Ryu and Agresti (2008) further evaluated methods for constructing confidence intervals for the *PS* when outcomes are ordinal categorical for the cases of independent groups and matched pairs. Wilcox (2005a) provided S-PLUS and R functions for the Brunner and Munzel (2000) method for testing H_0: $PS = .5$ and for constructing a confidence interval for the *PS* under conditions of heteroscedasticity and/or ties. For evidence that the Brunner–Munzel method performs well when each $n \geq 30$ consult Reiczigel et al. (2005). For further evaluation of the Brunner–Munzel method for constructing a confidence interval for the *PS*, including its inapplicability when $PS = 0$ or 1, consult Ryu and Agresti.

FURTHER DISCUSSIONS OF THE *PS* FOR ORDINAL CATEGORICAL DATA

Because of the limited number of outcome categories in the case of ordinal categorical data there is no opportunity for the most extreme outcomes to be shifted up or down by a treatment to a more extreme value (for which there is no outcome category). The result would be a bunching of tallies in the existing most extreme category (skew), obscuring the degree of shift in the underlying variable. Such bunching can cause an underestimation of the *PS* because ties are increased with respect to an existing extreme category when in fact some of these ties actually represent superior outcomes for members of one group with respect to the underlying variable. Again, such problems can be reduced by using the maximum number of categories into which participants can reliably be placed and by using either the Brunner and Munzel (2000) tie-handling method or the method that is the topic of the next section.

Cohen, Kolassa, and Sackrowitz (2004) proposed an application of the Mann–Whitney *U* statistic for choosing among four possible conclusions when comparing two groups with regard to an ordinal categorical outcome variable. The four possible conclusions from the results are (a) the two distributions of outcomes are the same, (b) $\Pr(Y_1 > Y_2)$, (c) $\Pr(Y_2 > Y_1)$, and (d) none of these three conclusions are supported. The fourth conclusion means that the two distributions differ, but not in the sense that $\Pr(Y_1 > Y_2)$ or $\Pr(Y_2 > Y_1)$. Figure 5.4 provides an example of such a result. Wellek and Hampel (1999) presented a method for testing equivalence of two treatments when applying the *PS* to noncontinuous data. Simulations indicated good control of Type I error, even when sample sizes are small. Statistical power was found to be negatively related to the number of ties between members of the two samples. Munzel and Hauschke (2003) presented a test for non-inferiority when outcomes are ordered categories. Equivalence testing and non-inferiority testing are discussed in Chapter 2.

In Chapter 8 we discuss the strong possibility that results vary for different subgroups, creating a need for subgroup analyses. Ryu and Agresti (2008) discussed extension of estimation and construction of confidence intervals for values of *PS* for each level of a subgroup variable at each level of another subgroup variable. The number of resulting separate $2 \times c$ tables for which there is estimation and construction of a confidence interval for the *PS* is the product of the number of levels of all subgroup variables. For example, if two treatments are being compared for the subgroups gender (two levels) and age group at, say, three levels, there are $2 \times 3 = 6$ of the $2 \times c$ tables, each one of which is associated with a value of the *PS*.

DOMINANCE MEASURE

Recall from the section entitled "The dominance measure" in Chapter 5 that Cliff (1993, 1996a) and Long et al. (2003) discussed an effect size for continuous dependent variables that is a variation on the *PS* concept that avoids allocating ties, a measure that we called the dominance measure and defined in Equation 5.8 as $DM = \Pr(Y_a > Y_b) - \Pr(Y_b > Y_a)$. Cliff (1993, 1996a) called the estimator of this effect size the dominance statistic, which we defined in Equation 5.9 as $ds = \hat{p}_{a>b} - \hat{p}_{b>a}$. When calculating the *ds* each $\hat{p}$ value is given by the sample's value of $U/n_a n_b$ with no allocation of ties, so each U is now given only by the S part of Equation 9.2. Although ties are not allocated, the denominator of each $\hat{p}$ value is still given by $n_a n_b$, so pairings that result in ties do not reduce $n_a n_b$. The application of the *DM* and the *ds* to an ordinal categorical dependent variable will be made clear in the worked example for the data of Table 9.1 in the next section.

Recall also from Chapter 5 that the *ds* and *DM* range from -1 to $+1$. If every member of Sample *b* has a better outcome than every member of Sample *a*, then $ds = -1$. If every member of Sample *a* has an outcome that is better than the outcome of every member of Sample *b*, then $ds = +1$. If there is an equal number of superior outcomes for each sample in the head-to-head pairings, then $ds = 0$. Agresti (2010) discussed the *DM* for matched-pairs designs.

Tips and Pitfalls
When $ds = -1$ or $+1$ there is no overlap between the two samples' distributions in the $2 \times c$ table, and when $ds = 0$ there is complete overlap in the two samples' distributions. However, because estimators of the *PS* and the *DM* are sensitive to which outcome is better in each pairing, but not sensitive to how good the better outcome is, reporting an estimate of these two effect sizes is not very informative

unless the contingency table is also presented. For example, with regard to a table with the column categories of Table 9.1 (but not the data therein), suppose that $\hat{p}_{a>b} = 1$ or $ds = +1$ (both results indicating the most extreme possible superiority of Therapy a over Therapy b in the samples). Such a result could mean that (a) all members of Sample b were in the Worse column whereas all members of Sample a were in the No Change column, Improved column, or in either the No Change or the Improved column or (b) all members of Sample b were in the No Change column whereas all members of Sample a were in the Improved column. Readers of a research report must be informed about which of these four importantly different results underlies $\hat{p}_{a>b} = 1$ or $ds = +1$. Similarly, when $\hat{p}_{a>b} = .5$ or $ds = 0$ (both indicating no superiority for either therapy), among other possible patterns of frequencies in the table the result could mean that all participants were in the Worse column, all were in the No Change column, or all were in the Improved column. One would certainly want to know whether such a result were indicating that in the samples both therapies were always possibly harmful (Worse category), always inefficacious (No Change column), always efficacious (Improved column), or that there were some other pattern in the table.

TESTING AND CONFIDENCE INTERVALS FOR DOMINANCE

Refer to Cliff (1993, 1996a), Feng and Cliff (2004), and Long et al. (2003) for discussions of significance testing for the ds and construction of confidence intervals for the DM for the independent-groups and the dependent-groups cases and for software to undertake the calculations. Wilcox (2005a) provided S-Plus and R software functions for Cliff's (1993, 1996a) method, which seems to control Type I error well even when there are many ties. Consult Vargha and Delaney (2000) and Delaney and Vargha (2002) for further discussions.

Feng and Cliff (2004) studied the performance of a modified method for constructing a confidence interval for the DM under violation of parametric assumptions. They found that the probability coverage was near the nominal $1 - \alpha$ level under most conditions that were simulated except for $DM > .7$. However, coverage was rarely above .93 for nominal .95 confidence intervals. When testing null hypotheses the modified method also improved the rate of Type I error, but with a slight loss of power. Test performance improved as sample sizes increased.

SOMERS' D, THE RISK DIFFERENCE, AND THE NNT

The ds is also known as the version of Somers' D statistic (Agresti, 2002) that is applicable to $r \times c$ tables in which both variables are ordinal and to $2 \times c$ tables with c ordinal outcomes (Cliff, 1996a; Long et al., 2003). Somers' D accommodates ties and has a symmetric form and an asymmetric form. Recall from Chapter 8 that the former, unlike the latter, relates the two variables without requiring a distinction between an independent variable and a dependent variable. Here we distinguish between the independent variable of group membership and the dependent variable of ordinal outcome, so the asymmetric form of Somers' D is the form that is relevant to our discussion. SAS PROC LOGISTIC outputs the asymmetric D. An exact p level for the statistical significance of Somers' D is provided by StatXact and IBM SPSS Exact. Woods (2007; Correction, 2008) reported simulations that indicated that several methods for constructing confidence intervals for Somers' D yield probability coverage close to the nominal confidence level when total $N > 25$.

The risk difference that is applicable to 2×2 tables for nominal variables (Chapter 8) is also applicable to 2×2 tables in which the outcome variable has two ordinal categories. Indeed, for 2×2 tables the risk difference is equivalent to dominance (Agresti, 2010; Hsu, 2004; Kraemer, 2006) and, therefore, to the asymmetric Somer's D. In the 2×2 case these indices are also related to Kendall's tau_b (Chapter 4) (Acion et al., 2006a,b). Note that tau_b might not be the version of tau that is outputted by all software.

Estimation of the effect size called the number needed to treat (NNT_{pop}), which was discussed in Chapter 8 and defined there as the reciprocal of the risk difference (RD_{pop}), can be extended to the present case of $2 \times c$ tables with c ordinal outcome categories. Recall from Chapter 8 that in studies of clinical outcome the risk difference can also be appropriately called the success rate difference (SRD). First, each participant's outcome is classified as (a) *better* instead of (b) *worse* or *tied* when compared to each other participant's outcome across all $n_a n_b$ possible pairings of a participant from one group with a participant from the other group. Then the estimated SRD (SRD_{est}) is defined as the difference between the proportion of pairings in which the participants in Sample 1 perform better than participants in Sample 2 and the proportion of pairings in which the participants in Sample 2 perform better than the participants in Sample 1. Consistent with Equations 8.14 through 8.16 and Equation 5.9, the estimate of NNT_{pop} is given by

$$NNT_{est} = \frac{1}{SRD_{est}} = \frac{1}{2\hat{p}_{a>b} - 1}. \qquad (9.6)$$

As in Equation 5.9, $\hat{p}_{a>b}$ is defined in Equation 9.6 without allocation of ties. In the present context NNT_{pop} measures the number of people on average who have to be given Treatment a per each person who will perform better having been given this treatment than if having been given Treatment b. A worked example follows.

WORKED EXAMPLE OF THE DOMINANCE STATISTIC AND NNT_{est}

Although we cite software, calculation of the ds manually is simple and clarifies the meaning of dominance. Calculating the ds for the data of Table 9.1 by starting with column "3," and not allocating ties, we note first that (as was found previously) Therapy 1 had $(4 \times 13) + (4 \times 12) + (22 \times 12) = 364$ superior outcomes in the $29 \times 26 = 754$ head-to-head comparisons. Therefore, $\hat{p}_{a>b} = 364/754 = .4828$. Starting again with column "3" one now finds that 1 patient in Therapy 2 had a better outcome than $22 + 3$ patients in Therapy 1, so thus far there are $1(22 + 3) = 25$ pairs of patients within which Therapy 2 had the superior outcome. Moving now to column "2" one finds that 13 patients in Therapy 2 had an outcome that was superior to the outcome of 3 patients in Therapy 1, adding $13 \times 3 = 39$ to the previous subtotal of 25 superior outcomes for Therapy 2. Therefore, $\hat{p}_{b>a} = (25 + 39)/754 = .0849$. Thus, $ds = \hat{p}_{a>b} - \hat{p}_{b>a} = .4828 - .0849 = .398$, another indication, now on a scale from -1 to $+1$, of the degree of superiority of Therapy 1 over Therapy 2. One can check our calculation of $25 + 39 = 64$ superior outcomes for Therapy 2 by noting that there were a total of 754 comparisons, resulting in 364 superior outcomes (i.e., S_a) for Therapy 1 and $T = 326$ ties; so there must be $754 - 364 - 326 = 64$ comparisons in which Therapy 2 had the superior outcome.

Recall that the dominance statistic is the same as the estimator of the risk difference and that the number needed to treat is the reciprocal of the risk difference (Equation 8.14). Therefore, because the risk difference was found to be .398 for the data of Table 9.1, the estimated number needed to treat is $1/.398 = 2.51$. Rounding up, one thus concludes from the current analysis of the data in Table 9.1 that it is estimated that on average three couples have to be given Therapy 1 per each couple who will perform better having been given that therapy than if having been given Therapy 2. Rounding NNT_{est} up is a common conservative approach regardless of the decimal values.

GENERALIZED ODDS RATIO

Recall from Chapter 5 an estimator of an effect size that results from the ratio of $\hat{p}_{a>b}$ and $\hat{p}_{b>a}$, the *generalized odds ratio* (also known as *Agresti's alpha*). The generalized odds ratio is also applicable to $2 \times c$ tables with c ordinal outcome categories. The sample generalized odds ratio estimates, for the $n_a n_b$ possible pairings of outcomes from a member of Population a and a member of Population b, how many times more pairings there are in which a member of Population a has the better outcome than pairings in which a member of Population b has the better outcome. Alternatively stated, what are being estimated are the odds (not the probability) that a randomly drawn outcome from one specified population will be superior to a randomly drawn outcome from the other population, assuming no ties. Recall that if one were defining the probability of superiority instead of the odds ratio, the word "probability" would replace the word "odds" in the previous sentence.

Because population generalized odds ratios are strictly ratios of wins for Population a and wins for Population b (in head-to-head comparisons), ties are ignored. Therefore, to calculate a sample generalized odds ratio one uses the same definitions of $\hat{p}_{a>b} = U_a/n_a n_b$ and $\hat{p}_{b>a} = U_b/n_a n_b$ that were used in the previous discussions of dominance; that is, ties are ignored when calculating the two values of U but one uses all $n_a n_b = 26 \times 29 = 754$ possible pair-wise comparisons for the two denominators. Therefore, the estimate of the generalized odds ratio (OR_g) is given by

$$OR_g = \frac{\hat{p}_{a>b}}{\hat{p}_{b>a}},\qquad(5.3)$$

ignoring ties.

From the values that were calculated in the section entitled "Worked example of the dominance statistic and NNT_{est}," with regard to the data of Table 9.1, one now finds that $\hat{p}_{a>b}/\hat{p}_{b>a} = .4828/.0849 = 5.69$. For these data the OR_g provides the estimate that in the population there are nearly six times more pairings in which patients in Therapy a have a better outcome than patients in Therapy b than pairings in which patients in Therapy b have a better outcome than patients in Therapy a. Alternatively worded, it is estimated that the odds are nearly $6:1$ that a randomly drawn outcome from a population that is given Therapy a will be superior to a randomly drawn outcome from a population that is given Therapy b. The estimated parameter is

$$OR_{gpop} = \frac{\Pr(Y_a > Y_b)}{\Pr(Y_b > Y_a)}. \tag{5.4}$$

Recall from Chapter 5 that the generalized odds ratio is unbounded. Also, Agresti (1980) discussed the case of matched pairs, for which the simple sign test can be used to test H_0: $OR_{gpop} = 1$ against H_{alt}: $OR_{gpop} \neq 1$, and extension of the generalized odds ratio to the case of ordinal $r \times c$ tables in which $r > 2$.

Accommodating Ties

Because ignoring ties can result in the estimated OR_g yielding an inflated impression of effect size, modifying the generalized odds ratio to break ties is appropriate. For the case of ordinal categorical data O'Brien and Castelloe (2007) discuss a simple modification of the data in a contingency table in which all ties are broken in such a manner that Agresti's generalized odds ratio with no ties is equivalent to the modified tie-breaking OR_g and Agresti's (1980, 2010) method for construction of a confidence interval for the OR_{gpop} is applicable to the tie-broken data.

CUMULATIVE ODDS RATIOS

Suppose that in a $2 \times c$ table with c ordinal categories, such as Table 9.2, one is interested in comparing the two groups with respect to their attaining *at least* some ordinal category. For example, with regard to the ordinal categories of the rating scale Strongly Agree, Agree, Disagree, Strongly Disagree, suppose that one wants to compare the college women and college men with regard to their attaining at least the category Agree. Attaining at least the category Agree means

---

TABLE 9.2

Gender Comparison with Regard to an Attitude Scale

	Strongly Agree	Agree	Disagree	Strongly Disagree
Women	62	18	2	0
Men	30	12	7	1

---

attaining the category Strongly Agree or the category Agree instead of the category Strongly Disagree or the category Disagree. Therefore, one's focus would be on the now combined categories Strongly Agree and Agree versus the now combined categories Strongly Disagree and Disagree. Thereby, Table 9.2 is temporarily collapsed (reduced) to a 2 × 2 table, rendering the odds ratio (OR) for 2 × 2 tables of Chapter 8 applicable to the analysis of the collapsed data.

A population OR that is based on clustering (i.e., combining) categories is called a population *cumulative odds ratio*, which we denote OR_{cumpop} and whose estimator we denote OR_{cum}. This effect size is a measure of how many times greater the odds are that a member of a certain group will fall into a certain set of categories (e.g., Agree and Strongly Agree) instead of another specified set of categories than those same odds for a member of another group. In the present example one calculates the ratio of (a) the odds that a woman Agrees or Strongly Agrees with the statement (instead of Disagreeing or Strongly Disagreeing with it) and (b) the odds that a man Agrees or Strongly Agrees with that statement (instead of Disagreeing or Strongly Disagreeing with it). The choice of which of the two or more categories to combine in a 2 × c ordinal categorical table should be made before the data are collected. Table 9.2 presents an example of an original complete table (before collapsing it into Table 9.3) using actual data, but the labels of the response categories have been changed somewhat for our purpose. The non-statistical details of the research do not concern us here.

Collapsing Table 9.2 by combining the Strongly Agree and Agree columns and by combining the Disagree and Disagree Strongly columns produces Table 9.3. One finds a bias-adjusted OR_{cum} by applying the data from Table 9.3 to the correcting Equation 8.22; $OR_{cumadj} = (f_{11} + .0.5)(f_{22} + 0.5)/(f_{12} + .05)(f_{21} + .05)$. As in Chapter 8 we have adjusted each observed f value by adding .5 to it to improve OR_{cum} as an estimator of OR_{cumpop}. One finds that $OR_{cumadj} = 80.5(8.5)/2.5(42.5) = 6.44$. Therefore, the odds that a college woman will Agree or Strongly Agree with the statement instead of Disagreeing or Disagreeing Strongly with it are estimated to be more than six times greater than the same odds for a college man. However, in order to avoid exaggerating the gender difference that was just inferred from these data, it is also important to observe in Table 9.3 that in fact a great majority of the men Agree or Strongly Agree with the statement (42/50 = 84%) although an even greater majority of the women Agree or Strongly Agree with it (80/82 = 97.6%).

Any of the measures of effect size that were discussed previously in this chapter are applicable to the data of Table 9.3, subject to the previously discussed limitations. If the two population cumulative odds are equal, $OR_{cum} = 1$. Recall from Chapter 8

TABLE 9.3

Collapsed Version of Table 9.2

	Agree or Strongly Agree	Disagree or Strongly Disagree
Women	$f_{11} = 80$	$f_{12} = 2$
Men	$f_{21} = 42$	$f_{22} = 8$

that a test of H_0: $OR_{pop} = 1$ versus H_{alt}: $OR_{pop} \neq 1$ can be conducted using the usual χ^2 test of association. If χ^2 is significant at a certain p level then OR_{cumadj} can be considered to be statistically significantly different from 1 at the same p level. The data of Table 9.3 yield $\chi^2 = 11.85$, $p < .001$. Consult Agresti (2010) and O'Connell (2006) for further discussions of cumulative odds ratios, the latter of which discusses the construction of a confidence interval for a population cumulative odds ratio.

COMPENSATING FOR MULTIPLE TESTING

Some readers may be concerned about conducting two tests of statistical significance on the same set of data. For example, there may be concern about proper interpretation of the p level that is attained by a χ^2 test of the statistical significance of OR_{cum} for the data of a collapsed table, such as Table 9.3, after one has already conducted a test of association between the rows and columns of the original complete table, such as Table 9.2, having used any of the methods that were previously discussed in this chapter. The simplest solution would be to compensate for giving oneself two chances to obtain a statistically significant result from the same data by adopting a more conservative alpha level than the usual .05 level both for the statistical test that is first applied to the original full table and for the statistical test for OR_{cum}. For example, one might use a Bonferroni–Dunn approach by adopting, say, the .025 alpha level for each of the two tests. Such alpha levels should be adopted prior to the collection of data. The present p level is so small, $p < .001$, that perhaps one need not worry about this issue for the current data.

PHI COEFFICIENT

Recall from Chapters 4 and 8 that phi_{pop} is the correlation between two dichotomous variables, such as the two variables of Table 9.3. For a final estimated effect size for the data of Table 9.3 we apply Equations 8.1 and 8.2 to find that phi $= (\chi^2/N)^{1/2} = (11.85/132)^{1/2} = .300$. Again, following the recommendation of Fleiss et al. (2003), when using χ^2 to calculate phi one should use the basic equation (Equation 8.1) for χ^2 instead of a version of the equation that is adjusted for small samples. Also note again that the use of phi as an estimator of effect size for the data of Table 9.3 assumes naturalistic sampling, as is described in Chapter 8.

FURTHER READING

Consult Vargha and Delaney (2000) and Brunner and Puri (2001) for application of what we call the probability of superiority to the cases of between-groups and within-groups one-way and factorial designs with ordinal dependent variables. Agresti (2010) discussed a variety of software for analyzing contingency tables with ordered and unordered categories. Updates about SAS and other packages are currently provided courtesy of Alan Agresti at www.stat.ufl.edu/~aa/cda/cda.html. Agresti also discussed analyses of matched-pairs data when categories are ordinal and Bayesian approaches to ordinal categorical data.

Serlin et al. (1982) proposed an estimator of effect size that is analogous to eta squared (discussed in Chapter 6) for the case of two ordered categorical variables. Also for such data a version of Kendall's tau correlation can be used for an effect size (Berry, Johnston, Zahran, & Mielke, 2009).

Baguley (2009, 2010) argues that an unstandardized difference-between-means effect size might be more informative than d (or r_{pb}) for rating-scale data. For example, consider the scale Agree Strongly, Agree, Disagree, Disagree Strongly, scored 4, 3, 2, 1, respectively. In this case an unstandardized mean difference of 2 points between two groups suggests a very important shift, for example, from Agree to Disagree Strongly.

SUMMARY

For the case of $2 \times c$ contingency tables with $c > 2$ ordinal outcome categories for two independent groups we generally recommend as effect sizes the probability of superiority, dominance measure (equivalent to the asymmetric version of Somers' D), the generalized odds ratio, and the number needed to treat, the latter for communicating with laypersons. However, we do not recommend the number needed to treat for the case of naturalistic sampling. The cumulative odds ratio is useful only when it addresses the kind of research question for which it is appropriate.

In Chapter 5 we touted the invariance of the probability of superiority under any monotonic transformation of the outcome variable (i.e., the use of alternative outcome measures that are monotonically related to each other). The risk difference and the number needed to treat also have this beneficial property. For $2 \times c$ ordinal categorical tables we prefer measures of effect size that do not require the arbitrary assigning of scores to the ordinal categories. For this and other discussed reasons the point-biserial r is problematic for the present case.

In the present case of ordinal categorical data χ^2 as a test statistic is insensitive to the ordinal nature of the data. However, if sampling has been naturalistic and there is justification for collapsing a larger $2 \times c$ ordinal table into a 2×2 table, the sample phi coefficient, which is based on χ^2, is an appropriate estimator of effect size. Applying parametric statistical tests to ordinal data is controversial, but methods for nonparametric testing and construction of confidence intervals for ordinal effect sizes are available for independent groups and matched pairs.

QUESTIONS

9.1   Define *ordinal categorical variable* and provide an example that is not in the text.

9.2   Discuss criteria for one's choice of the number of ordinal categories to be used for the dependent variable.

9.3   Why should one be cautious about comparing effect sizes across studies that involve attitudinal scales?

9.4   What do the authors mean by an *ordinal hypothesis*?

9.5   Why is a χ^2 test inappropriate to test an ordinal hypothesis?

9.6 Discuss possible limitations of the use of the point-biserial r in the case of ordinal categorical data.

9.7 Discuss the problem of choosing a scale of scores to replace ordinal categories.

9.8 Provide, discussing your reasoning, your own choice of a possible *sensible* numerical scale for the example of treatment for alcoholism in the text in which the four outcome categories were abstinence, 2–6 drinks per week, between 7 and 140 drinks per week, and more than 140 drinks per week.

9.9 Describe how a result similar to skew in opposite directions may occur in the case of $2 \times c$ tables involving attitude scales, and why may such a result be problematic for the point-biserial r?

9.10 What adjustment may improve the accuracy of an obtained significance level for a U test based on the normal approximation?

9.11 Calculate an estimate of the *PS* if there are 610 wins for therapy in head-to-head comparisons of the outcomes of 33 participants who received therapy and outcomes of 33 participants who received a placebo, and there are 79 ties.

9.12 What would be possibly problematic about applying the *PS* to 2×2 tables with an ordinal outcome?

9.13 Apply Equation 9.2 to the data of Table 8.1, and interpret the estimated effect size obtained.

9.14 Why is the negative value for the point-biserial correlation for the data of Table 9.1 not inconsistent with the estimate of $PS = .699$ for those data?

9.15 Why may the use of too few categories cause the *PS* to be underestimated?

9.16 Define (a) *dominance measure*, (b) *generalized odds ratio*, and (c) *cumulative odds ratio*.

9.17 Why may the estimation of the *PS* or the *DM* not be very informative to a reader of a research report unless the underlying contingency table is also presented?

9.18 What are three other names for the dominance statistic?

9.19 Calculate an estimate of the *DM* for the data of Table 9.1 as an exercise in calculation and state why it would not be advisable for a researcher to estimate the *DM* for such data.

9.20 Interpret a generalized odds ratio that is equal to 5.

9.21 Calculate and interpret an estimate of the generalized odds ratio for the data of Table 9.2.

9.22 Interpret a cumulative odds ratio that is equal to 2.

9.23 Calculate and interpret an estimate of a cumulative odds ratio for the data of Table 9.1. Discuss whether a cumulative odds ratio is as well suited to the case of Table 9.1 as it is to the case of Table 9.2.

9.24 Define the kind of *sensitivity analysis* that was discussed in this chapter.

9.25 Distinguish between the two forms of Somers' D.

9.26 What is the relationship between estimates of the NNT_{pop} and the *PS*?

10 Effect Sizes for Multiple Regression/Correlation

INTRODUCTION

This chapter mainly discusses correlational and proportion-of-variance-explained effect sizes when there is one continuous dependent variable, Y, and multiple independent variables, X_1, X_2, X_3 .... We assume that some readers have scant familiarity with the basic ideas of multiple regression and multiple correlation. Therefore, throughout this chapter we provide background review of those aspects of these methods that relate to the effect sizes that we discuss. We sometimes use notation for subscripts that is more mnemonically friendly for less experienced readers than is the common notation. Although more experienced readers may consider some of our subscript notation to be redundant, we chose clarity over conciseness of notation.

We begin by assuming that the conditional distributions (*residuals*) of the Y variable in the population at each level of an independent variable are normal and that they are of equal variance (i.e., homoscedastic). Serious distortions of results can occur if the assumptions are sufficiently violated.

We mainly and first consider what is called *least-squares regression*. Optimal weights (the B values in regression Equation 10.1) are given to the X variables (i.e., predictor variables) in the regression equation (also called the prediction equation) that relates the X variables to a predicted value of Y. The weight that is given to a given X variable depends on how much independent information that the X variable contributes to the predictability of Y. For example, an X variable that correlates highly with Y but does not correlate highly with any of the other X variables that correlate with Y is providing much independent information for the prediction of Y. Such an X variable would be given a relatively large weight. An X variable that does not correlate highly with Y, or correlates highly with Y but also correlates highly with one or more of the other X variables that correlate highly with Y, is not providing very useful independent information for the prediction of Y, so it would be given relatively little weight. These optimal weights minimize the sum of the squared deviations between each predicted value of Y and its actual value (thus, "least squares"), such a deviation being called an *error of prediction* ($Y' - Y$). Thus, software renders the squared errors of prediction of Y the least that they can be by applying the optimal value of B to each X variable. (The value e_i in Figure 4.4 is an example of an error of prediction.)

We focus on *standard regression*, which is atheoretical, wherein all X variables are entered into the regression equation at the same time, not according to one's theory or according to certain statistical criteria that are met by the sample at hand. Standard regression can be undertaken using a variety of programs, including SAS REG, SAS GLM, IBM SPSS REGRESSION, SYSTAT REGRESS, and SYSTAT GLM.

MULTIPLE COEFFICIENT OF DETERMINATION

Major statistical software programs output a form of R^2, the sample *multiple coefficient of determination*, as an estimate of a proportion-of-variance-explained (*POV*) measure of effect size, R^2_{pop}, in the population. The sample R (*multiple correlation coefficient*) estimates the association in the population between Y and the optimally weighted linear combination of the X variables. The weighting is optimal also in the sense that it maximizes the value of R. The sample R^2 estimates the proportion of the total variance of Y that is attributable to the composite of the X variables.

The multiple regression equation is

$$Y' = \alpha + B_1 X_1 + B_2 X_2 + B_3 X_3 + \cdots + B_k X_k + e, \tag{10.1}$$

where
  Y' is the predicted value of the dependent variable
  α is the Y intercept
  each B is the weight to be given to the X variable that it multiplies to enable the
     set of X variables to predict Y most accurately
  k is the number of X variables
  e quantifies the error made in using the set of weighted X variables to predict Y

The sign, magnitude, and statistical significance of the B for a given X variable depend on the characteristics of the sample and on which other X variables are included in the regression equation, so generalizations from results must be made with appropriate caution.

In the illustrative case in which there are only two X variables, X_1 and X_2, the sample multiple coefficient of determination is given by

$$R^2_{yx_1x_2} = \frac{r^2_{yx_1} + r^2_{yx_2} - 2r_{yx_1}r_{yx_2}r_{x_1x_2}}{1 - r^2_{x_1x_2}}, \tag{10.2}$$

where each lowercase r indicates a simple correlation between the two variables that are indicated by the subscripts. Note the effect on Equation 10.2 when there is no correlation between variables X_1 and X_2 (i.e., these variables are providing entirely independent information). In this case the denominator equals 1 and the subtracted term in the numerator drops out, leaving the multiple coefficient of determination to equal the sum of the two simple coefficients of determination. This sum will be greater the stronger the correlation between X_1 and Y and between X_2 and Y. Thus, Equation 10.2 also indirectly

TABLE 10.1

Correlation Matrix of Adolescents' Use of Eight Drugs

	1	2	3	4	5	6	7	8
1	1							
2	.447	1						
3	.422	.619	1					
4	.435	.604	.583	1				
5	.114	.068	.053	.115	1			
6	.513	.445	.365	.482	.186	1		
7	.101	.088	.074	.139	.279	.204	1	
8	.245	.199	.184	.293	.278	.394	.511	1

Source: Partial results from Huba, G.A. et al., *J. Person. Soc. Psychol.*, *40*, 180, 1981.

Notes: 1 = cigarettes, 2 = beer, 3 = wine, 4 = hard liquor, 5 = cocaine, 6 = marijuana, 7 = hallucinogens, 8 = amphetamines.

demonstrates that the predictability of Y from two (or more) X variables increases as the correlation between each X and Y increases and the correlation between each X decreases.

An outputted *correlation matrix* is a table that provides the needed correlation between each pairing of variables to enter into an equation such as Equation 10.2. Table 10.1 provides a real example of a correlation matrix involving eight variables and $N = 1634$. In the example that we work next involving three of the correlations in Table 10.1 a researcher might want to estimate the proportion of variance in adolescents' extent of consumption of hard liquor (i.e., variable 4 in Table 10.1 is Y) that is associated with variance in their extents of consumption of beer (variable 2 is X_1) and wine (variable 3 is X_2). Generally no useful comparison can be made between the R^2 values from two or more studies of the same variables because the value of R^2 depends on the amount of total variance in the study. Lacy (2006) discussed uses and limitations of R^2 and analogs of R^2.

In the current example from Table 10.1, Equation 10.2 yields $R^2_{yx_1x_2} = [.604^2 + .583^2 - 2(.604)(.583)(.619)]/(1 - .619^2) = .4357143 \approx .44$. Observe that the multiple correlation coefficient for these results is $(.4357143)^{1/2} = .66$, which, as should be expected, is greater than the simple correlations between Y and X_1 and Y and X_2 in Table 10.1.

ADJUSTING R^2 FOR SHRINKAGE

The value of R cannot be negative, so the sampling distribution of R cannot include negative values. Therefore, the R^2 as defined by Equation 10.2, or an extension of Equation 10.2 for the case of more than two X variables, is a positively biased (i.e., tending to overestimate) estimator of R_{pop}^2. The bias increases as the number of independent variables increases (even if the additional independent variables are not related to the Y variable). This fact should further motivate researchers to choose X variables very carefully. Bias also increases as effect sizes and sample sizes decrease (Voelkle et al., 2007). To reduce the positive bias one can use, for fixed effects, what is often called an *adjusted* or *shrunken estimator*, such as

$$R_{adj}^2 = 1 - \frac{(1 - R^2)(N - 1)}{N - k - 1}, \tag{10.3}$$

where

N is the sample size
k is the number of independent variables

Observe in Equation 10.3 that, consistent with what one would expect based on our previous comment, the equation reduces the overestimating R^2 more the greater the number of independent variables, k, at a given sample size. We recommend the use of an adjustment although it may not completely eliminate the bias. Software such as IBM SPSS, SAS, and SYSTAT output an adjusted estimator.

Suppose that for fixed effects $R^2 = .2500$, $N = 10$, and $k = 2$. In this case Equation 10.3 yields $R_{adj}^2 = 1 - [(1 - .2500)(10 - 1)/(10 - 2 - 1)] = .0357$. As should be expected, the adjusted R^2 is lower than the upwardly biased unadjusted R^2. However, we intentionally chose an extremely unwise small value of $N/k = 10/2 = 5$ for our example to illustrate the extreme inflation of unadjusted R^2 that is possible in such a case (.2500 versus .0357). The reader can verify using Equation 10.3 that if k remains 2 and R^2 remains .25, but $N = 100$, the adjusted R^2 will equal .2345, which is only slightly less than the value of unadjusted R^2, .2500.

Keating and Mason (2005) found that R_{adj}^2 is almost always a better estimator than is R^2. However, note that R_{adj}^2 can yield negative values and can greatly underestimate R_{pop}^2 if the number of X variables or number of levels of X variables (in the fixed-effects case) is unwisely chosen by the researcher to be too close to the sample size (Keating & Mason). Such a negative value is apparently generally treated as if it had been 0, although some data analysts object to such treatment of negative estimates of POV_{pop} because of their concern that the practice can lead to an additional positive bias in meta-analytic estimation of POV_{pop}. Small ratios of sample sizes to the number of X variables also render R and R^2 less replicable from study to study.

Consult Keating and Mason (2005) for discussions of additional characteristics of R_{adj}^2. A multiple correlation will be reduced by unreliable measurement of the involved variables. Also, the method of extreme groups may result in inflated estimation of the multiple correlation and its square if inference is to be made to the full range of a variable that has been sliced at its extremes (Preacher et al., 2005).

D. A. Walker (2007) simulated the performances of eight competing published formulas for adjusting R^2 for bias, including Equation 10.3, under some extreme conditions. All of the formulas resulted in biased estimates, including in some cases negative bias that can be expected when overcorrecting for the positive bias of unadjusted R^2. The two formulas that produced the least biased estimates were found generally to be those which replace -1 in the numerator of Equation 10.3 with -4 or -4.15. Tables in Walker can assist researchers in the choice of a method, but further research is needed regarding conditions that were not studied by Walker, including outliers and nonnormality. Consult Shieh (2008) for another recommendation.

Although adjusted and unadjusted R^2 should be reported, the confidence intervals for R^2_{pop} should be based on unadjusted R^2, as explained by Smithson (2003). Algina and Keselman (2008) currently provide freely downloadable IBM SPSS and SAS programs for constructing confidence intervals and estimating needed sample size for estimation and for testing of nil and non-nil null hypotheses regarding R^2_{pop}. The url is http://plaza.ufl.edu/algina/index.programs.html. (Multivariate normality, which is defined later in this chapter, is assumed.) For the case of random-effects predictor variables (i.e., levels of the predictor variable emerge randomly instead of being intentionally selected, "fixed," by the researcher) Kelley (2008) discussed the accuracy-in-parameter-estimation, AIPE, method for planning for needed sample size with the goal of constructing sufficiently narrow exact or approximate confidence intervals for R^2_{pop} with no less than a specified probability of attaining the intended width. Routines for implementing the methods in R software were included. The AIPE method is discussed in Chapter 2.

ADJUSTING R^2 FOR CROSS-VALIDATION

Equation 10.3 improves the estimation of R^2_{pop} by adjusting R^2 for N and k, but it does not adjust R^2 for the sampling variance (error) that is specific to the sample that provided the data. Therefore, Equation 10.3 does not provide a satisfactory estimate of R^2 in future samples from the same population, unless perhaps N/k is very large (St. John & Roth, 1999). In other words, Equation 10.3 often does not provide a good estimate of what is called population *cross-validated R^2*, denoted R^2_{cv}. There are many competing equations for estimating R^2_{cv}, several of which were discussed by Rozeboom (1978) and St. John and Roth. The review by St. John and Roth tentatively indicated that shrinkage in random-effects ordinary least-squares regression can be kept below 10% by (a) using $N > 250$ and $k < 8$ (in which case they recommended that only Equation 10.3 need be reported) or (b) using a nearly unbiased (but complex) estimating equation by Browne, which Rozeboom (1981) simplified and modified to include the case of fixed effects. A review by Cattin (1980) concluded that Rozeboom's (1978, 1981) modification and Browne's original equation provide equivalent results. This modification was also discussed by Cohen and Cohen et al. (2003). (Shieh, 2008, recommended another modification of Browne's formula to reduce bias and sampling variability.) Rozeboom's (1978) equation is

$$R^2_{cv} = 1 - \frac{(1 - R^2)(N + k)}{N - k}. \qquad (10.4)$$

Applying the example that we applied to Equation 10.3 (with the intentionally unwise choice of a small value for N/k for our pedagogical purpose) to Equation 10.4 yields $R_{cv}^2 = 1 - [(1 - .2500)(10 + 2)/(10 - 2)] = .1250$. Again observe the large shrinkage from .2500 to .1250 in this case with very small sample size even when $k = 2$. Again, we recommend the use of the R_{adj}^2 and R_{cv}^2 corrections for their intended purposes under all conditions. The calculations are simple, or R_{adj}^2 can be outputted using common software.

Consult Smithson (2003) regarding the construction of a confidence interval for R_{cv}^2. Algina and Keselman (2008) provided IBM SPSS and SAS programs for constructing confidence intervals and estimating needed sample size for accurate estimation of R_{cv}^2. The url for free downloading of the programs was presented at the end of the previous section. Shieh (2009) discussed the relationship between R^2 and R_{cv}^2, and extended methods for the former to the latter for construction of a confidence interval, power analysis, and estimation of needed sample size.

STATISTICAL SIGNIFICANCE AND CONFIDENCE INTERVALS

To test H_0: $R_{pop}^2 = 0$ against the alternative H_{alt}: $R_{pop}^2 \neq 0$ one can use an F test, where

$$F = \frac{R^2(N - k - 1)}{k(1 - R^2)}, \tag{10.5}$$

and for which the degrees of freedom for the numerator and denominator are $df_n = k$ and $df_d = N - k - 1$, respectively. (Note that R^2 is used in Equation 10.5, not R_{adj}^2.) Software for standard multiple regression will output this test. Observe in Equation 10.5 that the value of F increases as N increases and k decreases. Therefore, again, conducting research with a small value of N/k is unwise because of the resulting lower power of the F test. In our earlier example of the use of Equation 10.2, $R^2 = .4357143$, $N = 1,634$, and $k = 2$, so applying these values to Equation 10.5 yields $F = [.4357143(1634 - 2 - 1)]/2(1 - .4357143) \approx 630$, which far exceeds any practical standard for statistical significance. The very high value of F is not surprising considering the very high $N/k = 1634/2 = 817$.

Tips and Pitfalls
A relatively high value of R^2 does not imply a statistically significant value of F when N/k is small. Also, a statistically significant F does not require a high value of R_{pop}^2, only that $R_{pop}^2 > 0$ and that at least one X variable be statistically significantly related to the Y variable. As k decreases or N increases an ever smaller value of R^2 can render F statistically significant.

Tips and Pitfalls
Methods and tables used for estimating sample sizes needed to test a null hypothesis about R_{pop}^2 should not be used to determine sample sizes needed to estimate R_{pop}^2 because the goals of the two tasks are different. The researcher's sought level of statistical power determines the former whereas the researcher's sought precision of estimation determines the latter. Tables relating sample size and power when

one is testing can be found in Cohen (1988) under the fixed-effects model. Algina and Olejnik (2000) provided a method for determining sample sizes needed to estimate R^2_{pop} accurately for the random-effects model.

Algina's (1999) computer simulations supported the use of the noncentral F distribution for construction of approximate confidence intervals for R^2_{pop} in the fixed-effects model as was discussed by Smithson (2003). IBM SPSS scripts for constructing a noncentral confidence interval for R^2_{pop} under the fixed-effects model are currently provided, courtesy of Michael Smithson, at http://www.anu. edu.au/psychology/people/smithson/details/CIstuff/CI.html. Such a confidence interval can also be constructed using the Power Analysis add-on module for the STATISTICA software package; the free DOS program R2 by Steiger and Fouladi (1992) for random and fixed effects, which is currently available at http://www. statpower.net/page5.html; and R software functions provided by Kelley (2007) for random and fixed effects. Smithson also provided free routines for the fixed-effects case for R, SAS, S-PLUS, and IBM SPSS at http://psychology.anu.edu.au/people/ smithson/details/CIstuff/CI.html. For some values of N, k, and R^2_{pop} it is not possible to calculate a lower limit for a confidence interval for R^2_{pop}, in which case the lower limit is set to 0 (Algina & Keselman, 2008). Algina and Olejnik (2000) provided SAS script for the random-effects case. Also, when sample size is very large some software might output a confidence interval that does not contain the sample R^2.

For construction of the confidence intervals the large-sample method and the method based on the noncentral F distribution assume normality and homoscedasticity. Kelley and Maxwell (2008) discussed methods and software for estimation of needed sample size either to maximize power or minimize the length of a confidence interval for R^2_{pop} for the fixed-effects model.

SEMIPARTIAL CORRELATION

Recall that R estimates the *overall* association between a Y variable and a set of X variables. In a more focused analysis the simplest kind of sample *semipartial R* estimates the association between a given X variable, say X_i, and the Y variable when mathematically removing (i.e., semipartialling) the contribution of correlations between X_i and all other X variables. (The term *part correlation* is often used synonymously with semipartial correlation. Part correlation should not be confused with *partial correlation*, which is discussed in the next section.) The square of the simplest kind of sample semipartial correlation estimates the proportion of the total variance in Y that is accounted for by a given X variable when the contribution of the correlation between this set and another given set of X variables to this variance is removed. Thus, this sample squared semipartial correlation estimates the independent contribution of a given one of all of the X variables to the total variance of Y. In the case of two X variables, X_i and X_j, if one is interested in the semipartial R, which we denote in general R_{sp}, that relates X_i and Y, one form of the equation is

$$R_{spyx_i-x_j} = \frac{r_{yx_i} - r_{yx_j}r_{x_ix_j}}{\left(1 - r^2_{x_ix_j}\right)^{1/2}}, \tag{10.6}$$

where the minus sign in the subscript of the semipartial R indicates that one is removing the contribution of an association between variables X_i and X_j. In this chapter a subscripted minus sign that precedes a subscripted x_j indicates, as a mnemonic aid, that the X_j variable is being statistically excluded semipartially (Equations 10.6 and 10.10) or partially (Equations 10.7 and 10.9). Whereas we use such a minus sign to indicate which X variable is being semipartialed or partialed (next section), some other authors use a subscripted dot for this purpose or parentheses to indicate which X variable is *not* being partialed. Applying to Equation 10.6 the values from our earlier example of predicting adolescents' extent of consumption of hard liquor from their extents of consumption of beer and wine, but this time removing the association between extents of consumption of beer (X_1) and wine (X_2), yields

$$R_{spyx_2 - x_1} = [.604 - (.583)(.619)]/(1 - .619^2)^{1/2} = .3095566 \approx .31.$$

The case of more than two X variables is discussed later in the section on higher-order partial correlations. If assumptions are satisfied, within the kind of approach to regression that we address in this chapter (again, standard regression), the squared semipartial correlation coefficient estimates the amount by which POV_{pop} would be reduced if variance contributed by the semipartialed X_i variable were excluded from the variance contributed by the other independent variable(s). In the present example the squared semipartial correlation equals $.3095566^2 \approx .096$. Therefore, one estimates that POV_{pop} would be reduced by approximately .096 if the correlation between the extents of consumption of beer and wine were excluded from the multiple correlation in which the predicted variable is extent of consumption of hard liquor.

Squared semipartial correlation coefficients are provided by major software, some software labeling them something such as "the unique contribution made by a variable to R^2," as is also discussed later. Consult Table 5.9 on page 147 in Tabachnick and Fidell (2007) for procedures for outputting a squared semipartial correlation coefficient using IBM SPSS and SAS. When there is correlation among the X variables there is some redundant information (i.e., some shared variance) within the set of two or more X variables so the sum of all of the squared semipartial coefficients will be lower than the overall R^2 in many cases.

A semipartial correlation or its square can also be calculated indirectly if output includes partial correlation or its square, to which topics we turn in the next two sections. Recall that in some software outputted semipartial R is labeled simply "part" and note that a common denotation for a semipartial R is sr_i. Again, output from software such as IBM SPSS or SAS provides a correlation matrix containing the simple correlation for each pairing of all variables needed for Equation 10.6, or for an extension of this equation for the case of more than two X variables.

The simple correlations are called *zero-order correlations*. A report of research should include the matrix of all zero-order correlations (e.g., Table 10.1) for better future integration of a current study into the literature because a future primary researcher or meta-analyst may be interested in some variables that a current study does not emphasize. Algina, Moulder, and Moser (2002) discussed determination of sample size for accurate estimation of squared semipartial correlation coefficients. Furr (2004) provided additional discussion of a squared semipartial correlation as an effect size. Aloe and Becker (in press) proposed a new estimator of semipartial correlation.

PARTIAL CORRELATION

A sample *partial R* also estimates the association between a given set of one or more included X variables and the Y variable while removing the contribution of any association between the included X variables and all other X variables. However, the partial R, denoted by some form of R_p in general here, goes further than R_{sp} by also removing the contribution of the association between those excluded X variables and the Y variable. The sample squared partial correlation estimates the proportional contribution of a given set of one or more X variables to the part of the variance of Y that is not accounted for by another given set of one or more fully excluded (i.e., fully partialed) X variables. In the case of two X variables, X_i and X_j, in which a researcher is interested in the partial R between X_i and Y, denoted here $R_{pyx_i - x_j}$, one form of the equation is

$$R_{pyx_i - x_j} = \frac{r_{yx_i} - r_{yx_j} r_{x_i x_j}}{\left[(1 - r_{yx_j}^2)(1 - r_{x_i x_j}^2) \right]^{1/2}}, \tag{10.7}$$

where the minus sign in the subscript of the partial R indicates that one is partialling (again, removing) the contribution of an association between variable X_j and variable Y and the contribution of any association between variable X_j and variable X_i as one seeks the "pure" relationship between Y and X_i. Equation 10.7 can be extended to the case of more than two X variables.

For an example, applying the relevant values from Table 10.1 to Equation 10.7 to obtain the correlation between extent of adolescents' consumption of hard liquor (Y) and wine (X_2) while excluding the correlations between (a) extents of consumption of beer (X_1) and liquor and (b) extents of consumption of beer and wine yields $R_{pyx_2 - x_1} = [.583 - (.604)(.619)][(1 - .604^2)(1 - .619^2)]^{1/2} = .3340936 \approx .334$. This result estimates that the correlation between extents of consumption of hard liquor and wine is approximately .334 if extent of consumption of beer is statistically held constant (i.e., partialed). When extent of consumption of beer is not partialed the correlation between extent of consumption of hard liquor and wine is observed in Table 10.1 to be .583.

Inferences that are based on Equation 10.7 are incorrect unless the relationships are sufficiently linear. Also, if one wants to correct Equation 10.7 for unreliability of measurement of all of the involved variables, each of the five r terms in the equation should be multiplied by its correction for unreliability as is discussed in the section on that topic in Chapter 4.

Observe the similarity between Equations 10.6 and 10.7. The additional term is on the left side of the denominator of Equation 10.6. This term, $1 - r_{yx_j}^2$, is what makes the partial R different from the semipartial R, namely, the removal of the contribution of the correlation between Y and the X_j variable that is not of interest at the moment. Equation 10.7 provides what is known as a *first-order partial correlation coefficient* because it removes the contribution of only one momentarily excluded X variable. Table 5.9 on page 147 of Tabachnick and Fidell (2007) provides procedures for outputting the squared partial R in IBM SPSS and SAS in standard multiple regression. Statistical significance and confidence intervals for R_p^2 are discussed here in later sections. If output does not provide $R_{pyx_i-x_j}$ directly but provides a t or F test for the related β_i coefficient, $R_{pyx_i-x_j}$ can be calculated manually from the outputted value for such a t or F (where $t^2 = F$) using

$$R_{pyx_i-x_j} = \frac{t^2}{(t^2 + N - k - 1)^{1/2}}. \tag{10.8}$$

BETA COEFFICIENTS

A β_i (Greek letter B, beta) *coefficient* is a standardized *beta coefficient* (a weight in a standardized version of a regression equation, i.e., a z score version of Equation 10.1) that is used when units are arbitrary and may vary from study to study (e.g., inches versus centimeters, pounds versus kilograms) and, therefore, raw scores on the independent and dependent variables have been converted for comparability within and between studies so as to have means = 0 and standard deviations = 1, as in z scores (standard scores). In the case of multiple regression, z scores on Y are being predicted from z scores on X variables. Equation 4.20 provides an example of simple standardized regression involving predicting z scores on Y from z scores on just one X variable. A beta coefficient is a function of an appropriate kind of correlation coefficient. In the case of simple standardized regression the beta coefficient equals simply the correlation relating Y and X. Beta coefficients for partial correlation as estimators of effect sizes are discussed next.

Recall from Chapter 4 that a slope, B (or b, i.e., *unstandardized beta*), can estimate an informative effect size when scores are in familiar units in the case of simple linear regression. However, in the case of multiple regression the various X variables may be correlated, thereby providing somewhat redundant information. Therefore, each beta coefficient as an effect size for its X variable has to be based on that X variable's partial correlation with Y to estimate that predictor variable's "pure" contribution. Such beta coefficients are called *partial regression coefficients*. Each such beta coefficient indicates the weight to be given to its X variable when all of the other X variables are included in the regression equation. As an estimator of effect size each partial regression coefficient estimates the change in Y for each unit increase in a given X variable (a slope) when all of the other

X variables are statistically held constant. For further discussion consult Cohen et al. (2003). Furr (2004) discussed squared partial correlation coefficients as contrast effect sizes. Kelley and Maxwell (2008) discussed methods and software for estimating needed sample sizes either for maximizing power or minimizing the width of a confidence interval for beta coefficients for the fixed-effects model. Heteroscedasticity can greatly inflate the rate of Type I error of tests of hypotheses about regression coefficients.

STATISTICAL CONTROL OF UNWANTED EFFECTS

Becker (2005) and Spector and Brannick (2011) discussed serious problems that can arise when researchers partial variables whose effects they want to control statistically in nonexperimental studies. A simple example is controlling for gender by numerically coding the X variable of gender (e.g., female = 1, male = 2) and then partialling gender from the relationship between the Y variable and the other independent variables. To the extent that there are correlations between the X variable that is to be controlled and the predictors and the Y variable, a decision to control for that X variable when perhaps it should not have been controlled can reduce effect sizes and increase the rate of Type II error. (Becker also described how unwise partialling of certain X variables might sometimes increase Type I error.) That is, partialling a variable that actually has an inherent role in a relationship that is of interest converts part of the variance that should be explained to mere error variance. Categories of such possibly unwisely partialed variables are variables that actually have a causal, mediating, or moderating role in the relationship of interest. For example, suppose that a researcher is studying the relationship between scores on an attitude scale about women's rights (Y) and various demographic X variables. In such research partialling gender can greatly decrease the association between Y and the other X variables.

Tips and Pitfalls
Random assignment in experimental research is expected in the long run to control for all variables that are not of interest, whether such variables do or do not need to be controlled. However, in nonexperimental research that relies instead on statistical control the researcher cannot be sure that all variables that need to be controlled have been controlled. Also, partialling can have an effect so great as to reverse the sign of the original correlation coefficient. For example, suppose that for a certain disease there is a slight negative correlation surprisingly found between a measure of the quality of the hospitals that treat the disease and the success of treatment. If the hospitals that have the best reputations also tend to attract the most severely ill patients then partialling (controlling) severity of illness may reverse the correlation coefficient to a positive one. Reports of research that used partialling should report results with and without partialling to facilitate interpretation and integration of the results with earlier results by authors of review articles and meta-analyses.

HIGHER-ORDER CORRELATION COEFFICIENTS

Higher-order correlation coefficients remove the influence of more than one momentarily partialed or semipartialed X variable. For example, a partial R that removes all contributions of two X variables is called a *second-order partial correlation coefficient*. Thus, if one is interested in the partial correlation between X_1 and Y when removing the contributions of the associations between (a) X_2 and X_1, (b) X_3 and X_1, (c) X_2 and Y, and (d) X_3 and Y, the second-order partial R is given by

$$R_{pyx_1-x_2-x_3} = \frac{R_{pyx_1-x_2} - R_{pyx_3-x_2}(R_{px_1x_3-x_2})}{\left[(1-R^2_{pyx_3-x_2})(1-R^2_{px_1x_3-x_2})\right]^{1/2}}. \tag{10.9}$$

For a hypothetical example, suppose that at an English-speaking university Y is the score on a final examination in statistics, X_1 is the score on a mathematics achievement test, X_2 is the score on a test of English, and X_3 is the grade-point average in the students' major field (nonmathematical). Suppose further that the relevant partial correlations to apply to Equation 10.9 are $R_{pyx_1-x_2} = .7939$, $R_{pyx_3-x_2} = .4664$, and $R_{px_1x_3-x_2} = .2791$. Applying these partial correlations to Equation 10.9 to estimate the correlation between scores on the final examination in statistics and scores on the mathematics achievement test, while totally excluding the contributions of the other two variables, yields $R_{pyx_1-x_2-x_3} = [.7939 - (.4664)(.2791)]/[(1 - .4664^2)(1 - .2791^2)]^{1/2} = .7813868 \approx .78$. This second-order partial correlation coefficient estimates the correlation between statistics scores and mathematics scores for those students who would have the same scores in English and the same grade-point average in their major.

Tips and Pitfalls

If one uses Equation 10.9 to find instead the second-order partial correlation between statistics scores (Y) and English scores (X_2) using the current hypothetical results, one will find that this correlation is equal to 0. Such a result should not be interpreted to mean that students' knowledge of English is irrelevant to their statistics scores. The proper interpretation would be that students' knowledge of English is sufficiently reflected by one or both of the other two variables, major grade-point average and mathematics score.

A definitional formula for the semipartial R that involves the relationship between X_i and Y may be written as

$$R_{spyx_i} = (R^2_{yx_1x_2...i...k} - R^2_{yx_1x_2...(-i)...k})^{1/2}. \tag{10.10}$$

The presence of a subscripted minus sign for i associated with the second R^2 indicates that the contributions of correlations between variable X_i and the other X variables are being excluded there, whereas the absence of a subscripted minus sign for i associated with the first R^2 indicates that the contributions of correlations between variable X_i and the other X variables are not being excluded there. (Notation in other writing uses the subscripted parenthetical i without the minus sign that we add for clarity.) Thus, Equation 10.10 estimates the change or difference in a multiple correlation when variable X_i is semipartialed. Squaring both sides of Equation 10.10 yields a definitional equation for an estimate of the difference in the proportion of variance in Y that is accounted for when the variance that is shared between X_i and the other X variables is permitted to contribute to the result (i.e., the first R^2) and when this latter variance is excluded (i.e., by subtracting the second R^2). In other words, the squared semipartial correlation coefficient estimates the proportion of the population POV that is uniquely attributable to X_i.

If one's software program for multiple regression and correlation does not automatically provide a semipartial correlation coefficient or its square, these values can sometimes be found indirectly. For example, suppose that output provides a value of $1 - R^2_{i.12...(-i)...k}$, where the R is the correlation between X_i as the *predicted* variable (for the moment) and a composite of the X variables as predictors from the first to the last (kth) X variable, excluding X_i. (This kind of $1 - R^2$ is an estimator [called *tolerance*, e.g., IBM SPSS and SYSTAT] of the proportion of variance of an X variable that is *not* shared by the other X variables. The greater the correlation between an X variable and the other X variables the closer tolerance will be to 0.) Using the outputted value for tolerance, one can solve the above tolerance formula to obtain the value of the squared multiple correlation between X_i and the other X variables. Then one uses Equation 10.11 to find the semipartial correlation coefficient (corrected from an early printing of Cohen et al., 2003)

$$R_{spyx_i} = \beta_i(1 - R^2_{i.12...(-i)...k})^{1/2}, \tag{10.11}$$

where β_i is the outputted standardized partial regression coefficient involving X_i and Y (i.e., the standardized slope of the straight line that relates X_i and Y).

If software outputs partial R or squared partial R involving Y and X_i then the squared semipartial correlation coefficient can be found using

$$R^2_{spyx_i} = \frac{R^2_{pyx_i}(1 - R^2_{yx_1x_2...k})}{1 - R^2_{pyx_i}}. \tag{10.12}$$

Again, consult Table 5.9 on page 147 in Tabachnik and Fidell (2007) for procedures for finding semipartial R^2 in SAS and IBM SPSS. If output provides semipartial R^2 but not partial R^2, then the latter can be found using

$$R^2_{pyx_i} = \frac{R^2_{spyx_i}}{1 - R^2_{yx_1x_2...(-i)...k}}. \tag{10.13}$$

MORE STATISTICAL SIGNIFICANCE TESTING AND CONFIDENCE INTERVALS

We previously observed when discussing Equation 10.7 in relation to Equation 10.6 that a semipartial R and a partial R have the same numerators. Furthermore, the same test result arises when testing a null hypothesis that a population semipartial

R equals 0 or a null hypothesis that a population partial R equals zero, tested against the alternatives that they are not equal to 0. A t test or F test can be used. The applicable t statistic is

$$t = R^2_{spyx_i} \left(\frac{N-k-1}{1-R^2} \right)^{1/2},$$

(10.14)

for which $df = N - k - 1$.

IBM SPSS provides "Sig F Change" for testing H_0: $R^2_{spyx_i} = 0$ against H_{alt}: $R^2_{spyx_i} \neq 0$. Noncentral confidence intervals for partial R^2 can be constructed by using IBM SPSS scripts that are provided free by Michael Smithson, again at http://www.anu.edu.au/psychology/people/smithson/details/CIstuff/CI.html, or by using the previously cited free Steiger and Fouladi (1992) DOS program R2 that can be downloaded from http://www.statpower.net/page5.html

INCONSISTENT TEST RESULTS FOR OVERALL R^2 AND THE r^2 VALUES

Recall from Chapter 6 that in ANOVA there can be inconsistent results between an omnibus F test and paired comparisons. Similarly, there can be inconsistent results between the F test for the statistical significance of the overall R^2 (Equation 10.5) and the tests involving the contribution of each X variable to the proportion of explained variance (Equation 10.14). Cohen et al. (2003) discussed ways in which such inconsistency can occur. Those authors also argued that unless the F test for overall R^2 attains statistical significance the contribution of no X variable to explained variance should be considered to be statistically significant. This argument results in the *protected test strategy* wherein no test of the kind in Equation 10.14 (i.e., the t test there or equivalent F test) is to be conducted unless the overall F test of Equation 10.5 yields statistical significance. Some may argue against this strategy. However, we merely recommend that one attempt to avoid this problem by limiting the number of X variables to those that are of greatest interest and that can reasonably be assumed not to be correlated with each other, or to be only slightly so. (Reducing the number of X variables to the most important few will also reduce the problem of inflation of family-wise rate of Type I error across the set of significance tests of the semipartial correlation coefficients.)

COLLINEARITY

Correlation among the X variables, called *collinearity* or *multicollinearity*, is diagnosed in major software. Collinearity is particularly a problem for interpretation of results when the X variables are scores on tests that share one or more common elements. For example, suppose that Y is a measure of academic achievement, X_1 is a test of mathematical ability, and X_2 is a test of verbal ability. To the extent that the mathematics test contains word problems there will be correlation between that test and the verbal test. At the other extreme, there should not be collinearity among the X variables in the case of experiments because in that case there is random assignment of participants to levels of an X variable. Indeed, in this experimental case, unlike the case of possible collinearity, one can validly use the labels "predictor variables" and "independent variables" synonymously. In fact, mathematically, the phrase "independent variables" literally means variables that are independent of each other (i.e., not correlated with each other). Therefore, the phrase "collinear independent variables" would be an oxymoron mathematically.

Tips and Pitfalls
If there is sufficient collinearity the relative contributions of the correlated predictors to R^2 cannot be estimated using zero-order correlations, semipartial correlations, or standardized regression weights. Even moderate collinearity can be problematic. If there is enough collinearity it is possible for R^2 to be relatively large even if none of the predictors is found to make a statistically significant contribution. Also, if there is collinearity it is not informative to compare R^2, partial R^2, or slopes among two or more studies.

The changing contribution (weighting) of a given X variable with regard to R^2, depending on the extent to which there are one or more other X variables that correlate with the given X variable, can be illustrated with a rough analogy with cooking. Suppose that a recipe calls for a certain amount of butter and a certain amount of salt. Suppose further that the cook may use a "sweet" (i.e., unsalted) butter or a salted butter. If a salted butter is used there is then some redundancy (analogous to collinearity) between such butter and the separate salt that is to be added. In this case the cook may compensate for the salt in the butter by using less of the separately added salt (analogous to giving less weight to a somewhat redundant predictor variable). A traditional threshold for declaring data to be manifesting a problematic level of multicollinearity is tolerance $\leq.10$. (Tolerance was defined in the previous section.)

SETS OF INCLUDED AND EXCLUDED X VARIABLES

For greater generality we consider the cases in which there is a set of included X variables and a set of X variables that are all partially or entirely excluded when one is estimating proportions of explained variance of the Y variable. We first define some terms and modify some notation for the present cases.

Set A is the set of partially or entirely excluded X variables and a is the number of X variables in that set. Set B is the set of included X variables and b is the number of X variables in that set. The previously provided verbal definitions and interpretations of semipartial and partial correlations apply. As was previously discussed in more detail in the sections on semipartial correlation and partial correlation, when the R^2 that is of interest only excludes the contribution of the relationship between set A and set B the R^2 is a semipartial R^2, and when the R^2 that is of interest excludes the contribution of the relationship between set A and set B and also excludes the relationship between set A and the Y variable the R^2 is a partial R^2.

Notation, Definitions, and Testing

For clarity, using somewhat different notation from what is found in other writing, we begin by denoting and defining the current squared semipartial correlation coefficient:

$$R^2_{spyB-A} = R^2_{yA\&B} - R^2_{yA}. \tag{10.15}$$

After the equal sign in Equation 10.15 the term on the left side represents the R^2 that is the squared correlation between Y and sets A and B of the X variables, and the term on the right side is the squared correlation between Y and only set A of the X variables. Therefore, Equation 10.15 yields an estimate of the increase in proportion of explained variance when set B is included, versus when it is not included (semipartially). This increase (if any) represents the unique contribution that set B makes to the variance in Y and is another example of what is commonly called R^2 change. An F test can be used to test H_0: $R^2_{spyB-A} = 0$ against H_{alt}: $R^2_{spyB-A} \neq 0$. The applicable F statistic is

$$F = \frac{R^2_{spyB-A}(N - a - b - 1)}{b(1 - R^2_{yA\&B})}. \tag{10.16}$$

The degrees of freedom for the numerator and the denominator of the current F statistic are $df_n = b$ and $df_d = N - a - b - 1$, respectively. As is true in the case that was discussed in the previous section, the attained p level of the test of statistical significance of the semipartial R^2 would also apply to a partial R^2 in the current case of sets of X variables. Therefore, a second F test for the other of these two kinds of R^2 when based on the same sets A and B as before would be redundant. The squared partial correlation is equal to the right side of Equation 10.15 divided by $(1 - R^2_{yA})$. The R^2 change and the F test for its statistical significance are outputted by IBM SPSS REGRESSION and SAS REG.

Nonnormality

The interpretation of a partial R or partial R^2 may be very inaccurate under sufficient nonnormality, which causes parameters to be greatly overestimated. Kromrey and Hess (2001) conducted simulations on the effects of nonnormality on confidence intervals for R^2. A kind of normality on which the inferential use of partial R appears to be very dependent is *bivariate conditional normality*, which means that, when an X variable is partialed, at each value of an included X variable there is a bivariate normal distribution of the included X variable and the Y variable. Serlin and Harwell (1993) simulated the performances of various tests of the statistical significance of a partial R^2 that, unlike the F test, do not assume *multivariate normality*, which is the assumption that each variable and each linear combination of the variables is normally distributed. Choosing a method appeared to involve a trade-off between controlling Type I error and maintaining statistical power.

CONFIDENCE INTERVAL FOR SEMIPARTIAL R^2_{pop}

Algina, Keselman, and Penfield (2010) discussed construction of confidence intervals for semipartial R^2_{pop}. Smithson (2003) opined that for many purposes a partial R^2 and another effect size, f^2, provide sufficient information, and confidence intervals can readily be constructed for the population values of these measures instead of semipartial R^2_{pop}. First, information about partial R^2 provides information about semipartial R^2 because the two are related as follows:

$$R^2_{spyA-B} = R^2_{pyA-B}(1 - R^2_{yA}).$$ (10.17)

Second, the effect size f^2 is a function of R^2_{pyA-B} given by

$$f^2 = \frac{R^2_{pyB-A}}{1 - R^2_{pyB-A}}.$$ (10.18)

The f effect-size estimator at hand is closely related to the f that was discussed in Chapter 6 as an effect-size estimator for ANOVA, which is not surprising because of the relationship between ANOVA and multiple regression/correlation, to which we turn our attention in the next section. The f is squared here because multiple regression typically focuses on the proportion of explained variance, and f^2 estimates the ratio of (a) the variance in Y that is explained by a given source (the source in the numerator of Equation 10.18 being set B of the X variables) and (b) the proportion of variance in Y that is residual (i.e., error) variance. The sample f^2 can also be simply calculated using

$$f^2 = \frac{df_n F}{df_d},$$ (10.19)

where df_n and df_d are as previously defined with regard to Equation 10.15. Consult Cohen (1988) and Smithson for further discussions of f^2.

MULTIPLE REGRESSION AND ANOVA: DUMMY CODING

We now consider the case in which there are more than two levels of a qualitative (i.e., categorical) X variable, such as type of treatment or political affiliation, and these are numerically *dummy coded* for the purpose of obtaining the kinds of effect-size information that, as has been discussed in this chapter, develop from conducting a multiple regression analysis in place of an ANOVA. (Results of tests of statistical significance from ANOVA and multiple regression with dummy coding are identical when independent variables are qualitative.) (As in shown later, assigning the value 0 to a control, standard-treatment, or other well-defined reference group with respect to each numerically dummy-coded variable is often [not always] an appropriate first step.) The reference group should not be very small relative to the other groups. As is soon explained, where g is the number of groups, there will be $k = g - 1$ numerically coded dummy variables X_1 through X_k.

Each *dummy-coded variable* represents a dichotomy: membership in a particular group versus non-membership in that group, non-membership meaning membership somewhere in the set of all of the other groups. For example, suppose that there is a control group and Treatment groups 1 through 4. In this case the $k = g - 1 = 5 - 1 = 4$ dummy-coded variables, namely, X_1, X_2, X_3, and X_4 can represent, respectively, the dichotomies Treatment 1 versus the combined groups other than Treatment 1, Treatment 2 versus the combined groups other than Treatment 2, Treatment 3 versus the combined groups other than Treatment 3, and Treatment 4 versus the combined other groups. In this case the dummy codes for participants given Treatments 1, 2, 3, or 4 with regard to dummy-coded variables X_1, X_2, X_3, and X_4, respectively, could be, say, 1, 0, 0, 0; 0, 1, 0, 0; 0, 0, 1, 0; and 0, 0, 0, 1. The dummy codes for participants in the control or reference group then are 0, 0, 0, 0 because its members are in none of the treatment groups.

What has been done here thus far renders what could have resulted in a one-way ANOVA into a form that will be amenable to a forthcoming multiple correlation/regression analysis with its resulting types of correlational and *POV* effect sizes. We began with a qualitative independent variable (type of treatment) with five levels (Treatments 1, 2, 3, 4, and control). The qualitative five-level independent variable was then recast into four quantitative independent variables. One might call these four new quantitative independent variables logically (although linguistically abominably) "Treatment Oneness," "Treatment Twoness," "Treatment Threeness," and "Treatment Fourness." Participants in Treatment 1 "score" 1 on Treatment Oneness, and 0 on each of the other three variables (i.e., dummy codes 1, 0, 0, and 0 for new independent variables X_1, X_2, X_3, and X_4, respectively). Participants in Treatment 2 "score" 0 on Treatment Oneness, 1 on Treatment Twoness, 0 on Treatment Threeness, and 0 on Treatment Threeness. The "scores" for participants in Treatments 3 and 4 are then 0, 0, 1, and 0, and 0, 0, 0, and 1, respectively. No redundant fifth dummy-coded X_5 variable is needed for the control group because the existing dummy-coded variables provide unique coding for a control or other kind of reference group. In the present example the "scoring" for members of the control group is 0, 0, 0, and 0 because the control group does not receive Treatments 1, 2, 3, or 4. The dummy-coding method also applies to research that uses pre-existing X variables such as political affiliation (e.g., Democrat, Republican, Independent, and Other) instead of an experimentally manipulated independent variable (type of treatment).

POINT-BISERIAL *r*S AND THE SIMPLE COEFFICIENTS OF DETERMINATION

In the present example four point-biserial correlation coefficients (r_{yi}) and their squares (i.e., coefficient of determination estimators of POV_{pop}) can be calculated, if they are of interest, by correlating each of the four dichotomous X variables with Y, as was discussed in Chapter 4. For example, the r_{y1}^2 that arises from the point-biserial correlation between X_1 and Y estimates the proportion of the variance in Y that is accounted for by participants getting Treatment 1 versus not getting Treatment 1. One should also report the sign of each r_{yi} to determine the direction of each correlation that is of interest. As is noted in Chapter 4, because the grouping variable (type of treatment) is not a random variable, but is fixed by the researcher, what is called a point-biserial r here is not strictly a point-biserial r but is typically labeled as such by researchers.

When all of the sample sizes are equal the simplest way to find the point-biserial r between Y and membership in either the group that serves as the reference group throughout the analysis (e.g., the control group) or the combined remaining groups, an r that is denoted here r_{yc}, is to use

$$r_{yc} = -\Sigma r_{yi}. \tag{10.20}$$

For the case of unequal sample sizes we first define $P_c = n_c/N$, where N is the total sample size and n_c is the number of participants that are in the control group (or other kind of reference group), so P_c is the proportion of the total sample that is in this group. We also define $P_i = n_1/N$, where each of the k values of n_1 for each of the k dummy-coded variables is the number of participants who are coded 1 on that variable, so that each of the k values of P_i is the proportion of the total N participants who are coded 1 on a given dummy-coded variable. For example, using the codes from the previous paragraph, if there are $N = 100$ total participants and 30 of them are given Treatment 1 (i.e., coded 1 on variable X_1), then $P_i = n_1/N = 30/100 = .30$ for this sample. If 33 participants are given Treatment 2 (i.e., coded 1 on variable X_2), then $P_i = 33/100 = .33$ for this sample, and so on. One can then find r_{yc} in the case of unequal sample sizes using

$$r_{yc} = \frac{\Sigma r_{yi}[P_i(1-P_i)]^{1/2}}{[P_c(1-P_c)]^{1/2}}. \tag{10.21}$$

If an r_{yi} is positive then the mean of the sample that was coded 1 on the given dummy variable is higher than the overall mean of the combined other samples, and if r_{yi} is negative then the mean of the sample that was coded 1 on the dummy-coded variable is the lower of the two means.

Nature of the Sampling

A very important factor in the interpretation of an r_{yi} or its square in nonexperimental research is the manner of sampling or assigning the participants. Recall from Chapter 4 that an r is reduced by restricted range (i.e., reduced variability) of the X or Y variable. It can be shown that the more P_i departs from .5 the lower the standard deviation of a dummy variable. Therefore, the value of each r_{yi} is influenced by the proportion of the total N that is in the sample that is coded 1 for that particular calculation of an r_{yi}. This r_{yi} reaches its maximum when $P_i = .50$. This fact raises the question as to whether the sampling should be representative (e.g., random, if practical) or should a preplanned number of participants be sought for each sample (e.g., equal sample sizes). In experimental research sample sizes will often be equal or nearly so and the population sizes are considered to be equal because the research addresses the question "What would happen if the entire population of interest (e.g., depressives) were given Treatment 1, or all were given Treatment 2, etc.?" However, in nonexperimental research the subpopulations of interest are typically not of equal size (e.g., Democrats, Republicans, Independents, Other), but large enough representative sampling is expected to provide acceptable approximations in the samples of the proportions of the subpopulations that exist in the overall population. Imposing equal sample sizes will not accomplish this proportionality, but, as Cohen et al. (2003) and Pitts and West (2001) discussed, imposing equal sample sizes can sometimes be justified for theoretical purposes and to increase statistical power.

Tips and Pitfalls
Research reports must clearly describe the method of sampling or assigning participants so that meta-analytic or less formal comparisons of effect sizes across a set of related studies not be subject to estimates of effect size that are inconsistent because of different relative proportions of subpopulations in the samples from study to study.

(Finally, an alternative approach that uses *sample weighting* in a form of *weighted ordinary least-squares regression* can be used to estimate the parameters when the relative proportions of subpopulations are known [say, from a census]. However, the method should only be attempted by those with a thorough understanding of it because it is subject to the possibility of erroneous results. In some instances the traditional approach of ordinary least squares will yield estimates of parameters that are comparable to those yielded by the sample-weighting approach. However, the traditional approach may yield more accurate estimates of standard errors because it is possible that one's software, STATA being one exception, uses formulas for standard errors that are not applicable to the sample-weighting approach. Consult Winship and Radbill (1994) for an extensive discussion of the sample-weighting methodology and consult Hahs-Vaughn (2005) for a related discussion. Freels and Sinha (2008) extended R^2 for the case of sample weighting.)

MULTIPLE R AND POV WHEN DUMMY CODING

Equation 10.2 can be used to find the multiple R^2 estimate of POV_{pop} involving Y and the set of X variables or the square root of this R^2, that is, the multiple correlation between Y and this set ($R_{yC_1C_2...k}$). This kind of R^2 estimates the proportion of the variance in Y that is attributable to the fact that participants vary with regard to the original independent variable, namely type of treatment or political affiliation in our current examples. Also, the previously discussed procedures and equations for constructing a confidence interval for this R^2 and testing its statistical significance with an F test (Equation 10.4, with $k = g - 1$ now) apply here. Further, Equation 10.3 can be used to adjust the current R^2 for some of its positive bias, again with $k = g - 1$ now.

For the same set of data, the F found when testing the significance of R^2 using Equation 10.4 has the same value as the F from a traditional ANOVA omnibus test of the null hypothesis that all of the population means are equal. Also, the R^2 and adjusted R^2 involving dummy variables are equivalent to the estimators of

POV_{pop} in ANOVA, namely sample eta squared and epsilon squared, respectively, which were discussed in Chapter 6. Finally, the method of sampling or assigning the participants must be taken into account when interpreting the current R and R^2, with regard to the nature of the population to which these results generalize, in the manner that was discussed in the previous section.

SEMIPARTIAL AND PARTIAL CORRELATION WHEN DUMMY CODING

Much of the previous discussions of squared and unsquared semipartial and partial correlations in this chapter, and testing their statistical significance or constructing confidence intervals for them, are conceptually applicable to the present case of dummy-coded variables. In the case of dummy coding the implication of calculating a squared semipartial correlation coefficient, R^2_{spyi}, is that sample i is in effect being combined for the moment with the control group (or whichever group is used as the reference group throughout the analysis). For example, suppose that dummy variable X_1 is semipartialed. In our present example X_1 represents membership in Treatment 1 versus membership in any of the other groups. Recall that participants receiving Treatment 1 and participants in the control group have both been coded 0, 0 with respect to X_2 and X_3. Therefore, there is for now no distinction made between the Treatment 1 and control samples with regard to X_2 and X_3 when X_1 is semipartially excluded. Subtracting R^2_{spyi} from the overall $R^2_{yX_1X_2X_3X_4}$, yields an estimate of the reduction in the overall POV_{pop} if the sample given Treatment 1 and the control sample were combined.

When dummy coding, each partial correlation, R_{pyi}, reflects only the point-biserial correlation between Y and the dichotomous variable that is represented by sample i versus the control sample (or, more generally, the reference sample). Thus, in our current example R^2_{py1} estimates the proportion of the variance in Y that is attributable to participants being given Treatment 1 versus being in the control group. Again, interpretation of the semipartial and partial correlations, and their squares, when dummy coding is subject to the previously discussed considerations regarding the method of sampling or assigning the participants.

STATISTICAL SIGNIFICANCE AND CIs WHEN DUMMY CODING

Earlier in connection with Equation 10.14 we stated that the same F test or same t test can be used to test a null hypothesis regarding a semipartial correlation and a null hypothesis regarding a partial correlation. Equation 10.14 can also be used to test such null hypotheses when dummy coding has been used. Again the $df = N - k - 1$, but now $k = g - 1$. Equation 10.14, using the current df, can also be considered to provide a test of a null hypothesis about a regression coefficient, $H_0: \beta_i = 0$ or $H_0: B = 0$, where each β_i or B regression coefficient is the slope (standardized or unstandardized) of the regression line relating Y to the ith independent variable in the population. This fact about Equation 10.14 is so because a regression coefficient is a function of a correlation coefficient. (Only if the latter is 0 will the former be 0.)

Smithson (2003) noted that a confidence interval for R^2 will be somewhat narrower if a preplanned equal number of participants is assigned to each level of an independent (X) variable or factor than if participants are assigned randomly so that sample sizes in the design can vary by chance. Smithson called the former and latter approaches the *fixed-score* and *random-score* models, respectively, and he discussed the implications for the use of software to construct the confidence intervals. The distinction is not necessary when testing for the statistical significance of R^2.

WORKED EXAMPLE OF MULTIPLE REGRESSION/CORRELATION

Table 10.2 presents our dummy coding with regard to the data from the experiment that was used for the calculation of effect sizes for one-way ANOVA in Chapter 6. The levels of the independent variable (X) were five methods of presentation of material to be learned and the dependent variable (Y) was the number of items recalled. The study (Wright, 1946; cited in McNemar, 1962) preceded the time when the computing power necessary for rapid multiple regression/correlation analyses was available. (Although the levels of the independent variable consisted of several fixed quantitative values, we treat X as qualitative here for our illustrative purposes of demonstrating analysis of dummy-coded variables and interpreting effect sizes that arise from ANOVA and multiple regression/correlation analyses of the same data. We are not recommending treating quantitative independent variables as categorical as a general practice in actual analyses of data unless the interest is focused on certain fixed levels.) Non-statistical details of this study do not concern us here. In the example $N = 80$, each $n_i = 16$, $g = 5$, and $k = g - 1 = 4$. Sample number 5 is the control group that serves as the reference group that is dummy coded 0, 0, 0, 0.

OUTPUT

For our current purpose and because of constraint on space we discuss only limited output from IBM SPSS REGRESSION here. Raw score means and effect sizes for the data in Table 10.2 from the perspective of ANOVA are presented and discussed in Chapter 6 (data of Table 6.1 there). Identical to what is reported for the current data in Chapter 6 using ANOVA, in the current multiple regression analysis outputted omnibus $F = 24.6$ ($p < .0001$). Therefore, the currently outputted results of $R = .753$, $R^2 = .568$, and adjusted $R^2 = .545$ are statistically significantly different from 0 at the $p < .0001$ level. As should be expected, there is closeness of the current outputted adjusted $R^2 = .545$ and the $\omega^2 = .541$ that are reported from the ANOVA in Chapter 6 for the current data. (It can be proved that epsilon squared [Equation 6.9], which is slightly more biased than omega squared as an estimator of POV_{pop}, is equivalent to adjusted R^2. [The reader

TABLE 10.2
Dummy Coding the Method of
Presentation Where Y Is the Recall Score

Case	Sample	Y	C_1	C_2	C_3	C_4
1	1	5	1	0	0	0
2	1	5	1	0	0	0
3	1	1	1	0	0	0
4	1	5	1	0	0	0
5	1	8	1	0	0	0
6	1	1	1	0	0	0
7	1	2	1	0	0	0
8	1	2	1	0	0	0
9	1	2	1	0	0	0
10	1	8	1	0	0	0
11	1	4	1	0	0	0
12	1	1	1	0	0	0
13	1	3	1	0	0	0
14	1	4	1	0	0	0
15	1	4	1	0	0	0
16	1	2	1	0	0	0
17	2	8	0	1	0	0
18	2	7	0	1	0	0
19	2	4	0	1	0	0
20	2	4	0	1	0	0
21	2	7	0	1	0	0
22	2	7	0	1	0	0
23	2	5	0	1	0	0
24	2	6	0	1	0	0
25	2	8	0	1	0	0
26	2	14	0	1	0	0
27	2	8	0	1	0	0
28	2	5	0	1	0	0
29	2	1	0	1	0	0
30	2	5	0	1	0	0
31	2	8	0	1	0	0
32	2	5	0	1	0	0
33	3	9	0	0	1	0
34	3	3	0	0	1	0
35	3	9	0	0	1	0
36	3	10	0	0	1	0
37	3	5	0	0	1	0
38	3	11	0	0	1	0
39	3	9	0	0	1	0
40	3	6	0	0	1	0

(*continued*)

TABLE 10.2 (continued)
Dummy Coding the Method of
Presentation Where Y Is the Recall Score

Case	Sample	Y	C_1	C_2	C_3	C_4
41	3	7	0	0	1	0
42	3	6	0	0	1	0
43	3	16	0	0	1	0
44	3	12	0	0	1	0
45	3	11	0	0	1	0
46	3	15	0	0	1	0
47	3	13	0	0	1	0
48	3	4	0	0	1	0
49	4	11	0	0	0	1
50	4	12	0	0	0	1
51	4	15	0	0	0	1
52	4	11	0	0	0	1
53	4	10	0	0	0	1
54	4	8	0	0	0	1
55	4	13	0	0	0	1
56	4	13	0	0	0	1
57	4	5	0	0	0	1
58	4	7	0	0	0	1
59	4	11	0	0	0	1
60	4	12	0	0	0	1
61	4	12	0	0	0	1
62	4	9	0	0	0	1
63	4	16	0	0	0	1
64	4	7	0	0	0	1
65	5	17	0	0	0	0
66	5	16	0	0	0	0
67	5	18	0	0	0	0
68	5	11	0	0	0	0
69	5	15	0	0	0	0
70	5	9	0	0	0	0
71	5	18	0	0	0	0
72	5	13	0	0	0	0
73	5	12	0	0	0	0
74	5	15	0	0	0	0
75	5	8	0	0	0	0
76	5	13	0	0	0	0
77	5	7	0	0	0	0
78	5	15	0	0	0	0
79	5	15	0	0	0	0
80	5	13	0	0	0	0

$\overline{Y}_1 = 3.56$, $\overline{Y}_2 = 6.38$, $\overline{Y}_3 = 9.13$, $\overline{Y}_4 = 10.75$, $\overline{Y}_5 = 13.44$.

can demonstrate this fact, within rounding, by calculating epsilon squared by applying the values in Table 6.1 to Equation 6.9.])

Thus, as in Chapter 6, from the output from IBM SPSS one estimates that approximately 54% of the variance of the recall scores is associated with varying the method of presenting the material that is to be learned, *based on the current sample*. However, recall from earlier discussion that the adjusted R^2 does not provide the best estimate of R^2 in *future* samples from the same population unless N/k is very large. A better estimate can be had using Equation 10.4 to calculate cross-validated R^2. Applying the needed values of unadjusted $R^2 = .568$, $N = 80$, and $k = 4$ to Equation 10.4 results in cross-validated $R^2 = .523$. A confidence interval for the cross-validated R^2 can be constructed using IBM SPSS or SAS programs that were provided by Algina and Keselman (2008) at the url that we previously cited.

Output indicates that the point-biserial correlation between the recall scores and the dichotomy of participants not being in the control group versus being in the control group is equal to .231 ($p = .020$, one-tailed). (Note that in the present example what we label generically the control group merely for illustrative purposes was the reference group that was given the treatment that happened to result in the highest mean recall score.) In contrast, the point-biserial correlation between the recall scores and the dichotomy participants not being in the worst-performing group versus being in that worst group is equal to $-.560$ ($p < .0001$, one-tailed). (Of course, in a research report one would not present just the most extreme results.) Such point-biserial correlations were outputted identically as correlations and as zero-order correlations. All semipartial (labeled "part" in output) and partial correlation coefficients, and all standardized and unstandardized regression coefficients, are statistically significantly different from 0 at $p = .016$ or beyond. Consistent with previously discussed facts, all p levels for these statistics are identical for a given one of the X_i variables.

For one illustrative example of the interpretation of a squared semipartial correlation coefficient, consider variable X_1. Recall that by semipartially excluding this dummy-coded variable one is in effect for the moment combining the sample that received Treatment 1, which happened to be the least effective treatment, with the reference ("control") sample, which happened to perform best. The outputted semipartial correlation coefficient involving X_1 is $-.687$, so the squared semipartial r is $(-.687)^2 \approx .472$. Therefore, combining the sample that received Treatment 1 and the reference sample is estimated to reduce the estimated proportion of accounted-for variance by the amount of .472. Recall that the unadjusted, adjusted, and cross-validated estimates of POV_{pop} were .568, .545, and .523 respectively. Subtracting .472 from such estimates, as in Equation 10.15, would leave a much smaller proportion of the variance in recall scores accounted for. This is not surprising because the samples that were combined for illustrative purposes were those that performed best and worst.

Regression Coefficients and the Point-Biserial rs

For an example of interpreting the statistically significant values of the unstandardized regression coefficients, the B_is, consider the outputted $B_1 = -.869$.

(The outputted 95% confidence interval for B_{1pop} is -12.049 to -7.701, which does not include 0.) The statistically significant negative value of B_1 implies that the mean for the sample that received Treatment 1 is statistically significantly lower than the mean for the reference group. The means of raw scores for these two groups are approximately 3.563 and 13.438, respectively.

We previously discussed outputted values of point-biserial correlations between Y and the dichotomy of participants being in a specified group versus not being in that group (i.e., being in *any* other group). Another kind of point-biserial correlation involves the dichotomy of being in a specified group versus being in another *specified* group. Information about the latter point-biserial correlations can be obtained from outputted partial correlations. For example, the outputted statistically significant partial correlation coefficient involving variable X_1 equals $-.722$, which implies that if the only groups were the reference group and Treatment 1 there would be a statistically significant negative point-biserial correlation between the recall scores and the dichotomy of membership in the reference group or Treatment 1. In other words, if membership in the reference group were coded, say, 1 and membership in Treatment 1 were coded numerically more highly, say, 2 (hypothetically there now being only these two groups), the resulting point-biserial correlation between recall scores and this dichotomy numerically coded in such a fashion would be statistically significantly negative. Consistent with our previous interpretation of B_1 and the two reported means, this result also implies that the mean for Treatment 1 is statistically significantly lower than the mean for the reference group. We do not discuss the very favorable collinearity output because the current data arise from an experiment (i.e., random assignment renders X variables independent of each other).

NONLINEAR REGRESSION

Frequently, the relationship between X and Y is nonlinear (e.g., Figure 4.3). For example, the relationship between age (X) and performance on some task (Y) may exhibit a rapid increase in performance throughout childhood, a slower increase in the teenage years, a further slow increase during the third decade, a slow decline some time thereafter, and perhaps a faster decline in the most advanced years of life. In such examples of nonlinear relationships, again, r only estimates the strength of the linear component of the association between X and Y. Also, there may well be a much better fit to the data than the one provided by the linear Equation 4.14.

POLYNOMIAL REGRESSION

One of the approaches for the case of nonlinear regression is *polynomial regression*, in which the regression equation includes, in addition to the predictor X (for the linear component), predictor terms such as X^2 (pure *quadratic component* when the role of X to the first power is excluded), X^3 (pure *cubic component* when the roles of X and X^2 are excluded), and so forth. In the present case the exponent to which X is raised is called its *order*. The terms with exponents that are smaller than the highest exponent in the equation are called the *lower-order terms*. In order for lower-order terms to be interpreted the predictor variable X must have a true 0, such as age, dosage, or time, not an arbitrary 0, such as scores on tests of personality, aptitude, or achievement. When the X variable does not have a true 0 the X variable should be *centered*. *Centering* involves subtracting the mean of the X values from each X value (i.e., converting X values to deviation scores). Labeling the deviation scores x, the mean of x conveniently becomes 0 and the quadratic and cubic terms then become x^2 and x^3, respectively. Centering also eliminates harmful extreme collinearity.

Earlier R and R^2 were discussed as effect sizes that relate multiple predictors (in the present case $X_1 = X$, $X_2 = X^2$, and $X_3 = X^3$) to Y. The earlier conceptualizations and methods apply to the present case. A common sequential procedure for polynomial regression outputs R^2 in sequence: (a) when only X is included in the regression equation, (b) when only X and X^2 are included, and (c) when X, X^2, and X^3 are included. Typically, in such output R^2 will be found to be greater, sometimes only slightly so, the more of the powers of X that are included, but adding powers of X beyond X^3 to the regression equation usually adds little or nothing to the predictability of Y or to the magnitude of R^2.

When there are powers of X in addition to X to the first power in the regression equation R is not the correlation between X and Y. In this case R is interpreted as the correlation between Y and a composite of the optimally weighted included powers of X (e.g., X, X^2, X^3). The powers of X are optimally weighted by B coefficients for the purpose of best fitting the curve to the data and thereby most accurately predicting Y and maximizing R^2. (Recall from Chapter 4 that in the bivariate linear case the optimal weighting of X is given by the slope of the regression line, $r(s_y/s_x)$.) The current R can also be interpreted as the correlation between Y and Y'.

Equation 10.16 provides an F for testing the statistical significance of the increase in R^2 when a higher-order term is added to a regression equation that had included only terms of lower order. For example, when the highest order term is X^3, consistent with our earlier discussion of the three relevant outputted values of R^2 in the present case, one typically conducts multiple F tests for the situations in which only X is included, only X and X^2 are included, and X, X^2, and X^3 are included. If centering was required because X does not have a true 0, replace X, X^2, and X^3 with x, x^2, and x^3, respectively, in the previous sentence. Cohen et al. (2003) discussed the advantages and limitations of the *build-up procedure* that was just described and a reversal of the described sequence in which the three versions of R^2 are considered. Such a backward procedure is called a *tear-down procedure*.

Tips and Pitfalls

A sufficient change in effect size (i.e., change in R^2) between two adjacent polynomial equations is one of several criteria that one may use to decide which is the highest order of the predictor variable (e.g., quadratic or cubic) that one will retain in the regression equation. For this purpose one can inspect the outputted semi-partial R^2 or, if such output is not available, use Equation 10.17 for the semipartial R^2, to determine if this value at least attains a predetermined magnitude that would be of interest. Alternatively, Cohen et al. (2003) suggested using the change in adjusted R^2 from one polynomial equation to the adjacent polynomial equation (i.e., applying Equation 10.3 to each of the two regression equations), instead of the change in the unadjusted R^2, for the criterion for deciding which is the highest order of X that is sufficient for inclusion in the regression equation. Those authors also discussed steps to reduce the instability of polynomial equations caused by outliers, testing statistical significance and constructing confidence intervals for regression coefficients, and related topics.

HIERARCHICAL LINEAR MODELING (MULTILEVEL MODELING)

Examples of *multilevel* or *hierarchical data* include data on students (or workers or patients) at *level 1*, nested within classrooms (or job sites or clinics), a possible *level 2*, that are within schools (or companies or multisite hospital corporations), a possible *level 3*, that are within school districts (or industries or states), a possible *level 4*. Thus, the first *level* of this hierarchy of variables is often persons. Often there are only two levels, and the interest is in relating a dependent variable to predictor variables at the level of the persons and at the level of the groups. The second level is also often times or occasions, as in *longitudinal research*. Unlike single-level regression, multilevel modeling is intended to uncover relationships between variables at different levels. Volume 10, number 4, 2007, of the journal *Organizational Research Methods* was a special issue on multilevel methods and statistical analysis.

Schonfeld and Rindskopf (2007) discussed the application of multilevel modeling to organizational research. In this approach the size of the effect of an earlier working condition on a later outcome can be estimated. Kreft and Deleeuw (1998) discussed the conditions that must be satisfied for uncomplicated estimation of POV_{pop} in multilevel modeling. Roberts and Monaco (2006) provided an overview of effect sizes for multilevel modeling and proposed three new measures of overall POV_{pop} involving all of the X variables. Software for hierarchical linear modeling includes HLMv6.03 (Raudenbush, Bryk, Cheong, & Congdon, 2004). Tabachnick and Fidell (2007) compared the features of SAS MIXED, IBM SPSS MIXED, HLM, and MLwiN software for multilevel linear modeling. Currently, there is a LISTSERV for those interested in multilevel modeling at http://www.jiscmail.ac.uk/lists/multilevel.html

Again, in studies that do not use random assignment the word "effect" does not imply causality. However, hierarchical linear modeling can be applied to *cluster-randomized designs* for multisite studies, wherein sets of sites, such as schools or clinics, are randomly assigned to treatments. Hedges (2011) discussed five standardized-difference effect sizes, involving five different standardizers, for such designs. Estimators of these effect sizes were also presented together with their sampling distributions and standard errors.

O'Connell and Doucette (2007) discussed the application of cumulative odds in multilevel modeling for longitudinal studies with ordinal independent variables.

Cumulative odds is defined in Chapter 9. Agresti (2010) discussed multilevel modeling with ordinal categorical variables. Software for multilevel modeling with ordinal data includes MLwiN (Plewis, 2002) and the previously cited HLMv6.03 (Raudenbush et al., 2004).

PATH ANALYSIS AND STRUCTURAL EQUATION MODELING

PATH ANALYSIS

An approach to evidence of, but not proof of, causality is *path analysis*, which tests a theory about sequential causal relationships among multiple *observed variables* by searching for consistencies between their correlations and their theorized causal relationships. "Sequential causal relationships" means that each causal connection is in one direction. For an example of a causal connection that is not necessarily unidirectional, the relationship between parental emotional health and the emotional health and behavior of their children would not necessarily be causally connected in only one direction. It is possible that being raised by an emotionally disturbed parent can cause impairment of a child's emotional health, and it is also simultaneously possible that raising an emotionally disturbed child can impair the parent's emotional health. Traditionally the previously discussed regression coefficients have been used to estimate the effect sizes in terms of the strength of connections between the variables.

STRUCTURAL EQUATION MODELING

Path analysis is related to a very general family of statistical methods for large samples (often $N \geq 200$) called *structural equation modeling* (*SEM*). SEM attempts to explore relationships among multiple observed variables and relationships among the continuous latent variables that might underlie the observed variables. The purpose is often to discover if the relationships are a good fit with the causal connections that have been theorized for the variables. When the fit is good, the evidence for the theorized causal connections is convincing when the research is experimental and the results are replicated by additional experiments. In SEM the same variables can be independent variables in some equations that relate variables and dependent variables in other equations that relate variables. For example, parental emotional health scores may serve as an independent variable that is theorized to relate to the dependent variable of children's emotional health scores, which, in turn, may be theorized to be an independent variable that is related to the dependent variable of behavioral problems in teenagers. The measure of relationship in SEM was traditionally the correlation coefficient, but now it is often the covariance, $r_{xy}s_xs_y$, which is discussed in another form in Chapter 4. Consult Bentler's (2007) discussion of the use of correlations versus covariances in SEM.

Constraint on length prevents a detailed account of SEM and its effect sizes here. Differences between group means on observed variables and differences between means on supposed latent variables can be analyzed, but often the effect sizes (strengths of association) of interest in SEM are analogous to R^2. The typical purpose is to estimate the proportion of variance in the dependent variables that is attributable to variability in the independent variables and to estimate the relative contributions of the independent variables to the accounted-for variance in the dependent variables. For this purpose traditional SEM involves continuous variables.

When the observed variables are categorical SEM can proceed with different kinds of correlational analyses and correlational effect sizes. In the case of observed dichotomous variables that are assumed to have bivariate normally distributed variables underlying them, the tetrachoric correlation that is discussed in Chapter 4 is used.

One approach to categorical variables in SEM is to dummy code them as was previously discussed and then proceed with the usual analyses. In the case of relating two ordinal variables it is common to use the *polychoric correlation* (Chapter 9), which assumes bivariate normality of the latent variables supposedly underlying the two observed variables. Then, based on normality and the proportion of participants who fall into each ordinal category z scores are calculated, and these z scores become the scores for each participant. For a very simple example, if, with respect to the ordinal scale Agree strongly, Agree, Disagree, Disagree Strongly, .025 of the participants respond "Disagree Strongly," such respondents are assigned a z score of +1.96 because .025 of the area under the normal curve lies beyond $z = +1.96$.

In the case of relating a continuous and an ordinal variable the *polyserial correlation* is used. The polyserial correlation assumes bivariate normality for the variables. Kraemer (2006) discussed the polychoric and polyserial correlations. Preacher (2006) proposed a method for estimating Pearson, semipartial, and partial correlation coefficients in SEM. He also demonstrated testing for the equality of such coefficients across multiple groups in SEM with any number of variables partialed. For such testing Preacher also provided software syntax for LISREL. Based on simulations Cheung (2009) argued for the application of SEM when constructing approximate confidence intervals for the kinds of correlational effect sizes that are discussed in this book.

Hunter and Schmidt (2004) urged correcting correlations for attenuation (reduction) by unreliability and all other artifacts in multivariate research and cited examples. Thompson (2002) provided a concise "Ten Commandments" of SEM. Ullman's chapter on SEM in Tabachnick and Fiddel (2007) discussed estimation of two POV_{pop} effect sizes and compared features of four statistical programs for SEM: AMOS, EQS, LISREL, and SAS CALIS. Kline (2011) argues that SEM provides better estimates of effect sizes for observed variables than do ANOVA and multiple regression, both of which can be subsumed under SEM in a family of statistical methods (e.g., Maxwell and Delaney, 2004). Methodological developments in SEM are reported in *Structural Equation Modeling: A Multidisciplinary Journal*. Also consult SEMNET at www2.gsu.edu/~mkteer/semnet.html.

EFFECT SIZE FOR ORDINAL MULTIPLE REGRESSION

Long (2005) recommended that his Q^2 statistic be used, in place of the traditional F statistic that is used in the least-squares approach, for testing the omnibus null hypothesis in multiple regression when variables are ordinal. Long's method, which is called *dominance multiple regression*, relates to our discussions of the probability of superiority effect size and Cliff's dominance effect size in Chapter 5. The method uses as an estimator of an ordinal measure of effect size *Cliff's phi*, which reflects, across all of the X variables, the overall extent to which the order of Y values corresponds to the order of the X values. Cliff's phi (not related to the phi coefficient that was discussed in Chapters 4 and 8) is an extension of Kendall's tau to the case of multiple X variables. In the univariate case of an ordinal Y variable and one ordinal X variable tau is the difference between (a) the probability that two randomly sampled participants have the same relative position on X and Y and (b) the probability that their relative positions are different on X and Y. Cliff's phi serves as an estimator of an omnibus ordinal effect size as R serves as an estimator of omnibus effect size in least-squares regression. Based on his simulations, Long reported that, among other advantages of Q^2, the power of the Q^2 test can be greater than the power of the F test under extreme nonnormality.

ADDITIONAL TOPICS AND READING

Maxwell (2000) discussed traditional criteria for choosing sample sizes for multiple regression analysis, and he discussed various other criteria that are based on the kinds of effect size that are of interest to the researcher. Wilcox (2004, 2005a, 2007c, 2009b) addressed many topics in robust multiple regression. We cited free access to Wilcox's R code in Chapters 1 and 2.

The best methods of robust regression should yield estimates that are (a) unbiased; (b) unaffected by outliers, or skewed or heteroscedastic conditional distributions; (c) consistent; and (d) efficient even under normality. (We define *consistent estimator* in Chapter 5. Roughly, an *efficient estimator* is one with relatively low sampling variability.) Robust regression can be implemented using a variety of software, including R, SAS, S-Plus, and STATA. Also, recall from Chapter 4 that an outlier that has a distorting influence on a correlation coefficient is called a bad leverage point. Diagnoses of leverage in multiple regression can be undertaken in major software programs such as SAS REG, IBM SPSS REGRESSION, and SYSTAT REGRESS.

Renaud and Victoria-Feser (2010) proposed a robust estimator of population coefficient of determination that makes no assumptions about the distributions of X variables (or the marginal distribution of a Y variable), is consistent, is efficient under normality, and in simulations compares favorably with other robust estimators even for small N. Wilcox (2005a) discussed and provided R and S-Plus functions for *nonparametric regression*, which is regression in which there is no assumption of a particular form of function (linear, curvilinear) relating Y to the X variables.

Consult Cohen et al. (2003) and Maxwell and Delaney (2004) for discussions of analysis of data from factorial designs within multiple regression. Consult Myers and Well (2003) for a concise discussion of regression with repeated measures. Furr (2004) discussed the relationship between multiple regression analysis and correlational contrast effect sizes.

SUPPRESSOR VARIABLES

It would be beyond the scope of this book to provide a detailed discussion of the topic of *suppression*, in which a *suppressor variable* is often conceptualized as an X variable whose presence in a regression equation increases the overall R^2 by excluding (suppressing) the portion of variance in one or more of the other X variables that is not shared with the Y variable. The concept of suppression arose from the observation that a multiple correlation, $R_{yx_1x_2}$, can be higher than the simple correlation, r_{yx_1}, if X_2 correlates with X_1 but X_2 does not correlate with Y. For example, suppose that one wants to predict performance (Y) on a job that involves only motor skills using the score on a written test (X_1) that is administered to job applicants. Although verbal ability (X_2) does not correlate with such a Y, verbal ability is correlated with X_1. If X_2 is not included in the prediction equation the irrelevant contribution it makes to the variance of the scores on X_1 that causes a decrease in r_{yx_1} will not be taken into account (removed). However, if X_2 is included in the prediction equation the irrelevant variance it contributes to X_1 will be removed and such removal will increase (no longer suppress) the correlation of X_1 with Y. In this case $R_{yx_1x_2} > r_{yx_1}$. A suppressor variable is also called a *third variable*. A suppressor variable can even reduce r_{yx_1} to zero. Also, because the absence of correlation between two variables may be attributable to the presence of such a third variable, it is not correct to believe that the absence of correlation always indicates the absence of causation. Consult Shieh (2006) for discussion of different approaches to suppression.

INTERACTION

Often researchers are interested in the effect of a variable (a *moderator variable*) on the relationship between two other variables, an *interaction*. In *moderated multiple regression* a supposed moderator variable is placed in a regression equation together with a predictor variable and the product of these two variables. An interaction is inferred when that product is found to be statistically significant.

Tips and Pitfalls
It is inadvisable to standardize the X variables (i.e., to convert to z_X scores) in moderated multiple regression. Doing so can result in incorrect values for coefficients, slopes, and limits of confidence intervals. For further discussion consult, courtesy of Kristopher J. Preacher, http://people.ku.edu/~preacher/interact/interactions.htm. McGrath (2008) discussed the typically very small and difficult to detect, but possibly important, proportion of variance that is attributable to a moderator term (interaction term).

For the case in which a moderator variable is originally categorical, Aguinis and Pierce (2006) discussed and provided a computer program for calculating an effect size for such a variable. The program is freely available at http://carbon.cudenver.edu/~haguinis/mmr/fsquared. The effect size is a more robust version of the f^2 in Equation 10.18. An f^2 in the present case is the ratio of (a) the explained variance in the dependent variable that is accounted for by variance of the moderator variable and (b) the unexplained variance in the dependent variable.

EFFECT SIZES FOR LOGISTIC REGRESSION

Logistic regression can be used to relate a truly categorical or ordinal categorical dependent variable to a set of predictor variables of any type of scale or mixture of types of scale. Borooah (2002), Huynh (2002), Liao and McGee (2003), and Menard (2000) discussed analogs of R^2 within logistic regression for the case of an ordinal dependent variable. (Analogs of R^2 in logistic regression do not estimate proportion of variance accounted for as does R^2 in ordinary least-squares regression.) O'Connell (2006) and Tabachnick and Fidell (2007) discussed the use of output from IBM SPSS and SAS to estimate effect sizes in logistic regression. Lacy (2006) proposed an R^2 analog for ordinal dependent variables that compared favorably to other ordinal R^2 analogs in simulations.

Allen and Le (2008) proposed an overall odds ratio for logistic regression that, unlike analogs of R^2, is interpretable on the same scale as the effect sizes for individual predictor variables and is insensitive to base rates. (Sensitivity to base rates is discussed in Chapter 4.) Logistic regression has been proposed for adjusting the estimated odds ratio and relative risk for confounding variables (Li, 2006).

DATA THAT ARE COUNTS AND POISSON REGRESSION

Often in a regression analysis the dependent variable is a count. Examples of counts include numbers of days in a therapy, alcoholic drinks consumed, children in a family, and crimes committed. A common analysis of such data uses *Poisson regression*, an assumption of which is that the mean and variance of the distribution of the dependent variable are equal, which is a characteristic of a *Poisson distribution*.

MIXED-MODEL REGRESSION

Sometimes in linear regression the X variables are a mixture of random-effects and fixed-effects variables (defined in Chapter 6), resulting in *mixed-model regression*. Several versions of R^2 have been proposed to evaluate the contributions of the fixed X variables to the mixed model (Orelien & Edwards, 2007).

SUMMARY

Correlational and proportion-of-variance-explained effect sizes were discussed in the context of standard regression for the case in which there is one continuous dependent variable, Y, and more than one independent variable, the Xs.

The sample multiple correlation coefficient, R, estimates the overall association in the population between Y and an optimally weighted linear combination of the X variables. The sample multiple coefficient of determination, R^2, estimates the proportion of variance in the dependent variable that is explained by variance in the independent variables. The sample R^2 is a positively biased (i.e., tending to overestimate) estimator of R^2_{pop}, so in the fixed-effects model this bias should be reduced using what is called an adjusted or shrunken estimator. To provide a satisfactory estimate of R^2 in future samples from the same population, R^2 should be corrected using an equation for what is called the cross-validated R^2. Whether estimating R^2_{pop} or population cross-validated R^2, confidence intervals should be constructed. Collinearity (correlation among the X variables) in nonexperimental research can be problematic for interpretation of R^2.

For a more focused effect size, the sample semipartial R estimates the association between a given X variable and the Y variable while removing the contribution of association between that X variable and all of the other X variables. Semipartial R^2 estimates the proportion of the total variance in Y that is accounted for by a given set of one or more X variables when the contribution of the correlation between this set and another given set of one or more X variables to this total variance is statistically removed (i.e., semipartialed). A sample partial R goes further than a sample semipartial R by also removing the contribution of the association between those other X variables and the Y variable. The sample partial R^2 estimates the population proportional contribution of a given set of one or more X variables to the part of the variance of Y that is not accounted for by another set of one or more fully excluded (i.e., fully partialed) X variables. All of the variables can be corrected for unreliability. Sample size needed to construct a satisfactory confidence interval for the change in R^2_{pop} that is attributable to inclusion of a given X variable increases the more of the other X variables that are included.

Partialling variables to control their effects statistically in nonexperimental research requires caution. Controlling (partialling) for an X variable that should not be controlled may reduce effect sizes. Possibly unwisely partialed variables include variables that actually have a causal, mediating, or moderating role in a relationship of interest. Partialling can have an effect so great as to reverse the sign of a correlation coefficient. Complete reporting and discussion of all partialling are necessary in research reports. In some cases researchers should consider reporting and interpreting results with and without partialling.

Numerically dummy coding when there are two or more levels of a categorical independent variable permits ready estimation of correlational effect sizes by enabling conduct of a multiple regression analysis in place of an ANOVA. Numerically dummy-coding membership in a certain group versus membership in one of the set of other groups permits calculation of point-biserial correlations between group memberships and the dependent variable. For example, a squared point-biserial r between Y and membership in the group receiving Treatment 1 versus non-membership in that group estimates the population proportion of variance in Y that is accounted for by participants getting Treatment 1 versus not getting Treatment 1. Also, dummy coding permits estimation of population R, overall POV, semipartial Rs, and partial Rs.

When there are outliers, skew, or heteroscedasticity methods of robust regression are applicable. When the relationship between X and Y in simple regression is nonlinear the usual sample r and r^2 underestimate effect sizes in the population. A common approach to this problem is a form of multiple regression known as polynomial regression, in which a population R and R^2 can be appropriately estimated and interpreted. Nonparametric regression also accommodates nonlinearity.

Hierarchical linear modeling, also known as multilevel modeling, involves levels (layers) of participants and their subgroups and groups as the sources of data. For example, such research may target data on students nested within classrooms that are within schools that are within school districts that are within states, although often there are only two levels. A goal is to discover relationships between variables at the different levels. The method is also applicable to estimation of effect sizes for longitudinal or growth data, as was briefly discussed in Chapter 3. Caution must be taken when interpreting proportion of variance explained in multilevel modeling.

A path analysis tests a theory about the sequential causal relationships among observed variables, the strength of these relationships constituting the traditional effect sizes. In SEM, which can explore relationships among multiple observed variables and among possibly latent variables, differences between supposed latent variable means can be estimated, but often the effect sizes of interest are analogous to R^2. When variables are ordinal an alternative ordinal regression approach is applicable, including estimation of an ordinal effect size. When dependent variables are truly categorical or ordinal, logistic regression is applicable. In the ordinal case analogs of R^2 are available, but they are not estimating the same kind of proportion-of-variance-explained effect size as in traditional multiple regression. An overall odds ratio is also applicable. There are versions of R^2 available for mixed-model regression in which the X variables are a mixture of fixed-effects and random-effects variables.

What are called suppressor variables can influence the magnitudes of estimates of effect size. Moderator variables can also be important, but it may be difficult to detect the proportion of variance that is attributable to them. When a moderator variable is truly categorical a more robust version of Equation 10.18 provides an estimate of effect size.

QUESTIONS

10.1 Define (a) *least-squares regression*, (b) *multiple regression*, (c) *multiple coefficient of determination*, (d) *adjusted* or *shrunken estimator*, (e) *zero-order correlation*, (f) *first-order partial correlation*, (g) *higher-order correlation*, (h) *partial regression coefficient*, (i) *tolerance*, (j) *protected test*, (k) R^2 *change*, (l) *collinearity*, (m) *multivariate normality*, (n) *dummy coding*, (o) *polynomial regression*, (p) *hierarchical data*, (q) *robust regression*, (r) *efficient estimator*, (s) *suppressor variable*, (t) *path analysis* (briefly), (u) *structural equation modeling* (briefly).

10.2 Calculate $R^2_{yx_1x_2}$ if $r_{yx_1} = .5, r_{yx_2} = .6$, and $r_{x_1x_2} = .4$.

10.3 What is the purpose of adjusting R^2 for cross-validation?

10.4 Distinguish between *semipartial* and *partial* Rs (a) when not dummy coding and (b) when dummy coding.

10.5 What is the purpose of the squared semipartial R?

10.6 Discuss how the research hypothesis should determine whether or not a given variable should be partialed.

10.7 Applying the hypothetical results given in the text to Equation 10.9, confirm that the second-order partial correlation between statistics scores (Y) and English scores (X) is 0.

10.8 With Question 10.1, part 1, in mind give a literal definition of *independent variable*.

10.9 What dichotomy does a dummy-coded variable represent?

10.10 How does a point-biserial r arise from a dummy-coded variable?

10.11 What is the relationship between the F of Equation 10.4 and the omnibus F in ANOVA?

10.12 What is the relationship between R^2 involving dummy variables and the eta squared of Chapter 6?

10.13 Calculate (a) adjusted R^2 when $R^2 = .25$, $k = 2$, and $N = 100$, and explain why adjusted R^2 is only slightly less than R^2 in this case; (b) adjusted R^2 and cross-validated R^2 when $R^2 = .25$, $k = 2$, and $N = 251$, and explain why the results are not very different in this case; (c) adjusted R^2 and cross-validated R^2 when $R^2 = .25$, $k = 7$, and $N = 251$, and explain any difference between these results and those in part (b).

11 Effect Sizes for Analysis of Covariance

INTRODUCTION

This chapter discusses estimation of effect sizes in an *analysis of covariance* (ANCOVA), which is a common modification of ANOVA that attempts to reduce within-group variability and the effects of confounding variables on the group means that are being compared. We assume that some readers have only vague familiarity with the elements of ANCOVA so we provide a brief review before proceeding with discussions of effect sizes. Fixed-effects for the independent variable applies in this chapter. We begin with the one-way between-groups case and proceed to other designs.

INCREASING POWER AND NARROWING CONFIDENCE INTERVALS

One of the two main purposes of ANCOVA, especially in experimental studies, is to attain more powerful ANOVA F tests and narrower confidence intervals for differences between means by reducing within-group variability in the data that is attributable to one or more extraneous variables (*covariates*) that are correlated with the dependent variable. A covariate is a variable that is not of direct interest in a particular study but is still measured because the researcher believes that it influences the dependent variable and, therefore, that it should be taken into account in the analysis. For example, in an experiment that compares methods of teaching statistics one may want to eliminate the contribution made to within-group variability by differences in previous coursework in mathematics. In another example one may want to pretest the participants with respect to the dependent variable and then use ANCOVA to adjust for the effect of pretest score difference between the groups. (Liu, Lu, Mogg, Mallick, & Mehrotra, 2009, reported evidence of superiority of a longitudinal analysis to ANCOVA for this purpose. Longitudinal analysis [growth modeling] is discussed in Chapters 3 and 4 in the present book.)

The stronger the correlation between a covariate and the dependent variable the more ANCOVA reduces within-group variability. Reliable measurement of the covariate scores and the dependent variable scores helps in this regard, and so helps maintain statistical power. An unreliably measured covariate can bias a treatment effect in nonexperimental designs.

Tips and Pitfalls

The weaker the correlation between a covariate and the dependent variable the less the power advantage of ANCOVA over ANOVA. At some point of insufficient correlation between a covariate and the dependent variable, ANCOVA becomes less powerful than ANOVA. The use of multiple covariates that are too weakly related to the dependent variable can place ANCOVA into an even greater power disadvantage with regard to ANOVA, but the weaker the relationship between covariates the better. When there is a strong relationship between or among covariates much of the error variance that can be reduced by any one of the covariates is already reduced by use of the other covariate(s), so each covariate is not making much of a unique contribution to reduction of error variance. Keppel and Wickens (2004) went so far as to recommend that more than two covariates never be used. However, Stevens (2009) argued for the use of two or three covariates when sample sizes are small, and he discussed Huitema's formula for limiting the number of covariates based on the number of groups and total sample size. When there is more than one covariate their contribution to reduction of error variance increases with increase in their multiple correlation with the dependent variable.

ANCOVA IN NONEXPERIMENTAL RESEARCH

Consider a variable, say X_2, that is related to the dependent variable, Y (X_2 is a covariate), and also related to the independent variable, say X_1. If such an X_2 is intrinsically related to X_1 (e.g., height and gender) then, depending on the purpose of the research, X_2 may be considered to be a mediating variable and analyzed as such, including estimation of its effect size as is discussed in Chapters 4 and 10. However, if the X_2 is related to X_1, but not intrinsically (e.g., gender and political affiliation) and X_2 has no role in the purpose of the research, then X_2 is an undesirable confounding variable. One can attempt to control the effect of a confounding variable by partialling it (Chapter 10) or by adjusting means in ANCOVA. An uncontrolled confounding variable can render an estimate of a truly small or zero effect size involving X_1 and Y misleading larger. If X_2 is a continuous variable the existence of a relationship between X_2 and the categorical X_1 can be tested using an ANOVA F test, with X_2 in this analysis being treated as the dependent variable and X_1 as the independent variable. If X_2 is a categorical variable the existence of a relationship between X_2 and the also categorical X_1 can be tested using chi square. However, one cannot be confident that tests of statistical significance will be powerful enough to detect a degree of confounding that would importantly change the main results.

Tips and Pitfalls
Confounding variables are much more likely to be found in nonexperimental research, which uses intact (preexisting) groups, than in research that randomly assigns participants (experiments). Random assignment is expected, especially the larger the samples, to distribute values of an otherwise confounding variable about equally in the samples (or at least not *systematically* differently as in confounding). If one has an opportunity to conduct a study using random assignment one should not instead opt to use a nonexperimental study with the expectation that an ANCOVA will fully compensate for confounding variables. There is a history of literature arguing against the use of ANCOVA in nonexperimental studies (e.g., Sawilowsky, 2007b). Later sections of this chapter discuss how ANCOVA

attempts to adjust for confounding variables and the difficulty in interpreting ANCOVA in nonexperimental studies.

Choosing Covariates

Covariates ordinarily must be chosen *before* data are analyzed. Covariates should not be selected as "finalists" from a larger set of contending covariates on the basis of the results of a preliminary analysis of the data at hand. It is sensible to select covariates on the basis of results from earlier studies that sampled from similar populations or on the basis of plausible reasoning if there are no relevant prior studies.

When a covariate is selected after a treatment that might have had an effect on the covariate, Keppel and Wickens (2004) recommended a multivariate approach. For further discussion of choice of covariates consult Shadish, Cook, and Campbell (2002).

Adjustment for Preexisting Differences

ANCOVA also adjusts posttest group means on the dependent variable based on the extent of preexisting differences between groups on one or more covariates (confounding). The purpose of the adjustment is to estimate what the differences between group means would be if the groups had the same means on the covariates. Because of random assignment to groups, in experimental studies there should be less difference between *adjusted and unadjusted means* the larger the size of the groups. In nonexperimental studies such adjustment can have a greater impact on the ANCOVA results than does the reduction of within-group variance. In nonexperimental studies ANCOVA is used in an attempt to control for the biasing effects of relevant preexisting differences between groups by statistical adjustment, whereas experimental studies attempt such control mostly by random assignment to groups. However, even with very carefully chosen covariates ANCOVA cannot be expected to render groups perfectly matched with respect to extraneous variables. Also, unreliable measurement of the covariate can have more serious consequences for nonexperimental than for experimental applications of ANCOVA. Consult Culpepper and Aguinis (2011) for evaluations of common solutions for this problem.

Tips and Pitfalls
In general, interpretation of results from an ANCOVA on nonexperimental data can be exceptionally challenging. Sawilowsky (2007b) reported simulations that indicated that the known shortcomings of nonexperimental designs may greatly understate the problem. Berger (2005) discussed the possibility of biased selection of participants and the ensuing group differences on covariates even in supposedly randomized clinical trials.

Assumptions of ANCOVA

Traditional ANCOVA adds to the ANOVA assumptions of independence of scores (discussed in Chapter 1 and violation of which can inflate Type I error), homoscedasticity, and normality by imposing the additional assumption of homogeneity of regression. In ANCOVA homoscedasticity is assumed not only with regard to the dependent variable but also with regard to covariates. In the case of multiple covariates it is further assumed that any relationship between covariates is linear. Statistical power is lowered to the extent that assumptions are violated.

HOMOGENEITY OF REGRESSION

In the case of a single covariate the assumption of *homogeneity of regression* means that the slopes of the regression lines (further assumed to be straight in traditional ANCOVA) that relate the covariate and the dependent variable are assumed to be the same for each population. In other words, it is assumed that a covariate has the same linear relationship with the dependent variable in each population. Violation of this assumption distorts the supposed F distribution, resulting in inaccurate p levels. Nonlinear regression lines in traditional ANCOVA affect the size of error variances and also possibly the adjusted means.

(Stevens, 2009, discussed homogeneity of regression in the case of two covariates, for which the regression homogeneity assumption is an assumption of *homogeneity* (i.e., *parallelism*) *of regression planes*, and the case of three or more covariates, for which the assumption is *homogeneity of regression hyperplanes*. The graph of an equation that relates a dependent variable (Y) and one covariate (X) is an example of a *line* (a regression line) in the XY plane. When there are two covariates the graph of the regression equation is a *plane* that is perpendicular to the XY plane. When there are three or more covariates the graph of the regression equation is called a *hyperplane*.)

The traditional method for addressing the assumption of homogeneity of regression is by testing for the interaction between the independent variable and the covariate. This test can be conducted readily in major software such as IBM SPSS MANOVA. Tabachnick and Fidell (2007) discussed the use of IBM SPSS MANOVA and other software for this test. Norušis (2003) discussed an alternative ANCOVA approach using IBM SPSS when this assumption is violated. Maxwell and Delaney (2004) discussed testing for homogeneity of regression and accommodating ANCOVA to its violation. However, as is often the case with tests of assumptions, a researcher cannot be assured that a test for homogeneity of regression has been powerful enough to detect a degree of violation of this assumption that is sufficient to result in inaccurate results from the ANCOVA. (On the other hand, sample sizes that are large enough to provide good statistical power for rejecting main null hypotheses may sometimes also be large enough to detect of a degree of heterogeneity of regression that is too small to be of much consequence.) For such reasons Wilcox (2005a) discussed a robust method for ANCOVA, a method of which we make further mention later. Keppel and Wickens (2004) discussed the assumption of linearity between a covariate and the dependent variable. Funatogawa, Funatogawa, & Shyr (2011) discussed Type I error rate and probability coverage of confidence intervals when assumptions are violated in ANCOVA with random assignment.

NONPARAMETRIC APPROACHES

Vickers (2005) simulated the performances of the ANCOVA F test and the Mann–Whitney U test under nonnormality for data from a two-group randomized clinical trial with pretests and posttests. The U test was applied either to the difference scores or to the posttest scores. The ANCOVA F test was generally more powerful than the U test except under extreme skew, in which case ANCOVA also exhibited greatly biased estimation of effect sizes.

Schacht, Bogaerts, Bluhmki, and Lesaffre (2008) proposed a nonparametric method for adjusting for covariates in the two-group case in which the covariates and/or the dependent variable can be dichotomous, ordinal, or continuous. The method yields an unbiased and efficient estimate of effect size, a test statistic, and confidence intervals. (Efficient estimator is defined in Chapter 10.)

PROPORTION OF VARIANCE EXPLAINED OVERALL

Standard software output for ANCOVA typically includes estimates of R^2, adjusted and/or unadjusted, but these are the squared multiple correlations between the dependent variable and the combined independent and covariate variables, so such values are not estimates of the proportion of variance (POV) in the dependent variable that is explained by variation in the independent variables alone. Also, such R^2 values are descriptive statistics. If one is interested in estimating overall POV_{pop} one can use as the least biased estimate

$$\omega^2 = \frac{df_{effect}(MS_{effect} - MS_{error})}{SS_{total} + MS_{error}}. \tag{11.1}$$

Equation 11.1 is a generic form for estimating POV_{pop} for any effect in designs that have no within-groups factors. Equation 11.1 is applicable to ANCOVA when covariates are considered to be intrinsic (as defined in Chapter 7), as is generally true of covariates. Varying with respect to the covariate would generally be natural (intrinsic) in the parent population, not variability that is imposed by an experimental manipulation (extrinsic).

When Equation 11.1 is used one wants to generalize results to all members of the parent population, not just to members who have the same value on the covariate. Other, somewhat more biased, estimators of POV_{pop} (e.g., η^2) are often used in ANCOVA (and ANOVA in general) but bias decreases with sample size, so when samples are large the choice of estimator of POV_{pop} is less important. Equation 11.1 can readily be calculated from the information in output that is provided by programs in major statistical packages (e.g., IBM SPSS GLM and SAS GLM), as we demonstrate later in the section entitled "Worked examples of effect sizes".

The generalized formulas in Olejnik and Algina (2000, 2003) for estimating POV_{pop}, such as Equation 11.1, replace estimators of partial POV_{pop}, which, on the other hand, Keppel and Wickens (2004) considered to be the appropriate POV_{pop} for ANCOVA. (The choice between whole and partial POV_{pop} is discussed in Chapter 7, so it is not revisited here.) Partial eta squared is typically outputted by common software, such as IBM SPSS. Tabachnick and Fidell (2007) demonstrated the construction of a confidence interval for partial POV_{pop}, as estimated by partial eta squared, using the method in Smithson (2003).

PROPORTION OF VARIANCE EXPLAINED BY A CONTRAST

For estimation of POV_{pop} accounted for by a simple contrast such as $\mu_a - \mu_b$, or a complex contrast such as $.5(\mu_a + \mu_b) - \mu_{control}$, which compares the mean of the control group with the mean of two treatment-group means, one can use

$$\omega^2 = \frac{SS_{contrast} - MS_{error}}{SS_{total} + MS_{error}}, \qquad (11.2)$$

where

$$SS_{contrast} = \frac{\left[\sum(c_i \bar{Y}_i)\right]^2}{\sum(c_i^2/n_i)}, \qquad (11.3)$$

and where the means are the adjusted means and the c_i are the contrast weights.

A contrast weight (contrast coefficient) is a numerical value assigned to each group's mean depending on its role in the contrast. For example, if a group is not involved in a contrast its weight is zero, that is, the product of it and the mean that it multiplies (weights) in the numerator of Equation 11.3 is zero. We use positive and negative weights such that the weights sum to zero. For example, suppose that there were two treated groups and a control group, and one wanted to compare the two treated groups. In that case one assigns +1 as the weight to one treated group's mean and −1 for the other treated group's mean. If instead one wanted to compare the mean of the combined two treated groups with the mean of the control group, the mean of each treated group is assigned a weight of .5 and the mean of the control group is assigned a weight of −1. The estimator in Equation 11.2 is somewhat less biased than the commonly used η^2 that lacks the terms at the right sides of the numerator and denominator of Equation 11.2.

STANDARDIZED DIFFERENCE BETWEEN MEANS

As is the case when estimating POV in the population, one can use essentially the same rationales to estimate a standardized difference between means when using ANCOVA in the one-way between-groups case as when using one-way ANOVA (Chapter 6) and the version of factorial ANOVA (Chapter 7) in which a peripheral factor is considered to be intrinsic. Again, we consider a covariate's contribution to error variability to be intrinsic variability, which is natural and not to be controlled when calculating the standardizer. Therefore, if one assumes homoscedasticity, the MS_w whose square root is the standardizer should not control for variability that is contributed by a covariate, thereby rendering the square root of such an *unadjusted* mean square for error an MS_w the same standardizer as would be obtained by conducting an ANOVA instead of an ANCOVA. This approach renders effect sizes from ANOVAs and ANCOVAs comparable.

The difference between the adjusted sample means should be used in the numerator of the estimator of effect size. In the case of an experiment the difference between adjusted means and the difference between unadjusted means should be similar, whereas these alternative numerators may vary greatly in the case of nonexperimental research. In the present case in which we are at first assuming homoscedasticity across all of the populations, the estimator of a standardized-difference effect size when comparing any two of the groups is

$$d_{msw} = \frac{\overline{Y}_{adj_i} - \overline{Y}_{adj_j}}{MS_w^{1/2}}, \tag{11.4}$$

where
> the subscript "adj" indicates an adjusted mean
> $MS_w^{1/2}$ is the unadjusted mean square within from output for all groups

If one assumes homoscedasticity just for the two populations whose samples are being compared and whose samples' unadjusted variances are therefore the only ones that are being pooled, each with $n_j - 1$ in the denominator, to standardize with s_p (subscript p for pooled) the estimator is

$$d_p = \frac{\overline{Y}_{adj_i} - \overline{Y}_{adj_i}}{S_p}. \tag{11.5}$$

Finally, if one wants to compare a group with respect to a specific comparison group, such as a control group, and one is not assuming homoscedasticity, the estimator is

$$d_{comp} = \frac{\overline{Y}_{adj_i} - \overline{Y}_{adj_j}}{s_c}, \tag{11.6}$$

where s_c is the unadjusted s of the control group, with $n_c - 1$ in the denominator. Equations 11.4 through 11.6 are the adjusted-means versions of Equations 6.15, 6.14, and 6.13, respectively.

Tips and Pitfalls
The approach that we have taken here in which the covariate is ignored when calculating the standardizer for the present case was discussed by Glass et al. (1981), Maxwell and Delaney (2004), and Olejnik and Algina (2000). This approach is appropriate if the results are to be compared or meta-analyzed with estimates

of standardized differences from designs without covariates (ANOVAs) or with covariates whose correlation with the dependent variable is different from study to study. Refer to Cortina and Nouri (2000), Glass et al., and Maxwell and Delaney for alternative approaches. In ANCOVA when a standardizer is covariate-adjusted it becomes smaller, rendering the estimate of a standardized-difference effect size larger and not comparable to an effect size from ANOVA. In order to avoid creating pseudo-contradictory results in the literature, research reports must be clear about how the presented estimates of standardized-difference effect sizes, or POV_{pop} effect sizes, were calculated.

Consult Cortina and Nouri (2000) for discussion of a method for calculating standardized-difference effect sizes when there is more than one covariate. The method for calculating the standardizer for the estimator becomes much more complex when there are more than two covariates. We do not recommend this method for nonexperimental studies because assumptions are even less likely to be met in that case.

UNSTANDARDIZED DIFFERENCE BETWEEN MEANS

In the case of ANCOVA, one can construct approximate confidence intervals for the unstandardized difference(s) between populations' adjusted means as an effect size when the observed dependent variable is of direct interest (e.g., weight) instead of representing a latent variable (e.g., depression). However, a complication can arise depending on one's conception of the covariate. Currently, major statistical software packages construct confidence intervals on the basis of regarding the covariate as a fixed-effect variable. If a covariate is instead a random-effects variable, which we believe is usually the case, then the outputted confidence intervals using, say, the Tukey HSD (Honestly Significantly Different) approximate method may yield intervals that are narrower than they should be for this conception of the nature of the covariate. An improved method for the case of random-effects covariates by Bryant and Paulson applies to fixed independent variables and involves modified critical values that are generally somewhat larger than Tukey's critical values for multiple comparisons and construction of confidence intervals. The method assumes homoscedasticity and a joint normal distribution for the covariate and the dependent variable. (The Tukey HSD method is discussed in the context of ANOVA in Chapters 6 and 7.) Maxwell and Delaney (2004) and Stevens (2009) illustrated construction of such approximate confidence intervals when a covariate is regarded to be a random-effects variable and provided tables of the Bryant–Paulson critical values to be used to construct the intervals in this case.

Wilcox (2005a) provided R and S-PLUS functions for a robust ANCOVA method that constructs approximate confidence intervals for the difference between covariate-adjusted trimmed population means. The method does not assume a linear relationship between the covariate and the dependent variable, homogeneity of regression, normality, or homoscedasticity. The method is flexible so that any measure of location can be used instead of the trimmed mean and any measure of scale can be used (the variance or any more outlier-resistant measure). The method can also be extended to the case of multiple covariates and multiple groups (Wilcox, 2007c).

Wilcox (2006g) reported reasonably good control of Type I error in simulations of the performance of a robust bootstrap method applied to the medians of two independent groups in ANCOVA with one covariate. Wilcox (2009c) also reported good performance of his proposed robust analog of the traditional ANCOVA for comparing medians or 20% trimmed means using percentile bootstrapping and avoiding the usual assumptions about the regression lines. (All of the foregoing elements of the Wilcox method were defined earlier in this book.)

WORKED EXAMPLES OF EFFECT SIZES

Table 11.1 depicts partial real data (not ours) on anorectic girls' pretreatment and posttreatment weights. Pretreatment weight is the covariate. There were two treatments and a control. For our sole purposes of illustrating calculations and interpretations of estimates of effect sizes most simply, not for reaching conclusions about

TABLE 11.1
Weights of Anorectics (in lb)

Control		Therapy a		Therapy b	
Pre	Post	Pre	Post	Pre	Post
80.7	80.2	80.5	82.2	83.8	95.2
89.4	80.1	84.9	85.6	83.3	94.3
91.8	86.4	81.5	81.4	86.0	91.5
74.0	86.3	82.6	81.9	82.5	91.9
78.1	76.1	79.9	76.4	86.7	100.3
88.3	78.1	88.7	103.6	79.6	76.7
87.3	75.1	94.9	98.4	76.9	76.8
75.1	86.7	76.3	93.4	94.2	101.6
80.6	73.5	81.0	73.4	73.4	94.9
78.4	84.6	80.5	82.1	80.5	75.2
77.6	77.4	85.0	96.7	81.6	77.8
88.7	79.5	89.2	95.3	82.1	95.5
81.3	89.6	81.3	82.4	77.6	90.7
78.1	81.4	76.5	72.5	83.5	92.5
70.5	81.8	70.0	90.9	89.9	93.8
77.3	77.3	80.4	71.3	86.0	91.7
85.2	84.2	83.3	85.4	87.3	98.0

Source: Partial data adapted from Everitt, B.S. from Hand, D.J. et al., *A Handbook of Small Data Sets*, Chapman & Hall, London, U.K., 1994.

treatments for anorexia nervosa, we deleted data from the two larger samples to achieve equal sample sizes because sample sizes were originally very unequal for reasons unknown to us. Possibly there was differential attrition or differential parental selection into their preferred type of therapy for their daughters. Even if we retained the original unequal sample sizes, such differential attrition or biased self-selection into groups would render the example suitable only for demonstrating calculations and interpretation in general, not for reaching conclusions about treatments for anorexia.

Researchers should not delete data in their larger samples to render them the same size as the smallest sample. Tabachnick and Fidell (2007) discuss the problem of unequal sample sizes and the use of software for ANCOVA for this case. Unequal sample sizes may exacerbate the negative effects of heteroscedasticity as is discussed in Chapter 1.

We discuss selected effect-size-related output from IBM SPSS GLM and IBM SPSS MANOVA, and some manual calculations, for an ANCOVA of the data of Table 11.1. We present results in the order in which the equations for estimation of effect sizes were presented and discussed previously. For the purpose of this section we emphasize those aspects of the output that relate directly to effect sizes. For detailed discussions of tests and diagnostics that point to some possible violations of assumptions manifested by the full set of the data of which the data in Table 11.1 are a part consult Norušis (2003). •

DIAGNOSTICS

For a general discussion of diagnostics and tests of assumptions for ANCOVA using major software consult Tabachnick and Fidell (2007). We merely report here that output for the data of Table 11.1 indicates that (a) there is insufficient evidence of unequal variances using the Levene test ($p = .264$) but this test may not be powerful enough to detect an amount of heteroscedasticity that would be problematic for the ANCOVA (Grissom, 2000) and (b) there is evidence that the assumption of homogeneity of regression may be violated because the pretest weights-by-treatment interaction is statistically significant at the $p = .048$ level.

OVERALL PROPORTION OF VARIANCE EXPLAINED

First, applying Equation 11.1 one calculates from values in output that $\omega^2 = 2(299.893 - 55.298)/(3714.466 + 55.298) = .130$. The overall F test yields statistical significance at $p = .008$ so one can conclude that $\omega^2 = .130$ is statistically significantly different from 0 at the same p level. One estimates from this result that approximately 13% of the variance in posttreatment weights is associated with group membership. Because Equation 11.1 is generic the result can be compared or combined (meta-analyzed) with results on these levels of the treatment variable from any between-groups design that has no covariates. (For completeness and for our purposes we report an overall F test although, as was discussed in Chapter 6, those who are going to conduct Tukey HSD tests of multiple comparisons should not sacrifice statistical power by requiring a preliminary statistically significant F before proceeding with the Tukey tests.)

PARTIAL POV_{pop}

If one wants to compare one's results with a previously reported value of an estimate of partial POV_{pop} the outputted partial eta squared for treatment is .188 for the current data. Software calculates this estimate as the adjusted sum of squares for treatment divided by the sum of that value and the adjusted sum of squares for error. The adjustment involves taking the covariate into account. For details consult Tabachnick and Fidell (2007). Again, consult Chapter 7 for discussion of whole and partial POV.

POV_{pop} FOR CONTRASTS

Applying Equations 11.2 and 11.3 we next estimate POV_{pop} accounted for by each of the simple contrasts based on covariate-adjusted means. (Adjusted means are often labeled "Estimated Means" in output.) Equation 11.3 for $SS_{contrast}$ simplifies in the present case because sample sizes are equal: all $n_i = 17$. Thus, multiplying both sides of Equation 11.3 by $n_i/n_i = 17/17$, a little algebra reveals that $n_i = 17$ now appears in the numerator and departs from the denominator. Therefore, when contrasting group a and group b, $SS_{contrast} = 17[(+1)(85.506) + (-1)$ $(90.005) + (0)(81.524)]^2/[(+1)^2 + (-1)^2 + (0)^2] = 172.049$, so $\omega^2 = (172.049 - 55.298)/$ $(3714.466 + 55.298) = .031$ for this contrast. Output indicates that the comparison of the adjusted means of these two groups fails to attain statistical significance at the $p = .05$ level, so ω^2 is also statistically insignificant.

When contrasting group a and the control group, $SS_{contrast} = 17[(+1)(85.506) +$ $(-1)(81.524) + (0)(90.005)]^2/[(+1)^2 + (-1)^2 + (0)^2] = 134.779$, so $\omega^2 = (134.779 -$ $55.298)/(3714.466 + 55.298) = .021$ in this case. Output indicates that the comparison of the adjusted means of these two groups fails to attain statistical significance at the $p = .05$ level, so ω^2 is also statistically insignificant. When contrasting group b and the control group $SS_{contrast} = 17[(+1)(90.005) + (-1)81.524) + (0)(85.506)]^2/$ $[(+1)^2 + (-1)^2 + (0)^2] = 611.383$, so $\omega^2 = (611.383 - 55.298)/(3714.466 + 55.298) =$ .148 for this contrast. Output indicates that the comparison of the adjusted means of these two groups is statistically significant at $p = .002$. Therefore, one concludes that the estimate of POV_{pop} for this contrast is statistically significantly different from 0 at $p = .002$, and it is estimated that nearly 15% of the variance in posttreatment weight is accounted for by membership in group b versus membership in the control group.

CONFIDENCE INTERVALS

As should be expected, 95% confidence intervals for the two contrasts that fail to attain statistical significance at the .05 level contain the value 0 within them. The confidence limits for the one simple contrast that attains statistical significance (group *b* versus the control group) are 3.3 and 13.7 lb (limits of an interval that excludes 0) when an ANCOVA adjustment has been made based on baseline weight as a covariate. (Reports of actual research should provide confidence limits for all constructed intervals, not just those that do not contain 0 within them.) Interpretation further depends on how representative the samples are of the population. Some software output individual confidence intervals, but for multiple comparisons we generally prefer simultaneous confidence intervals, as was discussed previously, so that one may be, say, approximately 95% confident that all of the targeted population mean differences are captured by their respective intervals.

STANDARDIZED MEAN DIFFERENCES

Although the present example involves a familiar physical dependent variable, weight, for which we prefer the use of unstandardized mean differences, for completeness we estimate some standardized mean differences for adjusted means using Equations 11.4 through 11.6 in that order. For illustration, three of the possible examples of estimated standardized mean differences (using three different standardizers) for the current data involve the control group and group *b*. Recall that the contrast involving adjusted means of these two groups is statistically significant at $p = .002$. The adjusted posttest mean weights for the group that received treatment *b* and for the control group are 90.005 and 81.524 lb, respectively.

First, $d_{msw} = (90.005 - 81.524)/(61.65)^{1/2} \approx 1.08$, assuming homoscedasticity for all three groups so that the standardizer, as was previously discussed, is the square root of the unadjusted error term that can be found in an ANOVA output for the posttreatment data only. Next, $d_p = (90.005 - 81.524)/[(4.6195^2 + 8.4751^2)/2]^{1/2} \approx 1.24$, when making the previous comparison between adjusted means but assuming that only the two involved populations are homoscedastic, so that the standardizer is now the square root of the pooled unadjusted variances of the two involved groups. Finally, $d_{comp} = (90.005 - 81.524)/4.6195 \approx 1.84$, when making the previous comparison and using the control group's unadjusted *s* as the standardizer.

Tips and Pitfalls

There are differences among the sizes of the three standardized differences despite the facts that they all standardize a difference between the same pair of means and the Levene test yields insufficient evidence of unequal population variances. A researcher should make a reasoned a priori decision about which, if any, standardized difference or differences to report and clearly identify the nature and interpretation of any such reported value. Again, any calculated estimate must be reported. Assuming normality, the different values of *d* can be interpreted as in the examples in Chapters 3, 6, and 7. Again, such values of *d* that use unadjusted standardizers can be compared or meta-analyzed with values of *d* from other studies that had used no covariates. (One must distinguish between unadjusted standardizers and unadjusted means.) The unadjusted posttreatment mean weights are 85.465, 90.494, and 81.077 lb for group *a*, group *b*, and the control group, respectively.

SUMMARY

Standardized and unstandardized mean difference and proportion-of-variance-explained effect sizes can be estimated for ANCOVA, which modifies ANOVA by attempting to reduce within-group variability and the effects of confounding variables on the group means that are being compared. Thus, one purpose of ANCOVA is to attain more powerful *F* tests and narrower confidence intervals for differences between means by reducing within-group variability in the data that is attributable to one or more extraneous variables (covariates) that are correlated with the dependent variable. ANCOVA also adjusts posttest group means on the measure of the dependent variable based on the extent of one or more preexisting difference between groups on a covariate. The adjustment permits estimation of what the differences between group means would be if the groups had the same mean on the covariate(s). Interpretation of results from an ANCOVA that has been applied to nonexperimental data is problematic.

In addition to the assumptions of ANOVA, homogeneity of regression is also assumed in ANCOVA. In the simplest case of one covariate, homogeneity of regression means that the slopes of the (straight) regression lines that relate the covariate and the dependent variable are assumed to be the same in each population. There are nonparametric approaches to ANCOVA, especially to accommodate nonnormality, including estimation of an effect size and construction of confidence intervals.

In traditional parametric ANCOVA omega squared can be used to estimate the overall proportion of variance explained (POV_{pop}) with the least bias, but if samples are very large there is little difference in the values of the omega-squared and the eta-squared estimators. Some favor estimation of partial POV_{pop} instead of whole POV_{pop} for ANCOVA, and software output and confidence intervals for POV_{pop} are often based on such estimation. Estimation of POV_{pop} for simple or complex contrasts of covariate-adjusted means is also possible in ANCOVA using omega squared or eta squared.

For estimating POV_{pop} and a standardized difference between means in one-way between-groups ANCOVA, essentially the same rationales are used as when using one-way ANOVA and a factorial ANOVA in which a peripheral factor is an intrinsic variable (Chapter 7). The choice of standardizer for a *d* type of effect size depends on whether equal variances are assumed for all populations, just the two populations that are involved in the standardized comparison of means, or not at all. Also, a covariate can be ignored when calculating a standardizer if the *d* is to be compared with *d* values from studies that did not use covariates. Reports should be clear about which type of estimates of POV_{pop} or d_{pop} they are reporting and why.

Again, when the dependent variable is a familiar variable that is of interest in its own right, instead of representing a latent variable, unstandardized differences between covariate-adjusted means are informative effect sizes. Construction of confidence intervals is recommended for the population values of such effect sizes but a complication can arise (and be resolved) if a covariate is a random-effects variable.

QUESTIONS

11.1   Define (a) *covariate* and (b) *homogeneity of regression*.

11.2   What are the two main purposes of ANCOVA?

11.3   Ideally for ANCOVA, which correlations should be strong and which correlations should be weak?

11.4   When during the research process should covariates be chosen?

11.5   Discuss the limitations of ANCOVA applied to nonexperimental data.

11.6   List the assumptions of ANCOVA.

11.7   Why is an outputted R^2 in ANCOVA not a *POV* in the usual sense?

11.8   Why is the estimator in Equation 11.2 preferable to eta squared?

11.9   When planning research what should be considered regarding whether or not to ignore a covariate when calculating a standardizer?

11.10 Using available software construct and discuss, for the data of Table 11.1, 95% confidence intervals for the contrast of adjusted means of groups (a) *a* and *b* and (b) *a* and control.

11.11 Calculate and discuss, for the data of Table 11.1, d_{msw}, d_p, and d_{comp} for groups (a) *a* and *b* and (b) *a* and control.

11.12 What is the relationship between partialling in multiple regression (Chapter 10) and adjusting means in ANCOVA?

12 Effect Sizes for Multivariate Analysis of Variance

INTRODUCTION

This chapter discusses effect sizes for research in which there are two or more groups that are being compared with respect to multiple continuous dependent variables (multivariate analysis of variance, MANOVA). The number of dependent variables is represented by the letter p and the number of groups is represented by the letter k. We assume that some readers have only slight familiarity with the basic concepts of MANOVA and multivariate analysis of covariance (MANCOVA). For our purpose little use of matrix terminology and no use of matrix algebra are made here.

For those who are entirely unfamiliar with matrix terminology, a *matrix* is a two-dimensional table of numerical values, the rows and columns of which are called *vectors*. One example of a matrix consists of column vectors, each of which contains a group's mean for each of the dependent variables (*a vector of means* for a given group), and row vectors, each of which contains each group's mean on a given dependent variable (a vector of means for a given dependent variable). There are other important kinds of matrices. Each value in the table, such as a group's mean score on one of the dependent variables in the present case of a matrix of means, is called an *element*. In the simplest case of MANOVA in which there are only two dependent variables (dependent variables 1 and 2) and two groups (groups 1 and 2) the matrix of each group's population mean on each dependent variable is

$$\begin{bmatrix} \mu_{11} & \mu_{12} \\ \mu_{21} & \mu_{22} \end{bmatrix}.$$

In this example the columns might represent a treated group and a control group, and the rows might represent two measures of outcome. As is discussed in more detail later, the usual null hypothesis is that the p columns ($p = 2$ in this example) are equal (i.e., the vectors of means of the $k = 2$ populations are equal).

We begin with the simple case of between-groups MANOVA in which comparisons are made between $k = 2$ groups with respect to $p \geq 2$ dependent variables, then proceed to the cases of more than two groups, MANCOVA, factorial designs, mixed designs, and within-groups designs. All of our discussions of between-groups designs involve the fixed-effects model (as defined in Chapter 6).

Regarding the statistical tests for main effects and interactions we assume here that cell sizes are equal, but major software packages such as IBM SPSS GLM, IBM SPSS MANOVA, and SAS GLM adjust for unequal cell sizes.

There is some controversy regarding under which circumstances MANOVA should be used when there are multiple dependent variables—MANOVA or separate ANOVAs for each dependent variable. This chapter need not discuss this controversy because our main purpose is to describe effect sizes and their estimation. However, it is common to use MANOVA when there are correlations among the observed dependent variables and so the researcher believes that underlying them is a lesser number of dimensions. Using the intercorrelations, software for MANOVA extracts these dimensions by creating optimal composite variables (i.e., combined correlated variables) from the observed dependent variables. For example, in the case of two groups, an optimal combination of observed dependent variables is one that maximizes the difference between the vectors of means for the two groups. MANOVA is also used in situations in which dependent variables are not correlated but MANOVA would have greater statistical power than a set of separate ANOVAs.

ASSUMPTIONS OF MANOVA

The assumptions of MANOVA are generalizations of the assumptions of ANOVA. Interpretation of effect sizes is jeopardized if the test statistics on which they are based are not sufficiently robust to violations of the assumptions. Unfortunately, the literature on tests of assumptions and robustness of various statistical tests in MANOVA is vast without currently resulting in definitive conclusions that apply to all conditions. Such literature is vast because of the great number of possible combinations of violations of assumptions and conditions that can be simulated. For discussions of assumptions, consult Finch (2005), Olson (1974, 1976), Seir (2002), and von Eye (2005, 2006).

Recall from Chapter 1 that the sequential procedure of testing main null hypotheses only if prior tests of assumptions provide insufficient evidence of their violation can inflate overall Type I error for the sequence. Such inflation of Type I error should also occur in the multivariate case. References for more robust statistical testing are given in the next section.

STATISTICAL TESTS

Recall that the omnibus null hypothesis in ANOVA is that the centers (as measured by arithmetic means) of all of the populations are equal. The traditional omnibus null hypothesis in typical MANOVA is that all of the population vectors of means (called *group centroids*) are equal. In simplest terms the omnibus null hypothesis in typical MANOVA implies that for each dependent variable all populations have the same mean. The typical alternative hypothesis is that the population vectors of means are not all equal; that is, at least one population's vector of means is not equal to the others. Tests in MANOVA account for the number of dependent variables, so no adjustment of alpha for multiple testing is required. The four traditional tests of the omnibus null hypothesis are Wilks' lambda (the original and most widely used test), Roy's greatest characteristic root (also known by slight variations of this label), the Lawley–Hotelling trace (also known as the Hotelling–Lawley trace or Hotelling's trace, and not the same as Hotelling's T^2 statistic for the $k = 2$ case), and the Pillai–Bartlett trace (sometimes labeled the Bartlett–Pillai trace or Pillai trace). (A *trace*, which need not be discussed for our purpose, is the sum of the diagonal elements of a matrix.) Wilks developed MANOVA as a generalization of ANOVA. In the case of only one dependent variable Wilks' *lambda* reduces to an inverse function of the F statistic of ANOVA. Only if $k = 2$ (ANOVA or MANOVA) or $p = 1$ (ANOVA) will the significance levels attained by these four MANOVA tests necessarily be equal. There are also nonparametric and other robust multivariate tests (Cliff, 1996b; Finch, 2005; Liu, Bathke, & Harrar, in press; Lix & Fouladi, 2007; Van Aelst & Willems, 2011; Wilcox, 2005a). When the number of dependent variables is very large relative to total sample size (a condition called *high dimensionality*), traditional MANOVA is inapplicable.

TENTATIVE RECOMMENDATIONS

No strong recommendation about choice of a test is made because of the great variety of conditions that influence the performance of a test when data are multivariate. Researchers who are very concerned about violation of assumptions can restrict their choice to one of the reportedly robust methods. Major software packages such as IBM SPSS output results from the four major tests. If the results of the four tests are not consistent it is unacceptable to report the results selectively. In this case all outputted results should be reported. Huberty and Olejnik (2006) provided syntax for IBM SPSS and Tabachnick and Fidell (2007) provided syntax for IBM SPSS and SAS.

MULTIPLE COMPARISONS

Consider the case in which the purpose of conducting a MANOVA is to avoid decreased statistical power by possibly overcontrolling for accumulating experiment-wise Type I error if conducting a separate ANOVA for each dependent variable. (Controlling for such experiment-wise Type I error in multiple ANOVAs by using the Bonferroni–Dunn adjustment of alpha [discussed in Chapter 6 and later in this chapter] can overcontrol in the sense of lowering statistical power.) In this use of MANOVA when an omnibus multivariate test yields statistical significance it is appropriate to conduct finer-grained univariate tests (t or F) for separate dependent variables. Such finer-grained follow-up tests pinpoint the individual dependent variables that are the sources of the overall statistical significance. If such a test yields statistical significance one can conclude that an estimate of omnibus effect size that is based on the involved dependent variable is statistically significant. Also, selected univariate or multivariate simultaneous confidence intervals for pair-wise comparisons can also be of great interest, the former being more readily interpreted. The topic of planned and unplanned finer-grained analyses after a MANOVA was discussed by Bray and Maxwell (1985), Huberty and Olejnik (2006), Maxwell and Delaney (2004), and Stevens (2009). Imada and Yamamoto (2010) discussed a method of multivariate pairwise comparisons of treated groups with a control group.

Each of the four major omnibus MANOVA test statistics can be approximately converted to F. Because for a given set of data such F values will be the same for each test when $k = 2$ any of the tests can equivalently be used as a test for the statistical significance of a simple contrast of two of the $k > 2$ vectors of means. We make use of those traditional parametric tests in the equations for estimates of effect size that are discussed throughout the remainder of this chapter. The null-hypothesized value of each parametric effect size that is discussed is zero. An estimate of an effect size in MANOVA can be considered to be statistically significantly greater than zero at a given level of significance if the statistical test that compares the groups that are involved in the effect size attains statistical significance at that level.

Because our focus is on effect sizes and because of constraint on length we do not discuss the results of tests of the assumptions when interpreting the estimates of effect size that are calculated here. However, sufficient satisfaction of assumptions can be crucial for valid interpretation of estimates of effect size. Therefore, some of our worked examples were chosen to involve sets of data from references that did not estimate the same effect sizes that we estimate but provided the results of tests of assumptions for those data. A good source for the use of major software to test assumptions of MANOVA and MANCOVA is Tabachnick and Fidell (2007).

EFFECT SIZES FOR ONE-WAY MANOVA

CONTRASTS AND STANDARDIZED MEAN-DIFFERENCE CONTRASTS AS EFFECT SIZES

As is the case in univariate research, there is often interest in going beyond statistically significant omnibus test results and omnibus effect sizes to tests involving individual dependent variables and effect sizes that are focused on the important between-group contrasts in a set of multivariate data.

Following Omnibus Significance with Separate ANOVAs?

If the omnibus MANOVA statistical test indicates overall statistical significance, follow-up ANOVAs can be conducted on the individual dependent variables. (It can be argued that such follow-up testing is appropriate when the dependent variables are not highly correlated.) Again, if the omnibus MANOVA statistical test indicates overall statistical significance the same omnibus multivariate test (or Hotelling's T^2 test) can be used to test for the statistical significance between two of the groups' vectors of means at a time from the $k > 2$ groups (multiple comparisons). A Bonferroni–Dunn adjustment of the alpha level for each of the planned follow-up ANOVAs and planned multiple-comparison tests can be made to correct for inflation of overall Type I error. The adjusted α level is the customary (but perhaps conservative) $\alpha_{adj} = \alpha_{ew}/n_{tests}$, where α_{ew} is the overall adopted experiment-wise error rate (say, .05) and n_{tests} is the number of tests that are going to be conducted.

In many cases univariate contrasts and effect sizes will be more informative than multivariate contrasts and effect sizes. Our discussions of ANOVA in Chapters 6 and 7 are applicable to univariate follow-up tests after a statistically significant omnibus MANOVA result has been obtained. Bray and Maxwell (1985) and Tabachnick and Fidell (2007) provide concise discussions of multivariate follow-up testing, the latter reference providing syntax for this purpose when using IBM SPSS GLM, IBM SPSS MANOVA, and SAS GLM. This syntax can also yield tests of univariate contrasts. Recall from earlier chapters that, generally, contrasts of unstandardized means are informative effect sizes when the observed dependent variable is of interest in its own right and that standardized contrasts are informative when the observed dependent variable stands-in for an underlying variable that cannot be measured directly.

Mahalanobis Distance Statistic

The four previously discussed traditional omnibus tests can also be used to calculate a multivariate extension of the version of the univariate standardized mean-difference effect size estimate that standardizes based on the pooled variance of the two involved groups (d of Chapters 3, 6, and 7). This multivariate standardized-difference effect size for the $k = 2$ case, or the case of contrasts, is D_{pop} that is estimated by D, which is the square root of the *Mahalanobis D^2 distance statistic*. The distance statistic can be used to estimate the degree of separation between any two populations (i.e., the distance between the two vectors of means). Whereas the univariate d standardizes the difference between two means using a standard deviation, which is the square root of a variance, D analogously standardizes the difference between two vectors of sample means using the square root of the sample variance-covariance matrix.

A *variance-covariance matrix* is a square table in which the rows and columns represent each dependent variable and the elements represent the variance of each dependent variable (the values on the main diagonal of the table) and covariance of each pair of dependent variables (the values not on the main diagonal). (Unlike a correlation coefficient, which ranges from −1 to +1, a covariance is an unbounded measure of relationship between two variables. The formula for a population covariance is the numerator of Equation 4.1.) The Mahalanobis D assumes equality of variance-covariance matrices between the two groups that are being compared. This effect size is of use when none of the intercorrelations among the dependent variables is at or near zero. There is small-sample positive bias of D, but there are corrections for it (Rao & Dorvio, 1985).

In this chapter we consider the use of Wilks' lambda test statistic to calculate the effect size estimator D. At the time of this writing, Wilks' lambda is available for pair-wise contrasts in IBM SPSS GLM by running a separate program for each contrast, and in SAS as output from multivariate contrasts:

$$D = \left[\frac{df_{\text{error}}(1-\Lambda)\sum (c_i^2/n_i)}{\Lambda} \right]^{1/2}, \tag{12.1}$$

where

$df_{\text{error}} = N_{\text{tot}} - k$, N_{tot} is the total of the sample sizes (including samples that are not involved in the contrast)

Λ is Wilks' lambda for the contrast (or, in general, for the effect) from output the summation is over all of the groups, each c_i is a contrast coefficient each n_i is the size of a sample

In the case of designs with only two groups $\sum (c_i^2/n_i)$ becomes $(1/n_a + 1/n_b)$. Contrast coefficients (weights) are discussed in Chapter 11.

For the case of a simple contrast between the two treatment groups, groups a and b, with group c being the control,

$$D_{\text{simple}} = \left[\frac{(N_{\text{tot}} - 3)(1-\Lambda)\left[(1^2/n_a) + ((-1)^2/n_b) + (0^2/n_c) \right]}{\Lambda} \right]^{1/2}. \tag{12.1a}$$

(We included the unnecessary term with 0^2 in Equation 12.1a to emphasize that the current D, unlike the one represented next by Equation 12.1b, gives no weight to the control group.) Suppose in this case that $N_{\text{tot}} = 90$, each $n_i = 30$, and the outputted Λ for this contrast equals .9000. Applying these values to Equation 12.1a yields

$$D_{\text{simple}} = \left[\frac{(90-3)(1-.9000)[(1^2/30) + ((-1)^2/30)]}{.9000} \right]^{1/2} = .8027725 \approx .803.$$

Thus, the vectors of means of the two treatments are estimated to be approximately .8 units apart, where the unit of distance in a multidimensional space is analogous to a pooled standard deviation in the univariate case.

For the complex contrast involving the combined treatment groups versus the control group

$$D_{\text{complex}} = \left[\frac{(N_{\text{tot}} - 3)(1-\Lambda)\left[(.5^2/n_a) + (.5^2/n_b) + ((-1)^2/n_c) \right]}{\Lambda} \right]^{1/2}. \tag{12.1b}$$

Continuing the previous example, suppose that the outputted Λ for the complex contrast equals .8500. Applying the needed values to Equation 12.1b yields

$$D_{\text{complex}} = \left[\frac{(90-3)(1-.8500)[(.5^2/30)+(.5^2/30)+((-1)^2/30)]}{.8500} \right]^{1/2}$$

$$= .8761546 \approx .876.$$

Thus, the vector of means of the combined treatment groups and the vector of means of the control group are estimated to be nearly .9 units apart, where, again, the unit in a multidimensional space is a multivariate analog of a pooled standard deviation in the univariate case. In the present case of comparisons or contrasts Λ relates to the optimal composite (optimal weighting) of the dependent variables that results in the greatest difference for the two groups that are being compared.

Results of computer simulations of the accuracy (probability coverage) and precision (width) of confidence intervals for population D^2, based on sample D^2 and a bias-corrected D^2, under various distributional conditions (and violation of the assumption of homogeneity of variance-covariance matrices) were reported by Ferron, Hess, Hogarty, and Kromrey (2004). Additionally, uncorrected sample D^2 typically displayed much positive bias, especially when n_i/p was 10 as opposed to 20, and varied greatly in degree of bias across the various conditions of violation of assumptions. The corrected D^2 showed little bias and little variability in bias. Regarding generally attaining fairly good accuracy of confidence intervals when using uncorrected D^2 those authors tentatively recommended the method by Steiger and Fouladi (1992, 1997) and when using corrected D^2 they tentatively recommended a percentile bootstrap method. Unfortunately, the confidence intervals were generally extremely wide. Confidence limits for population D are found by taking the square roots of the limits for population D^2, so the width will be narrower for D_{pop} than for D_{pop}^2. Ferron et al. acknowledged that recommendations and conclusions from their study have to be tentative because of the limited number of conditions that were studied and the limited number of replications in their sampling. Also consult Hess, Hogarty, Ferron, and Kromrey (2007).

Tiku, Qamarul Islam, and Qumsiyeh (2010) proposed an apparently efficient and robust estimator of D_{pop}^2 under nonnormality. Reiser (2001) reported on confidence intervals for D_{pop}^2, using the noncentral F distribution, when assumptions are satisfied. Except for the case of $D_{\text{pop}}^2 = 0$, the probability coverage was found to be nearly exact.

COMBINING EFFECT SIZES WITHIN A STUDY FOR A SINGLE ESTIMATE

Hancock (2003) discussed a standardized effect size for the latent variable when a single construct underlies all of the observed dependent variables. The method is applicable to a smaller sample size than is traditional MANOVA. (When dependent variables are highly correlated it would be reasonable and parsimonious to estimate a single multivariate effect size for the presumed single construct that is being measured. If the dependent variables are subscales of a normed test or are scores on separate tests from a battery of standardized tests the intercorrelations may already have been published.) Later Choi, Fan, and Hancock (2009) further discussed construction of a confidence interval for the standardized difference between means of two independent groups with respect to a latent variable that is believed to underlie multiple measured dependent variables. The method assumes normality. Assuming homoscedasticity, this multivariate effect size can be interpreted in the same manner as a univariate d. Specifically, in this case d estimates how many standard deviation units apart two population means are with respect to the latent dependent variable. Sample LISREL code for implementation of the method was provided by those authors.

Marascuilo, Busk, and Serlin (1988) presented a manual large-sample method for pooling a study's separate pair-wise multivariate effect sizes after determining that there are no statistically significant differences among them. Timm (1999) proposed an overall standardized-difference multivariate effect size across all of the dependent variables for the case of two independent groups and a statistical test for it.

PROPORTION OF VARIANCE EXPLAINED BY CONTRASTS IN MANOVA

Wilks' lambda can also be used to calculate types of eta-squared and omega-squared estimates of strength of association in terms of what may roughly be called the proportion of (generalized) variance of the *composite* of the dependent variables that is associated with group-membership contrasts in MANOVA. (The generalized variance is measured by what are called the determinants of the variance-covariance matrix.) Such an estimate of POV_{pop} is very roughly a multivariate analog of a univariate POV (Chapter 7). Thus, the kinds of POV_{pop} that are discussed in this chapter do not relate directly to the variances of individual observed dependent variables. However, a type of multivariate POV_{pop} that does relate directly to the individual observed dependent variables is the *redundancy index*, which is the arithmetic mean of the univariate eta^2 values for all of the dependent variables. For discussions of the redundancy index consult Cramer and Nicewander (1979), Stevens (2009), and Tabachnick and Fidell (2007). (A thorough understanding of multivariate POV_{pop} requires a good grasp of the concepts of determinants and eigenvalues in matrix algebra, discussions of which here are not possible given the constraints on length.) Whether in the omnibus $k > 2$ case (discussed in the next section), the case of a total of only two groups, or in the current case of a simple or complex contrast when the total number of groups is greater than two, estimation of POV_{pop} assumes equality of the covariance-variance matrices. Also, when using the estimators in this section estimation of POV_{pop} is useful when none of the intercorrelations among the dependent variables is at or near zero.

Because, as is discussed in Chapter 6, ω^2 is somewhat less positively biased than η^2 we favor and present the equation for the former. (In the multivariate case bias decreases with decreases in k and p and with increase in sample sizes.) Also, we provide Tatsuoka's (1988) adjusting equation for further reducing the bias in ω^2. Consult Tatsuoka or Olejnik and Algina (2000) for equations for η^2 and

Tatsuoka's adjusted η^2. Also consult Cohen (1988), Kline (2004), and Steyn and Elllis (2009) for discussions of η^2. Thus, there are two major estimators of POV_{pop}, each one of which has an adjusted and an unadjusted form. (We discuss important, but less widely used, estimators later.)

Tips and Pitfalls

It is imperative that researchers specify which of the four equations was the basis for a reported estimate of POV_{pop} for a contrast because there can be large differences in the estimates. We recommend that adjusted estimators be used. If more than one kind of adjusted estimate has been calculated each must be reported. If only one estimator is to be reported that decision must be made prior to the analysis of the data, so as to avoid biased reporting. Reporting all outputted estimates also facilitates comparisons of results with those from studies that have reported estimators other than the preferred estimator of the author of the report.

The equations for unadjusted and adjusted multivariate omega^2 are, respectively,

$$\omega_{multt}^2 = 1 - \left[\frac{N_{cont} \Lambda}{df_{error} + \Lambda} \right] \tag{12.2}$$

and

$$\omega_{multadj}^2 = \omega_{mult}^2 - \left[\frac{(p^2 + q^2)(1 - \omega_{mult}^2)}{3N_{cont}} \right], \tag{12.3}$$

where
N_{cont} is the total of sample sizes for only those samples that are involved in the simple or complex contrast
$df_{error} = N_{cont} - k$
q is the df for the contrast

(The value of q is 1 in the case in which two groups are involved in a pair-wise comparison. The value of q is 1 also in the case in which three groups are involved in the complex contrast of the kind that we previously related to Equation 12.1b because two of the groups are combined into one larger group to be compared with the other group.) The values of k, p, and Wilks' Λ are as previously defined. Equation 12.2 is attributable to Sachdeva. Equation 12.3 is equivalent to the equation proposed for biased-reducing estimation of omnibus POV_{pop} by Tatsuoka (1988).

We now write Equation 12.3 for the case in which there are $k = 3$ groups, $p = 2$ dependent variables, and one wants to estimate the proportion of the total variance that is attributable to the complex contrast involving control group c versus the combined groups a and b:

$$\omega_{multadj}^2 = \omega_{mult}^2 - \left[\frac{(2^2 + 1^2)(1 - \omega_{mult}^2)}{3N_{cont}} \right]. \tag{12.3a}$$

Again, in the case represented by Equation 12.3a $N_{cont} = n_a + n_b + n_c$ because there are three samples involved in the complex contrast. However, in the case of the simple contrast of group a versus group b only two samples are involved, so $N_{cont} = n_a + n_b$ in that case. In the case of an effect size for a contrast the estimates from eta^2, tau^2, xi^2, and zeta^2 that are discussed in the next section will be the same.

To illustrate the use of Equations 12.2, 12.3, and 12.3a we again use the hypothetical example in which each $n_i = 30$ and the outputted Λ for the complex contrast of the two combined treated groups versus the control group equals .8500 (with $p = 2$ dependent variables). In this case

$$\omega^2_{mult} = 1 - \left[\frac{(90)(.8500)}{90 - 3 + .8500} \right] = .1291975 \approx .129$$

and

$$\omega^2_{multadj} = .1291975 - \frac{[(2^2 + 1^2)(1 - .1291975)]}{3(90)} = .1130716 \approx .113.$$

As should be expected, the adjusted estimate is smaller than the unadjusted upwardly biased estimate. One concludes that approximately 11% of the (generalized) variance of the composite of the dependent variables is associated with the contrast involving membership in the combined treated groups versus membership in the control group. If one wants to calculate adjusted multivariate omega^2 for the simple contrast between the two treated groups, in the previous calculation 90 is changed to $N_{cont} = n_a + n_b = 60$ and .8500 is changed to the outputted value for Λ for this simple contrast. Again, the multivariate measure is only roughly analogous to univariate POV_{pop}. Reviews of criticisms of strength of association (POV_{pop}) in general as a measure of effect size were provided in Chapters 4 and 6.

OVERALL PROPORTION OF VARIANCE EXPLAINED IN MANOVA

We discuss six estimators of overall strength-of-association (i.e., proportion-of-variance explained) effect size. Four of the estimators are the previously discussed adjusted and unadjusted omega^2 and adjusted and unadjusted eta^2 for contrasts. Therefore, we need not rewrite Equations 12.2 and 12.3 here. However, for the present case of estimation of overall POV_{pop}, instead of POV_{pop} for contrasts, the value of Wilks' lambda that is now used in Equation 12.2 is the value that is outputted for the omnibus statistical test of equality of *all* of the population vectors of means, N_{cont} is now the overall total N, and $df_{error} = N - k$. In the present case of using Equation 12.3 for less biased estimation of overall POV_{pop}, $q = k - 1$ and the overall total N replaces N_{cont}. Such a POV_{pop} in the case of only two total groups is very roughly a multivariate analog of a squared point-biserial correlation (the coefficient of determination that is discussed in Chapter 4).

Tau²

(Note that because some readers might not be familiar with the Greek letter tau, and more readers are likely to confuse the forthcoming similar-looking Greek letters xi and zeta, all squared Greek letters that represent estimators of effect sizes will hereafter be spelled out.) Whereas the previously discussed adjusted and unadjusted estimators of POV_{pop} that are based on eta² and omega² do not relate to the dimensions that may underlie the observed dependent variables (such underlying dimensions often being called latent variables or constructs), some estimators of multivariate association are intended to do so. We consider three such estimators, tau², xi², and zeta², which are outputted by IBM SPSS MANOVA as such. (However, as of the time of this writing, some software output these three estimators labeled "eta squared.") These estimators take into account the number of dimensions underlying the observed dependent variables.

The first estimator is another one that is based on Wilks' lambda omnibus test statistic (Cramer & Nicewander, 1979), tau (Greek τ) squared given by

$$\text{tau}^2 = 1 - \Lambda^{1/s},$$

(12.4)

where s is the smaller of (a) the number of dependent variables (p) or (b) $k - 1$ (except for the case of an interaction effect in factorial designs, as is discussed later). When there are two groups $k - 1 = 1$ and $s = 1$, so the present estimator will simplify to $1 - \Lambda$, which is the common unadjusted (for bias) eta-squared estimator of POV_{pop} in the present omnibus case and in the previously discussed case of contrasts.

An underlying dimension is an optimally weighted combination of two or more observed dependent variables, the weights being chosen by the software so as to maximize the intercorrelation of just those observed variables of which the dimension is a composite. Each dimension is also formed so as not to correlate with any other dimension. Tau² is intended to estimate the mean (specifically, the geometric mean) proportion of generalized variance in the underlying dimensions that is associated with group membership. (Very briefly, a geometric mean is used to average proportions when certain conditions of the data apply.) (Tau is not related to Kendall's tau measure of correlation that was discussed in Chapter 4.)

Because Λ estimates the proportion of *unexplained* variance it is natural to use $1 - \Lambda$, or some variant thereof, to estimate the proportion of *explained* variance, POV_{pop}. Also, $1 - \Lambda$ can be defined as the squared multiple correlation between a set of Y variables and a set of one or more X variables, which is a generalization of the R^2 that is discussed in Chapter 10. Van Der Linde and Tutz (2008) discussed generalizing R^2 to this case. (If the X variable is a $k > 2$ grouping variable that has been dummy coded into $k - 1$ quantitative variables as discussed in Chapter 10, then the grouping variable has become a set of X variables.)

To illustrate tau² we use real sociological data that Smithson (2003) used to demonstrate construction of a confidence interval for eta² in MANOVA. The study hypothesized that members of communities that had been settled earlier than other communities have a stronger sense of community. The independent variable was the time period during which the $N = 375$ respondents' communities had been settled, with $k_a = 2$ levels, which were earlier and later settlement. The $p = 3$ dependent variables were sense of community, quality of social support, and size of one's network. The omnibus F was statistically significant beyond the .001 level and the overall Wilks' Λ equaled .9486. Applying the needed values to Equation 12.4 yields $tau^2 = 1 - .9486^{1/1} = .0514 \approx .051$. One thus estimates that, on average (i.e., the geometric mean) approximately 5% of the generalized variance in the dimension(s) underlying the dependent variables is related to group membership.

Smithson (2003) demonstrated the use of the noncentrality parameter to construct a .90. confidence interval for POV_{pop} for this example. The interval is bounded by .0167 and .0863. What we label tau^2 in this example Smithson labeled η^2 because, as was previously noted, these two estimators are identical when $s = 1$. Raykov and Marcoulides (2010) proposed a large-sample method for constructing a confidence interval for a POV_{pop} for an underlying dimension when there are two or three measured dependent variables.

Xi²

Another estimate of POV_{pop} that relates to supposed underlying dimensions is

$$xi^2 = V/s, \tag{12.5}$$

where
  xi is the Greek letter ξ
  V is the Pillai–Bartlett omnibus statistic (sometimes denoted U)
  s is as defined previously

The sample xi^2 is intended to estimate the arithmetic mean proportion of generalized variance of the supposed underlying dimensions that is associated with group membership. Consult Cramer and Nicewander (1979) and Rencher (2002) for further discussions of xi^2. (The notation of Cramer–Nicewander and Rencher differs from ours, which agrees with much current notation.)

Zeta²

The next estimator of multivariate POV_{pop} that is intended to relate to underlying dimensions is based on the Hotelling–Lawley trace omnibus test statistic, an estimator that is called zeta (Greek ζ) squared,

$$zeta^2 = \frac{U}{s + U}, \tag{12.6}$$

where
  U (some authors use the letter V) is the Hotelling–Lawley trace statistic
  s is as previously defined for Equation 12.4

(Some authors use U instead to denote Wilks' lambda.) The U trace is a multivariate generalization of the univariate F ratio of between-groups and within-groups sums of squares, and zeta^2 is roughly a multivariate generalization of univariate eta^2.

Zeta^2 is a weighted mean of the estimated values of eta^2 for each discriminant function. A discriminant function is a mathematical expression optimally combining the dependent variables so as maximally to separate (i.e., distinguish, discriminate) the participants into the groups. For example, discriminant functions enable a data analyst to classify each participant into one of the treatment groups as accurately as possible given the data at hand. Multivariate data can yield one or more discriminant functions. Consult Huberty (1983), Shaffer and Gillo (1974), and Styn and Ellis (2009) for discussions of zeta^2.

Consult Steyn and Ellis (2009) for an equation that, for the two-group case, relates zeta^2 or tau^2 to the previously discussed Mahalanobis distance, D^2. What we and some others call zeta^2 and tau^2, Steyn and Ellis call estimators of $\eta^2_{k,p}$ and η^2_Λ, respectively.

Tips and Pitfalls

Unfortunately, there can be a wide range of estimates produced by the various estimators. Again, if one reports an estimate of POV_{pop} we prefer a bias-adjusted estimate as is discussed in the next section, but all outputted estimates should be reported to facilitate comparison of results with those from studies that have used estimators other than a given researcher's preferred estimator.

ADJUSTMENT FOR BIAS

Serlin (1982) recommended adjusting xi^2 for positive bias using

$$xi^2_{adj} = 1 - \frac{N-1}{N-b-1}\left(1 - \frac{V}{s}\right), \tag{12.6a}$$

where b is the larger of p and $k - 1$ (except for the case of interaction in factorial designs, as is discussed later). Huberty (1994) and Huberty and Olejnik (2006) discussed Serlin's adjustment.

Serlin's adjustment can also be applied to zeta^2 and to tau^2 in the two-group case, or in the multiple-group case when sample sizes are large, by replacing the term V/s with zeta^2 or tau^2 in Equation 12.6a. Kim and Olejnik (2005) conducted simulations that supported the use of Serlin's (1982) adjustment (Equation 12.6a) under most conditions and confirmed that unadjusted estimates can be positively biased when groups and dependent variables are numerous and sample sizes are small, especially when the effect size in the population is small. Those authors also observed that Equation 12.6a is analogous to Ezekiel's bias-adjusted R^2, which we discuss in Chapter 10. Because the simulations conducted by Kim and Olejnik were based on all assumptions of MANOVA being satisfied and balanced designs, it is not known if their results would change under different conditions. Consult Steyn and Ellis (2009) for further discussion of bias-adjusted estimation of multivariate POV_{pop}.

We apply Serlin's adjustment for bias to the previous sociological example in which we found that tau^2 = .0514, based on $k = 2$, $p = 3$, and $N = 377$. To apply Serlin's adjustment to tau^2 $1 - \Lambda^{1/s}$ replaces V/s in Equation 12.6a, where the notation has previously been defined. One finds that

$$\text{tau}^2_{adj} = 1 - \frac{377 - 1}{377 - 3 - 1}(1 - .0514) = .0437706 \approx .044.$$

(Because xi^2, zeta^2, and tau^2 are identical when $k = 2$, as are their Serlin-adjusted values, we only calculate Serlin's adjustment for tau^2 for the current two-group example.) The adjustment causes one to estimate that approximately 4%, instead of the previously estimated approximately 5%, of the generalized variance of the underlying dimension(s) is associated with group membership.

Recommendations and Further Discussions

All of the estimators that have been discussed thus far can also be used to estimate strength-of-association effect sizes from contrasts. Inspection of their equations reveals that identical results for contrasts would be obtained using eta^2, tau^2, xi^2, and zeta^2 because the degrees of freedom for a contrast is equal to 1. For this reason those four estimators are also identical when there are only two total groups.

We recommend the use of adjusted omega^2 when one is interested in estimating the proportion of generalized variance of the observed dependent variables that is associated with group membership. When instead one is interested in estimating an average of the proportions of generalized variance in supposed underlying dimensions that are associated with group membership, we tentatively recommend the use of a Serlin-adjusted tau^2. If one intends to use xi^2 or zeta^2 we tentatively recommend the Serlin-adjusted versions as were described previously. However, except for the combination of small sample sizes and small effect sizes, Steyn and Ellis (2009) found that in terms of bias and sampling variability tau^2 performed better than the Serlin-adjusted xi^2, and also zeta^2, but all of these estimators have somewhat different interpretations. Those authors also found that most of the estimators that were studied are only slightly biased when samples are very large or effect sizes are large. Steyn and Ellis also provide a SAS program for constructing an approximate confidence interval for an omnibus effect size that is based on a bias-adjusted eta squared. Methods for construction of confidence intervals for all measures of effect size should be developed. It can be argued that the chosen estimator of effect size should be one that lends itself to the construction of a confidence interval for the effect size parameter. Kline (2004) provides discussion of some topics in estimation of multivariate effect sizes that constraint on length does not permit discussing here.

Some might argue that the researcher's choice of the type of multivariate POV_{pop} that is to be estimated should be consistent with the choice of test statistic. Thus, according to this point of view one should use omega^2 or tau^2 when testing with Wilks lambda, xi^2 when testing with the Pillai–Bartlett statistic, or zeta^2 when testing with the Hotelling–Lawley statistic. Alternatively, one might choose zeta^2 if one believes that many discriminant functions contribute to the effect or perhaps xi^2 if only the first few discriminant functions mainly contribute to the effect (R. B. Kline, personal communication, June 7, 2011). We have no strong opinion on the foregoing criteria for choosing a measure. However, to accommodate readers who might not share the preference of the author of a research report, we again recommend the reporting of all outputted estimates.

Tips and Pitfalls

We reiterate that it is imperative that research reports clearly identify which estimator is being reported. For example, Olejnik and Algina (2000) reported seven major estimators of effect size for the same real data. Although there was little variation among tau^2, xi^2, and zeta^2, overall these yielded estimates that were approximately 50% lower than those from unadjusted eta^2.

Recall from the section entitled "Epsilon squared (ε^2) and omega squared (ω^2)" for the ANOVA case in Chapter 6 that although POV_{pop} cannot be below 0, an estimate of POV_{pop} can be below 0. This is also true of estimators in the MANOVA case. Recall also that although negative values for the estimates are often reported as 0, there is an argument for reporting the obtained negative numerical value (Fidler & Thompson, 2001). Consult the references on this topic that were cited in Chapter 6. Also, as Tatsuoka (1988) pointed out, the traditional terminology of "proportion of variance explained" is only roughly applicable to MANOVA in terms of the proportion of generalized variance of the set of observed dependent variables or underlying variables that is associated with the independent variable of group membership. Tatsuoka also discussed the rationale for the use of each of the four test statistics in the estimation of strength-of-association effect sizes.

Kim and Olejnik (2005) discussed many measures of overall strength of association for one-way fixed-effects MANOVA, including some that they did not recommend and that we do not discuss here. Those authors noted that many of these measures are based on different conceptualizations of a multivariate effect-size parameter and, therefore, have different interpretations.

The effect size f was discussed in Chapter 6 for the univariate case as a kind of standardized average effect in the population across all of the levels of the independent variable, and f was also related to POV_{pop} (i.e., η^2) there. Consult Steyn and Ellis (2009) for a review of the extension of f^2 to the case of one-way MANOVA.

MANCOVA

The discussions of MANOVA thus far in this chapter and of ANCOVA in Chapter 11 can be extended to MANCOVA. We assume that the reader has an understanding of ANCOVA at least at the level of our review of the topic in Chapter 11. Assumptions of MANOVA and multivariate extensions of the assumptions of ANCOVA must be sufficiently satisfied. Therefore, the burdens of valid application of MANCOVA are greater than for MANOVA. MANCOVA is applicable to analysis of data yielded by a design in which there are two or more dependent variables and there are pretest data or one or more relevant covariates.

MANCOVA addresses possible differences among the covariate-adjusted population vectors of means. The adjustment renders each group's vector of means what it would have been if all of the participants had the same score on a covariate. As with ANCOVA, the more reliable the scores on the covariate the greater the power of the statistical test of difference in population covariate-adjusted vectors of means in MANCOVA.

As was discussed regarding ANCOVA in Chapter 11, MANCOVA cannot be expected to compensate for nonrandom assignment to groups. It might seem that the more covariates that are used the better because of the greater compensation for nonrandom assignment. However, the greater the number of covariates the greater the chance that (a) one or more covariates will not correlate sufficiently with the dependent variables to compensate for the possible incremental reduction of statistical power from the additional covariate(s) and (b) the greater the chance of violation of the assumptions of MANCOVA.

When there is a reasonable ranking of the importance of the dependent variables the Roy–Bargmann stepdown analysis that was discussed by Stevens (2002, 2009) and Tabachnick and Fidell (2007) is applicable to MANCOVA. Tabachnick and Fidell discussed syntax and output for IBM SPSS MANOVA when conducting a MANCOVA, and they provided a checklist for the procedure and a sample results section.

In addition to the assumptions of MANOVA, MANCOVA assumes that there is a correlation (traditionally a linear relationship) in the population between covariates and dependent variables. It is also assumed that the correlation between dependent variables and covariates is the same in all of the populations (*homogeneity of regression*) so that there is justification for averaging the sample regressions for the purpose of adjusting the group vectors of means for the covariate(s). When there is heterogeneity of regression there would be no single adjustment for covariates that would be applicable across all groups, so MANCOVA would be inappropriate in this case. Also, distributions of covariates should not contain outliers. Consult Chapter 11 for references to discussions of univariate alternatives to ANCOVA. These can be applied to the separate dependent variables in place of MANCOVA.

For the case of three or more covariates Stevens (2009) discussed the assumption of homogeneity of regression hyperplanes, which we defined in Chapter 11 and which can be tested in some software such as IBM SPSS MANOVA. We will not further discuss the previously discussed assumptions of MANOVA and ANCOVA (Chapter 11), violation of which can reduce the statistical power of MANCOVA. Table 7.34 in Tabachnick and Fidell (2007) compares the output of some major software for MANCOVA. Also consult Huberty and Olejnik (2006) regarding IBM SPSS syntax and interpretation of MANCOVA tests of assumptions and omnibus testing of covariate-adjusted vectors of means.

As is the case for ANOVA and MANOVA, it is not necessary to precede selected pair-wise or complex contrasts with an omnibus MANCOVA test if these contrasts are selected a priori. In this case, but not in the case of comparisons selected *after* examining the data, a Bonferroni–Dunn or similar adjustment of alpha levels sufficiently justifies the approach. All of the previously discussed four major MANOVA omnibus tests will yield the same result for tests of contrasts of the covariate-adjusted vectors of means in MANCOVA. Huberty and Olejnik (2006) provided IBM SPSS syntax and interpretation for such contrasts. The syntax is the same as it is for MANOVA contrasts, but, in the present case of adjustments based on covariates, output includes covariate-adjusted eta^2 as the effect size. Output also includes the correlation between each observed dependent variable and the composite of all the dependent variables as an estimate of the relationship between each variable and a common dimension that may underlie the observed dependent variable measures.

Omnibus and Contrast Effect Sizes for MANCOVA

Equations 12.2 and 12.4 through 12.6 are also applicable to estimation of an overall strength-of-association effect size in MANCOVA. For these applications use the Wilks' lambda and its associated df_{error} (Equations 12.2 and 12.4), Hotelling–Lawley U statistic (Equation 12.5), or Pillai–Bartlett V statistic (Equation 12.6) from the outputted omnibus test of statistical significance of the difference among covariate-adjusted vectors of means (e.g., IBM SPSS MANOVA). Our previous statement about reporting all calculated estimates applies. The estimates of overall effect size from Equations 12.2 and 12.4 through 12.6 (and other estimators such as eta^2) may differ greatly. Also, as one should expect, the estimates of overall effect size using MANCOVA can differ greatly from estimates arising from the same data when there are no covariates (MANOVA). Differences between estimates that are based on different estimators, and differences between estimates that are based on MANOVA or MANCOVA, are exemplified by the results in Tables 14 and 16 in Olejnik and Algina (2000). Again, comparison of results from study to study is fruitless unless each report is clear in all relevant details about which kind of estimate of effect size is being reported from which kind of design.

Huberty and Olejnik (2006) provided examples of effect sizes for simple or complex contrasts in MANCOVA. Such effect sizes are outputted, for example, by IBM SPSS MANOVA. Again, such effect sizes can be based on any of the four traditional MANOVA test statistics. As was discussed regarding effect sizes for contrasts in MANOVA without covariates, all four of the traditional outputted effect sizes for contrasts in MANCOVA will have the same value because $df_{effect} = 1$ for all contrasts. Huberty and Olejnik also discussed the use of software output to estimate in MANCOVA the proportion of generalized variance of an underlying dimension that is accounted for by group membership.

FACTORIAL BETWEEN-GROUPS MANOVA

The assumptions of one-way MANOVA, and problems of violations thereof, apply to factorial MANOVA. Output for factorial MANOVA typically includes the results of tests of assumptions and tests of each main effect and interactions. Huberty and Olejnik (2006), Norušis (2003), Stevens (2009), and Tabachnick and Fidell (2007) provide examples.

When outputted interaction effects are statistically insignificant one should inspect and interpret the omnibus tests or contrasts. IBM SPSS outputs effect sizes for pair-wise and complex main effect contrasts. If there is insufficient support for interaction, then one inspects and interprets (a) simple effects in terms of differences among row cell vectors of means or column cell vectors of means or (b) contrasts among cell vectors of means. Huberty and Olejnik (2006) discussed IBM SPSS syntax and output for simple effects and contrasts among main effects and among cell vectors of means. Factorial MANOVA is ideally, but not necessarily, conducted with equal cell sample sizes (i.e., *orthogonal factorial designs*). For example, IBM SPSS MANOVA and IBM SPSS GLM accommodate MANOVA with nonorthogonal designs.

Another reason to limit p (the number of dependent variables) is that it is necessary that each $n_{cell} > p$. If one proceeds with MANOVA in the case of insufficient cell size the statistical power of the omnibus test will be lowered. The lesson is to derive the greatest use from total available sample size by restricting the number of dependent variables and minimizing the number of factors and levels of factors to the most important ones.

STANDARDIZED DIFFERENCE BETWEEN VECTORS OF MEANS IN FACTORIAL MANOVA

Equation 12.1 can be used to estimate the vector-of-means-difference effect size (i.e., the previously discussed Mahalanobis D) in the case of a factor of interest with $k = 2$ levels, or contrasts within a factor of interest in which $k > 2$, in a factorial MANOVA when the research is experimental. In the current factorial case the summation in Equation 12.1 involves only those cells in the design that are relevant to the contrast and

$$df_{error} = N_{tot} - k_a k_b.$$

This method is not appropriate for the case in which one or more of the peripheral factors is intrinsic (e.g., gender). (We define and discuss peripheral and intrinsic factors in Chapter 7.) The equation in the current case only reflects variability that is attributable to the targeted factor (i.e., the factor of interest). Therefore, if one or more of the peripheral factors is intrinsic the D in Equation 12.1 is ignoring variability that exists in the populations to which the contrasts are supposed to generalize.

Tatsuoka (1988) presented an example of statistical significance testing (but not the D effect size) for an experimental 2×3 factorial MANOVA in which $p = 2$, $k_a = 2$, $k_b = 3$, $n_{cell} = 10$, $N_{tot} = 60$, $\Lambda_A = .9077$, $\Lambda_B = .1341$, $\Lambda_{AB} = .6361$, and $df_{error} = N_{tot} - k_a k_b = 60 - 2(3) = 54$. Note that the interaction in the present data was statistically significant and that many data analysts would not proceed with tests of statistical significance of main effects in such a case. References and discussion on how to proceed when interaction is statistically significant are provided in Chapter 7, so the topic is not revisited here. Also, recall from Chapter 1 that many data analysts would not report an effect size when the underlying statistical test does not yield significance. Statistical significance was not attained for Factor A at the .05 level. However, we proceed with this worked example solely to demonstrate the calculation and interpretation of Equation 12.1 when justified.

Applying the needed values to Equation 12.1 to compare the two levels of Factor A yields

$$D_A = \left[\frac{54(1-.9077)((1^2/10)+(1^2/10))}{.9077} \right]^{1/2} = 1.0479523 \approx 1.048.$$

One concludes that the vectors of means for the two levels of Factor A are estimated to be approximately one unit apart, where the unit of distance is analogous in a multidimensional space to a pooled standard deviation in the univariate case. A value of D can also be calculated for simple or complex contrasts within the three levels of Factor B using Equation 12.1, but for his purposes Tatsuoka (1988) did not provide the values of lambda that are needed for such calculations for the example at hand, so we proceed instead to demonstrate the use of Equation 12.1 to calculate D for the interaction (not done by Tatsuoka). The current application of Equation 12.1 to the interaction between Factors A and B in a 2 × 3 design involves summation over six cells. Also, as before, $df_{error} = 54$. Therefore,

$$D_{AB} = \left[\frac{54(1-.6361)((1^2/10)+(1^2/10)+(1^2/10)+(1^2/10)+(1^2/10)+(1^2/10))}{.6361} \right]^{1/2}$$

$$= 4.3052743 \approx 4.305.$$

One concludes that the difference between a cell vector of means at one level of a factor and a cell vector of means at another level of that factor at one level of the other factor is estimated to be approximately 4 distance units away from the value of that difference at another level of the other factor. (Not surprisingly, a multivariate interaction is more difficult to comprehend than a univariate interaction.) As in the univariate case (Chapter 7), an interaction is a difference between differences, but in the multivariate case the unit of difference (distance) is, again, the analog in multidimensional space of a pooled standard deviation in the univariate case.

STRENGTH OF ASSOCIATION EFFECT SIZES FOR FACTORIAL BETWEEN-GROUPS MANOVA

Equations 12.2, 12.3, and 12.3a can be used to estimate strength-of-association effect sizes for contrasts within a factor, and Equations 12.4 through 12.6 can be used to estimate a multivariate rough analog of overall *partial POV*$_{pop}$ for the entire factor. Unadjusted and adjusted η^2 are also applicable, but we favor the less biased adjusted ω^2 (Equations 12.3 and 12.3a) although the latter may not be outputted by one's available software, so Equations 12.3 and 12.3a would have to be calculated manually. Also, an estimate of *POV*$_{pop}$ can be expected to be somewhat larger when a treatment factor appears in a factorial MANOVA than when it appears in a one-way MANOVA if the other factor is a subjects factor (intrinsic factor of Chapter 7) because the use of a subject factor reduces error variability. (That is, in this case the subject variability moves from error variability in the treatment factor to between-groups variability for the subjects factor.) Again, comparisons of estimates of effect size for a given factor are problematic for a factor that appears in different designs. In the present factorial case Equations 12.2, 12.3, 12.3a, and 12.6 estimate a multivariate analog of a partial POV_{pop} for a given factor because they exclude variance that is attributable to any other factor. (Univariate partial POV_{pop} was discussed in Chapter 7.) Again, what is called POV in MANOVA is only approximately analogous to POV in univariate analysis.

Roughly, a sample partial POV in factorial between-groups MANOVA estimates what proportion of the partial generalized variance is explained by the optimally combined scores on the dependent variables for the main effect, interaction, or contrast that is the object of the POV. The generalized variance is partial in the current case because it consists only of error variance and variance from the effect of interest, excluding variance from the other effects.

IBM SPSS GLM currently outputs the partial POV_{pop} estimate that is represented by Equation 12.4 for between-groups factorial MANOVA. Huberty and Olejnik (2006) provided syntax and interpretation of pair-wise and complex contrasts using IBM SPSS. Output also includes estimation of strength of association adjusted for bias.

Degrees of Freedom When Estimating Strength of Association

The degrees of freedom that are outputted for tests of significance in MANOVA are not the same as the ones to be used in equations that call for degrees of freedom when estimating POV_{pop} in factorial MANOVA (Equations 12.2, 12.3, and 12.6a). The degrees of freedom for the purpose of estimating POV_{pop} are as follows:

$$df_{maineffect} = k - 1, \tag{12.7}$$

where k is the number of levels of the involved factor.

For the case of interaction between two factors, A and B,

$$df_{ab} = (k_a - 1)(k_b - 1). \tag{12.8}$$

The degrees of freedom for error are given by

$$df_{error} = k_a k_b (n_{cell} - 1) = N - k_a k_b. \tag{12.9}$$

Worked Example of POV Effect Sizes for Factorial Between-Groups MANOVA

Norušis (2003) partly worked a real example of a 2×2 between-groups MANOVA, using IBM SPSS, for which we now add estimation of (partial) POV_{pop} effect sizes for Factors A and B. (Estimation of overall POV_{pop} for a factor that has only two levels is analogous to estimation of POV_{pop} for a simple contrast involving two groups.) For these data the provided $p = 3$, $N_{tot} = 20$, $k_A = 2$, $k_B = 2$, $n_{cell} = 5$, $\Lambda_A = .382$ (p level $= .003$), $\Lambda_B = .523$ (p level $= .025$), and $df_{error} = 16$ for our purpose of estimating POV_{pop}. Unadjusted estimates of (partial) POV_{pop} will often be outputted, so here we calculate and interpret adjusted partial omega^2 and adjusted partial tau^2 for each main effect. For the present example the interaction was reported to be statistically insignificant ($p = .302$ for all four major tests), which simplifies interpretation. (Of course, there may actually have been an interaction, but one that was of insufficient magnitude to have been detected.) For Factor A, applying the needed values to Equation 12.2 yields

$$\omega^2_{multA} = 1 - \left[\frac{20(.382)}{16 + .382} \right] = .5336345 \approx .534.$$

Adjusting omega^2 using Equation 12.3 yields

$$\omega^2_{multadjA} = .5336345 - \left[\frac{(3^2 + 1^2)(1 - .5336345)}{3(20)} \right] = .455907 \approx .456.$$

For Factor B,

$$\omega^2_{multB} = 1 - \left[\frac{20(.523)}{16 + .523} \right] = .3669431 \approx .367.$$

Again adjusting omega^2 using Equation 12.3,

$$\omega^2_{multadjB} = .3669431 - \left[\frac{(3^2 + 1^2)(1 - .3669431)}{3(20)} \right] = .2614337 \approx .261.$$

We interpret the adjusted omega^2 values together with interpretation of values of adjusted tau^2 after the latter is calculated for both factors.

Tips and Pitfalls

One should not compare the estimated omega^2 (or adjusted omega^2) for Factors A and B because, as was previously explained, these are estimates of partial POV_{pop} that are each based on proportions of different generalized variances.

Applying the needed values to Equation 12.4 to calculate tau^2 for Factor A yields $tau^2_A = 1 - .382^{1/1} = .618$. Using Equation 12.6a, with tau^2 replacing V/s as was previously discussed for Serlin's adjustment, one finds that

$$tau^2_{adjA} = \frac{20 - 1}{20 - 3 - 1}(1 - .618) = .546375 \approx .546.$$

Applying the needed values to Equation 12.4 for Factor B yields $\text{tau}_B^2 = 1 - .523^{1/1} = .477$. Applying Serlin's adjustment,

$$\text{tau}_{\text{adjB}}^2 = 1 - \frac{20-1}{20-3-1}(1-.477) = .3789375 \approx .379.$$

From adjusted omega^2 one estimates that for Factor A and for Factor B approximately 46% and approximately 26%, respectively, of the generalized variance of the totality of dependent variables is related to group membership. Again, because these are estimates of partial POV_{pop} the two values should not be compared with each other, but each can be compared with relevant results from strictly comparable single-factor studies. One further estimates from adjusted tau^2 that for Factor A and Factor B approximately 55% and approximately 38%, respectively, of the proportion of generalized variance in the underlying dimensions is related to group membership. Each of these values can be compared with relevant results from strictly comparable single-factor studies. A field of study is better served if research reports include both adjusted omega^2 and adjusted tau^2, which provide different perspectives. Further, because xi^2 and zeta^2 are also often outputted, and can be adjusted using the appropriate version of Equation 12.6a as was previously described, a field is better served if all four adjusted estimates are reported. Again, a reader of a research report may be very interested in a type of an estimator that is not of great interest to the author of the report. Therefore, one might also consider reporting the redundancy index. Finally, note that for each factor in the current example unadjusted tau^2 is greater than unadjusted omega^2. Such a result is not surprising because, as was previously stated, when $k - 1 = 1$ and $s = 1$ unadjusted tau^2 is equivalent to unadjusted eta^2, and the latter is more upwardly biased than is unadjusted omega^2.

ONE-WAY WITHIN-GROUPS MANOVA

We provide a minimal background review for those who need it. More knowledgeable readers may want to proceed directly to the section entitled "Effect Sizes for One-Way Within-Groups Analyses." Often when a multivariate approach is taken with within-groups data a single dependent variable has been measured on the same participants at different times (e.g., pretest, posttest, and, possibly, follow-up test, or trials 1 through p) or under different conditions, with the scores at each instance of measurement being treated in MANOVA as if they represented a separate dependent variable. Alternatively, sometimes two or more dependent variables are measured repeatedly on the same participants. For examples, a test of spelling and a test of grammar may be administered repeatedly during a class in English, or two tests of different aspects of mental health may be administered repeatedly during months of therapy. Such designs, called *doubly multivariate designs*, were discussed by Tabachnick and Fidell (2007) and are not discussed here. The label "doubly multivariate" arises from the fact that the design is multivariate in two ways: (a) there are two or more dependent variables and (b) the scores at each instance of repeated measurement are treated as an additional dependent variable.

SPHERICITY AND OTHER PRELIMINARY MATTERS

Recall from the section entitled "Within-Groups Designs" in Chapter 6 that even when there is only one main dependent variable MANOVA is often preferred to ANOVA. Unlike within-groups univariate ANOVA, in which participants constitute a second factor in the design, MANOVA does not make the assumption that is called sphericity (defined in Chapter 6). Tests in MANOVA are often (not always) more powerful than traditional ANOVA F tests or ANOVA F tests that have been sphericity-corrected by adjusting the df in the within-group case. However, when all assumptions are satisfied within-groups ANOVA may be more powerful than MANOVA. The assumptions in between-groups MANOVA apply in the present within-groups case.

Huberty and Olejnik (2006) provided IBM SPSS syntax and interpretation for testing sphericity and conducting omnibus tests. However, again, satisfaction of the assumption of sphericity is only relevant if one undertakes a univariate approach to within-groups data. Consult Keselman, Algina, and Kowalchuk (2001) for an informative review of different approaches for analyses of within-groups data. Consult Maxwell and Delaney (2004) for a detailed discussion of the multivariate F-testing approach to within-groups data. Wilcox (2005a) provided R and S-PLUS functions for a nonparametric method for making all pair-wise comparisons in the multivariate dependent-groups case.

EFFECT SIZES FOR ONE-WAY WITHIN-GROUPS ANALYSES

We now consider univariate and multivariate approaches to effect sizes for one-way within-groups analyses. We begin with estimates of univariate whole *POV* and partial *POV*, respectively, for one-way within-groups designs. (In later discussions we define partial POV_{pop} for each case in terms of which part of total variability is being excluded in that case.) However, for the purpose of estimating effect sizes it is customary to treat this nominal one-way design as if it were a two-way ANOVA design in which the subjects variable constitutes a random factor that is crossed with the fixed targeted factor of interest and the statistically insignificant mean square for interaction of these factors constitutes the error term.

There are estimates of univariate whole POV_{pop} and partial POV_{pop} using eta^2, epsilon^2, and omega^2. However, we only consider omega^2 here because it is a less biased estimator. Whole POV_{pop} includes subject variance in total variance to render an estimator of POV_{pop} from a within-subjects design comparable to an estimator from a between-subjects design, if this is the goal of the researcher. One kind of partial POV_{pop} excludes (partials) subject variance from total variance, if this is the goal of the researcher. To estimate *univariate whole POV_{pop}* we use Equation 6.17:

$$\omega^2 = \frac{(k-1)(MS_{effect} - MS_{txs})}{SS_{tot} + MS_{sub}},$$ (6.17)

where
   k is the number of levels of the fixed targeted factor with respect to which the
      effect size is being estimated
   $k-1$ is the df for the effect
   MS_{effect} is the mean square for the main effect of the targeted factor
   MS_{txs} is the mean square for treatment-by-subjects interaction
   SS_{tot} is the total sum of squares (i.e., $SS_{effect} + SS_{txs} + SS_{sub}$)
   MS_{sub} is the mean square for subjects

With regard to calculating Equation 6.17, currently in order to find SS_{tot} using IBM
SPSS, or to find SS_{tot} and MS_{sub} using SAS, data must be entered as if the within-
groups factor were a between-groups factor, so that there are only between-groups
factors. Calculation of Equation 6.17 was demonstrated in Chapter 6.

To estimate *univariate partial* POV_{pop} in which variability that is attributable to
the subject factor is excluded from total variability, there is again an omega^2 given by

$$\omega^2_{partial} = \frac{(k-1)(MS_{effect} - MS_{txs})}{(k-1)(MS_{effect}) + (N_{tot} - k + 1)MS_{txs}}. \tag{12.10}$$

For a set of hypothetical data Maxwell and Delaney (2004) thoroughly worked a
one-way within-groups ANOVA, including whole omega^2, to which we add partial omega^2 because it is instructive to compare these two approaches. The relevant values are $N_{tot} = 12$, $k = 4$, $MS_{effect} = 184.00$, and $MS_{txs} = 60.79$. Applying the
needed values to Equation 12.10 yields

$$\omega^2_{partial} = \frac{(4-1)(184.00 - 60.79)}{(4-1)(184.00) + (12 - 4 + 1)60.79} = .336299 \approx .336.$$

It is informative that Maxwell and Delaney reported that the whole omega^2 for
these data is .04, which is very much lower than our calculated partial omega^2
of .336. Such a very large difference between whole and partial estimates of
POV_{pop} is common, as is discussed in the following. (In Equation 12.10 the term
$(N_{tot} - k + 1)$ in the denominator represents $(N_{tot} - df_{effect})$, which, because in the
present case $df_{effect} = k - 1$, becomes $N_{tot} - (k-1) = N_{tot} - k + 1$.)

There are equations for multivariate estimated partial eta^2 and multivariate
estimated partial omega^2 for the current within-group case using Wilks' Λ. These
are outputted by IBM SPSS or can be calculated from SAS Repeated. We only
provide the equation for the less biased multivariate partial omega^2:

$$\omega^2_{multipart} = 1 - \frac{N_{tot}\Lambda}{df_{error} + \Lambda}, \tag{12.11}$$

where, again, $df_{error} = N_{tot} - (k-1) = N_{tot} - k + 1$. With regard to the current
data, for which we previously estimated using a univariate approach that partial

POV_{pop} = .336, Maxwell and Delaney (2004) reported that Λ = .5725. Applying the needed values to Equation 12.11 yields for the multivariate approach

$$\omega^2_{multpart} = 1 - \frac{12(.5725)}{(12 - 4 + 1 + .5725)} = .2823192 \approx .282.$$

Thus, the estimates of partial POV_{pop} based on the univariate approach (.336) and based on the current multivariate approach (.282) are different. Also, as is common, these two estimates are much higher than the estimate of whole POV_{pop} (.04) because univariate and multivariate partial POV_{pop} exclude subject variance from total variance.

Tips and Pitfalls
As we noted in the section entitled "Within-groups designs" in Chapter 6, Keppel and Wickens (2004) endorsed the use of partial POV_{pop} instead of total POV_{pop}. However, Maxwell and Delaney (2004) suggested whole POV_{pop} if one wants to render estimators of POV_{pop} from within-groups and between-groups designs comparable. Again, reports of research must include every estimate that has been calculated and be explicit about which kinds of estimator of POV_{pop} they are, because estimates of partial POV_{pop} can be very much larger than estimates of whole POV_{pop}. Again, the difference occurs because when partial POV_{pop} is being estimated explained variability is defined as a proportion of total variability from which subject variability has been excluded.

In the example provided by Maxwell and Delaney estimated partial POV_{pop} was approximately seven times larger than estimated whole POV_{pop}, and in examples provided by Olejnik and Algina (2000) estimates of partial POV_{pop} were nearly four times larger than estimated whole POV_{pop}. It would be unacceptable to favor reporting of estimates of partial POV_{pop} merely because they will be more impressive than estimates of total POV_{pop}. It is important to reiterate that when excluding subject variability to calculate an estimate of partial POV_{pop} for within-group data one is excluding a source of variability that would not ordinarily be excluded if the same independent variable were being studied in the context of a between-groups design. Consult Gaebelein and Soderquist (1978) for a review of the early history of the debate about the proper way to estimate POV_{pop} for within-groups variables.

RECOMMENDATIONS AND ADDITIONAL READING

In an area of research in which the relationship between a given independent variable and a given dependent variable is sometimes studied using a within-groups design and sometimes studied using a between-groups design, it is important that the kind of POV_{pop} that is estimated be comparable in each case if results from each kind of design are to be compared or meta-analyzed. In such areas of research a useful POV_{pop} for within-groups studies is one that includes the contribution of subject variability to total variability because subject variability is included in total variability when POV_{pop} is estimated for between-groups designs. An estimator for such a generalizable POV_{pop} for within-groups designs was given by Equation 6.17, which was repeated in this chapter. Estimators of within-groups POV_{pop} that are based on *lambda* in the MANOVA approach, such as the estimator in Equation 12.11, unlike the estimator in Equation 6.17, exclude subject variability from total variability. Such multivariate estimators should not be used by researchers who do not want to exclude subject variability.

For the univariate approach to one-way within-groups designs Chapter 6 provides recommendations for calculation of standardized-difference effect sizes, a reference for construction of a robust confidence interval for such an effect size, references for making traditional or robust pair-wise comparisons of unstandardized mean differences and constructing confidence intervals for them, and a reference for detecting the ordering of the population means. Maxwell and Delaney (2004) discussed univariate and MANOVA approaches for testing contrasts for the present design. Wilcox (2005a) presented R and S-PLUS functions for a nonparametric method for making all pair-wise comparisons in the multivariate dependent-groups case. Wilcox (2005e) proposed a rank-based multivariate method for comparing dependent groups that permits skew.

EFFECT SIZES FOR MIXED MANOVA DESIGNS

We now consider effect sizes for a *mixed design* with one between-groups and one within-groups factor. (Based on the heritage of applied statistics in agricultural research, this design is also called a *split-plot design*.) We label the between-groups Factor A and the within-groups Factor B. Both factors are considered to be fixed and extrinsic, as was defined in Chapter 7. The subjects factor (Factor S) is again a random factor. (Each participant represents a level of a subjects factor.) Analyses of the mixed design make the previously discussed (Chapter 6) assumptions of analyses of between-group and within-group designs and the assumption of independence of the vectors of scores across the groups.

UNIVARIATE AND MULTIVARIATE APPROACHES TO POV_{pop}

There are different approaches to POV_{pop} effect sizes for the present case. We first follow the univariate approach (e.g., Maxwell & Delaney, 2004), in which POV_A for the overall effect of between-groups Factor A is estimated as if Factor A were in a one-way design. This POV_A is a type of partial POV_{pop} in which variability that is attributable to Factor B is excluded from total variability. In this approach the effect size essentially averages POV_A across the levels of Factor B. However, in this approach, unlike the multivariate approach that is discussed next, variability between subjects is included as one of the sources of overall variance for which the researcher is attempting to account. This approach is intended to render the estimate of POV_{pop} comparable to an estimate from a between-groups design. From the current perspective an estimator of univariate partial POV_A is

$$\omega_{A\,part}^2 = \frac{SS_A - (k_a - 1)(MS_{S/A})}{SS_A + SS_{S/A} + MS_{S/A}},$$

(12.12)

where

k_a is the number of levels of Factor A

$MS_{S/A}$ and $SS_{S/A}$ are the mean square and the sum of squares, respectively, for error for Factor A

The subscript notation S/A indicates that the Subjects factor is nested under the between-groups Factor A

Nesting in this case means that each participant appears only at one level of Factor A, which has to be so because Factor A is a between-groups factor.

Consult Olejnik and Algina (2000) for an alternative to Equation 12.12 for univariate partial omega^2 for the between-subjects Factor A from another perspective. That equation may produce a very different estimate of partial POV_{pop}, so again research reports should be explicit about which equation has been used and alert readers to the rationale for the approach taken.

Univariate partial POV_{pop} for the main effect of within-group Factor B excludes variability that is attributable to Factor A, as if Factor B had been studied in a one-way design. In this case

$$\omega^2_{Bpart} = \frac{(k_b - 1)(MS_B - MS_{B\times S/A})}{SS_B + SS_{B\times S/A} + SS_{S/A} + MS_{S/A}},$$ (12.13)

where

k_b is the number of levels of Factor B

$MS_{B\times S/A}$ and $SS_{B\times S/A}$ are the mean square and sum of squares, respectively, for error for Factor B

the subscript notation B×S/A denotes the interaction between Factor B and the subjects factor that is nested under Factor A

Finally, the POV_{AB} for the interaction between Factors A and B is estimated by

$$\omega^2_{AB} = \frac{(k_a - 1)(k_b - 1)(MS_{AB} - MS_{B\times S/A})}{SS_{AB} + SS_{B\times S/A} + SS_{S/A} + MS_{S/A}},$$ (12.14)

where MS_{AB} and SS_{AB} are the mean square and the sum of squares, respectively, for interaction between Factors A and B.

Tips and Pitfalls

Simpler equations for estimating some of the current kinds of POV_{pop} within a univariate approach or within a multivariate approach are available using eta^2, but again we have provided estimators using the less-biased omega^2. Differences between eta^2 and omega^2 can be great, so again we urge full reporting.

The following two estimators for partial POV_{pop} are based on the multivariate approach taken by Olejnik and Algina (2000). These estimators assume no interaction between subjects and treatment in the population. Unlike the univariate approach of Maxwell and Delaney (2004) these estimators do not include the contribution of subject variability to the overall variance for which the researcher is trying to account. To estimate the proportion of partial variance that is attributable to within-subjects Factor B using a multivariate approach one can use

$$\omega^2_{Bmultpart} = 1 - \frac{N_{tot}\Lambda_B}{(N_{tot} - k_a)(k_b - 1) + \Lambda_B}, \tag{12.15}$$

where Λ_B is the outputted Wilks' lambda for Factor B.

To estimate the proportion of partial variance that is attributable to the interaction between Factors A and B using a multivariate approach one can use

$$\omega^2_{ABmultpart} = 1 - \frac{N_{tot}\Lambda_{AB}}{(N_{tot} - k_a)(k_b - 1) + \Lambda_{AB}}, \tag{12.16}$$

where Λ_{AB} is the outputted Wilks' lambda for interaction.

More on Partial POV_{pop} for Factors and Interaction

First we demonstrate the calculation and interpretation of results for estimation of a partial POV_{pop} for between-groups Factor A using Equation 12.12. Then it is instructive to apply the previously discussed univariate approach and equations for estimation of POV_{pop} for within-groups Factor B and the interaction to a set of data that was analyzed by Olejnik and Algina (2000) using their favored multivariate approach. We thereby demonstrate the calculations and the differences in results between univariate and multivariate approaches to estimation of effect sizes for within-groups Factor B and also for the interaction. (For our current limited purpose we ignore the statistical significance of the effect sizes.) The required values from the real data that were analyzed by Olejnik and Algina are, as were provided by those authors in their article or inferred by us from what was provided, $SS_A = 44.59$, $k_a = 3$, $k_b = 2$, $N_{tot} = 66$, $MS_{S/A} = 15.925$, $SS_{S/A} = 1003.295$, $MS_B = 96.735$, $MS_{B\times S/A} = 3.328$, $SS_B = 96.735$, $SS_{B\times S/A} = 209.659$, $MS_{AB} = 42.053$, $SS_{AB} = 84.106$, $\Lambda_B = .684$, and $\Lambda_{AB} = .714$.

Applying the needed values to Equation 12.12,

$$\omega^2_{Apart} = \frac{44.59 - (3-1)(15.925)}{44.59 + 1003.295 + 15.925} = .0119758 \approx .012.$$

One thus estimates that the between-subjects Factor A accounts for approximately 1% of the variance of the dependent variable, excluding any contribution made by within-groups Factor B to the variance of the dependent variable, as if Factor A were the only factor in the design.

We next calculate and compare the univariate-based and the multivariate-based estimates of partial POV_{pop} attributable to within-groups Factor B using Equations 12.13 and 12.15, respectively. From univariate Equation 12.13,

$$\omega^2_{Bpart} = \frac{(2-1)(96.735 - 3.328)}{96.735 + 209.659 + 1.003.295 + 15.925} = .0704631 \approx .070.$$

One thus estimates that approximately 7% of the variance in the dependent variable is attributable to within-groups Factor B when subject variability is included in the total variance to be explained. In contrast, multivariate Equation 12.15 yields

$$\omega^2_{Bmultpart} = 1 - \frac{66(.684)}{(66-3)(2-1)+.684} = .291125 \approx .291.$$

Therefore, one now estimates that approximately 29% of the variance in the dependent variable is attributable to within-groups Factor B when subject variability is not included in the total variance to be explained.

Tips and Pitfalls
The estimated values 7% and 29% are not contradictory; they are merely based on different conceptualizations of the baseline variance for a portion of which a researcher wants to account. The multivariate approach will almost always produce the greater estimate of partial POV_{pop} for a within-groups factor. Researchers should not choose the multivariate approach merely for the purpose of obtaining the more impressive estimate. Again, a report of research should indicate which approach has been used and the rationale for that approach.

We next calculate and compare the univariate-based and the multivariate-based estimates of POV_{pop} for interaction between Factors A and B using Equations 12.14 and 12.16, respectively. From Equation 12.14,

$$\omega^2_{AB} = \frac{(3-1)(2-1)(42.053-3.328)}{84.106+209.659+1003.295+15.925} = .0589877 \approx .059.$$

One thus estimates that approximately 6% of the total variance of the dependent variable is attributable to the interaction between Factors A and B, when total variance includes subject variability. In contrast, multivariate Equation 12.16 yields

$$\omega^2_{ABmultpart} = 1 - \frac{66(.714)}{(66-3)(2-1)+.714} = .2603824 \approx .260.$$

As expected, the multivariate approach results in the larger estimate of the proportion of the variance that is attributable to interaction, 26% versus 6%, because this approach excludes the contribution of subject variability to the total variance.

At the time of this writing the estimators of partial POV_{pop} that IBM SPSS provides as an option for the between-groups and within-groups factors, and the output that is provided by SAS to calculate estimates of partial and whole POV_{pop} that are based on omega^2, are the kinds of estimators that were presented by Olejnik and Algina (2000) and included here.

Tips and Pitfalls

The use of a univariate approach to estimate a more easily interpreted POV_{pop} with respect to within-groups variables may be considered by some data analysts (not all, and not the present authors) to be incompatible with using a multivariate approach to test for the statistical significance of the effects of those within-groups variables. The tests of whether the sample POV effect sizes are statistically significantly different from zero are the univariate (F) test or a multivariate test of the main effect or interaction (e.g., Wilks' lambda). However, because of the previously discussed assumption of sphericity, when there are more than two levels of the within-groups variable and the univariate approach is used the degrees of freedom for the F test must be corrected using one of the three traditional corrections (e.g., the Huynh–Feldt correction). Violation of sphericity can increase the rate of Type I error when conducting a univariate test (although apparently much less so if the optimal correction of df is used). This problem provides one of the motivations for using the MANOVA approach to significance testing, which avoids such correction, when a design includes a within-groups factor with $k > 2$ levels.

Tests of sphericity, and the three kinds of adjustments of df when sphericity is violated, are provided by IBM SPSS GLM and IBM SPSS MANOVA. SAS GLM provides two of the methods for adjusting df. Huberty and Olejnik (2006) provided IBM SPSS syntax and interpretation for mixed MANOVA designs with and without a covariate, including tests of assumptions, within-groups factors, interaction, a between-groups factor, and within-groups and between-groups contrasts. Output includes estimates of POV_{pop} and partial POV_{pop} as appropriate.

ADDITIONAL APPROACHES AND READING FOR MIXED DESIGNS

There are other univariate and multivariate approaches to the analysis of data from the current mixed design when assumptions are violated. For example, there is an adjusted mixed-model method that is available in SAS PROC MIXED under violations of the assumptions of homogeneity of variance-covariance matrices and multivariate normality.

For discussions of standardized and unstandardized mean-difference effect sizes for the between-groups factors and within-groups factors, and tests and construction of confidence intervals for such effect sizes, in a univariate context consult Chapters 6 and 7. Major software packages provide confidence intervals for unstandardized mean differences for pairs of levels of the within-groups factor.

Tips and Pitfalls

Recall that an unstandardized pair-wise difference can be an informative effect size when the dependent variable is of interest in its own right instead of representing an underlying dimension. If the Bonferroni–Dunn method is used to construct simultaneous confidence intervals for pairs of levels of the within-groups factor, IBM SPSS and SAS do not currently use the critical F values that are applicable to this method. Consult Maxwell and Delaney (2004) for the appropriate table of the needed critical values of F and an example of how to use output from IBM SPSS or SAS to construct such simultaneous confidence intervals.

Wilcox (2005a) provided R and S-PLUS functions for robust testing of hypotheses of interaction and main effects for the current mixed designs. Wilcox also presented R and S-PLUS functions for using ranks to make all pair-wise comparisons for the current design. In Chapter 7, we discuss the Wilcox extension of what we called the probability-of-superiority effect size to multiple comparisons for mixed designs.

There are different methods for testing multivariate interaction contrasts in mixed designs when assumptions are violated. (A simple example of a test of an interaction contrast would be a test to determine if the extent of difference between groups at level 1 and level 2 of the between-groups factor depends on whether that difference is examined at level 1 or level 3 of the within-groups factor.) A SAS/IML program to implement such a method and other methods is available in Keselman, Wilcox, and Lix (2003).

EFFECT SIZES FOR WITHIN-GROUPS MANOVA FACTORIAL DESIGNS

The assumptions and df corrections of the univariate approach to the factorial case of this section are similar to what was discussed earlier with regard to within-group variables. We assume that the goal is to render estimates of effect sizes comparable to what they would have been if the factor had been studied in a one-way between-groups design to permit comparison of effect sizes from both designs. The effect-size measure for each effect, such as a within-groups factor or interaction, is a partial POV_{pop} that excludes variance that is attributable to all other effects but includes variance that is attributable to subjects as would be the case in a between-groups design. Using the previously discussed univariate approach the estimator is

$$\omega^2_{\text{wgpartial}} = \frac{df_{\text{effect}}(MS_{\text{effect}} - MS_{\text{effect}\times S})}{SS_{\text{effect}} + SS_{\text{effect}\times S} + SS_S + MS_S}, \quad (12.17)$$

where wg represents within-groups, and $df_{\text{effect}} = k_A - 1$ or $k_B - 1$, for within-groups Factors A and B, respectively, or $(k_A - 1)(k_B - 1)$ for the interaction between Factors A and B. Equation 12.17 is a more general version of Equation 12.13 with a modification of notation.

Construction of confidence intervals for unstandardized differences between any two means (simple or complex comparisons) is straightforward in the present case if sphericity is satisfied. Well-known methods include the Dunn–Bonferroni method. When constructing a confidence interval for the unstandardized difference between the two means for a factor that only has two levels sphericity is not defined (i.e., is "satisfied"), so it is not an issue in this case. Huberty and Olejnik (2006) provide IBM SPSS syntax and interpretation for main effects and simple effects for within-groups factorial designs. Output includes estimation of POV_{pop} or partial POV_{pop} when appropriate.

ADDITIONAL ANALYSES

There are ongoing efforts to develop additional multivariate methods and effect sizes, including those that are more robust than the traditional ones. Taskinen, Oja, and Randles (2005) presented outlier-resistant multivariate extensions of the nonparametric Kendall's tau and Spearman's rho effect sizes for the $k = 2$ multivariate between-groups case. Brunner, Munzel, and Puri (2002) presented another nonparametric multivariate method for comparing two independent groups. The method is applicable to multivariate continuous and ordinal data and includes an estimator of an effect size that is related to the probability-of-superiority effect size that we discussed in Chapters 5 and 9. Consult Kawaguchi, Koch, and Wang (2011) for another method that uses the probability-of-superiority effect size for multivariate ordinal data and adjusts for covariates. In Chapter 5 we briefly discuss group overlap as an effect size. Natesan and Thompson (2007) simulated and discussed the robustness of an index of group overlap, the improvement-over-chance I effect size, for the case of small samples. The heteroscedasticity-robust I index is applicable to multivariate as well as univariate analyses.

SUMMARY

This chapter discussed overall effect sizes and effect sizes for contrasts for research in which there are two or more groups that are being compared with respect to multiple continuous dependent variables.

The assumptions of MANOVA are extensions of the assumptions of ANOVA. The sensitivity to violation of assumptions differs for the four traditional omnibus (overall) tests of the statistical significance of group difference in MANOVA (Wilks' lambda, Roy's greatest characteristic root, Lawley–Hotelling trace, Pillai–Bartlett trace), and no single method is superior under all conditions. There are alternative robust parametric and nonparametric methods. An estimate of an effect size in MANOVA can be considered to be greater than its null-hypothesized value of 0 at a given level of significance if the statistical test that compares the groups that are involved in the effect size attains statistical significance at that level.

For more focused results that involve important pairings of groups, contrasts, standardized mean-difference contrasts, and confidence intervals are informative. In many cases univariate contrasts (unstandardized or standardized) and confidence intervals for them are more informative than multivariate contrasts. A multivariate extension of a univariate d type of estimator of a standardized mean-difference effect size for the case of two groups in one-way or factorial MANOVA is D, the square root of the Mahalanobis D^2 distance statistic. Taking into account the fact that the dependent variables are on different scales and may be correlated, D estimates the extent of separation between two populations in the multidimensional space that represents the multiple dependent variables. D should be corrected for its positive bias, and it is applicable to simple comparisons and complex contrasts (e.g., control group versus combined treatment groups). Construction of confidence intervals for population D using bias-adjusted D^2 can be informative, although such confidence intervals may be very wide.

Population proportion of (multivariate generalized) variance explained (POV_{pop}) that is roughly analogous to univariate POV_{pop} can be estimated for contrasts and over all groups in between-groups MANOVA. When appropriate methods are available, confidence intervals should be constructed for such effect sizes. Whole and partial effect sizes are also applicable to one-way within-groups MANOVA, where each version has a different purpose and, importantly, a possibly greatly different value. Partial POV_{pop} can be estimated as an effect size in within-groups MANOVA factorial designs to yield an effect size that is comparable to one from a between-groups design. Construction of confidence intervals for simple or complex unstandardized contrasts involving any two groups in that design is straightforward in the univariate approach if the assumption of sphericity is satisfied.

The univariate and multivariate approaches to estimating partial POV_{pop} can yield very different results when applied to mixed MANOVA designs (designs with between-groups and within-groups factors). For this design standardized and unstandardized mean-difference effect sizes can be estimated, and confidence intervals constructed, in a univariate context using methods that are discussed in Chapters 6 and 7. There are also more robust parametric methods available to counter violation of assumptions for this design.

We favor the use of Tatsuoka's (1988) bias-adjusted omega-squared or eta-squared estimators over the unadjusted versions. We recommend Serlin's adjusted tau squared when estimating the average of the proportions of generalized variance in dimensions underlying the observed dependent variables that is explained by group membership. Reports must make clear which estimator is being reported because results can vary greatly, and any calculated estimate must be reported.

The discussions of ANCOVA (Chapter 11) and MANOVA can be extended to MANCOVA. The assumptions can be burdensome because assumptions of MANOVA and of multivariate extensions of univariate ANCOVA apply. As is the case for ANOVA, ANCOVA, and MANOVA, pair-wise or complex-contrast testing and estimation of effect sizes can be undertaken if chosen in advance without being preceded by an omnibus MANCOVA test of statistical significance. Covariate-adjusted eta square is often outputted as the estimate.

There are robust nonparametric multivariate methods for comparing two independent groups. One method yields an estimate of an effect size that is related to the probability of superiority that is discussed in Chapters 5 and 9.

QUESTIONS

12.1 Define *high dimensionality.*

12.2 What is the purpose of Hotelling's T^2?

12.3 What is the purpose of Wilks' *lambda*?

12.4 In the context of this chapter what is the purpose of Mahalanobis' D_{pop}?

12.5 Distinguish between the purposes of omega^2 and tau^2.

12.6 Will ANOVA or MANOVA typically yield the larger estimate of POV_{pop} from a within-groups factor, and why?

12.7 For one-way between-groups MANOVA calculate and interpret D_{simple} when $N_{tot} = 99$, $k = 3$, each $n_i = 33$, and the outputted Wilks lambda = .9500 for the contrast.

12.8 Calculate and interpret the Serlin-adjusted tau^2 for a one-way between-groups MANOVA when $N_{tot} = 300$, $k = 2$, $p = 4$, and the overall Wilks lambda = .9000.

12.9 Calculate and interpret adjusted omega^2 for a factor in a 2×2 between-groups factorial MANOVA when $N_{tot} = 40$, Wilks lambda for the factor = .4000, and $p = 4$. (Other needed values can be derived from what has been provided.)

12.10 Calculate and discuss the difference in interpretations of a univariate-based estimate of whole POV_{pop} and a multivariate-based estimate of partial POV_{pop} for interaction between the between-groups Factor A and the within-groups Factor B in a 2×3 mixed (split-plot) factorial design that yields the following values (assume no interaction between subjects and treatment): $k_a = 2$, $k_b = 3$, $N_{tot} = 60$, $MS_{AB} = 50.000$, $SS_{AB} = 100.000$, $MS_{B \times S/A} = 3.000$, $SS_{B \times S/A} = 348.00$, $MS_{S/A} = 20.000$, $SS_{S/A} = 1160.000$, $\Lambda_{AB} = .700$.

References

Abelson, R. P. (1985). A variance explanation paradox: When a little is a lot. *Psychological Bulletin, 97*, 129–133.

Abelson, R. P. (1995). *Statistics as principled argument*. Mahwah, NJ: Lawrence Erlbaum Associates.

Abelson, R. P. (1997). A retrospective on the significance test ban of 1999 (If there were no significance tests, they would be invented.) In L. L. Harlow, S. A. Mulaik, & J. H. Steiger (Eds.), *What if there were no significance tests* (pp. 117–141). Mahwah, NJ: Lawrence Erlbaum Associates.

Abelson, R. P., & Prentice, D. A. (1997). Contrast tests of interaction hypotheses. *Psychological Methods, 2*, 315–328.

Abu Libdeh, O. (1984). *Strength of association in the simple general linear model: A comparative study of Hays' omega-squared*. Unpublished doctoral dissertation, The University of Chicago, Chicago, IL.

Acion, L., Peterson, J. J., Temple, S., & Arndt, S. (2006a). Probabilistic index: An intuitive non-parametric approach to measuring the size of treatment effects. *Statistics in Medicine, 25*, 591–602.

Acion, L., Peterson, J. J., Temple, S., & Arndt, S. (2006b). Authors' reply. *Statistics in Medicine, 25*, 3946–3948.

Acion, L., Peterson, J. J., Temple, S., & Arndt, S. (2007). Correction. *Statistics in Medicine, 26*, 3524.

Afshartous, D., & Preston, R. A. (2010). Confidence intervals for dependent data: Equating non-overlap with statistical significance. *Computational Statistics & Data Analysis, 54*, 2296–2305.

Agresti, A. (1980). Generalized odds ratios for ordinal data. *Biometrics, 36*, 59–67.

Agresti, A. (1990). *Categorical data analysis*. New York: Wiley.

Agresti, A. (2002). *Categorical data analysis* (2nd ed.). Hoboken, NJ: Wiley.

Agresti, A. (2007). *An Introduction to categorical data analysis* (2nd ed.). Hoboken, NJ: Wiley.

Agresti, A. (2010). *Analysis of ordinal categorical data* (2nd ed.). Hoboken, NJ: Wiley.

Agresti, A. (2011). Score and pseudo-score confidence intervals for categorical data analysis. *Statistics in Biopharmaceutical Research, 3*, 163–172.

Agresti, A. (in press). Score and pseudo-score confidence intervals for categorical data analysis. *Statistics in Biopharmaceutical Research*.

Agresti, A., Bini, M., Bertacinni, B., & Ryu, E. (2008). Simultaneous confidence intervals for comparing binomial parameters. *Biometrics, 64*, 1270–1275.

Aguinis, H., & Pierce, C. A. (2006). Computation of effect size for moderating effects of categorical variables in multiple regression. *Applied Psychological Measurement, 30*, 440–442.

Aguinis, H., Pierce, C. A., & Culpepper, S. A. (2009). Scale coarseness as a methodological artifact: Correcting correlation coefficients attenuated from using coarse scales. *Organizational Research Methods, 12*, 623–652.

Alhija, F. N.-A., & Levy, A. (2009). Effect size reporting practices in published articles. *Educational and Psychological Measurement, 69*, 245–265.

Algina, J. (1999). A comparison of methods for constructing confidence intervals for the squared multiple correlation coefficient. *Multivariate Behavioral Research, 34*, 493–504.

Algina, J., & Keselman, H. J. (2003). *Confidence intervals for Cohen's effect size.* Paper presented at a conference in honor of H. Swaminathay. University of Massachusetts, Amherst, MA.

Algina, J., & Keselman, H. J. (2008). Population validity and cross-validity: Applications of distribution theory for testing hypotheses, setting confidence intervals, and determining sample size. *Educational & Psychological Measurement, 68,* 233–244.

Algina, J., Keselman, H. J., & Penfield, R. P. (2005a). An alternative to Cohen's standardized mean difference effect size: A robust parameter and a confidence interval in the two independent groups case. *Psychological Methods, 10,* 317–328.

Algina, J., Keselman, H. J., & Penfield, R. P. (2005b). Effect sizes and their intervals: The two-level repeated measures case. *Educational and Psychological Measurement, 65,* 241–258.

Algina, J., Keselman, H. J., & Penfield, R. D. (2006a). Confidence interval coverage for Cohen's effect size statistic. *Educational and Psychological Measurement, 66,* 945–960.

Algina, J., Keselman, H. J., & Penfield, R. D. (2006b). Confidence intervals for an effect size when variances are not equal. *Journal of Modern Applied Statistical Methods, 5,* 2–13.

Algina, J., Keselman, H. J., & Penfield, R. D. (2010). Confidence intervals for squared semipartial correlation coefficients: The effect of nonnormality. *Educational and Psychological Measurement, 70,* 926–940.

Algina, J., Moulder, B., & Moser, B. K. (2002). Sample size requirements for accurate estimation of squared semi-partial correlation coefficients. *Multivariate Behavioral Research, 37,* 37–57.

Algina, J., & Olejnik, K. S. (2000). Determining sample size for accurate estimation of the squared multiple correlation coefficient. *Multivariate Behavioral Research, 35,* 119–136.

Algina, J., Oshima, T. C., & Lin, W.-Y. (1994). Type I error rates for Welch's test and James's second-order test under nonnormality and inequality of variance when there are two groups. *Journal of Educational and Behavioral Statistics, 19,* 275–291.

Al-Kandari, N. M., Buhamra, S. S., & Ahmed, S. E. (2005). Estimating and testing effect size from an arbitrary population. *Journal of Statistical Computation and Simulation, 75,* 987–1001.

Al-Kandari, N. M., Buhamra, S. S., & Ahmed, S. E. (2007). Testing and merging information for effect size estimation. *Journal of Applied Statistics, 34,* 47–60.

Allen, J., & Le, H. (2008). An additional measure of overall effect size for logistic regression models. *Journal of Educational and Behavioral Statistics, 33,* 416–441.

Aloe, A. M., & Becker, B. J. (in press). An effect size for regression predictors in meta-analysis. *Journal of Educational and Behavioral Statistics.*

American Psychological Association. (2010). *Publication manual of the American Psychological Association* (6th ed.). Washington, DC: Author.

Anderson, D. R., Burnham, K. P., & Thompson, W. L. (2000). Null hypothesis testing: Problems, prevalence, and an alternative. *Journal of Wildlife Management, 64,* 912–923

Arceneaux, K., Gerber, A. S., & Green, D. P. (2010). A cautionary note on the use of matching to estimate causal effects: An empirical example comparing matching estimates to an experimental benchmark. *Sociological Methods Research, 39,* 256–282.

Austin, P. C. (2009). Some methods of propensity-score matching had superior performance to others: Results of an empirical investigation and Monte Carlo simulations. *Biometrical Journal, 51,* 171–184.

Austin, P. C., & Laupacis, A. (2011). A tutorial on methods to estimating clinically and policy-meaningful measures of effects in prospective observational studies: A review [Electronic version]. *The International Journal of Biostatistics, 7.* Retrieved January 10, 2011, from http://www.bepress.com/ijb/vol7/iss1/6. DOI: 10.2201/1557-4679.1285.

Baguley, T. (2009). Standardized or simple effect size: What should be reported? *British Journal of Psychology, 100*, 603–617.

Baguley, T. (2010). When correlations go bad.... *The Psychologist, 23*, 122–123.

Bakeman, R. (2005). Recommended effect size statistics for repeated measures designs. *Behavior Research Methods, 37*, 379–384.

Barchard, K. A. (in press). Examining the reliability of interval level data using root mean square differences and concordance correlation coefficients. *Psychological Methods*.

Barnette, J. J., & McLean, J. E. (1999, November). Empirically based criteria for determining *meaningful effect size*. Paper presented at the annual meeting of the Mid-South Educational Research Association, Point Clear, AL.

Baugh, F. (2002a). Correcting effect sizes for score reliability: A reminder that measurement and substantive issues are linked inextricably. *Educational and Psychological Measurement, 62*, 254–263.

Baugh, F. (2002b). Correcting effect sizes for score reliability. In B. Thompson (Ed.), *Score reliability: Contemporary thinking on reliability issues* (pp. 31–41). Thousand Oaks, CA: Sage Press.

Beal, S. L. (1987). Asymptotic confidence intervals for the difference between binomial parameters for use with small samples. *Biometrics, 43*, 941–950.

Beatty, M. J. (2002). Do we know a vector from a scalar? Why measures of association (not their squares) are appropriate indices of effect. *Human Communication Research, 28*, 605–611.

Becker, B. J. (1988). Synthesizing standardized mean change measures. *British Journal of Mathematical and Statistical Psychology, 41*, 257–278.

Becker, T. E. (2005). Potential problems in the statistical control of variables in organizational research: A qualitative analysis with recommendations. *Organizational Research Methods, 8*, 274–289.

Belia, S., Fidler, F., Williams, A., & Cumming, G. (2005). Researchers misunderstand confidence intervals and standard error bars. *Psychological Methods, 10*, 389–396.

Bendermacher, N., & Souren, P. (2009). Beyond kappa: Estimating inter-rater agreement with nominal classifications. *Journal of Modern Applied Statistical Methods, 8*, 110–121.

Benjamini, Y. (2010). Discovering the false discovery rate. *Journal of the Royal Statistical Society: Series B (Statistical Methodology), 72*, 405–416.

Berger, V. (2005). *Selection biases and covariate imbalances in randomized clinical trials*. New York: Wiley.

Berk, R. A., & Newton, P. J. (1985). Does arrest really deter wife battery? An effort to replicate the findings of the Minneapolis spouse abuse experiment. *American Sociological Review, 50*, 353–362.

Berry, K. J., Johnston, J. E., & Mielke, P. W., Jr. (2006). A measure of effect size for r × c contingency tables. *Psychological Reports, 99*, 251–256.

Berry, K. J., Johnston, J. E., & Mielke, P. W., Jr. (2007). An alternative measure of effect size for Cochran's Q test for related proportions. *Perceptual and Motor Skills, 104*, 1236–1242.

Berry, K. J., Johnston, J. E., & Mielke, P. W., Jr. (2010). Maximum-corrected and chance-corrected measures of effect sizes for the Mantel-Haenszel test. *Psychological Reports, 107*, 393–401.

Berry, K. J., Johnston, J. E., Zahran, S., & Mielke, P. W., Jr. (2009). Stuart's tau measure of effect size for ordinal variables: Some methodological considerations. *Behavior Research Methods, 41*, 1144–1148.

Bevan, M. F., Denton, J. Q., & Meyers, J. L. (1974). The robustness of the F test to violations of continuity and form of treatment population. *British Journal of Mathematical and Statistical Psychology, 27*, 199–204.

Bickel, P. J., & Lehmann, E. L. (1975). Descriptive statistics for nonparametric models: II. Location. *Annals of Statistics, 3*, 1045–1069.

Bird, K. D. (2002). Confidence intervals for effect sizes in analysis of variance. *Educational and Psychological Measurement, 62*, 197–226.

Biswas, A., & Park, E. (2008). Measures of association for nominal categorical variables. *Journal of the Korean Statistical Society, 38*, 247–258.

Bloom, H. S., Hill, C. J., Black, A. R., & Lipsey, M. W. (2008). Performance trajectories and performance gaps as achievement effect-size benchmarks for educational interventions. *Journal of Research in Educational Effectiveness, 1*, 289–328.

Blouin, D. C., & Riopelle, A. J. (2005). On confidence intervals for within-subjects designs. *Psychological Methods, 10*, 397–412.

Bond, C. F., Wiitala, W. L., & Richard, F. D. (2003). Meta-analysis of raw differences. *Psychological Methods, 8*, 406–418.

Bonett, D. G. (2006). Robust confidence interval for a ratio of standard deviations. *Applied Psychological Measurement, 30*, 432–439.

Bonett, D. G. (2007). Transforming odds ratios into correlations for meta-analytic research. *American Psychologist, 62*, 254–255.

Bonett, D. G. (2008). Confidence intervals for standardized linear contrasts of means. *Psychological Methods, 13*, 99–109.

Bonett, D. G. (2009a). Meta-analytic interval estimation for standardized and unstandardized mean differences. *Psychological Methods, 14*, 225–238.

Bonett, D. G. (2009b). Estimating standardized linear contrasts of means with desired precision. *Psychological Methods, 14*, 1–5.

Bonett, D. G., & Price, R. M. (2002). Statistical inference for a linear function of medians: Confidence intervals, hypothesis testing, and sample size requirements. *Psychological Methods, 7*, 370–383.

Bonett, D. G., & Price, R. M. (2006). Confidence intervals for a ratio of binomial proportions based on paired data. *Statistics in Medicine, 25*, 3039–3047.

Bonett, D. G., & Price, R. M. (2007). Statistical inference for generalized Yule coefficients in 2 × 2 contingency tables. *Sociological Methods & Research, 35*, 429–446.

Bonett, D. G., & Seier, E. (2003). Confidence intervals for mean absolute deviations. *The American Statistician, 57*, 233–236.

Borenstein, M., Hedges, L. V., Higgins, J. P. T., & Rothstein, H. R. (2009). *Introduction to meta-analysis*. Chichester, England: Wiley.

Borooah, V. K. (2002). *Logit and probit: Ordered and multinomial models*. Thousand Oaks, CA: Sage Press.

Bradley, M. T., Smith, D., & Stoica, G. (2002). A Monte-Carlo estimation of effect size distortion due to significance testing. *Perceptual and Motor Skills, 95*, 837–842.

Bray, J. H., & Maxwell, S. E. (1985). *Multivariate analysis of variance*. Newbury Park, CA: Sage Press.

Breaugh, J. A. (2003). Effect size estimation: Factors to consider and mistakes to avoid. *Journal of Management, 29*, 79–97.

Brown, L., & Li, X. (2005). Confidence intervals for two sample binomial distribution. *Journal of Statistical Planning and Inference, 130*, 359–375.

Browne, R. H. (2010). The t-test p value and its relationship to the effect size and $P(X > Y)$. *The American Statistician, 64*, 30–33.

Brownie, C. (1988). Estimating $Pr(X < Y)$ in categorized data using "ROC" analysis. *Biometrics, 44*, 615–621.

Brumback, B., & Berg, A. (2008). On effect-measure modification: Relationships among changes in the relative risk, odds ratio, and risk difference. *Statistics in Medicine, 27*, 3453–3465.

Brunner, E., Domhof, S., & Langer, F. (2002). *Nonparametric analysis of longitudinal data in factorial experiments.* New York: Wiley.

Brunner, E., & Munzel, U. (2000). The nonparametric Behrens-Fisher problem: Asymptotic theory and small-sample approximation. *Biometrical Journal, 42,* 17–25.

Brunner, E., Munzel, U., & Puri, M. L. (2002). The multivariate nonparametric Behrens-Fisher problem. *Journal of Statistical Planning and Inference, 108,* 37–53.

Brunner, E., & Puri, M. L. (2001). Nonparametric methods in factorial designs. *Statistical Papers, 42,* 1–52.

Bryk, A. S. (1977). Evaluating program impact: A time to cast away stones, a time to gather stones together. *New Directions for Program Evaluation, 1,* 32–58.

Bryk, A. S., & Raudenbush, S. W. (1988). Heterogeneity of variance in experimental studies: A challenge to conventional interpretations. *Psychological Bulletin, 104,* 396–404.

Bunner, J., & Sawilowsky, S. (2002). Alternatives to S_w in the bracketed interval of the trimmed mean. *Journal of Modern Applied Statistical Methods, 1,* 176–181.

Callaert, H. (1999). Nonparametric hypotheses for the two-sample problem. *Journal of Statistics Education, 7.* Retrieved August 5, 2005, from http://www.amstat.org/publications/jse/secure/v7n2/callaert.cfm

Campbell, I. (2007). Chi-squared and Fisher-Irwin tests of two-by-two tables with small sample recommendations. *Statistics in Medicine, 26,* 3661–3675.

Carlson, K. D., & Schmidt, F. L. (1999). Impact of experimental design on effect size: Findings from the research literature on training. *Journal of Applied Psychology, 84,* 851–862.

Carroll, J. B. (1961). The nature of the data, or how to choose a correlation coefficient. *Psychometrika, 26,* 347–372.

Carroll, R. M., & Nordholm, L. A. (1975). Sampling characteristics of Kelley's ε^2 and Hays' $\hat{\omega}^2$. *Educational and Psychological Measurement, 35,* 541–554.

Carter, N. J., Schwertman, N. L., & Kiser, T. L. (2009). A comparison of two boxplot methods for detecting univariate outliers which adjust for sample size and asymmetry. *Statistical Methodology, 6,* 604–621.

Carver, R. (1978). The case against statistical significance testing. *Harvard Educational Review, 48,* 378–399.

Cattin, P. (1980). Estimation of the predictive power of a regression model. *Journal of Applied Psychology, 65,* 407–414.

Chan, W., & Chan, W.-L. (2004). Bootstrap standard error and confidence intervals for the correlation corrected for range restriction: A simulation study. *Psychological Methods, 9,* 369–385.

Chen, X., & Luo, X. (2004). Some modifications on the application of the exact Wilcoxon-Mann-Whitney test. *Communications in Statistics – Simulation and Computation, 33,* 1007–1020.

Cheung, M. W.-L. (2009). Comparison of methods for constructing confidence intervals of standardized indirect effects. *Behavior Research Methods, 41,* 425–438.

Chinn, S. (2000). A simple method for converting an odds ratio to effect size for use in meta-analysis. *Statistics in Medicine, 19,* 3127–3131.

Chinn, S. (2002). Comparing and combining studies of bronchial responsiveness. *Thorax, 57,* 393–395.

Choi, J., Fan, W., & Hancock, G. R. (2009). A note on confidence intervals for two-group latent mean effect size measures. *Multivariate Behavioral Research, 44,* 396–406.

Christensen, R. (2005). Testing Fisher, Neyman, Pearson, and Bayes. *The American Statistician, 59,* 121–126.

Cleveland, W. S. (Ed.). (1988). *The collected works of John W. Tukey. Vol. V. Graphics.* New York: Chapman & Hall.

Cleveland, W. S. (1994). *The elements of graphing data* (2nd ed.). Summit, NJ: Hobart Press.

Cliff, N. (1993). Dominance statistics: Ordinal analyses to answer ordinal questions. *Psychological Bulletin, 114*, 494–509.

Cliff, N. (1996a). *Ordinal methods for behavioral data analysis.* Mahwah, NJ: Erlbaum.

Cliff, N. (1996b). Answering ordinal questions with ordinal data using ordinal statistics. *Multivariate Behavioral Research, 31*, 331–350.

Cohen, A., Kolassa, J., & Sackrowitz, H. B. (2004). A four action problem with ordered categorical data: Are two distributions the same, ordered, or otherwise? *Statistics and Probability Letters, 70*, 223–234.

Cohen, J. (1960). A coefficient of agreement for nominal scales. *Educational and Psychological Measurement, 20*, 37–46.

Cohen, J. (1973). Eta-squared and partial eta-squared in fixed factor ANOVA designs. *Educational and Psychological Measurement, 33*, 107–112.

Cohen, J. (1988). *Statistical power analysis for the behavioral sciences* (2nd ed.). Mahwah, NJ: Lawrence Erlbaum Associates.

Cohen, P., Cohen, J., Aiken, L. S., & West, S. G. (1999). The problem of units and the circumstance for POMP. *Multivariate Behavioral Research, 34*, 315–346.

Cohen, J., Cohen, P., West, S. G., & Aiken, L. S. (2003). *Applied multiple regression/ correlation analysis for the behavioral sciences* (3rd ed.). Mahwah, NJ: Lawrence Erlbaum Associates.

Cohen, A., Kolassa, J., & Sackrowitz, H. B. (2003). A four action problem with ordered categorical data: Are two distributions the same, ordered or otherwise? *Statistics and Probability Letters, 70*, 223–234.

Coin, D. (2007). A goodness-of-fit test for normality based on polynomial regression. *Computational Statistics & Data Analysis, 52*, 2185–2198.

Consumers Union. (2005, May). "50 percent decrease!" Dramatic statistics can be misleading. *Consumer Reports on Health, 17*(5), 9.

Correction. (2008). Correction to Woods (2007). *Psychological Methods, 13*, 72–73.

Cortina, J. M., & Landis, R. S. (2009). When small effect sizes tell a big story and when large effect sizes don't. In C. E. Lance & R. J. Vandenberg (Eds.), *Statistical and methodological myths and urban legends: Doctrine, verity, and fable in the organizational and social sciences* (pp. 287–308). New York: Routledge.

Cortina, J. M., & Landis, R. S. (in press). The earth is *not* round (*p* = .00). *Organizational Research Methods.*

Cortina, J. M., & Nouri, H. (2000). *Effect sizes for ANOVA designs.* Thousand Oaks, CA: Sage Press.

Cramer, E. M., & Nicewander, W. A. (1979). Some symmetric invariant measures of multivariate association. *Psychometrika, 44*, 43–54.

Credé, M. (2010). Random responding as a threat to the validity of effect size estimates in correlational research. *Educational and Psychological Measurement, 70*, 596–612.

Cribbie, R. A., & Keselman, H. J. (2003a). The effects of nonnormality on parametric, nonparametric, and model comparison approaches to pairwise comparisons. *Educational and Psychological Measurement, 63*, 615–635.

Cribbie, R. A., & Keselman, H. J. (2003b). Pairwise multiple comparisons: A model testing approach versus stepwise procedures. *British Journal of Mathematical and Statistical Psychology, 56*, 167–182.

Cribbie, R. A., Wilcox, R. R., Bewell, C., & Keselman, H. J. (2007). Tests for treatment group equality when data are nonnormal and heteroscedastic. *Journal of Modern Applied Statistical Methods, 6*, 117–132.

Crits-Christoph, P., Tu, X., & Gallop, R. (2003). Therapists as fixed versus random effects— Some statistical and conceptual issues: A comment on Siemer and Joormann. *Psychological Methods, 8*, 518–523.

Culpepper, S. S., & Aguinis, H. (2011). Using analysis of covariance (ANCOVA) with fallible covariates. *Psychological Methods, 16*, 166–178.

Cumming, G. (2007). Inference by eye: Pictures of confidence intervals and thinking about levels of confidence. *Teaching Statistics, 29*, 89–93.

Cumming, G. (2009). Inference by eye: Reading the overlap of independent confidence intervals. *Statistics in Medicine, 28*, 205–220.

Cumming, G., & Finch, S. (2001). A primer on the understanding, use, and calculation of confidence intervals that are based on central and noncentral distributions. *Educational and Psychological Measurement, 61*, 532–574.

Cumming, G., & Finch, S. (2005). Inference by eye: Confidence intervals and how to read pictures of data. *American Psychologist, 60*, 170–180.

Cumming, G., Williams, J., & Fidler, F. (2004). Replication and researchers' understanding of confidence intervals and standard error bars. *Understanding Statistics, 4*, 299–311.

D'Agostino, R. B. (1971). A second look at analysis of variance on dichotomous data. *Journal of Educational Measurement, 8*, 327–333.

Darlington, M. L. (1973). Comparing two groups by simple graphs. *Psychological Bulletin, 79*, 110–116.

Davies, L., Gather, U., & Weinert, H. (2008). Nonparametric regression as an example of model choice. *Communications in Statistics—Simulation and Computation, 37*, 274–289.

Dayton, C. M. (2003). Information criteria for pairwise comparisons. *Psychological Methods, 8*, 61–71.

Dayton, C. M., & Pan, X. (2005). JMASM21: PCIC_SAS: Best subsets using information criteria. *Journal of Modern Applied Statistical Methods, 4*, 621–626.

DeCoster, J., Iselin, A.-M. R., & Gallucci, M. (2009). A conceptual and empirical examination of justifications for dichotomization. *Psychological Methods, 14*, 349–366.

Delaney, H. D., & Vargha, A. (2002). Comparing several robust tests of stochastic equality with ordinally scaled variables and small to moderate sized samples. *Psychological Methods, 7*, 485–503.

DeMars, C. E. (2011). An analytical comparison of effect sizes for differential item functioning. *Applied Measurement in Education, 24*, 189–209.

Doksum, K. A. (1977). Some graphical methods in statistics: A review and some extensions. *Statistica Neerlandica, 31*, 53–68.

Donner, A., & Zou, G. Y. (2011). Estimating simultaneous confidence intervals for multiple contrasts of proportions by the method of variance estimates recovery. *Statistics in Biopharmaceutical Research, 3*, 320–335.

Duncan, B. W., & Olkin, I. (2005). Bias of estimates of the number needed to treat. *Statistics in Medicine, 24*, 1837–1848.

Emerson, J. D., & Moses, L. E. (1985). A note on the Wilcoxon-Mann-Whitney test for 2 × k ordered tables. *Biometrics, 41*, 303–309.

Fagerland, M. W., & Sandvik, L. (2009). The Wilcoxon-Mann-Whitney test under scrutiny. *Statistics in Medicine, 28*, 1487–1497.

Fahoome, G. (2002). Twenty nonparametric statistics and their large-sample approximations. *Journal of Modern Applied Statistical Methods, 2*, 248–268.

Fairchild, A. J., MacKinnon, D. P., Taborga, M. P., & Taylor, A. B. (2009). R^2 effect size measures for mediation analysis. *Behavior Research Methods, 41*, 486–498.

Fan, X. (2001). Statistical significance and effect size in education research: Two sides of a coin. *Journal of Educational Research, 94*, 275–282.

Fay, B. R. (2002). JMASM4: Critical values for four nonparametric and/or distribution-free tests of location for two independent samples. *Journal of Modern Applied Statistical Methods, 2*, 489–517.

Fay, B. R. (2003). *A Monte Carlo computer study of the power properties of six distribution-free and/or nonparametric statistical tests under various methods of resolving tied ranks when applied to normal and nonnormal data distributions.* Unpublished doctoral dissertation, Wayne State University, Detroit, MI.

Fay, B. R. (2006). The effect on Type I error and power of various methods of resolving ties for six distribution-free tests of location. *Journal of Modern Applied Statistical Methods, 5,* 22–40.

Feingold, A. (1992). Sex differences in variability in intellectual abilities: A new look at an old controversy. *Review of Educational Research, 62,* 61–84.

Feingold, A. (1995). The additive effects of differences in central tendency and variability are important in comparisons between groups. *American Psychologist, 50,* 5–13.

Feingold, A. (2009). Effect sizes for growth-modeling analysis in controlled clinical trials in the same metric as for classical analysis. *Psychological Methods, 14,* 43–53.

Feinstein, A. R. (1998). P-values and confidence intervals: Two sides of the same unsatisfactory coin. *Journal of Clinical Epidemiology, 61,* 355–360.

Feng, D. (2007). Robustness and power of ordinal *d* for paired data. In S. S. Sawilowsky (Ed.), *Real data analysis* (pp. 163–183). Charlotte, NC: Information Age Publishing.

Feng, D., & Cliff, N. (2004). Monte Carlo evaluation of ordinal *d* with improved confidence level. *Journal of Modern Applied Statistical Methods, 3,* 322–332.

Ferguson, C. F., & Brannick, M. T. (in press). Publication bias in psychological science: Prevalence, methods for identifying and controlling, and implications for the use of meta-analysis. *Psychological Methods.*

Ferron, J., Hess, M., Hogarty, K., & Kromrey, J. (2004, April). *Interval estimates of multivariate effect sizes: Accuracy and precision under nonnormality and variance heterogeneity.* Paper presented at the Annual Meeting of the American Educational Research Association, San Diego, CA.

Fidler, F., Faulkner, C., & Cumming, G. (2008). Analyzing and presenting outcomes. In A. M. Nezu & C. M. Nezu (Eds.), *Evidence-based outcome research: A practical guide to conducting randomized controlled trials for psychosocial interventions* (pp. 315–334). New York: Oxford University Press.

Fidler, F., Thomason, N., Cumming, G., Finch, S., & Leeman, J. (2005). Confidence intervals, still much to learn: Reply to Rouder & Morey. *Psychological Science, 16,* 494–495.

Fidler, F., & Thompson, B. (2001). Computing correct confidence intervals for ANOVA fixed-and-random effects effect sizes. *Educational and Psychological Measurement, 61,* 575–604.

Fielding, A. (1997). On scoring ordered classifications. *British Journal of Mathematical and Statistical Psychology, 50,* 285–287.

Finch, H. (2005). Comparison of the performance of nonparametric and parametric MANOVA tests statistics when assumptions are violated. *Methodology, 1,* 27–38.

Finch, W. H., & French, B. F. (in press). A comparison of methods for estimating confidence intervals for omega-squared effect size. *Educational and Psychological Measurement.*

Fleishman, A. I. (1980). Confidence intervals for correlation ratios. *Educational and Psychological Measurement, 40,* 659–670.

Fleiss, J. L. (1994). Measures of effect size for categorical data. In H. Cooper & L. V. Hedges (Eds.), *The handbook of research synthesis* (pp. 245–260). New York: Russell Sage Foundation.

Fleiss, J. L., Levin, B., & Paik, M. C. (2003). *Statistical methods for rates and proportions* (3rd ed.). New York: Wiley.

Fligner, M. A., & Policello, G. E., II. (1981). Robust rank procedures for the Behrens-Fisher problem. *Journal of the American Statistical Association, 76,* 162–168.

Fouladi, R. T., & Steiger, J. H. (2008). The Fisher transform of the Pearson product moment correlation coefficient and its square: Cumulants, moments, and applications. *Communications in Statistics—Simulation and Computation, 37*, 928–944.

Fowler, R. L. (1987). A general method for comparing effect magnitudes in ANOVA designs. *Educational and Psychological Measurement, 47*, 361–367.

Freels, S., & Sinha, K. (2008). R-squared for general regression models in the presence of sampling weights. *Statistics and Probability Letters, 78*, 1671–1672.

Frick, R. W. (1995). A problem with confidence intervals. *American Psychologist, 50*, 1102–1103.

Friedrich, J. O., Adhikari, N. K. J., & Beyene, J. (2008). The ratio of means method as an alternative to mean differences for analyzing continuous outcome variables in meta-analysis: A simulation study [Electronic version]. *BMC Medical Research Methodology, 8*. Retrieved August 13, 2008, from http://www.biomedcentral.com/1471-2288/8/32

Funatogawa, T., Funatogawa, I., & Shyr, Y. (2011). Analysis of covariance with pre-treatment measurements in randomized trials under the cases that covariances and post-treatment variances differ between groups. *Biometrical Journal, 53*, 512–524.

Furr, R. M. (2004). Interpreting effect sizes in contrast analysis. *Understanding Statistics, 3*, 1–25.

Gaebelein, J. W., & Soderquist, D. R. (1978). The utility of within-subjects variables: Estimates of strength. *Educational and Psychological Measurement, 38*, 351–360.

Gall, M. D., Borg, W. R., & Gall, J. P. (1996). *Educational research* (6th ed.). White Plains, NY: Longman.

Gao, G., Wan, W., Zhang, S., Redden, D. T., & Allison, D. B. (2008). Testing for differences in distribution tails to test for differences in 'maximum' lifespan [Electronic version]. *BMC Medical Research Methodology, 8*. Retrieved August 13, 2008, from http://www.biomedcentral.com/1471-2288/8/49

Gautam, S., & Ashikaga, T. (2003). Assessing the effect of an open-ended category on the trend in 2 × K ordered tables. *Journal of Data Science, 1*, 167–183.

Genest, C., & Lévesque, J.-L. (2009). Estimating correlation from dichotomized normal variables. *Journal of Statistical Planning and Inference, 139*, 3785–3794.

Gibbons, J. D. (1985). *Nonparametric statistical inference* (2nd ed.). New York: Dekker.

Gillett, R. (2003). The metric comparability of meta-analytic effect size measures. *Psychological Methods, 8*, 419–433.

Gilpin, A. R. (1993). Table for conversion of Kendall's tau to Spearman's rho within the context of measures of magnitude of effect for meta-analysis. *Educational and Psychological Measurement, 53*, 87–92.

Glass, G. V, McGaw, B., & Smith, M. L. (1981). *Meta-analysis in social research*. Thousand Oaks, CA: Sage Press.

Gleser, L. J. (1996). Comment on "Bootstrap confidence intervals." *Statistical Science, 11*, 219–221.

Goodman, S., & Greenland, S. (2007, April 24). Why most published research findings are false: Problems in the analysis [Electronic version]. *PLoS Medicine, 4*. Retrieved April 24, 2007, from http://medicine.plosjournals.org/perlserve/?request=get-document&doi=10.1371/journal.pmed

Gorecki, J. A. (2002). *A meta-analysis of the effectiveness of antidepressants compared to placebo*. Unpublished master's thesis, San Francisco State University, San Francisco.

Greenland, S. (2010). Simpson's paradox from adding constants in contingency tables as an example of Bayesian noncollapsibility. *The American Statistician, 64*, 340–344.

Grissom, R. J. (1994a). Probability of the superior outcome of one treatment over another. *Journal of Applied Psychology, 79*, 314–316.

Grissom, R. J. (1994b). Statistical analysis of ordinal categorical status after therapies. *Journal of Consulting and Clinical Psychology*, *62*, 281–284.

Grissom, R. J. (1996). The magical number .7 ± .2: Meta-meta analysis of the probability of superior outcome in comparisons involving therapy, placebo, and control. *Journal of Consulting and Clinical Psychology*, *64*, 973–982.

Grissom, R. J. (2000). Heterogeneity of variance in clinical data. *Journal of Consulting and Clinical Psychology*, *68*, 155–165.

Grissom, R. J., & Kim, J. J. (2001). Review of assumptions and problems in the appropriate conceptualization of effect size. *Psychological Methods*, *6*, 135–146.

Haddock, C. K., Rindskopf, D., & Shadish, W. R. (1998). Using odds ratios as effect sizes for meta-analysis of dichotomous data: A primer on methods and issues. *Psychological Methods*, *3*, 339–353.

Hadi, A. S., Imon, H. A. M. R., & Werner, M. (2009). Detection of outliers. *Wiley Interdisciplinary Reviews: Computational Statistics*, *1*, 57–70.

Hafdahl, A. R., & Williams, M. A. (2009). Meta-analysis of correlations revisited: Attempted replication and extension of Field's (2001) simulation studies. *Psychological Methods*, *14*, 24–42.

Hahs-Vaughn, D. L. (2005). A primer for using and understanding weights with national data sets. *The Journal of Experimental Education*, *73*, 221–248.

Hancock, G. R. (2003). Fortune cookies, measurement error, and experimental design. *Journal of Modern Applied Statistical Methods*, *2*, 293–305.

Hand, D. J. (1992). On comparing two treatments. *The American Statistician*, *46*, 190–192.

Hand, D. J., Daly, F., Lunn, A. D., McConway, K. J., & Ostrowski, E. (1994). *A handbook of small data sets*. London: Chapman & Hall.

Harris, D. N. (2009). Toward policy-relevant benchmarks for interpreting effect sizes: Combining effects with costs. *Education Evaluation and Policy Analysis*, *31*, 3–29.

Hasselblad, V., & Hedges, L. V. (1995). Meta-analysis of screening and diagnostic tests. *Psychological Bulletin*, *117*, 167–178.

Hays, W. L. (1994). *Statistics for psychologists* (5th ed.). Fort Worth, TX: Hartcourt Brace.

Hedges, L. V. (2011). Effect sizes in three-level cluster-randomized designs. *Journal of Educational and Behavioral Statistics*, *36*, 346–380.

Hedges, L. V., & Friedman, L. (1993). Gender differences in variability in intellectual abilities: A re-analysis of Feingold's results. *Review of Educational Research*, *63*, 94–105.

Hedges, L. V., & Nowell, A. (1995). Sex differences in mental test scores, variability, and numbers of high-scoring individuals. *Science*, *269*, 41–45.

Hedges, L. V., & Olkin, I. (1985). *Statistical methods for meta-analysis*. San Diego: Academic Press.

Hedges, L. V., & Pigott, T. D. (2001). The power of statistical tests in meta-analysis. *Psychological Methods*, *6*, 203–217.

Hemphill, J. F. (2003). Interpreting the magnitudes of correlation coefficients. *American Psychologist*, *58*, 78–80.

Heo, M. (2008). Utility of weights for weighted kappa as a measure of interrater agreement on ordinal scale. *Journal of Modern Applied Statistical Methods*, *7*, 205–222.

Hess, B., Olejnik, S., & Huberty, C. J (2001). The efficacy of two improvement over chance effect sizes for two-group univariate comparisons under variance heterogeneity and nonnormality. *Educational and Psychological Measurement*, *61*, 909–936.

Hess, M. R., Hogarty, K. Y., Ferron, J. M., & Kromrey, J. D. (2007). Interval estimates of multivariate effect sizes: Coverage and width estimates under variance heterogeneity and nonnormality. *Educational and Psychological Measurement*, *67*, 21–40.

Hess, M. R., & Kromrey, J. D. (2004, April). *Robust confidence intervals for effect sizes: A comparative study of Cohen's d and Cliff's delta under non-normality and heterogeneous variances*. Paper presented at the annual meeting of the American Educational Research Association, San Diego, CA.

Hess, M. R., Kromrey, J. D., Ferron, J. M., Hogarty, K. Y., & Hines, C. V. (2005, April). *Robust inference in meta-analysis: Comparing point and interval estimates using standardized mean differences and Cliff's delta*. Paper presented at the Annual Meeting of the American Educational Research Association, Montreal, Quebec, Canada.

Hill, C. J., Bloom, H. S., Black, A. R., & Lipsey, M. W. (2008). Empirical benchmarks for interpreting effect sizes in research. *Child Development Perspectives, 2,* 172–177.

Hill, C. R., & Thompson, B. (2004). Computing and interpreting effect sizes. In J. C. Smart (Ed.), *Higher education: Vol. 19. Handbook of theory and research* (pp. 175–195). Boston: Kluwer Academic.

Hogarty, K. Y., & Kromrey, J. D. (2001, April). *We've been reporting some effect sizes: Can you guess what they mean?* Paper presented at the annual meeting of the American Educational Research Association, Seattle, WA.

Hogarty, K. Y., & Kromrey, J. D. (2004, April). *Estimation of variance components in random effects meta-analysis: Impacts on inferences about mean effect sizes under non-normality and variance heterogeneity*. Paper presented at the Annual Meeting of the American Educational Research Association, San Diego, CA.

Howard, G. S., Lau, M. Y., Maxwell, S. E., Venter, A., Lundy, R., & Sweeny, R. M. (2009). Do research literatures give correct answers? *Review of General Psychology, 13,* 116–121.

Howard, K. I., Kraus, M. S., & Vessey, J. T. (1994). Analysis of clinical trial data: The problem of outcome overlap. *Psychotherapy, 31,* 302–307.

Hsu, L. M. (2003). Interrater agreement measures: Comments on kappa$_n$, Cohen's kappa, Scott's π, and Aicken's α. *Understanding Statistics, 2,* 205–219.

Hsu, L. M. (2004). Biases of success rate differences shown in binomial effect size displays. *Psychological Methods, 9,* 183–197.

Huberty, C. J. (1983). Some univariate-multivariate generalizations. *Educational and Psychological Measurement, 43,* 705–721.

Huberty, C. J (2002). A history of effect size indices. *Educational and Psychological Measurement, 62,* 227–240.

Huberty, C. J., & Olejnik, S. (2006). *Applied MANOVA and discriminant analysis* (2nd ed.). Hoboken, NJ: Wiley.

Hufthammer, K. A. (2005). *Some measures of local and global independence*. Unpublished master's thesis, University of Bergin, Bergin, Norway.

Humphreys, L. G. (1988). Sex differences in variability may be more important than sex differences in means. *Behavioral and Brain Sciences, 11,* 195–196.

Hunter, J. E., & Schmidt, F. L. (1990). *Methods of meta-analysis*. Thousand Oaks, CA: Sage Press.

Hunter, J. E., & Schmidt, F. L. (2004). *Methods of meta-analysis* (2nd ed.). Thousand Oaks, CA: Sage Press.

Hunter, J. E., Schmidt, F. L., & Le, H. (2006). Implications of direct and indirect range restriction for meta-analysis methods. *Journal of Applied Psychology, 91,* 594–612.

Hutton, J. L. (2004). Number needed to treat: Properties and problems. *Journal of the Royal Statistical Society A, 163,* 403–419.

Huynh, C. L. (2002, April). *Regression models of ordinal response data: Analytic methods and goodness-of-fit tests*. Paper read at the Annual Meeting of the American Educational Research Association, New Orleans, LA.

Imada, T., & Yamamoto, Y. (2010). Multivariate one-sided multiple comparison procedure with a control based on the approximate likelihood ratio test. *Biometrical Journal*, *52*, 771–783.

Ioannidis, J. P. A. (2005, August). Why most published research findings are false [Electronic version]. *PLos Medicine*, *2*. Retrieved May 8, 2006, from http://medicine.plosjournals.org/perlserv/?request-get-document&doi=10.1371/j

James, G. S. (1951). The comparison of several groups of observations when the ratios of the population variances are unknown. *Biometrika*, *38*, 324–329.

Kang, S.-H., Lee, Y., & Park, E.-S. (2006). The sizes of the three popular asymptotic tests for testing homogeneity of two binomial proportions. *Computational Statistics & Data Analysis*, *51*, 710–722.

Kawaguchi, A., Koch, G. G., & Wang, X. (2011). Stratified multivariate Mann-Whitney estimators for the comparison of two treatments with randomization based covariance adjustment. *Statistics in Biopharmaceutical Research*, *3*, 217–231.

Keating, J. P., & Mason, R. L. (2005). Pitman nearness comparison of the traditional estimator of the coefficient of determination and its adjusted version in linear regression models. *Communications in Statistics—Theory and Methods*, *34*, 367–374.

Kelley, K. (2005). The effects of nonnormal distributions on confidence intervals around the standardized mean difference: Bootstrap and parametric confidence intervals. *Educational and Psychological Measurement*, *65*, 51–69.

Kelley, K. (2007). Confidence intervals for standardized effect sizes: Theory, application, and implementation. *Journal of Statistical Software*, *20*, 1–24.

Kelley, K. (2008). Sample size planning for the squared multiple correlation coefficient: Accuracy in parameter estimation via narrow confidence intervals. *Multivariate Behavioral Research*, *43*, 524–555.

Kelley, K., & Maxwell, S. E. (2003). Sample size for multiple regression: Obtaining regression coefficients that are accurate, not simply significant. *Psychological Methods*, *8*, 305–321.

Kelley, K., & Maxwell, S. E. (2008). Sample size planning with applications to multiple regression: Power and accuracy for omnibus and targeted effects. In P. Alasuuta, L. Bickman, & J. Brannen (Eds.), *The Sage handbook of social research methods* (pp. 166–192). London: Sage Press.

Kelley, K., Maxwell, S. E., & Rausch, J. R. (2003). Obtaining power or obtaining precision: Delineating methods of sample-size planning. *Evaluation and the Health Professions*, *26*, 258–287.

Kelley, K., & Rausch, J. R. (2006). Sample size planning for the standardized mean difference: Accuracy in parameter estimation via narrow confidence intervals. *Psychological Methods*, *11*, 363–385.

Keppel, G. (1991). *Design and analysis: A researcher's handbook* (3rd ed.). Englewood Cliffs, NJ: Prentice Hall.

Keppel, G., & Wickens, T. D. (2004). *Design and analysis: A researcher's handbook* (4th ed.). Upper Saddle River, NJ: Pearson.

Keppel, G., & Zedeck, S. (1989). *Data analysis for research designs*. New York: Freeman.

Keselman, H. (1975). A Monte Carlo investigation of three estimates of treatment magnitude: Epsilon squared, eta squared, and omega squared. *Canadian Psychological Review*, *16*, 44–48.

Keselman, H. J. et al. (1998). Statistical practices of educational researchers: Analysis of their ANOVA, MANOVA, and ANCOVA analyses. *Review of Educational Research*, *68*, 350–386.

Keselman, H. J., Algina, J., & Fradette, K. (2005). Robust confidence intervals for effect sizes in the two group case. *Journal of Modern Applied Statistical Methods*, *4*, 353–371.

Keselman, H. J., Algina, J., & Kowalchuk, R. K. (2001). The analysis of repeated measures designs: A review. *British Journal of Mathematical and Statistical Psychology, 54*, 1–20.

Keselman, H. J., Algina, J., Lix, L. M., Wilcox, R. R., & Deering, K. N. (2008). A generally robust approach for testing hypotheses and setting confidence intervals for effect sizes. *Psychological Methods, 13*, 110–129.

Keselman, H. J., Wilcox, R. R., & Lix, L. M. (2003). A generally robust approach to hypothesis testing in independent and correlated groups designs. *Psychophysiology, 40*, 586–596.

Keselman, H. J., Wilcox, R. R., Lix, L. M., Algina, J., & Fradette, K. (2007). Adaptive robust estimation and testing. *British Journal of Mathematical and Statistical Psychology, 60*, 267–293.

Kieffer, K. M., Reese, R. J., & Thompson, B. (2001). Statistical techniques employed in AERJ and JCP articles from 1988 to 1997: A methodological review. *Journal of Experimental Education, 69*, 280–309.

Kim, S., & Olejnik, S. (2005). Bias and precision of measures of association for a fixed-effect multivariate analysis of variance model. *Multivariate Behavioral Research, 40*, 401–421.

King, J. E. (2003, February). *What have we learned from 100 years of robustness studies on r?* Paper presented at the Annual Meeting of the Southwest Educational Research Association, San Antonio, TX.

Kline, R. B. (2004). *Supplemental chapter: Multivariate effect size estimation.* Retrieved June 8, 2007, from http://www.apa.org/books/resources/kline

Kline, R. B. (2011). *Principles and practices of structural equation modeling* (3rd ed.). New York: Guilford.

Klingenberg, B. (2010). Simultaneous confidence bounds for relative risks in multiple comparisons. *Statistics in Medicine, 29*, 3232–3244.

Knapp, T. R. (2002). Some reflections on significance testing. *Journal of Modern Applied Statistical Methods, 1*, 240–242.

Knapp, T. R. (2003). Was Monte Carlo necessary? *Journal of Modern Applied Statistical Methods, 2*, 237–241.

Knapp, T. R., & Sawilowsky, S. S. (2001). Constructive criticisms of methodological and editorial practices. *The Journal of Experimental Education, 70*, 65–69.

Kowalchuk, R. K., Keselman, H. J., Wilcox, R. R., & Algina, J. (2006). Multiple comparison procedures, trimmed means and transformed statistics. *Journal of Modern Applied Statistical Methods, 5*, 44–65.

Koyama, T., Sampson, A. R., & Gleser, L. J. (2005). A framework for two-stage adaptive procedures to simultaneously test non-inferiority and superiority. *Statistics in Medicine, 24*, 2439–2456.

Kraemer, H. C. (2003). Reconsidering the odds ratio as a measure of 2×2 association in a population. *Statistics in Medicine, 23*, 257–270.

Kraemer, H. C. (2004). Reconsidering the odds ratio as a measure of 2×2 association in a population. *Statistics in Medicine, 23*, 257–270.

Kraemer, H. C. (2005). A simple effect size indicator for two-group comparisons? A comment on $r_{equivalent}$. *Psychological Methods, 10*, 413–419.

Kraemer, H. C. (2006). Correlation coefficients in medical research: From product moment correlation to the odds ratio. *Statistical Methods in Medical Research, 15*, 525–545.

Kraemer, H. C. (2008). Toward non-parametric and clinically meaningful moderators and mediators. *Statistics in Medicine, 27*, 1679–1692.

Kraemer, H. C. (2010). Epidemiological methods: About time. *International Journal of Environmental Research and Public Health, 7*, 29–45.

Kraemer, H. C., & Andrews, G. (1982). A non-parametric technique for meta-analysis effect size calculation. *Psychological Bulletin, 91*, 404–412.

Kraemer, H. C., & Kupfer, D. J. (2006). Size of treatment effects and their importance to clinical research and practice. *Biological Psychiatry, 59*, 990–996.

Kraemer, H. C., Periyakoil, V. S., & Noda, A. (2004). Kappa coefficients in medical research. In R. B. D'Agostino (Ed.), *Statistical methods in clinical studies* (pp. 85–105). New York: Wiley.

Kraemer, H. C., & Thiemann, S. (1987). *How many subjects? Statistical power analysis in research*. Thousand Oaks, CA: Sage Press.

Krantz, D. H. (1999). The null hypothesis testing controversy in psychology. *Journal of the American Statistical Association, 44*, 1372–1381.

Krauth, J. (1983). Nonparametric effect size estimation: A comment on Kraemer and Andrews. *Psychological Bulletin, 94*, 190–192.

Kreft, I., & Deleeuw, J. (1998). *Introducing multilevel modeling*. Thousand Oaks, CA: Sage Press.

Kromrey, J. D., & Coughlin, K. B. (2007, November). *ROBUST_ES: A SAS macro for computing robust effect estimates of effect size*. Paper presented at the Southeast SAS Users Group. Retrieved April 14, 2008, from http://analytics.ncsu.edu/sesug/2007/PO19.pdf

Kromrey, K. Y., & Hess, M. R. (2001, April). *Interval estimates of R^2: An empirical comparison of accuracy and precision under violations of the normality assumption*. Paper presented at the Annual Meeting of the American Educational Research Association, Seattle, WA.

Kruskal, J. B. (1978). Transformations of data. In W. H. Kruskal & J. M. Tanur (Eds.), *International Encyclopedia of Statistics* (pp. 1044–1056). New York: Free Press.

Kulinskaya, E., Dollinger, M. B., Knight, E., & Gao, H. (2004). A Welch-type test for homogeneity of contrasts under heteroscedasticity with application to meta-analysis. *Statistics in Medicine, 23*, 3655–3670.

Kulinskaya, E., Morgenthaler, S., & Staudte, R. G. (2010). Variance stabilizing the difference of two binomial proportions. *The American Statistician, 64*, 350–356.

Kulinskaya, E., & Staudte, R. G. (2006). Interval estimates of weighted effect sizes in the one-way heteroscedastic ANOVA. *British Journal of Mathematical and Statistical Psychology, 59*, 97–111.

Kuljanin, G., Braun, M. T., & DeShon, R. P. (in press). A cautionary note on modeling growth trends in longitudinal data. *Psychological Methods*.

Lacy, M. G. (2006). An explained variation measure for ordinal response models with comparisons to other ordinal R^2 measures. *Sociological Methods & Research, 34*, 469–520.

Laird, N. M., & Mosteller, F. (1990). Some statistical methods for combining experimental results. *International Journal of Technology Assessment in Health Care, 6*, 5–30.

Lambert, M. J., & Bergin, A. E. (1994). The effectiveness of psychotherapy. In A. E. Bergin & S. L. Garfield (Eds.), *Handbook of psychotherapy and behavior change* (4th ed., pp. 143–189). New York: Wiley.

Lane, D. M., & Sándor, A. (2009). Designing better graphs by including distributional information and integrating words, numbers, and images. *Psychological Methods, 14*, 239–257.

Lawson, R. (2004). Small sample confidence intervals for the odds ratio. *Communications in Statistics—Simulation and Computation, 4*, 1095–1113.

Le, H., & Schmidt, F. L. (2006). Correcting for indirect range restriction in meta-analysis: Testing a new meta-analytic procedure. *Psychological Methods, 11*, 416–438.

Lecoutre, B. (2007). Another look at confidence intervals for the noncentral T distribution. *Journal of Modern Applied Statistical Methods, 6*, 107–116.

Lecoutre, B., & Derzko, G. (2001). Asserting the smallness of effects in ANOVA. *Methods of Psychological Research Online, 6*, 1–32.

Lenth, R. V. (2001). Some practical guidelines for effective sample-size determination. *The American Statistician*, *55*, 187–193.

Lenth, R. V. (2006). Java applets for power and sample size [Computer software]. Retrieved October 3, 2007, from http://www.stat.uiowa.edu/~rlenth/Power

Leslie, D., Kohn, R., & Nott, D. (2007). A general approach to heteroscedastic linear regression. *Statistics and Computing*, *17*, 131–146.

Levin, J. R., & Robinson, D. H. (2003). The trouble with interpreting statistically non-significant effect sizes in single-study investigations. *Journal of Modern Applied Statistical Methods*, *2*, 231–236.

Levine, J. H. (2005). Extended correlation: Not necessarily quadratic or quantitative. *Social Methods and Research*, *34*, 31–75.

Levine, T. R., & Hullett, C. R. (2002). Eta-squared, partial eta-squared, and misreporting of effect size in communication research. *Human Communication Research*, *28*, 612–625.

Li, B. (2006). The *p*-value of the hypothesis testing about relative risks. *Statistics & Probability Letters*, *76*, 1731–1734.

Liao, J. G., & McGee, D. (2003). Adjusted coefficients of determination for logistic regression. *The American Statistician*, *57*, 161–165.

Liberman, A. M. (2005). How much more likely? The implications of odds ratios for probabilities. *American Journal of Evaluation*, *26*, 253–266.

Lin, Y., Newcombe, R. G., Lipsitz, S., & Carter, R. E. (2009). Fully specified bootstrap confidence intervals for the difference of two independent binomial proportions based on the median unbiased estimator. *Statistics in Medicine*, *28*, 2876–2890.

Lipman, M. M. (2008a, May). Placebos can be good medicine. *Consumer Reports on Health*, *21*, 11.

Lipman, M. M. (2008b, June). No safety in numbers. *Consumer Reports on Health*, *21*, 11.

Lipsey, M. W. (2000). Statistical conclusion validity for intervention research. In L. Bickman (Ed.), *Validity and social experimentation* (pp. 101–120). Thousand Oaks, CA: Sage Press.

Lipsey, M. W., & Wilson, D. B. (1993). The efficacy of psychological, educational, and behavioral treatments: Confirmation from meta-analysis. *American Psychologist*, *48*, 1181–1209.

Lipsey, M. W., & Wilson, D. B. (2001). *Practical meta-analysis*. Thousand Oaks, CA: Sage Press.

Liu, C., Bathke, A. C., & Harrar, S. W. (in press). A nonparametric version of Wilks' lambda–Asymptotic results and small sample approximations. *Statistics & Probability Letters*.

Liu, G. F., Lu, K., Mogg, R., Mallick, M., & Mehrotra, D. V. (2009). Should baseline be a covariate or dependent variable in analyses of change from baseline in clinical trials? *Statistics in Medicine*, *28*, 2509–2530.

Liu, O. L., & Wilson, M. (2009). Gender differences in large-scale math assessments: PISA trend 2000 and 2003. *Applied Measurement in Education*, *22*, 164–184.

Lix, L. M., & Fouladi, R. T. (2007). Robust step-down tests for multivariate independent group designs. *British Journal of Mathematical and Statistical Psychology*, *60*, 245–265.

Lloyd, C. J. (2010). Bootstrap and second-order tests of risk difference. *Biometrics*, *66*, 975–982.

Long, J. D. (2005). Omnibus hypothesis testing in dominance-based ordinal multiple regression. *Psychological Methods*, *10*, 329–351.

Long, J. D., Feng, D., & Cliff, N. (2003). Ordinal analysis of behavioral data. In I. B. Weiner (Editor-in-Chief), J. A. Shinka, & W. F. Velicer (Vol. Eds.), *Handbook of psychology: Vol. 2. Research methods in psychology* (pp. 635–661). New York: Wiley.

Louis, T. A., & Zeger, S. L. (2007, August). Effective communication of standard errors and confidence intervals [Electronic version]. Johns Hopkins University, Dept. of Biostatistics Working Papers, Working Paper 151. Retrieved August 29, 2007, from http://www.bepress.com/jhubiostat/paper151

Lui, K.-J., & Chang, K.-C. (2011). Test non-inferiority (and equivalence) based on the odds ratio under a simple crossover design. *Statistics in Medicine, 30,* 1230–1242.

Lunney, G. H. (1970). Using analysis of variance with a dichotomous dependent variable: An empirical study. *Journal of Educational Measurement, 7,* 263–269.

Maghsoodloo, S., & Huang, C.-Y. (2010). Comparing the overlapping of two independent confidence intervals with a single confidence interval for two normal population parameters. *Journal of Statistical Planning and Inference, 140,* 3295–3305.

Maity, A., & Sherman, M. (2006). The two-sample *t*-test with one variance unknown. *The American Statistician, 60,* 163–166.

Malgady, R. G. (2007). How skewed are psychological data? A standardized index of effect size. *Journal of General Psychology, 134,* 355–359.

Marascuilo, L. A., Busk, P. L., & Serlin, R. C. (1988). Large sample multivariate procedures for comparing and combining effect sizes within a single study. *Journal of Experimental Education, 57,* 69–85.

Martín Andrés, A., & Herranz Tejedor, I. (2003). Unconditional confidence interval for the difference between two proportions. *Biometrical Journal, 45,* 426–436.

Martín Andrés, A., & Herranz Tejedor, I. (2004). Exact unconditional non-classical tests on the difference between two proportions. *Computational Statistics & Data Analysis, 45,* 373–388.

Martín Andrés, A., Silva Mato, A., Tapia García, J. M., & Sánchez Quevedo, M. J. (2004). Comparing the asymptotic power of exact tests in 2 × 2 tables. *Computational Statistics & Data Analysis, 47,* 745–756.

Martín Andrés, A., Tapia García, J. M., & del Moral Ávila, M. J. (2008). Two-tailed unconditional inferences on the difference of two proportions in cross-sectional studies. *Communications in Statistics—Simulation and Computation, 37,* 455–465.

Matsumoto, D., Grissom, R. J., & Dinnel, D. L. (2001). Do between-culture differences really mean that people are different? A look at some measures of cultural effect size. *Journal of Cross-Cultural Psychology, 32,* 478–490.

Maxwell, S. E. (1998). Longitudinal designs in randomized group comparisons: When will intermediate observations increase statistical power? *Psychological Methods, 3,* 275–290.

Maxwell, S. E. (2000). Sample size and multiple regression analysis. *Psychological Methods, 5,* 434–458.

Maxwell, S. E. (2004). The persistence of underpowered studies in psychological research: Causes, consequences, and remedies. *Psychological Methods, 9,* 147–163.

Maxwell, S. E., Camp, C. C., & Arvey, R. D. (1981). Measures of strength of association: A comparative examination. *Journal of Applied Psychology, 66,* 525–534.

Maxwell, S. E., & Delaney, H. D. (1985). Measurement and statistics: An examination of construct validity. *Psychological Bulletin, 97,* 85–93.

Maxwell, S. E., & Delaney, H. D. (2004). *Designing experiments and analyzing data: A model comparison perspective* (2nd ed.). Mahwah, NJ: Erlbaum.

Maxwell, S. E., Kelley, K., & Rausch, J. R. (2008). Sample size planning for statistical power and accuracy in parameter estimation. *Annual Review of Psychology, 59,* 537–563.

May, K. (2003). A note on the use of confidence intervals. *Understanding Statistics, 2,* 133–135.

McGrath, R. E. (2008). Not all effect sizes are the same: Comments on Holden (2008). *Personality and Individual Differences, 44,* 1819–1823.

McGrath, R. E., & Meyer, G. J. (2006). When effect sizes disagree: The case of r and d. *Psychological Methods, 11*, 386–401.

McGraw, K. O., & Wong, S. P. (1992). A common language effect size statistic. *Psychological Bulletin, 111*, 361–365.

McNemar, Q. (1947). Note on the sampling error of the difference between correlated proportions or percentages. *Psychometrika, 12*, 153–157.

McNemar, Q. (1962). *Psychological statistics* (3rd ed.). New York: Wiley.

Meade, A. W. (2010a). A taxonomy of effect size measures for the differential functioning of items and scales. *Journal of Applied Psychology, 95*, 728–743.

Meade, A. W. (2010b). "A taxonomy of measurement invariance effect size indices." Correction to Meade (2010). *Journal of Applied Psychology, 95*, 943.

Mee, R. W. (1990). Confidence intervals for probabilities and tolerance regions based on a generalization of the Mann-Whitney statistic. *Journal of the American Statistical Association, 85*, 793–800.

Meehl, P. E. (1992). Factors and taxa, traits and types, differences of degree and differences in kind. *Journal of Personality, 60*, 117–174.

Menard, J. (2000). Coefficients of determination for multiple logistic regression analysis. *The American Statistician, 54*, 17–24.

Mends-Cole, S. J. (2008). Probability of coverage and interval length for two-group techniques assessing the median and trimmed mean. *Journal of Modern Applied Statistical Methods, 7*, 158–179.

Micceri, T. (1989). The unicorn, the normal curve, and other improbable creatures. *Psychological Bulletin, 105*, 156–166.

Mills, L., Cribbie, R. A., & Luh, W.-M. (2009). A heteroscedastic rank-based approach for analyzing 2 × 2 independent groups designs. *Journal of Modern Applied Statistical Methods, 8*, 322–336.

Mohr, D. C. (1995). Negative outcomes in psychotherapy: A critical review. *Clinical Psychology: Science and Practice, 2*, 1–27.

Morey, R. D., & Rouder, J. N. (in press). Bayes factor approaches for testing interval null hypotheses. *Psychological Methods*.

Morris, S. B. (2008). Estimating effect sizes from pretest-posttest-control group designs. *Organizational Research Methods, 11*, 364–386.

Morris, S. B., & DeShon, R. P. (1997). Correcting effect sizes computed from factorial analysis of variance for use in meta-analysis. *Psychological Methods, 2*, 192–199.

Morris, S. B., & DeShon, R. P. (2002). Combining effect size estimates in meta-analysis with repeated measures and independent-groups designs. *Psychological Methods, 7*, 105–125.

Moses, L. E. (1986). *Think and explain with statistics*. Reading, MA: Addison-Wesley.

Moses, L. E., Emerson, J. D., & Hosseini, H. (1984). Analyzing data from ordered categories. *New England Journal of Medicine, 311*, 442–448.

Mulaik, S. A., Raju, N. S., & Harshman, R. A. (1997). There is a time and place for significance testing. In L. L. Harlow, S. A. Mulaik, & J. H. Steiger (Eds.), *What if there were no significance tests* (pp. 65–115). Mahwah, NJ: Lawrence Erlbaum Associates.

Munk, A., Skipka, G., & Stratmann, B. (2005). Testing general hypotheses under binomial sampling: The two-sample case—Asymptotic theory and exact procedures. *Computational Statistics & Data Analysis, 49*, 723–739.

Munzel, U., & Hauschke, D. (2003). A nonparametric test for proving noninferiority in clinical trials with ordered categorical data. *Pharmaceutical Statistics, 2*, 31–37.

Murphy, K. R., & Myors, B. (2008). *Statistical power analysis: A simple and general model for traditional and modern hypothesis tests* (3rd ed.). Mahwah, NJ: Erlbaum.

Murray, L. W., & Dosser, D. A. (1987). How significant is a significant difference? Problems with the measurement of magnitude of effect. *Journal of Counseling Psychology, 34,* 68–72.

Myers, J. L., & Well, A. D. (2003). *Research design and statistical analysis* (2nd ed.). Mahwah, NJ: Lawrence Erlbaum Associates.

Nakagawa, S., & Cuthill, I. C. (2007). Effect size, confidence interval and statistical significance: A practical guide for biologists. *Biological Reviews, 82,* 591–605.

Nam, J. (2008). Comments on 'Confidence intervals for a ratio of binomial proportions based on paired data' by D. G. Bonett and R. M. Price, *Statistics in Medicine* 2006; 25:3039–3047. *Statistics in Medicine, 27,* 3209–3210.

Nanna, M. J. (2002). Hoteling's T^2 vs. the rank transformation with real Likert data. *Journal of Modern Applied Statistical Methods, 1,* 83–99.

Nanna, M. J., & Sawilowsky, S. S. (1998). Analysis of Likert scale data in disability and medical rehabilitation research. *Psychological Methods, 3,* 55–56.

Nashimoto, K., & Wright, F. T. (2007). Nonparametric multiple-comparison methods for simply ordered medians. *Computational Statistics & Data Analysis, 51,* 5068–5076.

Nasiakos, G., Cribbie, R. A., & Arpin-Cribbie, C. A. (2010). Equivalence-based measures of clinical significance: Assessing treatments for depression. *Psychotherapy Research, 20,* 647–656.

Natesan, P., & Thompson, B. (2007). Extending improvement-over-chance *I*-index effect size simulation studies to cover some small sample cases. *Educational and Psychological Measurement, 67,* 59–72.

Neuhäuser, M., Lösch, C., & Jöckel, K.-H. (2007). The Chen–Luo test in case of heteroscedasticity. *Computational Statistics & Data Analysis, 51,* 5055–5060.

Newcombe, R. G. (2006a). A deficiency of the odds ratio as a measure of effect size. *Statistics in Medicine, 25,* 235–240.

Newcombe, R. G. (2006b). Confidence intervals for an effect size measure based on the Mann-Whitney statistic. Part 1: General issues and tail area based methods. *Statistics in Medicine, 25,* 543–557.

Newcombe, R. G. (2006c). Confidence intervals for an effect size measure based on the Mann-Whitney test statistic. Part 2: Asymptotic methods and evaluation. *Statistics in Medicine, 25,* 559–573.

Newcombe, R. G. (2007). Comments on 'Confidence intervals for a ratio of binomial proportions based on paired data' by D. G. Bonett and R. M. Price, *Statistics in Medicine* 2006; 25:3039–3047. *Statistics in Medicine, 26,* 4684–4685.

Newcombe, R. G., & Nurminen, M. M. (in press). In defence of score intervals for proportions and their differences. *Computational Statistics & Data Analysis.*

Norušis, M. J. (2003). *SPSS 12.0 Statistical procedures companion.* Upper Saddle River, NJ: Prentice Hall.

Nugent, W. R. (2009). Construct validity invariance and discrepancies in meta-analytic effect sizes based on different measures. *Educational and Psychological Measurement, 69,* 62–78.

Nye, C. D., & Drasgow, F. (2011). Effect size indices for analyses of measurement equivalence: Understanding the practical importance of differences between groups. *Journal of Applied Psychology, 96,* 966–980.

O'Brien, P. C. (1988). Comparing two samples: Extensions of the *t*, rank-sum, and log-rank tests. *Journal of the American Statistical Association, 83,* 52–61.

O'Brien, R., & Castelloe, J. (2007). *Exploiting the link between the Wilcoxon-Mann-Whitney test and a simple odds statistic.* Paper 209-31. Retrieved April 4, 2007, from http://www.bio.ri.ccf.org/robrien/WMWodds/

O'Connell, A. A. (2006). *Logistic regression models for ordinal response variables.* Thousand Oaks, CA: Sage Press.

O'Connell, A. A., & Doucette, H. L. (2007). Modeling longitudinal ordinal response variables for educational data. *Journal of Modern Applied Statistical Methods, 6,* 304–319.

Odgaard, E. C., & Fowler, R. J. (2010). Confidence intervals for effect sizes: Compliance and clinical significance in the *Journal of Consulting and Clinical Psychology. Journal of Consulting and Clinical Psychology, 78,* 287–297.

Olejnik, S., & Algina, J. (2000). Measures of effect size for comparative studies: Applications, interpretations, and limitations. *Contemporary Educational Psychology, 25,* 241–286.

Olejnik, S., & Algina, J. (2003). Generalized eta and omega squared statistics: Measures of effect size for some common research designs. *Psychological Methods, 8,* 434–437.

Olson, C. L. (1974). Comparative robustness of six tests in multivariate analysis of variance. *Journal of the American Statistical Association, 69,* 894–908.

Olson, C. L. (1976). On choosing a test statistic in multivariate analysis of variance. *Psychological Bulletin, 83,* 579–586.

Onwuegbuzie, A. J., & Levin, J. R. (2003). Without supporting statistical evidence, where would reported measures of substantive importance lead? To no good effect. *Journal of Modern Applied Statistical Methods, 2,* 133–151.

Onwuegbuzie, A. J., & Levin, J. R. (2005). Strategies for aggregating the statistically nonsignificant outcome of a single study. *Research in the Schools, 12,* 10–19.

Onwuegbuzie, A. J., Levin, J. R., & Leech, N. L. (2003). Do effect size measures measure up?: A brief assessment. *Learning Disabilities: A Contemporary Journal, 1,* 37–40.

Orelien, J. G., & Edwards, L. J. (2007). Fixed-effect variable selection in linear mixed models using R^2 statistics. In C. R. Rao, J. P. Miller, & D. C. Rao (Eds.), *Handbook of statistics* (Vol. 27, pp. 1896–1907). Amsterdam, the Netherlands: Elsevier.

Ozer, D. J. (1985). Correlation and the coefficient of determination. *Psychological Bulletin, 97,* 307–315.

Pan, X., & Dayton, C. M. (2005). Sample size selection for pairwise comparisons using information criteria. *Journal of Modern Applied Statistical Methods, 4,* 601–608.

Parker, S. (1995). The "difference of means" may not be the "effect size." *American Psychologist, 50,* 1101–1102.

Pedersen, W. C., Miller, L. C., Putcha-Bhagavatula, A. D., & Yang, Y. (2002). Evolved sex differences in sexual strategies: The long and the short of it. *Psychological Science, 13,* 157–161.

Pezeshk, H., Maroufy, V., & Gittens, J. (2009). The choice of sample size: A mixed Bayesian/frequentist approach. *Statistical Methods in Medical Research, 18,* 183–194.

Pierce, C. A., Block, R. A., & Aguinis, H. (2004). Cautionary note on reporting eta-squared values from multifactor ANOVA designs. *Educational and Psychological Measurement, 64,* 916–924.

Pitts, S. C., & West, S. G. (2001). *Alternative sampling designs to detect interaction in multiple regression.* Unpublished manuscript, Department of Psychology, Arizona State University, Tempe, AZ.

Plewis, I. (2002). Modeling ordinal data using MIwiN. *Multilevel Modelling Newsletter, 14*(1). Available online at http://multilevel.ioe.ac.uk/publref/nesletters.html

Pradhan, V., & Banerjee, T. (2008). Confidence interval of the difference of two independent binomial proportions using weighted profile likelihood. *Communications in Statistics—Simulation and Computation, 37,* 645–659.

Preacher, K. J. (2006). Testing complex correlational hypotheses with structural equation models. *Structural Equation Modeling: A Multidisciplinary Journal, 13*, 520–543.

Preacher, K. J. (2008, August). *Effect size, practical significance, and graphical representation for mediation effects.* Poster presented at the annual meeting of the American Psychological Association, Boston.

Preacher, K. J., & Hayes, A. F. (2008). Contemporary approaches to assessing mediation in communication research. In A. F. Hayes, M. D. Slater, & L. B. Snyder (Eds.), *The Sage handbook of advanced data analysis methods for communication research* (pp. 13–54). Thousand Oaks, CA: Sage Press.

Preacher, K. J., & Kelley, K. (2011). Effect size measures for mediation models: Quantitative strategies for communicating indirect effects. *Psychological Methods, 16*, 93–115.

Preacher, K. J., Rucker, D. D., MacCallum, R. C., & Nicewander, W. A. (2005). Use of the extreme groups approach: A critical reexamination and new recommendation. *Psychological Methods, 10*, 178–192.

Prentice, D. A., & Miller, D. T. (1992). When small effects are impressive. *Psychological Bulletin, 112*, 160–164.

Price, R. M., & Bonett, D. G. (2008). Confidence intervals for a ratio of two independent binomial proportions. *Statistics in Medicine, 27*, 5497–5508.

Raju, N. S., Lezotte, D. V., Fearing, B. K., & Oshima, T. C. (2006). A note on correlations corrected for unreliability and range restriction. *Applied Psychological Measurement, 30*, 145–149.

Ramsey, P. H. (1980). Exact Type I error rates for robustness of Student's *t* test with unequal variance. *Journal of Educational Statistics, 5*, 337–350.

Ramsey, P. H., & Ramsey, P. R. (2007). Testing variability in the two-sample case. *Communications in Statistics—Simulation and Computation, 36*, 233–248.

Randles, R. H. (2001). On neutral responses (zeros) in the sign test and ties in the Wilcoxon-Mann-Whitney test. *The American Statistician, 55*, 96–101.

Rao, P. S. R. S., & Dorvio, A. S. (1985). The jackknife procedure for the probabilities of misclassification. *Communications in Statistics—Simulation and Computation, 14*, 779–790.

Raudenbush, S., Bryk, A., Cheong, Y. F., & Congdon, R. (2004). *HLM 6: Hierarchical linear and nonlinear modeling.* Lincolnwood, IL: Scientific Software International.

Raudenbush, S. W., & Bryk, A. S. (1987). Examining correlates of diversity. *Journal of Educational Statistics, 12*, 241–269.

Raudenbush, S. W., & Liu, X. (2001). Effects of study duration, frequency of observation, and sample size on power in studies of group differences in polynomial change. *Psychological Methods, 6*, 387–401.

Raykov, T., & Marcoulides, G. A. (2010). Multivariate effect size estimation: Confidence interval construction via latent variable modeling. *Journal of Educational and Behavioral Statistics, 35*, 407–421.

Reed, J. F., III. (2003). Solutions to the Behrens-Fisher problem. *Computer Methods and Programs in Biomedicine, 70*, 259–263.

Reed, J. E., III, & Stark, D. B. (2004). Robust two-sample statistics for testing equality of means: A simulation study, *Journal of Applied Statistics, 31*, 831–854.

Reichardt, C. S., & Gollob, H. E. (1997). When confidence intervals should be used instead of statistical tests and vice versa. In L. L. Harlow, S. A. Mulaik, & J. H. Steiger (Eds.), *What if there were no statistical tests?* (pp. 259–284). Mahwah, NJ: Lawrence Erlbaum Associates.

Reiczigel, J., Abonyi-Tóth, Z., & Singer, J. (2008). An exact confidence set for two binomial proportions and exact unconditional confidence intervals for the difference and ratio of proportions. *Computational Statistics & Data Analysis, 52*, 5046–5053.

Reiczigel, J., Zakariás, I., & Rózsa, L. (2005). A bootstrap test of stochastic equality of two populations. *The American Statistician, 59,* 156–161.

Reiser, B. (2001). Confidence intervals for the Mahalanobis distance. *Communications in Statistics—Simulation and Computation, 30,* 37–45.

Renaud, O., & Victoria-Feser, M.-P. (2010). A robust coefficient of determination for regression. *Journal of Statistical Planning and Inference, 140,* 1852–1862.

Rencher, A. C. (2002). *Methods of multivariate analysis* (2nd ed.). New York: Wiley.

Rice, M. E. (1997). Violent offender research and implications for the criminal justice system. *American Psychologist, 52,* 414–423.

Roberts, J. K., & Henson, R. K. (2003). Not all effects are created equal: A rejoinder to Sawilowsky. *Journal of Modern Applied Statistical Methods, 2,* 226–230.

Roberts, J. K., & Monaco, J. P. (2006, April). *Effect size measures for the two-level multilevel model.* Paper presented at the annual meeting of the American Educational Research Association, San Francisco, CA.

Robinson, D. H., & Levin, J. R. (1997). Reflections on statistical and substantive significance, with a slice of replication. *Educational Researcher, 26,* 21–26.

Ronis, D. L. (1981). Comparing the magnitudes of effects in ANOVA designs. *Educational and Psychological Measurement, 41,* 993–1000.

Rose, S., & van der Laan, M. J. (2008, July). Why match? Investigating matched case-control study designs with causal effect estimation [Electronic version]. U. C. Berkeley Division of biostatistics Working Paper Series, Working Paper 240. Retrieved August 6, 2008, from http://www.bepress.com/ucbbiostat/paper240

Rosenthal, R. (2000). Effect sizes in behavioral and biomedical research. In L. Bickman (Ed.), *Validity and social experimentation* (pp. 121–139). Thousand Oaks, CA: Sage Press.

Rosenthal, R., & Rosnow, R. L. (2008). *Essentials of behavioral research: Methods and data analysis* (3rd ed.). New York: McGraw-Hill.

Rosenthal, R., Rosnow, R. L., & Rubin, D. B. (2000). *Contrasts and effect sizes for Behavioral Research.* Cambridge, U.K.: Cambridge University Press.

Rosenthal, R., & Rubin, D. B. (1982). A simple general purpose display of magnitude of experimental effect. *Journal of Educational Psychology, 74,* 166–169.

Rosnow, R. L., & Rosenthal, R. (1989). Statistical procedures and the justification of knowledge in psychological science. *American Psychologist, 44,* 1276–1284.

Rosnow, R. L., & Rosenthal, R. (2003). Effect sizes for experimenting psychologists. *Canadian Journal of Experimental Psychology, 57,* 221–237.

Rosnow, R. L., & Rosenthal, R. (2008). Assessing the effect size of outcome research. In A. M. Nezu & C. M. Nezu (Eds.), *Evidence-based outcome research: A practical guide to conducting randomized controlled trials for psychosocial interventions* (pp. 379–401). New York: Oxford.

Rouder, J. N., & Morey, R. D. (2005). Relational and arelational confidence intervals: A comment on Fidler, Thomason, Cumming, and Leeman (2004). *Psychological Science, 16,* 77–79.

Rousson, V. (2011). Assessing inter-rater reliability when raters are fixed: Two concepts and two estimates. *Biometrical Journal, 53,* 477–490.

Rovine, M. J., & von Eye, A. (1997). A 14th way to look at a correlation coefficient: Correlation as the proportion of matches. *The American Statistician, 51,* 42–46.

Rozeboom, W. W. (1978). Estimation of cross-validated correlation: A clarification. *Psychological Bulletin, 85,* 1348–1351.

Rozeboom, W. W. (1981). The cross-validational accuracy of sample regressions. *Journal of Educational Statistics, 6,* 179–198.

Rudas, T. (1998). *Odds ratios in the analysis of contingency tables.* Thousand Oaks, CA: Sage Press.

Rupinsky, M. T., & Dunlap, W. P. (1996). Approximating Pearson product-moment correlation from Kendall's tau and Spearman's rho. *Educational and Psychological Measurement, 56*, 419–429.

Ruscio, J. (2008a). A probability-based measure of effect size: Robustness to base rates and other factors. *Psychological Methods, 13*, 19–30.

Ruscio, J. (2008b). Constructing confidence intervals for Spearman's rank correlation with ordinal data: A simulation study comparing analytic and bootstrap methods. *Journal of Modern Applied Statistical Methods, 7*, 416–434.

Ryu, E., & Agresti, A. (2008). Modeling and inference for an ordinal effect size measure. *Statistics in Medicine, 27*, 1703–1717.

Sánchez-Meca, J., Martín-Martínez, F., & Chacón-Moscoso, S. (2003). Effect-size indices for dichotomized outcomes in meta-analysis. *Psychological Methods, 8*, 448–467.

Satterthwaite, F. E. (1946). An approximate distribution of estimates of variance components. *Biometrics Bulletin, 2*, 110–114.

Sawilowsky, S. S. (1985). *Robust and power analysis of the 2 × 2 × 2 ANOVA, rank transformation, random normal scores, and expected normal scores transformation tests.* Unpublished doctoral dissertation, University of South Florida, Tampa, FL.

Sawilowsky, S. S. (2002). A measure of relative efficiency for location of a single sample. *Journal of Modern Applied Statistical Methods, 1*, 52–60.

Sawilowsky, S. S. (2003a). Trivials: The birth, sale, and final production of meta-analysis. *Journal of Modern Applied Statistical Methods, 2*, 242–246.

Sawilowsky, S. S. (2003b). Reliability as psychometrics versus datametrics. In B. Thompson (Ed.), *Score reliability: Contemporary thinking on reliability issues* (pp. 103–121). Thousand Oaks, CA: Sage Press.

Sawilowsky, S. S. (2003c). Reliability: Rejoinder to Thompson and Vache-Haase. In B. Thompson (Ed.), *Score reliability: Contemporary thinking on reliability issues* (pp. 149–154). Thousand Oaks, CA: Sage Press.

Sawilowsky, S. S. (2005). Abelson's paradox and the Michelson-Morley experiment. *Journal of Modern Applied Statistical Methods, 4*, 352.

Sawilowsky, S. S. (2007a). Effect sizes, simulating interaction versus main effects, and a modified ANOVA table. In S. S. Sawilowsky (Ed.), *Real data analysis* (pp. 191–212). Charlotte, NC: Information Age Publishing.

Sawilowsky, S. S. (2007b). ANCOVA and quasi-experimental design. In S. S. Sawlowsky (Ed.), *Real data analysis* (pp. 213–238). Charlotte, NC: Information Age Publishing.

Sawilowsky, S. S., & Fahoome, G. (2003). *Statistics through Monte Carlo simulation with Fortran.* Rochester Hills, MI: Journal of Modern Applied Statistical Methods.

Sawilowsky, S. S., & Spence P. R. (2007). Controlling experiment-wise Type I error: Good advice for simultaneous and sequential hypothesis testing. In S. S. Sawilowsky (Ed.), *Real data analysis* (pp. 155–162). Charlotte, NC: Information Age Publishing.

Sawilowsky, S. S., & Yoon, J. S. (2002). The trouble with trivials (p > .05). *Journal of Modern Applied Statistics, 1*, 143–144.

Schaarschmidt, F., Sill, M., & Hothorn, L. A. (2008). Approximate simultaneous confidence intervals for multiple contrasts of binomial proportions. *Biometrical Journal, 50*, 782–792.

Schacht, A., Bogaerts, K., Bluhmki, E., & Lesaffre, E. (2008). A new parametric approach for baseline covariate adjustment for two-group comparative studies. *Biometrics, 65*, 1110–1116.

Schmidt, F. L., Oh, I.-S., & Hayes, T. L. (2009). Fixed versus random effects models in meta-analysis: Model properties and an empirical comparison of differences in results. *British Journal of Mathematical and Statistical Psychology, 62*, 97–128.

Schmidt, S. (2009). Shall we really do it again? The powerful concept of replication is neglected in the social sciences. *Review of General Psychology, 13*, 90–100.

Schonfeld, I. S., & Rindskopf, D. (2007). Hierarchical linear modeling in organizational research. *Organizational Research Methods, 10*, 417–429.

Seir, E. (2002, January). Comparison of tests for univariate normality [Electronic version]. *InterStat*, 1–17. Retrieved June 16, 2006, from http://ip.statjournals.net.2002/InterStat/index/Jan02.html

Senn, S. (2011). U is for unease: Reasons for mistrusting overlap measures for reporting clinical trials. *Statistics in Biopharmaceutical Research, 3*, 302–309.

Serlin, R. C. (1982). A multivariate measure of association based on the Pillai-Bartlett procedure. *Psychological Bulletin, 91*, 413–417.

Serlin, R. C. (2002). Constructive criticism. *Journal of Modern Applied Statistical Methods, 1*, 202–227.

Serlin, R. C., Carr, J., & Marascuilo, L. A. (1982). A measure of association for selected nonparametric procedures. *Psychological Bulletin, 92*, 786–790.

Serlin, R. C., & Harwell, M. R. (1993). An empirical study of eight tests of partial correlation coefficients. *Communications in Statistics—Simulation and Computation, 22*, 545–567.

Serlin, R. C., Wampold, B. E., & Levin, J. R. (2003). Should providers of treatment be regarded as a random factor? If it ain't broke don't fix it: A comment on Siemer and Joorman (2003). *Psychological Methods, 8*, 524–534.

Shadish, W. R., Cook, T. D., & Campbell, D. T. (2002). *Experimental and quasi-experimental designs for generalized causal inference.* Boston: Houghton Mifflin.

Shaffer, J. P., & Gillo, M. W. (1974). A multivariate extension of the correlation ratio. *Educational and Psychological Measurement, 34*, 521–524.

Sharma, S., Durvasula, S., & Ployhart, R. E. (in press). The analysis of mean differences using mean and covariance structure analysis: Effect size estimation and error rates. *Organizational Research Methods.*

Shieh, G. (2006). Suppression situations in multiple linear regression. *Educational and Psychological Measurement, 66*, 435–447.

Shieh, G. (2008). Improved shrinkage estimation of squared multiple correlation coefficient and squared cross-validity coefficient. *Organizational Research Methods, 11*, 387–407.

Shieh, G. (2009). Exact analysis of squared cross-validity coefficient in predictive regression models. *Multivariate Behavioral Research, 44*, 82–105.

Shulkin, B., & Sawilowsky, S. (2009). Estimating a population median with a small sample. *Model Assisted Statistics and Applications, 4*, 143–155.

Siegel, S., & Castellan, N. J. (1988). *Nonparametric statistics for the behavioral sciences* (2nd ed.). New York: McGraw-Hill.

Siemer, M., & Joormann, J. (2003a). Power and measures of effect size in analysis of variance with fixed versus random nested factors. *Psychological Methods, 8*, 497–517.

Siemer, M., & Joormann, J. (2003b). Assumptions and consequences of treating providers in therapy studies as fixed versus random effects: Reply to Crits-Christoph, Tu, and Gallop (2003) and Serlin, Wampold, and Levin (2003). *Psychological Methods, 8*, 535–541.

Simon, S. (2007, March 14). Odds ratio versus relative risk [Electronic version]. *StATS*. Retrieved March 15, 2007, from http://www.childrensmercy.org/stats/journal/oddsratio.asp

Simonoff, J. S., Hochberg, Y., & Reiser, B. (1986). Alternative estimation procedures for $Pr(X < Y)$ in categorical data. *Biometrics, 42*, 895–907.

Singh, P., Goyal, A., & Gill, A. N. (2010). A note on comparing several variances with control variances. *Statistics & Probability Letters, 80*, 1995–2002.

Skinner, B. F. (1958). Teaching machines. *Science, 128*, 969–977.

Slavin, R., & Smith, D. (2009). The relationship between sample sizes and effect sizes in systematic reviews in education. *Educational Evaluation and Policy Analysis, 31*, 500–596.

Smith, M. L., & Glass, G. V (1977). Meta-analysis of psychotherapy outcome studies. *American Psychologist, 32*, 752–760.

Smithson, M. (2001). Correct confidence intervals for various regression effect sizes and parameters. *Educational and Psychological Measurement, 61*, 605–632.

Smithson, M. (2003). *Confidence intervals*. Thousand Oaks, CA: Sage Press.

Snedecor, G. W., & Cochran, W. G. (1989). *Statistical methods* (8th ed.). Ames, IA: Iowa State University Press.

Snyder, P., & Lawson, S. (1993). Evaluating results using corrected and uncorrected effect size estimates. *Journal of Experimental Education, 6*, 334–349.

Snyder, D. K., Wills, R. M., & Grady-Fletcher, A. (1991). Long-term effectiveness of behavioral vs. insight-oriented marital therapy: A 4-year follow-up study. *Journal of Consulting and Clinical Psychology, 59*, 138–141.

So, H.-S., & Sham, P. C. (2010). Effect size measures in genetic association studies and age-conditional risk prediction. *Human Heredity, 70*, 205–218.

Spector, P. E., & Brannick, M. T. (2011). Methodological urban legends: The misuse of statistical control variables. *Organizational Research Methods*.

Spies, R. A., & Plake, B. S. (2005). *The sixteenth mental measurements yearbook*. Lincoln, NB: Buros Institute.

St. John, H. C., & Roth, P. L. (1999). The impact of cross-validation adjustments on estimates of effect size in business policy and strategy research. *Organizational Research Methods, 2*, 157–174.

Staines, G. L., & Cleland, C. M. (2007). Bias in meta-analytic estimates of the absolute efficacy of psychotherapy. *Review of General Psychology, 11*, 329–347.

Steiger, J. H., (1999). *STATISTICA power analysis*. Tulsa, OK: StatSoft.

Steiger, J. H. (2004). Beyond the *F* test: Effect size confidence intervals and tests of close fit in the analysis of variance and contrast analysis. *Psychological Methods, 9*, 164–182.

Steiger, J. H., & Fouladi, R. T. (1992). R2: A computer program for interval estimation, power calculation, and hypothesis testing for the squared multiple correlation. *Behavior Research Methods, Instruments, and Computers, 4*, 581–582.

Steiger, J. H., & Fouladi, R. T. (1997). Noncentrality interval estimation and the evaluation of statistical methods. In L. L. Harlow, S. A. Mulaik, & J. H. Steiger (Eds.), *What if there were no significance tests?* (pp. 221–257). Mahwah, NJ: Erlbaum.

Stevens, J. P. (2002). *Applied multivariate statistics for the social sciences* (4th ed.). Mahwah, NJ: Lawrence Erlbaum Associates.

Stevens, J. P. (2009). *Applied multivariate statistics for the social sciences* (5th ed.). New York: Routledge.

Steyn, H. S., Jr., & Ellis, S. M. (2009). Estimating an effect size in one-way multivariate analysis of variance (MANOVA). *Multivariate Behavioral Research, 44*, 106–129.

Strahan, R. F. (1991). Remarks on the binomial effect size display. *American Psychologist, 46*, 1083–1084.

Subbiah, M., & Srinivasan, M. R. (2008). Classification of 2×2 sparse data sets with zero cells. *Statistics & Probability Letters, 78*, 3212–3215.

Tabachnick, B. G., & Fidell, L. S. (2007). *Using multivariate statistics* (5th ed.). Boston: Pearson Education.

Tang, M.-L., Ling, M.-H., Ling, L., & Tian, G. (2009). Confidence intervals for a difference between proportions based on paired data. *Statistics in Medicine, 29*, 86–96.

Tasdan, F., & Sievers, G. (2009). Smoothed Mann-Whitney-Wilcoxon procedure for two-sample location problem. *Communications in Statistics—Theory and Methods, 38*, 856–870.

Taskinen, S., Oja, H., & Randles, R. H. (2005). Multivariate nonparametric tests of independence. *Journal of the American Statistical Association, 100*, 916–925.

Tatsuoka, M. M. (1988). *Multivariate analysis: Techniques for educational and psychological research* (2nd ed.). New York: Collier Macmillan.

Taylor, M. J., & White, K. R. (1992). An evaluation of alternative methods for computing standardized mean difference effect size. *Journal of Experimental Education, 61*, 63–72.

Tchetgen Tchetgen, E. J., & Rotnitzky, A. (2011). Double-robust estimation of an exposure-outcome odds ratio adjusting for confounding in cohort and case-control studies. *Statistics in Medicine, 30*, 335–347.

Thoemmes, F. J., & Kim, E. S. (2011). A systematic review of propensity score methods in the social sciences. *Multivariate Behavioral Research, 46*, 90–118.

Thompson, B. (1991). Review of the book *Data analysis for research designs*. *Educational and Psychological Measurement, 51*, 500–510.

Thompson, B. (1993). The use of statistical significance tests in research: Bootstrap and other alternatives. *Journal of Experimental Education, 61*, 361–377.

Thompson, B. (1996). AERA editorial policies regarding statistical significance testing: Three suggested reforms. *Educational Research, 25*, 26–30.

Thompson, B. (1999, April). *Common methodology mistakes in educational research, revisited, along with a primer on both effect sizes and the bootstrap.* Paper presented at the Annual Meeting of the American Educational Research Association, Montreal, Canada.

Thompson, B. (2002, April). What future quantitative social science research could look like: Confidence intervals for effect sizes. *Educational Researcher, 31*, 25–32.

Thompson, B. (2003). Guidelines for authors reporting score reliability estimates. In B. Thompson (Ed.), *Score reliability: Contemporary thinking on reliability issues* (pp. 91–101). Thousand Oaks, CA: Sage Press.

Thompson, B. (2007). Effect sizes, confidence intervals, and confidence intervals for effect sizes. *Psychology in the Schools, 44*, 423–432.

Thompson, B., & Vacha-Haase, T. (2003). Psychometrics *is* datametrics: The test is not reliable. In B. Thompson (Ed.), *Score reliability: Contemporary thinking on reliability issues* (pp. 123–147). Thousand Oaks, CA: Sage Press.

Tiku, M. L., Qamarul Islam, M., & Qumsiyeh, S. B. (2010). Mahalanobis distance under non-normality. *Statistics: A Journal of Theoretical and Applied Statistics, 44*, 275–290.

Timm, N. H. (1999). A note on testing for multivariate effect sizes. *Journal of Educational and Behavioral Statistics, 24*, 132–145.

Timm, N. H. (2004). Estimating effect sizes in exploratory experimental studies when using a linear model. *The American Statistician, 58*, 213–217.

Trenkler, D. (2002). Quantile-boxplots. *Communications in Statistics—Simulation and Computation, 31*, 1–12.

Tryon, W. W. (2001). Evaluating statistical difference, equivalence, and indeterminacy using inferential confidence intervals: An integrated alternative method of conducting null hypothesis statistical tests. *Psychological Methods, 6*, 371–386.

Tryon, W. W. (2005, August). *Evaluating proportions for statistical difference, equivalence, and indeterminacy using inferential confidence intervals.* Paper presented at the Annual Meeting of the American Psychological Association, Washington, DC.

Tryon, W. W., & Lewis, C. (2007, August 20). *Evaluating independent proportions using inferential confidence intervals*. Paper presented at the Annual Meeting of the American Psychological Association, San Francisco, CA.

Tryon, W. W., & Lewis, C. (2008). An inferential confidence inference method of establishing statistical equivalence that corrects Tryon's (2001) reduction factor. *Psychological Methods*, *13*, 272–277.

Tryon, W. W., & Lewis, C. (2009). Evaluating independent proportions for statistical difference, equivalence, indeterminacy, and trivial difference using inferential confidence intervals. *Journal of Educational and Behavioral Statistics*, *34*, 171–189.

Ukoumunne, O. C., Williamson, E., Forbes, A. B., Gulliford, M. C., & Carlin, J. B. (2010). Confounder-adjusted estimates of the risk difference using propensity score-based weighting. *Statistics in Medicine*, *29*, 3126–3136.

Vacha-Haase, T., Kogan, L. R., & Thompson, B. (2000a). Sample compositions and variabilities in published studies versus those in test manuals: Validity of score reliability inductions. *Educational and Psychological Measurement*, *60*, 509–522.

Vacha-Haase, T., Nilsson, J. E., Reetz, D. R., Lance, T. S., & Thompson, B. (2000b). Reporting practices and APA editorial policies regarding statistical significance and effect size. *Theory and Psychology*, *10*, 413–425.

Vacha-Haase, T., & Thompson, B. (2004). How to estimate and interpret effect sizes. *Journal of Counseling Psychology*, *51*, 473–481.

Van Aelst, S., & Willems, G. (in press). Robust and efficient one-way MANOVA tests. *Journal of the American Statistical Association*, *106*, 706–718.

Van Der Linde, A., & Tutz, G. (2008). On association in regression: The coefficient of determination revisited. *Statistics*, *42*, 1–24.

van der Meulen, E. A. (2008). A nonrandomized, nonconservative version of the Fisher exact test. *Communications in Statistics—Theory and Methods*, *37*, 699–708.

Vargha, A. (2005). Sokágok összchasonlítósa új módszerekkel [Comparisons of populations with new methods.]. *Statisztikai Szemle*, *83*, 429–448.

Vargha, A., & Delaney, H. D. (1998). The Kruskal-Wallis test and stochastic homogeneity. *Journal of Educational and Behavioral Statistics*, *23*, 170–192.

Vargha, A., & Delaney, H. D. (2000). A critique and improvement of the CL common language effect size statistics of McGraw and Wong. *Journal of Educational and Behavioral Statistics*, *25*, 101–132.

Vargha, A., & Delaney, H. D. (2004). *Stochastic comparison of several independent groups*. Manuscript submitted for publication.

Vaughan, G. M., & Corballis, M. C. (1969). Beyond tests of significance: Estimating strength of effects in selected ANOVA designs. *Psychological Bulletin*, *72*, 204–213.

Vickers, A. J. (2005, November 3). Parametric versus nonparametric statistics in the analysis of randomized trials with non-normally distributed data [Electronic version]. *BMC Medical Research Methodology*, *5*, 35. Retrieved May 10, 2006, from http://www.biomedcentral.com/1471-2288/5/35

Vickers, A. J. (2006, November 3). Look at your garbage bin: It may be the only thing you need to know about statistics [Electronic version]. *Medscape*. Retrieved November 14, 2006, from http://www.medscape.com/view/article/546515

Vickers, A. J. (2008a, March 3). Statistics is unscientific! (As practiced by clinicians: Part II) [Electronic version]. *Medscape*. Retrieved March 11, 2008, from http://www.medscape.com/viewarticle/570072

Vickers, A. J. (2008b, January 7). Statistics is unscientific! (Well, as clinicians see it, anyway) [Electronic version]. *Medscape*. Retrieved January 15, 2008, from http://www.medscape.com/viewarticle/566912

Voelkle, M. C., Ackerman, P. I., & Wittman, W. W. (2007). Effect sizes and *F* ratios < 1.0: Sense or nonsense. *Methodology: European Journal of Research Methods for the Behavioral and Social Sciences, 3*, 35–46.

von Eye, A. (2005, October). Comparing tests of multinormality—A Monte Carlo study [Electronic version]. *InterStat, 1–24.* Retrieved June 23, 2006, from http://ipstatjournals.net:2002/InterStat/ARTICLES/2005/abstracts/0510001/html-ssi

von Eye, A. (2006, May). Comparing tests of multinormality under sparse data conditions—A Monte Carlo study [Electronic version]. *InterStat.* Retrieved June 9, 2006, from http://itp.statjournals.net:2002/InterStat/ARTICLES/2006/abstracts/0605005.html-ssi

von Eye, A., & Mun, E. Y. (2003). Characteristics of measures for 2 × 2 tables. *Understanding Statistics, 2*, 243–266.

von Eye, A., & von Eye, M. (2005). Can one use Cohen's Kappa to examine disagreement? *Methodology, 1*, 129–142.

von Weber, S., von Eye, A., & Lautsch, E. (2004). The Type II error of measures for the analysis of 2 × 2 tables. *Understanding Statistics, 3*, 259–282.

Walker, D. A. (2003). JMASM9: Converting Kendall's *tau* for correlational or meta-analytic analyses. *Journal of Modern Applied Statistical Methods, 2*, 525–530.

Walker, D. A. (2005). JMASM19: A SPSS matrix for determining effect sizes from three categories: *r* and functions of *r*, differences between proportions, and standardized differences between means. *Journal of Modern Applied Statistical Methods, 4*, 333–342.

Walker, E. L. (1947). *Factors in Vernier acuity and distance discrimination.* Unpublished doctoral dissertation, Stanford University, Stanford, CA.

Wampold, B. E., & Serlin, R. C. (2000). The consequences of ignoring a nested factor on measures of effect size in analysis of variance. *Psychological Methods, 5*, 425–433.

Wang, Z., & Thompson, B. (2007). Is the Pearson r^2 biased, and if so, what is the best correction formula? *The Journal of Experimental Education, Winter*, 109–129.

Warrens, M. J. (2008). On association coefficients for 2 × 2 tables and properties that do not depend on the marginal distributions. *Psychometrika, 73*, 777–789.

Warrens, M. J. (2010). Cohen's kappa can always be increased and decreased by combining categories. *Statistical Methodology, 7*, 673–677.

Weber, M., & Sawilowsky, S. (2009). Comparative power of the independent t, permutation t, and Wilcoxon tests. *Journal of Modern Applied Statistical Methods, 8*, 10–15.

Welch, B. L. (1938). The significance of the difference between two means when the population variances are unequal. *Biometrika, 29*, 350–362.

Wellek, S., & Hampel, B. (1999). A distribution-free two-sample equivalence test allowing for tied observations. *Biometrical Journal, 41*, 171–186.

Werner, M., Stabenau, J. B., & Pollin, W. (1970). TAT method for the differentiation of families of schizophrenics, delinquents, and normals. *Journal of Abnormal Psychology, 75*, 139–145.

Westfall, P. H., Troendle, J. F., & Pennello, G. (2010). Multiple McNemar tests. *Biometrics, 66*, 1185–1191.

Wickens, T. D. (1989). *Multiway contingency tables analysis for the social sciences.* Mahwah, NJ: Erlbaum.

Wilcox, R. R. (1987). New designs in analysis of variance. *Annual Review of Psychology, 38*, 29–60.

Wilcox, R. R. (1996). *Statistics for the social sciences.* San Diego, CA: Academic Press.

Wilcox, R. R. (1997). *Introduction to robust estimation and hypothesis testing.* San Diego, CA: Academic Press.

Wilcox, R. R. (2001). *Fundamentals of modern statistical methods: Substantially improving power and accuracy.* New York: Springer-Verlag.

Wilcox, R. R. (2003). *Applying contemporary statistical techniques*. San Diego, CA: Academic.

Wilcox, R. R. (2004). Some results on extensions and modifications of the Theil-Sen regression estimator. *British Journal of Mathematical and Statistical Psychology*, *57*, 265–280.

Wilcox, R. R. (2005a). *Introduction to robust estimation and hypothesis testing* (2nd ed.). Burlington, MA: Elsevier.

Wilcox. R. R. (2005b). Comparing medians: An overview plus new results on dealing with heavy-tailed distributions. *The Journal of Experimental Education*, *73*, 249–263.

Wilcox, R. R. (2005c). Estimating the conditional variance of *Y*, given *X*, in a simple regression model. *Journal of Applied Statistics*, *32*, 495–502.

Wilcox, R. R. (2005d). Within by within ANOVA based on medians. *Journal of Modern Applied Statistical Methods*, *4*, 2–10.

Wilcox, R. R. (2005e). An affine invariant rank-based method for comparing dependent groups. *British Journal of Mathematical and Statistical Psychology*, *58*, 33–42.

Wilcox, R. R. (2006a). Graphical methods for assessing effect size: Some alternatives to Cohen's *d*. *The Journal of Experimental Education*, *74*, 353–367.

Wilcox, R. R. (2006b). Testing the hypothesis of a homoscedastic error term in simple nonparametric regression. *Educational and Psychological Measurement*, *66*, 85–92.

Wilcox, R. R. (2006c). A note on inferences about the median of the distribution of difference scores. *Educational and Psychological Measurement*, *66*, 624–630.

Wilcox, R. R. (2006d). Comparing medians. *Computational Statistics & Data Analysis*, *51*, 1934–1943.

Wilcox, R. R. (2006e). Some results on comparing the quantiles of dependent groups. *Communications in Statistics—Simulation and Computation*, *35*, 893–900.

Wilcox, R. R. (2006f). Pairwise comparisons of dependent groups based on medians. *Computational Statistics & Data Analysis*, *50*, 2933–2941.

Wilcox, R. R. (2006g). ANCOVA: A robust omnibus test based on selected design points. *Journal of Modern Applied Statistical Methods*, *5*, 14–21.

Wilcox, R. R. (2007a). On flexible tests of independence and homoscedasticity. *Journal of Modern Applied Statistical Methods*, *6*, 30–35.

Wilcox, R. R. (2007b). Local measures of association: Estimating the derivative of the regression line. *British Journal of Mathematical and Statistical Psychology*, *60*, 107–117.

Wilcox, R. R. (2007c). An omnibus test when using a regression estimator with multiple predictors. *Journal of Modern Applied Statistical Methods*, *6*, 361–366.

Wilcox, R. R. (2008a). Sample size and statistical power. In A. M. Nezu & C. M. Nezu (Eds.), *Evidence-based outcome research: A practical guide to conducting randomized controlled trials for psychosocial interventions* (pp. 123–134). New York: Oxford.

Wilcox, R. R. (2008b). Estimating explanatory power in a simple regression model via smoothers. *Journal of Modern Applied Statistical Methods*, *7*, 368–375.

Wilcox, R. R. (2009a). Robust multivariate regression when there is heteroscedasticity. *Communications in Statistics—Simulation and Computation*, *38*, 1–13.

Wilcox, R. R. (2009b). Robust ANCOVA using a smoother with bootstrap bagging. *British Journal of Mathematical and Statistical Psychology*, *62*, 427–437.

Wilcox, R. R., & Keselman, H. J. (2002). Power analysis when comparing trimmed means. *Journal of Modern Applied Statistical Analysis*, *1*, 24–31.

Wilcox, R. R., & Keselman, H. J. (2003). Repeated measures one-way ANOVA based on a modified one-step M-estimator. *British Journal of Mathematical and Statistical Psychology*, *56*, 15–25.

Wilcox, R. R., & Keselman, H. J. (2006). Detecting heteroscedasticity in a simple regression model via quantile regression slopes. *Journal of Statistical Computation and Simulation, 76*, 705–712.

Wilcox, R. R., & Muska, J. (1999). Measuring effect size: A non-parametric analog of ω^2. *British Journal of Mathematical and Statistical Psychology, 52*, 93–110.

Wilkinson, L., & APA Task Force on Statistical Inference (1999). Statistical methods in psychology journals: Guidelines and explanations. *American Psychologist, 54*, 594–604.

Wilson, D. B., & Lipsey, M. W. (2001). The role of method in treatment effectiveness: Evidence from meta-analysis. *Psychological Methods, 6*, 413–429.

Winship, C., & Radbill, L. (1994). Sampling weights and regression analysis. *Sociological Methods and Research, 23*, 230–257.

Wood, M. (2005). Bootstrapped confidence intervals as an approach to statistical inference. *Organizational Research Methods, 8*, 454–470.

Woods, C. M. (2007). Confidence intervals for gamma-family measures of ordinal association. *Psychological Methods, 12*, 185–204.

Woolfe, R., & Cumming, G. (2004). Communicating the uncertainty in research findings: Confidence intervals. *Journal of Science and Medicine in Sport, 7*, 138–143.

Wright, S. T. (1946). *Spacing of practice in verbal learning and the maturation hypothesis.* Unpublished master's thesis, Stanford University, California.

Wylie, P. B. (1976). Effects of coarse grouping and skewed marginal distributions on the Pearson product moment correlation coefficient. *Educational and Psychological Measurement, 36*, 1–7.

Yalta, A. T. (2008). On the accuracy of statistical distributions in Microsoft® Excel 2007. *Computational Statistics & Data Analysis, 52*, 4570–4578.

Yelland, L. N., Salter, A. B., & Ryan, P. (2011). Relative risk estimation in randomized controlled trials: A comparison of methods for independent observations [Electronic version]. *The International Journal of Biostatistics, 7*. Retrieved January 10, 2011, from http:www.bepress.com/ijb/vol7/iss1/5. DOI: 10.2202/1557-4679.1278.

Yuan, K.-H., & Bentler, P. M. (2006). Mean comparison: Manifest variable versus latent variable. *Psychometrika, 71*, 139–159.

Yuen, K. K. (1974). The two sample trimmed *t* for unequal population variances. *Biometrika, 61*, 165–170.

Zakzanis, K. K. (2001). Statistics to tell the truth, the whole truth and nothing but the truth: Formulae, illustrative numerical examples and heuristic interpretation of effect size analyses for neuropsychological researchers. *Archives of Clinical Neuropsychology, 16*, 653–667.

Zheng, S., Shi, N.-Z., & Ma, W. (2010). Statistical inference on difference or ratio of means from heteroscedastic normal populations. *Journal of Statistical Planning and Inference, 140*, 1236–1242.

Zou, G. Y., & Donner, A. (2008). Construction of confidence limits about effect measures: A general approach. *Statistics in Medicine, 27*, 1693–1702.

Zumbo, B. D., Gadermann, A. M., & Zeisser, C. (2007). Ordinal versions of coefficients alpha and theta for Likert rating scales. *Journal of Modern Applied Statistical Methods, 6*, 21–29.

Author Index

A

Abelson, R.P., 126, 131, 143, 229
Abonyi-Tóth, Z., 261
Abu Libdeh, O.A., 183
Acion., L., 170, 300
Ackerman, P.I., 184, 310
Adhikari, N.K.J., 32
Afshartous, D., 57–58
Agresti, A., 155–156, 246, 251, 253–254,
            259, 262, 271–272, 276, 278–280, 287,
            291, 297–302, 304, 335
Aguinis, H., 127, 209, 289–290, 339, 345
Ahmed, S.E., 67, 88–89
Aiken, L.S., 86, 112, 143, 250, 311,
            317, 319–320, 323, 326,
            333–334, 338
Algina, J., 15–16, 48, 50–51, 53, 70, 72, 78, 80,
            82–83, 87, 89–90, 185, 188, 190, 192,
            194–195, 197–199, 210, 214–215,
            222, 224, 227–229, 232–234,
            311–313, 315, 323, 331, 347, 349, 364,
            371, 373, 379, 381, 383–385
Alhija, F.N.-A., 5
Al-Kandari, N.M., 67, 88–89
Allen, J., 339
Allison, D.B., 171
Aloe, A.M., 315
American Psychological Association, 9, 12, 33,
            118, 195
Anderson, D.R., 10
Andrews, G., 90, 169
Arceneaux, K., 262
Arndt, S., 152, 170, 300
Arvey, R.D., 183, 185, 210
Ashikaga, T., 291
Austin, P.C., 263–264

B

Baguley, T., 62, 67, 71, 125, 191, 305
Bakeman, R., 188, 198
Banerjee, T., 259
Barchard, K.A., 118
Barnette, J.J., 10, 188
Bathke, A.C., 359
Baugh, F., 120
Beal, S.L., 258

Beatty, M.J., 136–138
Becker, B.J., 91, 232
Becker, T.E., 317
Belia, S., 39–40, 58
Bendermacher, N., 246
Benjamini, Y., 194
Bentler, P.M., 61
Berg, A., 272
Berger, V., 345
Bergin, A.E., 18
Berk, R.A., 263
Berry, K.J., 277–280, 305
Bertacinni, B., 276
Bevan, M.F., 290
Bewell, C., 192
Beyene, J., 32
Bickel, P.J., 52
Bini, M., 276
Bird, K.D., 44, 194, 228, 232
Biswas, A., 280
Black, A.R., 4
Block, R.A., 209
Bloom, H.S., 4, 129–130, 132
Blouin, D.C., 197
Bluhmki, E., 347
Bogaerts, K., 347
Bond, C.F., 191
Bonett, D.G., 13, 21, 24, 37, 46, 51, 72, 79–80,
            83, 88–89, 195, 197, 217, 233,
            261–262, 269, 273
Borenstein, M., 13–15, 67, 78
Borg, W.R., 128
Borooah, V.K., 292, 339
Brannick, M.T., 317
Braun, M.T., 143
Bray, J.H., 360–361
Breaugh, J.A., 131, 140–141, 261
Brown, L., 54
Browne, R.H., 10, 81, 155, 161, 169, 311
Brownie, C., 172
Brumback, B., 272
Brunner, E., 152–153, 173, 195–196, 201, 228,
            232, 297, 304, 388
Bryk, A.S., 20, 334–335
Buhamra, S.S., 67, 88–89
Bunner, J., 50
Burnham, K.P., 10
Busk, P.L., 364

C

Callaert, H., 158, 162–165
Camp, C.C., 183, 185, 210
Campbell, D.T., 345
Campbell, I., 248–249, 254, 256
Carlin, J.B., 252
Carlson, K.D., 91
Carr, J., 195, 201, 280, 305
Carroll, J.B., 111, 250
Carroll, R.M., 182–183, 188
Carter, N.J., 25, 259
Carter, R.E., 259
Carver, R., 10
Castellan, N.J., 277
Castelloe, J., 156, 302
Cattin, P., 311
Chacón-Moscoso, S., 274
Chan, W., 126
Chan, W.L., 126
Chang, K.-C., 274
Chen, X., 157
Cheong, Y.F., 334–335
Cheung, M.W.-L., 144, 336
Chinn, S., 273
Choi, J., 364
Christensen, R., 16, 39
Cleland, C.M., 6, 10, 14, 64
Cleveland, W.S., 25, 172
Cliff, N., 115, 152–153, 166–167, 173, 195, 218,
        229, 232, 292, 298–299, 359
Cochran, W.G., 290
Cohen, A., 102, 112, 143, 250, 297,
        311, 317, 319–320, 326,
        333–334, 338
Cohen, J., 12, 68–69, 72, 86, 112, 128–129,
        141, 143, 160–161, 168–169, 179,
        194, 210, 243, 250, 259, 311, 313,
        317, 319–320, 323, 326, 333–334,
        338, 365
Cohen, P., 112, 143, 250, 311, 317, 319–320,
        326, 333–334, 338
Coin, D., 17
Congdon, R., 334–335
Consumers Union, 262
Cook, T.D., 345
Corballis, M.C., 184–185, 228, 234
Correction, 300
Cortina, J.M., 131, 196, 216, 218, 220,
        232–233, 350
Coughlin, K.B., 75, 159, 167, 169
Cramer, E.M., 364, 367–368
Credé, M., 118
Cribbie, R.A., 74, 192–193, 205
Crits-Christoph, P., 208

Culpepper, S.A., 127, 289–290
Cumming, G., 8, 39–40, 44, 58, 78, 81, 88,
        234, 257
Cuthill, I.C., 90, 92, 143

D

D'Agostino, R.B., 289
Daly, F., 42, 55
Darlington, M.L., 172
Davies, L., 111
Dayton, C.M., 191, 193–194, 198, 256
DeCoster, J., 86, 98, 206
Deering, K.N., 15, 48, 50, 53, 70, 72, 83, 87, 89,
        192, 195, 214, 232
Deleeuw, J., 334
del Moral Ávila, M.J., 252, 257, 281
Delaney, H.D., 67, 80, 152–153, 157, 159,
        161, 165, 173, 181–183, 192–193,
        195–197, 199, 201, 210, 228–229,
        231–234, 246, 290, 293, 297, 299,
        304, 336, 338, 346, 349–350, 360,
        379–383, 386
Deleeuw, J., 334
DeMars, C.E., 122
Denton, J.Q., 290
Derzko, G., 201
DeShon, R.P., 88, 143, 220
Dinnel, D.L., 4
Doksum, K.A., 171
Dollinger, M.B., 192
Domhof, S., 152
Donner, A., 259, 260
Dorvio, A.S., 361
Dosser, D.A., 185, 188
Doucette, H.L., 334
Drasgow, F., 122
Duncan, B.W., 265, 267, 271

E

Edwards, L.J., 339
Ellis, S.M., 369–371
Emerson, J.D., 293–294, 296

F

Fagerland, M.W., 153–154
Fahoome, G., 154, 229, 295
Fairchild, A.J., 144
Fan, W., 264
Fan, X., 10
Faulkner, C., 8, 58
Fay, B.R., 153–154, 293, 296
Fearing, B.K., 126

Feingold, A., 12, 92, 143, 171
Feinstein, A.R., 44
Feng, D., 115, 173, 229, 299
Ferguson, C.F., 14
Ferron, J.M., 81, 167, 363
Fidell, L.S., 314, 316, 319, 334, 339, 346–347, 352–353, 359–361, 364, 372–373, 378
Fidler, F., 8, 39–40, 44, 58, 78, 107, 183–184, 227, 371
Fielding, A., 291
Finch, S., 39, 44, 58, 78, 81, 88, 183, 234, 358–359
Fleishman, A.I., 179
Fleiss, J.L., 243, 245–246, 251, 253–254, 256–260, 262, 267, 272, 274, 278, 280, 282, 287, 304
Fligner, M.A., 152
Forbes, A.B., 252
Fouladi, R.T., 81, 108, 181, 194, 228, 313, 320, 359, 363
Fowler, R.J., 81
Fowler, R.L., 210
Fradette, K., 48, 51, 82, 192
Freels, S., 326
French, B.F., 183
Frick, R.W., 44
Friedman, L., 171
Friedrich, J.O., 32
Funatogawa, I., 346
Funatogawa, T., 346
Furr, R.M., 185, 201, 315, 317, 338

G

Gadermann, A.M., 287
Gaebelein, J.W., 381
Gall, J.P., 128
Gall, M.D., 128
Gallop, R., 208
Gallucci, M., 86, 98, 206
Gao, G., 171
Gao, H., 192
Gather, U., 111
Gautam, S., 291
Genest, C., 98
Gerber, A.S., 262
Gibbons, J.D., 162
Gillett, R., 210, 233
Gillo, M.W., 369
Gilpin, A.R., 114
Gittens, J., 12
Glass, G.V., 14, 63, 68, 72, 131, 349–350
Gleser, L.J., 42, 53
Gollob, H.E., 37
Goodman, S., 13
Gorecki, J.A., 79

Goyal, A., 20
Grady-Fletcher, A., 285
Green, D.P., 262
Greenland, S., 13, 272
Grissom, R.J., 4, 16–17, 19, 21, 64, 129, 149, 159, 161, 170, 178, 228, 352
Gulliford, M.C., 52

H

Haddock, C.K., 250, 272
Hadi, A.S., 19
Hafdahl, A.R., 108
Hampel, B., 153, 298
Hancock, G.R., 363–364
Hand, D.J., 42, 55–56, 173, 351
Harrar, S.W., 359
Harris, D.N., 4
Harshman, R.A., 9
Harwell, M.R., 322
Hasselblad, V., 273
Hauschke, D., 298
Hayes, A.F., 144
Hayes, T.L., 13
Hays, W.L., 183–184, 248, 278
Hedges, L.V., 10, 13–15, 67–70, 74, 76, 78–79, 90, 106, 171, 273, 334
Hemphill, J.F., 129
Henson, R.K., 10
Heo, M., 243, 287
Herranz Tejedor, I., 253, 259
Hess, B., 169, 322
Hess, M.R., 81–82, 167, 169, 322, 363
Higgins, J.P.T., 13–15, 67, 78
Hill, C.J., 4, 129–130, 132
Hill, C.R., 131
Hines, C.V., 81, 167
Hochberg, Y., 159
Hogarty, K.Y., 71, 81, 167, 363
Hosseini, H., 293–294
Hothorn, L.A., 259
Howard, G.S., 10
Howard, K.I., 157, 165–166, 169
Hsu, L.M., 135, 246, 268, 300
Huang, C.-Y., 39
Huberty, C.J., 9, 16, 169, 359–360, 369, 372–374, 376, 379, 386–387
Hufthammer, K.A., 101
Hullett, C.R., 210
Humphreys, L.G., 19
Hunter, J.E., 10, 13, 15, 55, 97, 99, 101, 120–122, 124, 141, 336
Hutton, J.L., 267
Huynh, C.L., 292, 339

I

Imada, T., 360
Imon, H.A.M.R., 19
Ioannidis, J.P.A., 13
Iselin, A-M.R., 86, 98, 206

J

James, G.S., 45
Jöckel, K.-H., 153
Johnston, J.E., 277–280, 305
Joormann, J., 208

K

Kang, S.-H., 253
Kawaguchi, A., 388
Keating, J.P., 310
Kelley, K., 54–55, 65, 78, 81–82, 144, 181, 183,
         311, 313, 317
Keppel, G., 20, 184–185, 194, 199, 201, 210,
         229, 233–234, 344–347, 381
Keselman, H.J., 15–16, 19, 48, 50–53, 70,
         72, 78, 80, 82–83, 87, 89–90,
         111, 182, 192–195, 197–198, 214–215,
         232, 311–313, 323, 331, 379, 387
Kieffer, K.M., 209
Kim, E.S., 264
Kim, J.J., 149, 159
Kim, S., 369, 371
King, J.E., 112
Kiser, T.L., 25
Kline, R.B., 365, 370–371
Klingenberg, B., 261
Knapp, T.R., 10, 37, 44
Knight, E., 192
Koch, G.G., 388
Kogan, L.R., 118
Kohn, R., 111
Kolassa, J., 143, 250, 297, 311, 317, 319–320,
         333–334, 338
Kowalchuk, R.K., 48, 192, 379
Koyama, T., 42
Kraemer, H.C., 12, 90, 98–101, 114, 152, 155,
         160, 169, 243, 246–248, 250, 260,
         266–268, 270, 272–273, 278, 281,
         287, 300, 336
Krantz, D.H., 38, 131
Kraus, M.S., 157, 165–166, 169
Krauth, J., 90
Kreft, I., 334
Kromrey, J.D., 71, 75, 81–82, 159, 167, 169,
         322, 363
Kromrey, K.Y., 71, 322
Kruskal, J.B., 83

Kulinskaya, E., 181, 184, 192, 259
Kuljanin, G., 143
Kupfer, D.J., 152, 160, 169, 266–268, 272

L

Lacy, M.G., 292, 309, 339
Laird, N.M., 75
Lambert, M.J., 18
Lance, T.S., 209
Landis, R.S., 10, 131
Lane, D.M., 25, 172
Langer, F., 152
Lau, M.Y., 10
Laupacis, A., 263
Lautsch, E., 251
Lawson, R., 54, 276
Lawson, S., 10
Le, H., 124, 339
Lecoutre, B., 32, 38, 44, 81, 84, 194, 201
Lee, Y.S., 253
Leech, N.L., 4
Leeman, J., 39
Lehman, E.L., 52
Lenth, R.V., 12, 41–42
Lesaffre, E., 347
Leslie, D., 111
Lévesque, J.-L., 98
Levin, B., 4, 10, 208, 243
Levin, J.R., 10
Levine, J.H., 210
Levine, T.R., 101
Levy, P., 5
Lewis, C., 42, 257, 276
Lezotte, D.V., 126
Li, B., 339
Li, X., 54, 339
Liao, J.G., 339
Liberman, A.M., 270
Lin, W.-Y., 16
Lin, Y., 259
Ling, L., 259
Ling, M.-H., 259
Lipman, M.M., 7, 262
Lipsey, M.W., 4, 10, 129, 169, 188, 235
Lipsitz, S., 259
Liu, G.F., 6, 92
Liu, O.L., 92, 143, 343
Liu, Q., 359
Liu, X., 12, 92, 143
Lix, L.M., 15, 48, 359, 387
Lloyd, C.J., 257
Long, J.D., 115, 167, 173, 195, 229, 232, 290,
         292, 298–299, 337
Lösch, C., 153
Louis, T.A., 40

Lu, K., 92, 343
Luh, W.-M., 205
Lui, K.-J., 274
Lundy, R., 10, 157, 165–166, 169
Lunn, A.D., 42
Lunney, G.H., 289
Luo, X., 157

M

Ma, W., 32
MacCallum, R.C., 86
MacKinnon, D.P., 144
Maghsoodloo, S., 39
Maity, A., 74
Malgady, R.G., 18
Mallick, M., 92, 343
Mantel, N., 279
Marascuilo, M.A., 195, 364
Marcoulides, G.A., 368
Marín-Martínez, F., 274
Maroufy, V., 12
Martín Andrés, A., 251, 253–254, 257, 259, 281
Mason, R.L., 310
Matsumoto, D., 4
Maxwell, S.E., 54–55, 67, 80, 181–183, 185,
        192–193, 195, 197, 199, 210, 228–229,
        231–234, 246, 313, 317, 336–338, 346,
        349–350, 360–361, 379–383, 386
May, K., 45
McConway, K.J., 42
McGaw, B., 63, 68–72, 131, 213, 349–350
McGee, D., 339
McGrath, R.E., 69, 100–101, 104, 106, 116,
        123, 338
McGraw, K.O., 149, 159
McLean, J.E., 10, 188
McNemar, Q., 102, 178, 199, 279–280, 328
Meade, A.W., 122
Mee, R.W., 152, 153
Meehl, P.E., 98
Mehrotra, D.V., 92, 343
Menard, J., 339
Mends-Cole, S.J., 51
Meyer, G.J., 69, 100–101, 104, 106, 116, 123
Meyers, J.L., 290
Micceri, T., 17
Mielke, P.W. Jr, 277, 279, 305
Miller, D.T., 131, 229
Miller, L.C., 19
Mogg, R., 92, 343
Mohr, D.C., 18
Monaco, J.P., 334
Morey, R.D., 39, 42, 234
Morgenthaler, S., 259
Morris, S.B., 88, 91–92, 220

Moser, B.K., 315
Moses, L.E., 290, 293–294, 296
Mosteller, F., 75
Moulder, B., 315
Mulaik, S.A., 9
Mun, E.Y., 248, 250–251, 254
Munk, A., 253, 274
Munzel, U., 152–153, 297–298, 388
Murphy, K.R., 12
Murray, L.W., 185, 188
Muska, J., 66, 169
Myers, J.L., 338
Myors, B., 12

N

Nakagawa, S., 90, 92, 143
Nam, J., 262
Nanna, M.J., 290
Nashimoto, K., 197
Nasiakos, G., 74
Natesan, P., 169, 388
Neuhäuser, M., 153
Newcombe, R.G., 152, 196, 201, 259, 262,
        272, 297
Newton, P.J., 263
Nicewander, W.A., 86, 364, 367–368
Nilsson, J.E., 209
Noda, A., 243
Nordholm, L.A., 182–183, 188
Norušis, M.J., 346, 352, 373, 376
Nott, D., 111
Nouri, H., 196, 216, 218, 220, 232–233, 350
Nowell, A., 171
Nugent, W.R., 122
Nurminen, M.M., 259
Nye, C.D., 122

O

O'Brien, P.C., 171, 302
O'Brien, R., 156
O'Connell, A.A., 304, 334, 339
Odgaard, E.C., 81
O'Grady, K.E., 285
Oh, I.-S., 13
Oja, H., 388
Olejnik, S., 169, 185, 188, 190, 198–199, 210,
        215, 222, 224, 227–229, 233–234,
        313, 347, 349, 359–360, 364, 369,
        371–374, 376, 379, 381, 383–387
Olkin, I., 10, 67–68, 70, 75–76, 78–79, 90, 106,
        265, 267, 271
Olson, C.L., 358
Onwuegbuzie, A.J., 4, 10
Orelien, J.G., 339

Oshima, T.C., 16, 126
Ostrowski, E., 42
Ozer, D.J., 91–92, 230

P

Paik, M.C., 243
Pan, X., 193–194, 198
Park, E.S., 253, 280
Parker, S., 44
Pedersen, W.C., 19
Penfield, R.D., 78, 82, 90, 323
Pennello, G., 279
Periyakoil, V.S., 243
Peterson, J.J., 152
Pezeshk, H., 12
Pierce, C.A., 127, 209, 339
Pigott, T.D., 67
Pitts, S.C., 326
Plake, B.S., 118
Plewis, I., 335
Policello II, G.E., 152, 155
Pollin, W., 66
Pradhan, V., 259
Pratt, J.W., 173
Preacher, K.J., 86, 124, 144, 310, 336, 338
Prentice, D.A., 131, 229
Preston, R.A., 57–58
Price, R.M., 46, 51, 261–262, 269
Puri, M.L., 152, 173, 195–196, 201, 228, 232,
      304, 388
Putcha-Bhagavatula, A.D., 19

Q

Qamarul Islam, M., 363
Qumsiyeh, S.B., 363

R

Radbill, L., 326
Raju, N.S., 9, 126
Ramsey, P.H., 16
Ramsey, P.R., 16, 45
Randles, R.H., 153, 388
Rao, P.S.R.S., 361
Raudenbush, S.W., 12, 20, 92, 143, 334–335
Rausch, J.R., 54–55, 78
Raykov, T., 368
Redden, D.T., 171
Reed III, J.F., 16, 50
Reese, R.J., 209
Reetz, D.R., 209
Reichardt, C.S., 37
Reiczigel, J., 152–153, 261, 297
Reiser, B., 159, 363

Renaud, O., 337
Rencher, A.C., 368
Rice, M.E., 18
Richard, F.D., 191
Rindskopf, D., 250, 334
Riopelle, A.J., 197
Roberts, J.K., 10, 25, 334
Robinson, D.H., 10
Ronis, D.L., 270
Rose, S., 263
Rosenthal, R., 10, 69, 83–85, 100–101, 106,
      108, 132, 135, 140, 169, 195, 201,
      234, 272, 280
Rosnow, R.L., 10, 69, 84, 100–101, 106,
      135, 280
Roth, P.L., 311
Rothstein, H.R., 13–15, 67, 78
Rotnitzky, A., 272
Rouder, J.N., 39, 42, 234
Rousson, V., 246
Rovine, M.J., 136
Rozeboom, W.W., 311
Rózsa, L., 152
Rubin, D.B., 10, 132, 140
Rucker, D.D., 86
Rudas, T., 272, 279
Rupinsky, M.T., 114
Ruscio, J., 18, 71, 98, 106, 115, 152–153, 161
Ryan, P., 260
Ryu, E., 276, 297–298

S

Sackrowitz, H.B., 297
Salter, A.P., 260
Sampson, A.R., 42
Sánchez-Meca, J., 274
Sánchez Quevedo, M.J., 253, 274
Sándor, A., 25, 172
Sandvik, L., 153–154
Satterthwaite, F.E., 45, 80
Sawilowsky, S.S., 10, 16–17, 21, 33, 44, 50–51,
      119, 131, 151, 191, 205, 229, 234,
      290, 344–345
Schaarschmidt, F., 259
Schacht, A., 347
Schonfeld, I.S., 334
Schwertman, N.L., 25
Seir, E., 17, 358
Senn, S., 169
Serlin, R.C., 21, 37, 42, 195, 201, 208, 280, 305,
      322, 364, 369–370, 377–378, 389
Shadish, W.R., 250, 345
Shaffer, J.P., 369
Sham, P.C., 280
Sherman, M., 74

Shi, N.-Z., 32
Shieh, G., 311–312, 338
Shulkin, B., 51
Shyr, Y., 346
Siegel, S., 277
Siemer, M., 208
Sievers, G., 157
Sill, M., 259
Silva Mato, A., 253
Simon, S., 272
Simonoff, J.S., 159
Singer, J., 261
Singh, P., 20
Sinha, K., 326
Skinner, B.F., 20
Skipka, G., 253, 274
Slavin, R., 5
Smith, D., 5, 76
Smith, M.L., 14
Smithson, M., 44, 53–54, 78, 81, 107, 143–144,
        183, 194, 227, 251, 260, 278, 288,
        311–313, 320, 323, 328, 348, 367–368
Snedecor, G.W., 290
Snyder, D.K., 10, 285
Snyder, P., 10
So, H.-S., 280
Souren, P., 246
Spector, P.E., 317
Spence, P.R., 21, 191
Spies, R.A., 118
St. John, H.C., 311
Stark, D.B., 16
Stabenau, J.B., 66
Staines, G.L., 6, 10, 14, 64
Staudte, R.G., 181, 184, 259
Steiger, J.H., 41–42, 81, 108, 181, 183, 194, 228,
        313, 320, 363
Stevens, J.P., 16–17, 344, 346, 350, 360, 364,
        372–373
Steyn, H.S. Jr, 365, 369–371
Stoica, G., 76
Strahan, R.F., 134
Stratmann, B., 274
Subbiah, M., 272
Sweeny, R.M., 10

T

Tabachnick, B.G., 314, 316, 334, 336, 339,
        346, 348, 352–353, 359–361, 364,
        372–373, 378
Taborga, M.P., 144
Tang, M.-L., 259
Tapia Garcia, J.M., 252–253
Tasdan, F., 157
Taskinen, S., 388

Tatsuoka, M.M., 364–365, 371, 374–375, 389
Taylor, A.B., 144
Taylor, M.J., 91, 144
Tchetgen Tchetgen, E.J., 272
Temple, S., 152
Thiemann, S., 12
Thoemmes, F.J., 264
Thomason, M., 39
Thompson, B., 10, 39, 44, 53, 70, 78–79, 81,
        107, 118–119, 131, 137, 169, 183–184,
        194, 209, 227, 336, 371, 388
Thompson, W.L., 10, 118, 209
Tian, G., 259
Tian, M., 259
Tiku, M.L., 363
Timm, N.H., 195, 228, 364
Trenkler, D., 25
Troendle, J.F., 279
Tryon, W.W., 42, 126, 257, 276
Tu, X., 208
Tukey, J.W., 172, 191–194, 196–197, 202, 228,
        256, 350, 352–353
Tutz, G., 367

U

Ukoumunne, O.C., 252

V

Vacha-Haase, T., 10, 70, 118–119, 209
Van Aelst, S., 359
van der Laan, M.J., 263
Van Der Linde, A., 367
van der Meulin, E.A., 254
Vargha, A., 152–153, 157, 159, 161, 165, 173,
        195–196, 201, 291, 293, 297, 299, 304
Vaughan, G.M., 184–185, 227, 234
Venter, A., 10
Vessey, J.T., 157
Vickers, A.J., 13, 19, 45, 347
Victoria-Feser, M.-P., 337
von Eye, A., 136, 246, 248, 250–251, 254, 358
von Eye, M., 246
von Weber, S., 251, 254

W

Walker, D.A., 14, 170, 310–311
Walker, E.L., 199
Wampold, B.E., 208
Wan, W., 171
Wang, X., 388
Wang, Z., 137
Warrens, M.J., 244, 246, 249–250
Weber, M., 151

Weinert, H., 111
Welch, B.L., 21, 45–47, 50–51, 58, 80,
      152, 205
Well, A.D., 338, 387
Wellek, S., 153, 298
Werner, M., 19, 66
West, S.G., 86, 326
Westfall, P.H., 279
White, K.R., 91
Wickens, T.D., 184–185, 199, 201, 210, 229,
      233–234, 279, 344–347, 381
Wiitala, W.L., 191
Wilcox, R.R., 15–17, 19–20, 22–24, 27, 39,
      45–46, 48, 50–53, 57, 66, 71, 73, 75,
      80, 90, 102, 107, 110–115, 125–126,
      136–137, 144, 152–153, 158–159,
      167, 169, 171, 173–174, 178, 180,
      191–193, 195–198, 205, 228–229,
      231–233, 253, 255, 259, 288, 297,
      299, 337, 346, 350–351, 359, 379,
      382, 387
Wilkinson, L., 12, 33, 118
Willems, G., 359
Williams, A., 39
Williams, J., 40
Williams, M.A., 108
Williamson, E., 252
Wills, R.M., 285
Wilson, D.B., 10, 129, 169, 188, 235
Wilson, M., 6
Winship, C., 326

Wittman, W.W., 184
Wong, S.P., 149, 159
Wood, M., 53
Woods, C.M., 114, 300
Woolfe, R., 40
Wright, F.T., 178, 328
Wright, S.T., 197
Wylie, P.B., 127

Y

Yalta, A.T., 35, 43, 62, 160
Yamamoto, Y., 360
Yang, Y., 19
Yelland, L.N., 260
Yoon, J.S., 10
Yuan, K.-H., 61
Yuen, K.K., 47–51, 58

Z

Zahran, S., 305
Zakariás, I., 152
Zakzanis, K.K., 9
Zedeck, S., 194
Zeger, S.L., 40
Zeisser, C., 287
Zhang, S., 171
Zheng, S., 32
Zou, G.Y., 259–260
Zumbo, B.D., 287

Subject Index

A

Agresti's alpha, *see* Generalized odds ratio
Association size *vs.* effect size, 263
Attitudinal scales, 285; *see also* Rating
    scale data
    problems in comparing effect sizes, 285
AUC (ROC), 155, 268

B

Base rate difference, 158
Beta coefficients, 316–317
    standardized and unstandardized, 316–317
Biased estimators of effect size, 347
Binomial effect size display (BESD),
    132–133, 252

C

Coefficient of determination
    interpretation, 135, 136, 140–141, 146,
        186, 261
    multiple
        for mediation analysis, 144
        R^2 change, 322
Coefficient of nondetermination, 141
Cohen's d_s, 68
Cohen's U_3, 168–169
Common language effect size statistic, 159, 174
Confidence intervals
    accuracy, 34–35, 43, 45, 54–55, 81, 257,
        311, 363
    AIPE method, 54, 311
    approximate, 37, 45, 52–53, 57, 76, 79, 107,
        108, 152, 183, 194, 197, 228, 232,
        251, 257–259, 261, 275, 288, 297,
        311, 313, 336, 350, 370
    asymmetric, 44, 45
    bootstrapping *vs.* noncentral distributions,
        78, 80–81, 183, 194
    Cohen's kappa, 245
    combining for d_{pop}, 78–80
    contingency coefficient, 278
    correlation coefficient, 85, 107, 114–115,
        137, 145, 246, 316, 317, 320, 332,
        336, 340
    Cramér's V_{pop}, 251, 277
    criteria for comparing methods, 54–55

difference between dependent means,
    40, 57, 88
difference between independent means, 40
difference between independent
    medians, 51
difference between two proportions,
    251–259
difference between two quantiles, 57
disappointingly wide width, 46, 76, 276
dominance measure, 173, 232, 236,
    299, 300
and effect sizes, 8, 31–59, 65, 108, 152, 181,
    210, 251, 288, 311, 343, 359
eta squared, 210, 355, 370
    whole or partial, 209
exact, 54, 81, 88, 194, 228, 259
factorial ANOVA POP_{pop}, 355
horseshoe-tossing analogy, 39
inferential, 42, 257, 276
interpretations, 35, 37, 39, 75, 78, 184, 189,
    236, 246, 332, 340, 354, 370, 387
    Bayesian and frequentist, 32, 39
for MANOVA effect sizes, 367, 382,
    386–389
for multiple regression effect sizes, 311–313,
    316–317, 319–321, 323, 326–328,
    331, 332, 334, 336, 338, 340
multivariate for difference between two
    latent means, 364
narrowing, 77–78, 343–344
for NNT_{pop}, 267–268
vs. null–counternull intervals, 85, 108, 145,
    251–259, 276–277, 288–289
for odds ratio
    contingency tables larger than 2 x 2,
        273, 276–278
one-sided, 41, 53
phi coefficient, 281, 305
point-biserial r_{pop} for ordinal categorical
    data, 292, 305
population d, charts, 79
population r, 107
precision, 31, 35, 37, 55, 58, 261, 363
for probability of superiority, 149, 152–154,
    158, 167, 173–174, 228, 232,
    388–389
for relative risk, 260, 276, 281
for reliability coefficients, 117
Satterthwaite procedure, 45, 80

simultaneous
    in ANCOVA, 354, 359
    in one-way ANOVA
        standardized differences, dependent
            groups, 191–192, 197, 228, 232,
            261, 276, 279
    standardized differences, independent
        groups, 33, 88
    transformation principle, 181
    unbiased, 34, 54, 57, 145, 155, 195, 201,
        202, 260, 347
    using noncentral distributions, 78, 81,
        183, 194
    vs. significance testing for effect sizes,
        267–268, 319–321
    Welch's method, 45–47, 50, 58
    width, 44–46, 51, 54, 78, 183, 184, 311,
        317, 363
        and statistical significance, 44
    Yuen's method, 47–51
Contingency coefficient, 277, 278
Correlation
    assumptions, 98, 103, 105–107, 109–115,
        120, 122, 132, 136, 138, 145, 146,
        174, 197
    attenuation by restricted range, 118, 123
    bivariate normality, 98, 110, 111, 145, 336
    correction for attenuation from
        dichotomizing, 97–98, 144
    curvilinearity, 113, 142, 145
    fine-grained, 101
    generalized, 123, 126, 135, 246, 364, 367
    heteroscedasticity, 102, 105, 106, 110, 111,
        113–114, 195, 197, 234, 290, 317, 341
    intraclass, 183, 246
    local and global, 101
    multiple, 140, 142, 307, 309, 310, 314, 319,
        324, 326, 338, 340, 344, 347, 367
    nonsense, 132
    partial, 313–318, 321, 322, 327, 331,
        332, 336
    point-biserial (*see* Point-biserial)
    polychoric, 290, 336
    polyserial, 336
    semipartial (part), 313–315, 319–322,
        327, 331
    spurious, 102, 146
Correlation coefficient
    base rates, unequal, 102–106
    bias and bias reduction, 70
    confidence intervals, 85, 107, 114, 115,
        137, 145, 246, 316, 317, 320, 332,
        336, 340
    correcting for artifacts, 121, 122
    first order, higher order, and zero order, 314,
        316, 318, 321, 331, 341

Kendall's tau, 114, 170, 305, 337
    nonparametric alternatives, 114
    null–counternull intervals, 84, 85,
        108–109, 288
    restricted range, 122–126, 143, 146
    robust alternatives, 111, 112, 145, 174, 195,
        290, 337, 338
    skew in opposite directions, 111, 113, 145
    Spearman's rho, 114
    success percentage difference, 133–135, 169
    tetrachoric, 98, 290, 336
Correlation ratio, 182
Counternull effect size, 83–85, 109
Cramér's V_{pop}, 251, 277
Cross-validation of R^2, 311–312
Cumulative odds ratio, 303–305

D

d and Δ
    interpretation under normality, 62–64
Difference between medians, 51, 158
Differential item (or scale) functioning, 122
Discriminant function, 369, 371
Dominance statistic and dominance measure
    for dependent measures, 167
    relationship with the *PS,* 167
    statistical significance, 166, 174, 298, 300–302

E

Effect sizes
    in ANCOVA, 344–348, 350, 351, 355,
        371, 372
    in ANOVA, 177, 320, 327, 328, 347, 350,
        354, 355, 358, 359, 361, 379
    applied *vs.* theoretical research, 10, 98
    categorical variables, 241–282, 285, 287,
        305, 335, 336
    comparing from continuous and categorical
        data, 251, 280, 292–295, 297, 302, 304
    D and D^2 in MANOVA, 346, 352, 357–388
    defined, 24, 31, 54, 57, 67, 75, 79, 82, 90,
        110, 111, 121, 139, 140, 149, 154,
        166, 168, 171, 172, 180, 181, 201,
        205, 224, 225, 261–263, 267, 268,
        276, 281, 292, 296, 298, 300, 309,
        311, 321, 323, 335, 339, 365, 367,
        368, 370, 372, 381, 387
    difference between dependent proportions,
        65, 257
    difference between independent
        proportions, 251, 256, 257, 260, 276
    different for different dependent variables, 61,
        68, 102, 142, 191, 197, 363, 364, 372
    estimation, biased, 70, 347, 366

f, 179–182, 194, 227, 242, 323, 371
factorial ANOVA, 181, 205, 211, 348, 355
    standardized interaction effect, 217
for factorial MANOVA, 373–376, 387–389
graphic, 25
Hedges–Friedman method, 171
longitudinal design, 195
for MANCOVA, 357, 360, 371–373, 389
misleading about relationships between
    distributions, 165, 170, 229,
    263–264, 268, 281
nonparametric for ANOVA, 195, 359, 389
one-way ANOVA, 177–201, 205, 228, 324,
    328, 348, 355
ordinal categorical dependent variable,
    298, 339
    Cliff's phi, 337
overlap and nonoverlap of distributions,
    5, 39, 40, 73, 79, 129, 159, 162,
    166–169, 257, 298, 388
percent of maximum possible score
    (POMP), 86–87
for pretest–posttest control-group designs,
    55, 87, 88, 90–93, 232
probability of superiority, 105, 149–165,
    172, 174, 196, 201, 218, 228, 229,
    232, 236, 268, 292–298, 301, 304,
    305, 337, 387–389
ratio of means, 31–32
relationships among different measures, 268
relationship with a test statistic, 2, 5, 15, 68,
    85, 151, 201, 254, 274, 286, 305, 347,
    361, 367, 368, 370
response ratio (*see* Ratio of means)
slopes as, 142–144
small, medium, and large designations
    problematic, 127–132, 146
standardized and unstandardized mean
    difference, 31, 33, 61–94, 149, 189,
    191–195, 202, 236, 305, 327, 331,
    350, 354, 355, 361, 382, 386, 389
when not comparing centers of two groups,
    15, 57, 64, 65, 77, 90, 129, 171, 257,
    262, 293, 297, 349
for within-groups designs
    in ANCOVA, 344–348, 350, 351, 355,
        371, 372
    in factorial ANOVA, 181, 205, 211,
        348, 355
    in MANOVA, 357, 358, 360, 364, 367,
        371, 373, 374, 376, 378, 379, 388
    in one-way ANOVA, 179, 197, 198, 205,
        324, 328
Epsilon squared, 182–183, 327, 328, 331, 371
    in one-way ANOVA, 179, 197, 198, 205,
        324, 328

Equivalence bound, 40
Equivalence testing, 40–42
ESCI, *see* Exploratory software for confidence
    intervals (ECSI)
Eta squared
    ANOVA, 181–182, 208, 327, 348, 355, 388
        factorial, 181, 205, 211, 348, 355
        and *f,* 182
        generalized, 210
        one-way, 181–182, 304, 355
Exploratory software for confidence intervals
    (ESCI), 40, 78–80

F

Fisher's Z_r transformation, 107–108, 288

G

Generalized odds ratio, 155, 156, 174,
    301–302, 305
Glass' *d,* 69
Good-enough values, 42

H

Hedges' *g,* 68, 69
Hunter-Schmidt meta-analysis programs
    package, 122

I

I^2, 13, 67

J

Journal editors, 6, 9, 11, 73, 77
    effect size reporting, 6, 9, 11, 73

L

Latent variables, 61, 153, 161, 167, 197, 335,
    336, 341, 367
    and MANOVA effect size, 346, 352, 363,
        364, 367
Longitudinal design, 195
    effect size for, 195, 280, 334, 341, 343

M

Mahalanobis *D, see* Effect sizes, *D*
MANCOVA, 357, 360, 371–373, 389
    POV effect sizes, 373
MANOVA
    factorial MANOVA POV effect sizes
        within groups, 387

standardized mean vector difference
effect size, 374–375
mixed design
effect sizes, 382
nonparametric, 359, 379, 382, 388
POV effect sizes
adjustment for bias, 369–370
eta², 364, 366, 367, 369–371, 373,
379, 383
omega², 365–367, 370, 377, 378, 380,
383, 385
tau², 366–371, 377, 378
xi², 366–371, 378
zeta², 366–371, 378
standardized mean difference contrasts
effect sizes, 360, 388
Mediation effect size, 144
Meta-analysis, 1, 9, 12–15, 74, 78, 79, 106, 109,
122, 184–186, 191, 259, 260
Minimal clinical importance, 20
Moderator variables, 13, 341
Multiple coefficient of determination, 142, 292,
308–313, 340
when dummy coding, 340

N

Nested designs, 208, 234
POV overestimation in, 208
Net clinical benefit, 4
Nocebo and placebo effects, 7, 55, 64, 65
Noninferiority trials, 256
Nonnormality, 15, 16, 21, 34, 46, 50, 51, 66, 71,
75, 80–83, 88, 93, 107, 151, 152, 167,
184, 193, 205, 288, 297, 311, 322,
337, 347, 355, 363
interpreting a standardized difference,
71, 83, 263
Nonoverlap, 166–169
Normed test and choice of standardizer,
74, 75, 87–88, 198–199, 202,
213–217, 224–225, 230–231, 236,
355, 364
Null–counternull intervals
for OR_{pop}, 276–277
for Phi_{pop}, 251
for point-biserial r_{pop}, 170
for r_{pop}, 108–109
Null hypothesis significance testing, 1–3, 9–11,
70, 76
controversy, 9–11
Number needed to harm (NNH), 267
Number needed to treat (NNT), 265–268,
299–300
confidence intervals, 267

O

Odds ratios
confidence intervals, 276
converting to r, 273–274
converting to standardized difference,
273–274
cumulative, 302–304
generalized, 156, 301–302
larger contingency tables, 278–279
limitations, 272, 273
Omega squared
in ANCOVA, 282–283
comparable for different designs
in factorial ANOVA
difficulty in comparing values, 209–210
interaction, 205
partial, 208
ratios of two values, 208
in MANOVA, 364–365, 371
in one-way ANOVA, 179, 197, 198, 205,
324, 328
and standardized difference, 179
ratios vs. standardized difference
ratios, 207
in specific comparisons, 210
Ordinal categorical dependent variables
scores, choice of, 290–291
skew, 291, 292, 297
sliced from continuous variables, 290, 292
spacing of conversions to "scores," 291
tests of significance on multiple estimates
of effect size, 228
ties, 288, 292–302
Ordinal dominance curve, 172
relation to the probability
of superiority, 172
Outliers, 19, 21–25, 28, 48, 51, 72–75, 82, 93,
111–115, 142, 145, 158, 167, 184,
198, 296, 311, 334, 337, 341, 372
and standardized-difference effect sizes,
72–73
Overlap, 5, 39, 40, 73, 79, 129, 157, 162, 166,
168, 169, 175, 257, 298, 388
as measure of effect size, 158, 167

P

Partial correlation, 313–318, 321, 322, 327, 331,
332, 336
Partial POV, 199–200, 202, 208–210, 220,
227, 232–236, 347, 348, 353, 355,
375–387, 389
Path analysis effect sizes, 335, 341
Percentage of nonoverlapping data, 167, 169

Percentile comparison graph, 172
Phi coefficient
    collapsed 2 x c ordinal categorical tables,
        302–304
    comparing from different studies, 243, 277,
        304–305, 337
    margin totals influence, 134, 249
    maximum value, 111–112
    for naturalistic studies only, 140, 248–250,
        252, 253, 281, 304, 305
Point-biserial r
    assumptions, 99, 106, 109–115, 132,
        250, 289
    attenuation from restricted range, 123, 146
    bias and bias reduction, 106
    calculation, 97, 99, 102, 106, 117, 127, 133,
        137, 288, 340
    conversion to t, 115
    ordinal categorical data
        confidence interval, 288, 298
        limitations, 289–290, 297
    unequal ns correction, 188
Power analysis, 1, 12, 41, 68, 106, 312, 313
Practical significance
    effect-size benchmark for educational
        significance, 129
Probability of superiority (PS)
    assumptions, 105, 150, 155–156,
        160–161, 166
    dependent groups, 172–174
    estimators, 149, 161, 293, 298
    exact test of H_0: PS = .5, 152, 159, 161,
        294–295
    homoscedasticity and normality, 105, 154,
        158–161, 228
    and medians, 158, 174
    ordinal data, 292–298, 388
    relation to d_{pop}, 151–152, 159–161
    robust methods, 152, 154, 174, 389
    robustness, 296–297
    $vs.$ standardized difference, 174, 268
    ties, 150, 151, 153, 156–157, 166, 173–174,
        292–298
Proportional reduction in error (PRE), 182
Proportion of variance explained (POV)
    in ANCOVA, 347, 348, 355
    comparable for different designs, 188, 210, 376
    factorial ANOVA, 348, 355
    multiple regression POV
        when dummy coding, 324, 326–327
    one-way ANOVA, 198, 324, 355
    partial, 199–200, 202, 208–210, 220,
        227, 232–236, 347, 348, 353, 355,
        375–387, 389
    sampling variability great, 183, 209, 210, 236

Proportions
    difference between two
        repeated measures, 255, 257
PS, see Probability of superiority

Q

Q_{max}, 280
Q statistic for homogeneity of effect sizes, 67

R

R^2
    adjusted for cross-validation, 311–312
    adjusted for shrinkage, 309–312
Range null hypothesis, 42
Rating scale data, 305
Ratio of means, 31–32
Regression
    coefficients, partial, 316, 319
    equation, 111, 142, 307, 308, 316, 332–334,
        338, 346
    increase-over-chance effect size, 388
    least-squares, 138, 144, 307, 311, 326,
        337, 339
    multiple
        nonlinear
            polynomial, 332–333, 341
        nonparametric
            robust, 337, 341
            semiparametric, 337, 341
        simple, 115
        standard, 307, 308, 312, 314,
            316, 339
Relative risk, 135, 251, 259–261, 264, 269,
    272–274, 276, 280, 281, 339
Reliability coefficients
    differences causing differences in
        effect-size estimates, 117, 118
Replication, 13–15, 40, 46, 62, 70, 79, 84, 131,
    335, 363
Risk difference, 243, 253, 261, 264, 265, 267,
    268, 272, 274, 280, 281, 300, 301,
    305

S

Scale coarseness
    correcting r for, 127, 289, 290
Semipartial correlation, 313–315, 319–322,
    327, 331
Sensitivity analysis
    spacing of "scores" converted from ordinal
        categories, 291
Shift model, 157–158, 171, 172, 174

Significance
  vs. confidence intervals for effect sizes,
    33, 267
  testing, controversy, 9–11, 70, 267
Simpson's paradox, 280
Small, medium, and large effect sizes,
    127–132, 146
Somers' *D*, 299–300, 305
Standardized difference between means
  in ANCOVA, 87, 90, 92, 348, 355
  in ANOVA, 361
  bias and bias reduction, 70
  control group and normality, 63–64, 93
  conversion from *t*, 69
  dependent groups
    standardizer choice, 87–88
  for normed dependent variables, 74
  pooling *vs.* not pooling, 69
  resistant estimators, 75
  standardizer from normative group, 74
  variances equal or unequal, 68–72, 89
  when there are outliers, 74–75
Standardized difference effect sizes
  Cohen, Glass, Hedges, 63, 67–72, 74, 76,
    78–79, 81, 83, 86, 90, 128–129, 179,
    210, 213, 232, 273, 334, 349–350
  confidence intervals, 65–67, 75–87, 89–90,
    94, 194–195, 197, 201, 229, 232, 382
  factorial ANOVA, 211, 348, 355
  one-way ANOVA, 178–179, 185–188, 191,
    194–198, 201, 205–206, 348, 355
  outliers, 72–75
  overall in one-way ANOVA, 178
  specific comparisons in one-way ANOVA,
    185, 349
  within-group ANOVA, 196–197, 355,
    379–380, 382

Standardizers
  outlier-resistant, 75
Stochastic superiority; *see also* Probability
    of superiority
Strength of association, *see* Proportion
    of variance explained (POV)
Structural equation modeling effect sizes,
    335–336
Success percentages
  rate ratio, 133, 260
Superiority, 40–42, 59, 128, 162, 166, 173–174,
    257, 274, 275, 287, 288, 296, 299,
    301, 343

T

Treatment
  effect on variabilities and centers, 11–12,
    20, 170–171
  effects throughout a distribution, 171
  exploring data for effect on variability,
    20–25
Trimmed means, 49, 51–53, 57, 75, 82–83,
    89–90, 197, 198, 205, 214, 351
Truncated range, 123
t statistic
  converted from point-biserial r, 99
Tukey sum-difference graph, 172

U

Ubiquitous effect-size index, 195, 228
Uncertainty coefficient, 278
Unreliability; *see also* Reliability
  attenuation of effect-size estimates, 115,
    118, 288